THE PAPERS OF ALEXANDER HAMILTON

Alexander Hamilton, *circa* 1796. Oil portrait by James Sharples
Bank of New York and Trust Company

THE PAPERS OF

Alexander Hamilton

VOLUME XIV

FEBRUARY 1793–JUNE 1793

HAROLD C. SYRETT, EDITOR

JACOB E. COOKE, ASSOCIATE EDITOR

Assistant Editors

JEAN G. COOKE   CARA-LOUISE MILLER

DOROTHY TWOHIG   PATRICIA SYRETT

 COLUMBIA UNIVERSITY PRESS

NEW YORK AND LONDON, 1969

FROM THE PUBLISHER

The preparation of this edition of the papers of
Alexander Hamilton has been made possible by
the support received for the work of the editorial and research staff from the generous grants
of the Rockefeller Foundation, Time Inc., and
the Ford Foundation, and by the far-sighted co-
operation of the National Historical Publications
Commission. To these organizations, the publisher expresses gratitude on behalf of all who
are concerned about making available the record
of the founding of the United States.

PREFACE

THIS EDITION of Alexander Hamilton's papers contains letters and other documents written by Hamilton, letters to Hamilton, and some documents (commissions, certificates, etc.) that directly concern Hamilton but were written neither by him nor to him. All letters and other documents have been printed in chronological order. Hamilton's legal papers are being published under the editorial direction of Julius Goebel, Jr., George Welwood Murray Professor Emeritus of Legal History of the School of Law, Columbia University. The first volume of this distinguished work, which is entitled *The Law Practice of Alexander Hamilton*, was published by the Columbia University Press in 1964.

Many letters and documents have been calendared. Such calendared items include routine letters and documents by Hamilton, routine letters to Hamilton, some of the letters or documents written by Hamilton for someone else, letters or documents which have not been found but which are known to have existed, letters or documents which have been erroneously attributed to Hamilton, and letters to or by Hamilton that deal exclusively with his legal practice.

Certain routine documents which Hamilton wrote and received as Secretary of the Treasury have not been printed. The documents that fall within this category are warrants or interest certificates; letters written by Hamilton acknowledging receipts from banks, endorsing margins of certificate of registry, and enclosing sea letters; letters to Hamilton transmitting weekly, monthly, and quarterly accounts, or enclosing certificates of registry and other routine Treasury forms; and drafts by Hamilton on the treasurer. Statements of facts from the judges of the District Courts on cases concerning violations of the customs laws and warrants of remission of forfeiture issued to Hamilton have generally been omitted unless they pertain to cases discussed in Hamilton's correspondence.

The notes in these volumes are designed to provide information concerning the nature and location of each document, to identify Hamilton's correspondents and the individuals mentioned in the text, to explain events or ideas referred to in the text, and to point out textual variations or mistakes. Occasional departures from these standards can be attributed to a variety of reasons. In many cases the desired information has been supplied in an earlier note and can be found through the use of the index. Notes have not been added when in the opinion of the editors the material in the text was either self-explanatory or common knowledge. The editors, moreover, have not thought it desirable or necessary to provide full annotation for Hamilton's legal correspondence. Perhaps at this point it should also be stated that arithmetical errors in Hamilton's reports to Congress have not been corrected or noted. Finally, the editors on some occasions have been unable to find the desired information, and on other occasions the editors have been remiss.

GUIDE TO EDITORIAL APPARATUS

I. SYMBOLS USED TO DESCRIBE MANUSCRIPTS

AD	Autograph Document
ADS	Autograph Document Signed
ADf	Autograph Draft
ADfS	Autograph Draft Signed
AL	Autograph Letter
ALS	Autograph Letter Signed
D	Document
DS	Document Signed
Df	Draft
DfS	Draft Signed
LS	Letter Signed
LC	Letter Book Copy
[S]	[S] is used with other symbols (AD[S], ADf[S], AL[S], D[S], Df[S], L[S]) to indicate that the signature on the document has been cropped or clipped.

II. MONETARY SYMBOLS AND ABBREVIATIONS

bf	Banco florin
V	Ecu
f	Florin
₶	Livre Tournois
medes	Maravedis (also md and mde)
d.	Penny or denier
ps	Piece of eight

£	Pound sterling or livre
Ry	Real
rs vn	Reals de vellon
rdr	Rix daller
s	Shilling, sou or sol (also expressed as /)
sti	Stiver

III. SHORT TITLES AND ABBREVIATIONS

Annals of Congress	*The Debates and Proceedings in the Congress of the United States; with an Appendix, Containing Important State Papers and Public Documents, and All the Laws of a Public Nature* (Washington, 1834–1849).
Annual Register (State Papers), 1792	*The Annual Register, or a View of the History, Politics, and Literature, for the Year 1792* (London, 1821).
Annual Register (State Papers), 1793	*The Annual Register, or a View of the History, Politics, and Literature, for the Year 1793* (London, 1821).
Arch. des Aff. Etr., Corr. Pol., Etats-Unis	Transcripts or photostats from the French Foreign Office deposited in the Library of Congress.
Archives Parlementaires	*Archives Parlementaires de 1787 à 1860* (Paris, 1868–).
ASP	*American State Papers, Documents, Legislative and Executive, of the Congress of the United States* (Washington, 1832–1861).
Boyd, *Papers of Thomas Jefferson*	Julian P. Boyd, ed., *The Papers of Thomas Jefferson* (Princeton, 1950–).
Carter, *Territorial Papers*	Clarence E. Carter, ed., *The Territorial Papers of the United States* (Washington, 1934–).
3 Dallas, *U.S. Reports*	A. J. Dallas, *Reports of Cases Ruled and Adjudged in the Several Courts of the United States, and*

	of *Pennsylvania, Held at the Seat of the Federal Government* (Philadelphia, 1793–1801).
Executive Journal, I	*Journal of the Executive Proceedings of the Senate* (Washington, 1828), I.
Ford, *Writings of Jefferson*	Paul Leicester Ford, ed., *The Writings of Thomas Jefferson* (New York, 1892–1899).
Fraunces, *An Appeal*	[Andrew G. Fraunces], *An Appeal to the Legislature of the United States, and to the Citizens Individually, of the Several States, Against the Conduct of the Secretary of the Treasury. By Andrew G. Fraunces, Citizen of the State of New-York, Late in the Treasury of the United States. "E tenebris elucidit lux." Printed for Andrew G. Fraunces, Esq.* (n.p., 1793).
Grotius, *The Rights of War and Peace*	[Hugo Grotius], *The Rights of War and Peace, in Three Books. Wherein are explained, The Law of Nature and Nations, and The Principal Points relating to Government. Written in Latin by the Learned Hugo Grotius, And Translated into English. To which are added All the large Notes of Mr. J. Barbeyrac, Professor of Law at Gröningen, And Member of the Royal Academy of Sciences at Berlin* (London: Printed for W. Innys and R. Manby, J. and P. Knapton, D. Brown, T. Osborn, and E. Wicksteed, 1738).
GW	John C. Fitzpatrick, ed., *The Writings of George Washington* (Washington, 1931–1944).
Hamilton, *Intimate Life*	Allan McLane Hamilton, *The Intimate Life of Alexander Hamilton* (New York, 1910).

HCLW — Henry Cabot Lodge, ed., *The Works of Alexander Hamilton* (New York, 1904).

Hogan, *Pennsylvania State Trials* — [Edmund Hogan], *The Pennsylvania State Trials: Containing the Impeachment, Trial, and Acquittal of Francis Hopkinson, and John Nicholson, Esquires* . . . (Philadelphia, 1794).

JCC — *Journals of the Continental Congress, 1774–1789* (Washington, 1904–1937).

JCH Transcripts — John C. Hamilton Transcripts. These transcripts are owned by Mr. William H. Swan, Hampton Bays, New York, and have been placed on loan in the Columbia University Libraries.

JCHW — John C. Hamilton, ed., *The Works of Alexander Hamilton* (New York, 1851–1856).

Journal of the House, I — *Journal of the House of Representatives of the United States* (Washington, 1826), I.

JPP — "Journal of the Proceedings of the President," George Washington Papers, Library of Congress.

Miller, *Treaties*, II — Hunter Miller, ed., *Treaties and Other International Acts of the United States of America* (Washington, 1931), II.

"Minutes of the S.U.M." — MS minutes of the Society for Establishing Useful Manufactures, City of Paterson, New Jersey, Plant Management Commission, Successors to the Society for Establishing Useful Manufactures.

Pennsylvania Statutes — James T. Mitchell and Henry Flanders, eds., *The Statutes at Large of Pennsylvania from 1682 to 1801* (Harrisburg, 1896–1915).

PRO: F.O., or PRO: C.O. — Transcripts or photostats from the Public Record Office of Great

	Britain deposited in the Library of Congress.
PRO: F.O., or PRO: C.O. (Great Britain)	Public Record Office of Great Britain.
Pufendorf, *Of the Law of Nature and Nations*	Samuel Pufendorf, *Of the Law of Nature and Nations. Eight Books. Written in Latin by the Baron Pufendorf, Counsellor of State to his late Swedish Majesty, and to the late King of Prussia. Done into English by Basil Kennett, D.D. late President of Corpus Christi College in Oxford. To which are added All the large Notes of Mr. Barbeyrac, translated from the best Edition; Together with large Tables to the whole. The Fourth Edition, carefully Corrected* . . . (London: Printed for J. Walthoe, R. Wilkin, J. and J. Bonwicke, S. Birt, T. Ward, and T. Osborne, 1729).
Simcoe Papers	E. A. Cruikshank, ed., *The Correspondence of Lieut. Governor John Graves Simcoe, with Allied Documents Relating to His Administration of the Government of Upper Canada* (Toronto, 1923–1931).
1 *Stat.*	*The Public Statutes at Large of the United States of America* (Boston, 1845).
6 *Stat.*	*The Public Statutes at Large of the United States of America* [Private Statutes] (Boston, 1856).
Turner, "Correspondence of French Ministers"	Frederick J. Turner, ed., "Correspondence of the French Ministers to the United States, 1791–1797," *Annual Report of the American Historical Association for the Year 1903* (Washington, 1904), II.

Vattel, *Law of Nations*   Emeric de Vattel, *Law of Nations; or Principles of the Law of Nature: Applied to the Conduct and Affairs of Nations and Sovereigns* (London, 1759–1760).

IV. INDECIPHERABLE WORDS

Words or parts of words which could not be deciphered because of the illegibility of the writing or the mutilation of the manuscript have been indicated as follows:

1. ⟨-----⟩ indicates illegible words with the number of dashes indicating the estimated number of illegible words.
2. Words or letters in broken brackets indicate a guess as to what the words or letters in question may be. If the source of the words or letters within the broken brackets is known, it has been given a note.

V. CROSSED-OUT MATERIAL IN MANUSCRIPTS

Words or sentences crossed out by a writer in a manuscript have been handled in one of the three following ways:

1. They have been ignored, and the document or letter has been printed in its final version.
2. Crossed-out words and insertions for the crossed-out words have been described in the notes.
3. When the significance of a manuscript seems to warrant it, the crossed-out words have been retained, and the document has been printed as it was written.

VI. TEXTUAL CHANGES AND INSERTIONS

The following changes or insertions have been made in the letters and documents printed in these volumes:

1. Words or letters written above the line of print (for example, 9th) have been made even with the line of print (9th).
2. Punctuation and capitalization have been changed in those instances where it seemed necessary to make clear the sense

of the writer. A special effort has been made to eliminate the dash, which was such a popular eighteenth-century device.

3. When the place or date, or both, of a letter or document does not appear at the head of that letter or document, it has been inserted in the text in brackets. If either the place or date at the head of a letter or document is incomplete, the necessary additional material has been added in the text in brackets. For all but the best known localities or places, the name of the colony, state, or territory has been added in brackets at the head of a document or letter.

4. In calendared documents, place and date have been uniformly written out in full without the use of brackets. Thus "N. York, Octr. 8, '99" becomes "New York, October 8, 1799." If, however, substantive material is added to the place or date in a calendared document, such material is placed in brackets. Thus "Oxford, Jan. 6" becomes "Oxford [Massachusetts] January 6 [1788]."

5. When a writer made an unintentional slip comparable to a typographical error, one of the four following devices has been used:

a. It has been allowed to stand as written.

b. It has been corrected by inserting either one or more letters in brackets.

c. It has been corrected without indicating the change.

d. It has been explained in a note.

6. Because the symbol for the thorn was archaic even in Hamilton's day, the editors have used the letter "y" to represent it. In doing this they are conforming to eighteenth-century manuscript usage.

1793

To Thomas Pinckney [1]

[Philadelphia] Febr. 5. 1793

My Dr. Sir

Inclosed is a packet for Mr. Short [2] which I beg you to forward. I leave it open for your perusal to save me the time it would require to repeat the subject to you. Inclosed is another Copy of the Letter for you. [3] I have the consolation of believing that the attempt will in the end do good to the Government & to myself. [4]

Yrs. respectfully & with true esteem   A. Hamilton

Mr. Pinckney

ALS, Pinckney Family Papers, Library of Congress.

1. Pinckney was United States Minister Plenipotentiary to Great Britain.

2. H to William Short, February 5, 1793. Short at this time was in Madrid where he was serving as co-commissioner with William Carmichael to settle the differences between the United States and Spain.

3. This was a copy of H's "Report on the Balance of All Unapplied Revenues at the End of the Year 1792 and on All Unapplied Monies Which May Have Been Obtained by the Several Loans Authorized by Law," February 4, 1793.

4. For the "attempt," see the introductory note to the report cited in note 3.

Report Exhibiting the Amount of All the Public Funds up to the End of 1792 and Statement of What Remains of Each Appropriation [1]

Treasury Department
February 5. 1793.
[Communicated on February 6, 1793] [2]

[To the President of the Senate]
Sir

In pursuance of the first part of the order of the Senate of the 23d of January past,[3] I have the honor to send herewith sundry statements marked A, AB, B, Ba, D, E, F, and I beg the permission of the Senate to add the Copy of a letter dated yesterday, which served to transmit duplicates of the same documents to the House of Representatives; and which contains some explanations of them; a repetition of which here will be thereby rendered unnecessary. The document C referred to in that letter was also sent to the House of Representatives, but being of considerable length, a duplicate is not yet ready; and I did not think it advisable to detain the other papers 'till it was ready.[4]

The documents now transmitted will answer the whole of the enquiry contained in the first part of the order above referred to, except what regards a distribution of the expenditures under each head of appropriation; which is in preparation and will be forwarded as soon as it can be ready.

The situation in which I am placed renders further delay absolutely necessary to the fulfilment of the second part of the Order.

There is a point in my letter of the 16th of January to the Senate concerning which some explanation is requisite.[5] I stated as one motive to the joint negotiation of the loans, under both Acts,[6] "an intimation from our Bankers in Holland [7] that a distinction might prove an embarrassment, being a novelty, the reason of which would not be obvious to the money lenders." This was done from memory, without recurrence to documents, and in a degree of hurry occasioned by my anxiety for the speedy passing of the Appropriation Bill,[8] and upon a revision proves to be not accurate. The mistake arose in the following manner. My original idea was to maintain a separation between the two Acts. This will appear from my letter of the 28th of August 1790 to our Bankers in which I express a desire that they would endeavour to place part of the first loan upon one Act and another part upon the other Act. But they did not carry this idea into execution for the reason assigned in their answer,[9] now before the Senate, which is that the subdivision proposed would under the circumstances of the case tend to excite speculations and doubts among the money lenders.

But prior to the receipt of their answer I had made further enquiry and had reflected more on the subject. The result of my enquiry was that the money lenders having been accustomed to lend on the general Credit of the Government borrowing, with a sort of general pledge of its revenues and resources, the attempt to bottom a loan upon any particular law, might, as a novelty, occasion some hesitation and embarrassment among them; especially as they are known to be a description of men much influenced by habit and precedent; and the conclusions from more full reflection were that the distinguishing of the loans with reference to each act, might not only embarrass the business, in the first stages of negotiation, but might interfere with an application of the proceeds of the loans in the most convenient and beneficial manner, according to circumstances.

On these considerations I abandoned my original intention, and in my first instruction to Mr Short[10] was silent on the point.

These different positions of the subject in the mind, at different times, and what actually took place with regard to the first loan, produced some confusion in the recollection of facts, and led me to assign as a cause what had been only a collateral circumstance, and to ascribe to the Bankers intimations, or rather information, which I had received from other quarters.

I submit this explanation of the matter to the candor of the Senate, and have the honor to be, with perfect respect,

Sir, Your Most Obedt Servant.   Alexander Hamilton

P S   I have the honor to return the original Bank Books and accounts which were withdrawn respecting my request that as soon as the use for them shall cease they may be returned.[11]

The Vice President of the United States
and President of the Senate.

LS, RG 46, Second Congress, 1791–1793, Reports of the Secretary of the Treasury, National Archives.

1. For background to this document, see the introductory note to "Report on the Balance of All Unapplied Revenues at the End of the Year 1792 and on All Unapplied Monies Which May Have Been Obtained by the Several Loans Authorized by Law," February 4, 1793.

A note accompanying this document reads: "Letter to the Vice President from the Secretary of the Treasury accompanying sundry documents in pursuance of an Order of Senate of the 23d. of January 1793, relative to his financial arrangements, together with a Copy of a Letter dated Feby 4th. 1793 transmitting duplicates of the same Documents to the House of Representatives containing some explanations. February 5th. 1793."

2. *Annals of Congress*, III, 640.

3. For this Senate order of January 23, 1793, see the introductory note to "Report on the Balance of All Unapplied Revenues at the End of the Year 1792 and on All Unapplied Monies Which May Have Been Obtained by the Several Loans Authorized by Law," February 4, 1793.

4. For the letter and enclosures mentioned in this paragraph, see "Report on the Balance of All Unapplied Revenues at the End of the Year 1792 and on All Unapplied Monies Which May Have Been Obtained by the Several Loans Authorized by Law," February 4, 1793. "Statement AB" was also enclosed in "Report on Bank Deposits, Surplus Revenue, and Loans," January 16, 1793, and is printed as an enclosure to that document.

5. "Report on Bank Deposits, Surplus Revenue, and Loans," January 16, 1793.

6. "An Act making provision for the (payment of the) Debt of the United States" (1 *Stat.* 138–44 [August 4, 1790]) and "An Act making Provision for the Reduction of the Public Debt" (1 *Stat.* 186–87 [August 12, 1790]).

7. Willink, Van Staphorst, and Hubbard.

8. On January 9, 1793, "An Act making appropriations for the support of Government for the year one thousand seven hundred and ninety-three" was approved in the House of Representatives and was submitted for the consideration of the Senate (*Journal of the House*, I, 665). The act was approved on February 28, 1793 (1 *Stat.* 325–29).

9. Letter not found.

10. H to William Short, September 1, 1790.

11. See H to John Adams, January 24, 1793.

Report on Foreign Loans[1]

Treasury Department
February 5. 1793.
[Communicated on February 6, 1793][2]

[To the President of the Senate]
Sir

By order of the President of the United States, I have the honor to transmit herewith.[3]

I. Copies of a power given by him to the Secretary of the Treasury for the time being dated the 28th of August 1790, for the negotiation of the loans authorised by the laws of the 4th and 12th of August 1790 and of certain instructions relative thereto dated on the same day.[4]

II. Copies of an authority founded upon the power of the President from me to William Short, Esquire, dated the 1st of September 1790,[5] and of sundry letters from me to the said William Short, of dates from the 29th of May 1790 to the 31st of December 1792, inclusively, relating to the negotiation and application of the above-mentioned loans.

III Originals of sundry letters from William Short to me under dates from the 2d. of December 1790 to the 2d of November 1792, inclusively, relating to the same subject.

IV Copy of an authority from me to Messrs Wilhem and John Willinks Nicholas and J van Staphorst and Hubbard, Bankers of the United States at Amsterdam, dated the 28th of August 1790, relating to the first of the loans, made under the above mentioned Acts,[6] and Copies of sundry letters to the said Bankers, of dates from the 28th of August 1790 to the 31st of December 1792, inclusively.

V Originals of sundry letters from the said Bankers to me of dates from the 25th of January 1790 to the 5th of November 1792.

VI Copies of sundry letters of dates from the 18th of June to the 24th of September 1792, inclusively, between G Morris[7] and W Short, Esquires, having relation to the above subjects.

The general power from the President to the Secretary of the Treasury of the 28th of August 1790 and the communications from William Short, Esquire, who has been the only Commissioner, would, it is presumed, have fulfilled the terms of the Resolution of the Senate of the 23d of last month;[8] and are transmitted pursuant to the request contained in that Resolution.

But the President has been pleased to direct the transmission of the other documents also, in the supposition, that they will serve to throw light upon the general subject of that Resolution.

With perfect respect, I have the honor to be, Sir, Your Mo. Obedt and humble Servant   Alex Hamilton

Secy of the Treasy

LS, RG 46, Second Congress, 1791–1793, Reports of the Secretary of the Treasury, National Archives.

1. For background to this document, see the introductory note to "Report on the Balance of All Unapplied Revenues at the End of the Year 1792 and on All Unapplied Monies Which May Have Been Obtained by the Several Loans Authorized by Law," February 4, 1793.

2. *Annals of Congress*, III, 640.

3. On January 23, 1793, the Senate *"Resolved,* That the President of the United States be requested to lay before the Senate, copies of the powers given by him for the negotiation of the loans authorized by the laws of the 4th and 12th of August, 1790, and of the communications from the Public Commissioners in Holland" (*Annals of Congress*, III, 633).

4. George Washington to H, August 28, 1790. The laws authorizing the loans were "An Act making provision for the (payment of the) Debt of the United States" (1 *Stat.* 138–44 [August 4, 1790]) and "An Act making Provision for the Reduction of the Public Debt" (1 *Stat.* 186–87 [August 12, 1790]).

5. This document is enclosed in H to Short, September 1, 1790.

6. This document is enclosed in H to Willink, Van Staphorst, and Hubbard, August 28, 1790.

7. In January, 1792, Gouverneur Morris was appointed United States Minister Plenipotentiary to France.

8. See note 3.

From William Short

[*Madrid, February 5, 1793.* On February 25, 1793, Short wrote to Hamilton: "I had the honor of writing to you on the 5th. inst from Madrid." *Letter not found.*]

To William Short [1]

(Private)   Philadelphia February 5th: 1793.

Sir:

The spirit of party has grown to maturity sooner in this country than perhaps was to have been counted upon. You will see a specimen of it in the inclosed speech of Mr. Giles, a member from Virginia. The House of Representatives adopted the resolutions proposed by him, *nemini contradicente*. The object with a majority was to confound the attempt by giving a free course to investigation.

I send you also a printed copy of a letter from me to the House of Representatives of yesterday's date, being the first part of an answer to those resolutions. The statements referred to in it could not yet be printed; but lest the thing should pass the Atlantic, and be made an ill use of, to the prejudice of our country, I send you the antidote to be employed or not as you may see occasion.

An investigation intended to prejudice me is begun with respect to the circumstances attending the last payment on account of the French debt; which, in its progress, may draw your conduct into question. I think, however, you need be under no anxiety for the result. Your hesitations, at a certain stage, were so natural, and your reasons so weighty for them, that they will give little handle against you, besides the coincidence in opinion here about the expediency of a suspension of payment.[2] The popular tide in this country is strong in favor of the last revolution in France; and there are many who go, of course, with that tide, and endeavour always to turn it to account. For my own part I content myself with praying most sincerely that it may issue in the real advantage and happiness of the nation.

With much esteem and regard,   I am   Your obedt Servt

A. Hamilton.

JCH Transcripts, Columbia University Libraries.

1. For background to this letter, see the introductory note to H's "Report on the Balance of All Unapplied Revenues at the End of the Year 1792 and on All Unapplied Monies Which May Have Been Obtained by the Several Loans Authorized by Law," February 4, 1793.

2. For the controversy over the payment of the installment on the French debt due in the summer of 1792, see Short to H, September 25, October 27, 1792; Gouverneur Morris to H, September 25, 1792; Thomas Jefferson to H, October 31, 1792.

To Thomas Willing

Treasury Department
February 5. 1793.

Sir

I request that the Bank will advance to Messrs. Young & Dannaker [1] Five hundred Dollars on account of their Cloathing with the Public on the same principles as the advances heretofore made.

With respectful consideration I have the honor to be   Sir   Your most Obed ser   A Hamilton

Thomas Willing Esqr
President of the Bank of the UStates

ALS, Historical Society of Pennsylvania, Philadelphia.
   1. See "Contract with George Dannacker and William Young," October 22, 1792.

To the President and Directors of the Bank of the United States

Treasury Department Febry 6th 1793

Gentlemen

I request that you will advance to Mr Philip Nicklin as agent to Samuel Smith, agent to Elliot & Williams [1] the sum of Ten thousand Dollars on account of the existing contract between the public and the latter Gentlemen; taking a proper receipt of Mr. Nicklin.

This affair is to be wound up together with the former advances hereafter.

As the money is intended to be remitted to Baltimore, to facilitate matters I have directed the Treasurer to lodge in the Bank a Bill upon the office of discount & Deposit in Baltimore for the sum above mentioned.

I have the honor to be   Gentlemen   Yr Ob Servt
                                                    Alexander Hamilton

The Presidt Directors &C
of the Bank of the U St

LS, Long Island Historical Society, Brooklyn, New York.
   1. The firm of Robert Elliot and Elie Williams had been contractors for supplying the western posts since the commencement of the Federal Government. Williams was a brother of Otho H. Williams, collector of customs at Baltimore. See H to John Kean, January 1, 1793.

From William Hull [1]

Niagara Feb.y. 6th. 1793.

Sir,

I arrived at this place on the 2d. instant, but was not able to see the Governor untill the 3d. on account of the vast quantity of Ice floating in the River.

On the 3d. instant I addressed myself to him, delivered Mr. Hammonds letter, and communicated the object of My mission.[2]

Copy, Massachusetts Historical Society, Boston.

1. Hull, a native of Derby, Connecticut, had served as a lieutenant colonel in a Massachusetts regiment during the American Revolution. After the war he settled in Newton, Massachusetts, where he practiced law. In 1784 Congress sent him to Canada on an unsuccessful mission to demand the surrender of the posts which the British held in violation of the 1783 treaty. In January, 1793, Hull was appointed agent to arrange with John Graves Simcoe, governor of Upper Canada, for the purchase of supplies for the proposed meeting with the western Indians in the spring.

For background to this letter, see "Draft of Instructions for William Hull," January 14, 1793. See also "Conversation with George Hammond," December 15–28, 1792; H to Hammond, December 29, 1792. For the proposed council with the western Indians, see "Conversation with George Hammond," November 22, 1792, note 4.

On December 29, 1792, H had requested Hammond, the British Minister to the United States, to facilitate preparations for the council with the western Indians in the spring of 1793, and in January, 1793, Hammond had forwarded accounts of his negotiations with the Americans to Simcoe. On January 21, 1793, Simcoe wrote to Hammond explaining his position on the proposed conference. In this letter he stated that it had been the long-standing policy of the British government in Canada to supply the Indians, and that, since the British held the posts "by their permission, from hence has arisen the constant Necessity that the Government of Canada has been under of supplying the Wants of any Assemblage of the Savages for any purpose whatsoever; and consequently the Standing Orders of these Posts have always been to this Effect" (*Simcoe Papers*, I, 277–78).

2. In a letter to Hammond, dated February 3, 1793, Simcoe described his meeting with Hull as follows: "General Hull has just delivered to me Your Excellency's Credentials. . . . I conceived it to be improper for me to admit the request of the United States to furnish the Indians with Provisions, I can only add that I have endeavoured to press upon the General that my declining the request is consequent to the Military Orders subsisting at this post, and in particular as upon a similar construction to that which I now place upon those orders, Colonel [Andrew] Gordon, my predecessor, refused the request of Colonel [Thomas] Proctor in 1791 to proceed with some Indian Chiefs in one of the King's Vessels to Sandusky for the purpose of Negociation,—which proceeding of Colonel Gordon's met with the full approbation of Lord Dorchester.

"Colonel Proctor's request was 'to be permitted to charter a freight in one of

He was engaged in preparing for a journey to the River Tranche, and from thence to Detroit and the next morning was fixed on for his departure.

He expressed much surprize that the British Minister should have imagined that the request I made could have been complied with by him.

1. Because the Indian affairs are under the direction of the Commander in Chief in his military character.

2. Because Lord Dorchester while in this country issued a standing order that no supplies should be conveyed to the Indians by the United States thro' the medium of these ports on any pretence whatever.

3. Because Genl. Clarke [3] is now the Commander in chief and continues the same regulations.

4. That an instance in point happened on the application of Colo.

---

our vessels for such Number of Indians as may accompany me to Sandusky.'—on Colonel Gordon's refusal the Answer of Lord Dorchester [Governor General of Canada] is, June 2nd 1791 'the Application of Mr. Proctor for the hire of one of the King's Vessels on Lake Erie, has to me an appearance of insult, 'tis impossible He could expect success—I take it for granted You have taken effectual means also to prevent his procuring any Vessel or Conveyance from any of the King's Subjects which Mr. [John] Butler mentions to have been his intention.' I read the substance of this transaction to General Hull to evince to him that I did not *Personally* throw any obstacles in the way of his Mission, but that I follow'd Instructions which I could not misinterpret as they had already been acted upon.

"At the General's request I have given him a Copy of the Message of the Western Indians to me, and that of the Six Nations with my Answers. He intimated to me in Conversation, that He had understood the Message must have been misinterpreted to the President as far as related to the place of meeting, which the President understood to be at the *Glaize*, and General [Israel] Chapin the Superintendant whom he met with on the road, had informed him was at Sandusky. Upon our recurrence to the above-mentioned Speeches He was confirmed that General Chapin was right in his assertion.

"I declined of course placing my refusal of the request upon any other Basis than my Obedience to the Military Orders of the Post, and whenever in Conversation, any observation called for animadversion, I took care constantly to observe, that what I then said was matter of discourse, and that my Subordinate Situation prevented me from entering into any discussion of what was not committed to my discretion. I also mentioned to him in strong terms the Obligation which had been imposed upon our Posts of always Supplying the Indians. . . ." (*Simcoe Papers*, I, 286–87.)

3. Alured Clarke, who had served as a brigadier general in the British army during the American Revolution, had been appointed lieutenant governor and administrator of the Province of Lower Canada on December 26, 1791.

Proctor to Colo. Gordon, which was refused, and Colo. Gordon's Conduct was highly approved by Lord Dorchester.[4]

5. Because the Indians, when they proposed the treaty applied to him for supplies, and he engaged to furnish them.[5]

6. Because it has been the invariable custom of the British Government to furnish them with provisions at all their meetings & treaties.

7. Because the Indians themselves have objected to the measure of being supplied by the United States, as they cannot treat on independent ground; while they daily receive their dinners from the party with whom they were treating.

As nearly as I recollect, these are all the reasons which the Governor stated against a compliance with our wishes.

At present it is unnecessary to communicate to you the reply which I made to these reasons. It is sufficient to say that they were unavailing. The next day the Governor began his journey, and expects to be absent six weeks.

Before his departure, he communicated to me the proceedings of the Indians at their Councils at the Au-glaise in Octobr. 1792, and at Buffaloe Creek in Novr. 1792.[6] as interpreted by the British Interpreters.

I have obtained copies of those proceedings and have enclosed them to the Secretary at War, being particularly within his department, and have stated the conversation which took place between the Governor and myself respecting the proposed treaty.

In the course of my journey, late at night, when I was much

4. See note 2. Proctor had been sent in 1791 on a mission to the Miami and Wabash Indians to persuade them to attend a council at Fort Washington. Henry Knox's "Instructions to Colonel Thomas Proctor," March 11, 1791, is printed in *ASP, Indian Affairs*, I, 145–46, and Proctor's account of his journey and his correspondence with Gordon, commandant at Niagara, are printed in *ASP, Indian Affairs*, I, 149–65.

5. On October 9, 1792, a deputation from the western tribes had announced to Simcoe their willingness to meet the representatives of the United States and requested that the British furnish the provisions for the meeting (*Simcoe Papers*, I, 229). Simcoe assured the Indians of the continued "assistance which has ever been afforded you, by the King your Father, & the provisions which you request shall be forwarded to Lower Sandusky" (*Simcoe Papers*, I, 231).

6. The proceedings of the council at the Auglaize are printed in *Simcoe Papers*, I, 218–29. An account of the Buffalo Creek council, dated November 13, 1792, may be found in *Simcoe Papers*, I, 256–60. A somewhat different version, dated November 16, 1792, is printed in *ASP, Indian Affairs*, I, 323–24. See also "Conversation with George Hammond," November 22, 1792, note 4.

fatigued, I wrote you several letters with respect to the supplies.[7]

I stated that my instructions did not fully authorize me to contract with Citizens of the United States to have the supplies furnished from the states. The instructions in fact did not give me that authority. But before I left Canadagua, I re-examined my power of attorney and found sufficient Authority in that for the purpose.

I therefore consulted with Genl. Chapin,[8] and it was his opinion that all the supplies could not be furnished in upper Canada. He recommended a Colo Taylor of that place, with whom I was well acquainted, as the most suitable person to contract with.

I applied to Colo. Taylor, and he with two of the Genls sons were willing to contract for the whole of the supplies. The Genl. engaged to Guarantee the contract on their part. We therefore made a memorandum of the terms of the contract, provided that Governor Simcoe would open the communication, and with this further provision, that I could not make a more advantageous contract in upper Canada.

Colo Taylor has accompanied me, with a view, if the contract had been made absolute, immediately to begin the operation.

A complete ration by this contract would have cost the United States, delivered at the place of treaty about fourteen Cents.

Mr. Hamilton,[9] the most respectable merchant in this place would have been concerned in the contract, as a part of the supplies could have better been supplied here than from the States.

As the Governor is absent and I can be of no use here, I have determined to return to Canadagua again and there wait for further instructions.

I should likewise have enclosed to you the proceedings of the Councils I have refered to, but I have not time to make out another set of Copies.

7. Letters not found.
8. Israel Chapin, a native of Grafton, Massachusetts, had served as a brigadier general in the Massachusetts militia during the American Revolution. In 1789 he was a member of the group that negotiated the Phelps-Gorham purchase in western New York, and in the same year he settled at Canandaigua, New York. In 1793 he was United States agent to the Six Nations.
9. Robert Hamilton was a merchant at Niagara and a member of the Legislative Council for the Province of Upper Canada.

The Secretary at War will doubtless communicate their contents to you, and likewise the informations I have given him relating to the treaty.[10]

During my short stay here, I have received every possible civility & respect, from the Governor his officers, and the Gentlemen of the place.

With every consideration of respect, I am your most obedt. servt.   William Hull

Secretary of Treasury

P.S. Since writing the above, I have considered whether under all circumstances, it is not most adviseable for me to remain at this place untill I receive further instructions. If I do not remain here, I shall not proceed further than Genl. Chapins. I am &c.   Wm. Hull

10. On February 24 the President submitted to the cabinet the documents which Hull sent to Knox. See Washington to H, Jefferson, Knox, and Randolph, February 24, 1793, note 3.

From Charles Lee

Collectors Office, Alexandria [Virginia] 7th. Febry 1793.

Sir!

In answer to your letter of the 31st. of last month[1] I am to inform you, that there were in the mail as I suppose at the time of the robbery on the 28th. of last month[2] a paid Treasury Draft of 1000 dollars, cancelled and receipted in the usual manner, a more description of which is contained in the annexed copy of the receipt now in this office; also a weekly return from my Office, a duplicate whereof is now enclosed.[3] I know of no other papers or documents sent by me, that were probably in that mail.

I am with respectfull consideration Your most Obedt. hum. Servt.   Charles Lee, Collector

Copy, RG 56, Letters to and from the Collector at Alexandria, National Archives.

1. Letter not found.

2. On January 28 the mail to Philadelphia "from the Southward" had been robbed "soon after it left Baltimore" ([Philadelphia] *Gazette of the United States,* January 30, 1793).

3. A copy of this receipt, signed "Hartshorne & Donaldson" and dated January 19, 1793, appears at the bottom of this letter.

To Alexander Dallas

Treasury Department
February 8. 1793

Sir

It is regretted that the pressing business of this Department has not till this time permitted a reply to the questions stated in Mr. Gallatin's letter of the 14th: of January respecting the new loan certificates of the State of Pennsylvania.[1]

It has been the uniform construction of the act making provision for the debt of the United States, that to render any certificates receivable on the loan, it was not only necessary that they should have been issued for services or supplies towards the prosecution of the late war; but also, that they should at the time of being subscribed be recognized by the existing laws of the States as *evidences of debts by them respectively owing.*[2]

It was not, till lately understood, that any doubts were entertained whether the new loan certificates were in fact debts due by the State of Pennsylvania, in every sense necessary to bring them within the meaning of the act of Congress; it is certain, that no such doubts were suggested to the Treasury.

The Commissioner of loans was accordingly advised in June 1791, that the certificates which had been received of the State in lieu of certificates of the United States were receivable on loan, though at the same time he was instructed, with a view to future convenience, to use his endeavours with the holders, to exchange them with the State.[3]

In consequence of an explanation which was rendered necessary by the provisions contained in the 18th. section of the act making provision for the debt of the United States, it appeared, that none of the new loan certificates of Pennsylvania had been subscribed to the loan of the United States—that only the sum of about forty thousand pounds of said certificates remained to be exchanged, and that adequate and final arrangements had been made for exchanging the remainder by the State.[4]

This being the state of the case, it became necessary to determine, whether the payment of interest on the assumed debt of Pennsylvania was to remain suspended, until a sum in certificates of the United States, equal to the amount of new loan certificates remaining unexchanged, was surrendered to the Treasury.

As the provision in the law was expressly designed to prevent interest from being twice paid on what originally constituted but one debt; an event which could not in this case happen; as it appeared inconsistent with equity, that the State should be required to surrender the certificates which were the sole consideration for which they had become indebted to their citizens, when no equivalent had been stipulated therefor by the United States; as such a surrender would defeat the arrangements made by the State, for effecting a reexchange of the outstanding certificates, and a just settlement with their Creditors—as a suspension of the payment of interest on the assumed debt of Pennsylvania, would prove highly injurious to the rights of Individuals. And lastly, as it appeared to me, that the terms and intent of the law could be satisfied without assuming a construction liable to the strong objections before stated, I could not hesitate to determine, that a surrender on the part of the State was not necessary.

I have been the more explicit in my reply to the first question proposed by Mr. Gallatin, as it appears to be the most important; and for the purpose of evincing, that as the case was then presented, no doubt was, or could be entertained, that the new loan certificates might have been subscribed to the loan of the United States. If however the new loan certificates are not by the laws of Pennsylvania to be considered as *debts*, but merely as receipts for certificates of the United States, which may be demanded at pleasure—then according to the general rule of construction, the new loan certificates of the State will not be considered as receivable on loan to the United States, and will be restored to the Subscribers.

As the engagements of the United States appear to be somewhat implicated in a right decision of this question, I shall take measures to have the case stated to the Attorney General of the United States, for his opinion. At the same time I suggest the expediency of some measures being taken on the part of the Government of the State, for expressing their sense, respecting the certificates in question.[5]

[With great consideration and esteem   I have the honor to be
Sir   Your obedient servant] [6]   Alexander Hamilton

Alexander J Dallas Esqr.
Secretary of the
Commonwealth of Pennsylvania.

LS, Historical Society of Pennsylvania, Philadelphia; two copies, Division of
Public Records, Pennsylvania Historical and Museum Commission, Harrisburg.
    1. See Dallas to H, January 15, 1793, which also includes Albert Gallatin's
letter of January 14, 1793, to Dallas.
    2. H is referring to Section 18 of this act (1 *Stat.* 144 [August 4, 1790]). For
this section, see Dallas to H, January 15, 1793, note 7.
    3. See "Treasury Department Circular to the Commissioners of Loans," June
6, 1791, and H to Thomas Smith, June 8, 1791.
    4. See Thomas Mifflin to H, December 27, 1791, note 1.
    5. A copy of H's letter to Dallas was enclosed in a letter that Dallas wrote to
Albert Gallatin on February 11, 1793, which reads in part as follows: "If you
think I can be of any further service to your enquiries, I beg you to suggest
the points, and to rely on a prompt and chearful attendance. In the mean time,
permit me to request, that you will pay particular attention to that part of Mr.
Hamilton's letter, which invites a declaration of the sentiments of the government, respecting the New-Loan Certificates" (Hogan, *Pennsylvania State Trials,*
79).
    6. The bracketed material is in the handwriting of H.

From Tobias Lear [1]

United States 8 Febry. 1793.

By the President's command T. Lear has the honor to transmit to
the Secretary of the Treasury, a letter from the Minister of France
to the Secretary of State, requesting to be furnished with a certain
sum by the Government of the United States; on account of the
Debt owing to France, to be laid out for provisions in the United
States to be sent to France; and to desire that the Secretary will,
tomorrow morning, give the President his opinion on the practicability of complying with the Minister's request.[2]

Tobias Lear.
S. P. U. S.

LC, George Washington Papers, Library of Congress.
    1. Lear was George Washington's secretary.
    2. Early in February, 1793, Jean Baptiste de Ternant, the French Minister to
the United States, received instructions dated September 19, 1792, from Pierre
Henri Hélène Marie Lebrun-Tondu, French Minister for Foreign Affairs,
ordering him to negotiate with the United States Government for supplies for

France. Ternant was instructed to obtain three million livres applicable to the debt owed France by the United States for the purchase of supplies of grain, flour, and salted beef to alleviate the serious shortage of these commodities in France (Ternant to Lebrun, February 13, 1793 [Turner, "Correspondence of French Ministers," 170–76]). On February 8, 1793, Ternant relayed these instructions to Thomas Jefferson, requested the three million livres, and stressed that this "mode of payment would procure to America a vent for superfluous commodities, useful to it's commerce as well as to it's agriculture & at the same time, an occasion of keeping up practical offices of friendship between two nations which the cause of liberty first united" (translation, letterpress copy, in the handwriting of Jefferson, Thomas Jefferson Papers, Library of Congress). According to JPP, on February 9 "The Secretary of the Treasury waited upon the President, this morning, agreeably to desire, and informed him that the practicability of complying with the request of the Minister of France could not be determined upon until the appropriation bill, now before the Senate, should be passed, which it was expected would be acted upon this day. The Secretary of State was therefore desired to inform the Minister of France, that an answer should be given in a few days on the subject of his letter" (JPP, 37).

While waiting for a decision on his request for three million livres, Ternant asked for an emergency advance of one hundred thousand dollars from the United States Treasury so that immediate shipments of supplies for France could be arranged (Ternant to Lebrun, February 13, 1793 [Turner, "Correspondence of French Ministers," 170–76]). On February 14 Jefferson informed Ternant: "It will require some few days yet to estimate the probable calls which may come on the treasury, and the means of answering them; till which is done a final answer can not be given to your application for the three millions of livres but in the mean time that your purchases of provision may be begun, arrangements may be made with the Secretary of the Treasury for the immediate payment of one hundred thousand dollars on account of our debt to France" (ALS, letterpress copy, Thomas Jefferson Papers, Library of Congress).

Report on Foreign Loans [1]

Treasury Department,
February, 13th. 1793.
[Communicated on February 13, 1793] [2]

[To the Speaker of the House of Representatives]
Sir,

In obedience to an Order of the President of the United States, founded upon the requests contained in two resolutions of the House

Copy, RG 233, Reports of the Treasury Department, 1792–1793, Vol. III, National Archives.

1. For background to this document, see the introductory note to "Report on the Balance of All Unapplied Revenues at the End of the Year 1792 and on All Unapplied Monies Which May Have Been Obtained by the Several Loans Authorized by Law," February 4, 1793.

2. *Journal of the House,* I, 702.

of Representatives, of the 23d of January last,[3] I have the honor to lay before the House—

I. The several papers, numbered I, II, III, IV,[4] being copies of the authorities, under which, loans have been negociated, pursuant to the Acts of the 4th. and 12th. of August 1790.

II. Sundry letters,[5] as per list at foot, from the Secretary of the Treasury to William Short, esquire, and to Wilhem and J: Willinks, N: and J: Van Staphorst and Hubbard, being copies of the authorities respecting the application of the monies borrowed.

III. Statement A, shewing the names of the persons, by whom, and to whom, the respective payments of the French debt have been made in Europe, specifying the dates of the respective payments, and the sums. With regard to the precise dates of the respective draughts, which may have been drawn, or Orders which may have been given by Mr. Short to our Bankers, for making these payments, they cannot be furnished, not being known at the Treasury. It is, however, to be inferred from the correspondence and circumstances, that they preceded, but a short time, the respective payments, to which they related.

Statement B, shewing by whom the payments have been made, on account of the Dutch loans, the dates and the sums. As to the persons, to whom the payments were made, no specification is practicable,

3. For these resolutions, see the introductory note to "Report on the Balance of All Unapplied Revenues at the End of the Year 1792 and on All Unapplied Monies Which May Have Been Obtained by the Several Loans Authorized by Law," February 4, 1793.

4. These documents, which are printed in these volumes under the dates on which they were written, are:
I. George Washington to H, August 28, 1790.
II. Washington to H, August 28, 1790.
III. Commission to Willink, Van Staphorst, and Hubbard, August 28, 1790. This document is printed as an enclosure to H to Willink, Van Staphorst, and Hubbard, August 28, 1790.
IV. Commission to William Short. This document is printed as an enclosure to H to Short, September 1, 1790.

5. The "sundry letters" are: Willink, Van Staphorst, and Hubbard to H, January 25, 1790; H to Willink, Van Staphorst, and Hubbard, April 7, July 17, August 28, and November 29, 1790, March 12, 18, June 30, and October 31, 1791, January 27, April 17, July 16, 26, September 19, October 16, November 26, and December 31, 1792; H to Short, August 29 and September 1, 1790, April 13, May 9, 24, November 1, 30, 1791, January 28, March 5, April 2, 10, June 30, July 25, September 13, October 16, November 26, and December 31, 1792. These letters are printed under the dates on which they were written.

these being the numerous subscribers to the several loans, their agents or assignees. It has never been considered, either, under the former or present government, as interesting to the Treasury, to know who those individuals were. Indeed, by the transfers always going on, they are continually changing. This demand for a communication of their names would have been unprecedented, and the disclosure, from time to time, would been attended with a great deal of useless, but expensive trouble.

The Statement desired, in reference to the Spanish debt,[6] cannot be furnished. In a note upon Statement, No. I, of my late report concerning foreign loans,[7] it is mentioned, "that advice had been received, that the payment of this debt was going on, though it had not been completed." This appears by letters from Mr. Short, now before the Senate, dated August 30th. and October 9th. and 22d.[8] No advice of the completion of the payment has since been received. All, that is known, is, that our Bankers were procuring Bills under orders from Mr. Short, for the purpose of remitting to Spain the sum necessary to discharge her debt.

There will be seen a difference in the Statement now presented and No. I, of my late report concerning foreign loans, as to the date of the last payment to France. In one, the 9th. of August is mentioned; in the other, the 6th. of September. The fact is, that it had its inception, some time in August, but was not perfected till the sixth of September. Mr. Morris,[9] who had been charged by Mr. Short, with endeavoring to adjust with the French Treasury, the rule, by which, the payments that had been and might be made, should be liquidated into livres, having regard to certain equitable considerations, made an arrangement with it provisionally, for the

6. The second resolution of January 23, 1793, directed the President to have information sent to the House of Representatives concerning the payment of the Spanish debt. For a description of this debt, see H to Short, September 1, 1790, note 19; Joseph Nourse to H, October 9, 1792; Short to H, February 25, 1793, note 13.

7. "Report on Foreign Loans," January 3, 1793.

8. H had transmitted these letters to the Senate on February 5, 1793. They are printed in these volumes under the dates on which they were written. The Short letter to which H is referring is dated October 27, 1792, rather than October 22.

9. Gouverneur Morris had arrived in Paris in May, 1792, to assume the duties of United States Minister, replacing William Short who, while holding the diplomatic rank of chargé d'affaires in Paris, had acted as United States Minister.

payment of 1,641,250* florins, and wrote to Mr. Short, requesting that he would direct the payment to be completed. There appear to have been two letters from Mr. Morris, on the subject, one dated the 6th, the other, the 9th of August.[10] But Mr. Short, for reasons, which he explains in his correspondence now before the Senate, did not consummate the payment, till the sixth of September. One Statement has reference to the beginning, the other, to the conclusion of the affair.

I am instructed by the President to observe, that there are some circumstances in the communications now made, which would render a public perusal of them not without inconvenience. With perfect respect, I have the honor, to be, Sir,

Your most obedient and most humble Servant

Alexander Hamilton
Secretary of the Treasury.

The Honorable The Speaker,
of the House of Representatives.

Statement A.

Statement shewing the dates and sums of the respective payments which have been made on account of the Debt due to France out of the Dutch and Antwerp Loans—and by whom and to whom the monies were remitted or paid.

		Livres tournois. s. d.	Florins. st:
1790 Decemr. 3.	Remitted by Wm. and J: Willink, N. and Jacob Van Staphorst and Hubbard of Amsterdam, to Monsr. du Fresne,	3.611.950.	1.500.104.
1791, June 10th.	Director of the royal treasury of France, by order of Wm. Short Esquire	2.696.629. 4	1.005.000.

* 1,625,000 Banco.

10. Both letters, as well as further correspondence between Short and Morris relating to this payment on the French debt, are printed as enclosures to Morris to H, September 25, 1792.

August 11th:			941.176. 9	358.187.10
Septemr. 12th:			642.896. 9. 9.	238.233. 6.
15th.			1.080.874.12. 6.	400.531.12.
22d:	Remitted by the same,		1.457.734.15. 4.	539.414.10.
	to the Commissioner of		907.280.15. 2.	335.726.14.
29th	the national treasury at		616.212.14. 7.	229.500.15.
October, 3d.	Paris, by order of William		220.680.10.	81.957.10.
6th:	Short Esquire.		806.420. 3. 3.	300.951. 9
13th:			1.139.053.14. 1.	429.550.16.
20th:			811.154. 2. 8.	302.291. 4
24th:			487.692. 2. 8.	108.608.13.

Do, by the same to Mr. Garat, Cashier of the national treasury at Paris, by order of William Short Esquire.   1.540.909. 2.   567.825.

Remitted from Antwerp by Mr. de Wolf to the national treasury at Paris, by order of William Short.

270.500.	
338.990.	9.
101.700.	
312.004. 6. 6.	
308.441. 6.	

from January to March — Payments made by Mr. De Wolf, to J. Broeta at Antwerp, by order of the Commissioners of the national treasury of France . .   4.581.413.15. 1.

from April 1st. to June 4th: — Do.   Do.   843.925.10. 6.

6.756.974.18.10.*   1.968.000.

Do, by Wm. and J. Willink. N. and Jacob Van Staphorst, and Hubbard, of Amsterdam, to Messrs. Hogguer, Grand and Company, bankers for the Commissioners of the national treasury of France, by order of William Short Esquire

6.000.000.   1.641.250.

29.717.639.13.10.   10.073.043. 8.

Treasury Department,
February 13, 1793.

Alexander Hamilton
Secretary of the Treasury.

* The amount of Livres here stated, exceeds somewhat that which was stated in No. I, of my last report,[11] It will be observed, that it was then mentioned, that the details of this transaction were wanting. They have since been received, and correspond with the present Statement. The difference arises from the real rates of exchange, at the times of the respective payments having been different from what was assumed by analogy, as a rule of computation.

11. "Report on Foreign Loans," January 3, 1793.

Statement B.

Statement, shewing the respective payments which have been made by William and John Willink, Nicholaas and Jacob Van Staphorst and Hubbard, in Amsterdam, to individuals, upon the several loans made in Holland, on account of the United States.

1791.			Florins. st. d
Febry. 1: Payment of 54 premiums drawn in the lottery, agreeably to the terms of contract, of the 4 per cent loan of 2.000.000. florins[12]	(a)		90.000.
Interest due this date on the said loan, at 4 per cent	(a)		80.000.
Ditto on the loan of 3.000.000 florins, commencing the 1st February 1790,[13] at 5 per cent	(b)		119.783. 6.
June. 1: Ditto on the loans of 7.000.000 florins at 5 per cent[14]	(a)		350.000.
1792 Febry. 1: Ditto on the loan of 2.000.000 florins at 4 per cent	(a)		80.000.
Ditto on the loan of 3.000.000 florins, commencing on the 1st. of February 1791, at 5 per cent			150.000.
Mar: 1st: Ditto on the loan of 2.500.000 florins, commencing on the 1st March 1791,[15] at 5 per cent	(b)		119.879. 4
June 1st: Ditto on the loans of 7.000.000 florins at 5 per cent	(a)		350.000.
Sept. 1st. Ditto on the loan of 6.000.000 florins, commencing on the 1st. September 1791,[16] at 5 per cent	(b)		294.566.13
Decr. 1st. Ditto on the loan of 2.050.000 florins,[17] made at Antwerp, at 4½ per cent			92.250.
1793. Janry. 1st. Ditto on the loan of 3.000.000 florins, commencing on the 1st. January 1792,[18] at 4 per cent	(b)		106.709.19. 8.
			1.833.189. 2. 8.

Note: (a) These loans were negociated under the late Government.

(b) The interest payable upon each of these loans, at the expiration of the first year, was not due upon the entire capital borrowed, but in proportion to the time, in which the loans were completed.

The sum of 1.833.189 florins, 2 Stivres and 8 deniers, here stated, is the same as reported to the House by the Secretary, on the 3d. instant,[19] in the Statement No. I.

Alexander Hamilton,
Secretary of the Treasury

Treasury Department,
February 13th. 1793.

Special reasons for drawing for the last sum of one million two hundred and thirty seven thousand five hundred guilders.[20]

Mr. Short, from his own view of the situation of French affairs, had concluded to suspend further payments in consequence of the Revolution of the 10th of August last, as appears by his letter of the 30th of that month, in possession of the Senate. This letter contains the following passage "It is impossible to say how long the position of affairs will last. There will probably be several changes before a permanent order is established. This of course will occasion a suspension in our payments." And in addition to this, he expresses in another place a wish to receive orders from hence for the disposition of the monies in hand.

The propriety of a suspension of payments under the *then* existing circumstances, was considered and admitted here by the executive; and a correspondent intimation was given both to Mr. Morris and Mr. Short.[21]

It remained for the Secretary of the Treasury to decide pursuant to the general discretion vested in him, what should be done with

---

12. The Holland loan of 1784. For a description of this loan, see H to Short, September 1, 1790, note 22.

13. The Holland loan of 1790. For a description of this loan, see H to Willink, Van Staphorst, and Hubbard, November 29, 1790, note 1. Although this loan was not formally authorized by the United States until August, 1790, the Dutch bankers had opened negotiations for it in January, 1790. See Willink, Van Staphorst, and Hubbard to H, January 25, 1790; H to Willink, Van Staphorst, and Hubbard, August 28, 1790.

14. This is a reference to the Holland loans of 1782, 1787, and 1788. For descriptions of these loans, see Willink, Van Staphorst, and Hubbard to H, January 25, 1790, note 15, and H to Short, September 1, 1790, notes 24 and 25.

15. The Holland loan of March, 1791. For a description of this loan, see Short to H, February 17, 1791.

16. The Holland loan of September, 1791. For a description of this loan, see Short to H, August 31, 1791.

17. The Antwerp loan of 1791. For a description of this loan, see Short to H, November 8, 1791, note 4, and November 12, 1791.

18. The Holland loan of December, 1791. For a description of this loan, see Short to H, December 23, 28, 1791.

19. "Report on Foreign Loans," January 3, 1793.

20. The remainder of this report was appended as a note to the copy of H's letter to Short of November 26, 1792. The letter was submitted to the House of Representatives with this report.

21. See H to Short, October 1–15, 1792. The instructions to Morris, sent by Thomas Jefferson on October 15, 1792, are printed in Ford, *Writings of Jefferson*, VI, 120–21.

regard to the monies undisposed of in the hands of our Bankers. It had so happened that they had already been a considerable time unemployed, at the expense of the United States. In the language of Mr. Short, it was impossible to say how long that position of affairs, which had induced the suspension of payment would last [22]—and every appearance at that time indicated that it would be of no inconsiderable duration. It might last six months, a year, or a much longer term.

When it would cease was altogether uncertain, but it was very certain, that the leaving the money unemployed would occasion further loss and involve some risk to the United States—as must always be the case in a degree when large sums are left long in the hands of private individuals engaged in extensive money operations.

Had it been left as it was, and had any accident happened, or had a long period elapsed before it could have been prudently applied, as was originally intended, it must have been very difficult to have justified the measure. This delay and loss which had been incurred served to enforce the motives which pleaded for putting the money in a train to be as speedily as possible useful. The past was calculated to inspire an anxiety that no further delay or loss should ensue.

A train of events, in favor of the change which took place, more rapidly prosperous than could reasonably have been expected, cannot impeach the prudence of having contemplated as possible a different course of things, and of having elected to proceed in a manner in which there was no doubt that the safety and interest of the United States would be consulted. This was evidently to put the money on hand in a train to be employed at home as early as might be; except so much of it as was wanted in Europe for other purposes, as for the payment to Spain &c.

This course was accordingly concluded upon. The remaining difficulty was how to effect it with security and advantage. It happened that there were some expressions in Mr. Shorts letter which appeared to me to render it not perfectly certain, though highly probable that orders from hence would in every event be waited for.

The unconditional sale of Bills to individuals in such a situation would have been unsafe and imprudent, besides that, a considerable fall of exchange at the moment, with a probability of a still greater fall interfered with an advantageous sale. It was known that the bank

22. See Short to H, August 30, 1792.

of the United States had contemplated a plan for regulating foreign exchanges so as to obviate the inconveniences to trade of sudden and violent fluctuations, and at the same time to check the exportation of specie, from momentary causes, occasioning a great rise in exchange.

It occurred that the Bank might be disposed to possess itself of a fund in Europe to begin the operation, and might be willing with this view to purchase and remit Bills *upon its own account*, with an understanding, that in case the fund upon which the Bills were drawn should happen to be applied otherwise, no inconvenience to the public was to ensue from their non-payment.

A proposition to this effect was made to the Bank and after consideration accepted. Bills for 1,237,500. guilders, equal at the rate of 36⁴⁄₁₁ nineteeths of a dollar, to 500,000 dollars were directed to be furnished which, if paid, are on the 1st of April next, to pass to the credit of the United States; unless provision by law shall be made, in the mean time, to convert that sum into a payment to the Bank.[23]

This disposition will be to the government equivalent to a sale for cash. It is now known that the fund will remain to answer the Bills— and as the punctual payment by the bank at the time may be absolutely relied upon, the public monies on hand or coming in, destined for the next quarterly payments, may be applied to any purpose to which the proceeds of the bills if received would be applicable, in the full assurance of finding a substitute in that fund at the moment it may be necessary.

It is however to be observed that prior to the receipt of Mr. Shorts letter of the 30th of August, and upon the arrival of the intelligence of the event of the 10th of that month, and those which shortly succeeded—I had entertained an opinion that a suspension of payments to France was adviseable 'till further light should be thrown upon the situation and prospects, and had expressed that opinion to Mr. Short.[24] The change that had taken place, was so great, and apparently attended with so much hazard; the circumstances that had accompanied it, were, in several respects, so inauspicious, as, in my then view, to render the issue extremely precarious. I reflected that should a reverse of fortune follow, not only the validity of

23. For a discussion of this transaction, see "Report on the Balance of All Unapplied Revenues at the End of the Year 1792 and on All Unapplied Monies Which May Have Been Obtained by the Several Loans Authorized by Law," February 4, 1793 (*Hamilton Papers*, XIII, 552).
24. H to Short, October 1–15, 1792.

further payments might be called in question; but questions of a still more delicate nature might be raised; especially as those payments would be anticipations of sums not yet due. The making of them, therefore, might be construed into taking part with the new order of things, and might not only commit the United States, with regard to the powers at War with France, but might interrupt the good understanding between them and France herself. Those who should possess the power in case of the restoration of the constitution just overturned, could not fail to take ill a voluntary payment of sums not due to those by whom it had been overturned. Such were the reflections that presented themselves upon the occasion and that induced the communication of the opinion which has been mentioned.

It need only be added, that at the time of *taking this step, the President was* absent from the seat of government—And it became my duty to act provisionally according to the best dictate of my judgment.

Report Relative to the Loans Negotiated Under the Acts of the Fourth and Twelfth of August, 1790 [1]

Treasury Department. [February 13–14, 1793]
[Communicated to the House on February 13, 1793 [2]
Communicated to the Senate on February 18, 1793] [3]

[To the Speaker of the House of Representatives and the President of the Senate]
Sir,

The next most important articles of enquiry, involved in the resolutions of the House of Representatives of the 23d of January last,[4]

Copy, RG 233, Reports of the Treasury Department, 1792–1793, Vol. III, National Archives; copy, RG 46, Second Congress, 1791–1793, Reports of the Secretary of the Treasury, National Archives.

1. For background to this report, see the introductory note to "Report on the Balance of All Unapplied Revenues at the End of the Year 1792 and on All Unapplied Monies Which May Have Been Obtained by the Several Loans Authorized by Law," February 4, 1793.

2. *Annals of Congress,* III, 875.

3. *Annals of Congress,* III, 650. The copy of this report which was sent to the Senate is dated February 14, 1793. The covering letter, dated February 18, may be found in RG 46, Second Congress, 1791–1793, Reports of the Secretary of the Treasury, National Archives.

4. For these resolutions, see the introductory note to "Report on the Balance of All Unapplied Revenues at the End of the Year 1792 and on All Unapplied

and in the observations, which have been [made] respecting the conduct of this department, relates to the loans which have been negociated under the Acts of the fourth and twelfth of August, one thousand seven hundred and ninety.[5]

The papers, which have been transmitted to the House, by order of the President, disclose the following particulars.

1st. That the immediate superintendance of the business of the loans was confided to the department of the Treasury, being naturally connected with it. This trust, besides the original instructions for regulating the execution of it, which have been communicated,[6] was, of course, subject to such directions, from time to time, as the President should think fit to give, or as occasions should require. A considerable latitude of discretion, nevertheless, from the very nature of the case, attended it; so as justly to leave on the head of this department, a complete responsibility in all instances, where special exceptions do not appear.

2d. That the first loan, which was obtained,[7] was undertaken and completed by the agency of Wilhem and Jan Willink, and Nicholaas and Jacob Van Staphorst and Hubbard, who, both under the former and present government, have been, and are the Bankers of the United States at Amsterdam.

3d. That with the single exception of the first loan, William Short, Esquire, then Charge des Affairs at the Court of France, now resident Minister at the Hague, was constituted the sole Agent of this department, for carrying into effect, the powers confided to it, with this qualification only, that if any negociation with a Prince of State, to whom any part of the debt to be discharged by the loans was due, shoud be requisite—the same was to be carried on through the person, who in capacity of Minister, Charge des affairs, or otherwise, then was, or thereafter might be charged with transacting the affairs of the United States, with such Prince or State.

Monies Which May Have Been Obtained by the Several Loans Authorized by Law," February 4, 1793.

5. "An Act making provision for the (payment of the) Debt of the United States" (1 *Stat.* 138–44 [August 4, 1790]) and "An Act making Provision for the Reduction of the Public Debt" (1 *Stat.* 186–87 [August 12, 1790]).

6. See George Washington to H, August 28, 1790. A copy of this letter was enclosed in H's "Report on Foreign Loans," February 13, 1793.

7. The Holland loan of 1790. For a description of this loan, see H to Willink, Van Staphorst, and Hubbard, November 29, 1790, note 1. See also Willink, Van Staphorst, and Hubbard to H, January 25, 1790.

4th. That all payments, which have been made out of the proceeds of the loans, have been made by the immediate and special order of Mr. Short, except those, upon the Bills of the Treasurer for the monies drawn to this country, and those to the money lenders in Holland; which were made in course by our bankers, at the periods they respectively became due. This consequently embraces all the payments to France; the very last of which, though agreed for by Mr. Morris, in consequence of his having been employed for a special purpose by Mr. Short, was not and could not be completed, but by the same immediate and special direction of Mr. Short.[8]

It moreover appears, from the same papers, and more fully from the correspondence at large, now before the Senate,[9] that except in the particular instance, which has been just stated, with regard to Mr. Morris, there has been no other agency in the whole business, than that of Mr. Short, and of the Bankers at Antwerp and Amsterdam, whom he necessarily employed, as instruments in the negociations with the money lenders, and in the receipt and disbursement of the monies borrowed. These, as already mentioned, were at Amsterdam, the two Houses of Wilhem and Jan Willink, and of Nicholaas and Jacob Van Staphorst and Hubbard; at Antwerp, a Mr. G: De Wolf [10] was the Banker.

It may not be without its uses, to add, that the monies proceeding from the loans have constantly remained in the hands of the respective Bankers, till they have been paid over to the creditors; namely, the French treasury, or their bankers, the money-lenders or their representatives, the holders of the bills drawn from this country by the Treasurer. Neither Mr. Short, nor Mr. Morris has ever had possession of a single guilder. The latter indeed has never even had power over one, excepting merely a sum of 105.000 guilders, by letters of mine, dated the 13th September last, placed at his disposal for paying it at Paris, according to stipulation, the interest on the debt due to foreign Officers. The fact is, and it is so demonstrated

8. Despite the fact that Gouverneur Morris had replaced William Short as United States representative in Paris in May, 1792, Short remained in charge of the payments on the French debt. See H to Short, June 14, 1792. For information on the payment of the installment of the French debt due in August, 1792, see Short to H, September 25, 1792, and Morris to H, September 25, 1792.

9. "Report on Foreign Loans," February 5, 1793.

10. The Antwerp loan of 1791 was negotiated through Charles John Michael De Wolf. See Short to H, November 8, 1791, note 4, and November 12, 1791.

by the correspondence already referred to, that I never wrote a line to Mr. Morris, on the subject of the loans or their proceeds, but in reference to the case just mentioned, of the interest payable to foreign officers; in respect to which, local situation governed.

One more circumstance only is necessary to be noticed in this place, with a view to the elucidation intended: It is this—that the last payment, though originating prior to the change in the political position of France, of the 10th of August last, not having been con-summated till the 6th of September following, fell, of course, under the disposition of those then in possession of the power of the nation.

It could not but have been unexpected to me, that exception should be taken to the report lately made by me on the subject of foreign loans,[11] for the omission of details, which I did not, at the time, and do not yet conceive to have been called for, by the terms of the resolutions, upon which it was founded. The request, addressed to the President by those resolutions, was, that he would cause to be laid before the House, a particular account of the sums borrowed under his authority by the United States, the terms, on which each loan was obtained, the applications, which had been made of the monies, agreeably to appropriations, the balances, if any, which remained unapplied, specifying also, at what times interest com-menced, on the several sums obtained, and at what times, it was stopped by the several payments made. It was not natural to imagine that these expressions were designed to comprehend a specification of the precise authorities under which the loans were negociated, of the names of the persons, by whom they were negociated, of the particular place or places, where the balance unexpended, of the sums that had been drawn for to the United States, were deposited. Still less natural was it for me to anticipate surmises, which could give to such particulars, the shadow of importance. But, as animad-versions have attended the omission of those details, I ought to regard it as an admonition to me, to be more full and precise in my present communication; a motive, which co-operates with my desire, to throw all possible light upon the subject.[12]

11. "Report on Foreign Loans," January 3, 1793.

12. For an explanation of the contents of this paragraph, see the introductory note to "Report on the Balance of All Unapplied Revenues at the End of the Year 1792 and on All Unapplied Monies Which May Have Been Obtained by the Several Loans Authorized by Law," February 4, 1793.

The first general circumstance, which requires to be noticed and explained, after the particulars, that have been communicated, is this —That all the loans, which have been hitherto obtained, have been made under the authority of both Acts, without particular reference to either.

The idea originally entertained, was to conduct them on a different plan, founding each loan upon one, or other of the Acts; as will be seen by my letter of the 28th of August 1790, to our Bankers at Amsterdam;[13] at the same time, that it will appear, from the same letter, that the separation did not appear to me a matter of consequence, and that I anticipated the possibility of a difficulty in adhering to it, in the particular case. That difficulty proved, in the opinion of the Bankers, to be of sufficient moment, to render the arrangement contemplated, under the circumstances of the case, unadvisable; as they inform me in their answer to the above mentioned letter.[14]

But prior to the receipt of that answer, further enquiry and reflection had determined me to abandon my original idea as likely to produce embarrassment and inconvenience, both in the negociation of the loans, and in the application of their proceeds. It was accordingly concluded to let the loans proceed indiscriminately, upon both Acts.

These loans were to have reference to two purposes—first, the reimbursement of the foreign debt, second, the purchase of the domestic debt, at its market price.

There were weighty reasons for carrying on both these operations concurrently. The arrears to France had been a considerable time accumulating. It was, in every sense, proper, that a reimbursement of them should begin without delay, and desirable, for obvious reasons, that it should go on, without any very considerable chasms or intermissions. This manner of proceeding could not but have the fairest chance of being the most satisfactory and convenient to France; unless, indeed, the business were to have proceeded upon the principle of an entire postponement of the domestic object, to that of the reimbursement.

But very cogent reasons rendered this course not the most eligible.

13. H to Willink, Van Staphorst, and Hubbard, August 28, 1790.
14. Letter not found.

The early commencement of purchases of the debt was a matter of real and great importance.

It was important in two relations; as it regarded the advantages of the government, from redeeming a portion of the debt at low prices; and still more, as it regarded the savings to the country, from raising the price of stock on foreign purchasers; the beneficial influence upon the credit of the nation, abroad and at home, to be expected from a quick appreciation of the public obligations; the benefit to the public creditors in general, and to the most meritorious classes of them, in particular, which would result from the same cause; all which objects were suggested from the treasury, as motives to the provision respecting purchases, and are evidently contemplated in the preamble of the Act, which makes that provision.

Exclusive of the other advantages, which have been cited, and which are of a nature truly precious and important, that of preventing foreigners from acquiring the property of our citizens at a great under-value, is too obvious, not to be estimated, as it ought to be, at first sight. It cannot require argument, to shew how great an evil it was, that foreigners should be able to acquire, with nine or ten, that, for which the country would ultimately have to pay them twenty, with full interest, in the interval; nor how much it merited the attention of the government to prevent or lessen so serious an evil.

But the influence, which the purchases by the government may have had upon this event, may not be equally obvious. Price naturally keeps pace with competition and demand; whatever encreases the latter, necessarily tends to an augmentation of the former. Merely, then, as another purchaser, by adding to the competition and demand, the purchases of the government were calculated to influence a rise of price. But they had an effect, more than proportioned to their real extent. Imagination has much to do in all such questions, and in scarcely any thing, so much, as in what relates to public funds. Experience proves, that it is here exerted with uncommon effort. The appearance of the government, as a purchaser, has not failed to excite the expectation of a greater demand than was real, because the extent of the resources to be employed might be very great, and was unknown; which, by stimulating the zeal of those, who wanted to buy, lest the price should rise suddenly and considerably upon them, and, by encouraging those, who wanted to sell, under the hope of a better price, to hold back the commodity, has, in both ways, generally contributed to give a spring to the market. Prices once raised, when founded on intrinsic value, tend to maintain themselves; because those, who have given them, are, for the most part, interested in keeping them up. And every new impulse, which they receive, serves to carry them rapidly to their just level.

Those, who have been most attentive to the operation of the public purchases, will have the least doubt, that they had a material agency in accelerating the appreciation of the public stock.

An enquiry naturally arises here. Were the monies, which were drawn from Europe on account of the foreign loans, the instruments of the purchases, to which these beneficial effects are ascribed?

I answer, that these purchases are to be attributed to the instrumentality of that fund—that, had it not been for this resource, they could not have been made at the early periods, when most of them were made. The course of the transaction will be fully, and with more propriety, explained in another place.[15]

An attention to both objects—to the reimbursement to France, and to the purchase of the debt, rendered expedient, even, a subdivision of the first loan. Considerations of the moment seconded those of a general nature, to induce an immediate payment to that country. The loan had been undertaken, without previous authority from hence, with a view to such payment. This was known, and a correspondent expectation excited. The immediate situation of the French finances rendered a payment, at the particular juncture, more than ordinarily interesting. In such a state of things, there could be no hesitation, about applying a large part of the loan to that object. Another part of it was, of necessity, applied to the payment of the sums, that were falling due on the Dutch loans. And, it is presumed, that the reasons, which have been assigned, will appear to have been sufficiently powerful, to have dictated the drawing of a part of it to the United States.

15. "Report on the State of the Treasury at the Commencement of Each Quarter During the Years 1791 and 1792 and on the State of the Market in Regard to the Prices of Stock During the Same Years," February 19, 1793 (see *infra*, pp. 114–18).

Accordingly, a million and a half of the three millions borrowed were appropriated to France, something more than 800.000 guilders, were drawn for here, and the remainder of the loan was left to be disbursed in Holland.[16]

It shall not be concealed, though I am aware that the acknowledgement may be a subject of criticism, that the conduct, which was pursued, both with regard to this and to the succeeding loan, was, in some degree, influenced by a collateral consideration. The government had but just adopted a plan for the restoration of public credit. The periodical payment of interest was to commence on the 1st of April 1791.[17] A considerable part of the revenue, out of which the monies were to arise, was only to begin to accrue on the first of January preceding.[18] This revenue was liable to credit of four, six, and twelve months.[19]

How far its eventual product would answer expectation—how far the punctuality of payments could be relied upon, were points unascertained, and which required, to their ascertainment, much more experience, than had been obtained. In such a situation, it was not only natural, but necessary for an Administrator of the finances, to doubt—and, doubting, it was his duty to call, to the aid of the public credit, every auxiliary, which it was in his power to command. He was bound to reflect, that a failure in any stipulated payment would be fatal to the dawning credit of the country—to the reputation of the government just beginning to rise. That a wound inflicted upon either, at so early a stage, under all the circumstances of opposition to the Constitution, which had existed in the community, would have been deeply felt, and might have either not have admitted of a cure at all, or not till after a length of time, and a series of mischiefs—that it could not but be an important service rendered to the country, to ward off so great a misfortune, by the temporary

16. See H to Willink, Van Staphorst, and Hubbard, August 28, 1790, and H to Short, August 29, 1790.

17. See Section 8 of "An Act making provision for the (payment of the) Debt of the United States" (1 *Stat.* 141 [August 4, 1790]).

18. See Section 1 of "An Act making further provision for the payment of the debts of the United States" (1 *Stat.* 180–81 [August 10, 1790]).

19. See Section 41 of "An Act to provide more effectually for the collection of the duties imposed by law on goods, wares and merchandise imported into the United States, and on the tonnage of ships or vessels" (1 *Stat.* 168 [August 4, 1790]).

use of any extraordinary resource, which might be at hand, till time was given for more effectual provision.

If, in the course of such reflections, a doubt had occurred, about the strict regularity of what was contemplated, as a possible resort, a mind sufficiently alive to the public interest, and sufficiently firm in the pursuit of it, would have dismissed that doubt, as an obstacle, suggested by a pusillanimous caution, to the exercise of those higher motives, which ought ever to govern a man, invested with a great public trust. It would have occurred, that there was a reasonable ground to rely, that the necessity of the case, and the magnitude of the occasion, would insure a justification, and that if the contrary should happen, there remained still the consolation of having sacrificed personal interest and tranquility, no matter to what extent, to an important public interest, and of having avoided the humiliation, which would have been justly due to an opposite, and to a feeble conduct.

The disposition, which was resolved upon, with regard to the first loan, involved necessarily a decision of the point, that the loans might be placed on the joint foundation of both Acts. That loan having been undertaken, as already mentioned, without previous authority, and consequently without a particular eye to either act, it was probable that it would be found too late, to make an apportionment of one part of the sum borrowed, to one Act, of another part to the other Act. In that case, the distributive application of the fund to the different objects was to be relinquished, or the possibility was to be admitted, of the loan being left to stand upon the authority of both Acts. The same disposition of the first loan will also illustrate the convenience and expediency of the plan, which was finally adopted, that is, of placing the loans on the basis of both Acts.

The idea of a concurrent execution of both the objects, to which the loans were destined, could not conveniently have been pursued, upon the plan of a separation of the loans; which, to be effectual, would include the strict application of the proceeds of each, to the purposes of the particular Act, upon which it was founded.

Amsterdam was naturally looked to, as the great scene of the intended loans. There, as every where else, there is but a certain quantity of money floating in the market, from time to time, beyond the necessary demands of trade and industry, seeking for employment in loans. This quantity, of course, varies at different periods, from a variety of causes. Of the quantity at any time afloat, but a certain proportion can be commanded by any one borrowing power; owing to the competition of other borrowers, who have, each, their connections through their bankers, with different sets of undertakers and money-lenders. Nor is it always, that considerable loans can be had at any rate. There are certain seasons only, when they are practicable.

To have brought two loans upon the market, at one time, as an opportunity of borrowing offered, which must have been the case, in order to make provision for both the objects in question, if the principle of a separation of the loans had been adopted, would have been to exhibit to the money-lenders a very unusual appearance. With men, known to be much influenced by prejudice and habit, such an appearance could not have failed to prove a source of speculation and conjecture; and might have led to a confused idea, that the wants of the United States were excessive; a supposition, by no means calculated to promote their credit. It would, moreover, have been a departure from that simplicity of procedure, which, where numbers are concerned, is always of moment to a right conception of the business to be accomplished, and ought not to be abandoned, but for reasons of real utility and weight.

To have instituted the loans successively, founding each upon one or the other of the Acts, would have had a tendency to occasion longer intervals between the payments to France, than was desirable. The intervention of a loan for the purpose of purchases, would have created, of course, a very considerable chasm. It may be objected, that such chasms did happen, on the plan which was pursued. This is true in two instances; but the most material of the two proceeded from casualties foreign to the plan itself; which are detailed in the correspondence more than once alluded to.[20]

20. A delay in payments by the United States on the French debt had been caused by the desire of the French government to convert the payments into supplies for the relief of Santo Domingo after the insurrection of August, 1791. For an account of the advances on the French debt for this purpose, see the introductory note to George Latimer to H, January 2, 1793. A further delay arose out of the French financial and political situation following the depreciation of the French currency in 1791 and 1792 and the suspension of the King on August 10, 1792. See Short to H, November 22, December 1, 30, 1791, May 14, June 28, August 6, 30, September 25, October 9, 27, November 29, 1792; H to Short, September 2, 1791, July 25, October 1–15, November 5, 1792; Gouverneur Morris to H, September 25, 1792.

It is possible too, that a separation of the loans might have rendered it less easy to take advantage of a state of the market, favorable to their extension at a particular juncture. The loan to be brought on the market might relate to the purchase of the debt. The moment might be favorable to a more considerable loan, than was within the limits prescribed for that object, and the opportunity might slip before a second could be instituted. In this business, moments are often of importance, and are to be embraced with promptitude and dexterity.

Thus it appears, that in different ways, the negociation of the loans might have been embarrassed by their separation.

But the most obvious, if not the most serious of the inconveniencies, which would have attended it, respects the application of the sums borrowed. This could not then have been moulded, as the interest or policy of the government might dictate. A loan for the purchase of the debt might have been made under prospects, promising a ready and beneficial investment of it; but before the investment was made, a change of the market might render it ineligible—involving the alternative, either of a disadvantageous investment, or of leaving perhaps a large sum of money a long time unemployed. Such a state of things might have produced to the Banks an advantage, and to the government a loss, of magnitude sufficient to give color to a surmise, that the public interest had been sacrificed to the profit of those institutions. The contrary course has essentially avoided that evil; which in this and in other instances, would have been incident, in a far greater degree, to the modes of proceeding, contrasted with those that have been pursued, than has in reality attended them.

Or political considerations might have rendered it advisable to transfer the application of the fund from one object to the other.

Of this, the case of St. Domingo presents an example. It might have happened on the plan of separate loans, that there was no fund in hand but for the purchase of the debt. Then, on the principle of that plan, there would have been no fund in the disposition of the Executive, applicable to the other object, which would have embarrassed the performance of a duty towards a friendly power, and in a way, which included the positive advantage to the country of paying directly a part of its foreign debt, in its own productions.[21]

Such were the embarrassments avoided, and such the conveniences secured, by the plan of making the loans indiscriminately upon the authority of both Acts.

In the opposite plan, I can discern no counterbalancing advantage nor convenience.

Consequently, if both are equally legal, there can be no doubt, which of them ought to have been preferred.

If there be any want of legality in the plan, which has been pursued, I was not, at the time, and am not yet sensible of it.

I know of no rule, which renders it illegal in an agent, having from the same principal two authorities to borrow money, whether for one or different purposes, to unite the loans he may make, upon the foundation of both authorities: Provided the terms of them be consonant with both or either of his commissions. If the purposes are different, it will be incumbent upon him, to take care that the application of the monies borrowed makes the proper separation, and doing this he will have fulfilled his trust. To test this position, it seems only necessary to ask, whether the principal in such case would not be fully bound to the lenders?

In reflecting originally upon the regularity of the proceeding meditated, there was but one source of hestitation; the difference in the funds, upon which the loans were to rest. But the following reasoning satisfied the scruple: The pledging of particular funds is for the security of the lenders. If they are willing to wave the special security, by lending on the general credit of the government, or to dispense with the preference of one fund to another, where two are pledged, by lending indiscriminately on the credit of both, the one or the other circumstance must be alike indifferent to the government. The authority will have been well executed, to the extent necessary for public purposes, and if any thing remains unexecuted, it will be in enlargement, not in abridgement of the public rights. It is, however, presumed, that the practical construction in the present case will be, that the two funds pledged will constitute an aggregate, for the joint security of the monies borrowed upon both Acts.

21. See note 20.

The second general circumstance respecting the foreign loans, negociated under the Acts of the 4th and 12th of August, which requires attention, relates to the terms, on which they have been obtained. These, it appears, have been represented, as neither honorable nor advantageous.

The following facts, witnessed by the correspondence before the Senate, more than once referred to, and well known to all who have had opportunities of information, demonstrate, that the terms of those loans have been both honorable and advantageous.

1st. There is not one of them, which originated under the Acts, that was not effected upon conditions equally favorable with those attending the loans of the cotemporary borrowing powers of the most tried resources and best established credit, and more favorable than were obtained by some powers of great respectability.

2nd. The United States took a lead in the market, with regard to the subsequent reductions of interest; having had, either earlier, or more complete success, than any other borrowing power.

3d. From a rate of five per cent interest, and four and a half per cent charges, which marked the level of market, when they begun their loans, they, in the course of a single year, brought down the terms to four per cent interest, and five per cent charges; that is, from an interest on the nett sum received (including an indemnification for charges) of 5.5012, something more than five and a half per cent, to an interest on the like sum of 4.4951, something less than four and a half per cent.

When this state of things is applied to a government, only in the third year of its existence, and to a country, which had so recently emerged from a total derangement of its finances, it would seem impossible to deny, that the issue is not only honorable, but flattering; unless indeed, it can be denied, that a sound and vigorous state of credit is honorable to a nation.

I forbear a comparison between the loans of the present and of the former government of this country, because an immense disparity of circumstances would render it an improper one—further than to take notice of a very great error, which has been, upon some occasions, advanced. It has been alleged, to disparage the management under the present, that the loans of the former government, in a situation comparatively disadvantageous, have been effected upon equal terms; and, in proof of this, an appeal has been made to the loan of 2.000.000. of guilders, at four per cent, which is of the 9th of March 1784.[22]

Nothing can manifest, more clearly than this, the very precipitate and superficial views, with which, suggestions on important public subjects are sometimes made. The last four per cent loan, obtained under the existing laws, including charges, is a real four and a half per cent loan, or, more exactly, a 4.4951 per cent loan.[23] The four per cent loan of March 1784 is a real 6.6468 per cent loan. The difference, which exceeds two per cent, arises principally from extra-premiums and gratifications, which were allowed upon this loan, and which are unknown to the other.

Much praise, no doubt, is due to the exertions, which effected the loans under the former government. A superiority of merit shall readily be conceded to them, from the circumstances, under which they were made, and their signal utility in the revolution. But it is not necessary to their eulogium, to affirm, that they were made upon equal terms, with those of the loans lately obtained, or to deny the goodness of the terms of the latter. Truth will not justify the one or the other.

The facts, which have been stated, prove, that the terms of the loans are advantageous, as well as honorable. They are comparatively advantageous, because they are as moderate as other powers, in the best credit, have allowed; and they are absolutely advantageous, because the highest real, not nominal rate of interest, which has been given, does not exceed 5.5012, a fraction more than 5½ per cent, while the lowest real rate is 4.4951, a fraction less than 4½ per cent.

If the question, whether advantageous or not, be tested by the purposes, for which the loans have been made, the conclusion is equally in their favor. The payments on account of the foreign debt were an indispensible obligation. Unless it can be shewn, that they might have derived from another, and more advantageous source, it will follow, that it was the interest of the government, to avail itself

22. For a description of this loan, see H to Short, September 1, 1790, note 22.

23. This is a reference to the Holland loan of 1792. For a description of this loan, see Short to H, June 28, 1792, note 17.

of the resource which has been employed, because it was its duty to discharge its obligations.

It is sometimes urged, that foreign loans, for whatever purpose are pernicious, because they serve to drain the country of its specie for the payment of interest, and for the final reimbursement of the principal—that it would be preferable, for that reason, to procure loans at home, even at a higher rate of interest.

To this, several answers may be given, some of a special, others of a general nature.

In reference to the reimbursement of the foreign debt, it may be observed, that as a debt had already been incurred abroad, upon which, interest was payable, the contracting of new loans there for the reimbursement of that debt, would leave us, as to the demand for the exportation of our specie, just where we originally stood.

Moreover, if the money could have been borrowed at home, for that reimbursement, the remittance of it would have been ruinous to the country. The mere necessity of remitting could not alone have encreased the foreign demand for our commodities; so as to deduce from an extra-exportation of them, the requisite means of payment, and if our specie was to perform the office, the country would speedily have been exhausted, to a degree inconsistent with the support of its commerce and industry. The quantity of coin in the United States has never been considerable enough for such an operation.

But this very state of things would have rendered the procuring of the money from domestic resources impracticable. These, it may be safely affirmed, are to limited for extensive loans, of any considerable degree of permanency.

In the last place, The expedient of domestic loans would not prevent the evil, which is desired to be prevented. Foreigners would either, in the first instance, bring their monies to subscribe them to the loans, or they would afterwards purchase the stock arising from them; and in either case, they would equally draw away the money of the country, on account of their interest and principal. The only consequence of giving a disproportionate rate of interest for domestic loans would be, that our specie would be carried away so much the faster.

Experience having shewn, that nations sometimes pay more regard to their external than to their internal credit, this consideration co-operates, with reasons of convenience to induce monied men abroad, to be content with a lower rate of interest, stipulated to be paid in their own country, than if the place of payment be in another country; making even a greater difference, than is an equivalent for the expense and risk of obtaining remittances.

The clear inference from these observations is, that with regard to the reimbursement of the foreign debt, no other expedient than that of foreign loans, was practicable or eligible.

The utility of that part of the loans, which has reference to the purchase of the debt, has already been explained in certain views. So far as their agency has been hitherto concerned in that operation, it is a sufficient demonstration of the advantage of the measure, to state, that the sum invested in purchases up to the period of the last report to Congress,[24] has redeemed what is equal to an annuity of 6.15 per cent, including also the advantage of sinking a capital more than 50 per cent greater than the sum expended.

A valuable profit will arise from the investment of the sums on hand, either in a payment to the Bank, or in the purchase of Stock. The liberation of an annuity of six per cent can be secured—while upon a great part of the fund, which is to effect it, no more than 4½ per cent is payable, and less than 5½ upon the other part. The mean of these rates being 5 per cent, an annual saving of one per cent may be effect[ed], which, upon 2.000.000 of dollars, interest at 5 per cent, is equal to a capital or gross sum of 400.000 dollars; an item certainly of no inconsiderable consequence.

Against the advantages, which are claimed in favor of the loans, it is natural to place the loss of interest incident to the delays, which have attended their application to the purposes, for which they were obtained. This leads to an examination of the cases of delay, their causes, the circumstances, if any, which counterbalance them.

There are three instances of delay—one respecting the first loan,[25]

24. "Report of the Commissioners of the Sinking Fund," November 17, 1792. The enclosures to this report are printed in *ASP, Finance*, I, 163–71.

25. The Holland loan of 1790. For a description of this loan, see H to Willink, Van Staphorst, and Hubbard, November 29, 1790, note 1.

another, the second loan,[26] and a third, a part of the two last loans.[27]

The first loan, it will be seen, was not applied, till a considerable time after its commencement. It has been already intimated, that it was undertaken without previous authority from this country. The motives to the measure are detailed in a letter from our Bankers, of the 25th. of January 1790, a copy of which accompanies the communications herewith made by order of the President.[28] A regard to those motives led to an acceptance of the loan. Nor could it have been deemed an unfortunate circumstance, that such an auxiliary to the operations of the Treasury had been previously prepared.

The laws, authorising the loans, passed the 4th and 12th of August. As early as the 28th of that Month, the acceptance above mentioned was communicated, and the application of 1.500.000 flori[n]s, in a payment to France, directed. So far, no time was lost, more than could not have been avoided.

But the bills for the sum to be brought here were not drawn till some months after. This proceeded from an unwillingness to risk the public credit, by drawing before there was a certainty of funds to answer the drafts. It was not impossible, that the great delay, which had attended the passing the law for borrowing, might have led the Bankers to come to some arrangement with the money-lenders, for surrendering the monies paid in, and terminating the loan. Independent of this source of apprehension, they had expressed themselves, in their letter, communicating the step they had taken, to this effect. "To spare the United States all possible advance of interest, while the money shall remain unappropriated, we shall issue the recipisses, at the option of the buyers to take them so late as they please, on the expectation the three millions would be placed in a few months." This, though it announced an expectation that the monies would be paid in, in a few months, did not render the event

26. The Holland loan of March, 1791. For a description of this loan, see Short to H, February 17, 1791.

27. The Holland loan of December, 1791, and the Holland loan of 1792. For a description of the loan of December, 1791, see Short to H, December 23, 28, 1791. The Holland loan of 1792 is described in Short to H, June 28, 1792, note 17.

28. A copy of this letter to H from Willink, Van Staphorst, and Hubbard was included in "Report on Foreign Loans," February 13, 1793.

certain. And as the Bankers appeared, from that precaution, to have adverted to the idea of saving the United States an advance of interest, it was supposable that they might have found means still further to procrastinate the payments, or a considerable part of them, till they had received a confirmation of the loan. This policy would have been the more natural, as they risked the loss of interest themselves, if the transaction should not have been finally ratified.

Under such circumstances, I thought it most prudent to defer the drafts till advice was received of the actual progress of the loans. There was no room to hesitate between the loss of a small sum in interest, and the danger of committing the public credit by a premature operation.

The second case of delay relates to the second loan. It was occasioned by a determination to suspend the orders for its application, till information was received of its having been contracted for.

One motive to this determination has been already intimated; namely, the yet untried and immature state of our fiscal arrangements. The general reasoning on this head was strengthened by an occurrence altogether unlooked for, which disclosed itself on the 23d of August 1790, eleven days after the rising of Congress; an occurrence, which they had not contemplated, in their pecuniary dispositions. I allude to the commencement of an Indian war, which was announced in a letter from Governor St. Clair, dated on the above mentioned day; [29] the progressive extent, and consequences of which, would of course not be foreseen. Under such circumstances, I judged it for the public interest and safety, to hold the resource, which the prospect of a loan presented, under the power of the Treasury, till advice should be received of the actual institution of the loan; with intention, then to dispose of it, as should appear advisable, under a better matured view of our pecuniary situation and prospects.

Hence, the delay, which attended the application of the second loan; the first in fact, that originated subsequent to the laws for borrowing. But after advice had been received of its having been set on foot, no time was lost in converting it, with due dispatch, to its

29. Major General Arthur St. Clair's letter, addressed to Henry Knox, is printed in William Henry Smith, ed., *The St. Clair Papers: The Life and Public Services of Arthur St. Clair* (Cincinnati, 1882), II, 155–62.

proper uses: There was only, not an anticipation of its application. As early as May 24th 1791, I wrote a letter to Mr. Short, (a copy of which is in possession of the House) [30] empowering him to apply the proceeds of all future loans, as they should accrue, in payments to France; except as to such sums, as therein were, or afterwards should be previously and specially reserved. This arrangement was calculated to obviate the inconvenience of leaving the proceeds of the loans, for any considerable time, unemployed. At the period of making it, and not sooner, the public prospects appeared to me sufficiently unfolded, to render a general and permanent disposition free from hazard. This instruction proceeded, in due season, all the loans subsequent to that of March 1791.

Whatever delay, therefore, may have attended succeeding investments for paying the French debt, is not attributable to this department: And, I think, it will not appear, that any has been incurred, in respect to the sums, which were destined for the public service here. In judging of this point, it will be proper to observe, that a latitude of six months for making their payments has been reserved to the money-lenders, though with liberty to make them earlier. It was, however, necessary for the Treasury, to regulate its bills, according to the possible delay, lest they should not meet adequate funds. The general policy adopted was to let them fall upon the rear of each loan; this giving a freer course for early payments to France, and best conciliating a certainty of funds for answering the bills, with as little double interest as possible.

It will appear, that notwithstanding the arrangement, which was made, a considerable time intervened between the two last payments to France, while there were funds in hand waiting for employment. It may be expected, that the causes of this procrastination, though, as I have said, not imputable to this department, should be unfolded to the House. Particular circumstances, however, induce me to confine myself to stating generally, that the delay proceeded in the first place, from an expectation to Mr. Short, and kept up, from time to time, by the French Minister of Marine, that a plan would be adopted, to which a decree of the National Assembly was requisite, for converting a large sum into supplies for St. Domingo, which Mr. Short

30. A copy of this letter was included in "Report on Foreign Loans," February 13, 1793.

concluded, must justly come out of the foreign fund, and consequently suspended its application in Europe. In the second place,
from a desire to settle, previously to further payments, a definitive
rule, by which the monies paid, should be liquidated and credited to
the United States.[31]

Both the one and the other appears to have been procrastinated,
from period to period, by the disordered state of French affairs, and
to have finally issued contrary to expectation. It would be an unnecessary commitment of my opinion to declare, how far the delay
appears to me to have [been] justified by the causes. But being led
by the occasion to take notice of it, I think it improper to send it
abroad, liable perhaps to misconstruction, without observing, that
the inducements appear to me to have been weighty—that the delays
naturally grew out of the circumstances, and that I am entirely persuaded of the goodness of the motives which governed. The correspondence before the Senate, contains the particulars of the transaction.[32]

Having pointed out the instances of material delay, which happened, and the causes of them, it remains to state what circumstances
there are to counterbalance the loss on that account.

These circumstances are of two kinds.

1st.   Gain by exchange in the sale of the Bills drawn by the Treasury, and upon the higher rate of interest on the credits which were
given for those bills, than was payable upon the fund, upon which
they were drawn.

2nd.   Gain by exchange in the payments to France.

According to my calculation, founded on the best information
extant, the real par of the metals between the United States and
Amsterdam, makes a current guilder equal to 35 $^{89}/_{106}$ ninetieths of a
dollar. The lowest rate, which has been obtained for the bills, has
been 36 $^{4}/_{11}$ ninetieths, with an allowance of sixty days credit, without
interest. Making a deduction for the interest, the bills were still sold
above the true par. In some instances they have been sold as high as
40 cents and 7 mills per guilder, with interest for the whole term of
the credit given.

31. See note 20. See also Short to H, January 26, March 24, May 14, 1792;
H to Short, March 5, 1792.
32. "Report on Foreign Loans," February 5, 1793.

The rate of interest for the credits allowed upon the bills was 6 per cent, the mean interest paid upon the fund 5 per cent, producing consequently a gain of one per cent.

With regard to the payments to France, if the current rate of exchange between Paris and Amsterdam, at the moment of each remittance or payment, were to govern, a large profit would result to the United States. But certain equitable considerations will produce deductions, which will greatly lessen this advantage; yet, making a liberal allowance for them, there is ground to calculate, that a saving may be made in this particular, more than sufficient to indemnify for the loss of interest.[33]

Hence, any positive advantage, which will have been otherwise gained, will probably be undiminished by that circumstance.

I proceed, in the next place, to state the views, which prevailed, respecting the sums, that have been, from time to time, drawn for; the purposes they have hitherto answered, and the further advantages to be expected from the measure.

The direct object of all the sums drawn for, prior to July 1792, was the purchase of the debt. A collateral consideration, which operated in the first stages of the drawing, has also been mentioned. It has likewise been stated, that the early purchases of the debt are to be ascribed to the instrumentality of the fund derived from the loans. This idea shall now be explained.

Two mistakes appear to have influenced the impressions, which have been entertained, in relation, directly or indirectly, to this subject. First, it seems to have been all along forgotten, that a considerable part of the duties is always outstanding on account of the credits which are given, whence the assertion, that the sinking fund has continually overflowed from domestic resources. Second, it seems to have been taken for granted, that the proceeds of the loans have remained apart, distinct from the mass of the money in the treasury; while in truth, the course of the business has been to turn them over to the Treasurer by warrants, as they have been received, so as to form a part of the aggregate, from time to time, appearing in his hands, and in his accounts. The Banks have been the agents employed for selling these bills. Sometimes warrants on account have issued

33. For the decision of the United States not to take advantage of the depreciation of the assignats in its payments to France, see H to Short, September 2, 1791, July 25, 1792; Short to H, May 14, August 6, 1792.

upon them, for the sums accruing from the sales, at other times, the warrants have been deferred, till the whole proceeds of any parcel have been received, and the accounts of the Banks settled at the treasury; as the state of the treasury has happened to render the one or the other most convenient.

The Banks of North America and New York were the agents for the sale of all the Bills, which were sold, prior to April 1792, amounting to 1.006.526 dollars and 36 cents. Of this sum, 361.391 dollars and 34 cents were passed over to the Treasury in 1791—327.126 dollars and 22 cents, in March 1792, and 140.000 dollars in June following—the residue having remained, as heretofore stated, in deposit with the Bank of North America, upon a special consideration.[34] This is exclusive of certain bills, furnished for the use of the department of State, amounting to 78.766 dollars and 67 cents.

The remainder of the bills which have been sold, beginning in April 1792, were sold by the Bank of the United States, and its branches at New-York and Baltimore. The accounts of the sales had been just made out for settlement, when the present enquiry began, but warrants had not yet issued for placing the proceeds in the Treasury. It will be remarked, that from the terms of credit allowed, they only began to be receivable in October last; the 26th day of which month, the first return made by the Bank shews a sum of 127.225 dollars and 53 cents received; and that the collection had not been completed, when the accounts of sales were rendered.

There are different views of the subject, which will enable the House to perceive, that the possession of the fund in question was necessary to enable the Treasury to furnish the means of making all the purchases, which were made prior to July 1792.

It is true, that there was a surplus of revenue to the end of the year 1790, equal to 1.374.656 dollars and 40 cents, which was appropriated to purchases of the debt, and from the credits then given upon the duties, this surplus would naturally come into the Treasury, in the course of the year 1791.

But the legislature foreseeing that the revenue of 1791, from the

---

34. This is a reference to the sum of $156,596.56 left on deposit in the Bank of North America to counterbalance an advance that the bank made to the War Department for the Indian campaign of 1791. See "Report on the Balance of All Unapplied Revenues at the End of the Year 1792 and on All Unapplied Monies Which May Have Been Obtained by the Several Loans Authorized by Law," February 4, 1793 (*Hamilton Papers*, XIII, 558).

same cause, could not actually be in the Treasury, within that year, to face the appropriations upon it (which, it is to be observed, were nearly commensurate with the fund) inserted a clause in the law appropriating the surplus of 1790, to the purchase of the debt, which authorised a reservation of so much of that surplus, as might be necessary to make the payments of interest during 1791, in case of a deficiency in the receipts into the Treasury, on account of the current revenue of the year.[35]

It will appear to the House, upon a recurrence to the Treasurer's quarterly account ending the 30th of September 1791, that the balance of Cash then on hand was 662,233 dollars and 99 cents.[36]

At that time, there had been paid into the Treasury, upon warrants, from the proceeds of the bills drawn upon the foreign fund, 361.391 dollars and 34 cents. Consequently, the balance of cash, had it not been for that auxiliary, would have been only 300.842 dollars and 65 cents; considering the whole balance in the treasury, as representing an equal sum of the proceeds of the Bills.

Even in a time of complete peace, in a country, where a small extent of monied capital forbids a reliance upon large pecuniary aids to be suddenly obtained, a prudent administrator of the finances could not feel entirely at ease, with a less sum at all times in the command

35. This is a reference to Section 1 of "An Act making provision for the (payment of the) Debt of the United States," which reads in part as follows: "*Be it enacted by the Senate and House of Representatives of the United States of America in Congress assembled,* That reserving out of the monies which have arisen since the last day of December last past, and which shall hereafter arise from the duties on goods, wares and merchandise imported into the United States, and on the tonnage of ships or vessels, the yearly sum of six hundred thousand dollars, or so much thereof as may be appropriated from time to time, towards the support of the government of the United States, and their common defence, the residue of the said monies, or so much thereof, as may be necessary, as the same shall be received in each year, next after the sum reserved as aforesaid, shall be, and is hereby appropriated to the payment of the interest which shall from time to time become due on the loans heretofore made by the United States in foreign countries; and also to the payment of interest on such further loans as may be obtained for discharging the arrears of interest thereupon, and the whole or any part of the principal thereof; to continue so appropriated until the said loans, as well those already made as those which may be made in virtue of this act, shall be fully satisfied, pursuant to the contracts relating to the same, any law to the contrary notwithstanding" (1 *Stat.* 138–39 [August 4, 1790]).

36. This account had been presented in the House of Representatives on December 5, 1791 (*Journal of the House,* I, 468). See also "Statement IV" appended to this report.

of the treasury, than 500.000 dollars, for meeting current demands and extra-exigencies, which, in the affairs of a nation, are every moment to be expected. But, with a war actually on hand, and a possibility of its extension to a more serious length, he would be inexcusable in leaving himself with a less sum at command; unless from an impracticability of doing otherwise. It would be always his duty to combine two considerations—the chance of extra-calls for money, and a possibility of some failure in the receipts which were expected. Derangements of various kinds may happen in the commercial circle, capable of interrupting, for a time, the punctual course of payments to the Treasury. It is necessary, to a certain extent, to be prepared for such casualties.

But during the year 1791, there was a circumstance, which operated as an additional reason for keeping a respectable sum always on hand. The loans of the domestic debt were going on, till the last of September of that year, while, at the same time, the interest was in a course of payment. It was, therefore, always uncertain, what sum would be payable, at the end of a quarter; this depending on the eagerness or backwardness of the public creditors in bringing forward their subscriptions, or their claims as non-subscribers. The omissions, at the end of a preceding quarter, might be expected to fall upon a subsequent one—and it was necessary to be prepared for that possibility; of course, to keep in hand a larger fund for contingent demands. This necessity extended to the termination of the period for receiving subscriptions; because the treasury was to be prepared, on a supposition, that the whole of the domestic debt would then be in a state to receive interest, either as subscribed or unsubscribed. But this did not, in fact, happen. A part of the sums, which were presented, were crowded into the last days of the quarter, and were too late for a dividend. A considerable sum remained ultimately in a form, which, according to the terms of the provision, did not entitle it to interest, either as subscribed or as unsubscribed debt.

Hence, the cash in the treasury, on the 1st of October 1791, was, by a considerable sum, greater than was to have been counted upon, or that might have happened.

The conclusion, which results from the foregoing observations, is this—that the purchases, which preceded the first of October 1791,

and which amounted to 699.984 dollars, and 23 cents in specie, could
not have been hazarded, but for the aid of the sums, which had actually accrued, from the proceeds of the bills, and the expectation of
those which were to accrue from the yet uncollected proceeds of
others.

Had it not been for this aid, the Treasury would have been left
more bare, than was consistent with the security of public credit, and
the certain execution of the public service.

There is, however, a later period in the state of the treasury, which
will more completely illustrate the idea intended to be established.
This is the 2nd of July 1792.

On that day, the balance of cash in the treasury, comprehending
the deposits in all the banks, and including a sum of 200.000 dollars,
received on loan of the Bank of the United States, together with a
sum of 220.900 dollars, in bills drawn upon domestic funds, the
proceeds of which had not been received, was 625.133 dollars and
61 cents.

Prior to this period, a further sum of 545.902 dollars and 89 cents,
arising from the sales of foreign bills, had been placed in the treasury,
by warrants, making, with the former sum placed there from the
same source, 907.294 dollars, and 23 cents.

Had it not been for this auxiliary, and that of the loan from the
Bank, the treasury would then have been in arrear, 484.160 dollars
and 62 cents. It, therefore, necessarily follows, that for the purchases
to that period, which amounted in specie, to 942.672 dollars and
54 cents, at least 484.160 dollars and 62 cents, must have come from
the foreign fund.

But when it is considered, for the reasons which have been stated,
and which will hereafter be fortified by others, tending, as I conceive, to give them conclusive force, that the sum in the treasury at
the period in question, was barely what ought to have been there,
for safety, and for a due supply to current demands—it will follow,
that the whole, or nearly the whole of the purchases, which were
made, previous to July 1792, were made by the means or instrumentality of the foreign fund.

A similar view, extended to the subsequent quarter, will exhibit
this point in a still stronger light. The balance then in the treasury

including a further loan from the Bank of 100.000 dollars, was only 420.914 dollars and 51 cents.

What then, it may be asked, became of the surplus of revenue to the end of 1790? What was the Office performed by that fund, during the period in question?

The answer is, that it served exactly the purpose, which was anticipated by the legislature. It came in aid of the current receipt, for satisfying the current expenditure of 1791, with particular reference to the interest of the debt. This will be easily comprehended, when it is recollected, that the appropriations, made during 1791, upon the revenues of that year, and some small surplusses of antecedent appropriations, amounted to three million six hundred and thirty seven thousand and fifty eight dollars and thirty four cents; that the revenues themselves amounted to no more than three million five hundred and fifty three thousand one hundred and ninety five dollars and eighteen cents; and that, at the end of 1791, there were outstanding in bonds for the duties on imports, besides the chief proceeds of the duties on spirits distilled within the United States, then also uncollected, 1.828.269 dollars and 28 cents.

On this point likewise, of the surplus of revenue to the end of 1790, it is presumable, a misapprehension has been entertained. It seems to have been supposed, that that surplus, as well as the proceeds of the foreign fund, have been kept separate and distinct from the common mass of the monies appearing, from time to time, to be in the treasury. It has been already observed, that this was not the case with regard to the foreign. It is now proper to add, that it has not been the case, either, with regard to the surplus in question. That surplus, as received by the Collectors of the Customs, has regularly passed into the treasury, and appears in the quarterly accounts of the Treasurer, for the periods, to which they relate.

It is the course of the treasury, resulting from the constitution of the department, for all monies, from whatever source, to be brought into it, to constitute an aggregate; subject to the dispositions prescribed by law. The monies to be employed in the sinking fund have, consequently, only been separated, as they have been called for, for actual investment. The only exception to this relates to that part of the sinking fund, which is created by the interest of the debt purchased. This has been included in the quarterly dividends, and covered by the warrants in favor of the Cashiers of the Banks, for paying those dividends, after which, they have passed into a distinct account, in the books of the Bank, opened with Samuel Meredith, as agent to the Commissioners of the sinking fund.

To the foregoing representation, it may seem an objection, that the purchases, to the end of 1791, appear to have been carried to the account of the surplus at the end of 1790.

The ultimate form, which, it has been judged convenient to give to the transaction, in the accounts of the treasury, cannot change what was truly the course of facts. The proceeds of the above mentioned surplus and of the foreign loans, formed together the fund for purchases. In the accounts of the treasury, the thing was susceptible of various modifications at pleasure. The two parts of the fund might have been united in one account, or divided into distinct accounts. Being separated, monies issued for purchases might have been legally carried to either of them.

It was judged most advisable, in the forms of the treasury, to place the purchases to the end of 1791, to the account of the domestic fund, because it was calculated to give greater latitude and energy to the sinking fund. Had not this course been pursued, the business would have taken the following shape—the foreign fund, to the extent of the purchases, would have been exhausted—the whole, or the greater part of the surplus of 1790, would have continued wrapt up in the expenditure of 1791, not liable to be liberated, till the receipts into the treasury should yield a correspondent surplus beyond the actual disbursements—which could not have been the case, while the war with the Indians continues to call for extraordinary expenditures.

From the form, into which the thing has been thrown, the foreign fund has been set free to be applied to further purchases; and a necessity produced of anticipating the outstanding duties, by temporary loans for the current service.

I trust, there can be no doubt, that the course pursued was regular and within the discretion of the department. I hope also, that it will appear to the House to have been the most eligible. The expediency of giving the earliest, and greatest possible extent and activity to whatever concerns the sinking fund, will, it is presumed, unite all opinions.

What has been said hitherto respecting the employment of the foreign fund, is applicable only to that part of it, which was drawn for prior to April 1792; the residue standing in a different situation, and requiring a separate examination.

From the statement, which has been given, it may be perceived, that the fund in question has neither been idle nor useless. A confirmation of this will be found in the following details.[37]

The whole sum successively received on account of Amsterdam bills, from August 17th 1791, to March 1st 1792, was 408.722 dollars and 69 cents. The amount of the monies invested in purchases between those periods, was 349.984 dollars, and 23 cents, chiefly in the month of September, and by anticipation of those receipts.

The whole sum successively received on account of Amsterdam bills, subsequent to the 1st of March, and prior to July 1792, was 235.412 dollars and 33 cents. The amount of the monies invested in purchases, between those periods, was 242.688 dollars and 31 cents.

It was stated in my last letter, that 177.998 dollars and 80 cents, of the proceeds of the foreign bills, were left in deposit with the Bank of North America; and in a note upon Statement B, accompanying that letter,[38] the occasion of it was shewn to be an advance without interest, made by that Bank, for the use of the department of War, which could not yet be covered, in consequence of a doubt still remaining, whether the fund, appropriated for satisfying the object, was adequate to it, the sufficiency of that fund depending, in part, on certain unexpended residues of antecedent appropriations, which, it was expected, would not be finally necessary for satisfying the purposes of those appropriations.

37. At this point in the copy of the report sent to the Senate the following paragraph was inserted:
"The whole sum successively received on account of Amsterdam Bills, up to the 17th of August, 1791, was 361,391 Dollars and 34 Cents. The amount of the monies invested in purchases prior to that day was 350,000 dollars, chiefly by anticipation of those receipts."
38. This transaction is described in "Statement B" of the "Report on the Balance of All Unapplied Revenues at the End of the Year 1792 and on All Unapplied Monies Which May Have Been Obtained by the Several Loans Authorized by Law," February 4, 1793.

It is to be remarked, that the delay of the employment of this part of the proceeds of the foreign fund has been compensated by a saving of interest on the sum advanced on the Bank, which otherwise must have been procured upon a loan with an allowance of interest, probably at the time of the advance, at a rate of 6 per cent; so that even in this particular, the fund, though temporarily suspended from its destination, has not been idle or unproductive. I reserve, for another place, some additional observations and statements, which will be calculated to shew, that opportunities of investing the monies, at any time on hand, applicable to purchases of the debt, were not suffered to pass unimproved, and that as much, in this respect was done, as the state of the treasury and the state of the market would permit.[39]

It has been said, that a distinct examination would be proper, with regard to the bills, which have been drawn upon the foreign fund, subsequent to March 1792. I proceed now to this examination.

The expediency of what has been, in this respect, done, seems to have been called in question, under a suggestion, that an application of the fund to the purchases had ceased to be advantageous.

The drawing of these bills has been, at different periods, influenced by various considerations. A leading motive was always a purchase of the debt. And a correct view of the subject will, I doubt not, satisfy the House, that the measure was recommended by an adequate prospect of advantage.

It is to be observed, that all these drafts were predicated upon the two four per cent loans; [40] being, as already stated, real 4½ per cent loans.

There was good ground to presume, that opportunities would be found of investing the monies drawn for in purchases, which would yield, at least, 5 per cent, with a possibility of doing still better. The difference of ½ per cent was alone an object of importance; but it would be coupled with the further benefit of reducing a principal sum materially exceeding the sum invested. When the three per cents are purchased at 12/ in the pound, there is not only a redemption of

39. See "Report on the State of the Treasury at the Commencement of Each Quarter During the Years 1791 and 1792 and on the State of the Market in Regard to the Prices of Stock During the Same Years," February 19, 1793.

40. The Holland loan of December, 1791, and the Holland loan of 1792. See note 27.

an annuity of 5 per cent, but a sinking of a capital of 20/ for 12. And though this might not be material, if the market rate of interest should never fall below 5, because, in that case, the 3 per cents might always be purchased at the same rate, yet if it should, at any time happen, that interest fell below 5, it would be a gain to the government to have purchased at 5, in exact proportion to the difference between 5, and the then market rate. Add to this, that the 3 per cents have generally a value in the market, more than proportioned to the income they produce, which arises from the capacity of the capital to appreciate, even to par. These observations are also, for the most part, applicable to the deferred, with this circumstance in addition, that when interest begins to be payable on that species of Stock, the money invested, and which, in the mean time, would have produced five, would then begin to produce to the government 6 per cent, with the advantage of having anticipated the redemption of a species of stock, of right only gradually redeemable. Combining these considerations, it appears to be clearly and even eminently for the interest of the government, to purchase within the limit suggested, with a fund which does not cost more than 4½ per cent.

That this was the view of the subject, which governed, is deducible, not only from the circumstances of the fact, but from my letter of the 2d of April 1792, to Mr. Short, announcing my intention to draw, in which I assign, as the ground of that intention, "that I considered it for the interest of the United States, to prosecute purchases of the public debt, with monies borrowed on the terms of the last loan," meaning the loan of the first of January 1792 at 4 per cent.[41]

If the event be taken as a criterion, the anticipation will be more than justified, the present juncture offering an opportunity for purchases peculiarly advantageous.

But without insisting on a state of things, occasioned by extraordinary circumstances, it was morally certain, that the common course of events would render the operation a beneficial one. And it would not argue peculiar foresight, if a calculation was even made on the effect, which the situation and probable progress of affairs in Europe might produce upon our market. A pretty general war there,

41. This is a reference to the Holland loan of December, 1791. See note 27.

by extending the demand for money, would naturally divert from our stocks, a portion of what might otherwise be employed upon them, and affect injuriously their prices. It is also a familiar fact, that during the winter in this country, there is always a scarcity of money in the towns; a circumstance calculated to damp the prices of stock.

A consideration, which collaterally influenced the drawing of the latter bills, was the situation of the French colony of St: Domingo.

This not only produced an early application for a considerable advance, which was promised; but it was to be foreseen that still further aids would be indispensible.

Indeed sundry letters from Mr. Short, the first dated at Paris, the 28th December 1791, announced the daily probability of an arrangement, requiring an advance here of 800.000 dollars, for the use of that colony. A sum of 4.000.000 of livres has, in fact, been successively stipulated for that object, the greatest part of which has been actually furnished.[42]

It is known, that these supplies could proceed from no other source, than the foreign fund.

The payment to the foreign officers of near 200.000 dollars, by which an interest of 6 per cent would be released, was another object, for which, provision was to be made out of the same fund.[43]

These several purposes conspired with the object of purchasing the debt, to induce the latitude of drawing, which took place.

But there was still a further inducement, which came in aid of the others. The time for reimbursing the first instalment of the two millions of dollars due to the Bank was approaching when, by positive stipulation, the government would have to pay two hundred thousand dollars,[44] for which there was no domestic fund, that could

42. See note 20.
43. For a description of the debt owed to foreign officers, see Short to H, August 3, 1790, note 5. Section 5 of "An Act supplementary to the act making provision for the Debt of the United States" (1 *Stat.* 282 [May 8, 1792]) authorized the President "to cause to be discharged the principal and interest of the said debt, out of any of the monies, which have been or shall be obtained on loan." For the negotiations on the payment of these officers, see H to Short, August 16, September 13, 1792; H to Washington, August 27, 1792; Washington to H, August 31, 1792; H to Gouverneur Morris, September 13, 1792.
44. See Section 11 of "An Act to incorporate the subscribers to the Bank of the United States" (1 *Stat.* 196 [February 25, 1791]). The sum borrowed was "reimbursable in ten years, by equal annual instalments." For the controversy over the payment of this installment, see H to the President and Directors of the Bank of the United States, January 1, 1793.

be spared from the current exigencies. I thought it incumbent upon this department, to have an eye to placing within the reach of the legislature, the means of fulfilling this engagement; the object of which bore a strict analogy to that, for which, the two millions, authorized by the Act making provision for the reduction of the public debt, were to be borrowed.

I did not even scruple to take into the calculation, that if from the extent of the draughts upon the foreign fund, there should happen to be found on hand a larger sum, than was necessary for, or could be advantageously employed towards the several purposes, which were the immediate and direct objects of the operation, the surplus would facilitate to the government a measure manifestly and unequivocally beneficial—an additional payment to the Bank, on account of a debt, upon which an annual interest of 6 per cent was payable; a measure by which a certain saving of one per cent, to the extent of the payment, that might be made, would be accomplished.

The possibility of this application of the fund afforded a perfect assurance, that the public interest could, in no event, fail to be promoted.

I felt myself the more at liberty to do it, because it did not interfere with a complete fulfilment of the public engagements in regard to the foreign debt. It could not be done, consistently with a full reimbursement of all arrears and instalments, which had accrued on account of that debt.

The detail, which has been given, comprehends a full exposition of the views and motives, that have regulated the conduct of this department; in relation to those parts of the proceeds of the foreign loans, which have been transferred to the United States, except as to the last sum of one million two hundred and thirty seven thousand five hundred florins, directed to be drawn for on the 30th of November last; in regard to which, circumstances of a special nature co-operated, as is explained in a note upon the copy of my letter of the 26th of that month, to Mr Short, forming a part of the communication herewith made by order of the President of the United States.[45]

45. In his letter to Short of November 26, 1792, H had informed him that the treasurer of the United States would draw upon the United States bankers in Amsterdam for 1,250,000 florins. The sum was later reduced to 1,237,500 florins. See H to Short, December 31, 1792, and H to Willink, Van Staphorst, and Hubbard, December 31, 1792.

The House will perceive, that the variety of matter comprised in this letter has not been collected and digested into its present form, without much labor, and an unavoidable expense of time. I trust, they will be sensible, that no delay has been unnecessarily incurred. It is certain, that I have made every exertion in my power, at the hazard of my health to comply with the requisitions of the House, as early as possible. And it has even been done with more expedition, than was desirable to secure the perfect accuracy of the communication.

Yet I have still to regret, that some part of the subject must remain to be presented in a subsequent letter.[46] To lessen, however, the inconvenience of this further delay, I shall transmit, with the present letter, the statements required by the first and second of the resolutions of the 23d. of January, which will be found in the Schedules herewith marked No. I to V; those required by the last of the resolutions,[47] having been already forwarded.

There remain, however, some particulars, to complete the information contemplated by those resolutions, that must be reserved for another communication. This, I may venture to assure the House, will not be deferred beyond the present, or at least the first day of the ensuing week.[48]

With perfect respect, I have the honor to be, Sir, Your most obedient and most humble servant   Alexander Hamilton
Secretary of the Treasury.
13th. February 1793.

The Honorable the Speaker
of the House of Representatives.

46. "Report on the State of the Treasury at the Commencement of Each Quarter During the Years 1791 and 1792 and on the State of the Market in Regard to the Prices of Stock During the Same Years," February 19, 1793.

47. For these resolutions, see the introductory note to "Report on the Balance of All Unapplied Revenues at the End of the Year 1792 and on All Unapplied Monies Which May Have Been Obtained by the Several Loans Authorized by Law," February 4, 1793.

48. See "Report on the State of the Treasury at the Commencement of Each Quarter During the Years 1791 and 1792 and on the State of the Market in Regard to the Prices of Stock During the Same Years," February 19, 1793.

A STATEMENT OF THE APPROPRIATION FOR REDUCING THE PUBLIC DEBT, CONSTITUTED BY THE ACT OF CONGRESS PASSED ON THE 12TH DAY OF AUGUST 1790.

	Dollars. Cts.			Dollars. Cts.
To the surplus of the products of duties on imports and tonnage to the last day of December 1790, after reserving a sufficient sum from said products to satisfy the appropriations made during [the first] and second Sessions of Congress, as ascertained at the Treasury	1.374.656. 40	**1790.** Dec: 15:	By warrant No.776, on the Treasurer, in his favor, to be applied in purchases of the public debt	200.000
		1791. Jan: 26.	By warrant No.856 do. do. do.	50.000.
		Feb: 5:	By do. No. 869, in favor of B. Lincoln, do.	50.000.
			By do. 870 do. in favor of Wm Heth do.	50.000.
		Sep: 30:	By do. 1265 do. in his favor do.	149.984. 23
			By do. 1266. do. in favor of Wm. Seton, do.	200.000.
		1792. Mar. 31.	By do. 1605 in his favor do.	28.915. 52
		June 30.	By do. 1864 do. do.	62.673. 90
			By do. 1867 do. in favor of Wm. Seton do.	151.098. 89
		Dec: 29:	By do. 2328. do. in his favor do.	15.098. 11
				957.770. 65.
			Balance, being the difference between the surplus of duties appropriated and the sum drawn therefrom	406.885. 75
Dollars,	1.374.656. 40.			1.374.656. 40.

Treasury Department, February 13th. 1793

A. Hamilton,
Secry. of the Treasy.

— II —

A STATEMENT OF THE APPLICATION OF THE FUNDS DRAWN
ON THE APPROPRIATION OF THE SURPLUS OF DUTIES TO
THE END OF THE YEAR 1790, FOR THE REDUCTION OF THE
PUBLIC DEBT.

					Dollars. Cts.

To appropriation for reducing the public debt, constituted by the
Act of Congress, passed on the 12th. day of August 1790,[49] for
the amount drawn from said Appropriation by Warrants on the
Treasurer from December 15th. 1790, to December 29th. 1792,
Viz:

1790. Dec: 15:	No. 776 in favor of Samuel Meredith,		Dollars. Cts.
	to be applied in purchases of the public		
	debt		200.000.
1791. Jan: 26:	No. 856	do. do.	do.	50.000.
" Feby: 5:	869	do of Ben. Lincoln	do.	50.000.
" "	870.	do. of Wm. Heth	do.	50.000.
" Sept: 30:	1265.	do. of S: Meredith	do.	149.984. 23.
	1266.	do. of Wm. Seton	do.	200.000.
1792. Mar: 31:	1605.	do. of S: Meredith	do.	28.915. 52.
June 30:	1865.	do. of do.	do.	62.673. 90.
	1867.	do. of Wm. Seton	do.	151.098. 89.
Dec: 29th:	2328.	do. of S: Meredith	do.	15.098. 11.

957.770.65

To this sum invested in purchases by Benjamin Lincoln, being in part of a sum of interest received by
him on Stock purchased   5. 51.

Dollars,   957.776. 16.

Treasury Department, February 13th. 1793.

49. 1 *Stat.* 186–87.

Dollars. Cts.

By Samuel Meredith's account of purchases, to the 7th. day of De-
cember 1790, as reported to Congress by the Commissioners for
reducing the public debt, on the 21st day of December 1790   150.239. 24
By sundry purchases reported by said Commissioners to Congress
on the 7th day of November 1791, Viz:
By Samuel Meredith, from the 7th of December 1790,
to 19th September 1791   248.984. 71.
By William Seton, from the 19th August 1791, to 12th
September, 1791   200.000.
By William Heth, from the 24th February 1791, to 2nd
April 1791   49.934. 9
By Benjamin Lincoln, from the 22d February 1791, to
3d March 1791   50.005. 51.
                                          548.924. 31.
By interest from January 1st to July 1st 1791, on Stock purchased
by Samuel Meredith, in August and September 1791   760. 28.
By sundry expenses attending purchases of public debt, charged by
William Heth, and admitted to his credit   4. 15.
By sundry purchases reported by said Commissioners to Congress,
on the 17th day of November 1792, Viz:
By Samuel Meredith, from the 21st March to 25th
April 1792   91.589. 42
By William Seton, from 2d. to the 17th. April 1792   151.098. 89.
                                          242.688. 31.
By purchases by Samuel Meredith, from the 15th to the 22d De-
cember 1792, as per account settled at the treasury   15.098 11.
By balance, being money remaining in the hands of William Heth,
of the sum advanced to him for making purchases, and for
which he is accountable   61. 76.

                 Dollars,   957.776. 16.

Alexander Hamilton,
Secry: of the Treasry.

— III —

STATEMENT OF THE APPLICATION OF THE FUND CONSTITUTED BY THE ACT OF CONGRESS, PASSED ON THE 8TH. OF MAY 1792, FOR REDUCING THE PUBLIC DEBT,[50] ARISING FROM THE INTEREST ON THE SUMS OF SAID DEBT PURCHASED, REDEEMED, AND PAID INTO THE TREASURY OF THE UNITED STATES.

	Dollars. Cts.		Dollars. Cts.
1791.		**1791.**	
April 1st. To interest due this day on the Stock purchased	4.230. 63.	July 1st. By balance to the credit of the Commissioners for reducing the public debt, deposited, as follows:	
July 1st. To ditto ditto	5.103. 2.	In the Bank of North America	8,711. 97.
		In the hands of the Commissioner of loans for the State of Massachusetts	531. 68.
	9.243. 65.		9.243. 65.
To balance	9.243. 65.		9.243. 65.
October 1st To interest due this day on the Stock purchased	8.635. 18.	**1792.**	
		January 1st. By balance to the credit of the Commissioners for reducing the public debt, deposited, as follows:	
1792		In the Bank of North America	23,830. 37.
January 1st. To ditto ditto	6.989. 1.	In the hands of the Commissioner of loans for the State of Massachusetts	531. 68.
		In the hands of the Commissioner of loans for the State of New York	505. 79.
	24.867. 84.		24.867. 84.
			24.867. 84.

50. 1 *Stat.* 281-83.

To Balance	24,867. 84.
April 1st. To interest due this day on the Stock purchased	6,989. 1.
1792. April 1st. To interest due this day on part of the Stock paid into the treasury by the state of Pennsylvania, for land on Lake Erie, purchased from the United States	48. 63.
July, 1st To ditto ditto on the Stock purchased	9,338. 76.
To do. do. on the Stock paid as above, for land on Lake Erie	48. 63.
To do. do. on the Stock paid into the treasury on account of the commutation of Willis Wilson	127. 30.
	41,470. 17.

1792. July 1st By balance to the credit of the Commissioners for reducing the public debt, deposited, as follows:	
In the Bank of North America	23,830. 37.
In the Bank of the United States	17,639. 80.
	41,470. 17.

	41,470. 17.
To balance	
October, 1st. To interest due this day on the Stock purchased	9,366. 24.
To do. do. on Stock as above, for land on Lake Erie	48. 63.
To do. do. on the Stock paid as above, on account of the commutation of Willis Wilson	21. 21.
1793 January 1st To do. do. on the stock purchased	9,420. 42.
To do. do. on the Stock paid as above, for land on Lake Erie	48. 63.
To do. do. on the Stock paid as above on account of the Commutation of Willis Wilson	21. 21.
To do. do. on the Stock paid into the treasury, by John Hopkins, for a balance due from him in indents of interest	159. 44.
	60,555. 95.

	41,470. 17.
By purchases made by Samuel Meredith, from the 29th to the 31st of October 1792, as reported to Congress by the Commissioners for reducing the public debt, on the 17th of November 1792	25,969. 96.
By purchases made by Samuel Meredith, from the 17th to the 26th of January 1793, inclusive, agreeably to his account rendered to the Treasury	34,585. 99.
Note—Interest stated per contra remained in the Bank of the United States, until expended.	
	60,555. 95.

Remarks.

In addition to the sums received as within stated, there remain to be received from the following persons, balances found to be due from them, on the settlement of their accounts at the Treasury, Viz:

	dollars.	Cts.
From William Heth, for interest received on Stock purchased by him,	658.83.	
From Benjamin Lincoln, for do. do.	154.49.	
From ditto for interest struck on Stock purchased by him, stated in his name in dividend accounts of Commissioner of loans for the State of Massachusetts; now transferred to the books of the treasury among unclaimed dividends	368.56.	

The fund is likewise liable to receive additions of interest on the following sums paid into the Treasury, upon which no dividend has yet been struck—Viz.

On 85. 032. $\frac{8}{100}$ dollars, unfunded Stock received from the State of Pennsylvania, for land on Lake Erie.

On 1.356. $\frac{87}{100}$ dollars, received from Jonathan Burrall, which had been paid to him, on a balance due in the Commissary department.

These sums at present stand on the books of the Treasury, in the name of Samuel Meredith, Treasurer of the United States, in trust for the United States.

Also, for the interest on the debt due to foreign Officers, now in a course of redemption.

Treasury Department,   Alexander Hamilton,
February 13th. 1793.   Secretary of the Treasury.

— IV —

QUARTERLY STATEMENT OF CASH IN THE HANDS OF THE
TREASURER OF THE UNITED STATES, FOR THE YEAR 1791.

Balance of Cash in my hands the 30th of June 1791, see below			533.638. 24
Balance of Cash in the Bank of North America		428.200.17.	
Ditto	New York	92.680.77.	
Ditto	Massachusetts	2.226.76	
Cash paid on account of Contingent expenses		490.54	
The[o]dosius Fowler & Company's Note		10.000.	
			533.638. 24

From the 1st of January to the 30th. June, two quarters.

Balance of Cash in my hands the 30th of September 1791, See below			622.233. 99
Cash in the Bank of North America		136.830.38.	
Ditto	New York	465.926.94.	
Ditto	Maryland	31.391.78.	
Ditto	Massachusetts	28.084.89.	
			622.233. 99.

Balance of Cash in my hands the 31st of December, 1791, see below			953.862. 75.
Cash in the Bank of the United States		133.000.	
Ditto	North America	471.972.28.	
Ditto	New York	224.677.35.	
Ditto	Massachusetts	65.578.22.	
Ditto	Maryland	50.665.29	
Ditto	Providence	7.969.61.	
			953.862. 75.

The previous sickness, and afterwards the death of Mr. Eveleigh
the last Comptroller,[51] which happened on the 15th of April 1791,
occasioned an accommodation between the Secretary of the Treasury and the Bank of North America, with respect to a number of
Warrants, which were not countersigned; the Bank agreeing to pay
them, and retain them in its possession, till the appointment of a
Comptroller, when they could be regularly countersigned, and
charged to my account. This caused an agreement with the Comptroller, that the two first quarters of the year 1791 might be included
in one account, in order that the different Offices in the Treasury
Department should correspond in their balances.

Samuel Meredith,

Treasury of the United States.   Treasurer of the United States

51. Nicholas Eveleigh.

— V —

STATEMENT OF CASH IN THE TREASURY, DURING THE YEAR 1792, SHEWING THE BALANCE ON HAND HALF MONTHLY.

Dates.	Bank of United States.	Office of Disc: and D: Boston.	Office of Disc: and D: New York.	Office of Disc: and D: Baltimore.	Office of Disc: and D: Charleston.	Bank of Massachusetts.
1792						
Jan. 1st.	133.000.					65.578.22.
15.	333.000.					66.453.22.
Feb: 1:	456.278.90					71.215.55.
15:	708.160.44.					24.115.55.
Mar: 1:	692.959. 6.					31.769. 5.
15.	618.503.69.					36.286. 4
April 1:	359.643.64					37.712.58.
15:	247.051.80.					50.785.24
May 1:	301.455.62.					50.785.24
15:	388.479. 1.					3.735.24
June. 1:	309.186.44		24.273.94.			3.735.24
15:	406.610.50.		43.257.65.			8.965.63
July. 2:	212.403.89.	111.343.44.	63.919.54.		43.850.13.	11.415.63.
15:	196.526.10.	111.343.44.	68.318.90.		55.559.99	11.415.63
August 1:	208.988. 3	99.538.42.	83.099.63.		49.133.25.	13.012. 6
15:	399.940.80	100.626.42.	90.867.54.	2.530.	27.682.33.	13.626.39
Sept. 1:	401.084.78.	110.139.92.	93.980.32.	3.454.36.	33.661. 3	13.626.39
15:	305.786.48	137.169.59.	105.280. 2.	5.889.98	37.381.73.	13.626.39
Octor. 1:	117.198.54.	77.666. 2.	14.103. 2	22.344.83.	36.970.18.	13.626.39
15:	110.991.29.	47.666. 2.	27.349.28.	26.044.83	36.970.18.	13.626.39
Nov: 1:	172.405.89.	116.686.48.	64.908.82.	43.644.83.	51.616.98.	13.626.39
15:	216.932.31.	101.763.23.	133.576.23.	59.051.72.	51.616.98.	13.626.39
Dec: 1:	247.139.33.	143.267.37.	223.321.29.	81.074.93.	69.354.43.	
15:	371.894.62.	135.052.41.	189.016.16.	40.738.12.	65.287.83.	
1793.						
Jan: 1:	109.169.45.	154.860.67.	224.473.51.	73.653.64.	62.015.85.	

Bank of New York.	Bank of N. America.	Bank of Providence.	Bank of Maryland.	Total Amount.	Sums in Bills at certain periods, as returned by The Bank U.S:	Specie Totals at said periods.
224.677.35.	471.972.28.	7.969.61.	50.665.29.	953.862.75.		
164.469.95.	254.134.47.	7.969.61.	52.198.58.	878.225.83		
128.708.21.	151.516.32.	7.969.61.	49.583.25.	865.271.84		
20.912.27.	91.516.32.	2.969.61.	29.583.25.	877.257.44		
32.352.52.	31.515.74.	8.404.94.	34.752.85.	831.754.16.		
295.717.44.	31.515.74.	7.656.65.	45.893.10.	1.035.572.66.		
254.930.41.	31.515.74.	7.156.65.	60.418.32.	751.377.34.		
259.099.60.	31.515.74.	1.156.65.	60.418.32.	650.027.35.		
305.854.35.	31.515.74.	1.156.65.	86.618.39.	777.385.99.		
293.827.35.	31.515.74.	1.156.65.	77.075.95.	795.789.94		
294.527.35.	31.515.74	5.856.65.	85.095.07.	754.191.33	157.508.33.	596.683.
294.527.35.	31.515.74.	5.356.65.	27.518.66.	817.752.18.	316.900. "	500.852.18.
62.628.46	61.601.30.	18.434.65.	37.581.57.	623.133.61.	220.900. "	402.233.61.
54.078.46.	61.601.30.	12.234.65.	37.581.57.	608.660. 4.	150.650. "	449.010. 4.
54.078.46.	61.601.30.	21.588.65.	2.723.13.	593.762.93.	73.650. "	520.112.93.
58.141.28.	61.601.30.	14.916.65.	9.800. "	779.732.21.	174.450. "	605.282.21.
54.259.43.	61.601.30	18.649.65.		790.457.18.	118.700. "	671.757.18.
71.070.75.	61.601.30	17.157.65.		754.963.89	28.200.	726.763.89
60.219.58.	61.601.30.	17.157.65.		420.914.51.	31.100.	389.814.51.
69.019. 8.	61.601.30.	11.157.65.		404.426. 2.	99.000.	305.426. 2
69.019. 8.	61.601.30.	28.452.87.		621.962.64.	88.700.	533.262.64.
69.019. 8.	61.601.30.	28.452.87.		735.640.11.	96.600.	639.040.11.
69.019. 8.	61.601.30.	45.957.87.		940.735.60.	58.300.	882.435.60.
69.019. 8.	61.601.30	30.157.87.		962.767.39.	209.200.	753.567.39.
69.019. 8.	61.601.30.	28.157.87.		783.212.37.	155.200.	682.012.37.

Total amount of quarter ending 31st December 1792, brought down	783.212.37.
Amount of Contingencies paid, for which there is no appropriation	142.14
Ditto, paid Samuel Brook, a Clerk in the Office, for which there is no appropriation	90.
Dollars,	783.444.51

Treasury of the United States,

Samuel Meredith,
Treasurer of the United States.

From Tench Coxe [1]

Treasury Department, Revenue Office, February 14, 1793. Encloses "a return from this Office, to enable you to make the report relative thereto required by the order of the Senate of the 7th day of May last." [2]

LC, RG 58, Letters of Commissioner of Revenue, 1792–1793, National Archives.
  1. Coxe was commissioner of the revenue.
  2. The Senate order reads as follows: "*Ordered,* That the Secretary of the Treasury do lay before the Senate, at the next session of Congress, a statement of the salaries, fees, and emoluments, for one year, ending the first day of October next, to be stated quarterly, of every person holding any civil office or employment under the United States, (except the judges,) together with the actual disbursements and expenses in the discharge of their respective offices and employments for the same period; and that he do report the name of every person who shall neglect or refuse to give satisfactory information touching his office or employment, or the emoluments or disbursements thereof" (*Annals of Congress,* III, 138).
  For the report, see "Report on the Salaries, Fees, and Emoluments of Persons Holding Civil Office Under the United States," February 27, 1793.

Report on Revenue, Appropriations, and Expenditures [1]

Treasury Department
Feby 14th. 1793
[Communicated on February 14, 1793] [2]

[To the President of the Senate]
Sir

I have the honor to transmit herewith in further pursuance of the order of the Senate of the 23rd of January past,[3] these several statements marked A.B.C.

A being a general account of revenue and appropriations; exhibit-

LS, RG 46, Second Congress, 1791–1793, Reports of the Secretary of the Treasury, National Archives.
  1. For background to this document, see the introductory note to "Report on the Balance of All Unapplied Revenues at the End of the Year 1792 and on All Unapplied Monies Which May Have Been Obtained by the Several Loans Authorized by Law," February 4, 1793.
  2. *Annals of Congress,* III, 647.
  3. For this order, see the introductory note to "Report on the Balance of All Unapplied Revenues at the End of the Year 1792 and on All Unapplied Monies Which May Have Been Obtained by the Several Loans Authorized by Law," February 4, 1793.

ing on one side all the Income of the United States, except from the proceeds of Loans foreign & Domestic, to the end of the year 1792, on the other the respective amounts of all the appropriations which have been made by law to the same period.

B being a general account of appropriations and expenditures to the same end of the year 1792. This statement takes up the excess of the appropriations beyond the Expenditure to the end of the year 1791 as contained in the Account of receipts and expenditures reported to the House of Representatives during the present session,[4] and, including all the subsequent appropriations and expenditures to the end of 1792, shews the balance unsatisfied of each head of appropriation.

C being an explanatory statement for the purpose of shewing a conformity between the aggregate of the balances of appropriations unsatisfied and the balance of the Public Income beyond the Public Expenditure, to the end of the year 1792, as represented in the Statement B heretofore reported.

It will be observed that the most considerable item among the balances of appropriations is for interest on the public debt amounting to 1,395,824 Dollars & 65 Cents. This happens in three ways—1 The interest on the foreign part of the debt has been paid in Europe out of the proceeds of the loans—the sum paid will consequently require to be replaced out of the domestic funds and will operate as if an equal sum had been transferred here by drafts. 2d. The payment of interest to certain States upon the difference between their quotas of the assumed debt and the sums subscribed upon the first loan has been suspended in consequence of the opening of the second loan to avoid a double payment of interest, first to the States and next to subscribers; which might otherwise happen. 3rd There is a part of the public debt which has continued in a form that has not entitled the holders under the existing laws to receive interest either as subscribers or non subscribers.[5]

4. "Report on the Receipts and Expenditures of Public Monies to the End of the Year 1791," November 10, 1792.

5. "An Act making provision for the (payment of the) Debt of the United States" (1 Stat. 138–44 [August 4, 1790]) had established the terms under which individuals holding certificates of debt issued under the Confederation might subscribe to the funded debt under the new government. Section 10, however, provided: "That such of the creditors of the United States as may not subscribe to the said loan, shall nevertheless receive during the year one thousand seven

There are certain arrears of interest on the part of the debt intitled to Interest which did not come into the accounts of the year 1792.

This balance of interest however will be a real future expenditure as indeed will be the case with regard to most of the other balances of appropriations. There will be surplusses, but these surplusses

---

hundred and ninety-one, a rate per centum on the respective amounts of their respective demands, including interest to the last day of December next, equal to the interest payable to subscribing creditors, to be paid at the same times, at the same places, and by the same persons as is herein before directed, concerning the interest on the stock which may be created in virtue of the said proposed loan. But as some of the certificates now in circulation have not heretofore been liquidated to specie value, as most of them are greatly subject to counterfeit, and counterfeits have actually taken place in numerous instances, and as embarrassment and imposition might, for these reasons, attend the payment of interest on those certificates in their present form, it shall therefore be necessary to entitle the said creditors to the benefit of the said payment, that those of them who do not possess certificates issued by the register of the treasury, for the registered debt, should produce previous to the first day of June next, their respective certificates, either at the treasury of the United States, or to some one of the commissioners to be appointed as aforesaid, to the end that the same may be cancelled, and other certificates issued in lieu thereof; which new certificates shall specify the specie amount of those in exchange for which they are given, and shall be otherwise of the like tenor with those heretofore issued by the said register of the treasury for the said registered debt, and shall be transferable on the like principles with those directed to be issued on account of the subscriptions to the loan hereby proposed."

Individuals, particularly foreign creditors, who had been unable to exchange their certificates because of the time limitation of "An Act making provision for the (payment of the) Debt of the United States" were relieved by an extension granted by "An Act supplementary to the act making provision for the Debt of the United States" (1 *Stat.* 281–83 [May 8, 1792]). During the operation of both acts, another class of creditors had consistently refused to surrender their certificates. These were the holders of certificates issued between September, 1777, and March, 1778, who were reluctant to exchange them, believing the value of their certificates exceeded their exchange rate at the Treasury. Since some states during the seventeen-eighties had assumed a part of the Continental debt owed to their own citizens and had issued their own securities in place of Continental certificates, further complications in the payment of interest arose out of the operation of Sections 17, 18, and 19 of "An Act making provision for the (payment of the) Debt of the United States," which defined the terms under which such creditors might become subscribers to the domestic debt.

cannot exceed, if they equal, the sum mentioned in my letter of the 4th instant to the House of Representatives.[6]

With perfect respect   I have the honor to be   Sir   Your obedt Servant   Alex Hamilton
                                          Secy of the Treasy

The Vice President of the
United States &
President of the Senate

6. "Report on the Balance of All Unapplied Revenues at the End of the Year 1792 and on All Unapplied Monies Which May Have Been Obtained by the Several Loans Authorized by Law," February 4, 1793.

STATEMENT OF THE REVENUE OF THE UNITED STATES AND APPROPRIA TIONS CHARGED THEREON TO THE END OF THE YEAR 1792.

Dr.

REVENUE	Dollars C
To Amount of Duties on Imports and Tonnage and of Fines Penalties and Forfeitures from the commencement of the present Government to the 31st Decr. 1791.	6,534,263
" Product of Duties on Spirits distilld within the United States for a half year ending the 31st of December 1791. as estimated	150,000.
" Product of Duties on Imports and Tonnage &ca. for the year 1792 heretofore estimated at	3,900,000
" Ditto on Spirits distilled within the United States for the same period as estimated	400,000
" Cash received into the Treasury from Fines Forfeitures & for Balances to the end of the year 1791	11.355
" Ditto recd for Arms & Accoutrements sold, Fines & Penalties, Balances of Accounts settled in the year 1792 and on accot. of the first dividend declared by the Bank of the United States	21.860
Dollars	11,017.460.

7. "An Act providing for the Expenses which may attend Negotiations or Treaties with the Indian Tribes, and the appointment of Commissioners for managing the same" (1 *Stat.* 54).

8. "An Act making Appropriations for the Service of the present year" (1 *Stat.* 95).   9. 1 *Stat.* 104–06.

10. 1 *Stat.* 128–29. This act was to "continue and be in force for the space of two years."

11. "An Act to satisfy the claims of John McCord against the United States" (6 *Stat.* 2–3).

12. "An Act providing for holding a Treaty or Treaties to establish Peace with certain Indian tribes" (1 *Stat.* 136).

13. "An Act making provision for the (payment of the) Debt of the United States" (1 *Stat.* 138–44).

14. Provision for the revenue cutters had been made in Section 62 of "An Act to provide more effectually for the collection of the duties imposed by law on goods, wares and merchandise imported into the United States, and on the tonnage of ships or vessels" (1 *Stat.* 175).

15. "An Act authorizing the Secretary of the Treasury to finish the Lighthouse on Portland Head, in the District of Maine" (1 *Stat.* 184).

16. "An Act for the relief of disabled soldiers and seamen lately in the service of the United States, and of certain other persons" (6 *Stat.* 3–4 [August 11, 1790]).

17. "An Act making certain Appropriations therein mentioned" (1 *Stat.* 185–86).   18. 1 *Stat.* 186–87.

19. "An Act making appropriations for the support of Government during the year one thousand seven hundred and ninety-one, and for other purposes" (1 *Stat.* 190).

20. "An Act making an appropriation for the purpose therein mentioned" (1 *Stat.* 214).

21. "An Act for raising and adding another Regiment to the Military Establishment of the United States, and for making farther provision for the protection of the frontiers" (1 *Stat.* 222–24).

Date of Acts		APPROPRIATIONS	Dollars	Cts.
1789				
Augst. 20	By.	Appropriation for Indian Treaties [7]	20.000	
Septr. 29	"	do. for sundry objects [8]	639.000	
1790				
Mar: 26	"	do. for support of Government [9]	754,658	99
July 1st.	"	do. Intercourse with Forn. Nations 90 & 91.	80,000.	
" "	"	do. do. for 1792 [10]	40,000	
" "	"	do. for the claim of John McCord [11]	1.309	71
" 22nd.	"	do. for Indian Treaties [12]	20.000	
Augst. 4th	"	do. Intert. on the Debt Forn. & Domst: for 91.	2.060 861	40
" "	"	do. do. for 1792 [13]	2.849 194	73
" "	"	do. for the Cutter Establishment [14]	10,000	
" 10	"	do. for Portland Lighthouse [15]	1.500	
" "	"	do. for disabled Seamen [16]	548	57
" 12	"	do. for sundry objects [17]	233 219	97
" "	"	do. for reduction of the public debt being surplus of revenue for 1790 [18] }	1.374 656.	40
1791				
Feb: 11	"	do. for sundry objects [19]	740.232	60
Mar: 3rd.	"	do. Recognition of the Treaty with Morocco [20]	20,000	
" "	"	do. the protection of the Frontiers [21]	312,686	20
" "	"	do. Officers of the Judicial Courts [22]	4 055	33
Decr: 23rd:	"	do. the support of Governmt. for 1792 [23]	1,059 222	81
1792.				
April 2nd:	"	do. for a Lighthouse on Baldhead [24]	4,000	
" "	"	do. Mint Establishment [25]	7 000	
" 13th.	"	do. Wilmington Grammar-School [26]	2 553	64
May 2nd:	"	do. for Protection of the Frontiers [27]	673,500	
" 8th.	"	do. for sundry objects [28]	84,497	90
" "	"	do. for compensation to Colo. Gibson [29]	1 000	
" "	"	do. the claim of John Brown Cutting [30]	2 000	
			10 995.698	25
		Surplus of Revenue above the appropriations to the end of the year 1792 }	21,762	39
		Dollars	11.017.460.	64

Treasury Department Febr. 14. 1793
Alexander Hamilton

22. "An Act providing compensations for the officers of the Judicial Courts of the United States, and for Jurors and Witnesses, and for other purposes" (1 *Stat.* 216–17).   23. 1 *Stat.* 226–29.

24. "An Act for finishing the Lighthouse on Baldhead at the mouth of Cape Fear river in the State of North Carolina" (1 *Stat.* 246).

25. "An Act establishing a Mint, and regulating the Coins of the United States" (1 *Stat.* 246–51).

26. "An Act to compensate the corporation of trustees of the public grammar school and academy of Wilmington, in the state of Delaware, for the occupation of, and damages done to, the said school, during the late war" (6 *Stat.* 8).

27. "An Act for raising a farther sum of money for the protection of the frontiers, and for other purposes therein mentioned" (1 *Stat.* 259–63).

28. "An Act making certain appropriations therein specified" (1 *Stat.* 284–85).

29. 6 *Stat.* 10.   30. 6 *Stat.* 10.

A GENERAL STATEMENT OF THE APPROPRIATIONS MADE BY LAW, AND OF THE EXPENDITURES OF THE UNITED STATES IN RELATION THERETO, FROM THE FIRST DAY OF JANUARY TO THE LAST DAY OF DECEMBER 1792.

Dates and Titles of the Acts of Appropriations.	For discharging the warrants issued by the late Board of Treasury	For the support of the Civil List under the late and present Government	For the support of the …
Balances remaining unexpended on the 31st. of december 1791, on appropriations made prior to the 23d. of said month, agreeably to the schedule annexed to the General account of Receipts and Expenditures rendered to the House of Representatives on the 10th: of November 1792.	32.210.06	189,706.55	314,•
1790 July 1: An Act providing the means of Intercourse between the United States, and Foreign Nations			
Aug. 4: An Act making provision for the debt of the United States			
1791 Mar: 3. An Act to incorporate the Subscribers to the Bank of the United States [31]			
Decr. 23: An Act making appropriations for the support of Government for the year 1792		329.653.56	444.•
1792 Apl. 2: An Act for finishing the Light house on Bald Head at the mouth of Cape Fear river in the state of No. Carola.			
" An Act establishing the Mint and regulating the coins of the United States			
" An Act to compensate the corporation of Trustees of the Public Grammar School & Academy of Wilmington in the State of Delaware, for the occupation of & damages done to the said School, during the late War			
May 2: An Act for raising a further sum of money for the protection of the frontiers & for other purposes therein mentd.			673
8 An Act supplementary to the Act making provision for the debt of the United States [32]			
" An Act making certain appropriations therein specified			
" An Act to compensate the services of the late Colonel George Gibson			
" An Act concerning the claim of John Brown Cutting against the United States			
Amount of Appropriations	32,210.06	519,360.11	1,432
Amount of payments during the year 1792	33.33	327,711.80	1,116
Balances unexpended on the 31st. of December 1792.	32,176.73	191,648.31	316

For paying the pensions due to Invalids.	For defraying the expences of negociations or treaties of peace with the Indian Tribes	For paying Interest due on temporary loans obtained by the Secretary of the Treasury.	For the support of the Ministers &c of the United States at foreign Courts & maintaining intercourse with Foreign Nations	For effecting a recognition of the Treaty of the United States with the new Emperor of Morocco	For the building, equipment, and support of ten revenue cutters.	Towards discharging certain debts contracted by Ab: Skinner, late commissary of Prisoners.	Towards discharging certain debts contracted by Colonel Timothy Pickering	For paying the Interest due on the Domestic debt of the United States.
104,629.44	13,000.—	2,401.88	78,266.67	7,000.—	32,757.50	209.62	38,545.92	229,452.94
			40,000.—					{A. 691,231.26} {B. 2,849,194.73}
87.463.60								
			50,000.—					
192,093 04 108.800.15	13,000.—	2,401.88	168,266.67 78,766.67	7,000.—	32,757.50 53.02	209.62	38,545.92 2,606.18	3,769,878.93 2,374,054 28
83,292.89	13,000.—	2,401.88	89,500.—	7,000.—	32,704.48	209.62	35,939.74	F. 1,395,824.65

Dates and Titles of the Acts of Appropriations.	For paying bills of exchange drawn on the late Commr. at Paris, for Interest due on loan office certificates.	For the support and repairs of lighthouses, beacons, buoys & public piers.	For defraying the contingent
Balances remaining unexpended on the 31st. of december 1791, on appropriations made prior to the 23d. of said month, agreeably to the schedule annexed to the General account of Receipts and Expenditures rendered to the House of Representatives on the 10th: of November 1792.	152.38.	43,089.15	8,7
1790 July 1: An Act providing the means of Intercourse between the United States, and Foreign Nations			
Aug. 4: An Act making provision for the debt of the United States			
1791 Mar: 3. An Act to incorporate the Subscribers to the Bank of the United States			
Decr. 23: An Act making appropriations for the support of Government for the year 1792			
1792 Apl. 2: An Act for finishing the Light house on Bald Head at the mouth of Cape Fear river in the state of No. Carola.		4.000.—	
" An Act establishing the Mint and regulating the coins of the United States			
" An Act to compensate the corporation of Trustees of the Public Grammar School & Academy of Wilmington in the State of Delaware, for the occupation of & damages done to the said School, during the late War			
May 2: An Act for raising a further sum of money for the protection of the frontiers & for other purposes therein mentd.			
8 An Act supplementary to the Act making provision for the debt of the United States			
" An Act making certain appropriations therein specified			
" An Act to compensate the services of the late Colonel George Gibson			
" An Act concerning the claim of John Brown Cutting against the United States			
Amount of Appropriations	152.38	47,089.15	8,7
Amount of payments during the year 1792	152.38	28,265.04	4
Balances unexpended on the 31st. of December 1792.		18,824.11	8,3

the public debt.	For defraying the expences [of the enumeration] 33 of the Inhabitants of the United States.	For satisfying miscellaneous claims.	For balances due to the French Government, to Oliver Pollock &ca. &ca.	For paying the debt due to Foreign Officers.	For payments on account of the French debt.	For effecting a subscription in behalf of the United States to the Bank of the United States	Total Amount
72.17	1,259.29	13,570.33					1,784,061.13
							40,000.—
					C. 726,000 —		4,266,425.99
						4,000,000.—	4,000,000.—
			197,119.49				1,059,222.81
							4,000 —
		D. 7,000.—					7,000.—
		2,553.64					2,553.64
							673,500.—
				E. 191,316.90			191,316.90
			34,497.90				84,497.90
		1,000.—					1,000 —
		2,000.—					2,000.—
72.17	1,259.29	26,123.97	231,617.39	191,316.90	726,000.—	4,000.000.—	12,115,578.37
86.42	1,259.29	14,652.61	202,773.14	18,354.79	G. 435,263.83	4,000.000.—	8,967,692.05
85.75		11,471.36	28,844.25	172,962.11	290,736.17		3,147,886.32

Balance of the appropriations brought down is   3,147,886.32
which deduct the following sums, being payable out of the Foreign
nds vizt.

    Balance payable to Foreign officers   172,962 11
    Balance due on account of the sum requested for St. Domingo   290,736.17   463,698.28

iinder being the unsatisfied appropriations charged upon the Revenue   2,684,188.04

A. The difference between the actual dividends declared on the public debt
to the end of the year 1791, as contained in the printed statement, and the
entire Interest for that year as estimated, including the Foreign Debt.
B. The Interest on the debt for the year 1792, as estimated.
C. The sum requested by the National assembly of France by their decree of
June 26th: 1792,[34] for the Colony of St. Domingo.   4,000,000 Livres.
D. The Sum actually advanced for the Mint Establishment, during the year
1792.
E. The debt payable to Foreign Officers contemplated in the fifth section of
the act supplementary to the act making provision for the Debt of the
United States.[35]
F. In this balance is included two years Interest on the Foreign Debt which
has been paid out of the Foreign Loans, the accounts of which remain unsettled also the Interest on that part of the Domestic Debt which has not
been funded, or registered at the Treasury so as to be entitled to a dividend
and also the Interest due to States on the unsubscribed balance of the
assumed debt, the payment of which is at present suspended.
G. Warrants for 445,263 Dollars and 83 Cents had been drawn on the 31st. of
december 1792, towards the debt due to France, as stated in the report of
the Secretary of the Treasury of the 3d. of January 1793   10,000 Dollars
of which however had not been paid by the Treasurer at that time, and
consequently not charged in his accounts.

Treasury Department February 14. 1793
Alex Hamilton
Secy of the Treasy

31. 1 *Stat.* 191–96 (February 25, 1791), 1 *Stat.* 196–97 (March 2, 1791).
32. 1 *Stat.* 281–83.
33. Material in brackets has been taken from *ASP, Finance,* I, 221.
34. *Archives Parlementaires,* XLV, 593–95.
35. Section 5 of this act reads as follows: "And whereas the United States are
indebted to certain foreign officers, on account of pay and services during the
late war, the interest whereof, pursuant to the certificates granted to the said
officers by virtue of a resolution of the United States in Congress assembled, is
payable at the house of [Ferdinand Le] Grand, banker, at Paris, and it is expedient to discharge the same. *Be it therefore enacted,* That the President of
the United States be, and he hereby is authorized to cause to be discharged the
principal and interest of the said debt, out of any of the monies, which have
been or shall be obtained on loan, in virtue of the act aforesaid, and which shall
not be necessary ultimately to fulfil the purposes for which the said monies are,
in and by the said act, authorized to be borrowed" (1 *Stat.* 282 [May 8, 1792]).

STATEMENT EXHIBITING THE DEBTS CHARGED UPON THE UNEXPENDED AND UNCOLLECTED INCOME OF THE UNITED STATES ON THE LAST DAY OF THE YEAR 1792

To the following Sums, which rested as Charges upon the Excess of Income stated ℔ Contra on the 31st. December 1792. Vizt:

Balances of unsatisfied Appropriations as specified in the Schedule herewith marked [B] [36] — 2,684,188. 04

Balance reserved to compleat the sum requested for St. Domingo — 290,736. 17

Balance reserved to compleat the payment of debts due to Foreign Officers — 172,962. 11

Debt due to the Bank of North America for a Loan without Interest — 156,595. 56

Debt due to the Bank of the United States for a Loan for the War Department — 400,000

3,704,481. 88

1,388,452. 23

Balance of the Foreign Fund not specially applied & subject to disposition — 21,762. 39

Surplus of Revenue above the appropriations to the end of 1792 agreeably to a statement marked A herewith

5,114,696. 50

By the Excess of Income beyond the actual disbursements of the Treasury to the end of the Year 1792, including all sums remaining uncollected at that time as also Dollrs. 2305,769.13 the proceeds of Bills of Exchange drawn on the Foreign Funds as stated in the account marked B. rendered to the House of Representatives on the 4th. of February 1793 [37]

5,114,696. 50

The Balance of the Foreign Fund as herein stated is thus deduced Vizt.

The total amount of bills drawn was — 2,305,769. 13

Deduct

Paid for the Colony of St. Domingo as ℔ Statement marked } 435,263. 83

Paid to Foreign Officers at ℔ ditto } 18,354. 79

Reserved to compleat the payment for St Domingo } 290,736. 17

Reserved to compleat the payment to Foreign Officers } 172,962. 11

917,316. 90

1,388,452. 23

Balance as before Stated

Treasury Department February 14, 1793
Alex Hamilton
Secy of the Treasury

36. The material in brackets has been taken from *ASP, Finance*, I., 222.

37. "Report on the Balance of All Unapplied Revenues at the End of the Year 1792 and on All Unapplied Monies Which May Have Been Obtained by the Several Loans Authorized by Law," February 4, 1793.

To Jean Baptiste de Ternant [1]

Departement de la tresorerie
le 14 fevr. 1793

Mr.

Conformément aux ordres du President,[2] et à l'information que vous en avez recue aujourdhuy de la part du secretaire d'etat, je mettrai à votre disposition une somme de cent mille piastres. Cette somme sera prete à etre acquittée le 1r. avril prochain, ce qui au cours des affaires de la place, équivaut à un payement immédiat.

J'ai l'honeur d'etre avec respect et estime Mr. etc.

Alexandre hamilton.

LC, *Arch. des Aff. Etr., Corr. Pol., Etats-Unis.*
    1. For background to this letter, see Tobias Lear to H, February 8, 1793.
    2. According to an entry in JPP for February 13, 1793, George Washington directed "Arrangements to be made at the Treasury for paying the Minister of France 100,000 dollars on Acct. of the French debt—the residue of his demand to remain until the balance on the last Instalment could be ascertained, which was presumed to be in a day or two" (JPP, 42).

From Edward Carrington [1]

Richmond Feb. 15. 1793

Dr Sir

I have been favored with a packet from you containing several Copies of your letter of the 4th. Instant to the Speaker of the House of Representatives.[2] I had fully anticipated the decided contradictions contained in this letter, to the suggestions which gave rise to it, having seen the Resolutions alluded to. The Copies of the letter are circulated as far as the Numbers would admit, and I think, if you could send me more, they might be distributed with good effect.

I cannot but be of opinion that you ought to rejoice in those attacks which lead to decided contradictions—both sides of the question get fairly presented to public view and truth must ultimately have its due effect.

I am with great regard   Your sincere Friend   & He st.

Ed. Carrington

ALS, Hamilton Papers, Library of Congress.
1. Carrington was supervisor of the revenue for the District of Virginia.
2. "Report on the Balance of All Unapplied Revenues at the End of the Year 1792 and on All Unapplied Monies Which May Have Been Obtained by the Several Loans Authorized by Law," February 4, 1793.

From Tench Coxe

Treasury Department,
Revenue-Office, February 15th. 1793.

Sir,

The fourth section of the Act of the 3d. of March, 1791 imposing duties upon domestic spirits, directs that the States shall be divided into districts by the President, in such manner that each district shall consist of one state.[1] But it is not clear on account of the limitation of the Number to *fourteen* that a newly created State can be erected into a District. Should this prove to be the case, it appears necessary that an act should be passed in regard to Kentuckey. The Compensations in that district will also require attention considering the exhausted state of the fund. When your leisure permits I will attend you on this subject and on that of my general Report on the excise.[2] If anything is to be done in this session there appears but little time to spare.

I have the honor to be, with great respect sir, your most Ob.
servant   Tench Coxe
                                          Commissr. of the Revenue.

The honorable,
The Secretary of the Treasury.

LC, RG 58, Letters of Commissioner of Revenue, 1792–1793, National Archives.
1. "An Act repealing, after the last day of June next, the duties heretofore laid upon Distilled Spirits imported from abroad, and laying others in their stead; and also upon Spirits distilled within the United States, and for appropriating the same" (1 *Stat.* 199–200 [March 3, 1791]).
2. Coxe's report, which was enclosed in H's "Report on Stills and Spirits Distilled Within the United States," March 2, 1793, is printed in *ASP, Finance,* I, 250–51.

From Tench Coxe

Treasury Department,
Revenue Office, February 15th. 1793.

Sir,

I have the honor to apprize you that "The act supplementary to the Act for the Establishment & support of Light Houses, Beacons, Buoys and public piers" will expire by its own limitations in regard to the unceded establishments of that Nature on the first day of July next.[1]

It appears necessary therefore that a New Act of continuance should be passed as several important instances of want of cession exist. It will be remembered that it has been found on Inspection, that the Jurisdiction of the establishments in Massachusetts has not been duly ceded.[2]

I have the honor to be, with great respect,   sir, your most Obedt. Servant   Tench Coxe.

Commissr. of the Revenue.

The honble.
The Secretary of the Treasury.

LC, RG 58, Letters of Commissioner of Revenue, 1792–1793, National Archives.

1. Section 1 of this act reads as follows: "That all expenses which shall accrue from the first day of July next, inclusively, for the necessary support, maintenance, and repairs of all lighthouses, beacons, buoys, the stakeage of channels, on the sea-coast, and public piers, shall continue to be defrayed by the United States, until the first day of July, in the year one thousand seven hundred and ninety-three, notwithstanding such lighthouses, beacons, or public piers, with the lands and tenements thereunto belonging, and the jurisdiction of the same, shall not in the mean time be ceded to, or vested in the United States, by the state or states respectively, in which the same may be, and that the said time be further allowed, to the states respectively to make such cession" (1 Stat. 251 [April 12, 1792]).

2. See Coxe to H, January 19, 1793.

From Joseph Nourse

Treasury Department
Register's Office 15. February 1793

Sir

The 11th. Section of the Act for registering and recording Ships or vessels [1] enacts that where a ship or vessel is in any other District than where the Owner, being a Citizen resides, The Collector of the Port in whose District the Vessel may be shall register the same provided that when the vessel shall return to the Port to which she belongs the said Register shall be delivered up and a New Register granted, upon which the Collector is directed to *transmit the Register so delivered up to the Collector of the Port where the same was issued.*

Having reflected upon the Opperation of the foregoing Clause I beg Leave to suggest for Consideration whether this Mode of forwarding the Registers from one Collector to another is not subject to Exception from the Information not being given to the Treasury and also from the Risque, to which they may be liable from various Casualties in transmissions from an Extreme Eastern to a southern Port and that as often as such Accidents happen the Records of the Treasury will be imperfect.

The foregoing Difficulties might be removed by directing that instead of transmitting the Certificate of Registry to the Collector who issued the same, that in all such Cases it be *forwarded to the Register of the Treasury to be by him cancelld and who shoud thereupon transmit Certificate thereof to the Collector who granted the said Register.*

The above Observation applies with equal Force to the 12th. Section,[2] to which as well as the foregoing the Secty. of the Treasury is very respectfully referred.

I have the Honor to be   Sir   Your mo: ob: hb: Servt.

Honble. Alexr. Hamilton Esqr
Secretary of the Treasury.

Copy, RG 53, Register of the Treasury, Estimates and Statements for 1793, Vol. "135-T," National Archives.

1. 1 *Stat.* 292–93 (December 31, 1792). The effective date for this act was March 31, 1793.

2. Section 12 of this act specified the method by which vessels purchased by agents were to be registered (1 *Stat.* 293–94).

To Jonathan Trumbull

Treasury   Department,
February   15th.   1793.

Sir,

I have reason to believe that in my letter of yesterday[1] No. 11, certain words were omitted in copying, necessary to the sense of the clause.

The clause alluded to probably stands thus.

"The laws authorizing the loans, passed the 4th. and 12th. of August. As early as the 28th. of that month, the acceptance above mentioned was communicated. So far no time was lost more than could not have been avoided."

The words supposed to be omitted, are these, "and the application of 1,500,000 florins in a payment to France directed."[2] These words ought to follow the word "communicated."

I request that the Clerk of the House of Representatives may be permitted to insert those words in their proper place.

With perfect respect,   I have the honor to be, Sir,   your obedient & humble servant.   A. Hamilton.

The Honorable the Speaker of
the House of Representatives.

Copy, RG 233, Reports of the Treasury Department, 1792–1793, Vol. III, National Archives.

1. "Report Relative to the Loans Negotiated Under the Acts of the Fourth and Twelfth of August, 1790," February 13–14, 1793.

2. The version of H's report printed above, taken from the copy in RG 233, Reports of the Treasury Department, 1792–1793, Vol. III, National Archives, does not contain this error.

To George Washington

[Philadelphia, February 15, 1793]

The Secretary of the Treasury has the honor to communicate, for the perusal of the President, a copy of his second Letter to the H: of Representatives;[1] which he will be obliged, if not inconvenient, to the President, to have returned on Monday morning, to be then sent to the Senate.[2]

Friday 15 feby: 1793.

LC, George Washington Papers, Library of Congress.
1. "Report Relative to the Loans Negotiated Under the Acts of the Fourth and Twelfth of August, 1790," February 13–14, 1793.
2. This report was submitted to the Senate on February 18, 1793 (*Annals of Congress*, III, 650).

From Caleb Gibbs [1]

Barre [Massachusetts] February 16, 1793. "The foregoing Duplicate [2] My Dear Friend I forward apprehensive that my Letters must have miscarried or otherwise I should certainly have heard from you ere this. Let me repeat my solicitations and ask an answer, feel for me, call up your esteem for me, Let me not be a cast off. . . ."

ALS, Hamilton Papers, Library of Congress.
1. Gibbs and H had been close friends during the American Revolution when both had been aides-de-camp to George Washington.
2. The enclosure was a duplicate of Gibbs to H, September 10, 1792.

From Gouverneur Morris [1]

Paris 16. February 1793

Dear Sir

My last was of the sixteenth of January of which I now enclose a Copy. It has so happened that a very great Proportion of the french Officers who served in America have been either opposed to the Revolution at an early Day, or felt themselves oblig'd at a later Period to abandon it. Some of them are now in a State of Banishment and their Property confiscated. Among these last there are a few who had entrusted to their Agents the Certificates received from our Treasury, and these last under the pressure of penal Decrees either detain those Certificates or have delivered them up to those Persons appointed by the Republic to take Charge of Confiscated Property. There certainly can be no question on this Subject under the Laws hitherto existing among Nations; but I shall not undertake to decide either on Rights or Pretensions to Right especially where I am not authorized to act; but it is proper that I lay before you a State of Facts for your ulterior Decision. The only one at present before me is the Case of Colo. Laumoy,[2] to whom I shall write in Answer to his Applications,[3] that I am not authorized to make Payment, but on Production of the Certificate, and therefore he must address himself on the Subject to you, in the full Confidence that Right and Justice will take place, such being the clear Determination of the United States.

LC, Gouverneur Morris Papers, Library of Congress.
1. For background to this letter, see H to Morris, September 13, 1792; Morris to H, December 23, 1792, January 16, 1793.
2. Jean Baptiste Joseph, Chevalier de Laumoy, had served as a colonel in the Corps of Engineers in the Continental Army during the American Revolution. In 1783, he had been brevetted brigadier general. When this letter was written, Laumoy, who was at The Hague, had written to Morris concerning the certificate which Laumoy, had left with his attorney in France (Morris to Laumoy, January 26, 1793 [LC, Gouverneur Morris Papers, Library of Congress]).
3. Morris to Laumoy, February 16, 1793 (LC, Gouverneur Morris Papers, Library of Congress).

From Samuel Paterson [1]

Edin[burg]h. 16 feby. 1793

Respectd. Sir

My desire to doe what I think may encrease the prosperity of a Free Country makes me *once more* adress you with the inclosed paper on *Cash accounts* as given out by the Banks in Scotland a measure that has been followed by the private Banks of England & what has added more to the prosperity of G Britain within the last 30 years that it has been adopted then any other operation in Banking— as well as given greater gains to the Banking Compys.

Understanding that the Same is not adopted or pursued by the

Two Banks in Philadelphia I have presumed theirfore to give you Some account of the practice, hoping if it is not adopted before this Comes to your hand you will fully Consider it & If you approve of it, get it adopted by the Bank of the United states, & the others will soon perceive the Benefit of it, & follow it.

Warr being now begun twixt Britain & France, It Certainly is the Intrest & duty of the Government of the United States of America, to get directly Packet Boats or Ships for Carrying the Letters, Bills of Exchange &c &c. twixt Britain & America—as well as twixt France Holland &c. & America—As the British Packets will be Captured by the French & the French Packets by the British.

It will be Needfull for the United States of America, to have a few Frigates or Ships of Warr, that their Flag may be respectd in the generall Convulsion of Europe.

Its Strongly reported & Confidently asserted in all the Ministeriall prints, that *Spain* has agreed to Join the Confedracy of Kings against France. If its *true* America Never had a better oppertunity to procure the Opening of the River Missisipie to her Vessells. And I hope the Wisdom of America will improve it, to that purpose.

I have Seen a Copy of your Report to Congress on the Encouraging of Manufacters &c. It has been printed I understand at Dublin,[2] destributed & Sold cheap. It Should be printed in the Dutch French & German Languages fix the price to it & get it Sold in these Countrys—the best premium you Can give to Encourage the poor distressed Subjects of these States to flock to America. Here if the price was Not fixed to a pamphlet the Booksellers would Not Sell it Cheap. I suppose the Booksellers thro Europe are the Same. Here the great people & Landed Intrest discourage Emigrations to America, as Well as government. I suppose its the Same in Holland France & flanders. Would it not be the Intrest of America to give Some Encouragement to Ships bringing over Passengers of Certain Descriptions?

I have Sent you the Speech of Mr. Erskine at London on the Liberty of the Press[3]—also a Translation on Legislation from the Italian of Filangieri[4] & an Acct. of the representation of the Burroughs Cinque Ports &c. of G Britain in 3 Vollumes.[5]

This letter is Not Sent out of assuming ambition. I dont wish you *on Any account* to Spend a Moment of *Your time in giving me any reply*. I Shall trouble you no More—only Consider & Read what I have said. I have always thought that bystanders might notice what a great man Engaged in the affairs of a Nation might have in his Numerous Engagements over looked. with Respect & Esteem I am Sr. Yr hb Ser   Sam. Paterson

To A Hamilton Esqr.
Philadelphia

P. S. The Banks of Scotland are greatly assisted by the trouble with which Gold passes, if the least light or Even Exact weight. Every Body on this account prefers a Bank Note of a Guinea to a gold Guinea. The Banks to Encourage this are very Nice about what Gold they take & its alledged they often refuse what Ought to Pass.
                                                                                S.P.

ALS, Hamilton Papers, Library of Congress.
    1. Paterson was an Edinburgh bookseller and bibliographer. See Paterson to H, February 10, 1791, note 1.
    2. *Report of the Secretary of the Treasury of the United States, On the Subject of Manufactures. Presented To The House of Representatives, December 5, 1791* (Dublin: Re-printed by P. Byrne, No. 108, Grafton-Street, 1792).
    3. Thomas Erskine, *The celebrated Speech of the Hon. T. E., in support of the liberty of the press. Delivered at Guildhall, December 18, 1792. To which is prefixed, a preface by a Scotch Member of Parliament* (Edinburgh, 1793).
    4. Gaetano Filangieri, *An Analysis of the science of Legislation.* Translated by W. Kendall (London, 1791).
    5. Thomas Hinton Oldfield, *An Entire and Complete History, political and personal, of the boroughs of Great Britain (together with the Cinque Ports); to which is prefixed, An original sketch of constitutional rights,* 3 Vols. (London, 1792).

To George Washington

[Philadelphia, February 16, 1793]

The Secretary of the Treasury presents his respects to the President, and has the honor to enclose the statement respecting the French debt.[1] He hopes to be able to wait upon the President on Monday, when he will give a further explanation.
                                                        Saturday 16 feby. 93.

LC, George Washington Papers, Library of Congress.
    1. This statement is described in JPP, 46, as "a statemt. of the balances of the Instalments of the French debt to the end of the last year." See Washington to

H, February 13, 1793. The enclosure may have been a statement entitled "the Government of France in Account with the United States, for Payment of Interest and Instalments to the 31 January 1793," signed by Joseph Nourse and dated February 9, 1793 (DS, RG 53, Register of the Treasury, Estimates and Statements for 1793, Vol. "135-T," Nation Archives).

From Angelica Church [1]

[London, February 17, 1793]

My dear Brother: You will receive this from a friend of mine and an admirer of your virtues and your talents. He goes to America to partake of that Liberty for which he has often exposed his life, and to render it all the services his knowledge of Europe and of the emigration about to take place to America, give the opportunity of doing.

The Count de Noailles [2] requires less recommendation than most people, because he is well known to you my friend. When you and he have talked over Europe and America, spare a few moments to the recollection of your faithful friend

And affectionate sister,   Angelica Church.

London, February 17th, 1793.
Alexander Hamilton, Esq.

Hamilton, *Intimate Life*, 294.
1. Angelica Church was Elizabeth Hamilton's sister and the wife of John B. Church.
2. Louis Marie, Vicomte de Noailles, Lafayette's brother-in-law, had served in the American Revolution as *colonel en second* of the Regiment Soissonnais. He had returned to France in 1781. Although he at first supported the French Revolution and served in the French Army in 1792, his disapproval of the increasing excesses of the Revolution led to his emigration first to England and then in early 1793 to the United States.

From George Washington [1]

United States, February 17 1793.
(Private)

Sir,

I transmit you a copy of a Letter from the Secretary of War to me, with the heads of instructions proposed to be given to the

Commissioners who may be appointed to hold a Treaty with the Western Indians in the Spring.[2]

As I intend in a few days to call for the advice & opinion of the heads of the Departments on the points touched upon in the enclosed paper, I must request you will give it an attentive and serious consideration, and note such alterations, amendments or additions in writing as may appear to you proper to be introduced into the Instructions proposed to be given to the Commissioners.

I shall likewise request the opinion of the same Gentlemen upon the expediency of asking the advice of the Senate, before the end of their present Session, as to the propriety of instructing the Commissioners to recede from the present boundary, provided peace cannot be established with the Indians upon other terms. I therefore desire you will turn your attention to this matter also, in order that you may be able to give a deliberate opinion thereon, when the Gentlemen shall be called together.

Go: Washington

The Secretary of the Treasury

LS, Connecticut Historical Society, Hartford; LC, addressed to H, Thomas Jefferson, and Edmund Randolph, George Washington Papers, Library of Congress.

1. For background to this letter, see "Conversation with George Hammond," November 22, 1792, note 4, December 15–28, 1792; H to Hammond, December 29, 1792; "Draft of Instructions for William Hull," January 14, 1793; Hull to H, February 6, 1792.

2. Copies of Henry Knox's letter, dated February 16, 1793, and of "the heads of the Instructions to the Commissioners for treating with the hostile Indians" are in the Connecticut Historical Society, Hartford, and in the Thomas Jefferson Papers, Library of Congress.

The "heads of the Instructions" read as follows:

"I. The Commissioners to be fully informed upon the subject of all the Treaties which have been held by the United States, or which have been held under their authority with the northern and western Indians—particularly of the Treaty of Fort Harmar in the year 1789, and of the boundaries then described. That the Commissioners possess themselves fully of all the proceedings of said Treaty, and of the tribes and principal Characters who formed the same. The Indians to be informed by the Commissioners that the United States consider the said Treaty to have been formed with the tribes who had a right to relinquish the lands which were then ceded to the United States. That, under this impression, part of the said lands have been sold to individuals, and parts assigned to the late Army of the United States.

"II. That the lands acquired by the said treaty were by purchase, as well as a confirmation of the former treaties. That if the consideration then given was inadequate, or if other tribes than those who formed the said Treaty, should have a just right to any of the said lands in question, a particular compensation should be made them. That, in both instances, the United States were disposed to be liberal in granting additional compensations.

"III. That the remaining lands of the Indians within the limits of the United States, shall be guaranteed solemnly by the general government.

"IV. That if the Commissioners can get the former boundaries established, they be directed, besides compensation in gross, to the amount of   dollars, to promise payment of ten thousand dollars per annum, in such proportions to the several tribes, as shall be agreed upon.

"V. That the Commissioners be directed further to relinquish the reservations marked upon the map as trading places—provid⟨ed⟩ the same would satisfy the Indians so as to confirm the remaind⟨er⟩ of the boundary, always, however, reserving as much land about the several British Posts, within the United States, as are now occupied by the several Garrisons, or which shall be necessary for the same.

"VI. That the Commissioners be instructed to use their highest exertions, to obtain the boundary now fixed, the reservation excepted, as before explained— and that for this purpose they be entrusted with   dollars to be used to influence certain white men to favour their measures.

"VII. But if, after every attempt, the assembled Indians should refuse the boundaries aforesaid—then the Commissioners are to endeavour to obtain from the Indians, a description of the best boundary to which they will agree, the Commissioners always endeavouring to conform the same, as nearly as may be, to the one described in the Treaty of Fort Harmar.

"VIII. On obtaining this information of the Indians, they are to be informed by the Commissioners, that the President of the United States, conceiving the boundary established by the Treaty of Fort Harmar, to have been made with the full understanding and free consent of the parties having the right to make the same, had not invested them (the Commissioners) with power to alter the same, excepting as to the reservations before described. But that now possessing the final & full voice of the Indians upon the subject, the same should be reported to the President, who would give a definitive answer thereon, at a period to be fixed, which period should not be earlier than four months after the Senate should be assembled at their next session, and this would fix the period about one year from the time the Commissioners should obtain this information.

"IX. The Commissioners should further inform the Indians, that until the answer should be received, a solemn truce should be observed on both sides. The Indians to be answerable for their Young Warriors—and the President to be answerable for our's.

"X. If the idea of a truce should be relished, perhaps it might be extended by the Commissioners to three or seven years, all things to remain in the same state. If so, the effect would be a peace to all intents and purposes.

"XI. The Commissioners to be particularly instructed to do nothing which should in the least impair the right of pre-emption or general sovereignty of the United States over the Country, the limits of which were established by the peace of 1783. But at the same time, to impress upon the Indians that the right of pre-emption in no degree affects their right to the soil, which the United States concedes unlimitedly, excepting that when sold it must be to the United States, and under their authority—and no otherwise." (Copy, Connecticut Historical Society, Hartford.)

On March 1, 1793, Washington appointed Benjamin Lincoln, Beverley Randolph, and Timothy Pickering as commissioners "on the part of the United States, for holding a conference or treaty with the hostile Indians." The Senate confirmed the appointment on March 2 (*Executive Journal*, I, 135-36).

From Tobias Lear

[Philadelphia] Monday 18 febry. 1793.

Dear Sir,

The President does not recollect the name of the person mentioned to succeed the Collector of Edenton (N:C.)[1] and wishes you to send it. Is it intended that the person mentioned should be appointed Inspector of Survey No. 2. which office was held by the Collector of Edenton? Inspector of the Port he will be of course. Is William Munson to be appointed Inspector as well as Surveyor of the Port of New Haven? And if so, how is the matter to be settled with the Collector,[2] who has heretofore held the Office of Inspector?[3]

The President is desirous that the nominations should go to the Senate today, which is the cause of my giving you this trouble. I call'd at your House & Office to mention these matters; but had not the pleasure to find you at either.

I am &c.   Tos: Lear
                                                           S. P U S

LC, George Washington Papers, Library of Congress.
    1. Thomas Benbury, collector of customs at Edenton, had died.
    2. Jonathan Fitch.
    3. At the bottom of this letter the following note is written: "Note—In answer to the above the Secretary of the Treasury returned that *Saml. Tredwell* (now Deputy Collector) is to succeed the Collector of Edenton. If Benbury was appointed Inspector of Survey No. 2. by the last arrangement of all, Tredwell is to be appointed also. Wm. Munson is to be Inspector & Surveyor of Nw. Haven. The Collector, who has heretofore held the office of Inspector, has been written to on the score of it's being a *general arrangement*."

To Jonathan Trumbull

Treasury Department,
February 18th. 1793

Sir,

It is with much regret, I find myself under an impossibility of presenting to day, conformably to the expectation given in my last,[1] the concluding communication in answer to the late resolutions of the House. I trust nothing will delay it beyond tomorrow. With perfect respect,

I have the honor to be, Sir,　Your most obedient and humble servant,　　　　　　　　　　　　　　Alexander Hamilton

The Honorable the Speaker
of the House of Representatives.

Copy, RG 233, Reports of the Treasury Department, 1792–1793, Vol. III, National Archives.
　1. "Report Relative to the Loans Negotiated Under the Acts of the Fourth and Twelfth of August, 1790," February 13–14, 1793.

From Joseph Ward [1]

[*Newton, Massachusetts, February 18, 1793.* On May 6, 1793, Hamilton wrote to Ward and acknowledged the receipt of Ward's "letter of the 18th of February last." *Letter not found.*]

　1. Ward was a Boston stockbroker and real estate dealer.

Report on the State of the Treasury at the Commencement of Each Quarter During the Years 1791 and 1792 and on the State of the Market in Regard to the Prices of Stock During the Same Years [1]

Treasury Department
February 19th. 1793.
[Communicated on February 20, 1793] [2]

[To the Speaker of the House of Representatives]
Sir,
　The last letter, which I had the honor to address to the House of Representatives,[3] contained, a pretty full exposition of the conduct and views of this department, in regard to the foreign loans. There remains, however, some incidental topics, which it may not be expedient to pass over in silence.

Copy, RG 233, Reports of the Secretary of the Treasury, 1784–1795, Vol. IV, National Archives.
　1. For background to this document, see the introductory note to "Report on the Balance of All Unapplied Revenues at the End of the Year 1792 and on All Unapplied Monies Which May Have Been Obtained by the Several Loans Authorized by Law," February 4, 1793.
　2. *Journal of the House*, I, 709.
　3. "Report Relative to the Loans Negotiated Under the Acts of the Fourth and Twelfth of August, 1790," February 13–14, 1793.

In order to carry the attention of the House immediately to a just application of the remarks which will be submitted, it is necessary to premise that it is known to have been suggested, that the proceeds of the foreign bills, drawn for to this country, had no object of public utility—answered none—and were calculated merely to indulge a spirit of favoritism towards the bank of the United States.

It has already been shewn, clearly I trust, that but for the instrumentality of the parts of the loan drawn for prior to April 1792, amounting nearly to one half of the whole sum; the purchases of the debt which were made to that time, could not have been made; and that these purchases, besides being the objects designated by law, for the application of the fund, were productive of possitive and important advantages.[4]

How far the operation could have been influenced by motives of favor to the bank of the United States, the following facts will still more completely decide.

That bank did not begin its operations till the 12th of December 1791.

The banks of North America and New York were agents of the treasury for the sale of the bills in question. They sold them, collected, and, with the exception which will be presently stated, disbursed the proceeds.

The receipts on account of these bills, began in March 1791, and concluded in March 1792.

On the 31st. of December 1791, as the Treasurer's accounts before the House will shew,[5] the public cash was deposited as follows

		Dollars	Cents
In the Bank of the United States,		133,000.	
Bank of North America,		471,972.	28.
Bank of New York,		224,677.	35.
Bank of Massachusetts,		65,578.	22.
Bank of Maryland,		50,665.	29.
Bank of Providence,		7.969.	61.
Making together,	Dollars	953,862.	75

4. "Report Relative to the Loans Negotiated Under the Acts of the Fourth and Twelfth of August, 1790," February 13–14, 1793.

5. "Report Relative to the Loans Negotiated Under the Acts of the Fourth and Twelfth of August, 1790," February 13–14, 1793, Enclosure IV.

There were then also some monies in the banks of North America and New York, in a course of receipt which had not been passed over to the Treasurer; but all the public monies of whatever kind, in the Bank of the United States, are included in the above sum of 133,000 dollars, which had arisen from the duties on imports and tonnage.

It appears then, that on the 31st. of December 1791, no transfer for the benefit of the bank of the United States had been made; and the deposits of government there (exclusive of the proceeds of the bills remaining in the two Banks of North America and New York) amounted to little more than one fourth of the deposits in the bank of North America, and little more than one half of those in the bank of New York.

As late as the 1st. of February, the State Banks continued to share with the bank of the United States a large proportion of the public deposits. The state of the Treasury then was as follows, Viz.

		Dollars	Cents
In the Bank of the United States,		456,278	90.
Bank of North America,		151,516.	32.
Bank of New York,		128,708.	21
Bank of Massachusetts,		71,215.	55
Bank of Maryland,		49,583.	25
Bank of Providence,		7,969.	61
Making together, Dollars		865,271	84

A concentration of the public deposits in the bank of the United States was a measure which grew out of the relation between that establishment and the government. Yet instead of hastening it through favor, it was resolved to let it have a gradual course; so as to consult in a due degree, the convenience of the other banks; and to effect it rather by letting the public disbursements fall upon the monies in those banks than by direct transfer.[6]

But a state of things took place in the month of February, between the banks of the United States and North America, which rendered a more expeditious transfer than was meditated, for the mutual convenience of the two institutions.

6. See H to the President and Directors of the Bank of the United States, January 28, 1792; H to William Seton, March 19, 1792.

The effect of this was, that the state of the Treasury on the 1st. of March, stood as follows.

	Dollars	Cents
In the Bank of the United States.	692,959.	6.
Bank of Massachusetts,	31.769.	5.
Bank of New York,	32,352.	52
Bank of North America,	31,515.	74.
Bank of Providence,	8,404.	94.
Bank of Maryland,	34,752.	85.
Making together, Dollars	381,754.	16

But at this time there was in the bank of New York, from the proceeds of the foreign Bills, 121,984 dollars and 71 cents, not transferred to the account of the Treasurer.

This accumulation, however, in the bank of the United States, was of very short duration.

On the 1st. of April ensuing, the State of the public cash was as follows.

	Dollars	Cents
In the Bank of the United States,	359,643.	64.
Bank of New York,	254,930.	41.
Bank of North America	31,515.	74.
Bank of Massachusetts,	37,712.	58.
Bank of Providence	7,156.	65.
Bank of Maryland	60,418.	32.
Making together, Dollars	751,377.	34

A similar state of things lasted to the 1st. of June, comparatively more disadvantageous to the bank of the United States. The receipts of public revenue continued to go into the bank of New York 'till the 1st. of April 1792, when a branch of the bank of the United States began to operate in that city—which is the reason of the sum in the bank of North America. By this time also, the balance of the proceeds of foreign Bills had been passed to the account of the Treasurer; yet still remaining in deposit in the bank of New York.

These views of the state of the public cash are conformable to the Treasurer's statement of half monthly balances, accompanying my letter of the 14th instant, No. V.[7]

The same statement will shew, that a proportion of the public deposits has continued since the 1st. of April 1792, in the banks of North America and New York down to the end of the period, which that statement embraces.

From these details the following inferences are deducible.

That as far as any advantages may have accrued from the deposits on account of foreign bills drawn prior to April 1792, they accrued substantially to the banks of North America and New York, not to the bank of the United States or to its branches.

That in transferring the pecuniary concerns of the government from the pre-existing banks to that of the United States and its dependencies, a cautious regard has been paid to the convenience of the former institutions, and the reverse of a policy unduly solicitous for the accommodation of the bank of the United States has prevailed. Indeed so much has this been the case, that it might be proved, if it were proper to enter into the proof, that a criticism has been brought upon the conduct of the department, as consulting less the accommodation of the last mentioned institution than was due to its relation to the government and to the services expected from it.

But further examination will demonstrate another point; which is, that none of the establishments in question have received any accommodations, which were not in perfect coincidence with the public interest, and in the due and proper course of events.

This examination will be directed towards two objects; one, the state of the Treasury at the commencement of each quarter, during the years 1791 and 1792; the other the State of the market in regard to the prices of stock during the same years.

These periods are selected because they afford the truest criterion of the State of the Treasury, from time to time, being those at which the principal public payments are made; and for which it is necessary to be prepared by intermediate accumulations.

The state of the Treasury at the periods in question was as follows:

7. "Report Relative to the Loans Negotiated Under the Acts of the Fourth and Twelfth of August, 1790," February 13–14, 1793.

		Dollars	Cents
In the year 1791	January 1st	569.886.	55.
	March 1st	373,434.	53
	June 1st	533,638.	24
	October 1st	662,233.	99.

In the year 1792.

		Dollars	Cents
	January 1st	953,862.	75.
	April 1st	751,377.	34.
	July 1st	623,133.	61.
	October 1st	420,914.	51.
1793.	January 1st	783,212.	37.

This appears from the statements No. IV and V, forwarded with my last letter.[8]

The state of the stock market, during the several quarters of the same years, was as follows—

First quarter of 1791	Six per cents, from	16/9 to 17/6.
	Three per cents, from	8/6 to 9/4.
	Deferred, from	8/6 to 9/4.
Second quarter of 1791	Six per cents, from	17/ to 17/9.
	Three per cents, from	9/ to 10/.
	Deferred, from	8/11 to 9/4.
Third quarter of 1791	Six per cents, from	17/10 to 21/3.
	Three per cents, from	9/9 to 12/5.
	Deferred, from	9/9 to 12/10

As early as the 6th of August, the six per cents had a temporary rise to 21/ but by the 16th they had fallen to 20/. on the 20th they had risen to 20/6. and were sometimes above that rate, but never lower during the rest of the quarter.

As early as the 23d of July, the three per cents had reached 12/. and were sometimes higher, but never lower during the rest of the quarter.

On the 23d of July, the deferred also reached 12/. and afterwards rose to 12/6.

Fourth quarter of 1791.	Six per cents, from	20/4 to 22/4.
	Three per cents, from	12/2 to 13/8.
	Deferred, from	11/8 to 13/6.

8. "Report Relative to the Loans Negotiated Under the Acts of the Fourth and Twelfth of August, 1790," February 13–14, 1793.

The prices were lowest in the early, and highest in the latter part of the quarter.

During the whole of the month of December, the deferred was at 12/8. and upwards; the greatest part of the time at 13/.

First quarter of 1792.	Six per cents, from	21/ to 25/.
	Three per cents, from	12/6 to 15/.
	Deferred, from	12/. to 15/.

The low prices were in the last ten days of March.

Second quarter of 1792.	Six per cents, from	20/ to 22/6.
	Three per cents, from	12/ to 13/9.
	Deferred, from	11/6 to 13/4.
Third quarter of 1792	Six per cents, from	21/ to 22/3.
	Three per cents, from	12/4 to 13/6.
	Deferred, from	12/3 to 13/7.
Fourth quarter of 1792	Six per cents, from	20/2 to 21/9.
	Three per cents, from	12/3 to 13/6
	Deferred, from	11/10 to 13/6.

In October the deferred was at the highest. The lowest prices were in the month of December.

This view of the subject is derived from a statement of prices pursuant to actual purchases and sales, furnished by a dealer of this City, respectable for his intelligence and probity, combined with the accounts from time to time published in the Gazette of the United States. The papers marked (Ax) and (By) are transmitted for the more particular information of the House on this head.

The market prices of stock no doubt varied at other places, at some may have been higher, at others lower. At Philadelphia too, 'tis believed, that no small sums were obtainable at particular periods from necessitous individuals, below the prices in the statement.

But there is good ground of reliance that it is substantially a just representation of the state of the stock market, during the periods to which it refers.

The state of the Treasury from the first of January to the first of October 1791, may be said to have been at its proper level, exhibiting none or an inconsiderable excess beyond the sum which has been mentioned as necessary to be there, and concerning which a further explanation has been promised, and will be given in the course of this letter. The public purchases in August and September 1791, amounted to 349.744 dollars and 99 cents.

In the last quarter of the year 1791, beginning with the month of November, and the first quarter of the year 1792, there appears to have been an excess of some magnitude in the Treasury, being from about 250,000 to about 450,000 dollars. Taking the first quarter of the year 1792 as the truest criterion; (which it certainly was, because at the expiration of that quarter the payment of interest on the assumed debt began and was to be provided for) the real excess ought to be considered as 250,000 dollars; with the addition of about 80,000 dollars then in the bank of North America, from the proceeds of Amsterdam bills beyond the advances of the bank for the public service; which had not been passed into the Treasurers account. It is proper to remark that the course of importations occasions large receipts in the latter part of each year, which circumstance contributed to the accumulation in question.

From the last of November to about the 21st of March, an investment of the excess on hand in purchases was impracticable.

To enable the House to understand what is meant by saying that purchases were impracticable during that period, it is necessary to add, that the price of stock exceeded the limits the commissioners of the sinking fund had prescribed to themselves. Indeed a large proportion of the time, those prices were manifestly artificial, and such as predicted a great fall not far distant. The delay incurred was accordingly well compensated by the prices at which investments were afterwards made.

From the 21st of March to the 25th of April, purchases were effected to the extent of 242,688 dollars and 31 cents, in specie; within 80, or 90,000 dollars of what could have been spared, consistently with the rule which has been mentioned, as proper to regulate the arrangements of the Treasury.

But two circumstances operated against a further investment—a sudden rise of prices and a state of temporary disorder [9] in the two principal mercantile scenes of the Country (occasioned by the excessive speculations that had preceeded) which admonished the Treasury to be cautious in its disbursements.

9. This is a reference to the financial panic of 1792. See William Duer to H, March 12, 1792, note 3; H to Duer, March 14, 23, 1792; Robert Troup to H, March 19, 1792; Seton to H, March 21, 1792.

It results from the foregoing view of the subject, that as far as any extraordinary sum may have remained unemployed in the banks a longer term than was desirable, it proceeded essentially from a state of things which did not permit its employment; and is in no degree attributable to that spirit of favoritism towards those establishments or any of them, which has been imagined, as the solution of appearances, not rightly understood, and much over-rated.

The only question, then, of which the matter is susceptible, is this way—Was not the state of things, that did take place, to have been foreseen, so as to have influenced the drawing for a proportionably less sum?

This question may safely be answered in the negative.

The Bills, the proceeds of which contributed to constitute the excess, which remained unemployed during the two quarters, were drawn in May 1791. In that month the highest prices of stock were 17/2 for six per cents, 9/2 for three per cents, and 9/3 for deferred.

No reasonable anticipation at this juncture, of the progressive rise of stock could have carried it in so short a time to the height which it attained, or beyond the limits within which purchases were deemed advantageous. The rapid and extraordinary rise, which did ensue, was in fact artificial and violent; such as no discreet calculation of probabilities could have pre-supposed. It therefore cannot impeach the prudence or expediency of having made provision, on a different supposition, for an extension of purchases.

The proceeds of the bills which were drawn subsequent to May, only began to be collected about the beginning of February, and continued in collection 'till the 29th of March. On the second of February the sum received amounted to no more than 13,431 dollars and 33 cents.

These last bills were drawn when the rapid rise of stock commenced, and were sold upon a credit of three months.

It was a natural conjecture, that a rise so sudden and violent could [not] be of long duration and that a declension would shortly succeed, would afford an opportunity of purchasing with advantage; and render the intervention of public purchases advantageous in more than one respect. The event fully corresponded with anticipation.

With regard to the bills drawn in April last, it has been stated that they were directed to be sold upon a credit of six months; that those drawn in July, August and October, were made payable, one moiety in two, the other moiety in four months. Hence, with a moderate allowance for delay in the sales, the period contemplated by the arrangement for the commencement of receipts was the month of October; that for their consummation the month of February.

The inducements to the drawing these bills have been stated. The present examination has relation merely to the question, whether the bank of the United States, by premeditation of this department, or subsequent omissions, had enjoyed any undue advantage from the deposits of the proceeds of the bills at the end of the year 1792, the point of time to which this enquiry has reference.

The Statement which has been made, as to the monies received to that period had remained in deposit, might alone be relied upon as a sufficient answer. If delinquency can be attached to the non-employ-ment of one or two hundred thousand dollars for a few weeks, in the money operations of a nation, it implies a minuteness of responsi-bi[li]ty, which could never be encountered with prudence, and never will be fulfilled in practice. The distractions of attention, in-cident to a great and complicated scene of business would alone disappoint the expectation.

But I have more than this to offer, upon the present occasion. The opportunity for investing the monies on hand during the period in question was not favorable. This was experienced by the Treas-urer['s] indeavors to invest the fund arising from the interest on the purchased debt. There was no part but the deferred, which could be had at all within the limits prescribed. Several indications of an ap-proaching season, more advantageous for purchases, were discern-able, and a better employment of the money than at the then prices presented itself to the option of the legislature. This mode of em-ploying it formed in my mind part of a general plan for the regular redemption of the public debt according to the right reserved to the government. The one per cent which might be saved, was regarded as one mean of constituting the proposed annuities.

Accordingly: On the 30th of November last, pursuant to a refer-ence of the 22d of that month, and connected with the plan of redemption contemplated, I submitted to the House of Representa-tives a proposition for applying the monies in question, towards discharging the debt which the government owes to the bank, and upon which an interest of six per cent is payable.[10] This was manifestly, at the time of the proposition, the most profitable use that could be made of the fund. It has been already stated that it would produce a saving, if extended to the whole two millions, worth to the government an annual sum of 20,000 dollars, equal to a capital of 400,000 dollars.

This proposition tended to accelerate the employment of the monies on hand in a way the most beneficial to the government; and consequently to shorten the duration of the advantage to the banks of holding them, by way of deposit. I submit it to the candour of the House, whether it be not full evidence, that there was no disposition, on my part, to prolong to those institutions a benefit, at the expense of the government.

The proposition itself has not yet received the decision of the House.

Another ground, upon which the suggestion of mismanagement and undue concession to the interests of the banks has been founded respects the domestic loans which have been obtained. Those of them which have been made of the bank of the United States are represented as unnecessary, tending to afford an emolument to that institution, for which the United States had no equivalent advantage.[11]

It will conduce to a correct judgment of this matter to resume a point already touched upon, and to add here the further illustration of it which have been promised; to wit, that it ought to be a general principle to have constantly in the command of the Treasury, at its different places of deposit, a sum of about 500,000 dollars; [12] a principle, too, which must be understood with reference to the beginnings of the quarters of a year, when the chief public payments are made and making.

The following observations will apply generally to the balances, which appear at the commencement of each quarter. The greatest

10. "Report on the Redemption of the Public Debt," November 30, 1792.

11. H is referring to remarks made by William B. Giles in support of his resolutions of January 23, 1793. See the introductory note to "Report on the Balance of All Unapplied Revenues at the End of the Year 1792 and on All Unapplied Monies Which May Have Been Obtained by the Several Loans Authorized by Law," February 4, 1793.

12. See "Report Relative to the Loans Negotiated Under the Acts of the Fourth and Twelfth of August, 1790," February 13–14, 1793 (*supra*, pp. 48–49).

part of the interest for the preceeding quarter will have then been deducted. But a part is always in a different situation.

The payment of interest upon a public debt, at thirteen different places, is an operation as difficult and complicated as it is new. In carrying it into execution, it is of necessity to lodge for some time previous to the expiration of each quarter, at several of the loan offices, drafts of the Treasurer for the sums estimated to be necessary at those offices, with blanks for the direction, and with liberty to the respective officers to dispose of them upon different places, as a demand accrues. This arrangement has an eye to two purposes; to avoid large previous accumulations at particular points; to facilitate the placing of the requisite sums, where they are wanted, without the transportation of specie. The allowing of the drafts to be disposed of on several places gives larger scope to a demand for them, and renders them more easily saleable. But it is a consequence of this, that a part of the drafts are often not placed and brought into the accounts of the Treasurer till some time after the expiration of the quarter. The fund for them of course appears on hand 'till the transaction is completed.

Connected with the circumstance of paying the interest upon the public debt at different places is this further consequence. The transfers continually going on from one office to another, render it impossible to know at any moment when provision for the payment of interest is to be made, what sum is requisite at each place. Estimate must supply the want of knowledge, and to avoid disappointment any where, the estimate must always be large, and a correspondent sum placed in the power of the commissioners. This circumstance alone requires an extra sum at the different places of payment, which ought not to be computed at less than 50,000 dollars.

Again—the sums payable on account of the civil list, at the end of each quarter, which amounts to about fifty thousand dollars, exclusive of what relates to the two House of Congress, are always in a course of payment for some time within the succeding quarter. The fund for them consequently appears in the monies on hand at the beginning of such quarter.

Again: There are constantly considerable arrears of existing appropriations, for which demands on the Treasury are at every moment possible—the times when they will be presented, and to what extent, at any given time, being in a great degree contingent. The arrears for the different objects of the War department, can seldom be estimated at less than 150,000 dollars.

It is presumed to be a clear principle, that the Treasury ought to be always ready to face such arrears, as may be claimed at every instant, or within any short period. An hour's distress or embarrassment, to make good a public payment, already due, would be baneful to public credit. It has been a uniform maxim of the present administration of the Treasury never to risk such distress or embarrassment.

Independently therefore of the weighty consideration of being prepared (especially with a War on hand liable every moment to greater extension)[13] for future casualities, the mere satisfaction of arrears, ought to cause the constant reservation of a sum, that would be moderately stated at half the sum which it has been alledged ought always to be in the treasury. It is to be observed that it does not often happen, that the current receipts to be expected in any immediately succeeding quarter, are likely to exceed the probable expenditure of the quarter. The reverse is as often the case. Hence the greater necessity of maintaining a constant surplus.

There are still other considerations of weight, in a just estimate of the point in question.

The sum stated, as necessary to be always in the command of the Treasury, is never in fact at the seat of the government, where far the greatest part of the public disbursements are to be made. The depositories of it are the several banks from Charleston to Boston. The whole sum therefore can never be brought into immediate action, for answering the claims upon the Treasury. No part can be properly viewed as in this situation, beyond New York on the one side and Baltimore on the other. Whatever part is more remote than

13. After the defeat of Major General Arthur St. Clair by the Indians in November, 1791, plans had been made for a new campaign against the western tribes. "An Act for making farther and more effectual Provision for the Protection of the Frontiers of the United States" (1 *Stat.* 241–43 [March 5, 1792]) had increased the forces on the frontier and provided for a virtual reorganization of the Army. In April, 1792, Major General Anthony Wayne was appointed commanding officer to superintend the reorganization and training of the Army in preparation for a new Indian campaign. Although Indian attacks continued on the frontier during 1792, the campaign was delayed awaiting the outcome of peace negotiations with the Indians at a proposed conference in the summer of 1793. See George Washington to H, February 17, 1793.

those points, ought not to be regarded as capable of being commanded in less time upon an average, than sixty days, making an allowance for the usual delays in the sale of the bills, and the usual terms of credit; which experience has shewn to be convenient.

In estimating the effective sum at any time on hand, in the bank of the United States, it is necessary to be known, that a practice for the simplification of the Treasurer's bank account, begun with the bank of North America, has been continued with the bank of the United States, of this nature—The bills drawn by the Treasurer upon distant places, and deposited with the bank for sale, are immediately passed to his credit as cash; though they are allowed to be sold at credits from thirty to sixty days; and it is understood, that the proceeds are not demandable of the bank, 'till they are collected. Hence the apparent sum in the bank of the United States is always greater than the real; sometimes to a large amount.

The deductions to be made for this circumstance are shewn in the Treasurer's half monthly statement of balances No V, beginning with the first of June 1792, and ending with the first of January 1793.[14] The period begun with is that, when the first instalment of the loan from the bank was payable; and has been selected for this reason.

The propriety of these deductions appears to have been objected to, by anticipation, on two grounds—one, that the bills deposited answer all the purposes of cash and ought to be credited as such, on the receipt of them—the other, that "there is a regular and constant influx of monies into the bank, by the operation of these bills—and that it is not very material whether a bill lodged in the bank today, should be paid today provided something like the sum should be paid in consequence of a bill lodged in bank one or two months ago, and the bill of today should be paid one or two months hence." [15]

Neither the one nor the other of these two positions is correct.

In no sense are the notes of the purchasers of the bills, which are

14. See "Report Relative to the Loans Negotiated Under the Acts of the Fourth and Twelfth of August, 1790," February 13–14, 1793, Enclosure V.

15. This is a quotation from a speech made by William B. Giles in support of his resolutions of January 23, 1793. See the introductory note to "Report on the Balance of All Unapplied Revenues at the End of the Year 1792 and on All Unapplied Monies Which May Have Been Obtained by the Several Loans Authorized by Law," February 4, 1793.

taken payable in 30, 45 and 60 days the same thing to a bank as cash. 'Tis evident it could not pay its own bills with those notes. In this primary particular therefore the comparison fails—neither could it make disco[u]nts upon the basis of those notes as cash. Because every discount gives a right to a borrower to call and receive in coin, if he pleases, the amount of the sum discounted. Notes are not coin nor do they confer an equal power to pay. It is true that a bank will in its discounts make some calculation on expected receipts, but it never can consider them as equivalent to cash, in hand nor operate upon them in any degree to the same extent as upon equal sums in cash. If notes payable at future periods were equivalent to cash, then every discount made by a bank would confer a faculty to make another for an equal sum; for there is always a note deposited for the sum discounted—and the power of discounting might by the mere exercise of it become infinite. An hypothesis of this kind will never be acted upon by any prudent directors of a bank, and could not be long acted upon without ruin to the institution. It is to be observed that the great profitable business of a bank consists in discounting.

There is but one light in which the position under examination is in any degree founded. It is this, that were it not for the instrumentality of the bills, the specie of the bank would sometimes be remitted for purposes which are answered by the bills. As often as this happens, they are a substitute to the bank for cash, because, they prevent equivalent sums being carried away.

But this only sometimes happens. In numerous instances the enterprizes to which the bills are subservient would not be undertaken at all, were it not for the power of anticipation, which the credits upon them afford. In many other instances the bills of the bank itself would be remitted instead of specie; in others private bills would be substituted; in others mutual credits between the merchants, to be liquidated in the course of mutual dealings, would supply the call.

Hence it is only true that Treasury bills some times answer the purpose of cash to the bank—whence it does not follow, that they ought always to be considered and credited definitively as cash. It is also true, though in a less degree, that notes deposited with the bank by individuals for collection, sometimes answer to it the purposes of cash—but it will be readily perceived that it would be inadmissable as a general rule, to receive and credit them as such.

The effect in both cases would be, that the bank would make an advance of a present sum without interest, for a sum to be received in future.

An arrangement indeed has been for some time depending between the bank of the United States and the Treasury, for securing to the government the advantage of an immediate absolute credit for the bills deposited, as so much cash to be coupled with some collateral accommodations to the bank.[16] But it has not yet been carried into effect. The fact heretofore, has been stated, and the reasoning, to be just, must proceed on that basis.

The last of the two positions which have been cited has still less foundation than the first.

A sum received to day, for a bill deposited two months past, can in no view be deemed a substitute for the amount of a bill deposited to day, to be received two months hence. It is to be remembered that the amount of the first bill was itself credited at the time of the deposit; and that the sum received to day on that account can only realize the antecedent credit. It cannot represent or be equivalent for the future receipt upon a different bill. To affirm that it could, is to make one sum the representative of two. The consequence of the reasoning would be, that the government ought to receive the money paid in to day as a satisfaction, as well for the bill deposited to day as for that which was deposited two months past.

Making the proper deductions on account of the bills, the amount of the effective cash in the banks at Philadelphia, New York and Baltimore was on the first of June, 587,091 dollars and 11 cents; in other banks, there was then also the further sum of 9,561 dollars and 89 cents, making together 596,683 dollars; the amount of the effective cash on the second of July in the banks at Philadelphia, New York, and Baltimore was 217,234 dollars and seventy six cents; there were then also in the other banks 184,998 dollars and sixty one cents; the amount of effective cash on the first of October in the banks at Philadelphia, New York, and Baltimore, was 244,394 dollars and 27 cents; there were then also in the other banks 145,420 dollars and 24 cents, making together 389,814 dollars and 51 cents.

The deductions for bills at the several periods were June 1st, 157,508 dollars and 33 cents   July 2d, 220,900 dollars, October 1st.

16. See "Report on Foreign Loans," February 13, 1793 (*supra*, pp. 24-25).

31,100 dollars; so that including the bills at that epoch, the whole sum in the banks at Philadelphia, New York and Baltimore, amounted to no more than 275,494 dollars and 27 cents; the sums in the other banks to 145,420 dollars & 24 cents.

On the first of June, there were paid on account of the debt due to France 100,000 dollars; the day following, the first instalment of 100,000 dollars, on account of the loan from the bank was received. On the 30th of June, the second instalment of 100,000 dollars was received. These two instalments, amounting to 200,000 dollars are included in the sum of 217,234 dollars and 76 cents, which, on the 2d of July, constituted the cash in all the banks at Philadelphia, New York and Baltimore.

About the beginning of August, another instalment on account of the loan of the bank was received, and on the 29th of September another; making with the preceding ones, 400,000 dollars. This sum was involved in the balance in the Treasury on the first of October, which, it has been seen, did not exceed in the banks at and near the seat of the government, including even unsold and unpaid bills, 275,494 dollars and 27 cents; and comprehending the sums in all the other banks, amounted to no more than 420,914 dollars and 51 cents.

From the foregoing detail it appears, that excluding the 200,000 dollars received on loan of the bank of the United States, in the month of June, there would have been, on the 2d of July 1792, in the command of the Treasury at those places, from which immediate supplies may be derived, no greater sum than 17,234 dollars and 76 cents; that excluding the 400,000 dollars, before that time received on loan of the same bank, there would have been on the 1st of October 1792, an absolute deficiency within the scene described of 124,505 dollars and 73 cents; that the whole balance then in the Treasury where soever deposited, amounted only to 420,914 dollars and 51 cents, and excluding the loan of the bank would not have been more than 20914 dollars and 51 cents.

There must be some very radical error in my conceptions of the proper condition of the Treasury, if it was not in a sufficiently low state, during the whole period under consideration; and it be not demonstrated, that the monies taken by the bank on loan were necessary for the public service, and were obtained with due regard to economy.

There are circumstances which still further manifest the attention which has been paid to this point. The powers given to make loans for domestic purposes at different times, up to the 8th of May 1792,[17] comprehend an aggregate of 1,053,355 dollars and 74 cents; the sums which have been actually obtained upon interest amount to no more than 455,000 dollars.

The contract upon which the 400,000 dollars were obtained was made the 25th of May 1792, extending to 523,500 dollars, and contemplating the payment of 400,000 dollars of that sum, by the bank in equal monthly instalments beginning on the 1st of June and ending the 1st of September; the residue on the 1st of January 1793.

Previous to the making of that contract there had been stipulated to be paid on account of the French debt, for supplies to St Domingo 400,000 dollars, of which one fourth was paid in March, another fourth was payable on the 1st of June, another fourth on the 1st of September, another fourth on the 1st of December.[18]

Particular causes rendered it an accommodation to the agents of France to postpone and subdivide the September instalment. A similar postponement took place, with regard to the instalment payable by the bank on the 1st of September, which was not demanded 'till the latter end of the month, and the remainder of the sum contracted for has not yet been demanded. The spirit of the precaution, which secured the public the privilege of making or forbearing its calls, according to circumstances, needs no comment.

There remain to be noticed two circumstances which will serve to throw additional light upon the conduct which has been observed with regard to the sums from time to time kept on hand. A comparison of the sums in the Treasury, during the years 1791 and 1792, will contradict the idea of any disposition to suffer the public monies to accumulate, for the benefit of the bank of the United States and its subdivisions, and will at the same time indicate the general rule which has governed. In this comparison, it is necessary to recollect that large operations were to [be] performed in 1792.

17. "An Act making provision for the (payment of the) Debt of the United States" (1 *Stat.* 138–44 [August 4, 1790]) had been amended on May 8, 1792, by "An Act supplementary to the act making provision for the Debt of the United States" (1 *Stat.* 281–83).

18. For the negotiations for the relief of Santo Domingo, see this introductory note to George Latimer to H, January 2, 1793.

It may be objected that rule laid down has been on several occasions exceeded. How this has happened at certain periods has been explained. But there is a view of the subject which will throw further light upon it.

The sums which appear on hand at the end of any quarter are always larger on a retrospective than on a previous view. This proceeds from the following cause.

The judgment to be formed beforehand of the sums which will be received within any future period, must of necessity be regulated by the returns in possession of the Treasury, at the time the examination is made. As these come forward with more or less punctuality, that judgment will be more or less accurate; but the appearance on the returns will always be short of the fact; because a certain number of returns at any period of examination, will necessarily be deficient. What does not appear must of course be essentially excluded from the calculation of the receipts to be expended within any near period. Because the extent of the sums which may have accrued, beyond those shewn by the returns in hand is unknown, and it is still more uncertain in what months the payments of them may fall—and the combinations of the Treasury, as to the means of fulfilling the demands upon it, ought to proceed as little as possible upon conjectures and uncertainties.

Monthly abstracts of the bonds taken at each port, are the documents which serve to inform the Treasury of the progress of the receipts upon the duties of imports. From these a general abstract is made up once a month at the Treasury, for the information of the head of the department, shewing the amount payable in each month.

But very considerable differences appear from one month to another. The statement (CZ) will serve as an illustration.

It contains a comparison of the sums shewn by two successive abstracts, one of the 7th of November, the other of the 7th of December last, for a term of ten months distributed into monthly subdivisions. The aggregate difference upon the whole term between the two abstracts is 495,308 dollars and seventy three cents, upon two months, beginning with November and ending in December, it is 151,789 dollars and forty cents; upon a quarter beginning with January and ending with March, it is 174,471 dollars and 66 cents;

upon a subsequent quarter it is 81,055 dollars and 81 cents; upon a still subsequent quarter it is 87,991 dollars and 86 cents.

Hence it is evident, that an arrangement founded upon the abstract of the 7th of November, would suppose a receipt during any part of the time embraced by it, even the most proximate, considerably less than would appear by the abstract only one month later; and must always happen, from this circumstance, that the actual receipts while punctuality is preserved, will exceed the anticipations of them, and that greater balances will be found to exist at any given period than could have been beforehand safely calculated or acted upon.

This circumstance, duly considered, will be a further and a powerful justification of the conduct pursued generally, in relation to the monies from time to time kept on hand, and particularly with regard to the loan of the bank. Low as the state of the Treasury appears to have been on a retrospective view, when the monies upon those loans were called for, the prospect, at each time, must have presented the appearance of a less competent supply, or a greater deficiency, than was afterwards realized.

I am not sure but that I owe an apology to the House for taking up so much of its time in obviating the Imputation of partiality or favoritism towards the banks—the aspect under which I view it admonishes me, that I may have annexed to it greater importance than was intended to be given to it by its authors.

That a disposition friendly to the accommodation of those institutions as far as might be consistent with official duty and the public interest, has characterised the conduct of the department will not be denied.

No man placed in the office of Secretary of the Treasury, whatever theoretic doubts he may have brought into it, would be a single month without surrendering those doubts to a full conviction, that banks are essential to the pecuniary operations of the government.

No man, having a practical knowledge of the probable resources of the country, in the article of specie (which he would with caution rate beyond the actual revenues of the government) would rely upon the annual collection of four million and a half of dollars, without the instrumentality of institutions, that give a continual impulse to circulation, and prevent the stagnation, to be otherwise expected from locking up from time to time large sums for periodical disbur[s]ements; to say nothing of the accommodations, which facilitate to the merchant the payment of the considerable demands made upon him by the Treasury.

No man, practically acquainted with the pecuniary ability of individuals, in this country, would count upon finding the means of those anticipations of the current revenue for the current service, which have been and will be necessary, from any other source, than that of the banks.

No prudent administrator of the finances of the country, therefore, but would yield to the disposition, which has been acknowledged, as a like essential to the interest of the government and to the satisfactory discharge of his trust; a disposition which would naturally lead to good offices, within the proper and justifiable bounds.

After the explanation which has been offered, to manifest the necessity and propriety of the loans made of the bank, it can scarcely be requisite to enter into a refutation of the process, by which it has been endeavoured to establish that the government pays seventeen per cent upon those loans.[19] The state of the Treasury rendered it expedient to borrow the sums which were borrowed; they have been duly received, and the rate of interest stipulated upon them is five per cent. The government then pays upon them five per cent and no more.

The history, which was given in my last letter of the course and situation of the foreign fund, proves that the supposition, from which the inference, of paying seventeen per cent upon the domestic loan, has been drawn, is erroneous.[20] The balances on hand at the respective periods in question, are the residues of the monies which have been received from every source, including the loans foreign and domestic.

But if the supposition, which appears to have been made, had been true, it was still impossible that seventeen per cent could have been paid. By no construction can the rate be extended beyond ten. The

19. This is a reference to remarks made by Giles in support of his resolutions of January 23, 1793. See the introductory note to "Report on the Balance of All Unapplied Revenues at the End of the Year 1792 and on All Unapplied Monies Which May Have Been Obtained by the Several Loans Authorized by Law," February 4, 1793.
20. "Report Relative to the Loans Negotiated Under the Acts of the Fourth and Twelfth of August, 1790," February 13–14, 1793.

mean interest of the money borrowed abroad including charges is five per cent—the interest stipulated to be paid on the loan from the bank is also five—the sum of the two is ten. It is immaterial for what purpose the foreign fund was obtained, whether to pay France or to purchase the debt—the worst consequence that can result is double not treble interest. The interest payable to France is payable for monies borrowed and spent during the war. It can never be truly said, that in[terest is] now payable on any existing fund, whether borrowed in Holland or borrowed in the United States, or borrowed there and reborrowed here. It can never serve to make an addition to the cost or charges of any such fund. 'Tis payable upon one, long since procured and used.

But it is not obvious how the supposition came to be entertained, that all the monies drawn here from the foreign fund had been borrowed for the payment of the debt to France. The presumption would seem to have been more natural, that they had been principally, if not wholly introduced with a view to purchases of the debt, and consequently had a more special reference to the Act authorizing a loan for that purpose.[21] And the fact is, that this was the destination of far the greatest proportion of the sums drawn for. It has been stated, that a part had an eye to the supplies to St. Domingo,[22] and that another part was introduced with a view to the payment of the foreign Officers.[23]

The additional observations to which I shall request the attention of the House will apply to the course and state of the sinking fund, concerning which, I transmitted with my last communications, three statements numbered I, II, and III.[24]

21. "An Act making Provision for the Reduction of the Public Debt" (1 *Stat.* 186–87 [August 12, 1790]).

22. See note 18.

23. For a description of the debt owed to foreign officers, see William Short to H, August 3, 1790, note 5. Section 5 of "An Act supplementary to the act making provision for the Debt of the United States" (1 *Stat.* 282 [May 8, 1792]) authorized the President "to cause to be discharged the principal and interest of the said debt, out of any of the monies, which have been or shall be obtained on loan." For the negotiations on the payment to these officers, see H to Short, August 16, September 13, 1792; H to George Washington, August 27, 1792; Washington to H, August 31, 1792; H to Gouverneur Morris, September 13, 1792.

24. "Report Relative to the Loans Negotiated Under the Acts of the Fourth and Twelfth of August, 1790," February 13–14, 1793.

To give a more collected view of this part of the subject, it may be of use to include here a recapitulation of some ideas, which have been stated in other places.

It is the course and practice of this department for all public monies, from whatever source proceeding, to pass into the Treasury, and there form a common mass; subject, under the responsibility of the officers of the department, to the dispositions which have been prescribed by law.

The surplus at the end of the year 1790 appropriated to the sinking fund and amounting to 1,374,656 dollars and 40 cents, went as it was received into the Treasury.

All the proceeds of the bills drawn upon the fund, prior to april 1792, except the sum of 177,998 dollars and eighty cents, left in deposit with the bank of North America, for reasons which have been explained,[25] passed from time to time into the Treasury. The whole amount of the sums paid in is 907,294 dollars and twenty three cents.

The proceeds of the bills drawn for, in and subsequent to April 1792, have not yet passed into the Treasury, for reasons which [have] been likewise assigned.[26] It would have been done before this time as far as the receipts had gone, but for the present inquiry, which temporarily suspended it. I thought it best to make no alteration in the state of things, as they stood when it began, at least 'till all the information desired had been given. Measures will now be taken for a settlement of the accounts and for a transfer of the proceeds. The whole amount of those bills paid and unpaid, including an estimated sum of interest will be as heretofore stated, 1,220,476 dollars and ten cents.

The whole amount of the bills drawn is 2,305,769 dollars and thirteen cents.

Out of the sinking fund composed of the surplus of the revenue, to the end of 1790, and the proceeds of the foreign bills, there were

25. "Report on the Balance of All Unapplied Revenues at the End of the Year 1792 and on All Unapplied Monies Which May Have Been Obtained by the Several Loans Authorized by Law," February 4, 1793; "Report Relative to the Loans Negotiated Under the Acts of the Fourth and Twelfth of August, 1790," February 13–14, 1793.
26. "Report Relative to the Loans Negotiated Under the Acts of the Fourth and Twelfth of August, 1790," February 13–14, 1793 (see *supra*, pp. 54–56).

issued from the Treasury, and expended in purchases to the end of the year 1792, 957,770. dollars and 65 cents.

For reasons which have been stated, it was finally deemed adviseable to place those purchases wholly to the account of the surplus of 1790.

Consequently there remained on the 1st of January, of the present year 416,885 dollars and 75 Cents, of the abovementioned surplus unapplied to purchases and the whole of the foreign fund, except the sum of 726,000 dollars paid and reserved to be paid, for the use of the colony of St Domingo, and the sum of 191,316 dollars and 90 cents paid, and reserved to be paid to the foreign officers, became free for future application. The balance of the proceeds of the bills after deducting for those reservations, is 1,388,452 dollars and 22 cents.

Since the 1st of January 1793, there have been issued on account of the foreign fund, for purchases, 284,901. dollars and 89 cents.

The practice has uniformly been not to separate any of the monies belonging to the sinking fund, from the common Mass of the monies in the Treasury, but in proportion to the occasions of investing them in purchases.

Hence the sum of 957,770 dollars and 67 cents, issued previous to the present year, and the sum of 284,901 dollars and eighty nine cents, issued during the present year, making together, 1,242,672 dollars and 54 cents, are all the monies, which have ever been separated from the common mass of the Treasury for the purpose of the sinking fund; the whole of which, except 49,282 dollars and 74 cents have been actually expended in purchases.

The unapplied sum remains deposited in the bank of the United States, except a small balance of 61 dollars and seventy six cents, in the hands of William Heth.[27]

From the above rule, the part of the sinking fund arising from the interest on the debt extinguished by purchases or otherwise, is to be excepted. The practice hitherto has been to include this interest in the general dividend of each quarter, and the warrant issued to the cashier of the bank for paying it. The statement No III accompanying my last letter, shews the application of this fund hitherto.[28]

27. Heth was collector of customs at Bermuda Hundred, Virginia.
28. "Report Relative to the Loans Negotiated Under the Acts of the Fourth and Twelfth of August, 1790," February 13–14, 1793.

The law directs that this fund should be invested within 30 days after each quarter.[29] This provision began to take effect on the 1st of July last.

But the investments was not made within the respective times prescribed. This proceeded partly from the state of the market, and partly from the regulations adopted by the commissioners, who were, the Secretary of State the Attorney general, and the Secretary of the Treasury.

Their regulations applying to the two first quarters, limited the prices to certain rates and prescribed the mode of sealed proposals. The Treasurer was appointed agent for the commissioners.[30]

The proposals, with regard to the first quarter were receivable 'till 28th of July inclusively—none were offered, as the Treasurer reported to me, and nothing was done.

The experiment of sealed proposals was again tried the second quarter, with somewhat more, though with but little success. The restriction to this mode of proceeding was rescinded, on the last day of the thirty allowed for purchasing and some further purchases were made, but the whole sum invested was only 25,969 dollars and 96 cents.[31]

The residue of this fund except some small sums noted at foot of the statement No III, was invested in January past.[32]

The unapplied part of the surplus of 1790, having been expended in aid of the receipts of 1791, according to the provision which was made for that purpose,[33] will remain suspended until the future receipts shall so far exceed the current disbursements as to produce a surplus for replacing it.

In computing the amount of the unapplied foreign fund it is necessary to take into the account, the payments made from it during

29. See Section 7 of "An Act supplementary to the act making provision for the Debt of the United States" (1 *Stat.* 283 [May 8, 1792]).

30. See "Meeting of the Commissioners of the Sinking Fund," August 15, 1791, March 26, April 4, 12, July 13, 1792; John Jay to the Commissioners of the Sinking Fund, March 31, 1792.

31. See "Meeting of the Commissioners of the Sinking Fund," October 31, 1792.

32. See "Meeting of the Commissioners of the Sinking Fund," January 16, 26, 1793.

33. See "An Act making appropriations for the support of Government during the year one thousand seven hundred and ninety-one, and for other purposes" (1 *Stat.* 190 [February 11, 1791]).

the years 1791 and 1792, on account of the interest of the foreign debt.

Provision having been made for paying this interest out of the domestic revenues, the sums which have been paid on that account from the foreign fund, are to be considered in the same light, as if they had been transferred here by drafts.

The amount paid at Amsterdam is 1,633,189 guilders and 2 stivers, equal to 36⅘₁₁ ninetieths per guilder, to 659,874 dollars and 34 cents.

There will be additions to be made, which are not at present ascertained.

Adding this sum to the proceeds of the bills and deducting the sums paid and to be paid for St Domingo, and the foreign officers and those applied to purchases during the present year, there will remain a sum of 1,763,424 dollars and 68 cents, subject to a future application.

Of this sum 1,715,098 dollars and 11 cents, will be properly applicable to the purchase of the debt. But circumstances may render it eligible to appropriate a part of it towards the discharge of the foreign debt.

From the plan, which has been pursued, it is also liable to this application.

I have the honor to annex to the statements heretofore transmitted those in the printed schedules marked A, B, and C.[34]

A, exhibits the relative state of the revenue and appropriations to the end of 1792. B, the relative state of appropriations and expenditures to the same period shewing the balance unsatisfied of each head of appropriation. C, applies these statements to an explanation of the demands or charges upon the excess of income, beyond the disbursements to the end of 1792.

In addition to these are two statements marked D and E. D, shewing what proportions of the balances unsatisfied of the several appropriations are likely to be real expenditures, and what part are not likely to be so. In this however in several instances probability must guide, the nature of the thing not admitting of certainty.

---

34. These statements were enclosed in "Report on the Balance of All Unapplied Revenues at the End of the Year 1792 and on All Unapplied Monies Which May Have Been Obtained by the Several Loans Authorized by Law," February 4, 1793.

E, shewing the cash on hand upon the first of January last, and likely to be received from that day to the first of April next, and the sums paid and payable during that period.

The result, founded upon facts contradicts very essentially that statement, which aims at shewing the ability of the Treasury, besides defraying the current expenses of the quarter, to pay off two millions to the bank, still leaving the balance in favor of the Treasury of 664,263 dollars and 54 cents.[35]

It shews that after satisfying the demands for which the Treasury is bound to be prepared, including a payment to the bank of only one tenth part of the 2,000,000. of which the statement alluded to supposes the complete payment, there would remain a balance in favor of the Treasury of no more than 664,180 dollars and 89 cents.[36]

It could answer no valuable purpose to delay the House with a particular examination of the various misapprehensions which have led to a result, so different from the true one. It will be sufficient as an example, to state a single instance.

It is assumed as an item in the calculation, that a sum of a million of dollars will come into the Treasury by the first of April, on account of the revenue of the current year—while the probability is, that the sum received may not exceed ten thousand dollars. This presumption of a million is evidently founded upon two mistakes. 1st It proceeds on the basis of an annual revenue of four millions of dollars, and supposes this sum equally distributed between the different quarters of the year, a million to each quarter, when in fact there are two seasons of the year incomparably more productive than the other parts of it, viz. Those portions of the spring and fall which are embraced by the second and third quarters, the first and fourth being far less productive. 2d It supposes all the duties which accrue are immediately paid; whereas the cases of prompt payment are confined to those in which the duties on particular articles im-

35. This statement was made by Giles in his speech of January 23, 1793, supporting his resolutions. See the introductory note to "Report on the Balance of All Unapplied Revenues at the End of the Year 1792 and on All Unapplied Monies Which May Have Been Obtained by the Several Loans Authorized by Law," February 4, 1793.

36. At this point in MS the following note is inserted: "Note—The sum here mentioned was omitted through hurry to be inserted in the original. The blank is here filled conformably to the statement (E)."

ported in one vessel, by one person or co-partnership, do not exceed 50 dollars; in all other instances, a credit not less than four months is allowed, which carries the payment on the importations, upon the very first day of the quarter, a month beyond the expiration of it.

If the whole amount of the duties, which accrued during the first quarter of 1792, in cash and bonds, was no more than 307,163 dollars and 84 cents, adding ½ for the additional duties, it ought by analogy to be the first quarter of the present year, 322,472 dollars and 94 cents; less, in totality, than the sum which it has been computed would be actually in money in the Treasury, by 677,527 dollars and 6 cents; and less by the whole million, nearly, than will probably be in money in the Treasury on that account. With perfect respect I have the honor to be Sir, your most Obedient and most humble servant   Alexander Hamilton,
                                              Secretary of the Treasury.
The Honorable
The Speaker of the House of Representatives

(Ax.)

MARKET PRICES OF PUBLIC STOCKS, TAKEN FROM ACTUAL
PURCHASES AND SALES.

Dates		6 per Cents.	3 per Cents.	Deferred.
1791 January	3d	17/.	9/.	8/9. to 9/.
	20th	17/3	9/	8/10. to 9/.
Treasurers purchases	24th	17/4		
	26th.			9/4
February	2d.	17/. to 17/4	9/1	9/2.
	8th.	17/4	9/1	9/2.
	14th.	17/6	9/2	9/4.
	21th.	17/2		9/2.
	28th	17/.		
March	5th	17/.		9/.
	12th	17/.	9/.	
	25th			9/.
April	2d	17/.	9/.	9/.
	7th.	17/1		
	20th	17/2		
	26th:	17/,	9/	8/11
	30th.	17/5	9/3	9/.
May	4th.		9/.	9/.
	14th	17/2		
	20th	17/2	9/2	9/1
	25th	17/2	9/1	9/.
	27th:	17/2		9/
June	7th	17/2	9/3	9/3.
	10th:	17/6	9/6	9/4
	15th.	17/6		
	25th	17/9	10/.	
July	1st.	17/10	9/9 to 9/10	9/9. to 9/10.
	5th	18/	10/.	10/.
	11th	18/7	9/9.	
	21st.	19/		
	23rd	19/3	12/	12/
	29th	20/		
August	1st	20/6		
	6th	21/		
	16th	21/	12/.	12/6.
Treasurer's price	17th	21/		12/6.
	20th	21/		
	25th	21/	12/5	12/10.
	30th			12/10
September	1st	21/3		12/9
	3rd	21/		12/9
Treasurer's price	8th to 14th		12/.	12/6
	16th	20/9	12/	12/6
October	1st to 14th	20/4 to 20/9	12/3	12/4 to 12/6
	25th	21/8	12/3	13/3.

Dates		6 per Cents.	3 per Cents.	Deferred.
November	2d.	21/7	12/3	13/3.
	12th		12/6	13/.
	16th	22/	12/7.	13/3
December	2d.	22/1		
	6th.	22/2	12/10	13/2
	12th		12/10	13/2.
	22d	22/4	13/	13/2.
1792 January	4th.	23/4		
	9th	23/9		
	20th.	24/3	14/6	14/6.
February	9th	24/9	14/6	15/.
	15th	24/7		
	21st.			15/.
	23d	24/	14/3	14/9
March	7th	24/	14/6	15/.
	15th	22/		
	26th.	21/3		
April	12th	20/	12/	12/6
May	12th	21/3		
	14th	21/6		
	25th to 29th	22/		
June	7th	22/		
	16th			13/.
July	2d	21/3	12/6	13/.
	14th	21/2		
	17th.		12/4	12/10 to 13/.
	20th	21/6	12/4 to 12/6	12/10 to 13/.
August	6th	21/11 }		12/10 to 13/
	9th	22/ }		
	13th.			13/3
September	12th	22/	13/1	13/6.
	22d	21/11		
	26th		13/1	13/7.
October	2d	21/9 to 21/11		
	5th to 8th		13/	
	23d to 26th	21/6	13/	13/6
December	7th.		12/5	
	14th.	20/2. to 3d.		

At the request of the Secretary of the Treasury of the United States, I do certify that the prices mentioned in the foregoing statement, are taken from entries made in my books of purchases and sales of public stocks, in this City, at the respective Dates therein mentioned.

Matthew McConnell.[37]

Philadelphia,, February 16th. 1793.

37. McConnell was a Philadelphia securities broker.

(B.y.)

PRICES OF THE PUBLIC STOCKS TAKEN FROM THE GAZETTE OF THE UNITED STATES.

Date			6 per Cent.	Deferred.	3 per Cent.
1791.	January	1st	17/6	8/6	8/6
		5th	17/3	8/6	8/6
		8th	17/3	8/9	8/6
		12th	17/	8/9	8/6
		15th	17/	8/9	8/6
		19th	17/	9/	8/9.
		22d	17/4	9/4	9/
		26th	16/9	9/	9/
		29th	17/	9/	9/
	February	2d	17/3	9/1	9/
		5th	17/3	9/1	9/
		9th	17/4	9/2	9/2
		12th	17/8	9/2	9/2
		16th	17/3	9/2	9/1.
		19th	17/6	9/2	9/1.
		23d	17/2	9/2	9/1
		26th	17/3	9/2	9/2
	March	2d	17/3	9/2	9/2
		5th	17/	9/1	9/1
		9th	17/	9/1	9/1
		12th	17/	9/	9/
		16th	17/1	9/	9/
		19th	17/1	9/	9/
		23d	17/	9/	9/
	March	26.	17/1	9/	9/
		30	17/1	9/	9/
	April	2	17/2	9/	9/
		6.	17/2	9/	9/
		9.	17/2	9/	9/
		13.	17/	9/	9/1
		16.	17/2	9/	9/2
		20.	17/	9/	9/
		23.	17/	9/	9/
		30.	17/2	9/1	9/2
	May	4.	17/2	9/1	9/2
		7.	17/2	9/1	9/2.
		11.			
		14.	17/2	9/1	9/2
		18.	17/2	9/1	9/2
		21.	17/2	9/1	9/2
		25	17/2	9/1	9/2
		28.	17/2	9/2	9/3

Date		6 per Cent.	Deferred.	3 per Cent.
June	1	17/2	9/2	9/4
	4	17/3	9/3	9/4
	8	17/6	9/4	9/5
	11	17/6	9/4	9/5
	15	17/6	9/4	9/5
	18	17/7	9/5	9/7
	22	17/7	9/5	9/7
	25	17/8	9/9	9/9
	29	18/	10/	10/
July	2	18/	10/	10/
	6	17/10	9/11	9/11
	9	18/	10/	10/
	13.	18/6	10/6	10/6
	16	18/9	10/9	10/9
	20	19/	10/9	10/9
	23	19/11	11/	11/
	27.	19/6	11/9	12/
	30	20/	12/	12/
August	3.	20/6	13/.	12/6.
	6	21/3	13/11	12/9.
	10	22/3	13/6	13/3.
	13	22/6	13/4	13/2
	17.	20/	12/6	12/6
	20	20/6	13/	12/6
	24	21/3	12/6	12/3
	27.	21/3	12/9	12/5
	31.	21/3	12/9	12/5.
September	3.	21/3	12/9	12/5
	7.	21/	12/9	12/5
	10	21/	12/6	12/
	14	21/	12/6	12/
	17.	20/6	12/6	12/
	21.	20/9	12/	11/9.
	24	20/9	12/	11/9.
	28	20/9	12/	11/9
October	1.	20/6	12/2	11/6
	5	20/6	12/3	11/6
	8	20/6	12/3	11/3.
	12	20/8	12/4	11/4.
	15	20/8	12/6	11/4
	19	21/	12/9	11/9.
	22	21/6	13/	12/
	26	22/	13/4	12/6.
	29	22/	13/4	12/6.
November	2	21/6	13/3	12/3.
	5.	21/8	13/3	12/6.
	9.	21/6	13/	12/3.
	12	22/	13/2	12/6.
	16	22/	13/2	12/6.
	19	22/2	13/4	12/6.

Date		6 per Cent.	Deferred.	3 per Cent.
	23	22/	13/	12/6.
	26	21/10	13/2	12/4.
	30	21/9	13/	12/5.
December	3	22/2	13/3	12/8.
	7.	22/2	13/3	12/10
	10	22/4	13/4	13/.
	14.	22/2	13/3	13/.
	17.	22/6	13/3	13/.
	21	22/3	13/3	13/.
	24	22/6	13/3	13/.
	28	22/9	13/6	13/4.
	31.	23/	13/8	13/6.
1792. January	4	23/4	14/2	14/.
	7	23/4	14/	13/10
	11	23/9	14/6	14/3
	14	24/	15/1	14/8
	18	24/9	15/3	15/
	21	24/8	15/2	15/
	25	25/9	15/8	15/4.
	28	25/	15/2	15/.
February	1	25/6	15/6	15/4
	4	25/3	15/3	15/
	8	25/1	15/3	15/
	11			
	15	24/7	15/	14/8
	18	24/2	15/	14/6
	22	24/1	14/8	14/5
	25	24/4	14/8	14/3
	29	24/6	14/10	14/4
March	3	24/8	15/	14/4
	7	25/	15/	14/6
	10	24/	14/9	14/
	14	22/	13/6	13/2
	17.	22/	13/6	13/2
	21.	22/	13/	12/6.
	24	21/4	12/6	12/
	28	21/	12/6	12/
	31	21/3	12/6	12/
April	4	21/	12/6	12/.
	7	21/	12/6	12/
	11	20/	12/6	12/
	14	20/	12/	11/6
	18			
	21	20/	12/	11/6
	25			
	28	21/	12/9	12/3.
May	2	21/	12/6	12/2.
	5	21/3	12/9	12/2
	9.	21/3	12/9	12/2
	12	21/6	13/	12/6

Date		6 per Cent.	Deferred.	3 per Cent.
May	16	21/8	13/	12/6
	19	21/8	13/	12/6
	23	22/	13/2	12/8
	26	22/	13/2	12/8
	30	22/6	13/9.	13/4
June	2	22/6	13/9	13/4
	6.			
	9	22/3	13/9	13/2
	13	22/2	13/6	13/
	16	22/	13/2	13/
	20	22/	13/2	13/
	23	21/7	13/	12/4
	27.	21/	13/	12/4
	30	21/	13/	12/4
July	4	21/4	13/.	12/6
	7.	21/4	13/	12/6
	11	21/3	13/	12/3
	14	21/3	13/	12/3
	18	21/	12/10	12/3
	21	21/3	13/	12/4
	25	21/4	13/1	12/6
	28	21/4	13/1	12/6
August	1	21/4	13/	12/6
	4	21/6	13/6	12/6
	8	22/	13/4	12/10
	11	21/9	13/	12/6
	15	21/9	13/2	12/10
	18	21/9	13/3	12/9
	22	22/	13/4	12/9
	25	22/	13/6	13/
	29	22/	13/6	13/.
September	1	22/	13/6	13/
	5			
	8	22/	13/6	13/
	12	22/2	13/7	13/1
	15	22/	13/7	13/1
	19	22/	13/6	13/
	22	22/	13/6	13/
	26	22/	13/6	13/
	29			
October	3	22/	13/7	13/1
	6	21/9	13/6	13/
	10	21/9	13/6	13/.
	12	21/9	13/6	13/
	17.	21/6	13/4	12/10
	20	21/6	13/4	12/10
	24	21/6	13/4	12/10
	27	21/4	13/4	12/9
	31	21/4	13/4	12/9
November	3	21/4	13/3	12/8

Date		6 per Cent.	Deferred.	3 per Cent.
	7	21/4	13/3	12/8
	10	21/2	13/2	12/6
	14	21/3	13/3	12/6
	17			
	21	21/3	13/3	12/7
	24	21/3	13/3	12/7
	28	21/3	13/3	12/6
December	1	21/3	13/3	12/6
	5	21/	13/	12/4
	8	20/9	13/	12/
	12	20/3	12/3	12/.
	15			
	19	20/2	12/4	12/
	22	20/	12/4	11/4
	26.	20/	12/4	11/10
	29	20/6	12/8	12/

Treasury Department
February 19th 1793.

John Meyer, P: Clk.

(CZ)

A COMPARATIVE STATEMENT OF BONDS FOR DUTIES BECOMING DUE FROM NOVEMBER 1792, TO SEPTEMBER 1793, INCLUSIVE AS PER MONTHLY ABSTRACTS THEREOF TAKEN 7TH NOVEMBER AND 7TH DECEMBER.

Date of Abstract	Due in 1792 November	Due in December	Due in 1793 January	Due in February	Due in March	Due in April	Due in May	Due in June	Due in July	Due in August	Due in September	Total
	Dolls. Cts.	Dolls. Cts	Dolls. Cts	Dolls Cts	Dolls Cts	Dolls Cts	Dolls Cts	Dolls Cts	Dolls Cts	Dolls Cts	Dolls Cts	Dolls Cts.
Amt: per Abstract taken 7th November	487,313.90	341,600.58	85,992.87	26,870. 3	83,168.12	78,843. 5	54,898.21	50,118.64	39,716.75	7,858. 1	13,953.66	1,270,333.82
Amt: per abstract taken 7th December	520,577.89	460,125.99	128,710.62	60,607.55	181,184.51	95,596.37	61,362.99	107,956.35	56,667.84	32,807.22	60,045.22	1,765,642.55
Excess of December Abstract	33,263.99	118,525.41	42,717.75	33,737.52	98,016.39	16,753.32	6,464.78	57,837.71	16,951. 9	24,949.21	46,091.56	495,308.75

February 19th 1793
L. Wood, junr.[38]

38. Leighton Wood was a clerk in the Treasury Department.

(D.)

STATEMENT SHEWING THE SUMS OF APPROPRIATION TO THE END OF THE YEAR 1792. WHICH WILL PROBABLY NOT BE REQUIRED TO SATISFY THE SAME.

	Balances of appropriation unexpended on the 31st December 1792.	Balance which will probably not be required.	Balance which will be required
	dolls: Cents.	dolls. Cts	dolls: Cents
For discharging the warrants issued by the late board of Treasury,	32,176. 73	20,000.	12,176. 73
For the support of the civil list under the late and present government,	191,648. 31.	50,000.	141.648. 31.
For the support of the army of the United States,	316,161. 77	150,000.	166,161. 77.
For paying the pensions due to invalids,	82,292. 89	43,017. 24	40,275. 65.
For defraying the expenses of negociations or treaties of peace with the Indians,	13,000.	13 000.	
For interest due on temporary loans obtained by the Secretary of the Treasury,	2,401. 88		2,401. 88
For the support of the Ministers, &c. of the United States at foreign courts, and maintaining intercourse with foreign nations,	89,500.		89,500.
For effecting a recognition of the treaty of the United States with the new emperor of Morocco,[39]	7,000.		7,000
For the building, equipment and support of ten revenue cutters (A)	32,704. 48	32,704. 48	
For discharging certain debts contracted by Abraham Skinner late commissary of prisoners,	209. 62	209. 62.	
Towards discharging certain debts contracted by Colonel Timothy Pickering,	35,939. 74	20,000.	15,939. 74.
For paying the interest due on the domestic debt of the United States	1,395,824. 65		1,395,824. 65.
For the support and repairs of lighthouses, beacons, buoys & public piers	18,824. 11	10,000.	8,824. 11.

39. A treaty had been negotiated with Morocco in 1787, but the death of the Emperor, Sidi Mohamet, made necessary a renewal of the treaty. In March, 1791, Congress appropriated twenty thousand dollars for the renewal of the treaty (1 Stat. 214 [March 3, 1791]). Thomas Barclay was authorized to conduct the negotiations (ASP, Foreign Relations, 288–89). A civil war between rival candidates for the throne of Morocco, however, prevented a renewal of the treaty until 1795.

	Balance of appropriation unexpended on the 31st December 1792.	Balance which will probably not be required.	Balance which will be required
	dolls: Cents	dolls. Cts	dolls: Cents
For defraying the contingent charges of government,	8,302. 50		8,302. 50.
For the reduction of the public debt,	416,885. 75		416,885. 75.
For satisfying miscellaneous claims,	11,471. 36		11,471. 36.
For balances due to the French government, to Oliver Pollock, &c.,	28,844. 25		28,844. 25.
For paying the debt due to foreign Officers,	172,962. 11		172,962. 11
For payments on account of the French debt	290,736, 17.		290,736. 17.
	3,147,886. 32.	338,931. 34.	2,808,954. 98

(A)   This sum has been adjusted in the accounts of the collectors, as a charge on the collection of the revenue.

Treasury department
February 19th, 1793.
Alexander Hamilton,
Secretary of the Treasury.

(E.)

Dr. PROBABLE STATE OF CASH FROM THE LAST OF DECEMBER 1792, TO THE 1ST OF APRIL 1793. **Cr.**

	Dollars	Cents		Dollars	Cents
To Balance of cash in the Treasury, per statement (A) [40]	783,444.	51.	By amount of warrants which were drawn prior to the 1st of January 1793, and not paid by the Treasurer,*	42,136.	33.
Cash in the banks on account of foreign bills, not passed to credit of the Treasurer, per statement (A.B.) [41]	605,883.	8.	Sums for which warrants have issued subsequent to the year 1792,	549,640.	91.
Amount of proceeds of ditto, deposited with the bank of North America, [41]	177,998.	80.	Sums which were payable to foreign officers on the 31st December last [42] 172,962.11		
Proceeds of Amsterdam bills, expected to be received by the 1st of April,	614,593.	2.	From which deduct payments made since that period included in the amount above stated, of warrants issued subsequent to the		
Cash in the hands of the collectors at the end of 1792, per abstract (D.) [43]	151,851.	25.	year 1792 9,985.27	162,976.	84.
Sums expected to be received during the present quarter, on account of duties prior to 1793	918,254.	82	Sums payable on account of the debt due to France, to the 1st of April inclusively,	165,000.	
Sums which may be received on account of duties of the current quarter,	10,000.		Arrears for the War Department,	50,000	
Excess of dividend beyond the interest on the stock of the government in the bank of the United States for the last half year,	20,000.		Other arrears to the end of 1792,	50,000.	

* These of course did not come into his account for the last quarter of 1792.

(E. Continued)

	Dollars	Cents
Quarters interest on the public debt,	712,298.	68
Quarter part of the expenditure for the current service,	404,196.	27.
Sum requisite for the proposed Indian Treaty [44]	75,000.	
Sum advanced by the bank of North America, included in the deposit of the proceeds of bills per contra, [45]	156,595.	56
Sum to be issued from the treasury to enable the Secretary of State to pay for the bills furnished to him for the purpose of the third section of the Act of last session making certain appropriations therein specified [46]	50,000.	
First instalment of 2,000,000 dollars due to the bank of the United States, [47]	200,000.	
Balance	664,180.	89
	3,282,025.	48

3,282,025. 48

Alexander Hamilton, Secretary of the Treasury.

Treasury Department, February 20th, 1793.

40. This statement is printed as an enclosure to "Report on the Balance of All Unapplied Revenues at the End of the Year 1792 and on All Unapplied Monies Which May Have Been Obtained by the Several Loans Authorized by Law," February 4, 1793.

41. "Statement AB" is printed as an enclosure to "Report on Bank Deposits, Surplus Revenue, and Loans," January 16, 1793.

42. See note 23.

43. This statement is printed as an enclosure to "Report on the Balance of All Unapplied Revenues at the End of the Year 1792 and on All Unapplied Monies Which May Have Been Obtained by the Several Loans Authorized by Law," February 4, 1793.

44. See note 13.

45. See "Report Relative to the Loans Negotiated Under the Acts of the Fourth and Twelfth of August, 1790," February 13–14, 1793, note 34.

46. Section 3 of "An Act making certain appropriations therein specified" reads as follows: "That a sum of fifty thousand dollars in addition to the provision heretofore made be appropriated to defray any expense which may be incurred in relation to the intercourse between the United States and foreign nations, to be paid out of any monies, which may be in the treasury, not otherwise appropriated, and to be applied under the direction of the President of the United States who, if necessary, is authorized to borrow, on the credit of the United States, the said sum of fifty thousand dollars; an account of the expenditures whereof as soon as may be, shall be laid before Congress" (1 *Stat.* 285 [May 8, 1792]).

47. See Section 11 of "An Act to incorporate the subscribers to the Bank of the United States" (1 *Stat.* 196 [February 25, 1791]).

To Samuel Hodgdon [1]

Treasury Department, February 20, 1793. "A warrant has this day issued on the Treasurer in your favor, as Attorney of James O Hara, Quarter Master General of the army of the United States, for 1800 Dollars to be applied by you to the payment of two bills, drawn on the Secretary of War by John Belli, Deputy Quarter Master General."

LS, University of Pennsylvania.

1. Hodgdon, who was in the commissary department of the Continental Army during the American Revolution, had served as quartermaster general of the United States Army from March, 1791, to April, 1792. At this time he was an Army storekeeper at Philadelphia.

To Jonathan Trumbull

Treasury Department
February 20. 1793.

Sir,

I have reason to conclude, that in copying my letter to the House of Representatives of yesterday,[1] the following passage has been omitted.

"Connected with the circumstance of paying the interest upon the public debt at different places is this further consequence. The transfer continually going on from one office to another render it impossible to know at any moment, when provision for the payment of interest is to be made, what sum is requisite at each place. Estimate must supply the want of knowledge, and to avoid disappointment any where, the estimate must always be large and a correspondent sum placed in the power of the commissioners. This circumstance alone requires an extra sum at the different places of payment which ought not to be computed at less than 50,000 dollars."[2]

I pray the House that the Clerk may be permitted to insert this clause immediately after the paragraph which ends with this sentence.

"The fund for them of course appears on hand 'till the transaction is completed."

With perfect respect, I have the Honor to be, Sir, your most obedient humble Servant,   Alexr. Hamilton.

The Honble.
The Speaker of the House of Representatives.

Copy, RG 233, Reports of the Secretary of the Treasury, 1784–1795, Vol. IV, National Archives.
    1. "Report on the State of the Treasury at the Commencement of Each Quarter During the Years 1791 and 1792 and on the State of the Market in Regard to the Prices of Stock During the Same Years," February 19, 1793.
    2. The version of H's report of February 19 that is printed above, taken from the copy in RG 233, Reports of the Secretary of the Treasury, 1784–1795, Vol. IV, National Archives, contains this paragraph.

Meeting of the Commissioners of the Sinking Fund

[Philadelphia, February 21, 1793]

At a meeting of the trustees of the sinking fund, in the committee room of the Senate, February 21st, 1793,

Present: The Vice President, Chief Justice, Secretary of State, Secretary of the Treasury, and Attorney General.

The Vice President laid before the Board, a resolution of the House of Representatives of the 19th instant,[1] directing the Board to lay before them a statement of all their proceedings not heretofore furnished; Whereupon,

Resolved, That a copy of the journal of the Board, and a statement of the purchases made, since the last report to Congress,[2] be prepared and forwarded.[3]

ASP, Finance, I, 238.
    1. Journal of the House, I, 708.
    2. "Report of the Commissioners of the Sinking Fund," November 17, 1792.
    3. See "Report of the Commissioners of the Sinking Fund," February 25, 1793.

Treasury Department Circular
to the Collectors of the Customs

Treasury Department Febry 22d [–March 5,] 1793

Sir,

I have made the following arrangement with the Bank of the united States [1] for the accommodation of the merchants whose bonds for duties shall become payable between this date and the last day of the ensuing march.[2]

The Bank will discount during the period mentioned, the notes of such merchants as are endebted to the Custom house, for 30 days, for the respective sums that shall become payable. The Bank will receive those notes from you as cash; they must therefore be drawn in *your favour only*.

You will please to furnish the Bank with an abstract of the Bonds which will fall due within the time the arrangement is to continue; specifying, names, sums, and times when due. You will make known this arrangement *in conversation*.[3]

I am with great consideration   Sir   Your obedt Servt

Alexander Hamilton

LS, dated February 22, 1793, to Sharp Delany, Chicago Historical Society; LS, dated March 5, 1793, to William Ellery, Columbia University Libraries; L[S], dated March 5, 1793, to Benjamin Lincoln, RG 36, Collector of Customs at Boston, Letters from the Treasury, 1772–1818, Vol. 6, National Archives; copy, dated March 5, 1793, to Benjamin Lincoln, RG 56, Letters to the Collector at Boston, National Archives; copy, dated March 5, 1793, to Benjamin Lincoln, RG 56, Letters to Collectors at Small Ports, "Set G," National Archives; LS, dated March 5, 1793, to Jeremiah Olney, Rhode Island Historical Society, Providence; copy, dated March 5, 1793, to Jeremiah Olney, RG 56, Letters to the Collector at Providence, National Archives; copy, dated March 5, 1793, to Jeremiah Olney, RG 56, Letters to Collectors at Small Ports, "Set G," National Archives; LS, dated February 23, 1793, to Otho H. Williams, Columbia University Libraries.

1. The name of the bank varied with the area to which the letter was sent.

2. See "Treasury Department Circular to the Presidents and Directors of the Offices of Discount and Deposit of the Bank of the United States," February 23–March 5, 1793.

3. This sentence is in H's handwriting.

To Jonathan Trumbull

Treasury Department
February 22d. 1793.

Sir

I have the honor to transmit, herewith, a certain statement, which was intended to have accompanied my late communications to the House, but was by accident mislaid.[1]

With perfect respect, I have the honor to be, Sir, your most obedient, and humble servant. A: Hamilton.

The Honorable the Speaker of the
House of Representatives.

Copy, RG 233, Reports of the Secretary of the Treasury, 1784–1795, Vol. IV, National Archives.

1. At the bottom of this letter is written: "See reference D, accompanying the communication of 19th February 1793." This statement is printed as an enclosure to "Report on the State of the Treasury at the Commencement of Each Quarter During the Years 1791 and 1792 and on the State of the Market in Regard to the Prices of Stock During the Same Years," February 19, 1793.

Treasury Department Circular to the Presidents and Directors of the Offices of Discount and Deposit of the Bank of the United States

Treasury Department February 23d [–March 5] 1793

Gentlemen

I have made the following arrangement with the Bank of the united States for the accommodation of the merchants of Philadelphia whose bonds for duties shall become payable between this date and the last day of the ensuing month of march.

The Bank will discount during the period mentioned the notes of such merchants as are indebted to the Custom house, for 30 days, for the respective sums that shall become payable. The Bank will receive those notes from the Collector as cash; they must therefore be drawn in *favour of the Collector only*.

If a similar arrangement should appear to you, from any existing circumstance requisite to the accommodation of the merchants of New york,[1] I think it proper to mention to you as a facilitation of it, that I will not draw for the sums that have relation to this transaction until about the middle of may next.

I enclose you a letter to the Collector [2] desiring him to furnish you with an abstract of the Bonds which will fall due within the time the arrangement is to continue, specifying names, sums and times when due.[3] This letter may be delivered to the Collector if it should be thought proper to adopt the arrangement; if otherwise it may be suppressed.

I have the honor to be very respectfully Gentlemen Your obedt Servt   A Hamilton

LS, dated February 23, 1793, to the President and Directors of the New York Office of Discount and Deposit, Henry W. and Albert A. Berg Collection of The New York Public Library; copy, dated March 5, 1793, to the Presidents and Directors of the Boston and Providence Offices of Discount and Deposit, Connecticut Historical Society, Hartford.

1. The name of the city varies in each circular.
2. See "Treasury Department Circular to the Collectors of the Customs," February 22–March 5, 1793.
3. A note at the bottom of the copy in the Connecticut Historical Society indicates that the circular sent to the branch bank at Providence also enclosed letters for William Ellery, collector of customs at Newport, and Jeremiah Olney, collector at Providence.

Conversation with George Hammond [1]

[Philadelphia, February 24–March 7, 1793] [2]

At Governor Simcoe's [3] desire I have the honor of inclosing the copy of a despatch, which I have received from that Gentleman, explanatory of the reasons that prompt him to decline a compliance with the request of the American Ministers (conveyed through me as stated in my No: 3) [4] that he would contribute his assistance to their agent in the attempts to procure in that quarter a supply of provisions for the Indians at the approaching Council.

In communicating the contents of this dispatch to Mr. Hamilton, who had also received information to the same effect from General Hull,[5] I endeavoured to enforce the propriety of the motives that had dictated Governor Simcoe's refusal, as proceeding from the circumstances of his official situation, and not from any disposition to impede the progress or effect of the negociations. Mr. Hamilton expressed his regret at the refusal itself and his apprehension, that whatever might be his own personal sentiments, it would be difficult to impress the inhabitants of this country with a proper conviction of the real cause in which it had originated.

From the point immediately under discussion, our conversation naturally diverged into a more extensive investigation of the general subject to which it referred. In the course of which Mr. Hamilton assured me that it was a source of the deepest concern to this government that it had not hitherto been able to come to an understanding with the court of Great Britain on the particular matters that still remained undecided between the two countries. To this I replied, that the pressure of temporary business alone had hitherto prevented his Majesty's Ministers from attending to this object, but that I expected to receive in a very short time some further instructions respecting it.

As Mr. Hamilton's general reasoning in this conversation was similar to that which he has employed upon former occasions, it is unnecessary for me to trouble your Lordship with a repetition of it at present.

D, PRO: F.O., Series 5, Vol. I.
  1. This conversation has been taken from Hammond to Lord Grenville, March 7, 1793, Dispatch No. 8. For background to this conversation, see "Conversation with George Hammond," November 22, December 15–28, 1792; H to Hammond, December 29, 1792; "Draft of Instructions for William Hull," January 14, 1793; Hull to H, February 6, 1793; George Washington to H, February 17, 1793.
  2. Hammond did not give the date on which this conversation took place, but he states in the second paragraph of his letter of March 7 to Grenville that H "had also received information from . . . General Hull." As Hull's communication announcing the failure of his negotiations with John Graves Simcoe was laid before the President on February 24, this conversation presumably took place between that date and March 7, 1793.
  3. Simcoe had written to Hammond on February 3, 1793, announcing his refusal to comply with the request of the United States to purchase supplies in Canada to provision the proposed Indian-American council (*Simcoe Papers*, I, 286–87). He had also announced his opposition to the request in an earlier letter to Hammond, dated January 21, 1793. See Hull to H, February 6, 1793.
  4. Hammond's Dispatch No. 3, dated February 4, 1793 (PRO: F.O., Series 5, Vol. I), does not mention this matter. He may have intended to refer to his Dispatch No. 2, dated January 1, 1793 (MS Division, New York Public Library), which does discuss the United States request for provisions. See "Conversation with George Hammond," December 15–28, 1792.
  5. Hull to H, February 6, 1793.

George Washington to Alexander Hamilton, Thomas Jefferson, Henry Knox, and Edmund Randolph

United States 24 Feb: 1793.

The President of the United States requests the attendance of the ¹ at *Nine o'Clock tomorrow morning;* at the President's house, on the subject of the note sent to the   on the 17~. inst: ² and that the   will bring with him such remarks as he may have committed to writing in pursuance of said note.

At the same time the President will lay before the Heads of the Departments & the Attorney General some communications which he has just received from General Hull.³   Ge Washington

LC, George Washington Papers, Library of Congress.

1. This and the other spaces in this letter were left blank in MS.

2. See Washington to H, February 17, 1793.

3. An entry in JPP for February 24, 1793, describes these "communications" as follows:

"The following dispatches from Genl. [William] Hull were this day laid before me.

"Letter to the Secy of the Treasury, dated at Niagara 6th Feby 1793. Gives the reasons offered by Govr. [John Graves] Simcoe for not permitting supplies for the Indians, at the ensuing treaty, to be purchased by the U.S. in the British Territory or to be carried through it to the place of treaty.

"Letter to the Secretary of War, place & time of the foregoing. Gives an Acct. of his proceedings with respect to the six nations, & Governor Simcoe. Indians dislike the idea of changing the place of treaty. The language held by Govr. [Arthur] St. Clair at the Treaty at Muskingum, disagreeable to the Indians. The language of the President different, and pleasing to the Indians. Govr. Simcoe seems to think that by proper management, the Indians might be brought to recede from their demands with respect to the boundary. Proceedings at the Treaty, to be shewn to the British Minister.

"Proceedings of the General Council at AuGlaze from Septr. 30th to Octr. 9th. Representatives from 20 nations present. Union among all the Indians. Will hold a treaty with the U.S. at lower Sandusky in the Spring; but it seems to be expressed that if the U.S. are desirous of peace they must signify it by demolishing the forts &c. on the North of the Ohio before the treaty in the spring. Ohio to be the boundary between the U.S. & the Indians.

"From the Complexion of these proceedings which were noted by the British & attested by Mr McGee [Alexander McKee] A.I.A. it appears that the Indians look up to the British for council, & support.

"Answer of Govr. Simcoe to the General Confederacy.

"Proceedings of the Council of the six nations at Buffaloe Creek in November 1792.

"Answer of Govr. Simcoe to the six nations." (JPP, 55–56.)

Cabinet Meeting. Opinion on Furnishing Three Million Livres Agreeably to the Request of the French Minister [1]

[Philadelphia, February 25, 1793]

Feb. 25. 1793. The President desires the opinions of the heads of the three departments and of the Attorney General on the following question, to wit.

Mr. Ternant having applied for money equivalent to three millions of livres to be furnished on account of our debt to France at the request of the Executive of that country, which sum is to be laid out in provisions within the US. to be sent to France, Shall the money be furnished?

The Secretary of the Treasury stated it as his opinion that making a liberal allowance for the depreciation of assignats, (no rule of liquidation having been yet fixed) [2] a sum of about 318,000 Dollars may not exceed the arrearages equitably due to France to the end of 1792. and that the whole sum asked for may be furnished, within periods capable of answering the purpose of mr Ternant's application, without a derangement of the Treasury.

Whereupon the Secretaries of State & War & the Attorney General are of opinion that the whole sum asked for by mr Ternant ought to be furnished: the Secretary of the Treasury is of opinion that the supply ought not to exceed the abovementioned sum of 318,000. Dollars.

Th: Jefferson
Alexander Hamilton
H Knox
Edm: Randolph.

DS, in the handwriting of Thomas Jefferson, George Washington Papers, Library of Congress; DS, letterpress copy, Thomas Jefferson Papers, Library of Congress.

1. For background to this letter, see Tobias Lear to H, February 8, 1793.

Jefferson's account of the discussion at this meeting on the advance to France reads as follows:

"Qu. whether we should furnish the 3. millns of livres desired by France to procure provns?

"I was of opn we ot to do it, the one part as an arrearage (abt 318,000) the residue as an advance towards our payments to be made in Paris in Sep. & Nov. next.

"E. R. was for furnishing the whole sum asked but under such blind terms, that if the present French government should be destroyed & the former one reestablished, it might not be imputed to us as a proof of our taking part with the present, but might be excused under a pretext that we thought we might owe it. Knox of the same opn.

"Hamilton saw the combinn of powers agt France so strong as to render the issue very doubtful. He therefore was agt. going beyond the 318,000. D. understood to be in arrear." (AD, Thomas Jefferson Papers, Library of Congress.) Jefferson's account is printed in the "Anas," Ford, *Writings of Jefferson*, I, 220.

2. The assignats or interest-bearing notes had been issued by the French government in 1789, which used as security confiscated church land. By 1791 the value of these notes had begun to depreciate, and by the end of the year they had fallen between twenty and thirty percent. Despite the decision of the United States not to take advantage of the depreciation of the assignats in repaying the debt owed to France (H to William Short, September 2, 1791), a major problem facing Short and his successor at Paris, Gouverneur Morris, was to reach some agreement with the French government on assigning a value to the assignats before payments could be made on the French debt.

Cabinet Meeting. Opinion Respecting the Proposed Treaty with the Indians Northwest of the Ohio [1]

[Philadelphia, February 25, 1793]

The President having required the attendance of the heads of the three departments and of the Attorney general at his house on Monday the 25th. of Feb. 1793. the following questions were proposed and answers given.

1. The Governor of Canada having refused to let us obtain provisions from that province or to pass them along the water communication to the place of treaty with the Indians,[2] and the Indians having refused to let them pass peaceably along what they call the bloody path, the Governor of Canada at the same time proposing to furnish the whole provisions necessary, Ought the treaty to proceed?

    Answer unanimously, it ought to proceed.

2. Have the Executive, or the Executive & Senate together authority to relinquish to the Indians the right of soil of any part of the lands North of the Ohio, which has been validly obtained by former treaties?

    The Secretary of the Treasury, Secretary at war & Attorney

general are of opinion that the Executive & Senate have such authority, provided that no grants to individuals nor reservations to states be thereby infringed. The Secretary of State is of opinion they have no such authority to relinquish.

3.   Will it be expedient to make any such relinquishment to the Indians if essential to peace?

The Secretaries of the Treasury & War & the Attorney general are of opinion it will be expedient to make such relinquishment, if essential to peace, provided it do not include any lands sold or reserved for special purposes (the reservations for trading places excepted). The Secretary of state is of opinion that the Executive and Senate have authority to stipulate with the Indians and that if essential to peace it will be expedient to stipulate that we will not settle any lands between those already sold or reserved for special purposes, and the lines heretofore validly established with the Indians.

Whether the Senate shall be previously consulted on this point?

The Opinion unanimously is that it will be better not to consult them previously.   Th. Jefferson
                                                    Alexander Hamilton
                                                    H Knox
                                                    Edm: Randolph

DS, in the handwriting of Thomas Jefferson, George Washington Papers, Library of Congress; letterpress copy, Thomas Jefferson Papers, Library of Congress.

1. For background to this document, see "Conversation with George Hammond," November 22, 1792, note 4, December 15–28, 1792, February 24–March 7, 1793; H to Hammond, December 29, 1792; "Draft of Instructions for William Hull," January 14, 1793; Hull to H, February 6, 1793; George Washington to Alexander Hamilton, Thomas Jefferson, Henry Knox, and Edmund Randolph, February 24, 1793.

Jefferson's account of this cabinet meeting reads as follows:

"1st. Question. We were all of opinion that the treaty shd. proceed merely to gratify the public opinion, & not from an expectation of success. I expressed myself strongly that the event was so unpromising that I thought the preparations for a campaign should go on without the least relaxation, and that a day should be fixed with the Commss. for the treaty beyond which they should not permit the treaty to be protracted, by which day orders shd. be given for our forces to enter into action. The President took up the thing instantly after I had said this, and declared he was so much in the opn that the treaty would end in nothing that he then in the presence of us all gave orders to Genl. Knox not to slacken the preparns for the campaign in the least but to exert every nerve in preparing for it. Knox said something about the ultimate day for continuing the negocians; I acknoleged my self not a judge on what day the campaign should begin, but that whatever it was, that day should terminate the treaty. Knox said he thought a winter campaign was always the most efficacious against the Indians. I was of opn since Gr. Britain insisted on furnishing provns, that we should offer to repay. Hamilton thot we should not.

"2d. Question. I considered our right of preemption of the Indian lands, not as amounting to any dominion, or jurisdn, or paramountship whatever, but merely in the nature of a remainder after the extingmt of a present right, which gave us no present right whatever but of preventing other nations from taking possession and so defeating our expectancy: that the Indians had the full, undivided & independent sovereignty as long as they chose to keep it & that this might be for ever: that as fast as we extended our rights by purchase from them, so fast we extended the limits of our society, & as soon as a new portion became encircled within our line, it became a fixt limit of our society: that the Executive with either or both branches of the legislature could not alien any part of our territory: that by the L. of nations it was settled that the Unity & indivisibility of the society was so fundamental that it could not be dismembered by the Constituted authorities except 1. where *all power* was delegated to them (as in the case of despotic govmts) or 2. where it was expressly delegated. that neither of these delegations had been made to our general govmt, & therefore that it had no right to dismember or alienate any portion of territory once ultimately consolidated with us: and that we could no more cede to the Indians than to the English or Spaniards, as it might accding to acknolegd principles remain as irrevocably and externally with the one as the other: but I thought that as we had a right to sell & settle lands once comprehended within our lines, so we might forbear to exercise that right, retaining the property, till circumstances should be more favorable to the settlement, and this I agreed to do in the present instance if necessary for peace.

"Hamilton agreed the doctrine of the law of nations as laid down in Europe, but that it was founded on the universality of settlement there, conseqly. that no lopping off of territory cd. be made without a lopping off of citizens, which required their consent: but that the law of nations for us must be adapted to the circumstance of our unsettled country, which he conceived the Presidt. & Senate may cede: that the power of treaty was given to them by the constn. without restraining it to particular objects, conseqly. that it was given in as plenipotentiary a form as held by any sovereign in any other society. E. R. was of opn there was a difference between a cession to Indns. & to any others, because it only restored the ceded part to the condn in which it was before we bought it, and consequently that we might buy it again hereafter. Therefore he thought the Exec. & Senate could cede it. Knox joined in the main opn. The Presidt. discovd. no opn, but he made some efforts to get us to join in some terms which could unite us all, and he seemed to direct those efforts more towards me: but the thing could not be done.

"3d. Qu. We agreed in idea as to the line to be drawn, to wit so as to retain all lands appropriated, or granted or reserved.

"4th. Qu. We all thought if the Senate should be consulted & consequently apprised of our line, it would become known to Hammond, & we should lose all chance of saving any thing more at the treaty than our Ultimatum." (AD, Thomas Jefferson Papers, Library of Congress.)

This account is printed in the "Anas," Ford, *Writings of Jefferson*, I, 218–20.

2. See Hull to H, February 6, 1793; "Conversation with George Hammond," February 24–March 7, 1793.

Report of the Commissioners of the Sinking Fund

Philadelphia, February 25, 1793.

Sir,

In pursuance of a resolution of the House of Representatives, bearing date of the 19th of this instant, we lay before them a copy of the journal of our Board, and a statement of the purchases [1] made since our last report to Congress.[2]

We have the honor, sir, to be, your most obedient servants,

John Adams,
Th. Jefferson,
Alexander Hamilton,
Edm. Randolph.

To the Speaker of the House of Representatives.

ASP, Finance, I, 234.
1. The "journal" of the commissioners of the sinking fund consists of the minutes of the various meetings of the commissioners. The "journal" and other enclosures to this report are printed in *ASP, Finance,* I, 234-48.
2. "Report of the Commissioners of the Sinking Fund," November 17, 1792.

From William Short

Aranjuez [Spain] Feb. 25. 1793.

Sir

I had the honor of writing to you on the 5th. inst from Madrid [1] informing you that on my arrival there. I was overtaken by a letter sent from our Commissioners at Amsterdam, dated the 14th. of Janry.[2] & covering your two letters to me of Nov. 5 & 26. They inclosed at the same time your letter to them of Nov. 5. authorising them in the case of my absence to open that addressed to me which they had done.

As yours to me of the 26th. of Nov. circumstanced that of the

ALS, letterpress copy, William Short Papers, Library of Congress.
1. Letter not found.
2. Willink, Van Staphorst, and Hubbard to Short, January 14, 1793 (LS, Short Family Papers, Library of Congress).

5th. & was consequently also open to them, by which they observed your notification of having passed draughts on them to the amount of f1,250,000. they informd me with some degree of anxiety that that sum together with the interest payable the 1st. of March would exceed the amount of cash in their hands & that which they were still to recieve in the remaining bonds of the last loan. They had hoped to have found in your letter to me, an authorisation to open a loan at an higher rate of interest than the last which they would imme-diately have proceeded to have done, conceiving that delay tended to endanger the success of a loan on any terms & at least to render them more disadvantageous. As no mention was made of an increase of the rate [of] interest in your letter, & as they had long ago taken up of themselves, as I have already informed you,[3] an idea that your powers had limited it to 4 p. cent. they did not chuse to take on themselves to surpress it.

The object of their letter to me therefore was to present to me the present situation of affairs as to loans—your presumable disposi-tion as to remittances as early as the 1st. of June next—the extreme necessity of punctuality in those payments—& to urge me therefore to authorize them to open a new loan immediately extending the authority to 5 p. cent, relying that their duty & a point of honor would compel their every exertion to obtain the lowest terms possible.

After reflecting on the present state of affairs in Europe & par-ticularly those most influential on the Amsterdam market & being unable to judge of the extent of those which have changed your dis-positions as to remittences, & finding even that you would draw for additional sums if on hand, I could not hesitate in determining that it would be your expectation & choice, that provision should be made in Europe for payments up to the 1st. of June inclusive & therefore that not a moment was to be lost in taking measures for securing this provision. It would have given me much satisfaction to have been able to have waited until I could have heard from you, whether from the considerations mentioned in my late letter,[4] you would have thought it expedient to make exertions for remitting from America to satisfy the rising demands in Europe, during the present un-

3. Short to H, November 29, 1792.
4. Short to H, December 17, 1792.

favorable state of the market or at least until the U.S. by some delay should have so established their credit, as not to have been subjected to the rise in the rate of interest wch. other powers are obliged to submit to. The time of the next payments at Amsterdam did not admit of my waiting for your advice & it seems to me under the expressions of your letter of Nov. 26. that it would be highly improper to place these payments on that contingency. My letters however from the Hague will have given you my sentiments on this subject & shew how disadvantageous I consider it for the U.S. to be now forced on the markets.[5] There is one circumstance also which made me suppose you did not consider the U.S. being forced to make a retrograde step in the rate of interest, in as prejudicial a light as I do. In my letter of Aug. 30. I informed you of Russias having opened a loan at 4½ p. cent. interest & consequently of the difficulty if not impossibility of any other power obtaining one at a lower rate. In your letter of Nov. 26. you acknowlege the reciept of mine of Aug. 30. & still express no determination of efforts by remittances to prevent the U.S. from going on the market, to supply the demands of June next. As it is well known that they have large payments to make then, I had hoped if they could have satisfied them without coming on the market that this would have given such a confirmed idea of that determination never to raise their interest, as to have enabled them in fact to have kept up to it.

Independent of the several reasons given by the commissioners, in their letter [6] of which I hope they will have sent you a copy, for

5. Short to H, October 27, November 29, December 17, 1792.

6. In their letter to Short on January 14, 1793, Willink, Van Staphorst, and Hubbard wrote: "We have the honor to inclose you, a Letter We received for you under cover of One addressed to us the 26 Novbr last by the Secretary of the Treasury of the United States, Wherein He advises to have directed further Drafts on us to the Amount of...1,250,000, Which Sum with the Interest payable the First March next, will exceed the Amount of Cash in our hands, and what We have still to receive for the remaining Bonds of the last Loans.

"The Secretary ordering these Drafts upon us, but a very short time indeed, before He would have to make us Remittances for the One Million Guilders of Reimbursement and the Interest due the 1 June next, We were in the fullest persuasion His intention was to provide for said Reimbursement and Interest by a New Loan; Which, combined with the hope of succeeding in a Loan at this Moment for the United-States at 4½ per Cent Interest, while It may be difficult to obtain One at Five per Cent Interest, after Hostilities shall have commenced between Great-Britain and France...The Letter to you, having

losing no time in authorising them to open the loan—there was another which presented itself here from the present critical situation of the post. It was impossible to say how long it might remain open for the conveyance of letters from this country & it therefore became urgent to convey to them my ideas as fully & as expeditiously as possible. Had I been on the spot, or within corresponding distance I should of course have tried every gradation before consenting to the extreme of 5 p. cent. Situated as I was I thought it would be imprudent to risk delay on the possibility of obtaining lower terms. Although the expressions of their letter held out in a faint manner this possibility, yet I was convinced from the reason of the letter that it would not be realized. In this I have not been mistaken, as a letter from them of the 24th. of Jan.[7] received since my last informs me

---

been eventually destined to be opened by us, could not contain any Information, or direct any Measures, that You would have scrupled to confide unto us; Wherefore, after revolving the Subject in our Minds, and examining it maturely on all Sides, We judged ourselves impelled by the Duty of our Relation towards the United States, to open said Letter, not doubting but We should find therein, the Authority to open a new Loan at a higher Interest, to face the Interest and Reimbursement due the First of June next, and in the determination to execute it if possible immediately, to secure the Money, before the Fall that will take place in the English Stock after the breaking out of the War, shall have attracted the attention of our Money-Lenders, Which You may depend will take place in a considerable degree, by the prejudices People entertain of the Solidity of the English Stocks, and the recent Remembrance of the large profits made by those, who purchased them during the last War; And this Step of Our's would have been the more prudent, as You well know, the Monies for Loans are not paid down upon the fixing of the Engagement, but are stipulated to be furnished at different Instalments, Which Instalments even are not compulsory upon Recipisse, but solely when Bonds are deliverable, A Circumstance that could happen only after your Return here, So that We should have had to depend, only upon the good Will and the Chance of its being the Interest of the Money-Lenders to receive the Recipisse: A strong Motive, for our wishing the new Loan to commence so early as possible, in order to augment the Number of the Chances for the Money being paid unto us.

"Having in consequence opened the Letter addressed to you...to our Surprize and Regret, altho' It recommends as adviseable, your endeavoring to contract for a Loan of Two Millions of Florins, there is no fixation of the rate of Interest, or even authority to extend the rate paid for the last Loan, At which however, It is utterly impossible to borrow more Monies; We doubt greatly if It will be practicable to obtain any for the United-States at 4½ per Cent, Money being extremely scarce, and We having some Surmise, that a Loan will soon be offered for Russia at Five per Cent: If so, You may rely that the United-States will be obliged to pay that rate, should We not be able to conclude a Loan for them before Russia comes upon the Market...." (LS, Short Family Papers, Library of Congress.)

7. LS, Short Family Papers, Library of Congress.

that discount on bills of exchange has risen to 5 p. cent & upwards—
that the Financier of Holland has opened a loan for twelve millions
at 4 p cent & that people keep up their money in the hope of employing it advantageously in the English funds &c. so as to preclude
all thoughts of their being able to procure a return for the U.S. under
five p. cent interest.

I cannot better explain to you the authorisation I gave them & the
occasions in which I desired it to be acted under than by inclosing to
you copies of my two letters on that subject of Feb. 4. & 12.[8]—of the
first a copy was also sent in my last of the 5th. inst. I have since then
recieved no further information from them—nor shall I be able to
know for some time even supposing no interruption in the post, what
steps they may have taken in consequence of my letter of the 4th.
I still hope you will consider it proper for the reasons mentioned
formerly; to give your orders to the commissioners, in some more
direct way [9]—the unsettled state of the post & the possibility of its
being interrupted soon between this & the northern parts of Europe
by the way of France, render this still more necessary.

The commissioners wrote to me on the 10th. of Jan.[10] merely to
inform me that they had remitted on acct. of the Spanish debt [11] a
further sum of £30332.10.10 which has been recieved here. I have
not yet been able to get from M. Gardoqui,[12] any information respecting our debt. As in conversation he told me it amounted far
beyond what you had stated, I observed to him that I supposed there
must exist a specified debt of about 170,000 Dollars principal—& that
it was that debt alone with the interest on it that I considered myself
authorized to pay, not having powers to liquidate unsettled claims.
He has promised me to examine into this, but as yet it is only a
promise. Mr. Carmichael has been trying for months past to obtain
the ascertainment of this—but has never been able to get more than
promises to satisfy him. He thinks Mr. Jay did give a receipt for the

8. Neither of these letters from Short to Willink, Van Staphorst, and Hubbard has been found.
9. See Short to H, December 17, 1792.
10. LS, Short Family Papers, Library of Congress.
11. For a description of this debt, see H to Short, September 1, 1790, note 19;
see also Joseph Nourse to H, October 9, 1792.
12. Diego de Gardoqui, former Spanish envoy to the United States, had been
delegated by the Spanish government to negotiate with Short and William
Carmichael on Spanish-American problems.

sum of 170,000 dollars.[13] Of course I see no risk in going on with the payment to the amount of that sum with the interest to the present time. As the bankers have found difficulty for some time past in obtaining good bills & on good terms to any amount, it has been my intention ever since being here to make an arrangement with M. Gardoqui for his recieving this money at Amsterdam. I have not as yet been able to settle any thing whatever with him, or even to get an answer from him, so much delay is there here in every thing &

13. Spain's aid to the United States after the outbreak of the American Revolution had been in the form of secret loans and subsidies because of Spain's policy of non-recognition of American independence. For this reason the exact amount owed to the Spanish court by the former American colonies was uncertain. In an account of the foreign debt sent on January 4, 1783, by Robert R. Livingston, Secretary for Foreign Affairs, to William Greene, governor of Rhode Island, Livingston placed the amount owed to Spain as a result of a grant to John Jay at $150,000 (Francis Wharton, ed., *The Revolutionary Diplomatic Correspondence of the United States* [Washington, 1889], VI, 195). This sum is confirmed by an entry in the accounts of the register's office, Papers of the Continental Congress, National Archives, which is entitled "Loans and Grants from the Royal Treasury of Spain to the U. States" and lists the sum of $150,000 as the amount received by John Jay and 375,000 livres as the sum received by Arthur Lee "through the hands of Gardoqui and Son." The latter sum was given by Spain as a subsidy, but the $150,000 received by Jay was considered a loan. From Jay's correspondence it appears that, in addition to the $150,000 loan from Spain, he also secured supplies of clothing from the Spanish government. See Jay to Samuel Huntington, September 16, 1780 (LC, The Huntington Library, San Marino, California); Jay to Huntington, March 22, 1781 (LC, Papers of the Continental Congress, National Archives); Jay to Count Floridablanca, April 2, 1781 (copy, Archives des Affaires Etrangères, Correspondance Politique, Espagne, Paris).

In 1784 when Thomas Barclay, agent for settling the accounts of Congress in Europe, settled this account, his ledgers showed the sum of $174,010 owed to Spain rather than the amount of Jay's loan of $150,000 (D, RG 39, Foreign Ledgers, Public Agents in Europe, 1776–1787, f. 198). The "Statement of the Account of the Government of Spain with the United States" in the accounts of the register of the Treasury indicates that $174,011 was the amount finally accepted by the United States as the principal of the sum "By Foreign Debt incurred by the late Government. . . due to the Spanish Nation on the 21st. March 1782" (D, RG 217, Miscellaneous Treasury Accounts, 1790–1894, Account No. 6072, National Archives). The account of the Spanish debt submitted by Nourse to H is printed as an enclosure to Nourse to H, October 9, 1792. Although it is not clear which of the sums enumerated by Nourse were included in the $150,000 dollars borrowed by Jay, it is indicated in William Carmichael's "Acct. of Money paid his Excellency J. Jay by Mr. Gardoqui," May 16, 1781 (D, Columbia University Libraries), and in Richard Harrison's account in Barclay's books (D, RG 39, Foreign Ledgers, Public Agents in Europe, 1776–1787, f. 188) that the discrepancy of $24,000 between the sum debited to Jay and the amount of final settlement may be accounted for by clothing purchases which had been negotiated through Harrison at Cadiz.

so much are they occupied at this moment particularly in more pressing European business.

On my passage through Antwerp I asked M. de Wolf [14] what he then thought of US credit & he told me the American credit was still the best, but that the moment was unfavorable for business of any kind—all men's minds being totally occupied by the unsettled state of affairs. I easily inferred from his manner of speaking that he did not then think a loan at 4. p. cent could be effected. I did not dilate on this subject however & merely observed to him that there was no intention of going on the market, with which he seemed much pleased. This letter will be sent by duplicate by Libson & Cadiz.

I have the honor to be most respectfully sir, your most obedt. servt.

W Short

The Honble
Alexander Hamilton Secretary of the Treasury

14. Charles John Michael de Wolf was the Antwerp banker who negotiated the 1791 Antwerp loan for the United States.

To Jonathan Trumbull

Treasury Department
February 25th. 1793.

Sir,

I beg leave through you, to observe to the House of Representatives, that the statements communicated by my first and second letter in answer to their resolutions of the 23d. of January last which were printed by order of the House, have been printed in an incorrect and very confused manner.

In page 4 of my first letter,[1] a sum of 605,883 dollars and eight cents is expressed as 60583 Dollars and eight cents.

The Mercantile form of Debtor and Creditor sides, which was observed in the Accounts transmitted, and which is material to perspicuity, has been dropped and a statement in succession; of the oposite sides of the account substituted. In addition to this, *headings* have been introduced, which are not in the originals, and these *headings* have been in one important case inverted.

In statement A, transmitted with my first letter, *Receipts* have been put for *Expenditures,* and *Expenditures* for *Receipts.* Other inaccuracies, less material, might be noticed.

The effect of relinquishing the mercantile form of an account current will be perceived at once, upon an Inspection of either of the statements, but it will be particularly striking in statement No II of my second letter,[2] shewing half yearly the application of the fund for reducing the public debt, constituted by the Act of the 8th. of May last.[3]

It was the practice 'till the present session to send to the Treasury proof sheets of the reports from the Department, which were printed by direction of the House, in order to their being examined and corrected, before they were finally struck off. This useful practice, however has been discontinued, during the present session.

The House will be at no loss to perceive that their own satisfaction, on any point of inquiry, the due information of the public, and the reputation of the department, from which any report or statement proceeds, are alike concerned in the accuracy of the form, under which it is presented.

With a particular eye to the last consideration, I take the liberty to express a wish to the House, that some regulation may be adopted to enable the head of this department, to secure the fidelity and correctness of the printed copies of the reports, which shall hereafter be made to the House and shall be committed to the press by their order.[4]

With perfect respect, I have the honor to be Sir your most obedient & humble servant   Alexander Hamilton,

Secretary of the Treasury.

The Honble
The Speaker of the House of Representatives.

Copy, RG 233, Reports of the Secretary of the Treasury, 1784–1795, Vol. IV, National Archives; copy, RG 233, Reports of the Secretary of the Treasury, Second Congress, National Archives.

1. "Report on the Balance of All Unapplied Revenues at the End of the Year 1792 and on All Unapplied Monies Which May Have Been Obtained by the Several Loans Authorized by Law," February 4, 1793.

2. "Report Relative to the Loans Negotiated Under the Acts of the Fourth and Twelfth of August, 1790," February 13–14, 1793.

3. "An Act supplementary to the act making provision for the Debt of the United States" (1 *Stat.* 281–83).

4. This letter was referred to a committee of the House of Representatives, which issued the following report on March 2, 1793:

"That they have examined into the circumstances stated in the letter, and find

"That the standing order of the Clerk of this House to the printer is, to send the proof sheets of all reports and statements to the department from whence they were made; and that this practice has been generally followed.

"That it has been discontinued during the present session (so far as respects the Secretary of the Treasury) from an opinion of the printer, that the delay which the examination would occasion might interfere with the intention of the House, of having the business speedily accomplished.

"It did not appear to the Committee that any unnecessary delay had taken place at the office of the Comptroller, by reason of the examination of the proof sheets, nor in the printer, in the transaction of his business.

"The Committee are of opinion, that it is not necessary for them to recommend any new regulation for the future execution of this business, but in order to rectify the errors which have taken place in the printed reports and statements, the Committee recommend the following resolution:

"Resolved, that there be printed, under the direction of the Secretary of the Treasury, three hundred copies of the reports and statements made by him, during the present session; and that the same be delivered to the Clerk of this House." (Copy, RG 233, Reports of Select Committees, Second Congress, National Archives.)

From Wilhem and Jan Willink, Nicholaas and Jacob Van Staphorst, and Nicholas Hubbard

[*Amsterdam, February 25, 1793*. On April 4, 1793, Willink, Van Staphorst, and Hubbard wrote to Hamilton: "We had the honor to address you the . . . 25 February." *Letter not found.*]

To the President, Directors, and Company of the Bank of the United States

Treasury Department February 26th
1793

Gentlemen,

I have to request that you will be pleased to advance to The Honorable Jonathan Trumbull Esqr. the sum of Thirty Thousand Dollars; on Account of the compensations due to the Members of the House of Representatives of the United States.

As I have been informed, that the Bill making appropriations for the present year has passed both Houses of Congress,[1] I hope to have it in my power very shortly to replace this sum, as well as, the Monies which have been hitherto advanced by you for the Public service, in compliance with my several requisitions for that purpose.

I am with great Consideration   Gentlemen   Your Most Obedient
Servant   A Hamilton

The President, Directors & Company
of the Bank of the United States

LS, Hamilton Papers, Library of Congress.
    1. On February 23, 1793, the House agreed to the Senate's amendments to
"An Act making appropriations for the support of Government for the year
one thousand seven hundred and ninety-three" (*Journal of the House*, I, 716).
The act was approved on February 28 (1 *Stat.* 325–29).

To the President and Directors of
the Bank of the United States

Treasury Department, February 26, 1793. Requests "a further advance of one thousand Dollars to Young and Dannacker . . .[1] on
account of their Clothing Contract with the Public."

LS, St. Mary of the Lake Seminary Library, Mundelein, Illinois.
    1. See "Contract with George Dannacker and William Young," October 22,
1792; H to Thomas Willing, February 5, 1793.

From William Bingham [1]

Philada Feby. 26th 1793
Dr sir
    Whilst resident in Martinico, as agent of the United States, I had
committed to my Trust, in my official character, by the Government
of that Island, the 1st Proceeds of one thousand Barrels of Flour,
being the Cargo of the Danish Brig Hope, loaded at Cork on Account & Risk of Portuguese Merchants at Lisbon, which Vessel was
captured by an american Privateer & carried into Martinico.[2]
    The Vessel & Cargo being Neutral Property, Restitution was
formally demanded of the Government, by the Captain of the
Danish Vessel. There were no Courts at that Time instituted in
Martinico, which could take Consignment of American Captures and
no Powers ever were much wanted in the Island. The General
ordered the Cargo to be disposed of, the Freight &c to be paid to

the Captain & the Nt Proceeds to remain in my Hands, subject to the orders of Congress.

I immediately presented to Congress a particular account of the Transaction & transmitted at the Same time all the Papers that were found on board, in order that Congress might be enabled to determine the future destination of the Property.[3]

When the Business was thus placed in a Train of Settlement that had the appearance of being Satisfactory to all Parties, I was Surprized to find by Advices from my Correspondents that my Property in their Hands had been attached & a Suit commenced against me, for the Recovery of the Proceeds of the Cargo.[4]

In Consequence thereof I exhibited to Congress, various Documents concerning this Transaction, which included therein as evidence the Several Resolves, under Date of Nov 30 1779[5] & June 20th 1780,[6] expressive of their entire Satisfaction with ⟨my⟩ Conduct in relation to the affair & ordering the Navy Board at Boston to Sanction the Suit, & direct the Counsel employed in its defense.

Being thus exonerated from all Claims, I paid no further Attention to the Business. On Enquiry I now find that the Cause was brought to Trial in the inferior Court of Massachusetts in January 1781, where Verdict was found for the Defendant. Notwithstanding these adverse Decisions, the Plaintiffs instead of appealing to the Justice of Congress, who alone have the disposal of the Property, have again commenced a suit in the federal Court for its Recovery.

I shall be obliged to you to inform me, whether thro the Interference of the Executive, this Suit, that is now commenced against me, will be Sust⟨ain⟩ed by the United states, in Compliance with the Engagements of Congress, or whether it is necessary to make a fresh Application to Congress.

I have the honor to enclose you Copies of my Letters wrote to Congress on the subject & of the Resolutions entered into in Consequence thereof & of being with Respect & Esteem

sir, Your obedt hble ser   Wm Bingham

Honble Alexr Hamilton Esqr

ALS, letterpress copy, Historical Society of Pennsylvania, Philadelphia.
   1. Bingham, a prominent Philadelphia merchant and banker, was a member of the Pennsylvania legislature. From 1776 to 1780 he had served as agent of

the Continental Congress at Martinique and as consul at St. Pierre in the West Indies.

2. This case concerned an American ship, the *Pilgrim*, which in January, 1779, brought into Martinique as a prize the brig *Hope*, which she had captured in November, 1778. Upon examination the brig proved to be of Danish ownership carrying a cargo belonging to Portuguese merchants. Because no court of admiralty in Martinique was capable of deciding prize cases concerning American vessels, Bingham, acting on the direction of the governor of the island, the Marquis de Bouille, sold the disputed cargo, paid the expenses of the vessel, and placed the remainder of the sum to the credit of the Commercial Committee of Congress to be used in discharging advances which he had made at Martinique on the account of Congress. The American owners of the *Pilgrim*, who objected to this disposition of the cargo of the *Hope*, in October, 1779, brought action against Bingham in the Common Pleas Court of Suffolk County, Massachusetts, attaching Bingham's property, which was in charge of his agent, Thomas Russell of Boston. In a letter dated October 6, 1779, to the Commercial Committee of Congress, Bingham requested the intervention of Congress on his behalf in the suit (copy, RG 267, Appellate Case Files of the Supreme Court, 1792–1831, Case No. 5, National Archives). Congress agreed to assume the responsibility, and both in this action and in an appeal brought to the Supreme Court of Massachusetts in February, 1784, judgment was found in favor of Bingham (3 Dallas, *U.S. Reports*, 19–21). In early 1793, however, Bingham learned that the case was being reopened by the owners of the *Pilgrim*.

3. Bingham to the Committee of Commerce of the Continental Congress, February 2, 1779 (extract, Papers of the Continental Congress, National Archives).

4. Suit was brought against Bingham by the owners of the *Pilgrim*, "*John Cabot*, of *Beverly*, in the district of *Massachusetts*, merchant, and surviving co-partner of *Andrew Cabot*, late of the same place, merchant, deceased, *Moses Brown*, *Israel Thorndike*, and *Joseph Lee*, all of the same place, merchants, *Jonathan Jackson, Esq.*, of *NewburyPort*, *Samuel Cabot*, of *Boston*, merchant, *George Cabot* of *Brooklyn*, *Esq. Joshua Wood*, of *Salem*, merchant, all in our said district of *Massachusetts*, and *Francis Cabot*, of *Boston*, aforesaid, now resident at Philadelphia aforesaid, merchant" (3 Dallas, *U.S. Reports*, 382–83).

5. On November 24, 1779, a committee of the Continental Congress was appointed to consider and report on a letter from Bingham to the Commercial Committee of Congress, dated October 6, 1779, containing an "account of his proceedings relative to a vessel said to be Danish property, captured by the sloop *Pilgrim*, and carried into Martinique," and a statement that a suit was being brought against him in the Massachusetts courts. On November 30, 1779, the committee reported, and Congress resolved that a letter should be written to the legislature of Massachusetts suggesting that as "courts are now instituted at Martinique for the trial of such causes, Congress submit it to you whether it would not be advisable to stop the suit already commenced till judgment is obtained upon the principal question; after which it will be in Mr. Bingham's power to discharge himself by delivering to the true owners the property placed in his hands for their use" (*JCC*, XV, 1302, 1332).

6. On June 20, 1780, the Continental Congress considered Bingham's memorial concerning the *Hope* and the *Pilgrim* and "*Resolved*, That the general of Martinique, in ordering the cargo of the brig *Hope* to be sold, and the money to be deposited in the hands of Mr. W. Bingham, till the legality of the capture could be proved, (no courts being at that time instituted for the determining of such controversies . . . in that island) shewed the strictest attention to the rights of the claimants, and the highest respect for the opinion of Congress:

"That Mr. W. Bingham, in receiving the same, only acted in obedience to the commands of the general of Martinique, and in conformity with his duty as agent for the United States.

"*Resolved,* That Congress defray all the expences that Mr. W. Bingham may be put to by reason of the suits now depending, or which may hereafter be brought against him in the State of Massachusetts Bay, on account of the brig *Hope* or her cargo, claimed as prize by the owners, master and mariners of the private ship of war called the *Pilgrim.*

"And whereas the goods of the said William Bingham, to a very considerable amount, are attached in the said suits now depending in the hands of the factors of the said W. Bingham, to his great injury:

"*Resolved,* That the general court of the State of Massachusetts Bay, be requested to discharge the property of the said William Bingham from the said attachment; Congress hereby pledged themselves to pay all such sums of money, with costs of suit, as may be recovered against the said William Bingham in either or both the above actions.

"*Resolved,* That the navy council at Boston be directed to give such security, in the name of the United States, as the court may require, and to direct the counsel now employed by Mr. Bingham in the defence of the said actions." (*JCC,* XVII, 533–34.)

To Tobias Lear

Treasury Department, February 26, 1793. Encloses "a small account against the United States, for a Seal for the use of the District Court of the State of Vermont." Requests "the President's permission for paying it."

LC, George Washington Papers, Library of Congress.

Report on the Salaries, Fees, and Emoluments of Persons Holding Civil Office Under the United States

[Philadelphia, February 26, 1793
Communicated on February 27, 1793] [1]

[To the President of the Senate]

The Secretary of the Treasury, in obedience to the order of the Senate of the 7th of May last,[2] respectfully transmits herewith sundry statements of the Salaries fees and Emoluments for one Year ending the first of October 1792, of the Persons holding civil offices or employments under the united States (except the Judges) as far as

Returns have been rendered—together with the disbursements and
Expences in the discharge of their respective offices and employments for the same Period.[3]

No I.	relating to the Department of State
No. II	Treasury Department.
	A Office of the Secretary of the Treasury
	B Ditto Comptroller
	C Ditto Commissioner of the Revenue
	D Ditto Auditor
	E Ditto Register
	F Ditto Treasurer
No III	Department of war
No IV	Board of Commissioners
No V	Mint Establishment
No VI	Office of the Secretary of the Senate
No VII	Ditto Clerk of the House of Representatives
No VIII	Letter from the Governor of the Territory North-west of the Ohio
No IX	Letter from the Attorney General
No X	District Attornies
No XI	Marshalls of the Districts
No XII	Clerks of the District Courts
No XIII	Offices of the Commissioners of Loans
No XIV	Collectors of the Customs
	Naval officers
	Surveyors
	Cutter Establishment
	Inspectors, Gaugers, weighers, measurers and Boat-men employed by the Collectors
No XV	Supervisors of the Revenue
No XVI	Inspectors of the Revenue for Surveys
No XVII	Superintendents of Lighthouses
No XVIII	Keepers of Lighthouses

The Statements numbered from I to IX inclusively, and the letters
relating to the object, are transmitted in their original state, as rendered by the several officers.

No. X to XVIII inclusively are stated under each particular head,

from the accounts which have been received from the offices to
which they respectively relate.

No 19 is a List, specifying the Persons of whom no information
has yet been received on the subject.

All which is humbly submitted

Alexander Hamilton
Secy of the Treasury

Treasury Department
February 26 1793

DS, RG 46, Second Congress, 1791–1793, Reports of the Secretary of the Treasury, National Archives.

1. The communicating letter, dated February 27, 1793, may be found in RG 46, Second Congress, 1791–1793, Reports of the Secretary of the Treasury, National Archives.

2. For the Senate order of May 7, 1792, see Tench Coxe to H, February 14, 1793, note 2.

3. This enclosure, consisting of ninety manuscript pages, has not been printed. For an abbreviated version of it, see *ASP, Miscellaneous*, I, 57–68.

Report on Supplementary Sums Necessary to Be Appropriated for the Services of the Year 1793

Treasury Department,
February 26th. 1793.
[Communicated on February 27, 1793] [1]

[To the Speaker of the House of Representatives]

The Secretary of the Treasury respectfully reports to the House
of Representatives a suplementary estimate of certain sums for
which appropriations are necessary.

These appropriations may be charged upon any monies, which
shall have come into the Treasury of the United States, to the end
of the present year, not proceeding from the duties on imports and
tonnage and not heretofore appropriated, and also upon the surplus,
if any, of the duties on imports and tonnage during the present year,
as an auxiliary fund.

The Secretary embraces this Opportunity of observing that a provision is requisite, to the orderly conducting of the business, for

Copy, RG 233, Reports of the Secretary of the Treasury, 1784–1795, Vol. IV, National Archives.

1. *Journal of the House*, I, 721.

paying the interest on the two millions of Dollars borrowed of the bank [2] out of the dividends from time to time declared upon the Stock of the United States in the said bank.

All which is respectfully submitted   Alexander Hamilton,
Secretary of the Treasury.

[ENCLOSURE]

A Suplementary estimate of sums necessary to be appropriated for the services of the year 1793.

Mint of the United States.

For defraying certain expences which have been incurred by the institution of the Mint, under a resolution of Congress of 3rd March 1791,[3] and the Act for establishing a Mint and regulating the coins of the United States, passed 2d April 1792.[4]

Purchase of a House, and two lotts of ground erecting two new brick buildings, furnaces &c, and two new frame buildings, paying Workmen employed in making Machines for brass and Iron castings, Barr Iron steel coals, firewood &c for the Mint   12,079 78

Salaries of the Officers to 31st December 1792

Directors Salary from July 1st to December 31st, 1792.	1000.	
Coiners ditto from June 1st to December 31st 1792 @ 1500. dollars	875.	
His Clerks from August 13th to December 31st @ 312. dollars Pr. Annum	119. 88.	
Treasurers Salary from June 1st to December 31st @ 1200 dollars Pr. Annum	700.	
		2 694.88

	Dollars Cents	Dollars Cents
Salaries of the Officers for 1793.		
Director of the Mint	2,000	
Assayer	1,500	
Chief Coiner	1,500	
Engraver	1,200	
Treasurer	1,200	
Three Clerks @ 500 dollars	1,500	
Workmens wages about 50 dollars Per week	2,600	
		11,500

2. See Section 11 of "An Act to incorporate the subscribers to the Bank of the United States" (1 *Stat.* 196 [February 25, 1791]).

3. This resolution reads as follows: "Resolved *by the Senate and House of Representatives of the United States of America in Congress assembled,* That a mint shall be established under such regulations as shall be directed by law.

"*Resolved,* That the President of the United States be, and he is hereby authorized to cause to be engaged, such principal artists as shall be necessary to carry the preceding resolution into effect, and to stipulate the terms and conditions of their service, and also to cause to be procured such apparatus as shall be requisite for the same purpose." (1 *Stat.* 225.)

4. 1 *Stat.* 246–51.

For bringing forward to the seat of government the votes of the Electors in the several States for President and Vice President of the United States, as provided for by the Act of the 1st March 1792 [5]

To Ezra Bartlet; for New Hampshire

Pr. acct. settled at the Treasury 18th December 1792	105.75
John S. Tyler for Massachusetts Pr. acct. settled at the Treasury 26th December 1792	87.
Lott Hall for Vermont Pr. acct. settled at the Treasury 2d January 1792	90.25
" Daniel Updike for Rhode Island Pr. Acct. settled at the Treasury 26th Decr. 1792.	80.
" Enoch Parsons, for Connecticut Pr. Account settled at the Treasury 14th Decr. 1792	52.25
" Robert Williams for New York Pr. acct settled at the Treasury 12th December 1792	44.50
Estimated for New Jersey acct not settled at the Treasury 30 Miles @ 25 Cents	7.50
Stephen Stephenson for Pennsylvania Pr. acct settled at the treasury 11th Decr: 1792	26.
Gunning Bedford, for Delaware Pr. acct. settled at the Treasury 14th Decr 1792.	19.
E. Valette, for Maryland Pr act settled at the Treasury 17th December 1792	35.
Samuel Peters, for Virginia, Pr. acct settled at the Treasury 17th December 1792	69.50
Notley Conn for Kentucky Pr. acct settled at the Treasury, 8th January 1793	234.25
Stephen White for North Carolina Pr. acct settled at the Treasury 27th Decr. 1792	134.
Thomas Fitzpatrick, for South Carolina Pr. acct. settled at the Treasury 29th Decr 1792	168.25.
Anderson Watkins for Georgia Pr. account settled at the Treasury 31st December 1792	195.75
	1349.

For the discharge of a claim founded on a resolution of Congress of the 28th September 1785, granting two hundred dollars (but not paid) to Return Jonathan Meigs late a Colo. in the service of the United States, and to the legal representatives of

5. See Section 7 of "An Act relative to the Election of a President and Vice President of the United States, and declaring the Officer who shall act as President in case of Vacancies in the offices both of President and Vice President" (1 Stat. 240).

	dollars cents	
Christopher Green deceased	200.[6]	

Also for interest thereon from 16th May
1776, in pursuance of an Act of Congress
of the United States for that purpose
passed the 14th January 1793 [7] is 16 years
8 Months @ 6 Pr. Ct. Pr. Annum   200

                                                                                    400.

For the amount of the Secretary at War
his estimate dated 26th November 1792
of pay, subsistence and Forage due
to Wynthrop Sergeant as Adjutant
General to the troops late under the
command of Major General St. Clair,
the pay and emoluments of a Lieutenant
Colonel

    Pay from the 16th June to 31st Decr. 1791   }
        6½ months @ 60 dollars Pr. Month.   }   390.

    Forage for the same period @ 12   }
        dollars Per Month   }   78.

    Subsistence Vizt.

Fort Washington, from 16th June to 19th Octr
    126. days at 6 rations Pr. day is 756 rations
    @ 6¾ Cents   56.70.

On the March to the Miami Village
    from the 20th October to the 9th Novr.
    126 rations at 15¼ Cents   21.35.

Fort Washington,
    from the 10th Novr. to the 31st December
    312 rations @ 6¾ Cents   23.40   101. 45

                                                                                    569 45

For the payment of Dunlap and Claypoole, printers their ac-
    count of printing work done under the direction of a
    Committee of the Convention of the United States for
    1320 Copies of the Constitution &c   420.

For the Clerk of the House of Representatives his estimate
    for the payment of certain extra expences of the Door
    keeper this session, and also for defraying the expence of
    attending Witnesses and Clerk hire, to the late committee
    of the House on their enquiry into the causes of the failure
    of the expedition under General St. Clair   400

For so much short estimated for the principal
Clerk to the Secretary of the Senate for his
services from 1st July to 4th November 1792
127 days @ 3 dollars Per day   381.
Also for his services to 31st December 1793. the former

6. *JCC*, XXIX, 776.

7. "An Act to provide for the allowance of interest on the sum ordered to
be paid by the resolve of Congress, of the twenty-eighth of September, one
thousand seven hundred and eighty-five, as an indemnity to the persons therein
named" (6 *Stat.* 11).

estimate having been for only 6 months; whereas
the Secretary of the Senate estimates full employment throughout the year 365 days @ 3 dol:

℔ day		1095	
Deduct 6 months already estimated		547.50	
		547.50	
Ditto for engrossing Clerk 365 days @ 2 dol-lars Per day	730		
Deduct 6 Months already estimated	365	365.	
Also for the payment of Extra services of the Door keeper this session 183 days at 50 Cents Per day	91 50		1,385.

To defray the expence which will attend the stating and printing the public accounts for 1792, in compliance with the
order of the House of Representatives of the 30th Decr.
1791 [8]   800

For the payment of the Trustees of Wilmington public Grammar school & Accademy for damages done to the same by
the troops of the United States during late war according
to a settlement thereof, made at the Treasury under the
Act of the United States passed the 13th April 1792 [9]   2,553. 64

Light Houses.

To make good so much deficient in the appropriation for 1791	}	955.66
For building a lighthouse on Montok point agree-ably to the Act of Congress of 12 August 1792 (not yet ceded) [10]	}	20,000.
For building a pier at Sandy Hook in the State of New Jersey	}	1,625.
For building a pier at the Town of New Castle in the State of Delaware	}	8,000
For compleating the lighthouse on Bald-head at the mouth of Cape fear River	}	2,000

For three Clerks to be employed (so far
as necessary) in the Office of the
Commissioner of the Revenue upon
documents for the public service
relative to imports, exports,
Tonnage &c. @ 500 dollars Per Annum   1,500.

34,080. 66

8. On December 30, 1791, the House "*Resolved,* That it shall be the duty of
the Secretary of the Treasury to lay before the House of Representatives, on
the fourth Monday of October in each year, if Congress shall be then in session,
or if not then in session, within the first week of the session next following the
said fourth Monday of October, an accurate statement and account of the receipts and expenditures of all public moneys, down to the last day inclusively
of the month of December immediately preceding . . . and shall be shown the
sums, if any, which remain unexpended . . ." (*Journal of the House,* I, 484).
9. 6 *Stat.* 8.
10. 1 *Stat.* 251. See Tench Coxe to H, January 3, 1793; Edmund Randolph to
H, January 7, 1793.

For the printing of ships registers, and other Marine papers at
the Treasury, and for books of record in the Registry
office, incident to the Acts for "Registering and recording
ships and other vessels" [11] and for "enrolling and licencing
ships and vessels employed in the coasting trade and Fisheries." [12]

$$\frac{350}{}$$

Dollars   68,582 41

Treasury Department,
Registers Office, 27th February 1793.   Joseph Nourse Regr.

11. 1 *Stat.* 287–99 (December 31, 1792).
12. 1 *Stat.* 305–18 (February 18, 1793).

From Jean Baptiste de Ternant [1]

Philadelphie 26 fevr. 1793
l'an 2 de la Répe. francaise

Le M. d. f. au secretaire de la trésorerie

J'ai l'honneur de vous addresser cy-jointe la copie d'une lettre du
secretaire d'état,[2] en vous priant de me faire connoitre à quelles
époques le reste des trois millions mentionés dans cette lettre pourra
etre acquitté par la tresorerie des Etats unis. Vous sentirez in-
dubitablement, combien il importe au bien du service à effectuer
avec ces fonds, que les payemens en soient immédiats ou au moins
très prochains.

LC, *Arch. des Aff. Etr., Corr. Pol. Etats-Unis,* Supplement Vol. 20.
    1. For background to this letter, see Tobias Lear to H, February 8, 1793, and
"Cabinet Meeting. Opinion on Furnishing Three Million Livres Agreeably to
the Request of the French Minister," February 25, 1793.
    Following the agreement of the cabinet at its meeting on February 25, 1793,
to advance the money, the President wrote to Thomas Jefferson on February 26
that "The Minister of France may, as soon as he pleases, make arrangements
with the Secretary of the Treasury for the payment of Three Million of Livres
on account of the debt due from the U: States to France (including the one
hundred thousand dollars already ordered, in part) . . ." (ALS, Thomas Jefferson Papers, Library of Congress).
    2. Although H in his letter to Ternant of February 26, 1793, refers to this
enclosure as "also of this date," it is presumably the letter dated February 25,
1793, from Jefferson to Ternant. This letter reads as follows: "In my letter of
the 14th. inst. I had the honor to mention to you that it would take some days
to estimate the probable calls on the treasury of the U. S. and to judge whether
your application for three millions of livres to be laid out in provisions for the
supply of France, could be complied with, but that in the mean time an hundred
thousand dollars could be furnished in order to enable you to commence your
operations. I have now to add that the residue of the three millions can be

furnished on account, if you will be so good as to arrange with the Secretary of the Treasury such epochs as may be accomodated to the circumstances of the Treasury and to your operations also. We have very sincere pleasure in shewing on every possible occasion our earnest desire to serve your nation, and the interest we take in it's present situation" (ALS, letterpress copy, Thomas Jefferson Papers, Library of Congress).

From Jean Baptiste de Ternant [1]

Philadelphie 26 fevrier 1793.

Je viens de recevoir la reponse par laquelle vous m'informez des termes auxquels sera acquitté le reste des trois millions accordés par votre gouvernement pour me mettre en état de faire des envois de vivres en france. Je me trouve obligé de vous représenter encore que cet interessant objet de service ne peut être convenablement rempli sans des payemens immédiats ou au moins très rapprochés, et que c'est me mettre à la merci du commerce, et par conséquent diminuer, la somme des approvisionnemens nécessaires à ma nation que de trop reculer la libre disposition des moyens pecuniaires destinés à l'achat et à l'expédition de ces approvisionnemens. Pour peu que vous considériez l'extrême désavantage de payemens trop differés dans une opération urgente telle que celle dont je suis chargé, je ne doute pas, que vous ne sentiez comme moi la nécessité d'accélerer ces payemens, et que dans le cas où ceux de votre trésorerie ne pourroient absolument pas être immédiats vous ne vous prètiez, de tout votre pouvoir à les rapprocher au moins assèz pour faciliter le service délicat, que la nation française attend de mon Zèle. Le Succès des arrangemens définitifs que j'ai à prendre avec les négocians americains devant dépendre de votre response à cette lettre, je vous prie instament de me la faire parvenir le plutot possible.

Ternant.

Copy, *Arch. des. Aff. Etr., Corr. Pol., Etats-Unis,* Vol. 37; copy, *Arch. des Aff. Etr., Corr. Pol., Etats-Unis,* Supplement Vol. 20. The second copy is dated February 28 and differs slightly in wording from the copy printed above.

1. For background to this letter, see Tobias Lear to H, February 8, 1793; "Cabinet Meeting. Opinion on Furnishing Three Million Livres Agreeably to the Request of the French Minister," February 25, 1793; Ternant's first letter to H, February 26, 1793; H to Ternant, February 26, 1793.

To Jean Baptiste de Ternant [1]

Treasury Department February 26 1793

Sir

I have the honor of your letter of this date inclosing one to you from the Secretary of State also of this date.

Towards carrying into execution the arrangment, which has been directed by the President of the united States, and which is announced to you in the abovementioned letter from the Secretary of State I shall be ready to pay, on account of the Debt to France, in addition to the sums heretofore stipulated, the further sum of four hundred & forty four thousand and five hundred Dollars [2] in six equal installments—the first on the fifteenth of April next, the second on the first of may following—the third on the fifteenth of that month, the fourth on the first of June following, the fifth on the fifteenth of that month, and the sixth on the first of July following.

With esteem & respect   I have the honor to be   Sir   Your Obedt & humble Servt   Alexander Hamilton

De Ternant minister of France

LS, *Arch. des Aff. Etr., Corr. Pol., Etats-Unis,* Supplement Vol. 20; copy, *Arch. des Aff. Etr., Corr. Pol., Etats-Unis,* Vol. 37.
  1. For background to this letter, see Tobias Lear to H, February 8, 1793; "Cabinet Meeting. Opinion on Furnishing Three Million Livres Agreeably to the Request of the French Minister," February 25, 1793; Ternant to H, first letter of February 26, 1793.
  2. One hundred thousand dollars of the three million livres requested by Ternant had already been advanced. See George Washington to H, February 13, 1793.

From Wilhem and Jan Willink, Nicholaas and Jacob Van Staphorst, and Nicholas Hubbard

Amsterdam 26 February 1793.

Sir

We had the honor to address You the 25 Ulto.[1] and have now to advise you that owing to the attack made upon this Country by France The circulation of Money has been so checked as to render it excessively nay unparalleled scarce: The natural Consequence is a great depression in the prices of all Stocks and Bonds, to such a Degree indeed that they may be said to be unsaleable. Any fresh Undertakings are utterly impossible in this State of Things and We cannot foresee how long it will last. But we assure You that while it exists, no loans are to be raised here at any rate, even for the United States.

You will therefore please, not calculate upon any Resources here to face the Engagements of the United States falling successively due,[2] before You learn from us a favorable Change of Circumstances: To communicate which, will be a most pleasing task to us.

We are &c.   W. & J. Willink
                              N. & J. van Staphorst & Hubbard
Alexr. Hamilton Esqr.

Copy, Short Family Papers, Library of Congress.
1. Letter not found.
2. See William Short to H, February 25, 1793, note 6.

To Nathaniel Appleton [1]

Treasury Department, February 27, 1793. Has directed the treasurer of the United States to furnish Appleton with a draft for fifty-five thousand dollars to be applied "towards discharging the Interest which will become due the 31st of the ensuing month, on the several Species of Stock standing on your books."

LS, The Huntington Library, San Marino, California.
1. Appleton was commissioner of loans for Massachusetts.

Report on Exports for the Year Ending September 30, 1792, and the Import and Tonnage Duties to December 31, 1791

Treasury Department
February 27th. 1793
[Communicated on February 27, 1793] [1]

[To the Speaker of the House of Representatives]
Sir

I have the honor to transmit to you an abstract of the goods wares and merchandize exported from the United States during one year, ending on the 30th day of September last, and exhibiting the precise quantity of each article thereof exported from each State. Also two returns of impost and tonnage to the end of the year 1791.[2] A part of the necessary documents, for the year 1792 have not yet been received from the Custom houses.

I have the honor to be with perfect respect Sir your most obedient and   very humble servant   Alexr. Hamilton,
                                                          Secy of the Treasury.

To the Speaker of House of
Representatives of the United States.

Copy, RG 233, Reports of the Secretary of the Treasury, 1784–1795, Vol. IV, National Archives.
    1. *Journal of the House,* I, 721.
    2. The enclosures consist of three tables, which are printed in *ASP, Commerce and Navigation,* I, 157–66, and are entitled: "Abstract of Goods, Wares, and Merchandise, exported from each State, from 1st October, 1791, to 30th September, 1792"; "Abstract of Duties Arising on Goods, Wares, and Merchandise, imported into the United States, commencing the 1st of October, 1791, and ending on the 31st of December following"; and "Abstract of Duties arising on the Tonnage of Vessels entered into the United States, Commencing the 1st October, 1791, and ending on the 31st December following."

George Washington to Alexander Hamilton and Henry Knox

[Philadelphia] 27 February 1793.
Sir,

As the day is near at hand, when the President-elect is to take the oath of qualification, and no mode is pointed out by the Constitution or law; I could wish that you, mr Jefferson (Genl. Knox, or Colo. Hamilton) and mr Randolph could meet tomorrow morning, at any place which you may fix between yourselves; & communicate to me the result of your opinions as to time, place & manner of qualification.

Geo: Washington.

P.S. Mr. Jefferson & mr Randolph have suggested the idea of meeting at the war-office at *nine o'Clock* tomorrow morning; if this is convenient & agreeable to you, you will be there accordingly—if otherwise you will be so good as to let me know.

G: w.——n

LC, George Washington Papers, Library of Congress; Df, in the handwriting of Thomas Jefferson, RG 59, Miscellaneous Letters, 1790–1799, National Archives.

From Jonathan Burrall [1]

[*New York, February 28, 1793.* On March 2, 1793, Hamilton wrote to Burrall and referred to "your letter of the 28th ulto." *Letter not found.*]

1. Burrall was cashier of the New York branch of the Bank of the United States.

Cabinet Meeting. Opinion on the Time, Place, and Manner of the President-Elect Taking the Oath of Office [1]

[Philadelphia, February 28, 1793] [2]

If the qualification is to be in private, T.J, A.H H.K and E.R, are of opinion, that Mr. Cushing [3] should administer the oath to the President at his own house, where such officers, or others, as he may notify, will attend. T.J. and A.H. think, that it ought to be in private.

H.K. and E.R. on the other hand think, that the qualification ought to be in public: and that the Marshal of the district should prepare the house of Representatives for the purpose where Mr. Cushing shall administer the oath. The Prest. to go without form, accompanied with such gentlemen, as he thinks proper, and return preceded by the Marshall.

Monday, 12 o'clock, is presumed to be the best time.

But as the mode will be considered by the public, as originating with the President, it is submitted to him for his decision.

D, in the handwriting of Edmund Randolph, George Washington Papers, Library of Congress.

  1. For background to this document, see George Washington to H and Henry Knox, February 27, 1793.
  Jefferson's account of this meeting reads as follows: "Feb. 28. Knox, E. R. and myself met at Knox's where Hamilton was also to have met, to consider the time manner & place of the President's swearing in. Hamilton had been there before & had left his opn with Knox. To wit, that the Presid. shd. ask a judge to attend him in his own house to administer the oath in the presence of the heads of deptmts, which oath should be deposited in the Secy. of state's office. I concurred in this opn. E. R. was for the President's going to the Senate chamber to take the oath, attended by the Marshal of the U.S. who should then make proclmn &c. Knox was for this and for adding the house of Repr. to the presence, as they would not yet be departed. Our individl. opns were written to be communicated to the Presidt. out of which he might form one . . ." (AD, Thomas Jefferson Papers, Library of Congress).
  This account is printed in the "Anas," Ford, *Writings of Jefferson*, I, 221–22.
  2. This document is incorrectly dated February 27. According to Jefferson and Washington the cabinet met on February 28 (AD, Thomas Jefferson Papers, Library of Congress; JPP, 61, 63).
  3. William Cushing, associate justice of the Supreme Court.

From Peter Colt [1]

Paterson [New Jersey] 28 Febuy. 1793

Sir:

On examining mr. Pearce's acct. I find he has recieved a considerable Sum of Money from you [2] & that mr. Parkinson [3] has also been furnished with Some Money in part of his act. There is no charges made by the Society against you to cut up this act. except three Hundred Dollars which mr Walker [4] paid to your Order—neither is there any documents in this office which can serve to shew if you have been reimbursed your advances, or from what Quarter the Money has come. I can only conjecture it has been had through Colo Duer, the former Governor; [5] from whom I am told no accounts can be obtained. I must therefore pray you to cause a copy of your accounts with the Society to be made out & sent me here, as soon as can be conveniently done; that I may be enabled to lay before the Board of Directors a compleat Statement of their Funds &c. An acct. from the Bank of the united States up to this time is also wanted; as the cashier may not know of my appointment he may not choose to make me the return. I must therefore, for this once, request your interferance in procuring this return; as the orders for drawing out the Monies of the Banks have never been registered *here* it will be necessary that the Bank name the persons to whom Monies have been paid.

When I arrived at Paterson I found Messrs. Hall, Marshall[6] & Pearce, totally dissatisfied with their Situation & prospects—the two latter requesting to be discharged. Mr. Marshall has demanded that his Salary be raised to £200 Sterlg ℔ annum, without which he declares he will not continue in the Service of the Society. As I do not find I am authorised to make any contracts of this nature I have referd him to mr Low.[7] He went to New York yester day to bring this Business to a close. I have been told that mr. Pearce is dissatisfied with his Salary; but he has said nothing to me on the Subject. I have this moment learned that he leaves this with mr Hall, this day, for Philadelphia. I presume therefore you will be informed of his demand. Marshall & Pearce appear, as far as I can judge of their Branches, perfectly masters of their Business; & very valuable Men to the Society, & that they cannot be discharged without the Society Sustaining great loss. They will be ready with their work Sooner than we can get command of the water.

Several Buildings which have been ordered for manufactures, are extremely wanted, as well as a durable building for the purposes of general Magazine or Store House; but Majr. L'.Enfant,[8] to whom this part of the Business has been confided, not being here, nothing can be done; and our weavers are working by the *day* in such wretched Sheds, that they loose half their time. In short no arrangments can be made for puting things on a more durable & advantagious footing untill the Majr. returns on the ground.

Knowing how much you have the success of this institution at heart has induced me to make you this communication.

I am, Sir most respectfully your obedient humbl. Servant

P. Colt

Alexr. Hamilton Esquire
Secretary of the Treasury

ALS, Hamilton Papers, Library of Congress.
1. Colt, a resident of Hartford, Connecticut, had served during the American Revolution as deputy commissary general of purchases for the eastern depart-

ment. After the Revolution he became the agent in Hartford for Jeremiah Wadsworth's commercial enterprises and during the seventeen-eighties was active in the Hartford Woolen Manufactory. On February 19, 1793, he was appointed superintendent of the factory of the Society for Establishing Useful Manufactures.

Although H had no official connection with the society, he maintained an active role as its unofficial adviser, and in 1791 and 1792 he had assumed the responsibility for negotiating contracts with workmen for the society's projected establishment in New Jersey and for advancing money for the development of machinery.

2. William Pearce, an English artisan, had come to the United States in July, 1791, and was employed by H on behalf of the Society for Establishing Useful Manufactures to build and improve textile machines. H had advanced various sums of money to Pearce for the construction of machines for the society ("Receipt from William Pearce," August 20, September 7, 17, 1791, May 26, 1792).

3. George Parkinson was an English mechanic employed as a foreman by the Society for Establishing Useful Manufactures.

4. Benjamin Walker, who was a New York financier and speculator, was a director of the Society for Establishing Useful Manufactures. In January, 1792, he was "appointed to act as Accomptant to the Society, until a proper Person be appointed for that purpose" ("Minutes of the S.U.M.," 21). This appointment made him in effect the treasurer of the society.

5. William Duer had served as governor of the society in 1791 and 1792.

6. Thomas Marshall and William Hall had been employed by the society as mechanics.

7. Nicholas Low had been elected governor of the society on October 12, 1792.

8. Pierre Charles L'Enfant had been a French volunteer in the Corps of Engineers during the American Revolution. In 1789 he had designed Federal Hall in New York City. He had been hired to plan the new Federal City on the banks of the Potomac, but because of a dispute with the commissioners of the Federal District he stopped working on this project. In July, 1792, he was employed by the directors of the Society for Establishing Useful Manufactures to lay out the society's manufacturing center at the falls of the Passaic River in Paterson, New Jersey.

From Jeremiah Olney

Custom-House,

Providence 28th. February 1793.

Sir.

I have received your circular Letter of the 22nd. of January, covering the "Act concerning the Registering and Recording of Ships or Vessels." [1] Your Instructions relative to which, and the lost Certificate of registry, shall be carefully attended to.

I observe, that in the execution of the above mentioned Act, several different Oaths are required, which are to be so formed as to embrace a variety of Cases; and that no Form is pointed out for the

Register Bond: As a uniformity in these, as well as in all other Matters, relative to the Revenue Laws, is very desirable, I beg leave, respectfully, to suggest the propriety of such Forms being transmitted from the Treasury, as will be essential in respect to those Two particulars.

The Certificate of admeasurement, when a Vessel has been altered in *burthen*, is the Voucher for a Collector to register her anew; but what is to be his Voucher, or from whom is it proper the information should come, when any alteration is made in her *Form?* I also wish to be informed, Sir, whether the Certificates of registry, which may be granted agreeable to the 11th. and 12th. Sections, are to be transmitted by the Collector who issues them to the Register of the Treasury? The Seventh and Fourteenth Sections being so explicit, with respect to the transmission to him of all Certificates delivered up on the several occasions therein mentioned, that I am at a loss to know whether it was intended the others should be transmitted or not.

With my Return of Cash No. 134, I enclose a duplicate Receipt No. 38, of the Providence Bank, for Two Thousand Dollars, which I have charged to the United States.

I have the Honor to be &c.   Jereh. Olney Collr.

Alexander Hamilton Esquire
Secretary of the Treasury.

Copy, Rhode Island Historical Society, Providence.
  1. 1 *Stat.* 287–99 (December 31, 1792).

Report on the Exports of the United States for One Year Ending September 30, 1792

Treasury Department
February 28th 1793
[Communicated on February 28, 1793] [1]

[To the President of the Senate]
Sir,

I have the honor to transmit to you a return of the Exports of the United States for one year ending on the 30th. day of September 1792, exhibiting the Quantity of the various Articles thereof exported to the home dominions, and to the Colonial Dominions of all the foreign nations with whom the United States have commercial intercourse.[2]

I have the honor to be,   With perfect Respect, Sir   Your most Obedient and most humble Servant   Alexander Hamilton
                                                                 Secy of the Treasy

The Vice President of the United States,
and President of the Senate

LS, RG 46, Second Congress, 1791–1793, Reports of the Secretary of the Treasury, National Archives.
  1. *Annals of Congress*, III, 660–61.
  2. These enclosures are printed in *ASP, Commerce and Navigation*, I, 219–48.

From William S. Smith [1]

[*Philadelphia, February 28, 1793.* The account of a cabinet meeting on March 2, 1793, reads: "The President communicated to the Secretary of State, the Secretary of the Treasury, the Secretary of War and the Attorney General of the United States, a letter from William S. Smith Esqr. of the 28th of February past, to the Secretary of the Treasury." *Letter not found.*]

  1. Smith, who was John Adams's son-in-law, had served as George Washington's aide during the American Revolution and successively as Federal marshal and supervisor of the revenue for New York. At this time he had recently returned from a European tour.

From William Short

Aranjuez [Spain] Feb. 29. 1793.[1]

Sir

Since my last of the 25th. (of which a duplicate is inclosed) I have had the honor of recieving from Amsterdam yours of the 31st. of Dec. acknowleging the reciept of mine up to the 9th. of Oct. inclusive.

I have nothing at present to add to the contents of my last letter having as yet recieved no further advice from the commissioners at Amsterdam. No answer from them to my letter of the 4th of this month[2] can be expected here before the 10th of the next month even if there should be no interruption in the post. They will of course give you the earliest information of any measures they may take.

Should they succeed in the loan of two millions I have authorized [3] they will be able to answer to all calls at least as far as regard the interest & reimbursements of the foreign debt, up to June 1 inclusive. The market being likely to remain bad for the present year at least, perhaps even subject to such convulsions as not to be to be depended on at all, I cannot help repeating how much it is to be desired that such remittances should be made from home, as to not to expose the U.S. to the risk of that dependence. The sums that will be wanted at Amsterdam for the remaining part of the year, being known to you I shall add nothing further on the subject, except to mention the importance of your intentions being known as soon as possible.

I know not whether the commissioners will engage to furnish these sums in the manner & on the conditions you proposed. As soon as I can learn I will not fail to inform you. Perhaps the fear of its being done by others may induce them to make an exertion—though that is much more in the English than the Dutch way.

I am

The Honbl. Alexa: Hamilton   Secretary of the Treasury

ALS, letterpress copy, William Short Papers, Library of Congress.
  1. The date is incorrect. There were only twenty-eight days in February, 1793.
  2. Short's letter to Willink, Van Staphorst, and Hubbard has not been found.
  3. See H to Short, November 5, 1792, and Short to H, February 25, 1793.

To George Washington

[*Philadelphia, February, 1793.*] Sends list of recommendations for positions as Indian commissioners.[1]

AD, George Washington Papers, Library of Congress.
  1. This list, which consists of twenty-six names arranged by states, is entitled "Characters for consideration as Commissioners."
  On March 1, 1793, Washington nominated Benjamin Lincoln of Massachusetts, Beverley Randolph of Virginia, and Timothy Pickering of Pennsylvania "to be Commissioners on the part of the United States, for holding a conference or treaty with the hostile Indians" (*Executive Journal*, I, 135). Both Lincoln and Pickering were on H's list of recommended names. For information concerning the proposed conference, see "Conversation with George Hammond," November 22, December 15-28, 1792; H to Hammond, December 29, 1792; "Cabinet Meeting. Opinion Respecting the Proposed Treaty with the Indians Northwest of the River Ohio," February 25, 1793.

Cabinet Meeting. Opinion on the Time, Place, and Manner of the President-Elect Taking the Oath of Office [1]

[Philadelphia, March 1, 1793]

It is our opinion,

1. that the President ought to take the oath in public.

2. that the time be on Monday next at 12 o'clock in the forenoon.

3. that the place be the Senate-chamber.

4. that the Marshal of the district inform the Vice-President, that the Senate-chamber, being the usual place of the president's public acts, is supposed to be the best place for taking the oath; and that it is wished, the chamber be open.

5. that it may be informally notified to the Vice President governor and foreign ministers, that the oath is to be taken at the time and place abovementioned.

6. that Mr. Cushing be requested to attend; and administer the oath.

7. that the President go without form attended by such gentlemen, as he may choose, and return without form, except that he be preceded by the Marshal.　　　　　　H Knox

Edm: Randolph

March 1. 1793.

My opinion given yesterday was founded on prudential considerations of the moment; though I think it right in the abstract to give publicity to the Act in question. If this is to be done on the present occasion, I see no objection to the above form. I am not, however, satisfied that prudential considerations are not equally ballanced.

A Hamilton [2]

DS, in the handwriting of Edmund Randolph and H, George Washington Papers, Library of Congress.

1. This was the second of two cabinet meetings on the manner in which the President should take the oath of office. For the first meeting, see "Cabinet Meeting. Opinion on the Time, Place, and Manner of the President-Elect Taking the Oath of Office," February 28, 1793.

2. The final paragraph is in H's handwriting. The preceding paragraphs were written by Randolph.

From Tench Coxe

Treasury Department
Revenue Office March 1st. 1793

Sir,

I have the honor to transmit to you a general state of Revenue on domestic distilled spirits exhibiting as far as returns have been received at the Treasury, the several objects contemplated by the House of Representatives in their order of the 8th of May last.[1] The Supervisors of those Districts, wherein the distillation is principally from domestic materials in the Country, were in many instances unable to establish Collectors by reason of the smallness of the compensations under the first act,[2] and you will remember that from that and other causes, the detailed information was necessary to enable the President to make the final distributions of the funds assigned for compensations and expences could not be collected so as to complete that business 'till the end of October.

The appointments have since been generally made; and consequently this Revenue will now take a more orderly course.

I have the honor to be With great respect, Sir, Your most obedient Servant.   Tench Coxe,
                                        Commissioner of the Revenue.

The Honble
The Secretary of the Treasury.

Copy, RG 233, Reports of the Secretary of the Treasury, 1784–1795, Vol. IV, National Archives. This letter was enclosed in H's "Report on Stills and Spirits Distilled Within the United States," March 2, 1793.

1. See "Report on Stills and Spirits Distilled Within the United States," March 2, 1793.

2. Section 58 of "An Act repealing, after the last day of June next, the duties heretofore laid upon Distilled Spirits imported from abroad, and laying others in their stead; and also upon Spirits distilled within the United States, and for appropriating the same" provided "That the aggregate amount of the allowances to all the said supervisors, inspectors and other officers, shall not exceed seven per cent. of the whole product of the duties arising from the spirits distilled within the United States: *And provided also,* That such allowance shall not exceed the annual amount of forty-five thousand dollars, until the same shall be further ascertained by law" (1 *Stat.* 213 [March 3, 1791]). The compensation was changed by Section 16 of "An Act concerning the Duties on Spirits distilled within the United States," which authorized the President "to

make such allowances for their respective services to the supervisors, inspectors and other officers of inspection, as he shall deem reasonable and proper, so as the said allowances, together with the incidental expenses of collecting the duties on spirits distilled within the United States, shall not exceed seven and an half per centum of the total product of the duties on distilled spirits, for the period to which the said allowances shall relate, computing from the time the act, intituled 'An Act repealing after the last day of June next, the duties heretofore laid upon distilled spirits imported from abroad, and laying others in their stead, and also upon spirits distilled in the United States, and for appropriating the same,' took effect: *And provided also,* That such allowance shall not exceed the annual amount of seventy thousand dollars, until the same shall be further ascertained by law" (1 *Stat.* 270–71 [May 8, 1792]).

On October 31, 1792, Coxe had written to the supervisors of the revenue transmitting the order of May 8, 1792, of the House of Representatives and requesting them to send information on distilled spirits in their districts (LC, RG 58, Letters of Commissioner of Revenue, 1792–1793, National Archives).

To John F. Mercer [1]

Philadelphia March 1. 1793

Sir

You will readily comprehend, without explanation, the occasion of my having left your letter of the 31 of January unanswered, 'till this time.

You acknowlege that what Mr. Key states is the fact, as far as he states facts; and that *in general* the Conversation related by Mr. Campbell is such as really passed; though you recollect to have declared, that you never had said, or thought, that I was any how personally or pecuniarily interested with Duer; stating as your Idea that *Duer* was *favoured* from motives of personal friendship in whatever transactions he was concerned in that were connected with my Office.

Upon this acknowlegement, I conceive myself bound to declare, that the suggestions, which I understand to be avowed by you are gross misrepresentations, from whatever sources they may have been derived; and until the authorities, to which you allude, shall be made [to] appear to have been such as to justify on your part a belief of the matters alleged, I must consider your conduct in propagating them as wanton and unwarrantable. In the mean time, I aver that the allegations which have been made cannot be substantiated; and I add, that it is not in your power to shew that I ever unduly favoured Mr. Duer, from whatever motives, in any transactions of his with the Department under my care. I feel confident, that in no instance, did he experience from me, in my official character, any more favourable treatment, than it has been usual with me from considerations of public utility, to extend to others, in similar cases. Indeed, except as Assignee or Agent of Mr. Fowler,[2] I recollect no transactions, he has had with the Department, which have fallen under my cognizance or direction. And in regard to that, the strictest scrutiny would issue in a conclusion different from the one, which you seem to have drawn.

You observe, that you have been led into the present business, without provocation, & that the attack has not been on your side. Surely, Sir, you will not say, that any was made by me. I have good ground to believe, that you have before this learnt of General Heister [3] that the story of my opposition to your election, (which is traced to him) is without foundation. This he declares to me to be the case; and I understand from him, that he has communicated the same thing to you.

To the concluding passage of your letter I can make no reply; because I can annex to it no definite meaning.

I am Sir   Your humble servant

ADf, Hamilton Papers, Library of Congress.
    1. For background to this letter, see the introductory note to H to Mercer, September 26, 1792. See also H to Mercer, November 3, December 6, December, 1792; Mercer to H, October 16–28, December, 1792, January 31, 1793; H to David Ross, September 26, November 3, 1792; Ross to H, October 5–10, November 23, 1792; Uriah Forrest to H, November 7, 1792.
    2. See "Contract for Army Rations," October 28, 1790, note 2; H to William Duer, April 7, 1791, note 4.
    3. Daniel Hiester. In his newspaper article of September 26, 1792, Mercer had stated: "a young gentleman . . . told Mr. [Richard] Sprigg, my father-in-law, that gen. Heister, (whose reputation is well known) told him at Hagar's-town, that there certainly would be a great opposition made against my re-election . . . and that the secretary of the treasury was at the bottom of it" (The [Annapolis] Maryland Gazette, September 27, 1792).

To Samuel A. Otis [1]

[Philadelphia, March 1–2, 1793]

The Secretary of the Treasury here incloses a letter of request to the Bank of the U States for an informal advance to Mr Otis of

Fifteen thousand nine hundred & seventy two dollars & ninety cents
—on accot of the Compensations due to the Senators of the U States.

Copy, RG 46, Records of the Office of the Secretary of the Senate, National Archives.
1. Otis was secretary of the Senate.

Report on the Petition of Lewis Garanger

[Philadelphia, March 1, 1793
Communicated on March 2, 1793] [1]

[To the Speaker of the House of Representatives]

The Secretary of the Treasury to whom was referred by an order of
the House of Representatives of the 12th. of February, the Petition
of Lewis Garranger, on behalf of himself and his brother Charles
Garranger,[2] thereupon respectfully makes the following Report:

The petition among other objects sets forth that the interest due
upon certain certificates which had been issued in favor of Lewis
Garanger in November 1783, when he was in confinement for debt,
and upon those issued in favor of Charles Garanger in July 1784
having been mortgaged to the Creditors of the two Brothers, was on
that account not put upon the same footing with the certificates
granted to other foreign Officers, upon which the interest was
payable at the House of Mr. Grand [3] banker at Paris. The Petitioner
now prays payment of principal and interest of the said certificates
in specie, under the regulation made in favor of certain foreign
Officers.[4]

It appears that the accounts of the Petitioner and his brother for
pay and subsistence were liquidated by the commissioner of Army
accounts and final settlements issued to them, which were afterwards
exchanged for certificates of Registered debt.

If it was in the option of the petitioner either to take certificates
upon which the interest was payable at Paris in specie, or to prefer
the other certificates of the register of the Treasury, it appears that
the election was made in favor of the latter. The Petitioner is at
present a holder of Registered debt. Any other modification, except
the funding of it, if once admitted would form a precedent, which
might in many other cases be productive of consequences fraught
with inconvenience.

The Secretary therefore submits it as his opinion that so far as the petition relates to the special object in question, no legislative interference will be adviseable. As it relates to other objects, the Secretary on account of the lateness of the present session begs leave to defer his opinion until the meeting of the next Congress.

All which is humbly submitted.   Alexander Hamilton.
                                                  Secy of the Treasury.

Treasury Department
March 1st. 1793

Copy, RG 233, Reports of the Secretary of the Treasury, 1784–1795, Vol. IV, National Archives.

1. *Journal of the House*, I, 730. The communicating letter, dated March 1, 1793, may be found in RG 233, Reports of the Secretary of the Treasury, 1784–1795, Vol. IV, National Archives.

2. On February 12, 1793, "A petition of Lewis Garanger, in behalf of himself and his brother, Charles Garanger, was presented to the House and read, praying that the amount of the certificates of debt granted to the petitioner and his said brother, for their services in the late Army of the United States, and of the interest which has accrued thereon, may be paid in specie at the Treasury; also, that a claim for balance of subsistence due to them while prisoners of war, and for their passage to France, and travelling expenses to Paris, may be allowed and paid, with interest from the date of the said certificates" (*Journal of the House*, I, 700).

3. Ferdinand Le Grand.

4. See H to Gouverneur Morris, September 13, 1792.

To Jean Baptiste de Ternant

Treasury Department
March 1st. 1793.

Sir,

I have to assure you, in answer to your letter of the 26th. of February, that fully impressed with the importance to your Object, of speedy advances, it has been my aim to shorten the period of making them; as far as could consist with the general arrangements and prospects of the Treasury; having due regard to other Objects of expenditure which are indispensable.

In consequence of your last application, I have reexamined the subject with a strong desire to find it possible to abridge the periods which have been communicated; but the result is a confirmation of the conviction, that I ought not to promise more than has been already promised. The success of some arrangements which are meditated, may enable me hereafter to contract some of the more remote periods. In such an event it will give me pleasure to do it. And you will be duly informed of the possibility.

With Respect & Esteem   I have the honor to be   Sir   Your Most Obedient &   Humble Servant   Alexander Hamilton

Mr. Ternant
Minister Plenipotentiary of France

LS, *Arch. des Aff. Etr., Corr. Pol., Etats-Unis,* Supplement Vol. 20; LC, *Arch. des Aff. Etr., Corr. Pol., Etats-Unis,* Vol. 37.

To George Washington

[Philadelphia, March 1, 1793]

The Secretary of the Treasury presents his respects to The President, and has the honor to transmit a communication this morning received from Colo. Smith [1]—another from mr Ternant; [2] concerning both of which he will wait upon the President tomorrow.

March 1st 1793

LC, George Washington Papers, Library of Congress.
 1. William S. Smith's letter, which has not been found, was dated February 28, 1793. The letter is described in an entry in JPP for March 1, 1793, as "containing propositions from the French Ministry to the Government of the U.S. respecting the payment of the debt from the latter to the former" (JPP, 64).
 In November, 1792, Smith, who at that time was traveling in France, proposed a plan to the French Provisional Executive Council for using the American debt to France for the purchase of supplies for France in the United States. In a letter to Edmond Charles Genet, the new French Minister to the United States, Smith described the conditions of his proposals as follows: "I proposed to Supply provisions, arms & military Stores from America at the Market price charging only the Common Commission, and the Extra expences attending the Execution of the business. You will observe that the Minister of the Public Contributions; in his letter of the 7th November 1792 conveys to me the full approbation of the executive Council on the Subject of my propositions" (Smith to Genet, May 8, 1793, ALS, *Arch. des Aff. Etr., Corr. Pol., Etats-Unis,* Supplement Vol. 24). In his "Report of the Minister of Public Contributions, on the liquidation of the American debt" Etienne Clavière stated that Smith's offers had been approved by the Provisional Executive Council and were "to procure to the republic not only the reimbursement of what remains due from the United States, although not yet payable, but for the application of it, either for supplies for the army, or wheat, flour, and salted provisions, in augmentation of our internal supplies" (*ASP, Foreign Relations,* I, 144). Smith arrived in Philadelphia in February, 1793. On February 20 he called on Thomas Jefferson

and informed him that the French Ministry desired "our debt to be paid in provns, and have authorized him to negotiate this" (Ford, *Writings of Jefferson*, I, 216–17).

2. Jean Baptiste de Ternant to H, February 26, 1793.

To Jonathan Burrall

Treasury Department
March 2nd. 1793

Sir

I find that my letter of the 23rd ultimo (which was written in haste) proposing an arrangement for the accomodation of Merchants who are indebted to the Custom house, does not correctly express the idea which was contemplated.[1]

The mode of transacting the business as mentioned in your letter of the 28th ulto.[2] is the true one to be pursued, that is, Notes of the parties indebted will be presented for discount to the amount of the respective sums due to the Custom house—the Directors judge of the safety of the Notes, and take the risk of non payment upon themselves. When notes are accepted the proceeds are subject to checks in favor of the *Collector only*, which checks the Bank receives from the Collector as Cash

Your account concerning the purchase of Debt for the Commissioners of the sinking fund will be adjusted in a few days.

I am with consideration   Sir   your obedt Servant   Alex Hamilton

Jonathn Burral Esqr
Cashier of the Office of D & D
New York

LS, MS Division, New York Public Library.

1. "Treasury Department Circular to the Presidents and Directors of the Offices of Discount and Deposit of the Bank of the United States," February 23–March 5, 1793. See also "Treasury Department Circular to the Collectors of the Customs," February 22–March 5, 1793.

2. Letter not found.

Cabinet Meeting. Opinion on Proposals Made by William S. Smith Relative to the French Debt

[Philadelphia, March 2, 1793]

The President communicated to the Secretary of State, the Secretary of the Treasury, the Secretary of War and the Attorney General of the United States, a letter from William S. Smith Esqr. of the 28th of February past,[1] to the Secretary of the Treasury, with sundry Papers—No. I. II. III & IV. relating to a negotiation for changing the form of the debt to France; and required their opinion what answer should be returned to the Application.[2]

The opinion unanimously is, that the Secretary of the Treasury shall inform Mr. Smith that the Government of the United States have made engaged payments to France to the extent which is at present consistent with their arrangements; and do not judge it adviseable to take any measures on the subject of his Application.

Th: Jefferson
Alexander Hamilton
H Knox
Edm: Randolph.

March 2nd. 1793

DS, George Washington Papers, Library of Congress.
1. Letter not found.
2. For information on Smith's proposals, see H to George Washington, March 1, 1793.

From James Hillhouse [1]

[*Philadelphia, March 2, 1793.*] Recommends Melancthon Lloyd Woolsey "As a proper person to be Appointed Collector of the New District on Lake Champlain." [2]

AD, George Washington Papers, Library of Congress.
1. Hillhouse was a member of the House of Representatives from Connecticut.
2. Woolsey was appointed collector of "the District of Champlain, in the State of New York" on March 4, 1793 (*Executive Journal*, I, 138).

Report on Stills and Spirits Distilled Within the United States

Treasury Department
March 2d 1793.
[Communicated on March 2, 1793] [1]

[To the Speaker of the House of Representatives]
Sir,

Pursuant to an order of the House of Representatives of the 8th of May last,[2] I have the honor to transmit a general state of the Revenue on stills and spirits distilled within the United States, exhibiting the several particulars indicated by the said order, so far as returns have been received at the Treasury;[3] to which I beg leave to add, the Copy of a letter of yesterday from the Commissioner of the Revenue, transmitting the same to me.[4]

With perfect respect   I have the honor to be   Sir your obedient servant.   Alexander Hamilton,
Secy of the Treasury.

The Honble
The Speaker of the House of Representatives.

Copy, RG 233, Reports of the Secretary of the Treasury, 1784–1795, Vol. IV, National Archives.
  1. *Journal of the House*, I, 733–34.
  2. On May 8, 1792, the House "*Resolved*, That the Secretary of the Treasury report to this House, as early in the next session as may be practicable, the number and capacity of the stills in the respective districts and States; the nett product of revenue of the respective districts and States, particularizing the drawbacks, and distinguishing foreign from American materials, and the product paid by the gallon, month, and year; also, the number of officers and the amount of their salaries" (*Journal of the House*, I, 604).
  3. This enclosure is printed in *ASP, Finance*, I, 250–51.
  4. Tench Coxe to H, March 1, 1793.

From William S. Smith

[*Philadelphia, March 2, 1793*. According to an entry in JPP for March 2, 1793, Hamilton submitted to the President "a letter from Colo. W. S. Smith of this date respecting the debt of the U.S. to France[1]—with a Copy of a letter wh. he had written to Mr. Ternant on the subject[2]—and an Extract of a Communication from the Minister of Contributions at Paris to Colo. Smith dated Novr. 1792." [3] *Letter from Smith not found.*] [4]

JPP, 66.

1. For background to Smith's proposals concerning the debt owed to France by the United States, see H to George Washington, March 1, 1793, note 1; "Cabinet Meeting. Opinion on Proposals Made by William S. Smith Relative to the French Debt," March 2, 1793.

2. See H to Jean Baptiste de Ternant, March 1, 1793.

3. This letter from Etienne Clavière to Smith was dated November 7, 1792. See H to Washington, March 1, 1793, note 1.

4. The entry in JPP for March 2 notes that "Colo. Smith states to Mr. Ternant that according to the arrangemts. which had been made between him (Colo. S) and the Executive Council of France, he (Colo. S.) ought to receive the sum of 3 millions of Livres for which Mr Ternant had applied to the U.S. by order of the French Governmt., to purchase provisions &c. to send to France" (JPP, 66). For Ternant's application for this sum, see Tobias Lear to H, February 8, 1793; "Cabinet Meeting. Opinion on Furnishing Three Million Livres Agreeably to the Request of the French Minister," February 25, 1793.

From John Bard [1]

New york March 4 1793.

Sir

I dined a few days ago with a large Company at Judge Duanes,[2] In the course of the after noon, you became the Subject of general Conversation. It gave me the greatest pleasure to hear that Just and greatfull applause which all the Company bestowed upon ⟨y⟩ou. Your Friend General Gates [3] declared when ever ⟨y⟩our Idea was present to his mind, he could not help ⟨ap⟩plying to you the Beautifull Epitaph, Mr Pope wrote ⟨t⟩o the memory of his Friend Mr Secretary Craggs

> Statesman yet Friend to truth, of Soul Sincere,
> In Action Faithfull, and in Honour Clear!
> Who broke no Promise, Serv'd no Private end,
> Who gaind no Title, and who lost no Friend,
> Ennobled by Himself, by all approved
> Praised, wept, and Honourd, by the Muse he lov'd.[4]

It was Unanimously, & Heartily agreed by this Respectable Company, that these lines exibited an Exact and perfect portraid of Coll Hammiltons Character; The delight I felt at this Just and greatfull Ulogium has prompted me to Communicate it to the only Gentleman, who will probably feel less Sensibility on the Occasion, than any of his Numerous Friends Tho I presume, a Just Tribute of praise, which flows from a greatfull sense of those great and essential Benefits, a man derives to his Country, by Superiour abilities, and unremitting devotion to its real Interests, cannot be Ungreatfull to the Generous Donor himself.[5]

I am Sir   With Real Respect & affection   Your most Humble Servt.   John Bard

ALS, Hamilton Papers, Library of Congress.
1. Bard was a New York City physician.
2. James Duane was Federal judge for the District of New York.
3. After the American Revolution Horatio Gates had settled in Virginia. In 1790 he moved to New York and took up residence at "Rose Hill Farm," which was just outside New York City.
4. The quotation is Alexander Pope's epitaph "On James Craggs, Esq.; In Westminster-Abbey."
5. H endorsed this letter "Answered wirh thanks &c." Letter not found.

From George Cabot [1]

[Philadelphia, March 4, 1793]

My dear Sir

The People of Massachusetts entertain the idea that a balance is due to the State more than sufficient to cover her State debt, & some anxiety has been excited in the legislature of that state lest she shou'd finally fail of receiving it. After the failure of the Assumption bill [2] I intended to have had five minutes conversation with you on the subject, but saw that your time seemed to be overcharged with other business.

I hope you will find leisure & inclination to furnish me soon with your ideas on the interesting subject of commercial policy & that you will say definitively whether my continuance in the bank is to be desired or not since it furnishes so copious a topic for complaint.[3] I called this morning to bid you farewell but you were absent.

May God bless you!   G Cabot

Eveg March 4. 93

ALS, Hamilton Papers, Library of Congress.
1. Cabot was a member of the United States Senate from Massachusetts and a director of the Bank of the United States.
2. On December 12, 1792, the House of Representatives resolved "That a loan

to the amount of the balances which, upon a final settlement of accounts, shall be found due from the United States to the individual States, be opened at the Treasury of the United States" and that "the sums to be subscribed to such loans be payable in the principal or interest of the certificates or notes issued by any such of the said States, as, upon the final settlement of accounts, shall have a balance due to them from the United States" (*Journal of the House*, I, 637). On January 28, 1793, the House passed a bill entitled "An act to authorize a loan in the certificates or notes of such States as shall have balances due to them, upon a final settlement of accounts with the United States" (*Journal of the House*, I, 683–84). On February 4, 1793, the Senate rejected the measure (*Annals of Congress*, III, 638–39).

3. The "complaint" is a reference to an amendment to Article 1, Section 9, of the Constitution proposed in the Senate on March 2, 1793. It was suggested that "At the end of the section, add, 'no member of Congress shall be eligible to any office of profit under the authority of the United States, nor shall any person intrusted with the management of any bank or other moneyed corporation within the United States, be capable of a seat in either House of Congress'" (*Annals of Congress*, III, 663, IV, 23, 26–31). Cabot resigned as director and sold his stock in the bank in December, 1793.

From Benjamin Lincoln [1]

Boston March 4th. 1793

Sir

I had too little time with you when in Philadelphia. Your particular engagments forbid my calling on you as often as under different circumstances I should have called.

One question in particular was left unsettled the application of Mr. Joseph Blake [2] respecting the quallity of some wines he imported. The Comptroller [3] was in opinion that there could not any consideration be made for its being of an inferiour quallity. Mr Blake wishes you would look of his statement of the business as in the hands of the Comptroller and give your opinion after as soon as it shall be convenient.

Cap Williams [4] has an acct some where in your department, for expressing before the last Cutter was finished. He wishes it might be taken up & settled.

We shall want a few registers before April.

LC, Massachusetts Historical Society, Boston; LC, RG 36, Collector of Customs at Boston, Letter Book, 1790–1797, National Archives; copy, RG 56, Letters from the Collector at Boston, National Archives.

1. Lincoln was collector of customs at Boston.
2. Blake was a Boston merchant.
3. Oliver Wolcott, Jr.
4. John Foster Williams was master of the revenue cutter for Massachusetts.

From Nicholas Low [1]

New york 4 March 1793

Dr. Sir

The foregoing is extract of a Letter from Mr. Colt of 1 Instt.[2] What can be the Cause of Maj. L Enfants extraordinary long Absence? Will you speak to him and advise him to come forward immediately. I suspect that strong Efforts will be made to take Pearse out of our Employ and at the same Time I do not beleive we can do well without him. His & Marshalls [3] Salaries at £100: Stg are both too low and must at the next Meeting be raised. I wish you would find out pearse & converse with him.

I am Dr. sr. yours very sincerely   Nichs Low

ALS, Hamilton Papers, Library of Congress.

1. Low was a director of the Society for Establishing Useful Manufactures.
2. The extract from Peter Colt's letter to Low reads as follows: "The Absence of Maj. [Pierre Charles] L Enfant of whom I get no Intelligence becomes every Day more distressing not a day passes without Applications for Employmt. of Mechaniks & for House Lotts &ca. I do not feel myself at Liberty to take a single Step in this Business without consulting him as I am totally uninformed as to his Plans of the Town and the general Arrangements made for Building thereon.

"Yesterday Mr. [William] Hall and Mr. [William] Pearse both set out for Philada. Mr Halls Business I am not made acquainted with. I presume however on his own private Concerns. Mr. Pearse was sent for by the Secretary of State respecting his Patents and of Course is partly on his own Account and partly on that of the Society. Since he left Paterson I have been informed that Mr. [William] Bingham of Philada. has offerred him a Capital of £30,000 to be employ'd by Pearse in the Cotton Business. I am not without hope that this may not prove true as it must render him still more uneasy with his present Situation." (Copy, Hamilton Papers, Library of Congress.)
3. Pearce and Thomas Marshall were artisans employed by the Society for Establishing Useful Manufactures.

From John F. Mercer [1]

Baltimore Mar 5. 1793.

Sir

I was surprizd by a letter from you [2] at the moment I was about to leave Philadelphia with Mrs. Mercer very much indisposed & still more astonished to find on my arrival here, that Major Ross had brought this subject again before the public in the Newspapers,[3] in a manner calculated to make the falsest & most injurious impressions, where the progress of this business was altogether unknown. It woud have been more candid & honorable to have settled this in Philadelphia where we were all on the spot. My intention in my last [4] was to place this controversy, on such neutral ground that you might with propriety put an end to the correspondance on the principles you had yourself declard "that if I did not impeach your integrity, you woud not have concluded an attack on your public conduct a sufficient ground to adopt this mode of discussion." [5] But since you have thought proper to reject this mode you will make the best of that which you have prefered. I will now abide by what has already passed & as matter of opinion only is disputed. I shall deem all further explanation unnecessary on my part & risk a return of the gross expressions of your last. I shall wait any further communication from you 8 days in Annapolis.

I am &c.   John F Mercer

ALS, Hamilton Papers, Library of Congress.

1. For background to this letter, see the introductory note to H to Mercer, September 26, 1792. See also H to Mercer, November 3, December 6, December, 1792, March 1, 1793; Mercer to H, October 16–28, December, 1792, January 31, 1793; H to David Ross, September 26, November 3, 1792; Ross to H, October 5–10, November 23, 1792; Uriah Forrest to H, November 7, 1792.

2. H to Mercer, March 1, 1793.

3. The following notice, dated March 2, 1793, and signed by David Ross, appeared in *The Maryland Journal and Baltimore Advertiser* on March 5, 1793: "In Messieurs Goddard and Angell's Paper of the 30th of October, the Public are informed, that Colonel Mercer had given a *full, explicit,* and direct answer to the letter of the Secretary of the Treasury, calling on him to state what he really did say of him, if he had been misunderstood; but they are not yet informed whether Colonel Mercer disavows or justifies the charges he was understood to have made: I am induced, therefore, to observe, if the person that gave this information is sufficiently informed, and had consulted his candour, he would have found that justice to the Secretary required he should, by this time, have let the Public know, as I now do, that Colonel Mercer disavows his ever having impeached the integrity of the Secretary, or that he had charged him with being privately interested in the contract for supplying the western army with provisions, or that he had ever charged him with offering to him a bribe, or money, to vote for the assumption, and explicitly acknowledges what passed between him and the Secretary, on this subject, was altogether in jest, it being in the presence of Mr. Samuel Sterett, and several other gentlemen; and Colonel Mercer not only disavows that he had ever charged the Secretary with being privately interested in the purchases made by the Commissioners for buying up the public debt; but, in Colonel Mercer's own language to the Secretary, he says *he neither did, directly or indirectly, represent him as any wise pecuniarily concerned in purchasing or selling stock, or im-*

peach his honour or honesty. The Public are also assured, that General Hiester informed me, there was no foundation for the information Colonel Mercer alleged he had received of General Hiester's being the author of the report that the opposition to Colonel Mercer's election could be traced up to the Secretary; and so far from it, that General Hiester had not himself heard of even any suggestion of such an opposition being instituted by the Secretary. This communication is rendered the more necessary, in justice to the Public, it relating to an officer of theirs so highly intrusted, as well as in justice to the Secretary himself, since it has been circulated, in some parts of the State, that the Secretary *had admitted every one of the charges brought against him by Colonel Mercer;* and since others, as well as myself, understood Colonel Mercer very differently, indeed, from what he now states to the Secretary to have been said by him, respecting several of these subjects; and it affords also, I hope, a laudable gratification thus to be enabled to assure the Public, that I have not been mistaken in the high opinion I had formed of the Secretary's honour and integrity, from a personal acquaintance with him, and the impeaching of which, at least as I understood Colonel Mercer, was one of the principal inducements for taking a part against him in the late election."

Mercer answered Ross's observations in a statement dated March 7, 1793, which was published in *The Maryland Journal and Baltimore Advertiser,* March 12, 1793. This statement, addressed to James Angell, publisher of *The Maryland Journal,* reads as follows: "A Publication in your paper of Tuesday last, requires some transient animadversion. The repeated and unprovoked attacks I have experienced from this character, are unpleasant. When they have been addressed to me in private life, I have ever deemed them unworthy of reply; but while I remain a Representative of Maryland, I shall not disdain a public charge from even the meanest of my constituents. On my return, during this session, to Annapolis, where the legislature of the state were then convened, I was apprized that some treasury scouts or runners had spread a report similar to the one in your paper. In other words, they had repeated, that '*I had denied in Philadelphia, what I had asserted in Maryland.*' I immediately placed in the hands of Mr. George Mann every paper that had passed relative to the controversy between Mr. Hamilton and myself (the whole has been committed to writing) with directions to permit any person to peruse them, on whom he could rely for their return. Many read them, and their contents became, I believe, generally known. A similar conduct may, perhaps, be most advisable now —it is all that time, and I believe propriety, will admit. I shall therefore leave with you every paper that has hitherto passed on this subject, for the perusal of any person in whose honor you can confide for their return; or you have my leave to publish the whole transaction in the order it occurred, provided I am subjected to no expense: In either case, those that desire it may form their judgments from the whole of the documents; and from the perusal of them, I trust, it will unequivocally result, that Mr. Hamilton does not directly deny any one fact that I have *really,* at any time, asserted. It is true that the discussion has not yet ceased; but it will appear that the issue now joined is not a matter of fact but a matter of opinion only. I am sensible that motives of delicacy would have forbid the disclosure of a correspondence, at so critical a period of its progress; but I must plead the boring nonsense of this officious intermeddler, if not as a justification, at least as an excuse."

4. Mercer to H, January 31, 1793.
5. H to Mercer, December 6, 1792.

From William Seton [1]

New York 5 March 1793

Permit me My dear sir among the great number of your friends who rejoice at the Triumph you have gained to assure you that no one more sincerely feels the pleasure than myself; I never doubted the result, but the infamous manner of the attack gave us all uneasiness & particularly from its being so near the close of the Sessions.[2] I hope your Health has not suffered from the confined close attention you have been obliged to pay to get rid of these varlets.

All the Letters you have enclosed to me have been duly forwarded, those for General Schuyler [3] delivered as he was in Town. My friend in London writes me that he is very attentive to the delivery of the Letters for the Minister.[4]

Distress for Money is universal, and Usury prevailing. The great fall of Stocks is much to be lamented, for notwithstanding the low rate of Exchange, Foreigners will draw & are almost the only purchasers much to the loss of our own Citizens.

Our Specie is draining from us very fast for operations to the Southward & every week we get more & more into the power of the Branch,[5] the vast sum of Duties payable this month will still make this worse, however there is no help for it we must bear up as well as we can.[6]

I am with the sincerest esteem & respect   Dear sir   Your Obliged Obed Hule Servt   Wm Seton

Alex. Hamilton Esqr

ALS, Hamilton Papers, Library of Congress.
1. Seton was cashier of the Bank of New York.
2. For H's "Triumph," see the introductory note to "Report on the Balance of All Unapplied Revenues at the End of the Year 1792 and on All Unapplied Monies Which May Have Been Obtained by the Several Loans Authorized by Law," February 4, 1793.
3. Philip Schuyler, H's father-in-law.
4. Seton sent the letters that H had written to Thomas Pinckney, the United States Minister Plenipotentiary to Great Britain, to Joseph Hadfield, a London banker and businessman, for delivery to Pinckney.
5. See Seton to H, January 22, December 20, 1792.
6. H endorsed this letter "Answered the 22d." Letter not found.

To Tench Coxe

Treasury Department March 6th. 1793

Sir

I request your attention to the enclosed Resolution of the House of Representatives of the 2 instant, requiring certain Returns relative to the Revenue, to be furnished to Congress on the first monday in January next.[1]

I am Sir　Your obedt Servt　　　　A Hamilton

Commissioner of the Revenue
Tench Coxe Esquire

LS, RG 58, General Records, 1791–1803, National Archives.
1. The House resolution reads as follows: "*Resolved*, That the Secretary of the Treasury report to Congress, on the first Monday of January next, the number of stills in the respective districts, distinguishing those that are employed in distilling spirits from materials of the growth of the United States; and also the nett product of revenue arising from the respective Districts and States, particularizing the drawbacks, and distinguishing the foreign from American materials, and the product by the gallon, month, and year. Also, the number of officers, and amount of their salaries" (*Journal of the House*, I, 733).

Conversation with George Hammond [1]

[Philadelphia, March 7–April 2, 1793]

Since I last had the honor of addressing your Lordship, I have had several conversations with Mr Hamilton on the subject of the probable conduct which this government may be induced to observe in the case of a war between Great Britain and France, of the commencement of which we have indeed received here some vague information, though through uncertain channels. From the uniform tenor of these conversations I perceive clearly that that Gentleman remains immoveable in his determination whenever that event may occur, of employing every exertion in *his* power to incline this country to adopt as strict a neutrality as may not be directly contrary to its public engagements: and I learn that the President perfectly concurs in sentiment with Mr Hamilton not only on the propriety, but on the indispensable necessity of pursuing that line of conduct. . . .

I have not been able, through Mr. Hamilton's conversations, to ascertain *precisely* the nature of the reception which the officers of this administration may give to Mr Genêt [2] himself (when he arrives) or to any propositions that he may be instructed to offer. I can however collect that their actual intention is—to acknowledge that Gentleman as the Minister of the government of France *de facto*—to admit the principle that the treaties entered into with the former executive government of France, are binding upon the two nations— but to declare explicitly that, previous to the contracting of any *new* engagements, this country may deem it expedient to wait until the national will of France be expressed by some organ more competent efficient and permanent than the present provisional council. With respect to the *existing* engagements between the two nations, I have said above that "Exertions would be employed to incline this country to adopt as strict a neutrality *as may not be directly contrary*" to them. I deem myself fully justified in using so *loose* an expression by an assurance of Mr. Hamilton's that although these engagements could not be considered as null, yet that they would not be enforced to such an extent as that the observance of them might involve the United States in any difficulties or disputes with other powers.

How far subsequent events may effect an alteration in these resolutions, I cannot pretend to predict. But I have learnt from a *confidential* quarter [3] an important fact, which not only proves their present existence, but also in some measure elucidates the principle upon which they are founded. Your Lordship will recollect that in the course of the war the United States contracted a considerable debt with France. Very shortly after the peace, the old Congress formed an arrangement of discharging it by installments at stated periods. This arrangement has been punctually executed. Exclusive of a sum of two hundred thousand dollars, left due from the last installment, which has been since within the last month paid to a person authorized to receive it (and to which as well as the mode of applying it I shall have occasion to advert in another dispatch) [4] there still remains a balance against the United States of about three millions of dollars. The first installment of this balance becomes due in September next; and the residue at different settled intervals. But the provisional Council being solicitous to gain *immediate* possession of the whole, submitted to this government, either through the present

French Minister or their confident agent Colonel Smith,[5] a proposition for that purpose. viz—to convert the whole sum owen to France into a fund upon the same terms as the other American stocks—to allow the French government to dispose of this fund to individuals—and to appropriate the whole proceeds to the purchase of American flour and wheat to be sent to France. This proposition underwent a long discussion in the American Cabinet when it was at length finally determined to reject it, and to inform the provisional council that this government would make no change whatever in the nature and form of the debt, but would pay the installments to the executive government of France, however it might be constituted, existing *de facto* at the periods at which they might be respectively due. This determination of the American Cabinet appears to me decisive of its views relative of the actual position of France; for surely had it been solicitous to promote the success of the present system in that nation, it would have embraced this offer so specious in its principle, and so highly beneficial to this country in *all* its collateral relations.

D, PRO: F.O., Series 5, Vol. I.

1. This conversation has been taken from Hammond to Lord Grenville, April 2, 1793, Dispatch No. 11.

2. Edmond Charles Genet had been appointed in late December, 1792, to replace Jean Baptiste de Ternant as French Minister to the United States. He did not arrive in the United States until April, 1793.

3. At the end of this letter Hammond wrote in code: "P.S. The confidential Quarter from which I obtained the knowledge of the French Proposal above mentioned was Mr. Hamilton himself."

4. Hammond to Grenville, April 2, 1793 (copy, MS Division, New York Public Library).

5. For information concerning William S. Smith's proposals, see H to George Washington, March 1, 1793; "Cabinet Meeting. Opinion on Proposals Made by William S. Smith Relative to the French Debt," March 2, 1793.

From Henry Knox

[*Philadelphia, March 8, 1793.* On March 18, 1793, Hamilton wrote to Knox: "I have before me your letter of the 8th. instant." *Letter not found.*]

George Washington to Alexander Hamilton, Thomas Jefferson, and Henry Knox

[Philadelphia, March 9, 1793]

Sir,

Expecting that my private affairs will call me to Virginia on or before the 25 of this month, I have to request that you will lay before me, previous to that time, such matters within your Department as may require my attention or agency before I set out, as well as those which might be necessary for me to know or act upon during the time of my absence from the Seat of Government (which will be about four weeks) so far as such things may come to your knowledge before my departure.   Geo: Washington

United States
9 March 1793.

LC, George Washington Papers, Library of Congress.

To Edmund Randolph

Treasury Department
March 12. 1793

Sir

I had taken it for granted, from the general spirit of the transaction, that the first installment to the Bank of the United States of the loan mentioned in the within Agreement of the 25 of June last [1] became payable on the 1st of January of the present year. But upon examining the Agreement, a doubt arises whether that intention be consistent with the tenor of the Instrument or how far the Act of Congress of the second instant gives a construction and authorises immediate Payment.[2]

I request then, as a guide, your opinion, whether an immediate payment of the whole first installment of the two millions borrowed will be conformable to the general spirit of the Agreement and to the Act of Congress just referred to—and if not the whole, whether of any part and how much—and in general at what period or periods the first installment may be considered as payable.

It is indubitably the interest of the Government to pay the whole sum without delay because the Bank at present understands the installment to have been payable at the time I have mentioned, and will I doubt not, if that construction can be pursued, consider an equivalent sum of interest as ceasing from the first of January last; but if the legal construction be taken to be different, the Interest will of course go on against the Public till the payment is made. And as the Treasury must be prepared for it, a correspondent sum must be kept in deposit to answer the demand, when the period of payment arrives.[3]

These considerations however can only operate as motives to give as liberal a construction as can be fairly supported.

With respectful consideration   I am Sir   Your Obed ser

Ed Randolph Esqr
Atty General

ADf, Connecticut Historical Society, Hartford.

1. See "Agreement with the President and Directors of the Bank of the United States," June 25, 1792.

2. "An Act providing for the payment of the First Instalment due on a Loan made of the Bank of the United States" provided "That the President of the United States be, and he hereby is authorized and empowered to apply two hundred thousand dollars, of the monies which may have been borrowed, in pursuance of the fourth section of the act, intituled 'An act making provision for the reduction of the public debt,' in payment of the first instalment, due to the Bank of the United States, upon a loan made of the said bank, in pursuance of the eleventh section of the act for incorporating the subscribers to the said bank" (1 *Stat.* 338 [March 2, 1793]).

For Section 11 of "An Act to incorporate the subscribers to the Bank of the United States" (1 *Stat.* 196 [February 25, 1791]), see H to the President and Directors of the Bank of the United States, January 1, 1793, note 1.

3. No reply from Randolph to this letter has been found. On February 28, 1794, the House of Representatives "Resolved, That the Secretary of the Treasury be directed to furnish the House with . . . a copy of any opinions which may have been given by the Attorney General, relative to a construction of the said contract . . ." (*Journal of the House,* II, 76). In his "Report on the Contract Made with the Bank of the United States for a Loan of Two Million Dollars," April 25, 1794, H did not furnish the requested document. A statement in this report, however, reads as follows:

"According to the intent of this Contract as understood by the Secretary of the Treasury and the Bank, the first instalment of 200,000 dollars was payable on the first of January 1793. The Secretary in a report to the House of Representatives of the 30th. of November, 1792, submitted a provision for reimbursing the loan to the Bank. None was made 'till the time for reimbursing the first instalment as understood between the Treasury and the Bank, had elapsed on the first of January 1793. The Secretary by Letter informed the Bank that he would leave on deposit, as an offset against that instalment a Sum of 200,000 dollars, 'till Legislative provision should be made concerning the Matter. An Act of Congress of the 2d of March 1793, authorised the payment of this Instalment out of the proceeds of the Foreign Loans. But the then Attorney General being of Opinion that upon the legal Construction of the Contract compared with the words of the Act, the payment could not be made 'till the 25th. of June 1793; the Completion of the business accordingly remained suspended 'till the 20th. of July following, when a Warrant issued to pay over the proceeds of the Bills in deposit to the Treasurer, and another Warrant to pay an equal Sum to the Bank. Interest upon the Instalment ceased on the 31st. of December 1792, by Virtue of the Deposit" (copy, RG 233, Reports of the Secretary of the Treasury, 1784–1795, Vol. IV, National Archives).

To George Washington [1]

Treasury Departmt. 12 Mar: 1793.

Sir,

By an Act entitled "an Act providing for the payment of the first installment, due on a Loan made of the Bank of the U. States" [2] the President of the United States is authorised & empowered to apply two hundred thousand Dollars of the money which may have been borrowed, in pursuance of the 4th. section of the Act entitled, "an Act making provision for the reduction of the public debt," [3] in payment of the first installment due to the Bank of the United States, upon a Loan made of the said bank, in pursuance of the eleventh section of the Act for incorporating the subscribers to the said Bank. [4]

As the installment above alluded to has been due for some time, I have to request your authority to issue a Warrant for the payment thereof, agreeably to the provision of the Law.

I have the honor to be &c.   Alex: Hamilton
                                                        Secy. of the Treasury

LC, George Washington Papers, Library of Congress.
   1. For background to this letter, see H to the President and Directors of the Bank of the United States, January 1, 1793; H to Edmund Randolph, March 12, 1793.
   2. 1 *Stat.* 338 (March 2, 1793).
   3. 1 *Stat.* 187 (August 12, 1790). This section provided "That the President of the United States be, and he is hereby authorized to cause to be borrowed, on behalf of the United States, a sum or sums not exceeding in the whole two millions of dollars, at an interest not exceeding five per cent., and that the sum or sums so borrowed, be also applied to the purchase of the said debt of the United States. . . . Provided, That out of the interest arising on the debt to be purchased in manner aforesaid, there shall be appropriated and applied a sum not exceeding the rate of eight per centum per annum on account both of principal and interest towards the repayment of the two millions of dollars so to be borrowed."
   4. For Section 11 of this act, see H to the President and Directors of the Bank of the United States, January 1, 1793, note 1.

Observer

[Philadelphia, March 13–15, 1793]

Among the publications which have appeared as containing the Debates in Congress respecting the Official Conduct of the Secretary of the Treasury [1] Mr. Findley is represented as having made the following assertions "That the Secretary of the Treasury had *acknowleged* that he had *not applied* the money borrowed in Europe *agreeably to the legal appropriations of the President.* That he had *acknowleged* his having drawn to this Country and applied in Europe *to uses for which other monies were appropriated three millions* of Dollars. That he had *acknowleged* his having drawn from Europe more money than the law *authorised him to do.* That he was influenced to do so by motives not contemplated by the law and had either applied it or drawn it from Europe with the design of applying it to uses not authorised, and that he had *broken in* upon the fund appropriated for the discharge of the French Debt." [2]

Before I read this Speech I had carefully perused the different communications made by the Secretary of the Treasury to the House of Representatives and after reading it I was led to revise them. The result has been, that I have found all these assertions, attributed to Mr. Findly, either direct untruths or palpable misrepresentations and I challenge Mr. Findly or any of his friends to produce the passages which will warrant them. The truth is that Mr. Findley has palmed upon the Secretary his own reasoning and inferences for points conceded by him. The *commentary* has been substituted for the text.   OBSERVER

ADf, Hamilton Papers, Library of Congress.
1. See the introductory note to "Report on the Balance of All Unapplied Revenues at the End of the Year 1792 and on All Unapplied Monies Which May Have Been Obtained by the Several Loans Authorized by Law," February 4, 1793.
2. William Findley was a member of the House of Representatives from Pennsylvania. With very minor changes in wording this statement is a quotation from a speech made by Findley on March 1, 1793 (*Annals of Congress*, III, 920).

Remarks on Thomas Jefferson's Draft of an Address to the Indians

[*Philadelphia, March 13, 1793.*] "Recd. from . . . [the Secretary of State] a draft of an Assurance of friendship & protection & an Extract from the law regulating trade & intercourse with the Indian Tribes,[1] proposed to be given to the several Indian Tribes. . . . The drafts intended for the Indians, mentioned above, were put into the hands of the Secry of the Treasury for his opinion; who thought the extract from the laws might be given them in the way proposed without any inconvenience; but doubted whether the promise of protection &c. might not at some time produce inconveniencies."

JPP, 75.

1. The draft of this proclamation and the extracts may be found in the Thomas Jefferson Papers, Library of Congress. The extracts consist of Sections 4, 5, 8, and 10 of "An Act to regulate Trade and Intercourse with the Indian Tribes" (1 *Stat.* 329-32 [March 1, 1793]). The proclamation provided that the Indian tribe to which it was issued was "under the Protection of the United States of America: And all Persons citizens of the United States and others of whatever country or condition are hereby warned not to commit any Injury, Trespass or Molestation whatever on the persons, lands, Hunting-grounds, or other Rights or Property of the said Indians."

From David Ross [1]

Bladensburgh [Maryland] March 13. 1793

Dear Sir

You have been so much harrassed that I am sorry to trouble you so soon—but as I see a Note in the Baltimore Paper that Co Mercer intends to answer my Publication [2] I am induced to request you will favor me, as soon as you conveniently can, with a Copy of the Statement to the President respecting the Bribe,[3] and of the other Communications you promised me—for I shall not be surprised if Co Mercer should deny his language to you which I have quoted since I see he still holds out in his Speeches some insinuation of Corruption.

If you have made any observations on the last resolutions that were moved for,[4] I shall be glad of a Copy of them as also of any communications between you & Co Mercer that may have taken place since I left Philadelphia marking such as you may think has no rela-

tion to the subjects between us and which you would not wish me
to disclose.

Compts to Mrs Hamilton from   Your friend & obedt Servt

David Ross

PS The Patronage of Messrs. Jefferson & Maddison to Freneaus
Paper [5] was avowed when Subscriptions were solicited in this Neighbourhood and was held up as an inducement to subscribe but I did
not hear of this circumstance till today.

ALS, Hamilton Papers, Library of Congress.
  1. For background to this letter, see the introductory note to H to John F.
Mercer, September 26, 1792. See also H to Mercer, November 3, December 6,
December, 1792, March 1, 1793; Mercer to H, October 16–28, December, 1792,
January 31, March 5, 1793; H to Ross, September 26, November 3, 1792; Ross
to H, October 5–10, November 23, 1792; Uriah Forrest to H, November 7, 1792.
  2. This notice appeared in *The Maryland Journal and Baltimore Advertiser*,
March 8, 1793.
  3. See the introductory note to H to Mercer, September 26, 1792.
  4. For these resolutions, see the introductory note to "Report on the Balance
of All Unapplied Revenues at the End of the Year 1792 and on All Unapplied
Monies Which May Have Been Obtained by the Several Loans Authorized by
Law," February 4, 1793.
  5. Philip Freneau's *National Gazette* had been established in Philadelphia in
October, 1791, as an opposition newspaper to the Federalist [Philadelphia]
Gazette of the United States.

Treasury Department Circular to the Collectors of the Customs

Treasury Department,
March 13, 1793.

Sir,

Proof has been filed in the office of the Collector of Newbury
Port,[1] agreeably to the 13th section of the act, entitled, "An act for
registering and clearing Vessels, regulating the coasting Trade, &c." [2]
of the loss of two Certificates of registry, of the following numbers
and description, viz.

No. 42, dated Newbury Port the 19th of April 1790, granted to
Benjamin Joy, owner and master of the Ship Eliza, measuring
four hundred and twenty-one Tons.

No. 16, dated Newbury Port the 6th of February 1790, granted
to John Pettingal and Leonard Smith, owners of the Schooner
Hope, measuring ninety four Tons, John Couch, master.

This information is therefore given with a view to put the Officers of the Customs upon their guard, in order to prevent any fraudulent disposal of the said Certificates, in case they should be found again.

Enclosed is an act which will take effect from and after the last day of May next, entitled, "An act for enrolling and licensing Ships or Vessels to be employed in the coasting Trade and Fisheries, and for regulating the same."[3] The forms of Certificates relating to the object, will be prepared and transmitted by the Register of the Treasury.

With great consideration, I am, Sir, Your obedient Servant,

A Hamilton

LS, MS Division, New York Public Library; LS, Office of the Secretary, United States Treasury Department; L[S], RG 36, Collector of Customs at Boston, Letters from the Treasury and Others, 1789–1809, Vol. 1, National Archives; LC, RG 56, Circulars of the Office of the Secretary, "Set T," National Archives; copy, United States Finance Miscellany, Treasury Circulars, Library of Congress; copy, Essex Institute, Salem, Massachusetts.

1. Edward Wigglesworth.
2. 1 *Stat.* 58 (September 1, 1789).
3. 1 *Stat.* 305–18 (February 18, 1793).

From George Washington

United States 13 March 1793.

Sir,

In compliance with an Act passed during the last Session of Congress entitled, "an Act providing for the payment of the first installment due on a loan made of the Bank of the United States,"[1] I hereby desire that you will cause the payment of the first instalment to be made conformably to the said Act.[2]   Geo: Washington

LC, George Washington Papers, Library of Congress.
1. 1 *Stat.* 338 (March 2, 1793).
2. See H to Washington, March 12, 1793.

To Jonathan Burrall

Treasury Department
March 14. 1793

Sir

I request that you will immediately invest in the purchase of Bills on London or Amsterdam, on account of the Government, fifty thousand Dollars; to enable you to do which, I inclose you a letter to the President and Directors of the Office of Discount & Deposit at New York.[1] But as the advantageous purchasing of the bills will depend on secrecy, you had better not make use of your letter to the Directors 'till you have engaged the Bills—and You will be cautious to keep the Government out of sight.

I rely on your using the greatest circumspection as to the Drawers of the Bills that there may be no possible question about their goodness. If Mr Daniel Ludlow[2] or Messrs. Le Roy & Bayard[3] are drawing, upon the basis of their Dutch concerns, I should prefer their bills. And You will observe that I had rather pay an additional price for unexceptionable Bills than run the least risk. Houses much engaged in other than Mercantile Speculations, except those above-mentioned, whose bottom is known, are to be avoided. Perhaps you will even find it adviseable to keep yourself out of view and operate through a third person.

You may have the bills filled up in the name of Samuel Meredith Treasurer of the United States, if you should complete the intire purchase in one sum; otherwise you will take them in your own name and indorse them to him. This last will avoid the disclosure to which the other mode would be subject, if the purchases are successive. The bills are immediately to be forwarded to me.

For Your Agency in this matter you will be allowed ¼ ℀ Centum. Should you have occasion to indorse the Bills, it is to be understood that you are to incur no responsibility by it.

With esteem   I am Sir   Your Obed ser   A Hamilton

Jonathan Burrall Esqr

ALS, Independence National Historical Park Collection, Old Custom House, Philadelphia.

1. H to the President and Directors of the New York Office of Discount and Deposit of the Bank of the United States, March 14, 1793.
2. Ludlow, a former Loyalist, was a New York City merchant.
3. Herman Le Roy and William Bayard were partners in the New York City mercantile firm of Le Roy and Bayard.

From Tobias Lear

United States 14 March 1793.

By the President's command T. Lear has the honor to return to the Secrey. of the Treasury, the papers respecting the case of Hezekiah & George D. Usher,[1] which have been submitted to him; and to inform the Secretary that the President has no doubt, from the statement of facts in the above papers, of the intention to defraud the Revenue; but if it shall appear to the Secretary, from his information on the subject, that the said Ushers have suffered by the loss of their goods, and expences attending the suit, enough to answer the intention of the Law [2]—the President leaves it to his judgment, to remit the penalty in such way as, upon consulting the Attorney General of the Ud. States, shall appear best.   Tos. Lear.
S. P. US.

LC, George Washington Papers, Library of Congress.
1. See William Ellery to H, February 15, May 9, October 4, 1791; Henry Marchant to H, February 14, 1791.
2. An entry in JPP for March 13, 1793, reads as follows: "The Secy of the Treasury put into the President's hands certain papers respectg H. & G. Usher —the Captn. & Mate of a Vessel belonging to Rhode Island, who had been guilty of a breech of the Revenue Laws—to see if the President wd. approve of his & the Atty Genl. devising some mode to stop the levying the fine inflicted by law" (JPP, 75–76). On June 19, 1793, Washington sent to Thomas Jefferson pardons for George and Hezekiah Usher (LC, RG 59, George Washington's Correspondence with Secretaries of State, National Archives).

To John F. Mercer [1]

Philadelphia
March 14. 1793

Sir

I received yesterday your letter dated at Baltimore.[2] You will, on reflection, be sensible, that mine, to which it is an answer, could with difficulty, owing to peculiarity of situation, have reached you sooner than it did. It was left at your lodgings on Sunday Morning. My attention had been too much engaged on other matters, from the time your letter of the 31st of January was handed me, to have admitted of the requisite review of papers, in order to a reply earlier than was done.

As to Major Ross's publication 'tis an affair between You and him.

The issue, which I now conceive to be invited by you will not be declined; though it will necessarily be a considerable time, before a final eclarcissement can take place.

Indispensable Duties both of a public and personal Nature claim a prior attention. These satisfied, you will receive from me a further and more explicit communication.

At the same time I cannot forbear expressing my surprise at your assertion, that "matter of opinion only is now disputed between us" when there has been a general denial of the facts which are the basis of the exceptionable suggestions on your part. There is not one of them which is not either wholly or substantially unfounded.

    I am Sr   A Hamilton

John F Mercer Esqr

ADfS, Hamilton Papers, Library of Congress.
  1. For background to this letter, see the introductory note to H to Mercer, September 26, 1792. See also H to Mercer, November 3, December 6, December, 1792, March 1, 1793; Mercer to H, October 16-28, December, 1792, January 21, March 5, 1793; H to David Ross, September 26, November 3, 1792; Ross to H, October 5-10, November 23, 1792, March 13, 1793; Uriah Forrest to H, November 7, 1792.
  2. Mercer to H, March 5, 1793.

To the President and Directors of the New York Office of Discount and Deposit of the Bank of the United States

Treasury Department, March 14, 1793. "I request You to advance to Mr. Jonathan Burrall, Cashier of your Office, Fifty thousand Dollars, on account of the Government. . . ."[1]

LS, Washington's Headquarters (Museum), Newburgh, New York.
  1. See H to Burrall, March 14, 1793.

From Jeremiah Olney

Custom-House,
Providence 14th March 1793.

Sir.

Your Letter of the 5th Instant, was transmitted to me yesterday
by the President of the Providence Bank;[1] and agreeable to your
directions, I have furnished him with an Abstract of the uncancelld
Bonds, payable this Month, being only the one in Suit, (noted in the
enclosed Return of Cash) and another due to the 30th for 523
Dollars & 60 Cents.

I have the Honor to be &c.   Jereh. Olney Collr.

N.B.   The Bond in suit was given by Edward Dexter in Novr. last,
in consequence of a collusive Transfer, for Duties on the Cargo of
the Brigantine Neptune, the property of Welcome Arnold Esqr.[2]

Alexr. Hamilton Esqr.
Secy. of the Treasury.

ADfS, Rhode Island Historical Society, Providence.
 1. "Treasury Department Circular to the Collectors of the Customs," February 22–March 5, 1793. The copy of the circular sent to Olney was dated
March 5. See also "Treasury Department Circular to the Presidents and Directors of the Office of Discount and Deposit of the Bank of the United States,"
February 23–March 5, 1793. John Brown was president of the Providence Bank.
 2. For background concerning Welcome Arnold's collusive transfers, see
William Ellery to H, September 4, October 9, 1792; Olney to H, September 8,
13, October 4, 25, November 7, 28, December 10, 13, 27, 1792; H to Olney,
September 19, 24, October 12, November 27, 1792.

To William Short

Treasury Department
Philadelphia March 15th 1793

Sir

You will find inclosed a duplicate of a letter from me to you of
the 1st of February, and a copy of one from me of this date to our
Bankers at Amsterdam.[1]

I was not insensible to the judicious views, which led you to desire,
that the united States might not place themselves in a situation to be

obliged to retrograde, with regard to the rate of Interest. And I shall be sorry, if the arrangements made here have interfered with the execution of them; as appears to be now probable. An expectation of a more favourable state of the market, and a reluctance to incur a further loss of interest on the monies which remained on hand of former loans has led to the course which has been pursued.[2]

The present price of Bills enables me to invest monies for the intended remittance with a gain of about seven per cent which will be a partial indemnification for other disadvantages.

The enclosed extract from the minutes of the House of Representatives will inform you of the result of the affair, about which I wrote to you not long since by way of England.[3] 'Tis to be lamented, that already the spirit of party has made so great a progress in our infant Republic. But it is at the same time a source of consolation, that it, as yet, has its bounds—and that there are many who will only go a certain length in compliance with its dictates.

With much real consideration & esteem   I am   Sir   Your obedient Servant   Alex Hamilton

William Short Esqr
Minister Resident at the Hague

LS, William Short Papers, Library of Congress.
    1. H to Willink, Van Staphorst, and Hubbard, March 15, 1793.
    2. See Short to H, October 27, November 29, December 17, 1792, for Short's discussion of the rate of interest.
    3. H to Short, February 5, 1793. H is referring to the votes on February 28 and March 1, 1793, by which the House of Representatives rejected the resolutions of censure of his conduct. These resolutions had been introduced by William B. Giles. See the introductory note to H's "Report on the Balance of All Unapplied Revenues at the End of the Year 1792 and on All Unapplied Monies Which May Have Been Obtained by the Several Loans Authorized by Law," February 4, 1793.

To Wilhem and Jan Willink, Nicholaas and Jacob Van Staphorst, and Nicholas Hubbard

Treasury Department
Philadelphia March 15th 1793

Gentlemen

I received, two days since, the letter which You did me the honor to write me of the 14 of January last,[1] inclosing the copy of one of the same date to Mr Short.

I regret the state of things as there exhibited, and my regret will be increased, if circumstances shall have rendered it necessary, to allow the high rate of five per cent for the contemplated loan. I hope, nevertheless, a better issue, from your zeal and intelligent exertions. And in time to come, every effort must be made here to avoid a like necessity. If the thing were in my power, I should decline the loan altogether.

Lest a disappointment should attend the obtaining of a loan, I have taken measures to arrest in your hands 495,000 Guilders of the sum which I last advised you would be drawn for.[2] The sale having been made to the Bank of the united States has left this expedient in my power. I shall, in addition to this, cause to be remitted to you between this time and the third of next month when the British Packet sails, the further sum of 975000 Guilders in Bills upon London and Amsterdam; unless I should in the mean time hear of a loan having been undertaken. I cannot doubt, that it will be at all events in your Power to make temporary arrangements to face the exigency, should any delays ensue which may prevent these means being in measure for the demand.

With much consideration & esteem　I am Gentlemen　Yr obedt Servant　　　　　　　　　　　　　　　　　Alexander Hamilton

Messrs Wm & J. Willink　N & J. van Staphorst & Hubbard Bankers
Amsterdam

Copy, William Short Papers, Library of Congress.
　1. Letter not found, but presumably the contents were similar to the letter which Willink, Van Staphorst, and Hubbard wrote to William Short on the same day. See Short to H, February 25, 1793, note 6.
　2. See H to Willink, Van Staphorst, and Hubbard, December 31, 1792.

From Jean Baptiste de Ternant [1]

[Philadelphia] du 16 mars [1793]

Le Ministre soussigné prie le secretaire de la trèsorèrie de faire avancer à Conyngham Nesbit et Compe.[2] cinq mille piastres de plus à compte des cent mille payables au 1r. avril prochain.

T.

LC, *Arch. des Aff. Etr., Corr. Pol., Etats-Unis*, Supplement Vol. 20.

1. For background to this letter, see Tobias Lear to H, February 8, 1793; "Cabinet Meeting. Opinion on Furnishing Three Million Livres Agreeably to the Request of the French Minister," February 25, 1793; H to Ternant, February 26, 1793; Ternant to H, February 26, 1793.

2. The Philadelphia merchant and shipping firm of David H. Conyngham and John M. Nesbitt.

To Wilhem and Jan Willink, Nicholaas and Jacob Van Staphorst, and Nicholas Hubbard

[*Philadelphia, March 16, 1793.* On May 1, 1793, Willink, Van Staphorst, and Hubbard wrote to Hamilton: "We received your Respected favors of 1 February, 15 & 16 March." *Letter of March 16 not found.*]

From Gulian Verplanck [1]

Newyork March 17. 1793

Dr Sir

My second payment to You for the House in Wall Street has been due since the first day of the last Month & I have been waiting Your directions respecting it. In a former Letter [2] I requested the Deed, which will oblige Me, as I am preparing to Build on the Lot this Spring. Your late triumph over the malice of Your Enemies,[3] has given the most heartfelt satisfaction to Your friends in this City & to no One more than

Your Obt. Hume Sert   Gulian Verplanck

ALS, Hamilton Papers, Library of Congress.

1. Verplanck, president of the Bank of New York, had purchased H's house at 58 Wall Street.

2. Verplanck to H, September 10, 1792.

3. For H's "triumph," see the introductory note to H's "Report on the Balance of All Unapplied Revenues at the End of the Year 1792 and on All Unapplied Monies Which May Have Been Obtained by the Several Loans Authorized by Law," February 4, 1793.

From Tench Coxe

[*Philadelphia, March 18, 1793.* On March 22, 1793, Hamilton sent to George Washington "a Communication from the Commissioner of the Revenue, of the 18 instant." *Letter not found.*]

From William Ellery

Colles Office [Newport, Rhode Island] March 18 1793

Sir,

On the 16th of this month I recd. yours of the 5th.[1] inclosed in a letter from the President of the Providence Bank.[2] No bonds for duties will fall due in this District this present month.

I should very much regrett that no report was made on my Petition [3] during the last Session of Congress, was I not sensible that besides other important business your attention was called to one engaged in a matter in which your reputation and the public interest were concerned.[4] The honorable manner in which you acquitted yourself, and was acquitted has given great satisfaction to all your friends in this quarter and to no one more than to your most obedt. servt.   Wm Ellery Collector

A Hamilton Esqr Sec Treasy.

LC, Newport Historical Society, Newport, Rhode Island.
    1. "Treasury Department Circular to the Collectors of the Customs," February 22–March 5, 1793. The copy of the circular which was sent to Ellery is dated March 5.
    2. John Brown. See "Treasury Department Circular to the Presidents and Directors of the Offices of Discount and Deposit of the Bank of the United States," February 23–March 5, 1793.
    3. See Ellery to H, December 3, 1792.
    4. See the introductory note to H's "Report on the Balance of All Unapplied Revenues at the End of the Year 1792 and on All Unapplied Monies Which May Have Been Obtained by the Several Loans Authorized by Law," February 4, 1793.

From Thomas Jefferson

Philadelphia March 18. 1793.

Sir,

The contingent account of the Department of State down to the 9th. instant, having been delivered to, and passed by the Auditor, and being at present in want of a further sum to satisfy demands against my office, I must request the favor of you to order a warrant to issue payable to George Taylor Junior [1] for Twelve hundred Dollars, and am, with respect   Sir,   Your most obedt. servt.

The secretary of the Treasury of
the United States of america

Letterpress copy, in unidentified handwriting, Thomas Jefferson Papers, Library of Congress; LC, RG 59, Domestic Letters, 1792–1795, Vol. 5, National Archives.
  1. Taylor was chief clerk of the State Department.

To Henry Knox

Treasry Department
March 18. 1793

Sir

I have before me your letter of the 8th. instant,[1] transmitting sundry accounts for supplies at Post Vincennes, during the year 1791, to the neighbouring Indians.

From the nature of the case, it appears to me proper to request your more explicit opinion concerning the propriety of allowing these claims.

Though I entertain a favourable opinion of the Officers concerned and readily accede to the idea that the situation of things, at the period, called for measures to conciliate the Indians in question which would of course involve expence—Yet I cannot help thinking the expence which is stated to have been incurred, compared with the occasion, is considerable; and there are several items which, on different accounts, appear to me in a shape rather questionable.

As the business originated, without due authority, as there is in every such case a natural tendency to abuse, I submit whether if the claims, on general consideration, should appear to you to be such as to require admission—some middle course cannot be adopted, embracing the ideas of a partial advance on account, and a further examination on the spot into the propriety of the charges.

It is observable that the principal account has no other voucher than a general Certificate from Capt Prior.[2]

Very respectfully   I have the honor to be Sir   Your Obed servt

P.S. The papers are sent back for your further inspection.

The Secy at War

ADf, Connecticut Historical Society, Hartford.
  1. Letter not found.
  2. Abner Prior of New York was a captain in the Third Sub-Legion of the United States Army.

From Joseph Nourse

Treasury Department
Registers Office 18 March
1793.

Sir

I have the Honor to transmitt for your Inspection sundry Statements No. 1 to 12 which have been made out at the Request of the
Hon: W. Smith of So. Carolina.[1] Permit me to intimate that Mr.
Smith woud wish to be furnishd with them some time Tomorrow as
he Expects to sail for Charlestown on Wednesday morning.[2] I have
not conceived it necessary to render these Statements under Signature, as Mr. Smiths view is confind to his own Information, But shoud
this be requisite, I presume it might be safely done. With the greatest
Respect, I am Sir,

your mo: ob. Sert.

Hon: Alexander Hamilton Esqr.
Secretary of the Treasury

Copy, RG 53, Register of the Treasury, Estimates and Statements for 1793,
Vol. "135-T," National Archives.
  1. Statements 1 through 11 may be found in RG 53, Register of the Treasury,
Estimates and Statements for 1793, Vol. "135-T," National Archives. Statement
12 has not been found. The following list of the statements requested by William Loughton Smith, member of the House of Representatives from South
Carolina, is attached to Nourse's letter:

		Annual Int. on	
"1. Amount of Debt proper. 6 p. Cents			
do. do. 3 p. Ct.	do. ⎫		
do. do. Deferred			
2. Amount of Assumed 6 p. Cts.	do. ⎬ No. 1.		
do. 3 p. Cts.	do.		
do. Deferred.	⎭		
3. Amount of Debt supposed unsubscribed		2	
4. Amount of Debt purchased up vizt.		3	
6 p Cents			
3 p. Cents			
Deferred			
5. Amount of sinking fund arising from Surplus of 1790.		4	
Of which, applied			
Unapplied			
6. Amount of sinking Fund arising from the Interest of purchased Stock		5	
7. Annual Income from fines, Penalties and forfeitures		6	
Ditto of Public Lands sold			

8. Amount French Debt in 1789.
                Paid in part
    Amount of Dutch do.
                Paid in part
    Amount of Spanish do.
                pd. in part
    Amount to foreign Officers do.
                Paid in part."
2. After his reelection to Congress in February, 1793, Smith returned to South
Carolina to obtain support for Federalist policies among the newly elected
Congressmen from the backcountry of South Carolina.

From Jonathan Ogden

New Jersey   Morris town 18 March 1793
Sir,
    The following will I make no dout appologise for the fredom here
taken of writing to a Stranger as to personal acquaintance. I have
lately heard in a particular manner the sentiments of many people of
this County & State respecting your objects of revenue. I believe I
speak safe when I say not more than one person in five hundred dis-
agrees in sentiment with the present plans—the excise that glorious
act [1] is advocated by those who once oppos'd. As for Giles's malitious
efforts a few days a go in the House of Representatives [2] some people
say they have put you in danger of the curse denounced against him
who every one speaks well of. These are the Ideas of people universally here and who has no more acquaintance with your Self
than I have. My sincere wish is that you may long continue to fill
that august office you now occupy & your Virtues be imbraced by
those who Labour to tarnish them—being a Farmer you will excuse
incorrectness. I am with much Esteem your humble servant.
                                            Jonathan Ogden

Alexr. Hammilton, Esqr [3]

ALS, Hamilton Papers, Library of Congress.
    1. "An Act repealing, after the last day of June next, the duties heretofore
laid upon Distilled Spirits imported from abroad, and laying others in their
stead; and also upon Spirits distilled within the United States, and for appropriating the same" (1 *Stat.* 199–214 [March 3, 1791]).
    2. See the introductory note to "Report on the Balance of All Unapplied
Revenues at the End of the Year 1792 and on All Unapplied Monies Which
May Have Been Obtained by the Several Loans Authorized by Law," February
4, 1793.
    3. H endorsed this letter "1793 Answered April 1 with *thanks* &c." Letter not
found.

From Jeremiah Olney

Custom House
District of Providence 18th. March 1793.

Sir

I do myself the Honor to Transmit, for your information, the enclosed Impeachment against me Signed on the 31st. January last by Twenty Seven respectable Merchants and others, which was con- templated to have been Transmitted to the President of the United States, togeather with my Letter to the Committee, and my Vindica- tion of the particular Charges; which last was intended merely as an Individual explanation of my official Conduct.[1] This malicious im- peachment has been brought about through the artfull and per- severing address of Welcome Arnold Esquire, my avowed and in- veterate enimy (and was drawn up by his Brother Thomas Arnold A man professing the Quaker Religion and possessing great abilities and I wish I could add an Honest Heart) and for no other reason than because I will not dispence with the Law whenever it may Suite his convenience! Many of the Signees to the Petition have shewn so much candor as to Confess that they were deceived into the measure, and Since upon examination, they find some of the charges are malicious and Totally unfounded while others are unfairly and un- candidly Stated, have declared their determination to withdraw their names from the Petition, should the promoters of it attempt to Transmit it to the President. The Signees were furnished on the

---

ADfS, Rhode Island Historical Society, Providence.

1. As collector of customs at Providence, Olney was involved in numerous disputes and subsequent litigation with Welcome Arnold, a Providence merchant, over Olney's enforcement of the revenue laws. See Olney to H, May 19, November 28, 1792; H to Olney, September 19, October 12, Novem- ber 27, 1792. In a document dated November 20, 1792, Olney presented a defense of his official conduct against "the unwearied endeavours of Welcome Arnold Esquire, of this Town, Merchant, calculated to prejudice the minds of the good People, in this and the District of Newport, against my official Character" (Olney to H, December 10, 1792).

By the "Impeachment" Olney was referring to the following document ad- dressed to the President and dated January 31, 1793:

"The Merchants Sea Captains, & other Citizens in the district of Providence, most respectfully Shew.

"Whilst your Petitioners have been chearfully struling in the discharge of

23rd. Ulto. with a Copy of my vindication but they have had no meeting in consequence of it, that I can learn, nor do I believe they will, as the greater part of the Gentlemen are dissatisfied with the proceedings. My wish has uniformly been (and which I fully ex-

---

duties for the support of A Government wich they Venerate, and wich they used every exertion to induce this State to Adopt—whilst they have been labouring under a heavy increase of those duties not yet eqallized upon the Consumers at large—whilst they have been looking for the mild and fostering principles of the Constitution; they have been harrassed in this district with a rigorous and severe execution of the Revenue Laws; contrary as they Apprehend, to the True Intent, & meaning of them, and unexampled, & unparell'd in Other destricts in the United States.

"A. The Laws really doubtfull in their Construction in some cases and attended with forms in their Executions, in many Instances not fully understood by the Citizens or the Collector himself, have been uniformly so construed by him, as to render them in the highest degree penal, and attended with a variety of unessary and perplexing Embarresments to the great Injury of the Commerce of this district.

"We have long waited in hopes that further experience and a knowledge of the mode in wich the like Business is conducted in Other States, particularly in the principal Towns, & Citys, accompanied, with a Conduct on our part respectfull and attentive, to the laws in every substantial particular, would remove the Grounds of our Complaint & the nescessity of Troubling the President with our application for redress. But Time has proved the reverse to be True—And we regret that Justice to ourselves Obliges us to say that a Conduct bordering on Insult has been in some Instances, Added to Official Rigour, & Oppression. We are Confident it was the intention of the Legislature to afford every aid and accomodation to Commerce consistant with an exact, & punctual Collection of the Revenue; and that we shall entertain injustice in Our minds toward the Supreme Executive if we should longer remain Silent, thro' distrust of obtaining redress of the Greveiances under wich we have laboured.

"The Schedule accompanying this with Alphabetical referances States a number of Instances wich may serve as an examplification of the Conduct Complain'd off.

"B. We have been refused certain allowances upon the quantities, & Qualities of Goods Imported here, customary in Other States and Warrented as we apprehend by Law. Our Vessells arriving in the Winter season and Confined in the Isce, are Compelled to give Bond bearing Instant Date, and the time of Credit running has sometimes nearly expired before the Goods could be Unladen. And having been compelled to enter and pay the fees of Office in the district below, whilst So Confined in the Ice, or Otherwise by distress, have been here Compelled to pay them over again.

"C. We have often been Subjected to the great disadvantage of loss of fair Winds, & Sometimes maney days, detention of our vessells, Thro' the Critical, & unaccomodating disposition of the Collector in Clearing Them Out. Altho our Vessells are liable to Seisure and Confiscation for breaking bulk, without entry, to lighten when cast on Shore in Cases of extremity, yet in no cases of Urgency or extremity to our knowledge have we been able to Obtain a Vessell Cleared or Entere'd Out of the hours, of Office, wich he has been pleased to appoint.

"D. The delays and embaressments attending the Shipment of Goods intitled

pressed to the Committee who waited upon me),[2] that the impeachment might be Transmitted, as I should then have an opportunity of vindicating my official Conduct before the President of the United States to whom alone I am ameniable on impeachment, and for this I am the more desirous, as it seems to leave an implied or indirect Censure upon me, and from a conciousness that I have done my duty consonant to Law, and at the same time, with an upright impar-

---

to Drawback, such as Salted Provissions, Fish &c., have been so great Thro' the Introduction of Unessary and Absurd forms (introduced in no Other District within our knowledge) and Calculated to increase The fees of Office by multyplying the number of Entries permitts &c. as in a great measure to defeat the Benifit thereof and to Induce some wholly to forego, the Benifit rather than submitt to the disadvantages attending such Procedure.

"E. The Commanders of Coasting Vessells & others have been perplex'd with penal prossecutions in a number of Cases of deviation from the Letter of the Law *merely;* wich have been passed by in the neighbouring States, as not being within the intention of the law: tho' in no Instance of the maney prossecutions in this District of a Merchant or Commander of Vessell has the Charge of a disposition to defraud the Revenue or *Intentional* deviation from the Law been suggested; yet in several Instances they may be said to have been led into the deviation for Want of the Communication of that knowledge wich it was the duty of the Office to give: and altho in every Instance where application to the Secretary of the Treasury has been made a remission of that part of the fine or forfeiture payable to the United-States has been Obtained, yet the remainder being uniformly exacted, with the Costs of Court and nesscessary fees for Council to Conduct the Business thro' its various Stages, has in many Instances proved the remedy to be equal to the disease.

"The Excise duty wich has been submitted to with so much reluctance in some parts of the Union and wich falls with great weight On this small State; it having paid upwards of 50,000 Dollars the last year, has nevertheless been Collected with the utmost harmony.

"We have no personal objection to the Collector, as a Citizen he is a native of this Town, & otherwise Connected with some of your Petitioners; but experience has Convinced us that from *his past* mode of Conduct, the Trade of this Town must Languesh under maney embaressments, unknown to Our fellow Citizens in Other Districts, during his administration of the Revenue Laws here; and must soon be attended to with the loss of some of Our most Active, & valueable Citizens, unless an alteration takes place. We have no desire to defeat the reward wich may be tho't Justly due to aney One for former Services; but we trust that the Commerce of this District will never be made subservant to the Caprices of the Collector of its Revenue; or that the Citizens thereof be subjected to the mortification of Submitting to *Incivilities* in an Office where the Law has made it their duty to repair *daily* to hand in their Contributions for the Support of the Government under wich they live." (Copy, Rhode Island Historical Society.)

Another statement by the "Merchants of Providence and Newport," which is undated and unaddressed and which complains about the operation of customs regulations, may be found in the Hamilton Papers, Library of Congress.

2. Olney's letter to the merchants' committee is dated February 4, 1793, and addressed to John Mason, Joseph Nightingale, and Cyprian Sterry. A second letter is addressed to the committee on February 6. Both letters may be found in the Rhode Island Historical Society, Providence.

tiallity. A Second copy of my vindication has been presented to his Excellency Governor Fenner[3] who is a Firm and influential Friend and Supporter of the Revenue Laws, having uniformly advocated my official Conduct against the present and every other attack made upon me with a design to effect a deviation from the Law. It has been Circulated also, among the respectable Citizens of this Town and I am happy to add it has met with general approbation. Having long waited in expectation that the Gentlemen would have gratified my desire by Transmitting the impeachment to the President, and finding they are disposed to keep it back, I have upon due Consideration deemed it expedient to make you (as the principle officer of the revenue department) acquainted with the reason of its detention, as well as the real state of this Transaction, lest some misrepresentation has or should reach you, and possibly make, on your mind, an unfavourable impression, and respectfully to request Sir your Friendship and Support so far as my official Conduct shall (upon a full and Critical investigation) appear to you to have been dictated by principles consonant to law and my instructions from you. I could very soon Silence the opposition long carried on against me, through the persevering Temper of Mr. Arnold, provided I would descend to the base and unworthy principle of deviating from the plain Letter of the Law and my instructions, to serve on all occasions his, and the unwarrantable desires of a few restless Characters under his particular influence, but this neither he, nor they, can ever drive me to. Tho' it may be possible, by persevering in a misrepresentation of Facts, he may raise an influence to effect my removeal from office—but this could never afford any unpleasant reflections while I should carry along with me the Supporting consolation that I had done my duty according to the best of my skill and abilities, and with an honest Zeal to promote the public Interests.

I have the Honor to be very respectfully Sir Your Most Obed. and Most Hum Servt.   Jereh. Olney Collr.

Alexander Hamilton Esquire
Secretary of the Treasury

P. S. In justice to Mr. Geo. Benson and Mr. Thomas P. Ives of the House of Brown Benson & Ives, I feel a pleasure of mentiong. that

3. Arthur Fenner was governor of Rhode Island from 1790 until his death in 1805.

they have uniformly been against the impeachment, and the Signature of that firm on the Petition was made, contrary to their wish
and even advice, by the principle of the house, Mr. Nicho. Brown,
and wch. was effected through the instigation of W. Arnold Esqr,
but Mr. Brown has since declared his intention to withdraw his name.

To George Washington

Treasury Department 18 March 1793.

The Secretary of the Treasury respectfully makes the following
Report to the President of the United States.

The Act, entitled "an Act making appropriations for the support
of Government for the year one thousand seven hundred and ninety
three," empowers the President to borrow, for the purposes therein
specified, any sum or sums, not exceeding in the whole Eight hundred thousand Dollars, at a rate of interest not exceeding five per
centum per annum, and reimbursable at the pleasure of the United
States.[1]

In order to enable the president to judge how soon, and to what
extent it will be necessary to carry the above mentioned power into
execution, the following statements & facts are submitted.

1st. Statement (No. 1.) being the Copy of one lately reported to
the House of Representatives; which shews the probable situation of
the public Cash from the last of December 1792, to the 1st of April
1793; leaving a balance in the Treasury of 664,180 Dollars and 89
Cents.[2]

II. Statement (No. 2.) shewing the probable situation of the Account
between the United States & their Bankers at Amsterdam, on the first
of the present month, on the supposition of a full payment of the
Spanish Debt;[3] which statement is deduced from an account of the

LC, George Washington Papers, Library of Congress.

1. 1 *Stat.* 325–29 (February 28, 1793). The reference is to Section 3.

2. This statement is printed as Enclosure E to "Report on the State of the
Treasury at the Commencement of Each Quarter During the Years 1791 and
1792 and on the State of the Market in Regard to the Prices of Stock During
the Same Years," February 19, 1793.

3. For a description of this debt, see H to William Short, September 1, 1790,
note 19. See also Joseph Nourse to H, October 11, 1792; Short to H, February
25, 1793, note 13.

Bankers dated the 1st of January 1793, and exhibits a balance against the United States of 72,265 florins or Guilders. Besides this balance, requiring a provision, there will on the first of June next be payable at Amsterdam;

On Accot. of the principal of the Dutch loans		1000000
„ for interest on Do		470000
	Guilders	1470000.

which, being added to the above balance of 72,265. Guilders, at the rate of 36 ⁴⁄₁₁. ninetieths ⅌ guilder, will be equal to Dollars 623,137 and 37 Cents.

There are competent powers and instructions in Holland for making a further Loan, out of which the payment of the above sum might be effected; but it is problematical whether one can be obtained upon admissible terms, in time, to answer the purpose.[4]

That the public Credit may not be in jeopardy of suffering a wound, it is necessary to remit the whole, or the greatest part of the requisite sum without delay. Bills are now purchasing with a view to this object. The rate of exchange, which is at present more than seven per Cent below par, will afford an indemnification for the suspension of this fund from employment; in case it should turn out in the event that a Loan has been procured.

Deducting this sum from the balance, as per statement No. 1., there would remain only 41,053 Dollars & 52 Cents; which would be much too small a sum to be in the Treasury, if all the demands, for which it is liable, as expressed in the said statement, were likely to fall upon it within the period.

But 'tis probable, some of the calculated disbursements will not take place within the present quarter; particularly a part of the sums due to foreign Officers [5]—part of the Expenditure for the War De-

4. See H to Short, November 5, 1792; Short to H, February 25, 1793; H to Willink, Van Staphorst, and Hubbard, March 15, 1793.

5. For a description of this debt, see Short to H, August 3, 1790, note 5. Section 5 of "An Act supplementary to an act making provision for the Debt of the United States" (1 *Stat.* 282 [May 8, 1792]) authorized the President "to cause to be discharged the principal and interest of the said debt, out of any of the monies, which have been or shall be obtained on loan." For the negotiations on the payment of these officers, see H to Short, August 16, September 13, 1792; H to Washington, August 27, 1792; Washington to H, August 31, 1792; H to Gouverneur Morris, September 13, 1792.

partment—the sum stated for the expences of the Indian-Treaty; [6] which together may amount to about 300000 Dollars. To this may likewise be added about 150,000 dolls. of the Interest on the public Debt; of which the greatest part will be included in the sum to be paid the first of June in Holland, and which is comprehended in the sum stated as necessary to be remitted.

This circumstance will enable the Treasury to be in measure for the payments, which will accrue in the succeeding quarter on account of the Debt to France, and, together with the current receipts, to keep pace with other demands in the early part of that quarter.

But the aid of a Loan, during this second quarter, will probably be indispensable. The suspended disbursements of the first quarter ought to be calculated upon, as falling within the second; and the Treasury ought, at all events, to be prepared for them.

Statement No. 3. shews the probable state of the public Cash during the second quarter, that is, from the last of March to the 1st of July, shewing a balance against the Treasury of 672023 Dollars & 26 Cents. This balance ought to be provided for in due time by a Loan. And it will appear from Statement No. 4, that the same auxiliary will be necessary to the operations of the third quarter of the present year.

In the fourth quarter the Receipts may be expected to be amply sufficient, so as to afford a surplus towards reimbursing the Loan of the last year.

It is submitted, as the result of the foregoing data, that immediate measures be taken to engage of the Bank the loan of the 800,000 Dollars, authorised by the Act herein before mentioned.

It will be desirable to have the whole sum immediately passed to the credit of the United States, upon an agreement that none of it *shall* be *actually called for* 'till the first of June; and that it shall be payable in four equal monthly instalments; each to bear interest from the time stipulated for the payment.

The reason of endeavouring to have the whole sum immediately carried to the credit of the Treasury is, the better to conform to the *strict* theory of appropriations, which supposes that there is always a

6. See "Conversation with George Hammond," November 22, December 15–18, 1792; H to Hammond, December 29, 1792; "Draft of Instructions for William Hull," January 14, 1792; Hull to H, February 6, 1793; "Cabinet Meeting. Opinion Respecting the Proposed Treaty with the Indians Northwest of the Ohio," February 25, 1793.

representative in the Treasury, for any sums which may have come into it, and may not have been applied according to their legal destination.

By making the instalments commence only with the first of June, there would be a deficiency in the Treasury, if all the calculated disbursements were to take place within the time; but this seldom or never happens—and should a deficiency be experienced it may safely be counted upon that the Bank would accelerate it's latter instalments. And, as it may turn out, that a Loan may have been procured in Europe, it seems to be the most prudent mean to postpone the commencement of the instalments to the first of June, as proposed.

If the Bank will, as heretofore, leave it in the discretion of the Treasury to call for the money as wanted, which will be attempted, it will obviate all difficulty; but it is hardly to be expected they will repeat a practice so little provident on their part.

All which is respectfully submitted.   Alexander Hamilton
                                                  Secy. of the Treasy.

No. II.[7]
Wm & J. Willink, N. & J. van Staphorst, and Hubbard, Amsterdam.

Dr.

1793.		
Jan: 1st.	To balance in their hands	1.744.750.
	" Residue of the last 3/m loan,[8] to be recd:	360.000.
	" balance for which the Commissioners will be in advance on the 1st March 1793.	72.265.
	Flo.	2,177,015.

1793.	Contra—Cr.—	
	By premium on the residue of the 3/m loan at 5 ⅌ Cent[9]	18,000.
	" Interest due to foreign officers[10]	105,000.
Feb: 1st	" Interest on 3/m 5 per Ct.	150.000.
	" Do. on 2/m[11] 4 pr Ct.	80.000.
	" Premium on Do.	100.000.
	" Gratuity on Do. 8 pr. Ct.	28,000.

7. LC, George Washington Papers, Library of Congress.
8. The Holland loan of 1792. For a description of this loan, see Short to H, June 28, 1792, note 17.
9. The Holland loan of 1790. For a description of this loan, see Willink, Van Staphorst, and Hubbard to H, January 25, 1790, and H to Willink, Van Staphorst, and Hubbard, November 29, 1790, note 1.
10. See note 5.
11. The Holland loan of 1784. For a description of this loan, see H to Short, September 1, 1790, note 22.

Mar: 1st.   " Interest on 2½/m [12]   5 pr.ct.   125.000
             " Commission on paying interest 355,000 florin 1 p. ct.   3,550
1792.
Nov: 30.   " Draughts of the Treasurer   1.237.500.
Nov. 28   " Ditto   24,750.
            " Remittance to be made to Spain estimated
                                                    Flo. 680.000
             on accot. of which have been remittd.   374.785   305.215

                                                                    Flo   2.177,015

No. III.[13]
Probable state of Cash from the 1st of April
to the 1st of July 1793.

Dr.
To balance of Cash, per statement No. 1   664,180.89.
To amount of Sums expected to be received during this quarter
   on Accot. of the duties of Imports & tonnage Vizt:
      per returns to the 7 March 1793.   747,691.96.
      per estimate in the cases of deficient returns. 200.000.

                                                                        947,691.96.
To amount of sums expected to be received on account of duties
   on spirits distilled within the Ud. States.   100,000.
To balance against the Treasury, to be supplied by Loan   672,023.26.

                                                                     2,383,896.11.

Contra—Cr.
By this sum invested & expected to be invested towards the pay-
   ments which will become due in Holland on the 1st of June
   next   623,137.37.
By this sum to complete the advances for St. Domingo [14]   149,763.79.
By this sum promised in addition to 100,000 Dolls. payable the 1st
   of April, & credited in statement No. I. for supplies to France.[15] 444,500.
By amot. of one quarters interest.   712,298.68.
By ¼ of the current expenditure for 1793.   404,196.27.
By probable demands for arrears of appropriations antecedent to
   1793.   50.000.

                                                                     2,383,896.11.

12. The Holland loan of March, 1791. For a description of this loan, see Short
to H, February 17, 1791.
13. LC, George Washington Papers, Library of Congress.
14. For the negotiations concerning advances for the relief of Santo Domingo,
see the introductory note to George Latimer to H, January 2, 1793.
15. See Tobias Lear to H, February 8, 1793; "Cabinet Meeting. Opinion on
Furnishing Three Million Livres Agreeably to the Request of the French
Minister," February 25, 1793; Jean Baptiste de Ternant to H, February 26, 1793;
H to Ternant, February 26, 1793.

No. IV.[16]
Probable state of Cash From the 1st of July
to the 1st of October 1793.

	Dollars	Cts
Dr.		
To amount of sums expected to be receiv'd this quarter on accot. of Imports & Tonnages, per return to the 7 of March		
Drs 391,047.67.		
Ditto per Estimate 200,000	591,047.67.	
To amot. of sums expected to be received on account of spirits distilled within the Und: States	200,000	
To balance against the Treasury	325,447.28.	
	1,116,494.95.	
Contra—Cr.		
By amount of one quarters Interest	712,298.68.	
By ¼ of the current Expenditure for 1793	404,196.27.	
	1,116,494.95.	

16. LC, George Washington Papers, Library of Congress.

To Oliver Wolcott, Junior

Treasury Department
March 18. 1793

Sir

The XXXIV Section of the Collection law [1] provides that certain rates *per Cent.* shall be allowed for the Tares of Coffee Pepper and Sugar, other than loaf Sugar. Upon this provision, a doubt has existed whether the per centage ought not, in certain cases to be computed on the Cwt. or long hundred; or ought *in all cases* to be computed on the 100 lb or short hundred. The practice at different ports has on this point been and continues to be dissimilar.[2] It is necessary to produce uniformity.

As the subject is not free from ambiguity I wished to avoid interposing a construction from the Treasury by some Legislative explanation. But none having taken place it becomes a duty to put an end to the Question & establish a general rule.

Let it therefore be made known to the officers, by a circular instruction that in time to come the per Centage is in all cases to be computed on the 100 pounds.[3] In a doubtful case, this construction is preferred as most accommodating to the Merchant.

I believe at some ports the proviso at the end of the Section has been misconstrued.[4] It seems to have been taken for granted that Invoices are to govern in all cases *where desired by the Merchants.* This is not a just interpretation. The option is mutual. And if there is reason to suppose the tares, as expressed in the Invoices, are excessive, the Officer may follow the specific rates, in respect to articles to which such rates are applied. An intimation on this point will not be improper.

With much consideration & esteem   I am Sir   Your Obed ser

Oliver Woolcott Esq

ADf, Connecticut Historical Society, Hartford.

1. "An Act to provide more effectually for the collection of the duties imposed by law on goods, wares and merchandise imported into the United States, and on the tonnage of ships or vessels" (1 *Stat.* 166 [August 4, 1790]). H is actually referring to Section 35 rather than Section 34 of this act. For an explanation of the mistake in the numbering of the sections of this act, see "Treasury Department Circular to the Collectors of the Customs," August 6, 1792.

2. For H's attempt to obtain information concerning the different practices for the allowance for tare, see H to Sharp Delany, April 5, 1791; "Treasury Department Circular to the Collectors of the Customs," May 13, 1791; William Ellery to H, May 23, June 6, 13, 1791, March 5, 1792; Jeremiah Olney to H, May 24, 1791, December 6, 1792; Otho H. Williams to H, May 26, 1791; Joseph Whipple to H, June 16, 1791; Charles Lee to H, July 3, 1791; John Daves to H, November 1, 1791.

3. Wolcott sent a circular letter to the collectors of the customs on this subject on March 22, 1793 (LS, to James Lingan, Office of the Secretary, United States Treasury Department).

4. The "end of the Section" reads as follows: "*Provided always,* That where the original invoices of any of the said articles are produced, and the tare or tares appear therein, it shall be lawful, with the consent of the importer or importers, consignee or consignees, to estimate the said tare or tares according to such invoice" (1 *Stat.* 166).

To Edmund Randolph [1]

Treasury department March 20. 1793

Sir

I have the honor to inclose for your consideration Sundry papers relative to certain Certificates of the Commonwealth of Pennsylvania, originally issued in lieu of Continental Certificates and lately offered to be subscribed to the Loan in state debt continued by an Act of the 8th. of March 1792, entitled "An Act Supplementary to the Act making provision for the debt of the United States." [2]

The Question which arises is Wether these Certificates can legally be received upon Loan *as contended for by the UStates*? Upon this point I request your Opinion after mature examination and reflection. The papers now sent you may all serve to throw Light upon the Subject. They were furnished me on this Supposi[ti]on. But those which go most directly to the Object are those Marked A B C D E F.

With respectfull Consideration   I am Sir   Your Obedt. Servant
Alexander Hamilton

Edmund Randolph Esquire
Attorney General of the United States

Copy, Division of Public Records, Pennsylvania Historical and Museum Commission, Harrisburg.
1. For background to this letter, see John Nicholson to H, July 26, 1792, note 1; Alexander Dallas to H, January 15, 1793; and H to Dallas, February 8, 1793.
2. 1 *Stat.* 281–83 (May 8, 1792).

From George Washington

United States March 20 1793.

Sir,

It appears from your Report to me of the 18 instant, and the Statements accompanying it, that it will be proper to take measures for securing a Loan of Eight hundred thousand Dollars; as authorised by the Act, entitled "an Act making appropriations for the support of Government for the year 1793." [1] I have therefore to request that you will cause such a Power to be prepared for my signature as will be necessary for your authorization to effect said Loan in the time & manner stated in your Report.   Geo: Washington

LC, George Washington Papers, Library of Congress.
1. 1 *Stat.* 325–29 (February 28, 1793).

To George Washington

Treasury Departmt. 20 Mar: 1793.
Sir,

I have the honor to submit a letter from Wm. Bingham Esqr. of the 26 of febry. last, together with the papers which it enclosed.

It would seem that the United States in Congress assembled have already put the affair in a situation to make the consequences of the Suit a public concern; in which case it would appear adviseable that measures should be taken for a regular defence on behalf of the Government; so at least, that what is just may be finally done, and no more.

With perfect respect,   I am &c.   Alex: Hamilton

LC, George Washington Papers, Library of Congress.

To George Washington

Treasury Departmt. 20 Mar: 1793.

The Secretary of the Treasury has the honor to submit to The President of the United States the Draft of a Power to make the Loan of Eight hundred thousand Dollars.[1] In this, there is no reference to the ideas lately submitted to the President,[2] and which appear, by his note of to-day, to be approved by him; because it seems most proper, & is most usual for Powers to be simple & general. But it will be of course understood that it's application will be conformable to the views communicated; unless the President should otherwise direct.   Alexander Hamilton.

LC, George Washington Papers, Library of Congress.
   1. See Washington to H, March 20, 1793.
   2. H to Washington, March 18, 1793.

From George Washington [1]

[Philadelphia, March 21, 1793]

For carrying into execution the provisions in that behalf made by the Act, entitled, "An Act making appropriations for the support of

Government for the year one thousand seven hundred & ninety three"; [2]

I do hereby authorise you the said Secretary of the Treasury to agree and contract with the President, Directors and Company of the Bank of the United States for a loan or loans to the United States, of any sum or sums, not exceeding in the whole Eight hundred thousand dollars; to be advanced and paid in such proportions and at such periods as you shall judge necessary for fulfilling the purposes of the said Act. Provided that the rate of Interest of such loan or loans shall not exceed five per centum per annum, and that the principal thereof may be reimbursed at the pleasure of the United States. And I do hereby promise to ratify what you shall lawfully do in the premises.

In testimony whereof I have hereunto subscribed my hand at the City of Philadelphia the twenty first day of March in the year One thousand seven hundred & ninety three.

George Washington

LC, George Washington Papers, Library of Congress.
1. For background to this document, see Washington to H, March 20, 1793; H to Washington, March 18, second letter of March 20, 1793.
2. 1 *Stat.* 325–29 (February 28, 1793).

George Washington to Alexander Hamilton, Thomas Jefferson, Henry Knox, and Edmund Randolph

United States, March 21st [–22] [1] 1793

(Circular)

To The Secretary of State—The Secretary of the Treasury—The Secretary of War and The Attorney General of the United States.

Gentlemen,

The Treaty which is agreed to be held on or about the first of June next at the Lower Sandusky of Lake Erie,[2] being of great moment to the interests and peace of this Country; and likely to be attended with difficulties arising from circumstances (not unknown to you) of a peculiar and embarrassing nature; it is indispensably

necessary that *our* rights under the Treaties which have been entered
into with the Six Nations—the several tribes of Indians now in
hostility with us—and the claims of others, should be carefully investigated and well ascertained, that the Commissioners who are appointed to hold it [3] may be well informed and clearly instructed on
all the points that are likely to be discussed: thereby knowing what
they are to insist upon (with or without compensation, and the
amount of the Compensation, if any) and what, for the sake of
peace, they may yield.

You are not to learn from me, the different views which our
Citizens entertain of the War we are engaged in with the Indians,
and how much these different opinions add to the delicacy and embarrassments alluded to above—nor the criticisms which, more than
probably, will be made on the subject, if the proposed Treaty should
be unsuccessful.

Induced by these motives, and desireous that time may be allowed
for a full and deliberate consideration of the subject before the departure of the Commissioners, it is my desire that you will, on the
25th of this month, meet together at the War Office (or at such other
time and place as you may agree upon) where the principal documents are, with whatever papers you may respectively be possessed
of on the subject, and such others as I shall cause to be laid before
you, and then and there decide on all the points which you shall conceive necessary for the information and instruction of the Commissioners.[4] And, having drawn them into form, to revise the same
and have them ready, in a finished State, for my perusal and consideration when I return [5]—together with a digest of such references
as shall be adjudged necessary for the Commissioners to take with
them.

And, as it has been suggested to me, that the Society of Quakers
are desireous of sending a deputation from their Body, to be present
at the aforesaid Treaty [6] (which, if done with pure motives, and a
disposition accordant with those sentiments entertained by Government respecting boundary, may be a mean of facilitating the good
work of peace) you will consider how far, if they are approved
Characters, they ought to be recognized in the Instructions to the
Commissioners,[7] and how proper it may be for them to participate
therein or to be made acquainted therewith.   Go: Washington

LS, Thomas Jefferson Papers, Library of Congress; ADf, RG 59, Miscellaneous Letters, 1790–1799, National Archives; copy, RG 59, State Department Correspondence, 1791–1796, National Archives.

1. The letter in the Thomas Jefferson Papers is dated March 21; the draft and the copy in the National Archives are dated March 22.

2. For information concerning the proposed treaty with the western Indians, see "Conversation with George Hammond," November 22, December 15–28, 1792, February 24–March 7, 1793; H to Hammond, December 29, 1792; "Draft of Instructions for William Hull," January 14, 1793; Hull to H, February 6, 1793; Washington to H, February 17, 1793; "Cabinet Meeting. Opinion Respecting the Proposed Treaty with the Indians Northwest of the Ohio," February 25, 1793.

3. The commissioners appointed to meet with the western tribes were Beverley Randolph, Benjamin Lincoln, and Timothy Pickering.

4. A cabinet meeting was held on March 25 on "the subject of the proposed Treaty with the Indians" (JPP, 90).

5. Washington was going to Mt. Vernon. See Washington to H, Jefferson, and Knox, March 9, 1793.

6. On March 12, 1793, Knox wrote to Washington reporting that "the request made by the Indians of having some of 'the friends' called Quakers to attend the treaty at Sandusky seems to deserve consideration. I presume that some of those Citizens would chearfully accompany the Commissioners. . . . It might also conduce considerably to the success of the treaty were Mr. John Heckewelder to accompany the Commissioners. This amiable and intelligent Man is a teacher of the sect called Moravians, and for several Years resided with the Indians belonging to that sect of the Wyandot and Delaware Tribes, who inhabited the Waters of Muskingum—he well understanding their language. The influence he will have with the said Tribes may be expected to be very considerable . . ." (LS, George Washington Papers, Library of Congress). On the same day Washington informed Knox "that it would be well at all events to have the sd. Hackewelder to attend on acct. of his knowledge of the language & Customs of the Indians, altho he declines acting as an Interpreter. And that some of the Quakers should also be allowed to go—and if any could be found who were able & willing to act as Clerks or Secretaries they might go in that capacity. . . . Their exps. to be borne by the public as their attendg is for the public good & by the desire of the Indians" (JPP, 74–75).

7. In the instructions sent to the commissioners Knox stated: "The society of Friends have, with the approbation of the President of the United States, decided to send some of their respectable members, in order to contribute their influence to induce the hostile Indians to a peace. They are not, however, to confer with the Indians upon any subject of importance, until they shall have previously communicated the same, and received your approbation" (ASP, Indian Affairs, I, 341).

To Jonathan Burrall

Treasury Department
March 22d. 1793

Sir

You will, if you can, invest the fifty thousand Dollars heretofore put under your disposition [1] in the purchase of good bills on London or Amsterdam, if they can be obtained within the limit of four per Cent below par; so as to be forwarded to me by the first of April; I mean to *reach me* on that day by the Post.

I will thank you in the mean time to advise me dayly of the price of bills.

I am with consideration   Sir   Your obedient serv   Alex Hamilton

Jonathan Burrall Esquire

ALS, Historical Society of Pennsylvania, Philadelphia.
   1. See H to Burrall, March 14, 1793; H to the President and Directors of the New York Office of Discount and Deposit of the Bank of the United States, March 14, 1793.

From Tench Coxe

Treasury Department
Revenue Office March 22d 1793

Sir

A Contract with a person to finish the lighthouse at Bald head being expected from Jedediah Huntington Esqr.[1] in a few days for the purpose of submission to the President, it appears necessary that the pleasure of the President be also known in regard to the appointment of a person who shall have such a Supervision or Inspection, as was deemed necessary in the case of the Chesapeak Establishment.[2] An enquiry in general terms for a suitable person, and a particular enquiry in regard to the several gentlemen whose pretentions the state of North Carolina had countenanced by appointing them Commissioners for pilotage[3] and for this Work, has been made of Mr. Johnston, Mr. Hawkins,[4] and Mr. Iredell.[5] They all agreed that William Campbell, or George Hooper, two of the late Commissioners may be confided in and they added that they knew no person there more suitable. Mr Campbell and Mr. Hooper are both residents in Wilmington, from whence there is an easy passage by land and Water. The expediency of selecting some one Individual is suggested by the greater responsibility and expedition and by œconomy, as it is probable, that an allowance will be expected. Four dollars ⅌ day for expences and services were allowed to Mr Newton and Mr. Alibone[6] when they were appointed to visit and inspect in this and the Virginia case. It appears probable that an Allowance not exceeding that Sum would satisfy any Gentleman to whom the proposed duty may be assigned. The Supervisor or Inspector it is presumed need not make more than four or five occasional visits, when only he would be paid such Sum as it may be deemed proper to allow.[7]

I have the honor to be with great respect. Sir, Your Most Obedient Servant   Tench Coxe
                                   Commissioner of the Revenue

The Honble
The Secretary of the Treasury

LS, RG 217, Segregated Documents, "Famous Names," Hamilton, National Archives.

1. Huntington was collector of customs at New London, Connecticut.

The contractor who had started to build the lighthouse at Bald Head on Cape Fear Island at the mouth of the Cape Fear River in North Carolina had died before the building had been completed. On January 10, 1793, Coxe wrote to various collectors of the customs and supervisors of the revenue requesting them to suggest the names of builders qualified to complete the construction of the lighthouse at Bald Head (LC, RG 58, Letters of Commissioner of Revenue, 1792–1793, National Archives).

2. The contract for the Cheaspeake Lighthouse had been assigned to John McComb, Jr., a New York contractor. See "Agreement with John McComb, Junior," March 31, 1791. Thomas Newton, Jr., inspector of Survey No. 4 in Virginia, was in charge of inspecting McComb's work, although direct supervision of the construction of the lighthouse was in the hands of Lemuel Cornick. See Coxe to H, October 17, 1792.

3. See William Campbell *et al.* to H, April 18, 1791, and H to Campbell *et al.*, June 11, 1791.

4. Samuel Johnston and Benjamin Hawkins were United States Senators from North Carolina.

5. James Iredell, a resident of North Carolina, was an associate justice of the United States Supreme Court.

6. William Allibone was superintendent of lighthouses, beacons, buoys, public piers, and stakage for Philadelphia, Cape Henlopen, and Delaware.

7. On the back of this letter H wrote the following:

"For Mr. Coxe

"The President authorises the appointment of either of the persons mentioned. From the information which you communicated there are some reasons for preferring Mr. Hooper.

"It is the President's wish that an indication be given of the number of visits ꝑ week or ꝑ Month which may probably be found necessary. For this Newton's case may serve as a guide.   A H."

To Henry Lee [1]

Treasury Department
March 22. 1793

Sir

It has been communicated to me that the Commonwealth of Virginia, by an act not long since passed, authorized the reissuing of Certain Certificates which had been redeemed by the operations of the Sinking Fund of that Commonwealth and that there is every probability that the certificates so reissued, or a considerable part of them, have been subscribed to the loan payable in the Debt of the Commonwealth, which closed on the first of the present month.[2]

It has been settled after full deliberation at The Treasury in conformity with the opinion of the Attorney General of the United States, that the Certificates or evidences of debt of any state which had been once paid off or redeemed could not legally be received on Loan; upon the plain principle that they thereby ceased to constitute any part of the existing debt of a State.[3]

And though a state may by a subsequent act restore to such certificates the quality of *debt* which they had lost—this would plainly amount to the creation of a new debt, not in existence when the Act of Congress passed, not contemplated by it, and manifestly intended to be excluded by its provisions; particularly that which restricts the Certificates capable of being subscribed to those of a date prior to the 1st of January 1790.[4]

This construction has governed generally though it was in two cases drawn into question, one relating to N. Carolina,[5] the other to Georgia.[6]

It is therefore necessary, as well to equal justice, as to a correct execution of the laws of the Union, that it should continue to prevail.

The want of means to discriminate the *reissued* Certificates causes serious embarrassment. It operates as an obstacle to the granting of new certificates to all those Creditors, who subscribed subsequent to the passing of the Act which authorises the reissuing of redeemed certificates—among whom it is understood there are many who are the proprietors of certificates which had never been redeemed, and which are of course rightfully receivable upon the loan, and who consequently must be prejudiced by a suspension of their rights.

I learn that application has been made by the Commissioner of loans[7] to the proper Officer of the Commonwealth to obtain such indications as would enable him to distinguish the reissued certificates, from those of another description, and that a communication of them has been refused.

Feeling as I do an entire confidence, that the Commonwealth of Virginia does not desire to secure to itself an advantage not intended by the laws of the Union, or to impede their operations according to their true intent, I freely indulge a hope that upon mature reflection the Executive will think fit to direct the proper Offices to furnish the Commissioner of Loans with the information of which he stands in need for the execution of his duty in a manner consistent with justice and propriety. And accordingly request that such directions may be given.

If the Executive of Virginia should eventually disagree with the construction of the law, which has been adopted of the Treasury, I shall with pleasure concur in any proper arrangement for revising, and, if found wrong upon further examination for rectifying it. In the mean time however I should be glad that all impediment to the claims of Creditors, who ought not to be affected by the Question, may be removed by the requisite disclosure, on the part of the Commonwealth.

I shall be obliged by as speedy an answer to this application as may be practicable.

With high respect, I have the honor to be   Sir &ca.   A.H.

Copy, Sparks Transcripts, Harvard College Library.
  1. Lee was governor of Virginia.
  2. This is a reference to "An Act for appropriating the public Revenue" passed by the Virginia legislature on December 26, 1792. Section 4 of this act reads: "That it shall be lawful for the treasurer to pay to the agent of Caron de Beaumarchais, on warrant or warrants from the auditor, military or other certificates of the sinking fund dated prior to the first day of January, one thousand seven hundred and ninety, to the amount of the liquidated claim of the said De Beaumarchais, and in like manner to any other public foreign creditor willing to accept of such payment; and also to exchange certificates of the said fund of a prior date to the said period, for any of the certificates of this commonwealth, dated subsequent to the first day of January one thousand seven hundred and ninety, and bearing an interest of six per centum" (*Acts Passed at a General Assembly of the Commonwealth of Virginia. Begun and Held at the*

Capitol, in the City of Richmond, On Monday, the First Day of October, One Thousand Seven Hundred and Ninety-Two [Richmond, 1793], 6).

3. See Benjamin Hawkins to H, November 26, 1791; H to Hawkins, December 9, 1791; and Edmund Randolph to H, November 9, 1791. See also "Treasury Department Circular to the Commissioners of Loans," November 1, 1790.

4. Section 13 of "An Act making provision for the (payment of the) Debt of the United States" provided "That a loan be proposed to the amount of twenty-one million and five hundred thousand dollars. . . . And that the sums which shall be subscribed to the said loan, shall be payable in the principal and interest of the certificates or notes, which prior to the first day of January last, were issued by the respective states, as acknowledgments or evidences of debt by them respectively owing . . ." (1 *Stat.* 142 [August 4, 1790]).

5. See William Skinner to H, July 22, August 11, 29, 1791, and H to Skinner, August 12, September 8, 1791.

6. Oliver Wolcott, Jr., had written as follows to Richard Wylly, commissioner of loans for Georgia, on July 13, 1792, concerning a proposal before the Georgia legislature to reissue certificates: "It is suggested that application has or will be made to subscribe in your office on account of the State of Georgia, a sum of State Certificates which have been absorbed in Tares or otherwise discharged by the State, and that the Treasurer & Auditor of the State, have declared it as their opinion that in case such a subscription should be rejected by the United States, the State would be warranted in taking means to regain an adequate sum, *by negociating any of their Funds.*

"Though it is confidently presumed that the State Legislature cannot be influenced to adopt a measure so injurious to its dignity & the interests of the public as to permit Certificates which have been discharged to be thrown again into circulation, yet I judge it necessary to apprize you of the opinion which has been expressed by the Audr. & Treasurer & to request your most vigilant attention to this subject.

"In case any Certificates shall be reissued from the State Treasury, you will not fail to reject them as they shall be presented at your Office, and also to transmit immediate notice thereof to this Office." (ADf, Connecticut Historical Society, Hartford.)

7. John Hopkins.

To William Seton

[*Philadelphia, March 22, 1793.* On the back of a letter which Seton wrote to Hamilton on March 5, 1793, Hamilton wrote: "Answered the 22d." *Letter not found.*]

From William Short

Aranjuez [Spain] March. 22. 1793

Sir

My late letters of the 4th.[1] 25th. & 29th. of febry will have informed you of the state of the American affairs at Amsterdam as far as they were then known to me. I have been for some time in expectation of an answer from the commissioners[2] that I might know what they had done or were like to do in consequence of my authorisation to open a loan for two millions of florins & in case of absolute necessity to go as high as 5 per ct.[3]

As yet I have heard nothing, & it was only on the 19th. that this letter from them of the 14th. of febry. was recd. here wch. shows there must be some interruption between Amsterdam & this place. I enclose you a copy of that letter & my answer[4] to it as it will serve to inform you of all I know on the subject of the loan which had been counted on. You will find they consider one even at 5. p. cent as impracticable at present. I take it for granted you will have counted on this resource for the re-imbursement, notwithstanding my former letters as to the actual state of the market at Amsterdam. I never doubted myself that the U.S. could obtain money there by retrograding in their rate of interest unless the trouble at Amsterdam should become such either from domestic or foreign causes as to suspend all kinds of business therein and it still seems to me very extraordinary that should be the case. But the commissioners must be much better judges than I am, & particularly at this distance. Shd it be found impracticable to renew the million re-imburseables by giving new bonds at 5. p. cent which however I know not how to believe as yet, I really see not what mode can be adopted of answering the demands arising on the 1st of June, a circumstance of such

ALS, letterpress copy, William Short Papers, Library of Congress.
1. No letter from Short to H of February 4, 1793, has been found. Presumably Short is referring to a letter he wrote to H on February 5 (see Short to H, February 25 and October 17, 1793). The letter of February 5 has not been found.
2. Willink, Van Staphorst, and Hubbard.
3. See Short to H, February 25, 1793.
4. See enclosures.

momentous concern, that it is impossible to be without anxiety respecting it.

The bills of exchange for Spain mentioned in their letter were immediately indorsed to the Minister of finance, from whom I have even to this day found it impossible to get a state either of our debt[5] or of the payments he has already recd. from Amsterdam & which would have been made in mass long ago, if his consent to have recd. them at Amsterdam could have been obtained.

I am disabled from going into any other particulars at present from the actual state of my health—having been for some time past confined to my room by an indisposition of the climate & which does not yet admit of a due application to business. Still you may count on learning from me without delay whatever may be done to protect the credit of the U.S. at Amsterdam. You will however I hope be much more early informed from the commissioners of the state of things there, as their letters would get to you, about as soon & with as much certainty as to me, in the present state of the post.

I have the honor to be most respectfully   sir   Your most obedient & most humble servant   W Short

P.S. Since writing the above I have recd. from the commissioners a letter of the 19th of febry.[6] They had not at that date recd. any letters from me, although if there had been no interruption mine of the 4th. of febry. would have reached them. Their letter says nothing on the state of affairs there & seems merely to inclose seconds of the bills for Spain sent with their precedent letter.

The Honble. Alexr. Hamilton Sec. of the Treasury Philadelphia

[E N C L O S U R E]

Wilhem and Jan Willink, Nicholaas and Jacob Van Staphorst, and Nicholas Hubbard to William Short [7]

Amsterdam 14th Feby. 1793

Sir

We have the honour to inform you that it has not been possible to procure such Bills upon Spain as we could have wished, and it was

5. See Short to H, February 25, 1793.
6. LS, Short Family Papers, Library of Congress.
7. LS, Short Family Papers, Library of Congress.

only today that we got the 23 inclosed [8] amounting in all as ℔ particulars annexed to f17650.8.9—which we forthwith remit you, and shall continue our exertions to add to the same on every favorable opportunity. You are no doubt acquainted that War has taken place between England & France, in consequence of which, as we had formerly suspected, Money is become extremely scarce and even if we receive your directions to open a Loan in behalf of the United States at 5 ℔ Cent, We are almost certain that we could not succeed therein.[9] We therefore look for your instructions how to proceed to make due provision for the payment of f1,000,000 which becomes due the 1 of June next, together with the Interest which will then also be wanted. American 4 ℔ Cent Bonds were actually sold this day at 87½ ℔ Ct. a fact which strongly confirms the opinion just given that a new Loan would not succeed at 5 ℔ Cent.

We anxiously wish to be authorised to pursue some plan that may be likely to answer the desired end, and earnestly request you will not delay to give as such authority, as the period approaches fast when the above payments must be made. In expectation of speedily receiving full instructions upon the above subject We have the honour to be very truly

Sir   Your mo: obedt. & hble Servt

Wilhem & Jan Willink
N & J. Van Staphorst & Hubbard

Wm. Short Esqr Madrid

[ENCLOSURE]

*William Short to Wilhem and Jan Willink, Nicholaas and
Jacob Van Staphorst, and Nicholas Hubbard* [10]

Aranjuez [Spain] March 22. 1793

Gentlemen

I recd. on the 19th. your letter of the 14th. of febry. inclosing 23. bills of exchange on acct. of the debt to this country wch. were immediately indorsed & given to the Minister of finance. By yesterday's French post I acknowleged & answered you letter. To day I

8. The list of bills enclosed may be found in the Short Family Papers, Library of Congress.
9. See Short to H, February 25, 1793, note 6.
10. ALS, letterpress copy, William Short Papers, Library of Congress.

recd. your letter of the 19th. of febry. covering the secod. of the said bills. The length of time your two letters have been in route shew there must be some stoppage in the way—otherwise I shd. also certainly have recd. letters from you of a much later date & in answer to those or some of those I have written to you from hence.

For additional security I send this via Lisbon. The contents of your letter of feb. 14. much surprized & astonished me. As to instructions you say you expect from me, I can really give none in such a case. My powers are only competent to a particular business & you inform me that kind of business is now unpracticable—of course my powers are of no avail. I count much however on your efforts & abilities in this very important case. You will know what you may expect from the Sec. of the treasury from the dates of your letters to him informing him of this unexpected state of the business. As to myself I do not think that quarter to be counted on in the present instance, as he could not have been warned in time. The distance I am removed & the uncertainty of getting your letters & writing to you induce me to renew to you that I count altogether on your abilities & efforts to effect what is desirable. It might be necessary for you perhaps to consult or advise with Mr. Pinckney & Mr Morris [11] as it might so happen that all correspondence might be interrupted or reduced to much uncertainty between this part of Europe & Amsterdam. Whatever those Gentlemen may think advisable under such circumstances I should consider it my duty to subscribe to, not being able to dictate from hence for myself. I shd. suppose also & do not doubt the Government would approve whatever they shd. advise. I wait with much anxiety to hear further on these subjects & particularly to learn that you have recd. some of my letters at least relative thereto & am Gentlemen, yours sincerely

W Short

Messrs Willink & V Staphorst & Hubbard—Amsterdam

11. Thomas Pinckney, United States Minister Plenipotentiary to Great Britain, and Gouverneur Morris, United States Minister Plenipotentiary to France.

To George Washington

Treasury Department, March 22, 1793. Submits "a Communication from the Commissioner of the Revenue, of the 18 instant; [1] con-

cerning certain proposals for the maintenance and repairs of Buoys
moored at & near the entrance of Charlestown Bay in South Carolina." Discusses the merits of the proposals. Also encloses "Another
communication from the Commissioner of the Revenue respecting a
Clerical mistake in a late Act of the President concerning the revenue district of North Carolina." [2]

LC, George Washington Papers, Library of Congress.
   1. Tench Coxe's letter to H has not been found.
   2. Washington's "late act" was a letter, dated January 23, 1793, from the
President to the Senate and the House of Representatives presenting a plan "to
revise and amend the arrangements . . . in regard to certain Surveys and the
officers thereof in the District of North Carolina" (*GW*, XXXII, 311–12). See
also Coxe to H, December 13, 1792, January 12, 1793; H to Washington, January 4, 20, 1793.

George Washington to Edmund Randolph [1]

United States
22d March 93.

Sir

   I send you a letter of the 26 Ulto from William Bingham Esquire
to the Secretary of the Treasury together with the documents accompanying it.

   I desire your opinion on the following points arising upon these
papers.

   I   Whether the proceedings heretofore by the UStates in Congress assembled have transferred from Mr. Bingham to the public the
consequences of the transaction in question so as to make the suit
now depending properly an affair of the Government.

   II   Whether the Executive is competent to the requisite measures
of defence and security against any unfounded pretensions of the
claimants Plaintiffs or Prosecutors, or whether further special provision by law is necessary.

   III   If the Executive be so competent—What is the proper course
under the existing circumstances to be pursued.

G W

The Attorney Genl of the U. S.

Df, in the handwriting of H, RG 59, Miscellaneous Letters, 1790–1799, National
Archives.
   1. For background to this letter, see William Bingham to H, February 26,
1793, and H to Washington, March 20, 1793.

An entry in JPP for March 20, 1793, reads as follows: "The Secy of the Treasury laid before me a lettr. from Mr. W. Bingham with sundy documents —relative to a suit concerg a danish vessel captured during the War by an American Privateer—an act. of wh. a Suit has been brot agt. Mr. Bingham, which he wishes to know if the U. S. will sustain, as was done under the former congress. The Secy desired to bring the merits of the Case to the view of the atty. Genl. & obtain his opinion thereon" (JPP, 81). On March 25, 1793, "The Attorney General laid before me a lettr stating the opinion of the Secy of State —the Secy of the Treasury—& himself on the subject of a suit instituted agt. Mr. Bingham—and suggesting the measures proper to be pursued in that case" (JPP, 90). Although this letter has not been found, Washington's letter to Randolph, dated March 27, 1793, indicates that the opinion was favorable to Bingham (copy, RG 59, Miscellaneous Letters, 1790–1799, National Archives).

From Thomas Jefferson

Philadelphia Mar. 23. 1793 Saturday.

Sir

The Attorney general has just informed me that on a conversation with you it has been found convenient that we should meet at 9. oclock tomorrow at his house as Commissioners of the Sinking fund. I will attend there and shall hope the honor of meeting you. I have that of being Sir

your most obedt. servt.   Th: Jefferson

The Secretary of the Treasury.

ALS, letterpress copy, Thomas Jefferson Papers, Library of Congress; copy, Thomas Jefferson Papers, Library of Congress.

From Thomas Jefferson

Philadelphia Mar. 23. 1793.

Sir

I inclose you the order of the President [1] for 39,500. Dollars to complete the third year's allowance under the act concerning intercourse with foreign nations,[2] which third year will end on the last day of June next.

I have the honor to be Sir   your very humble servt   Th: Jefferson

The Secretary of the Treasury.

ALS, letterpress copy, Thomas Jefferson Papers, Library of Congress; LC, RG 59, Domestic Letters, Vol. 5, National Archives.
   1. George Washington to H, March 23, 1793.

2. "An Act providing the means of intercourse between the United States and foreign nations" (1 *Stat.* 128–29 [July 1, 1790]) provided the sum of forty thousand dollars annually for the expenses of the State Department abroad. This act was amended and extended by "An Act to continue in force for a limited time, and to amend the act intituled 'An act providing the means of intercourse between the United States and foreign nations'" (1 *Stat.* 299–300 [February 9, 1793]). On March 23, 1793, Jefferson wrote to Washington: "Before your departure it becomes necessary for me to sollicit your orders on the Treasury for the third year's allowance under the act concerning intercourse with foreign nations. This act commenced July 1. 1790. Two years allowance have been furnished and a sum of 500. Dollars over. Nine months of the 3d. year are now nearly elapsed, and according to an estimate I had the honor of giving in to you the 5th. of Nov. last, the expences to the 3d. of Mar. last probably amounted to about 90,785.09 D. from which deducting the sums received, to wit 80,500 D. the bankers would be in advance at that day upwards of 10,000 D. and near 20,000 D. by the time this remittance can reach them. They could feel no inconvenience from this because they had in their hands the Algerine funds but now that that is to be drawn for by Colo. [David] Humphreys, it becomes necessary to pay up the arrearages of the foreign fund, & to put them moreover in cash to answer the current calls of our ministers abroad, in order to prevent any risque to the honor of Colo. Humphreys's bills. I must therefore sollicit your orders for 39,500 D. which will compleat the allowance for the 3d. year, ending June 30 . . ." (ALS, RG 59, Miscellaneous Letters, 1790–1799, National Archives).

From George Washington

United States March 23d. 1793.

Pay, or cause to be paid to the Secretary of State or to his order, the sum of Thirty nine thousand five hundred Dollars, which, in addition to five hundred Dollars furnished to Colo. Humphreys[1] on the 14 of Augt. 1790, will complete the sum of forty thousand Dollars for the third year's allowance under the Act concerning intercourse with foreign Nations.[2]   Geo: Washington

LC, George Washington Papers, Library of Congress.
1. David Humphreys, a native of Connecticut, had served as Washington's aide-de-camp during the American Revolution. In 1790 Washington had sent him on a diplomatic mission to London, Madrid, and Lisbon, and on February 21, 1791, he was appointed United States Minister Resident at Lisbon. On March 21, 1793, Humphreys was appointed to succeed Thomas Barclay, who had been in charge of negotiations with Algiers and who had died.
2. See Thomas Jefferson to H, March 23, 1793, note 2.

To George Washington

Treasury Departmt. March 23d. 1793.

The Secretary of the Treasury has the honor to submit to The President of the United States the enclosed communication from the Commissioner of the Revenue.[1]

From the nature of the circumstances represented it appears to the Secretary advisable to embrace the offer which is made by Joseph Anthony & son.[2]   Alexander Hamilton

LC, George Washington Papers, Library of Congress.
  1. Tench Coxe's letter to H has not been found.
  2. The offer is described in an entry in JPP for March 26, 1793, as follows: "The Secretary of the Treasury laid before me a proposal of Josh. Anthony & Son to furnish 1000 Galls. of Oil for the Light-Ho. on Cape Henry @ 3/3 per Gal. The Commissr. of the Revenue states the *immediate* want of Oil at that establishmt. & that the above is the lowest for wh. it can now be purchased in this City. Upon these considerations I approved of purchasing sd. oil" (JPP, 90–91).

From Thomas Jefferson

[*Philadelphia, March 24, 1793*. On March 24, 1793, Hamilton wrote to Jefferson: "I have the honor of your two notes of yesterday and today." *Letter of March 24 not found.*]

To Thomas Jefferson

Philadelphia March
24. 1793

Sir

I have the honor of your two notes of yesterday and today, respecting a proposed Meeting of the Commissioners of the Sinking Fund.[1] The first came to hand only within a half hour.

As you mention, that the Attorney General has informed you, that "*on a conversation with me*, it has been *found convenient*" that a Meeting should take place—I cannot help inferring, there has been some misapprehension: Since it certainly is not my opinion, that a Meeting at the present moment is necessary; there being several depending and undecided circumstances which put it out of my power at this time, to pronounce that there are monies to be invested in purchases. Add to this that a Meeting must *of course* take place within the ensuing Month of April when further information may afford better data for operation.

I understood on Saturday from the Attorney General, that it was your wish a Meeting should be had—to which I replied, in substance, that I considered it as in your power to convene one; and should attend if called upon; but that I did not perceive the utility of one at this time.

As we shall meet at the War Office tomorrow on another business,[2] there will be an opportunity for further explanation.

I have the honor to be Sir   Your Obedient servant   A Hamilton

The Secretary of State

ALS, Thomas Jefferson Papers, Library of Congress.
    1. Jefferson's note of March 24, 1793, has not been found.
    2. See George Washington to Alexander Hamilton, Thomas Jefferson, Henry Knox, and Edmund Randolph, March 21–22, 1793.

From Jeremiah Olney [1]

Custom House
District of Providence 25th March 1793

Sir

I have the Honor to acquaint you that the Suit of Welcome Arnold Esqr. against me in the case of the Brigantine Neptune [2] was Tryed before the Superior Court of this State on the 23th Instant, the pleadings lasted Seven hours and being closed at 10 Clock P.M. the Court deferred giving their opinion in the Cause untill they meet here again by adjournment on the Eleventh day of April of Next, when I have reason to expect as favourable an Issue as was rendered in this Cause, at the last December Term of the Court of Common pleas. For want of time the Tryal of the Suit of Edward Dexter in the case of Said Brigantine Neptune was postponed untill the adjournment of the Court.

I have the Honor to be   very respectfully   Sir   your Most Obed
He. ser.   Jereh. Olney Collr.

Alexander Hamilton Esqr.
Secretary of the Treasury.

ADfS, Rhode Island Historical Society, Providence.

1. For background to this letter, see William Ellery to H, September 4, October 9, 1792; Olney to H, September 8, 13, October 4, 25, November 7, 28, December 10, 13, 27, 1792, March 14, 1793; H to Olney, September 19, 24, October 12, November 27, 1792.

2. In a decision on the case of *Olney* v *Arnold* handed down by the Supreme Court in 1796 the facts of the case were given as follows: "Olney, the Plaintiff in error, was the collector of imposts for *Rhode Island;* [Welcome] *Arnold,* the Defendant in error, was owner of the ship *Neptune;* and a citizen of the name of [Edward] *Dexter,* as the declaration alledged, was owner of the cargo of the ship; which arrived from *Surinam,* at *Providence,* about 4 o'clock P.M. on the 6th of *November,* 1792. On that day, the parties applied for a permit to land the cargo, and offered bonds to pay the duties; but the collector refused, or neglected, to accept the bonds and grant the permit. On the 7th of November, a second application was made for a permit, and bonds, actually executed, were tendered for the payment of the duties; but the collector again peremptorily refused to accept the bonds, or to grant the permit; in consequence of which the vessel, with the cargo on board, remained at a heavy expense from the 6th to the 13th of *November;* and *Arnold* laid his damages at £200" (3 Dallas, *U.S. Reports,* 308).

Under the terms of Section 41 of "An Act to provide more effectually for the collection of the duties imposed by law on goods, wares and merchandise imported into the United States, and on the tonnage of ships or vessels," duties on merchandise imported into the United States "shall be paid or secured to be paid, before a permit shall be granted for landing the same." In cases where the amount exceeded fifty dollars the duties could be secured by a bond given by the owner to the collector but no further credits could be given for duties until the bond was discharged (1 *Stat.* 168 [August 4, 1790]). In the case concerning the *Neptune* Olney maintained that "on the 17th of *January,* 1792, *Arnold* being indebted for duties, gave a bond for the amount, payable on the 17th of *May,* ensuing; that on the 5th of *November* 1792, the term for payment of the bond was elapsed, but the same remained unpaid and undischarged; that *Arnold* was the real owner of the cargo, but had fraudulently transferred it to *Dexter,* in order to obtain a credit at the Custom-house; that, though *Dexter* had tendered a bond on the 7th of *November,* it was rejected . . . and that a permit had been refused until the duties of the cargo were paid, or *Arnold's* old bond was discharged" (3 Dallas, *U.S. Reports,* 309).

In December, 1792, the case was heard before the Court of Common Pleas for Providence County and a decision was given in favor of Olney. Arnold then appealed to the Superior Court.

From George Washington

United States 25 March 1793

Pay to the Director of the Mint,[1] or to his order, five thousand Dollars for the purposes of that establishment.

Geo: Washington

LC, George Washington Papers, Library of Congress.
1. David Rittenhouse.

To the President and Directors of the Bank of the United States

[*Treasury Department, March 26, 1793.* "I am authorized by the President of the United States to borrow on account of the Government Eight Hundred Thousand Dollars. . . .[1] As the Public Service will in the course of the summer require a temporary anticipation of the current revenues, I request to be informed whether it will be convenient to the Bank of the United States to make the above mentioned loan. . . . I shall be willing to stipulate that the sum to be lent shall not be called for otherwise than in equal Monthly installments of Two hundred thousand dollars each . . . and that each installment shall be reimbursed, at furthest, within six months. . . . The experience I have had of the disposition of your Institution leaves me under no hesitation to count upon its cooperation in the present instance. . . ."[2] *Letter not found.*]

LS, sold by Paul C. Richards, Catalogue No. 3, Lot 78.
1. See H to George Washington, March 18, second letter of March 20, 1793; Washington to H, March 20, 21, 1793.
2. Extract taken from dealer's catalogue.

From Elisha Boudinot[1]

Newark [New Jersey] 26th. March 1793

Dear Sir

After passing through a fiery ordeal, I suppose you have a few moments to breathe a milder air. The part the Country in general take in your triumph over the envious and malicious, enemies to the Government as well as yourself; must convince you that the influence of these *beings* extend but a little way out of their own selfish narrow circle.[2]

Mr Low [3] has been over with me, and we have concluded to put off the meeting of the Directors till the 16th April, as then we should have a full board in all probability, and be more likely to have your attendance. In fact if you do not wish to forsake your child, it is ab[s]o[l]utely necessary for you to attend at that time. Mr Low informed Major L'Enfant,[4] Mr. Colt [5] and myself that Col. Ogden would make an offer at that time to deliver the water at Vrelandts point, purchase the lands necessary for the Canals for £20.000 and if he did he should be of opinion that it ought to be complied with.[6] The Major then said he would not begin any part of his plan that was not in actual operation until then and they concluded to discharge the laborers that applied and give out that they would not be wanted till the 20th April. This will occasion a delay that I am sorry for. Mr Colt goes home and will return by the time of our meeting. He is I think every way qualified for the business and I have no doubt of its success under his management as soon as the works can be set in motion. He is very much pleased with Peirce & Marshall [7] and they with him, and harmony is fully restored. Do not let these pompous, high minded, *would be King's*, though under the false garb of republicans—draw your attention from this great object—but look forward to those tranquil days when this child will be an Hercules, and you settled on the beautiful and peaceful banks of the Passaic, enjoying the fruits of your labor.

I am with respect   Dr. Sir   Yours sincerely   Elisha Boudinot

JCH Transcripts.

1. Boudinot, a lawyer and businessman in New Jersey, was a director of the Society for Establishing Useful Manufactures.

2. For H's "triumph," see the introductory note to "Report on the Balance of All Unapplied Revenues at the End of the Year 1792 and on All Unapplied Monies Which May Have Been Obtained by the Several Loans Authorized by Law," February 4, 1793.

3. Nicholas Low, governor of the Society for Establishing Useful Manufactures.

4. Pierre Charles L'Enfant had been employed in August, 1792, to superintend the construction of the society's manufactory. For L'Enfant's plan for a canal, see L'Enfant to H, September 17, 1792.

5. Peter Colt.

6. At the meeting of the directors of the society on April 16, 1793, "The Governor laid before the Board a letter from Colo. Samuel Ogden, relative to the conducting the Waters of the Passaick to Vreelandt's brook and Vreelandt's Point—the same being taken into consideration it is agreed that the Society has proceeded too far in their present plan to receed or adopt any other" ("Minutes of the S.U.M.," 86).

7. William Pearce and Thomas Marshall were artisans employed by the Society for Establishing Useful Manufactures.

From Edward Carrington

Richmond March 26. 1793

My dear Sir

With very great pleasure I have complied with your request in getting the final proceedings of the House of Representatives inserted in the most public and generally circulating paper of this place, and sent them to Norfolk Petersburg Alexandria & Winchester with a request through my friends at these places, that they be inserted in their papers, which will certainly be done.[1]

The votes of Colo Griffin upon this occasion[2] was caught at by the Enemies of the Government at the late election which took place just about the time of their appearing, and, as will always be the case, a dangerous effect was produced amongst the people in every County of his district, but the activity of better Men on the day, produced what the great body of the people I think are always ready to possess, a reasonable disposition, and his election was fortunately secured to the great mortification of some of our most active demagogues; and I am well assured that at this day, many who were carried away by the Storm, are much ashamed of their Conduct.

You are, my good Friend, too well acquainted with mankind, to expect that you are to proceed in the Administration of an Office so efficatious in the operations of Government as yours, without being constantly exposed to attacks; all that you can do, is to shield yourself, as you have done, against ultimate injury, by a steady exercise of your best abilities, and manifesting in every act an integrity that even your enemies have not, in all their complaints of pernicious tendency in your measures ventured to call in question.

You have this consolation, that do as they will with the further progress of your systems, they have proceeded far enough to wide(n) the solidity of the principles on which they were laid, and the ability

with which they wer⟨e⟩ set in motion; if they continue in their natural course they will at last be your most certain vindicators; if they
meet with such interruptions as to destroy them, worse measures, I
apprehend, will often force the reflections of the people back upon
them.

I am with very great regard   Dr sir   your afft Freind   & He Ser.

Ed. Carrington

Alexander Hamilton Esq [3]

ALS, Hamilton Papers, Library of Congress.

1. The letter in which H made this request has not been found. By the "final
proceedings of the House of Representatives" Carrington is referring to the
defeat of the Giles resolutions in the House. See the introductory note to H's
"Report on the Balance of All Unapplied Revenues at the End of the Year
1792 and on All Unapplied Monies Which May Have Been Obtained by the
Several Loans Authorized by Law," February 4, 1793.

2. Samuel Griffin of Richmond County, Virginia, was a member of the House
of Representatives in 1793. Unlike most of the Representatives from Virginia,
Griffin refused to support all of Giles's nine resolutions censuring H.

3. H endorsed this letter "Answered April 10. 1793." Letter not found.

From Pierre Charles L'Enfant

paterson [New Jersey] 26 March 1793.

dear sir

I have fund Everything at Paterson in as good a state as I had
promised from the arrangment made previous to my leaving the
place and Judging from the progress making in reducing the Rock I
would Continue to indulge the flatering hope of happily Ending the
opperations of this season was it not that I Feel a Sudden discourag-
ment in the prosecution of them owing to a Intimation I had that
the best of my Schems may yet by chance to be left aside and that
my whole labour is likely once more to be made a mean to gratify
the petit Interest of some men to the Expulsion of me and the Subversion of all my views.

at a meeting, last Sunday Evening, of Messrs. low, Boudinot, Colt
and myself Mr low brought forward a proposal from *Saml* Ogden to
carry the water from the fall dow[n] to vree land point,[1] and this
proposal the motive of which is obvious—and which in the first Instance of the business had been made and rejected Mr low now declared he would patronise at the next quarterly meeting. He said

Saml Ogden had assured him he would effect the purpose of a Coton Manufacture at that place for *ten thousand* Pounds—that to facilitate an agreement he, Mr low, had offered to give him 80,000 Pounds. You will observe that I was told 30,000 dollars would be the utmost I could Expect for Continuing and accomplishing the whole of my plan, which made me see with surprise the gratter sum offered for the other, but the observations naturally arrising from this and from the Consideration of the great advantages my plan had compared with any other as also of the discredit an attempt to part from a plan half accomplished would reflect upon the whole business at this moment. Nothing being noticed, I cannot but at best Conjecture an Intention to bring the society to a dissolution which I conceive is worked in different ways from Speculating motive as also from Ecinomical purpose.

disagreably situated wishing to take no resolution nor make any Steps Injurious to the grand project but at the same time unwilling to serve the view of any other sistem but the one in which I Engaged, Mr low making no reserve in saying that part of what I had done would facilitate *Saml Ogden* plan and that I might continue the work in consequence I declared that all what I could do consistently with my feeling and with the confidence I remained in that the Body of director could not but disapprove the adoption of a new plan—Was to suspend all work, until they had determined upon the proposal—and that consequently on the following day, yesterday, I should adjourn all hands until after the 20. of april—the Meeting of the directors being postponed to the 16.[2]

Wishing for your Opinion on this Business I hasten to communicate the whole to you without other remark. Beging you will favour me with it as soon as Convenient and in as confidential a manner as I hope your trust in me may Induce.

I have the Honor to be with respect, dear sir Your Most Humble & obedient servant   P Charles. L'Enfant

allexander Amilton Esqr
secretary to the treasuray

ALS, Hamilton Papers, Library of Congress.

1. See Elisha Boudinot to H, March 26, 1793.

2. For information on the rejection of the plan proposed by Samuel Ogden, see Boudinot to H, March 26, 1793, note 6.

From John F. Mercer [1]

Fredericksburg [Virginia] Mar. 26. 1793.

Sir

I have now to acknowledge the receit of yours of the 14th. of March which was handed to me on my way from Annapolis to this place. Your own discretion will determine you what course you are to pursue—confining myself as I have hitherto done to a line purely defensive, I shall assuredly not refuse any summons I may receive from you.

As the last paragraph however of your letter contradicts what I have both written & published: viz. "That matter of opinion only & not matter of fact was now at issue between us."—I shall not decline any explanation that may enable others & the public if judged expedient by either party (to whom this assertion has been thus committed) to determine with whom & on whom any departure from veracity may rest. I do therefore now recapitulate that the original & sole basis of your first letter to me [2] & that to Major Ross published in an hand bill,[3] rested, as I understood on this single fact—*That I had accused you of buying & selling stock on your private account.* This assertion was fully & unequivocally disprov'd by the Certificates of six as respectable Characters as any in the Union,[4] & as far as I recollect not one of the numerous Certificates procur'd by Major Ross [5] from the most avowed & bitter partizans against me, furnishes the slightest evidence of a fact that formed the ground work of a very exceptionable procedure; but on the contrary they as to that fact, fully corroborate the Certificates I had forwarded: Afterwards in reply to yours & stating what I actually did say (which it is to be ever understood was in reply to an attack made upon me in public & private for my opposition to your public measures as Secretary of the Treasury as appears by Capt. Campbells own Certificate) [6]—I then asserted two other facts—the one, *that of the public Money laid out in the purchase of Stock on account of the sinking fund, under your immediate direction, more had been given, than others had purchased for at the same time.* For this fact I quoted as my sole authority the public News papers, which I read extracts from in

Congress in my place to this effect & I added that this fact was not then contraverted or denied. *The other fact that when three parcels of Stock were offered under sealed proposals at these different prices that part was taken of each of the three & part returned.*[7] I have lodged with Mr. Beckley,[8] a Certificate of Mr. Hawkins,[9] a Senator from No. Carolina, substantially to this effect. And that Gentleman, will I have no doubt, also add if requisite, that he gave me fully the information I have above stated with regard to the three parcels at the three different prices—altho' when he gave me the partial Certificate mentioned as he could not perfectly recollect his authority, he did not insert it: Your interference in my Election previous to the first letter, became also collaterally a fact disputed, in a very exceptionable mode by the disclosure of a private conversation. At the time I mentioned my authority,[10] which altho' good ground for my belief & consequent conduct was improperly brought before the public. My information may & I believe has proved erroneous in its first source, yet it was a justification of my conduct & belief that your sentiments were not witheld with regard to my election, I believe I have from your own acknowledgement in one instance. There are still some farther facts that have been interwoven in the discussion respecting the payment for my Horse killed at Green Spring. Of this a full statement authenticated entirely by others—men of unexceptionable probity has been furnished, with which your own account of the transaction does I believe exactly correspond.[11] These are All the facts that I ever recollect to have been the subjects of enquiry between us. As to any other suggestions—they are I conceive Matters of opinion only—particularly what you observe respecting Mr. Duer & which seems the only ground of remaining discussion selected by yrs. of the 1st. of March. In my opinion of a preference, I conceive I am fully justified by the Report of the Committee of enquiry,[12] by which it appears that the transfer notified to you & lodged in your Office as the basis of the public Connexion with Duer was posterior to the correspondence with that Gentleman in character of Contractor & a Consultation between yrself, Genl. St. Clair & Genl. Knox & Mr Duer previous to Genl. St. Clair's departure. Saying this I am free to admit that private information of which I coud not doubt & on which I entirely relied respecting your interference in favor of this Gentleman Mr. Duer, appears by a Letter receiv'd from Mr. Baldwin [13] since my last to you, to be without any good foundation.

It is my wish now to be furnished with an exact copy of my Letter to you of the 31st. of January, as the one I have retaind is I am sensible inaccurate in expression, altho' I belive entirely correct in sentiment.

I am Sir &c.

John F Mercer

ALS, Virginia Historical Society, Richmond.

1. For background to this letter, see the introductory note to H to Mercer, September 26, 1792. See also H to Mercer, November 3, December 6, December, 1792, March 1, 14, 1793; Mercer to H, October 16–28, December, 1792, January 31, March 5, 1793; H to David Ross, September 26, November 3, 1792; Ross to H, October 5–10, November 23, 1792, March 13, 1793; Uriah Forrest to H, November 7, 1792.

2. H to Mercer, September 26, 1792.

3. H to Ross, September 26, 1792, was circulated as a broadside.

4. See Mercer to H, October 16–28, 1792.

5. See Ross to H, November 23, 1792.

6. For William Campbell's statement, see Ross to H, November 23, 1792, note 6.

7. See Mercer to H, October 16–28, 1792.

8. John Beckley, clerk of the House of Representatives.

9. Benjamin Hawkins served as Federalist Senator from North Carolina from 1789 to 1795.

10. Mercer attributed this information to Daniel Hiester. See H to Mercer, September 26, 1792, March 1, 1793.

11. See the introductory note to H to Mercer, September 26, 1792, and H to Mercer, December, 1792.

12. For an account of the report of the House committee of inquiry into the causes of the failure of Major General Arthur St. Clair's expedition against the western Indians, see H to William Duer, April 7, 1791, note 2.

13. Presumably Abraham Baldwin, member of the House of Representatives from Georgia.

From John Nicholson [1]

Compl Genl. Office [Philadelphia]
March 26th 1793

sir

As an enquiry which required some time was made after the closure of the Loan with Sep: 1791 whether or not Certificates of this State might not have been subscribed which had been granted for Continental Certificates [2]—And as it is probable the like enquiry will be made respecting the subscriptions to the Loan which closed the 1st Instant [3] before payment of interest or transfers will be allowed—and as there are some such Certificates included in the subscriptions to the last loan, I take the liberty to mention this now, and that I will prepare an equal quantity of principal & interest respectively to be delivered for the others when you shall think proper to make the necessary arrangements for performing the business.

I am with great respect   Your obt ser   JN

A Hamilton Esqr
secty Treasy
Ustates

LC, Division of Public Records, Pennsylvania Historical and Museum Commission, Harrisburg.
    1. For background to this letter, see Nicholson to H, July 26, 1792, note 1.
    2. See Thomas Mifflin to H, December 27, 1791; Nicholson to H, December 29, 1791, January 16, 17, 18, 1792; H to Nicholson, January 16, 1792.
    3. The Federal loan had been reopened under "An Act supplementary to the act making provision for the Debt of the United States" (1 *Stat.* 281–83 [May 8, 1792]).

To George Washington

Treasury Department, March 26, 1793. Submits "a communication from the commissioner of the Revenue, relating to a Contract for the building of a Beacon boat for the use of the River and Bay of Delaware." [1] Concurs in the views of the commissioner. [2]

LC, George Washington Papers, Library of Congress.
    1. The letter from Tench Coxe to H has not been found.
    2. An entry in JPP for March 26, 1793, reads: "A Contract for buildg, a Beacon-Boat for the use of the River & Bay of Delaware, for 264 Dolls.—which being represented by the Commissr. to be upon the lowest terms that the object can be completed—and that it is necessary—I approved the same" (JPP, 91).

From Peter Colt [1]

Paterson [New Jersey] 27th March 1793

Sir,

Some weeks past I wrote you by Mr. Hall [2] requesting to be favoured with the copy of your accts. with the Society for establishing useful Manufactures. By the Books which I have opened, you appear a Creditor for upwards of two thousand Dolls, advanced Pearce [3] & others. As I am without your answer, I cannot ascertain if you are Still in advance to the Society that sum, or if it has been repaid, from what quarter the Money has been received.

I find on the records of the Society, that Mr. Jos. Mort [4] is retained in their pay at £ 100 Sterling ⅌ Ann. I have never seen him here; & am assured he is in Virginia pursuing Business no ways essential to the Interest or views of this Society. Will there be any hazard in discharging him altogether? It is prety certain he cannot be useful to us this Season.

I find Mr. Hall also retained on a Salary of £ 300 Sterlg. It is worthy of some consideration if his salary should not be reduced untill such time as he is able to render Some Service to the Factory. I see no prospect of bringing his abilities in play under a Year from this time, in any manner that will justify such compensation.

I presume you will have been informed by Mr Low [5] that the quarterly meeting of the Directors is posponed untill the 16th April. Should you be prevented attending that Meeting, your Sentiments respecting those work men would be very acceptable to the Board.

Majr. L'Enfant is now with us. Presuming he will write you on the Subject of a proposition lately made respecting the mode of geting possession of the waters of the Passaic & constructing a Canal,[6] I shall forbare troubli⟨ng⟩ you on that Subject. This however may render your attendance at the meeting the more necessary.

I am Sir   Your most obedient   & very humble   Servant   P. Colt

Hone Alexr Hamilton Esqr.

ALS, Hamilton Papers, Library of Congress.
  1. When the directors of the Society for Establishing Useful Manufactures appointed Colt superintendent of the society on February 19, 1793, they authorized him "to act for the Society in the same manner as if the Works were his own property, and that if he should find from examination that any of the Salaries and Wages given by the Society should be inadequate to the merits of any one employed, that he report the same to the Board and if any of them should appear to be too high in proportion to the services rendered, that he reduce the same, and discharge every Person whose services are not profitable to the Society" ("Minutes of the S.U.M.," 79–80).
  2. Colt to H, February 28, 1793. William Hall was an artisan employed by the Society for Establishing Useful Manufactures in August, 1791, for "the business of printing staining and bleaching of Cotton and Linnens." See "Contract with William Hall," August 20, 1791.
  3. William Pearce.
  4. Joseph Mort was employed as an "Assistant in the Manufactory." See H to the Directors of the Society for Establishing Useful Manufactures, December 7, 1791.
  5. Nicholas Low.
  6. See L'Enfant to H, March 26, 1793, and Elisha Boudinot to H, March 26, 1793.

From Thomas Jefferson [1]

Philadelphia Mar. 27. 1793.

Sir

In compliance with the desire you expressed, I shall endeavor to give you the view I had of the destination of the loan of three millions of florins obtained by our bankers in Amsterdam previous to the acts of the 4th. & 12th. of Aug. 1790. when it was proposed to adopt it under those acts.[2] I am encouraged to do this by the degree of certainty with which I can do it, happening to possess an official [3] paper whereon I had committed to writing some thoughts on the subject, at the time, that is to say, on the 26th. of Aug. 1790.[4]

The general plan presented to view, according to my comprehension of it, in your Report & Draught of instructions,[5] was 1. to borrow, on proper terms, such a sum of money as might answer all demands for principal & interest of the foreign debt due to the end of 1791. 2 to consider *two* of the three m⟨illions⟩ of florins already borrowed, as if borrowed under the act of Aug. 4. and so far an execution of the operation beforementioned. 3. to consider the *third* million of florins so borrowed, as if borrowed under the act of the 12th. of Aug. and so far an execution of the powers given to the President to borrow two millions of Dollars for the purchase of the public debt.[6] I remember that the million of Dollars surplus of the Domestic revenues, appropriated to the purchase of the public debt, appeared to me sufficient for that purpose *here*, for probably a considerable time. I thought therefore, if any part of the three millions of florins were to be placed under the act of the 12th. of Aug. that it should rather be employed in purchasing our *foreign paper* at the market of Amsterdam. I had myself observed the different degrees of estimation in which the paper of different countries was held at that market, & wishing that our credit there might always be of the first order, I thought a moderate sum kept in readiness there to buy up any of our *foreign paper*, whenever it should be offered below par, would keep it constantly to that mark, & thereby establish for us a sound credit, where, of all places in the world, it would be most important to have it.

The subject however not being within my department, & therefore having no occasion afterwards to pay attention to it, it went out of my mind altogether, till the late enquiries brought it forward again. On reading the President's instructions of Aug. 28. 1790.[7] (two days later than the paper beforementioned) as printed in your Report of Feb. 13. 1793.[8] in the form in which they were ultimately given to you, I observed that he had therein neither confirmed *your* sentiment of employing a part of the money *here*, nor *mine* of doing it *there*, in purchases of the public debt; but had directed the application of the whole to the *foreign debt:* & I inferred that he had done this on full & ⟨just de⟩liberation, well knowing he would have time enough to weigh the merits of the two ⟨opini⟩ons, before the million of dollars would be exhausted *here*, or the loans for the foreign debt would overrun their legal measure *there*. In this inference however I might be mistaken; but I cannot be in the fact that these instructions gave a sanction to neither opinion.

I have thus, Sir, stated to you the view I had of this subject in 1790. and I have done it because you desired it. I did not take it up then as a Volunteer, nor should now have taken the trouble of recurring to it, but at your request, as it is one in which I am not particularly concerned, which I never had either the time or inclination to investigate, and on which my opinion is of no importance. I have the honor to be with respect, Sir,[9]

Your most obedt humble servt   Th: Jefferson

Colo. Hamilton.

ALS, Hamilton Papers, Library of Congress; ALS, letterpress copy, Thomas Jefferson Papers, Library of Congress; ADf, James Madison Papers, Library of Congress. A second ADf, letterpress copy, marked "not sent" and varying in some details from the draft and the receiver's copy, is located in the Thomas Jefferson Papers, Library of Congress. The draft sent to Madison was the original of the letterpress draft in the Thomas Jefferson Papers marked "not sent." Jefferson made a number of alterations and deletions on this copy before forwarding it to Madison. The amended copy sent to Madison agrees substantially with the version sent to H.

1. This letter can be understood only when placed in the context of the orders of the House of Representatives and the Senate directing H to submit information on his handling of the finances of the United States and of the resolutions of censure introduced in the House by William B. Giles. See the introductory note to "Report on the Balance of All Unapplied Revenues at the End of the Year 1792 and on All Unapplied Monies Which May Have Been Obtained by the Several Loans Authorized by Law," February 4, 1793.

2. Jefferson's account of H's request for a letter from the Secretary of State is contained in the following extract from a letter that Jefferson wrote to James Madison on March 31, 1793: "I inclose you the rough draught of a letter I wrote on a particular subject on which the person to whom it is addressed de-

sired me to make a statement according to my view of it. He told me his object was perhaps to shew it to some friends whom he wished to satisfy as to the original destination of the 3. mill of florins, and that he meant to revive this subject. I presume however he will not find my letter to answer his purpose" (AL, letterpress copy, Thomas Jefferson Papers, Library of Congress). Jefferson apparently also requested Edmund Randolph's views on this letter. The Attorney General's opinion, dated March 26, 1793, may be found in the Thomas Jefferson Papers, Library of Congress.

The "three millions of florins" mentioned by Jefferson constituted the first loan made by the new government under the Constitution. Bearing five percent interest, the loan commenced on February 1, 1790, but was not authorized until August, 1790, when Congress passed "An Act making provision for the (payment of the) Debt of the United States" (1 *Stat.* 138–44 [August 4, 1790]) and "An Act making Provision for the Reduction of the Public Debt" (1 *Stat.* 186–87 [August 12, 1790]). For a discussion of the terms of this loan, see Willink, Van Staphorst, and Hubbard to H, January 25, 1790; H to Willink, Van Staphorst, and Hubbard, November 29, 1790. For H's defense of his conduct respecting this loan, see "Report Relative to the Loans Negotiated Under the Acts of the Fourth and Twelfth of August, 1790," February 13–14, 1793.

3. The word "official" was omitted in the letter marked "not sent" in the Thomas Jefferson Papers.

4. A copy of "Jefferson's Opinion on Fiscal Policy," August 26, 1790, may be found in RG 59, Copybooks of George Washington's Correspondence with the Secretaries of State, 1789–1796, Vol. 21, National Archives. It is printed in Boyd, *Papers of Thomas Jefferson,* XVII, 425–27.

5. See H to George Washington, August 26, 1790. See also "Report on Foreign Loans," February 13, 1793, and "Report Relative to the Loans Negotiated Under the Acts of the Fourth and Twelfth of August, 1790," February 13–14, 1793.

6. In the letter marked "not sent" this paragraph is worded somewhat differently.

7. Washington to H, August 28, 1790.

8. "Report on Foreign Loans," February 13, 1793.

9. The last paragraph was omitted in the letter marked "not sent."

From John Brown

[*Providence, March 28, 1793.* On April 5, 1793, Hamilton wrote to Brown: "Your letter of the 28th. of March came to hand yesterday." *Letter not found.*]

From Thomas Smith [1]

[*Philadelphia*] *March 28, 1793.* Transmits "account of Stock remaining on the Books of this Office Subject to Interest for the quarter ending March 31st. 1793."

LC, RG 53, Pennsylvania State Loan Office, Letter Book, 1790–1794, Vol. "615-P," National Archives.

1. Smith was commissioner of loans for Pennsylvania.

To the President and Directors of the Bank of the United States

[*Philadelphia, March 29, 1793*. In "Report on the Periods at Which Moneys Were Received by the Banks for the Sale of Bills on Amsterdam and the Date of the Warrants for Passing the Said Moneys to the Credit of the Treasurer of the United States," March 29–May 12, 1794, Hamilton referred to "bills repurchased and surrendered, ⅌ Secretary's letter to the Bank March 29: 1793." *Letter not found.*]

To Pierre Charles L'Enfant [1]

[Philadelphia] March 29. 1793

Private & *Confidential*

Dear Sir

The ideas you have communicated give me pain. I wish you had not adopted the idea of adjourning the hands, unless you had been legally directed so to do. I cannot imagine that the Directors will adopt the change. If you are still in a situation to go on with propriety I wish you by all means to do it. You may be assured I shall not be *unmindful* of the business.

Yrs. truly

A Hamilton

ALS, Hamilton College Library, Clinton, New York.
1. For background to this letter, see Elisha Boudinot to H, March 26, 1793; L'Enfant to H, March 26, 1793; Peter Colt to H, March 27, 1793.

From Herman Le Roy

New york 29 March 1793.

Dear sir!

A part of the Estate wch. my Father has left consists in French Funds, wch. from the distracted situation that Country is in, neither principal or interest can be procured upon same. Since the United states are indebted to France, and they are now actually discharging same, pray would it not be possible to indemnify us, as American Citizens, out of the debt due them, by producing the Funds at their

Charge, wch. can be proved have been in the family for upwards of half a Century? Some of our Law Characters here have suggested the possibility of such a scheme being practicable, wch. alone induces me to sollicit the favor of your giving me your kind advice and opinion upon the subject, in doing of wch. you will render me a particular service, wch. on all occasions I shall be always happy to repay with sincere gratitude.[1]

I am ever with sincere esteem & respect   Dear sir   Your humble Servant   Herman LeRoy

Alex. Hamilton Esqr.

ALS, Hamilton Papers, Library of Congress.
    1. On the envelope of this letter H wrote "answered." The answer has not been found.

Treasury Department Circular to the Collectors of the Customs

Treasury Department,
March 29th, 1793.

Sir,

A question has been made—"What is to be the voucher to a Collector, for entering anew a Vessel which has been altered in *form* only?"[1] The 6th Section of the Act, concerning the Registering and Recording of Ships or Vessels, having made provision only for the case of an alteration in burthen.[2]

I answer, that the form of a Certificate of Registry, prescribed by the 9th Section of that Act, supposes a Certificate from the Surveyor, or person acting in his stead, for the special occasion, in every instance, except, merely, that of a transfer of property, when provision is made for referring to the former Certificate of Registry, as a substitute. It follows, then, that in the case of an alteration in *form* as well as *burthen*, such a Certificate is necessary, as an official description of the Vessel and a voucher for her Registry.

The only difference will be, that, when altered in burthen, a Vessel *must* be actually *measured* anew, to ascertain her tonnage—when only altered in form, so as not to affect her burthen, the tonnage *may be* certified from her old Register. And, in the first place, a fee for *admeasurement* will be due, in the last, none.

As an arrangement, which will conduce to the mutual convenience of the Officers of the Customs and of the Treasury—I am to request that all communications, which may be requisite after the receipt of this letter, relating to matters arising under either of the two Acts— the one entitled, "An Act concerning the Registering and Recording of Ships and Vessels," the other, entitled, "An act for enrolling and licensing Ships or Vessels to be employed in the Coasting Trade and Fisheries and for regulating the same," [3] may be addressed to the Comptroller of the Treasury, and that the instructions which shall be transmitted by him, in relation to these laws, may be considered of the like force, as if proceeding directly from the Head of this Department. It is, however, not intended by this to prevent an immediate recourse to the Secretary of the Treasury in any special case or circumstance, which may be thought to render it necessary.

All documents, directed by either of these acts to be transmitted to the Treasury, are to be forwarded immediately to the Register of the Treasury.

It appears that some of the Collectors have put a construction upon my circular letter of the 2d of January 1792, which precludes the Cash notes and Post notes of the Branch Banks, or Offices of Discount and Deposit, from being received for duties, and exchanged for specie. This is contrary to the design of that instruction—These notes being, in fact, notes of the Bank of the United States, signed by their President and Cashier, and having the same leading marks for distinguishing counterfeits from the genuine, as have been already communicated to you, are to be received and exchanged in like manner as heretofore directed.

With consideration and esteem,   I am, Sir, your obedient Servant,
A Hamilton

LS, to Charles Lee, Charles Lee Papers, Library of Congress; L[S], to Benjamin Lincoln, RG 36, Collector of Customs at Boston, Letters from the Treasury and Others, 1789–1809, Vol. 1, National Archives; LS, Circulars of the Treasury Department, 1789–1814, Library of Congress; LS, sold by Parke-Bernet Galleries, Inc., October 8, 1963, Lot 101; LC, United States Finance Miscellany, Treasury Circulars, Library of Congress; LC, RG 56, Circulars of the Office of the Secretary, "Set T," National Archives; copy, Office of the Secretary, United States Treasury Department.

1. See Jeremiah Olney to H, February 28, 1793.

2. 1 *Stat.* 287–99 (December 31, 1792). This act was to take effect on the "last day of March," 1793.

3. 1 *Stat.* 305–18 (February 18, 1793).

From Edmund Randolph

Philadelphia, March 30, 1793.

Sir,

The question which I had the honor of receiving in your letter of the 20th of March instant, is, Whether certain certificates of the commonwealth of *Pennsylvania*, originally issued in lieu of Continental certificates, and lately offered to be subscribed to the Loan in State debt, according to the Act supplementary to the Act, making provision for the debt of the United States, can be legally received upon loan, as contended for by the holders?

What may be the result of a contest between the holders of those certificates, and the state of *Pennsylvania*,[1] I presume, not to determine—But between the United States and that state I have no great difficulty in deciding—I am of opinion that the Acts of the *Pennsylvania* Assembly of the 27th March, 1789,[2] and of the 30th March, and 1st of April 1790,[3] abolished these certificates as debts of the State, except for the purpose of being re-exchanged for continental certificates, and therefore that the former, as wanting the due recognition from that state, cannot be legally received upon loan.

I have the honor to be, &c.   Edmund Randolph.

The Secretary of the Treasury.

Hogan, *Pennsylvania State Trials*, 81–82.
1. Randolph is referring to the controversy between John Nicholson and the Pennsylvania legislature. See Nicholson to H, July 26, 1792, note 1; Alexander Dallas to H, January 15, 1793; H to Dallas, February 8, 1793.
2. "An Act to Repeal So Much of Any Act or Acts of Assembly of This Commonwealth as Directs the Payment of the New Loan Debt or the Interest Thereof Beyond the First Day of April Next, and for Other Purposes Therein Mentioned" (*Pennsylvania Statutes*, XIII, 263–67).
3. "An Act to Enforce the Due Collection of the Revenues of the State and for Other Purposes Therein Mentioned" (*Pennsylvania Statutes*, XIII, 486–93).

From William Short

Aranjuez [Spain] March 30. 1793

Sir

I recieved yesterday from the commissioners at Amsterdam a letter dated the 26th. of february.[1] It came by the way of England &

Lisbon, the communication by post between Holland & France being intercepted. They had not therefore recieved the letters I had written to them by that route & they had not had time to have recieved such as had been written to them by precaution by the way of Lisbon. Their letter to me was merely to confirm the contents of that which they wrote to you the same day, & of which they inclosed me a copy, shewing that there is no possibility of making a loan at this time at Amsterdam for any power whatever.

This unexpected situation of affairs will have rendered their not recieving my letters, of no consequence as they were only to authorize them to open a loan, with an augmentation of interest if necessary. As neither the commissioners or any person on earth could have foreseen this so as to have given you notice of it on time, I fear it may be attended with very serious consequences. My former letters stated to you the disadvantages I apprehended from the U.S. being forced on the market at this time,[2] but I never contemplated the impossibility of their making a loan on increasing the rate of interest. I hoped however rather than do this you could make provision for the monies wanted either by leaving a part of the money which was on hand or by remittances from home. When I left Holland considerable sums remained on hand which have been absorbed by your draughts that arrived afterwards.

Hoping at that time that means would be taken for preventing the necessity of increasing the rate of interest I did not consider myself authorized to leave a power with the commissioners to do it, & particularly as there seemed no such urgent necessity at that time, from the interval subsisting between that period & the 1st of June—from the facility which the greater part being a re-imbursement seemed to give—& above all from my hope that you would on knowing I had left that country, authorize the minister at Paris or London[3] to act therein.

I have written to the commissioners long ago to desire them to correspond with these gentlemen on the subject & to them, asking them to give their aid & counsel. I have pressed the commissioners also by all the means in my power to make their personal exertions on this unexpected crisis—which I have been the more founded in doing, as they themselves had represented to me against transferring the loans elsewhere, the advantage of concentrating them in the same houses of great capital, on account of the assistance they could give in any emergency. I hope they will do whatever is in their power, as well from this consideration as motives of their own interest.

They suggest in their last letter (of Feb. 26) my making use of every discretional power I may have to provide them with funds & particularly by directing remittances to be made them from the correspondents in London of the bank of the United States. I have informed them that I had no other power than that of making loans & that as to the correspondents of the bank they were not known to me even by name. Whatever can be done by the means or by the exercise of any other discretional power I trust will be done by Mr. Pinckney & Mr. Morris. I do not venture to hope that you will have time to have furnished funds so early as the 1st. of June, from the date of their letter informing you that their market must not be looked to.[4] I observe in their letter to you, they state the situation in Holland as the cause of this—if that be the only cause we may consider the market as again open to us from the late events in that quarter & of which you will unquestionably have been informed.[5] But it should not be relied on exclusively until the experiment shall have been made. You will receive from them much earlier information than from me on all these subjects. In the present situation of Europe, communication between Amsterdam & this place is as precarious & almost as dilatory as between Amsterdam & America.

This letter will be sent both by Cadiz & Lisbon, the mode which I used of forwarding to you my late letters of Feb. 4th.[6] 25th. 29th & March 22d. The last letter which I have recieved from you was Dec. 31. acknowleging the reciept of mine to Oct 9 inclusively, & observing that time did not permit you to enter into any discussion upon the contents.

I have the honor to be most respectfully   Sir,   your most obedient & most humble servant   W: Short

The Honble
Alexander Hamilton Secretary of the Treasury.

ALS, letterpress copy, William Short Papers, Library of Congress.
    1. Willink, Van Staphorst, and Hubbard to Short, February 26, 1793 (LS, Short Family Papers, Library of Congress).
    2. Short to H, February 25, 29, March 22, 1793.
    3. Gouverneur Morris and Thomas Pinckney.
    4. Willink, Van Staphorst, and Hubbard to H, February 26, 1793.

5. Willink, Van Staphorst, and Hubbard wrote to H on April 4, 1793, concerning the situation in Holland.

6. No letter from Short to H of February 4, 1793, has been found. Short may be referring to a letter he wrote to H on February 5, 1793. See Short to H, February 25 and October 17, 1793. The letter of February 5 has not been found.

Treasury Department Circular [1]

Treasury Department, March 30th 1793

Sir,

I take the liberty to inform you, that the President, Directors and Company of the Bank of the United States have consented to accept Powers of Attorney from such persons as may have demands upon the Treasury, and to hold the monies which they may be authorised to receive, subject to drafts to be made upon their Cashier.

I have therefore prepared a Power of Attorney for that purpose; and in case the proposal meets with your approbation, you are requested to execute and acknowledge the same before some proper Magistrate, or Notary, and transmit it to this Office.

The blank in the Power of Attorney you will be pleased to have filled in such a manner, as to respect your compensation for the period subsequent to that for which you shall have previously made other arrangements.

Though the Power of Attorney is so drawn as to constitute in the Bank a general authority to receive all sums of money which may be due to you by the United States, yet, if you judge proper, it may be limited to such special objects as you shall choose to confide to their management.

To avoid risque from forgeries, you are desired to transmit your signature on several pieces of paper, and to make your drafts payable to order, according to the form herewith transmitted.

As some time will be necessary after your compensation falls due before the accounts can be settled at the Treasury and the money placed to your credit in the Bank, it is desired, that your drafts may be so regulated, that they will not be presented until ten days after the end of the quarter for which they may be drawn.

In case you consent to this arrangement, your salary will be regularly placed to your credit in the Bank, without the formality of an account thereof being transmitted to the Treasury for settlement.

If it shall be more agreeable to you, the Cashier of the Bank will, at your risque, remit through the Post Office the monies drawn on your account, either in Bank Notes payable to bearer, or in Bank Post Notes payable to your order, or drafts on the Collectors of the Revenue in your vicinity, when such drafts shall be at the disposal of the Bank. It will however be necessary that you should signify your election of this mode, and confine yourself thereto, until advice of a contrary intention shall be notified to the Bank.

As the President and Directors of the Bank will make no charge against you for their agency, it is expected by them, that the postage on such letters as you may have occasion to address to their Cashier will be paid at the offices in which they may be lodged.

This arrangement has been concerted essentially for the accomodation of the public officers, to facilitate to them the receiving of their dues with expedition and without expence.

I am, very respectfully,   Sir,   Your obedient Servant,

Copy, Connecticut Historical Society, Hartford.
1. Although no signed copy of this circular has been found, on August 30, 1793, William Cushing, one of the associate justices of the Supreme Court, wrote to H concerning the matter discussed in this circular and referred to "your favor relative to the accomodation of public officers in the receit of their salaries."
On a separate sheet appended to this circular is a list of names, apparently of the persons to whom the circular would be sent. It includes the judges of the district courts, the justices of the Supreme Court, the Attorney General, and the governors and judges of the Northwest Territory and the Southwest Territory.

From William Wiatt [1]

Fredericksburg [Virginia] 30th March 1793

Sir!

As the Patron of the Manufactures, now carrying on in the Town of Patterson in the Jerseys, I am desired by a Mr Robert Brownlow of this place, to write you, to be informed what wages are given to persons well skilled in spinning Cotton for Muslins and weaving Manchester Goods.

Mr Brownlow is a native of Lancashire, England, has had an opportunity of acquiring a considerable knowledge in the above mentioned branc[h]es, and I believe, if properly encouraged, wou'd prove a valuable acquisition to the Manufactory.

Your answer will oblige him, & I am   with every respect   Sir
Yr. Mo. Obt. St   Wm. Wiatt

Alexander Hamilton Esqr.

ALS, Hamilton Papers, Library of Congress.
    1. Wiatt was postmaster at Fredericksburg, Virginia.
    On the envelope of this letter H wrote the following: "William Wiatt.
answered. Things not yet prepared. Further inquiry to be made & information
given." H's reply has not been found.

From Thomas Jefferson [1]

[Philadelphia, March 31, 1793]

Th: Jefferson presents his compliments to the Secretary of the
Treasury. & is obliged to recall to his mind the order of the President
inclosed to him on the 23d. inst. Tuesday being the last day allowed
Th: J. for transmitting bills by the packet.

Mar. 31. 1793.

AL, Thomas Jefferson Papers, Library of Congress.
    1. For background to this letter, see Jefferson to H, March 23, 1793; George
Washington to H, March 23, 1793.

To Thomas Jefferson [1]

[Philadelphia, March 31, 1793]

Mr. Hamilton presents his Compliments to Mr. Jefferson. The
warrant for the sum in question will be forwarded to him tomorrow.[2]
Mr. J may therefore count on finding the money ready to pay for
the bills which he may engage, as early as he pleases tomorrow.

Sunday   March 31. 1793

AL, Thomas Jefferson Papers, Library of Congress.
    1. See Jefferson to H, March 23, 31, 1793; George Washington to H, March
23, 1793.
    2. In a report dated April 18, 1793, on "his proceeding of the present year for
transferring to Europe the annual fund of 40,000 Dollars appropriated to the
department of state," Jefferson stated that "he received from the Secretary of
the Treasury Mar. 31. a warrant on the Treasurer for 39,500 Dollars" (ADS,
RG 59, Miscellaneous Letters of the Department of State, National Archives).

For the Gazette of the United States [1]

[Philadelphia, March–April, 1793]

The late War with Great Britain produced three parties in the UStates, an *English* party a *French* Party, and an *American* party, if the latter can with propriety be called a party. These parties continue to the present moment. There are persons among us, who appear to be more alive to the interests of France, on the one hand, and to those of Great Britain, on the other, than to those of the UStates. Both these dispositions are to be condemned, and will be rejected by every true American.

A dispassionate and virtuous citizen of the UStates will scorn to stand on any but purely *American* ground. It will be his study to render his feeling and affections neutral and impartial towards all foreign Nations. His prayer will be for peace, and that his country may be as much as possible kept out of the destructive vortex of foreign politics. To speak figuratively, he will regard his own country as a wife, to whom he is bound to be exclusively faithful and affectionate, and he will watch with a jealous attention every propensity of his heart to wander towards a foreign country, which he will regard as a mistress that may pervert his fidelity, and mar his happiness. Tis to be regretted, that there are persons among us, who appear to have a passion for a foreign mistress; as violent as it is irregular—and who, in the paroxisms of their love seem, perhaps without being themselves sensible of it, too ready to sacrifice the real welfare of the political family to their partiality for the object of their tenderness.

These reflections are suggested by an attempt which appears to be making under different shapes to diffuse among the people an opinion, that in certain events the United States are bound to take part with France, in the expected War with G Britain. This effort is not prudent, is not commendable. It tends unnecessarily to hazard the public peace, by holding out to Great Britain an appearance, that a disposition to take such a part exists in this Country. It tends to embarrass the Councils of the Country, by leading the public opinion to prejudge the question. Discussions on one side will produce discussions on the other; and in one way or the other impressions may be formed contrary to the true policy of the Nation.

The treaty between France and the UStates is in possession of the public. But whether there be any secret article, defining the extent and force of any of its stipulations—whether there have been any official explanations, respecting their true import and application, which may give a complexion, different from that which the words may seem to bear—these, and perhaps other circumstances necessary to a right judgment, are unknown.

But without knowing them, it may justly be doubted, whether there be any thing in the Treaty, as it appears, that under the *existing circumstances* of the parties can oblige the UStates to embark.

It is understood, that *general guarantees*, where no precise stipulations point out special succours or special duties, have the least force of any species of National engagement; leaving much to reciprocal convenience. It is moreover a good excuse for not fulfilling a stipulation, especially if not very definite or precise, that it would *uselessly* expose the party, who is to perform, to a *great extremity* of danger.

If all or nearly all the maritime powers shall be combined against France, what could the UStates do, towards preserving her American possessions against Attacks of those Powers, which is the object of the guarantee on their part—and who could say to what they would expose themselves by embarking in a War on the side of France, in her present situation? [2]

But a still more serious question arises. Are the UStates bound to fulfil to the *present ruling powers* of France in the midst of a *pending* and *disputed* revolution, the stipulations made with the former government—with a Prince who has been dethroned and decapitated?

It may be answered that treaties are made between *Nations* not between *Governments*, and that the obligations they create attach themselves to the contracting Nations, whatever changes in the form of their Government take place. This, as a general principle, is true. But it is true only in reference to a *change*, which has been finally *established* and *secured*, not to one which is *depending* and *in contest*, and which may never be consummated. Such is the condition of France at this time. It is therefore in the discretion of the UStates to judge when the new Government is so established, as to be a proper organ of the National Will, in claiming the performance of any stipulations, which have been made with the late sovereign of France.

These considerations at least justify a suspension of the Public Opinion, on the points in question, and afford a good ground of hope, that if the Powers at War with France will act with moderation & Justice, towards this Country, we shall be able to continue in our present happy condition, and avoid the terrible calamities of War. Which that God may grant must be the fervent prayer of every good Citizen!

ADf, Connecticut Historical Society, Hartford; copy, Hamilton Papers, Library of Congress.

1. If this essay appeared in the [Philadelphia] *Gazette of the United States,* the issue of that paper in which it appeared has not been found.

2. Article 11 of the Treaty of Alliance of 1778 between France and the United States stipulated that the "two Parties guarantee mutually from the present time and forever, against all other powers, to wit, the united states to his most Christian Majesty the present Possessions of the Crown of france in America as well as those which it may acquire by the future Treaty of peace: and his most Christian Majesty guarantees on his part to the united states, their liberty, Sovereignty, and Independence absolute, and unlimited . . ." (Miller, *Treaties,* II, 39).

To John Armstrong, Junior [1]

Philadelphia April 1

1793

Dear Sir

The President has left here a Blank Commission for Supervisor of New York, with his signature, & with instruction to fill it up either in your name or that of Nicholas Fish, giving you the first option.[2]

I am therefore to request, that you will inform me as speedily as possible, whether the appointment is acceptable to you.

The present *gross* emoluments of it may amount to about 1300 Dollars of which 900 is salary. The whole duties of it may be performed by one person and in this case the nett emolument may be computed at 1200 Dollars. But as there is a considerable deal of Clerkship, the time of the person would then be pretty fully occupied. If the hire of a Clerk is to be defrayed out [of] the compensation, it would of course constitute a material deduction.

You will perceive that the emolument is not tempting. A main inducement therefore to the acceptance of the office would be the probability of growing importance. I contemplate that all future *interior* taxes are to be put under the superintendence of the Supervisor. The office will consequently become more important (now very respectable) and more lucrative. But how speedy the progress would be a very loose conjecture.

It is deemed necessary that the residence of the Supervisor should be at New York.

As Mr Morris[3] is impatient to be released, I request your prompt decision. I need not add that it will give me pleasure, if in favour of acceptance.

With much esteem & regard   I remain Dear Sir   Your obedient servant   Alex Hamilton

PS   It is the President's wish that the offer may remain a secret, for a time at least, if not accepted.

[John] Armstrong [junr][4]

ALS, from the Rokeby Collection, Barrytown, Dutchess County, New York, courtesy of Mr. Richard Aldrich and others; Df, Connecticut Historical Society, Hartford; copy, George W. Campbell Papers, Library of Congress.
    1. After service in the Continental Army during the American Revolution, Armstrong became secretary of the Supreme Executive Council of Pennsylvania. In 1789 he married Alida Livingston, a sister of Chancellor Robert R. Livingston, and settled in Red Hook, New York, where he became a farmer. In spite of the steadily increasing enmity between his wife's family and the Federalist Administration in the early seventeen-nineties, Armstrong remained for some years a stanch Federalist. On April 8, 1793, Tobias Lear wrote to George Washington concerning Armstrong's appointment: "Colo. Hamilton asked me some days ago whether I heard you mention the mode which you wished should be pursued with respect to the Commissions for the Supervisor of New York. I told him I had heard you say that you should desire him to write to Mr. Armstrong offering him the appointment and at the same time enclose a letter for Colo. [Nicholas] Fish, in Mr. Armstrong's, with a request that he would cause it to be delivered to Colo. Fish in case he should himself decline the appointment. Colo. H. observed that he had understood something of that Kind from you; but that he was not certain whether you had desired him to write or not—however he was now convinced from what I observed that you intend he should do so and that he would accordingly do it" (ALS, George Washington Papers, Library of Congress). On April 23, 1793, Thomas Jefferson sent to Armstrong his commission as supervisor of the revenue for New York (LC, RG 59, Domestic Letters of the Department of State, Vol. 5, February 4, 1792–December 31, 1793, National Archives). A copy of the commission is also in the Rokeby Collection, Barrytown, Dutchess County, New York.
    2. An entry in JPP for April 26, 1793, reads as follows: "The Secretary of the Treasury laid before me a letter from Mr John Armstrong—in which he

resigns his late appointmt. of Supervisor of New York—and assigns as a reason therefor, the increased expense of living in the City, which would more than swallow up the Salary & his own income" (JPP, 101). Armstrong's letter to H has not been found. Fish, a prominent New York Federalist, was then appointed to the position.

3. Richard Morris had been appointed supervisor of the revenue for New York in March, 1792.

4. The two bracketed words in this line are not in H's handwriting.

To the President and Directors of the Bank of the United States

Treasury Department
April 1. 1793.

Gentlemen

The Government has a considerable payment to make at Amsterdam in June next.[1] The provision for the purpose hitherto made falls short of the object; and it is desirable for perfect safety not to delay the remitting of funds from hence beyond the Packet of the present month—though I have great reason to believe that a loan at Amsterdam will have furnished the requisite means independent of remittances from the United States.[2]

In this situation, I am unwilling to place out of the power of the Treasury for current exigencies a greater sum than has been already applied to the purpose, and yet I wish to avoid every species of embarrassment to our Commissioners[3] in the event of a loan not having been made.

I have thought that an arrangement of the following kind—while it would answer my purpose, might not be inconvenient to the Bank—viz

That the Bank should furnish me with bills upon their Correspondents, in London, at Par, for 100.000 Dollars. These Bills to be remitted to the *Commissioners* of the United States at Amsterdam with instruction to cancel and return them in case *they* should be otherwise possessed of adequate funds, and to give immediate notice to your Agents in London that this has been done. The *Credit* to the United States for the amount to be suspended, until I receive advice concerning the expected loan. If one has been negotiated so as to render it certain that the bills will not be wanted, the Bank, upon notice of this, to cause the Credit which had been suspended to be given; upon a stipulation from this Department that the bills shall not be made use of, but shall be returned cancelled and surrendered to the Bank.

If in the mean time the *current market* price of Bills should rise to par, so as to afford an opportunity to the Bank of selling at that rate —it shall then be in the option of the Bank to consider the bills as absolutely sold to the Treasury at Par; giving notice to me of their having made this election.

If desired by the Directors, I shall be willing to agree that if the bills shall be made use of, the Credit to be given to the Bank for them shall correspond with the amount of guilders which they shall produce at Amsterdam at the rate of 36¾₁₁ Ninetieths of a Dollar per Guilder.

I shall think it reasonable also to fix a period (say sixty days) within which the information that the bills are to be returned shall be given or the purchase on account of the Government become absolute.

I have the honor to be   Gentlemen, with respectful consideration, Your Obedt Servt.   Alexander Hamilton

The President and Directors
of the Bank of the United States.

LS, Columbia University Libraries.
1. For an explanation of the payments due in Amsterdam in June, 1793, see H to George Washington, March 18, 1793.
2. For a description of the problems encountered in attempting to raise this loan in Amsterdam, see William Short to H, February 25, 29, March 22, 30, 1793.
3. Willink, Van Staphorst, and Hubbard, the bankers of the United States in Holland.

From Jonathan Burrall

[*New York, April 1, 1793.* On April 4, 1793, Hamilton wrote to Burrall and acknowledged receipt of "your letter of the 1st instant." *Letter not found.*]

To Jonathan Ogden

[*Philadelphia, April 1, 1793.* Hamilton endorsed a letter which Ogden sent to him on March 18, 1793, as follows: "1793 Answered April 1 with *thanks* &c." *Letter not found.*]

Conversation with George Hammond [1]

[Philadelphia, April 2–May 17, 1793]

Since my last [2] I have had several communications with Mr. Hamilton on the present critical state of affairs, from which I infer that he continues stedfast in his adherence to the opinions I have uniformly ascribed to him. In one of our most recent conversations I entered pretty largely into the exposition of those principles which your Lordship has been pleased to state to me in your last dispatch, as those that will actuate the conduct of his Majesty's government in regard to the commerce carried on by neutral vessels.[3] In the justice of these principles Mr. Hamilton perfectly coincided, and assured me that he would be responsible for the concurrence of all the members of this administration in the admission of their propriety [4] to the fullest extent.

D, PRO: F.O., Series 5, Vol. 1, Library of Congress.

1. This conversation has been taken from Hammond to Lord Grenville, May 17, 1793, Dispatch No. 14.

2. Since Hammond's Dispatch No. 13 to Grenville is also dated May 17, 1793, presumably the "last" dispatch refers to Dispatch No. 12, April 2, 1793 (copy, MS Division, New York Public Library).

3. On March 12, 1793, Grenvile had written to Hammond:

"I have great reason to believe, that one principal Object of Mons. [Edmond Charles] Genet's Mission is to procure a Supply of Corn and Provisions from the States of America and that for this Purpose he has been instructed to open a Negotiation with the American Government for liquidating the Payment of their loan to France by transmitting to the Ports of that Country a Supply of Corn and Provisions equal to the amount of the Outstanding Debt. It will therefore be proper for You to use every means in your power to ascertain whether any such Negotiation is going forward. Should you be able to discover that such a Proposal has been made it would be of the utmost Importance to inform me as early as possible, of the particulars of it. If in the result of any such Negotiation, Provisions and Grain should be actually shipped on board American Vessels, on the account of the French Government, they would evidently be French Property, and, as such, liable to Capture.

"It is indeed necessary to state on this occasion that the Principle of free Ships making free Goods, is one which never has been recognized by this Country and that it undoubtedly will not be allowed in the present case. . . .

"With respect even to American Property, bonâ fide such and which is carried to French Ports, on board American Vessels, it must be observed, that the Exemption from Capture does not extend to any of the Articles comprized under the Description of Contrebande de Guerre, and which are of such a Nature as to enable the Enemies of this Country to carry on the War against Us. . . .

"Another Principle to be attended to on this Occasion, is that (universally recognized) which prevents the carrying any Goods, tho' clearly Neutral Property and innocent in their Nature, to such Parts of an Enemy's Dominions as are besieged or blocked up. And it is the more necessary that You should explain this Point, and cause it to be generally understood, because of the very great Probability which there is, that, at no very great distance, this Mode of preventing the French from receiving Supplies of any Sort, from several of their Ports, will be resorted to. And it is therefore extremely likely that, even if such Articles should, bonâ fide, be shipped by American Merchants in Voyages of Speculation to those Ports, they may on their arrival in Europe be precluded from entering into those Ports by the Circumstances of their being blocked by His Majesty's Vessels. . . ." (Bernard Mayo, ed., "Instructions to the British Ministers to the United States, 1791–1812," *Annual Report of the American Historical Association for the Year 1936* (Washington, 1941), III, 37–39.)

4. In MS this word reads "property."

To Rufus King [1]

Philadelphia April 2d 1793

My Dr Sir

When you are acquainted with all the facts, I think you will alter the opinion you appear to entertain. My application comes literally within your rule. The loan is necessary for the current expenditure independent of any new advance to France or of purchases of the Debt. This has arisen from my having been under the necessity of remitting to Holland for a payment in June of 1000,000 of Guilders as an installment of the Principal, and 470 000 Guilders for interest, of the Dutch Debt. Late advices rendering it problematical whether a loan could be obtained for the purpose of the installment, it became necessary to make this remittance to avoid danger to the public Credit. Hence without a loan from the Bank, I ought to calculate upon a deficiency in the present Quarter (remember we are in April) of 672023 Dollars and 26 Cents and in the next of 325447 Dollars & 28 Cents.[2]

This is the result of as accurate a view of receipt and expenditure as can now be taken. You will anticipate, that by all the expenditures not falling *actually* within the periods, to which they are applicable, the real deficiency would not be as great as the calculated; but you will at the same time perceive that the view given supposes a state of the Treasury which renders an auxiliary indispensable.

At the same time, I cannot think but that you apply your principle too rigorously. I ought not to be forced to *divert for a length of time* funds appropriated for other purposes *to the current* expenditure. To compel this, would be in substance to withold the means necessary for the *current service*. For it would oblige the Treasury to employ an adventitious resource, which ought not to be so employed, and *that too* at a time when it could be employed advantageously according to its original and true destination. I therefore think, independent of the real exigency, the Bank ought to make the loan.

The loans to the Government stand on very different considerations from those to Individuals. Besides the chartered privileges, which are the grant of the Government—The *vast deposits* constantly in hand, and which ordinarily exceed the loans from the Bank, frequently very greatly, are an advantage which generally speaking bear no proportion to the advantages of the dealings between Individuals & the Bank.

Consider what has been the state of things for some time past—and the real *sacrifices* which have been made not to distress the Institution.

If for such accommodations equivalent services are not to be rendered they could not easily be defended.

Besides, from the necessity of having a considerable sum on hand in the Treasury and the natural course of the business The Bank is pretty sure of having always, in deposit a large part of what it lends to the Government. This does not exist, in any thing like the same degree in the case of Individuals.

You seem to calculate that the past advances will not be replaced. On the contrary it is my intention pursuant to stipulation to repay as fast as the funds come in applicable to it & in the *last Quarter* of the year I hope to make a considerable progress in the reimbursement. Till then it will not be practicable.

I do not know, whether Mr Kean [3] stated to you the nature of my proposal. It was that the payments should be made in 4 equal Monthly installments—the first on the 1st of June and that each installment should be reimbursed in six months. The real advance of the Bank will be very temporary indeed before greater sums will come into its vaults from the duties. In the last quarter of the present & the 1st of the ensuing year very large Receipts may be expected.

You are sure that while I seek to put myself in a proper posture, I shall not fail to have a due regard to the safety & interests of the Institution.

It is much to be wished that I could be enabled to make some purchases though this will not be the case with the loan in question unless a loan shall also have been obtained in Europe.

A meeting of the Commissioners has lately been called by Mr. Jefferson [4] out of the course heretofore practiced, in which I have been pressed to declare whether *I had or had not funds applicable to purchases*. I answered so as to be safe. But you readily perceive the design of this movement. There is no doubt in my mind that the next session will revive the attack [5] with more system and earnestness. And it is surely not the interest of any body or any *thing* that a serious *handle* should be furnished.

On the whole I am persuaded that the Bank can do what I ask without real inconvenience to itself and my situation is such that I shall be compelled to find an auxiliary.

All the cry here is for Peace. How is it with you? Adieu

Truly & Affecy Yrs   A Hamilton

R King Esq

ALS, New-York Historical Society, New York City.
  1. This letter was written to King in his capacity as a director of the Bank of the United States. For background to this letter, see H to George Washington, March 18, second letter of March 20, 1793; Washington to H, March 20, 21, 1793; H to the President and Directors of the Bank of the United States, March 26, 1793.
  2. See H to Washington, March 18, 1793.
  3. John Kean, cashier of the Bank of the United States.
  4. See Thomas Jefferson to H, March 23, 1793; H to Jefferson, March 24, 1793.
  5. For the 1793 "attack" on H's fiscal policy, see the introductory note to "Report on the Balance of All Unapplied Revenues at the End of the Year 1792 and on All Unapplied Monies Which May Have Been Obtained by the Several Loans Authorized by Law," February 4, 1793.

To Jeremiah Olney [1]

Philadelphia April 2. 1793

Private

My Dear Sir

You will receive by this opportunity an official Letter.[2] The present you will consider as a private and friendly one.

You will readily believe me, when I assure you, that all my prepossessions are in your favour, and that if there have been any faults on your side, I am ready to ascribe them to the *excesses* of virtues and good qualities, rather than to their *opposites*.

But you will, I am sure, consider it as an act of friendship when I tell you that some good men, who esteem you and think highly of your conduct, in the main, have expressed to me an idea that it has been in some instances too *punctilious*, and not sufficiently accommodating.

I am aware that in a scene where they have been accustomed to much relaxation, a spirit of exactness is particularly necessary, and that *only* a due degree of it may seem rigour. And I have thus construed the intimations alluded to.

But on the other hand I have considered it as possible that your ideas of precise conformity to the laws, may have kept you from venturing upon relaxations in cases in which, from *very special* circumstances, they may have been proper.

My own maxims of conduct are not favourable to much descretion, but cases do sometimes occur in which a little may be indispensable. The exercise of it must always be at the peril of the officer, and therefore ought to stand on manifest ground. But wherever it should appear to have been discreetly and prudently exercised, upon an *urgent* occasion, due allowances would be made for it.

I should be cautious in making such a remark to many officers— because I should fear an abuse—but with you, I have no apprehension, as I am sure your byass is, as it ought to be, towards a strict execution of the laws and your instructions.

The good will of the Merchants is very important in many senses, and if it can be secured without any improper sacrifice or introducing a looseness of practice, it is desireable to do it. Tis impossible for me to define the degree of accommodation which will avoid one extreme or another. This your own judgment, as *special* cases arise, must point out to you. I only mean to convey to you a general sentiment.

With real esteem & Regard   I rema[i]n Dear Sir   Your obedient servant   Alex Hamilton

Jeremiah Olney Esqr

ALS, Rhode Island Historical Society, Providence.
  1. This letter is a reply to Olney to H, March 18, 1793.
  2. Letter not found. The contents of this letter are described in Olney to H, April 18, 1793.

To Jeremiah Olney

[*Philadelphia, April 2, 1793.* On April 2, 1793, Hamilton wrote to Olney: "You will receive by this opportunity an official Letter." *Letter not found.*]

To Wilhem and Jan Willink, Nicholaas and Jacob Van Staphorst, and Nicholas Hubbard

[*Philadelphia, April 2, 1793.* On July 1, 1793, Willink, Van Staphorst, and Hubbard wrote to Hamilton: "and on the 9th: Ulto. only received your respected favor of 2 April." *Letter not found.*]

From Edmund Randolph [1]

Philadelphia April 3. 1793.

Dear Sir

I am extremely thankful to you for your readiness to accommodate me on the subject of the bills; but find, that the negotiation of the gentleman, to whom you alluded, was not for me. I must therefore make an arrangement for myself.

The sum, which I want to sell, is much less than £2600 stg. It is only 1300 £; as I prefer waiting for a rise. For the money to be raised on this latter sum I Am bound for *tomorrow*. This caused me to apply to that gentleman for bills to that amount; but he replied, that he is assured, the exchange will rise before the 18th. of this month, and holds it to be his duty in consequence of the trust, reposed in him to hold up until that time. Now, my dear sir; as you do not mean to send the bill off immediately, I will give you my own bill, indorsed by an able merchant here, (which would be paid if necessary) but to lie with you 'till the 18th. to be then redeemed by Mr. Ross's. Did I not suppose, that this would answer your object, I would not propose it; nor indeed would I ask the favour, but for the painful and unexpected dilemma into which I am thrown; and a belief, that I have not overated the degree of friendship, which I have experienced from you.

I am dear sir   Yr. friend & serv.   Edm: Randolph

Colo. Hamilton

ALS, Hamilton Papers, Library of Congress.

1. This letter presumably concerns a negotiation of foreign bills of exchange for a private payment which Randolph wished to make abroad. A series of entries in Robert Morris's account books indicate a part of Randolph's stock transactions as well as his financial relations with William Bell, a Philadelphia merchant. On April 1, 1793, Morris had agreed to pay twenty thousand dollars to Bell on behalf of Randolph. Morris's notes in favor of Bell paid fifteen thousand of the twenty thousand dollars. Morris also obtained Bell's signature on Randolph's note of April 1, 1793, payable at sixty and ninety days sight for approximately three thousand dollars. In addition Morris engaged to pay Antoine Hubert $2,625 on April 1, 1794, for seven thousand dollars worth of six percent funded stock which Randolph deposited with Hubert. Morris himself purchased an additional $2,660 of Randolph's six percent stock (D, partly in the handwriting of Robert Morris, Wastebook, 1792–1796, Historical Society of Pennsylvania, Philadelphia).

Randolph was undoubtedly injured by the financial panic in London during the spring of 1793. On August 21, 1793, he attached the stock standing on the books of the Treasury of John Warder, a partner of a London brokerage house (copy, RG 217, Oliver Wolcott's "Explanation of Accounts, 1792–1794," Comptroller of the Treasury, National Archives). Randolph's involved financial affairs are suggested by his appeal on August 5, 1793, to Thomas Jefferson for an endorsement on a note (Jefferson to Randolph, August 5, 1793 [ALS, letterpress copy, Thomas Jefferson Papers, Library of Congress]). Jefferson declined, and the following day he described Randolph's difficulties to George Washington: "The embarassments in his private affairs had obliged him to use expedts. which had injured him with the merchts. & shop-keepers & affected his character of independence: that these embarassments were serious, & not likely to cease soon" (AD, Thomas Jefferson Papers, Library of Congress).

To Jonathan Burrall

Treasury Department April 4th 1793

Sir

I have to acknowlege the receipt of the Bills on London for £6740 sterling, transmitted in your letter of the 1st instant.[1]

The account [2] has also been received and sent to the Auditor for settlement.

I am with consideration   Sir   Your obedt Servt   Alex Hamilton

Jonathan Burrall Esqr
Cashier of the office of Discount & Deposit
New York

LS, St. Mary of the Lake Seminary Library, Mundelein, Illinois.
1. Letter not found.
2. This statement of Burrall's purchases on behalf of the commissioners of the sinking fund may be found in RG 217, Miscellaneous Treasury Accounts, Account No. 3896, National Archives. The account was settled on April 15, 1793.

To Thomas Jefferson

[Philadelphia, April 4, 1793]

The Secretary of the Treasury presents his respects to the Secretary of State, and proposes, if convenient to him, a Meeting of the Commissioners of the Sinking Fund, on Saturday.[1] The Secretary of State will please to name the hour and place.

Thursday April 4th.

AL, Thomas Jefferson Papers, Library of Congress.
1. See Jefferson to H, March 23, 1793; H to Jefferson, March 24, 1793.

To Jeremiah Olney

Treasury Department, April 4, 1793. "Your letter of the 28th of February has been . . . received. The forms of oaths you allude to were transmitted from the Comptroller's Office. . . on the 23rd Ultimo. A Circular letter from this, of the 29th of the same month . . . contains an answer to your other enquiry."

LS, Rhode Island Historical Society, Providence; copy, RG 56, Letters to the Collector at Providence, National Archives; LC, RG 56, Letters to Collectors at Small Ports, "Set G," National Archives.

From Wilhem and Jan Willink, Nicholaas and Jacob Van Staphorst, and Nicholas Hubbard

Amsterdam 4 April 1793

Sir

We had the honor to address you the 25 Jany.[1] and 25 February,[2] since when we have [not] received any of your respected favors.

Mr. Short in answer to the Letter we wrote him the 24 January[3] to Madrid, of which we forwarded you copy, has authorised us to

open a Loan of Two Million of guilders for the United States at Five
per cent Interest, to face the Reimbursment and Interest due the 1
June next to the amount of ƒ1.470.000.[4]

The successes of the Allies, rendering certain the Evacuation of
this country and Brabant by the French Troops, confidence has
begun to recover; and will probably gain ground further, so as to
enable us to negotiate the Loan at Five p ct. Interest, but we cannot
flatter ourselves to obtain it at a Lower rate. Should there however
be a possibility to succeed at 4½ p ct, our Exertions shall not be
wanting to accomplish that desirable end, and we shall not fail to
give you immediate advice by different channels of the business
being concluded.

Mr Short having directed us some months ago;[5] not only to with
hold pressing the undertakers to receive their Bonds for the last loan
of the united States at the periods fixed, but even to inform them,
they would not be called upon to fulfill their Engagements punctually, one of them has 50 Bonds yet remaining in our hands, and his
circumstances being reduced, we cannot foresee, He will soon have
in his power to call for them, those Bonds selling for 90 p ct. we will
take the necessary measures, to effect a settlement with him, upon
the best footing we can stipulate for the United States.

The low price of all kinds of Public effects is no doubt chiefly
owing to political causes, but is in some measure occasioned, by the
many heavy failures that have lately happened both here, and in
England which create a temporary extraordinary Demand for money
in the commercial Line; We thank God are exempt from any loss,
With the Houses that have been obliged to suspend their payments,
and if we should suffer in an indirect manner, It can only be for
Triffles.

Such a juncture you Sir, will naturally conceive, to be extremely
unfavorable, to the execution of your plan, to engage Houses by a
Premium [6] to hold themselves ready to make large advances for the
United States, and we are certain, none would assume the Engagement now: we will revolve the proposal well in our minds, and inform you and Mr. Short the Result, after the return of calm and
confidence in the commercial World. In the mean while you may
rely, that we are penetrated with every disposition to accede to your
wishes, as far as is consistent with the Prudence we owe to our

Families, and to our own tranquility, which are Blessings paramount with us to every consideration of gain.

We transmit you inclosed the account current of the United States with us, up to the 30 Ulto. the Balance whereon due by us Holld. cy. ƒ486.506.18.8 we carry to their credit in a new account. Please have it examined, and on its proving right, pass same in conformity.

We are respectfully Your most Obedient and very Hhble Servants. Sir   Wilhem & Jan Willink

                    N. & J. Van Staphorst & Hubbard
Alexr. Hamilton Esqr.

LS, Connecticut Historical Society, Hartford; LS, marked "copy," Short Family Papers, Library of Congress.
    1. Letter not found.
    2. Presumably Willink, Van Staphorst, and Hubbard are referring to their letter of February 26, 1793, to H.
    3. LS, Short Family Papers, Library of Congress.
    4. The problems encountered in the attempt to negotiate a loan in Amsterdam in early 1793 are discussed in Short to H, February 25, 29, March 22, 30, 1793.
    5. See Short to H, November 29, 1792.
    6. See H to Short, November 5, 1792.

From Oliver Wolcott, Junior

[Philadelphia] 4th April 1793

Sir

The 25th: Section of the act entittled "an Act concerning the registering & recording of Ships & Vessells" [1] provides for the payment of the following fees to the Officers of the Customs.

	Cents
For the admeasurement of a Ship encluding 200 Tons	200.
For a Certificate of Registry	200.
For a Bond	25
	$4.25.

In Districts where there is no Naval Officer, two thirds of the fees, are to be recd. for the use of the *Collector* & the other third for the use of the *Surveyor*. Where there is more than one Surveyor in any district, each of them is to receive *his proportionable part of such fees as shall arise in the Port for which he is appointed.*

The 10th. Section directs that all Certificates of registry shall be *countersigned* by Surveyors in ports where there is no Naval Officer; as well from the terms of the Law as from the great inconvenience which would result from a different practice. It is presumed that the *Surveyor of the Port where the Collector resides,* is the person contemplated by the Law to perform this service.

The following case is supposed. A Vessell is *admeasured* at an out port, the Certificate of Registry is filled up by a Collector, & *countersigned* by the Surveyor of the Port where the Collector resides.

The whole fee for this service is supposed to be 425 Cents, and the point to be determined; respects the distribution to be made between the two Surveyors—one of whom has *admeasured* the Vessell, & the other *countersigned* the Certificate of Registry.

The 25th. section of the Act also provides for the payment of 100 Cents as a fee, for every *endorsement* upon a Certificate of Registry. This service of making endorsements is performed solely by the *Collectors.* A question has been made whether the fee for *endorsements* is to be divided solely among the *Officers of the Port at which the Collectors reside*—though the Vessells are *around at other Ports in the District at which there are Surveyors.*

These points being somewhat doubtful, I take the liberty to submit them to your consideration & to request a determination thereon.

I have the honour to be with the greatest respect   Sir

Hon AH.

ADf, Connecticut Historical Society, Hartford.
1. 1 *Stat.* 287–99 (December 31, 1792).

To John Brown

Treasury Department
April 5. 1793

Sir

Your letter of the 28th. of March came to hand yesterday.[1]

I regret much every embarassment which is experienced by the Mercantile Body—whether arising from the public operations, from accidental and unavoidable causes, or from a spirit of enterprise beyond the Capital which is to support it. That valuable class of

Citizens forms too important an organ of the general weal not to claim every practicable and reasonable exemption and indulgence.

I do not perceive however that I can at the present moment contribute to this end otherwise than by encouraging the Bank to continue its aids as liberally as shall be consistent with its safety under an assurance that I shall for some time to come forbear drafts upon them as much as shall be practicable. The deposits of the Government will during this period be proportionably considerable.

In making this declaration, I confide in the prudence of the Directors not to overstrain the faculties of the Bank by which the Institution and the public Interest might both suffer.

With consideration & esteem   I am Sir   Your Obedient serv

A Hamilton

John Brown Esqr
President of the B of Providence

ADfS, Connecticut Historical Society, Hartford.
   1. Letter not found.

To James Duane [1]

Treasury Department
April 5 1793

Sir.

I return herewith the statement sent me in the case of Lemuel Toby and the Ship Lydia,[2] in order that a further enquiry & statement may be had.

I am not at present satisfied of the innocence of the transaction, as it respects all the parties, who may be concerned, and as it is a shape in which fraud may present itself with great success, I am solicitous for a pretty strict scrutiny.

A Hogshead such as those we use with us is an Article so very distinguishable from a pipe, so different in the handling & stowage, that it is scarcely supposeable that the Captain could have been ignorant that the h'hds in question were on board & that they were not pipes.

It is still less supposeable that the Shippers of them could have considered them as pipes which it is presumable, (from their having been called so in the manifest) was the denomination given them.

The following particulars for different reasons appear to me desirable to be known

1 The Owner or Owners of the Ship
2 The Owner, Shipper & Consignees of the Geneva in question.
3 The denomination in the bills of lading & invoices of the Vessells containing it whether h'hds or pipes
4 The position of the H'hds in the Ship in relation to the use of the Cargo, as whether low down—midway—or at the top
5th The behaviour of the Ship upon her arrival on the Coast or within the Hook, whether she loitered or came immediately up— whether at the time of her arrival the Cutter was on the Coast or near the hook & had communication with her or not.

If the Ship was within reach, I should request an inspection of the Account of her Cargo while taking in, and of her log book, to ascertain the denomination there given to the H'hds.

I observe, it is stated, there were no certificates with the H'hds. If this has only been inferred negatively, a revision of the fact, with a more critical eye may be found useful.

It will readily occur that if they had been in possesion of the master, or any other person they may have been suppressed—and if any fraud was intended, the Oath of a party liable to suspicion would not be conclusive respecting such a point.

It would be reasonable in such a case to ask of the Consignee a production of his Correspondence.

It is with reluctance, I at any time give the trouble of a revision or restatement, but the present Case is in my opinion of a nature to require particular vigilance & circumspection. I doubt not the aditional attention requisite will be chearfully bestowed.

With respectful Consideration   I have the honor to be Sir   Yr Obdt Servt   A Hamilton

The Honble
James Duane Esq
New York

Copy, New-York Historical Society, New York City.
    1. Duane was Federal judge for the District of New York. This letter was enclosed in H to Richard Harison, April 5, 1793.
    2. This case was referred to H under the terms of Section 1 of "An Act to provide for mitigating or remitting the forfeitures and penalties accruing under

the revenue laws, in certain cases therein mentioned" (1 *Stat.* 122–23 [May 26, 1790]), which reads in part as follows: *"Be it enacted by the Senate and House of Representatives of the United States of America in Congress assembled,* That whenever any person who now is, or hereafter shall be liable to a fine, penalty or forfeiture, or interested in any vessel, goods, wares or merchandise, or other thing which may be subject to seizure and forfeiture, by force of the laws of the United States now existing, or which may hereafter exist, for collecting duties of impost and tonnage, and for regulating the coasting trade, shall prefer his petition to the judge of the district in which such fine, penalty or forfeiture may have accrued, truly and particularly setting forth the circumstances of his case, and shall pray that the same may be mitigated or remitted; the said judge shall inquire in a summary manner into the circumstances of the case, first causing reasonable notice to be given to the person or persons claiming such fine, penalty or forfeiture, and to the attorney of the United States for such district, that each may have an opportunity of showing cause against the mitigation or remission thereof; and shall cause the facts which shall appear upon such inquiry, to be stated and annexed to the petition, and direct their transmission to the Secretary of the Treasury of the United States, who shall thereupon have power to mitigate or remit such fine, penalty or forfeiture, or any part thereof, if in his opinion the same was incurred without wilful negligence or any intention of fraud. . . ."

This act was extended by "An Act to continue in force the act intituled 'An act to provide for mitigating or remitting the Penalties and Forfeitures accruing under the Revenue Laws in certain Cases,' and to make further Provision for the payment of Pensions to Invalids" (1 *Stat.* 275 [May 8, 1792]).

On May 23, 1793, H issued a warrant of remission in this case. In the warrant Toby's first name is given as Samuel. The warrant reads in part as follows: "And whereas I, the said Secretary of the Treasury, have maturely considered the said statement of facts and petition and although it doth appear to me most probable that there was no intention of fraud nor wilful negligence in the said Samuel Toby, yet the case is not wholly free from circumstances of suspicion, and the practice is in itself dangerous. Now therefore know ye that I, the said Secretary of the Treasury, in consideration of the premises, and by virtue of the power and authority to me given . . . have decided to remit and by these presents do remit to the said Samuel Toby all the right, claim and demand of the United States and of all others whomsoever to the said forfeiture; he, the said Samuel Toby, first paying one half of the appraised value of the nine Casks of gin forfeited, for the benefit of such parties other than the United States, who may be interested in the said forfeiture, together with all reasonable costs and charges attending the proceedings . . ." (DS, RG 21, Records of the United States District Court for the Southern District of New York, Warrants of Remission, National Archives).

To Uriah Forrest [1]

[*Philadelphia, April 5, 1973.* On the back of Forrest's letter to Hamilton on November 7, 1792, Hamilton wrote: "Answered April 5. 1793 with thanks &c." *Letter not found.*]

1. Forrest was a Federalist member of the House of Representatives from Maryland.

To Richard Harison

Treasury Department
April 5 1793

Sir

I enclose you a copy of a Letter from me to the district Judge of this date [1] requiring a revision in the Case of Lemuel Toby and the Ship Lydia.

You will see that I am not at present satisfied of the innocence of the transaction. The Invoice & Bill of Lading ought to be seen before there is time for fabrication.

I request your particular attention to a scrutinous investigation of the transaction.

With great Consideration   I am Sir   Yr Obed Servt   A Hamilton

Richard Harrison Eq
Atty for the District
of New yorke

LS, New-York Historical Society, New York City.
1. H to James Duane, April 5, 1793.

To Thomas Jefferson

[Philadelphia, April 5, 1793]

Mr. Hamilton presents his Compliments to the Secy of State—elects his office as likely to be most convenient to him where Mr. H will accordingly attend tomorrow at 10 oClock.[1]

Friday   April 5

AL, Thomas Jefferson Papers, Library of Congress.
1. See H to Jefferson, April 4, 1793.

To James McHenry [1]

Philadelphia
April 5. 1793

It is a good while My Dear Mac since I have either written to or received a line from you. I embrace the first moment I have been really able to spare to say some things to you which have for some time "lain heavy on my mind."

I have been conscious that I owed you an explanation concerning the issue of a certain Inspectorship [2] and I have meditated it ever since that issue took place.

In giving it now, I must rely on your discretion and delicacy; for you know I have no occasion to make enemies—and I must confide to you what in truth are in the nature of official secrets.

The Supervisor [3] named Perry Richardson and Chamberlain; [4] laying most stress on *Perry*. I had a conversation with Mr. Coxe (a matter of course in reference to his office) and it was agreed to recommend Perry. The three names were given in to the President (he always chooses to have more than one) with a decided recommendation of *Perry*. I thought his appointment certain.

Coxe spoke to Murray [5] or Murray to Coxe about this appointment. Murray recommended Richardson and Eccleston [6] preferring rather the latter. I believe, but I do not know it, that he rather spoke lightly of Perry. A Gentleman from Maryland (I think of the name of Hammersly) said to Coxe several things very disadvantageous of Perry. It seems he had opposed Mr. Tilghmans election [7] & through different channels Tilghmans Friends had approached Coxe—who from his connection with the family [8] was not difficult to be impressed against him.

Coxe came to me with his tone entirely altered on the subject of Perry. He was [9] a man not respected by respectable men—an intriguing and rather crooked character &c. &c. I perceived the influence of the election story & no impression was made. My byass towards Perry continued & Coxe perceived it.

The next morning I received a letter from him of which the inclosed is a copy.[10] This after the full conversations we had had was rather an officious proceeding. The design of it was not difficult to be understood.

The same morning I had occasion to call on the President. He had received a letter from Murray recommending strongly *Richardson* and *Eccleston* and I found he had through some Channel been approached disadvantageously to Mr. Perry.

He expressed a wish that I should make further Inquiry & particularly of Mr. Henry.[11]

I called on Mr. Henry. He was strong in favour of Richardson & Eccleston and *unusually decided* against Mr. Perry.

Having then no clue to it and having been led from former communications to entertain a favourable opinion of Henry's Candor I was much struck with his decision against Perry & I own a good deal shaken.

It was my duty to state facts to the President.

The Argument with him stood thus "Perry is strongly objected to by some; Richardson is recommended by every body—Ergo Richardson is the safest appointment."

Much could not be said by way of direct opposition. My *own* mind had been put in doubt. I took the course of recommending delay for further Inquiry & I understood that this idea would be pursued. I therefore wrote to you & I believe to Mr. Gale.[12] I received letters from both [13] which threw light upon the subject—but to my surprise the nomination was sent in before either Letter came to hand.

I flatter myself this detail will give you a correct idea of the business and that you will be satisfied that I have neither been wanting to you nor to Mr. Perry.

But this explanation is sacredly for your own breast. Mr. Henry's communications in particular were made under the most precise sanction of Confidence.

Nothing but a desire to vindicate the propriety of my conduct towards a friend could induce me to disclose it at any rate.

Affecty & truly Yrs   A Hamilton

What say your folks as to Peace or War in reference to the UStates?

J Mc.Henry Esqr

ALS, The Huntington Library, San Marino, California.
1. McHenry, like H, had been an aide-de-camp to George Washington during the American Revolution. He had served as a delegate from Maryland to the Constitutional Convention, as a member of the Maryland Ratifying Convention, and from 1783 to 1786 as a member of the Continental Congress. Before his election to the Maryland Senate in the fall of 1791, he had been in the state Assembly. At the time this letter was written McHenry was living in Baltimore.
2. The inspectorship was for Survey No. 3 in Maryland. See Tench Coxe to H, December 14, 1792. William Richardson had been appointed to this position on December 19, 1792.

3. George Gale.

4. William Perry, William Richardson, and James Chamberlaine. For information on these men, see Coxe to H, December 14, 1792, and McHenry to H, November 18, 1792.

5. William Vans Murray was a member of the House of Representatives from Maryland.

6. John Eccleston. See Coxe to H, December 14, 1792.

7. In the Maryland elections in the fall of 1792 James Tilghman and William Hindman were the candidates for Congress from the upper district of the Eastern Shore of Maryland. Hindman was elected.

8. See Gale to H, December 20, 1792, note 6.

9. In MS this word reads "has."

10. Coxe to H, December 14, 1792.

11. John Henry was a United States Senator from Maryland.

12. Letters not found.

13. See Gale to H, December 20, 1792. McHenry's letter to H has not been found.

From John Nicholson [1]

[Philadelphia] April 5 1793

sir

I have this morning seen Mr. Randolph who informed me he gave you his opinion just before on the question whether New Loan debt of this State was subscribable and that it was in the negative.[2] It appears to have been thus decided principally to avoid any difficulty with the State. Inclosed is a Copy of a letter I addressed to the Committe on Ways & means, and should be glad you would suspend any decision on Mr. Randolphs opinion untill I have an opportunity of seeing you thereon. If the mode I propose be adopted you will have the difficulty removed.[3]

I am Yr ob servt   J N

The Honble Alexr. Hamilton Esqr
secty Treasy

LC, Division of Public Records, Pennsylvania Historical and Museum Commission, Harrisburg.

1. For background to this letter, see Nicholson to H, July 26, 1792, note 1.

2. See H to Edmund Randolph, March 20, 1793; Randolph to H, March 30, 1793.

3. On April 1, 1793, Nicholson wrote to John Swanwick, chairman of the committee on ways and means of the Pennsylvania House of Representatives, proposing that court proceedings be instituted to determine whether the "new loan" certificates were redeemable under the Pennsylvania act of April 10, 1792, "An Act to Provide for Paying and Redeeming Certain Public Debts, and for Defraying the Expenses of Government" (Pennsylvania Statutes, XIV, 305–12).

Nicholson concluded his letter to Swanwick: "I am so well established in my opinion, that if the decision should be in the negative, I will go as far as to hold myself responsible to the state for the recovery and re-payment of all money paid by the state to the several creditors of that description" (Hogan, *Pennsylvania State Trials*, 82). On April 5, 1793, the Pennsylvania House of Representatives adopted a resolution "That the Attorney-General be directed to institute a suit against the said *John Nicholson*, to recover for the use of the commonwealth, the amount of the New-Loan certificates, which have been redeemed and paid at the Treasury of this State" (Hogan, *Pennsylvania State Trials*, 89).

To George Washington

Philadelphia April 5. 1793

Sir

The Ship *John Buckeley* is just arrived here from Lisbon, which place she left on the 23. of February.

The Messrs. Walls [1] a respectable Mercantile House here have received a letter from Mr. John Buckeley a respectable Merchant of Lisbon, after whom the Ship is named, of which the following is an extract.

"By letters from France by this day's Post, we find, that an Embargo took place there the 2d. instant on all English Russian and Dutch Vessels, which is certainly the prelude of War." This letter is dated the 22d of February.

Messrs. Walls, in addition, inform that on the 23 of Febry the moment the Ship was getting under way Mr. Buckeley came on board with a letter from Mr. Fenwick of Bourdeaux,[2] informing him that War had been declared by France against England Russia & Holland.[3] The foregoing particulars I have directly from the *Walls*.

The Report in the City is that the War was declared on the 8th of Febry.

Combining this with the Letter of Lord Grenville to Mr. Chauvelin requiring his departure [4] & the Kings Message to the House of Commons founded upon [5]—there seems to be no room for Doubt of the existence of War.

With perfect respect & the truest Attachment   I have the honor to be   Sir   Yr. Most Obed serv   A. Hamilton

The President of the UStates

P.S. I this instant learn that there are English Papers in Town by way of St Vincents which mention that on the 8th of February The late Queen of France was also put to Death after a Trial & Condemnation.[6]

ALS, George Washington Papers, Library of Congress; copy, Hamilton Papers, Library of Congress.

1. John and Joseph Wall.

2. James Fenwick was United States consul at Bordeaux.

3. This is a mistake. On February 1, 1793, France declared war on Great Britain, Holland, and Spain, but not on Russia.

4. Bernard François, Marquis de Chauvelin, was French Minister to Great Britain. Following the news of the execution of Louis XVI on January 21, 1793, Chauvelin was ordered by Lord Grenville to leave England.

5. On January 28, 1793, George III sent to Parliament copies of the correspondence between Chauvelin and Lord Grenville. In an accompanying message he declared it necessary to increase the British armed forces (*Annual Register* [State Papers], 1793, 128).

6. This is incorrect. Marie Antoinette was executed on October 16, 1793.

Meeting of the Commissioners of the Sinking Fund

[Philadelphia, April 6, 1793]

At a Meeting of the Trustees of the Sinking fund, at the Office of the Secretary of State on the 6 of April 1793.

Present, The Secretary of State,

        The Secrey. of the Treasury, and

        The Atty. Genl. of the U States.

It appears by a Certificate from the Register, bearing date this day, that there are at the disposal of the Board 25,445d.76Cts arising from the dividends of Interest payable on the 31st of March 1793. Whereupon it is,

Resolved, that the same be expended by Saml. Meredith, Agent, in the purchase of the several species of Stock, constituting the Debt of the United States, at their respective market prices, not exceeding the par or true value thereof, and as nearly as may be in equal proportions.

The Attorney Genl being of opinion that in fixing the par or true value of the 3 pr. Cent stock—a calculation according to the rate of Interest prescribed by the Resolution of the 15 of August 1791 [1]—

ought to govern; and the Secretary of the Treasury being of opinion, that it is not now expedient or necessary, that the said calculation should be exceeded;

It is further Resolved, that the price to be given for the said 3 pr. Ct. Stock, shall not exceed the limit prescribed by the said resolution of the 15 of Augt. 1791—the Secretary of State continueing to dissent from any estimate of the true value of the said 3 pr. Ct. stock at more than 10/— in the pound.   Edmd Randolph

Aproved
April 12 1793,
Go. Washington.

LC, George Washington Papers, Library of Congress.
    1. See "Meeting of the Commissioners of the Sinking Fund," August 15, 1791.

To John Cochran [1]

Treasury Department, April 8, 1793. "Enclosed is a List of certificates of transfers issued by the commissioner of Georgia [2] in which the time from which they bear interest has been altered, from the 1st of January to the 1st of April 1792. . . . I have thought proper to give You this information in order to remove any scruple which might arise on account of the alteration."

LS, The American Swedish Historical Museum, Philadelphia.
    1. Cochran was commissioner of loans for New York.
    2. Richard Wylly was commissioner of loans for Georgia.

From William Ellery

[*Newport, Rhode Island*] *April 8, 1973.* ". . . Inclosed is the declaration of Aaron Usher late master of the Sloop Flying Fish of Bristol of the burthen of nineteen and an half tons. It is true that he took passage from Cape Francois in the Brig Sally of Newport Elisha Brown master, arrived here on the twenty ninth day of March last, and on the same day delivered up his License; and I believe the other part of his declaration is equally true. One of the Owners of said Sloop was at the Custom House a few days before his arrival, and informed me of his Sloop being driven by distress of weather to

Hispaniola and expressed apprehensions least Usher through ignorance of the Law might import some merchandize in her from that Island. There doth not appear to have been any intention in the parties to counter act the Law. Please to favour me with your direction in this case."

LC, Newport Historical Society, Newport, Rhode Island.

From David Ross [1]

Bladensburgh [Maryland] April
8. 1793

Dear Sir

I expected before this Copies of your and Co Mercers Communications & the Statement to the President with the Certificates respecting the Bribe [2]—& I need say nothing farther than that particular circumstances render me more anxious for them than ever. It is still asserted here that you attended the Coffee House on the Evenings the Purchases were made and that it was a common mode of expression that the Secretary would be in Market and that Certificates was sure to rise in consequence of it: so that you see, the Journals of the Commissioners will not convince some of Co Mercers advocates.[3]

By insisting on it we have at least got Co Mercers *Detail* which he referred to in one of his publications. It would not be sufficiently interesting to you to send a Copy of it, but if you should desire it from the nature of the enclosed answers you shall have it from

Your friend & obedt Servt   David Ross

ALS, Hamilton Papers, Library of Congress.

1. For background to this letter, see the introductory note to H to John F. Mercer, September 26, 1792. See also H to Mercer, November 3, December 6, December, 1792, March 1, 14, 1793; Mercer to H, October 16–28, December, 1792, January 31, March 5, 26, 1793; H to Ross, September 26, November 3, 1792; Ross to H, October 5–10, November 23, 1792, March 13, 1793; Uriah Forrest to H, November 7, 1792.

2. See the introductory note to H to Mercer, September 26, 1792, and H to Mercer, December, 1792.

3. The "Journal" of the commissioners of the sinking fund had been submitted to Congress with the "Report of the Commissioners of the Sinking Fund," February 25, 1793. It was subsequently published in the newspapers ([Philadelphia] *Dunlap's American Daily Advertiser*, March 7, 1793).

To Simeon Theus [1]

Treasry Department
April 8. 1793

Sir

I have collected and reviewed the Papers relating to Mr. Prioleaus Petition.[2] If you persist in your request, those which came from you will be returned to you; but as I shall certainly report on the case at the next session of Congress, which is the course the business must have—I wish to retain them 'till that is done.

The claim appears to be of a nature, that I should reluctantly feel myself under a necessity of reporting against it and I am therefore desirous of preserving in my possession whatever may throw light upon the final consideration to be bestowed upon it. I am Sir

Your obedient Servt   A Hamilton

Simon Theus Esq

ALS, RG 217, Segregated Documents, "Famous Names," Hamilton, National Archives.

1. During the American Revolution Theus, who was a resident of Charleston, South Carolina, had served as a captain in the First South Carolina Regiment. At the time this letter was written he was the South Carolina agent to present the state's claims against the United States before the commissioners to settle the accounts between the United States and the individual states.

2. Samuel Prioleau, Jr., was a Charleston merchant and a member of a prominent South Carolina family. In the *Journal of the House* Prioleau's name is incorrectly given as "Prideau." The petition is cited as "the petition of Samuel Prideau, Junior, of the city of Charleston, praying to receive compensation for the value of certain wharves and houses which were taken from him, and appropriated to the use of the American Army at the siege of that place." The petition was referred to H on December 15, 1790 (*Journal of the House*, I, 337). H did not report on it until February 27, 1794, when he gave an opinion favorable to Prioleau's petition.

To George Washington

Philadelphia
April 8th. 1793

Sir

The papers of to day, which I take it for granted are forwarded to you [1] will inform you of a confirmation of the War between France

England & Holland [2] & of such other leading particulars, as are contained in the English Papers brought by the Packet.

The object of this Letter is merely to apprize you that the whole current of *Commercial Intelligence,* which comes down to the 11 of February, indicates, thus far, an *unexceptionable* conduct on the part of the British Government towards the Vessels of the UStates.

This information is received here with very great satisfaction as favourable to a continuance of peace—the desire of which may be said to be both universal & ardent.

With the highest respect & the truest attachment I have the honor to be   Sir   Your obedt & humb servant   A Hamilton

P.S   Lest the papers may not be regularly transmitted I enclose the two of this morning.

The President of the UStates

ALS, George Washington Papers, Library of Congress; copy, Hamilton Papers, Library of Congress.
    1. Washington had left for Mt. Vernon on March 27, 1793.
    2. See H to Washington, April 5, 1793, note 3.

From William Bingham

Philada April 9th 1793
Dear sir

The Committee of the Board,[1] (on the subject of the Loan) were unfortunate in not finding you at your Office or House, when they had the Honor of waiting on you this Morning.

They were instructed to confer with you on a Point, which is the Object of the inclosed Letter, & to which I request your early Reply, as the Board are desirous of terminating this Business, at an adjourned Meeting to Morrow Morning, at ten oClock.

The Reasons that influenced this Application, will naturally occur to you—they are not unfavorable to the Success of your Views.

I have the Honor to be   Your &c   Wm Bingham

Honble Alexr Hamilton Esqr

ALS, letterpress copy, Historical Society of Pennsylvania, Philadelphia.
    1. Bingham was a member of a committee of the board of directors of the Bank of the United States. This letter is in reply to H to the President and

Directors of the Bank of the United States, March 26, 1793. For further background to this letter, see H to George Washington, March 18, second letter of March 20, 1793; Washington to H, March 20, 21, 1793; H to Rufus King, April 2, 1793.

From Tench Coxe

[*April 9, 1793.* On April 11, 1793, Hamilton sent to George Washington "a communication of the 9 instant from the Commissioner of the Revenue." *Letter not found.*]

To John Jay

Philadelphia April 9
1793

Dear Sir

When we last conversed together on the subject we were both of opinion that the Minister expected from France should be received.[1]

Subsequent circumstances have perhaps induced an additional embarrassment on this point and render it adviseable to reconsider the opinion generally and to raise this further question—Whether he ought to be received *absolutely* or with *qualifications?*

The King has been decapitated. Out of this will arise a Regent, acknowleged and supported by the Powers of Europe almost universally—in capacity to Act and who may himself send an Ambassador to the United States. Should we in such case receive both? If we receive one from the Republic & refuse the other, shall we stand on ground perfectly neutral?

If we receive a Minister from the Republic, shall we be afterwards at liberty to say—"We will not decide whether there is a Government in France competent to demand from us the performance of the existing treaties. What the Government in France shall be is the very point *in dispute.* 'Till that is decided the *applicability* of the Treaties is suspended.[2] When that Government is *established* we shall consider whether such changes have been made as to render their continuance incompatible with the interest of the U States." If we shall not have concluded ourselves by any Act, I am of opinion, that we have at least a right to hold the thing suspended till the point in dispute is decided. I doubt whether we could *bona fide* dispute the ultimate obligation of the Treaties. Will the unqualified reception of a Minister conclude us?

If it will ought we so to conclude ourselves?

Ought we not rather to refuse receiving or to receive with qualification—declaring that we receive the person as the representative of the Government *in fact* of the French Nation reserving to ourselves a right to consider the applicability of the Treaties to the *actual situation* of the parties?

These are questions which require our utmost Wisdom. I would give a great deal for a personal discussion with you. *Imprudent things* have been already done; which renders it proportionably important that every succeeding step should be well considered.

With true attachment   Dr sir   Your obedt Ser   A Hamilton

ALS, Columbia University Libraries.

1. Edmond Charles Genet was appointed in November, 1792, to replace Jean Baptiste de Ternant as French Minister to the United States. Genet arrived in Charleston, South Carolina, on April 8, 1793.

2. A number of the provisions of the two 1778 American treaties with France complicated the diplomatic position of the United States after the outbreak of the European war in 1793. Most serious was Article 11 of the Treaty of Alliance, which provided that the "two Parties guarantee mutually from the present time and forever, against all other powers, to wit, the united states to his most Christian Majesty the present Possessions of the Crown of france in America as well as those which it may acquire by the future Treaty of peace: and his most Christian Majesty guarantees on his part to the united states, their liberty, Sovereignty, and Independence absolute, and unlimited, as well in Matters of Government as commerce and also thair Possessions, and the additions or conquests that their Confederation may obtain during the war, from any of the Dominions now or heretofore possessed by Great Britain in North America, conformable to the 5th. & 6th articles above written, the whole as their Possessions shall be fixed and assured to the said States at the moment of the cessation of their present War with England." Article 12 of the same treaty provided that the guarantee in Article 11 should take effect in the event of war between France and Great Britain (Miller, *Treaties*, II, 39-40).

In addition to this American guarantee of the French West Indies, the following articles of the Treaty of Amity and Commerce concerning the mutual rights and obligations of the two powers in time of war were considered most likely to affect the United States position in relation to other European nations: Articles 14 and 23 (originally Articles 16 and 25), by which the signatories subscribed to the rule of free ships–free goods, enemy ships–enemy goods; Article 17 (originally Article 19), which provided that "It shall be lawful for the Ships of War of either Party & Privateers freely to carry whithersoever they please the Ships and Goods taken from their Enemies, without being obliged to pay any Duty to the Officers of the Admiralty or any other Judges; nor shall such Prizes be arrested or Seized, when they come to and enter the Ports of either Party; nor shall the Searchers or other Officers of those Places search the same or make examination concerning the Lawfulness of such Prizes, but they may hoist Sail at any time and depart and carry their Prizes to the Places express'd in their Commissions, which the Commanders of such Ships of War shall be obliged to shew: On the contrary no Shelter or Refuge shall be given in their Ports to such as shall have made Prize of the Subjects, People or Property of either of the Parties; but if such shall come in, being forced by Stress of Weather or the Danger of the Sea, all proper means shall be vigorously used that they go out and retire from thence as soon as possible"; Article 19 (originally Article 21), which provided for the supply and reparation of ships forced into the ports of either power by disaster; Article 21 (originally Article 23), which provided that no subjects of either power should "apply for or take any Commission or Letters of marque for arming any Ship or Ships to act as Privateers" against the other, "And if any Person of either Nation shall take such Commissions or Letters of Marque he shall be punished as a Pirate"; Article 22 (originally Article 24), which provided that "It shall not be lawful for any foreign Privateers, not belonging to Subjects of the most Christian King nor Citizens of the said United States, who have Commissions from any other Prince or State in enmity with either Nation to fit their Ships in the Ports of either the one or the other of the aforesaid Parties, to sell what they have taken or in any other manner whatsoever to exchange their Ships, Merchandizes or any other lading; neither shall they be allowed even to purchase victuals except such as shall be necessary for their going to the next Port of that Prince or State from which they have Commissions"; Article 24 (originally Article 26), which defined contraband goods; and Article 25 (originally Article 27), which concerned the issuance of passports to ships of the signatory powers (Miller, *Treaties*, II, 12–24).

The Treaty of Amity and Commerce originally contained thirty-three articles but, as Hunter Miller points out, soon after 1779, "and certainly from 1781 on, the prints of the treaty omit Articles 11 and 12 [concerning a reciprocal commercial arrangement] from the text and renumber the articles following so that original Article 13 becomes 11, and so on; indeed the signed treaty has, in pencil, a marginal note to Articles 11 and 12, reading 'to be omitted, & the subsequent numbers changed accordingly.' . . . The congressional ratification of May 4, 1778, was complete and unconditional. The next day, however, Congress . . . expressed the desire that Articles 11 and 12 'be revoked and utterly expunged.' . . . While the American Commissioners were instructed accordingly, their formal authority was not at hand on July 17, 1778, and the ratifications then exchanged recited the entire treaty; although at that time the omission of the two articles received the verbal assent of Count de Vergennes. . . . Under date of September 1, 1778, Articles 11 and 12 were formally suppressed . . ." (Miller, *Treaties*, II, 32–33). References in documents written during the seventeen-nineties to specific articles of the Treaty of Amity and Commerce frequently reflect this confusion in numbering.

To John Jay

Philad April 9. 1793

My Dear Sir

I have already written you by this Post. A further Question occurs. Would not a proclamation prohibitting our citizens from taking Comns. &c on either side be proper?

Would it be well that it should include a declaration of Neutrality?

If you think the measure prudent could you draft such a thing as you would deem proper? I wish much you could.

Truly as Ever   A Hamilton

Chief Justice Jay

ALS, Columbia University Libraries.

From Thomas Jefferson

Philadelphia Apr. 9. 1793

Sir

Having received full authority from mr William Short to super-intend & controul the disposal of his property in the public funds,[1] I take the liberty of desiring that no property of his of that kind, whether standing in his own name or in that of mr James Brown [2] or any other person in trust for him may be permitted to be transferred or to [be] paid to any person whatever. I have the honor to be Sir

Your most obedt. humble servt   Th: Jefferson

The Secretary of the Treasury.

ALS, letterpress copy, Thomas Jefferson Papers, Library of Congress; copy, University of Virginia.
    1. In addition to serving as Jefferson's secretary in Paris during the seventeen-eighties, Short was a protégé and close friend of the Secretary of State.
    On at least two occasions in the spring of 1792 Jefferson wrote to Short that he was disturbed by the manner in which Short's public securities were being handled by Short's agent in the United States (Jefferson to Short, March 18, April 24, 1792, ALS, letterpress copies, Thomas Jefferson Papers, Library of Congress). On November 30, 1792, Short authorized Jefferson to supervise his financial interests in the United States (ALS, Thomas Jefferson Papers, Library of Congress).
    2. James Brown of Richmond, a merchant and stockbroker, was Short's business agent in the United States.

To _____

[Philadelphia, April 10, 1793]

Mr. Winstanlly [1] brought me a letter of Introduction from Chief Justice Jay; stating him to be a Young Gentleman from England, who, without having made it a profession, had made some promising essays in Landscape Painting.

There are two views of situations on Hudson's River painted by Mr Winstanly, in the drawing Room of Mrs. Washington, which have great intrinsic merit—and considered with reference to his opportunities, as related, announce a very superior genius in this branch of painting, worthy of encouragement.

A Hamilton

Philadelphia April 10. 1793

ALS, Mr. Hall Park McCullough, North Bennington, Vermont.

1. William Winstanley. Soon after the sale of his Hudson River landscapes to the President, Winstanley visited the area of the newly created Federal City to paint several landscapes of the Potomac which were also purchased by Washington. In 1795 he settled in New York City where he became a prominent portrait painter.

To William Bingham [1]

Treasury Department
April 10th. 1793

Gentlemen

The computed probable exigencies of the Treasury were my guide in asking of the Bank an accommodation to the extent of the sum applied for. Nor would any less sum leave me at perfect security against the possibility of embarrassment.

In this state of the business I shall hope that the Bank will endeavour to go the full length of my request. The Directors know my invariable attention to the due convenience of the Institution—and that in availing myself of the resource they may put within my power, I shall be careful to avoid as much as possible any obstruction to their necessary operations.

If in the progress of things, a less sum shall appear to be sufficient, I shall be glad to abrige my call, so as to accommodate to the views of the Directors.

With consideration & esteem   I have the honor to be   Gentlemen
Your Obedient servant   Alexander Hamilton

William Bingham Esqr
Chairman [2]

ALS, Historical Society of Pennsylvania, Philadelphia.
    1. This letter was written in reply to Bingham to H, April 9, 1793. For further
background to this letter, see H to George Washington, March 18, second
letter of March 20, 1793; Washington to H, March 20, 21, 1793; H to the
President and Directors of the Bank of the United States, March 26, 1793; H to
Rufus King, April 2, 1793.
    2. Bingham was chairman of a committee of the board of directors of the
Bank of the United States.

To Edward Carrington

[*Philadelphia, April 10, 1793.* On April 26, 1793, Carrington wrote
to Hamilton: "I am favored with your[s] of the 10th. Instant."
Letter not found.]

To Peter Colt

Philadelphia
April 10. 1793

Sir

    I have received two letters from you of the 28th. of Feby & the 27
of March—which the urgency of official avocations has prevented
my acknowleging sooner.

    I received five hundred Dollars from Mr. Duer, by an order upon
his Agent in the City [1] (whose name I at this moment forget) which
with the money received of Mr. Walker [2] is the whole that ever
came to my hands on account of the Society, and leaves me in advance all the difference between those two sums & my disbursements
for the Society:

    As soon as I can find leisure I will make out and render an exact
account. I should not be sorry however, if a provisional order was
made by the Directors, for paying such sum as should be found due
to me, as a reimbursement will be at this time convenient to me.

    The affairs of the Society would appear to require a termination
of Mr. Morts [3] salary. With regard to Mr. Hall [4] I think it will
depend on the evidence he may have given by this time of zeal for
the interests of the Society & capacity to promote them. If these
stand as might be wished I should imagine there would be objections
to a *temporary* reduction of his salary. It will however deserve consideration if under the prospects of the society, they can afford

permanently the salary intended for Mr. Hall and still more whether his conduct hitherto has been such as to justify the retaining of him in the employment of the Society.

I express myself thus—because I have heared suggestions of a delicate nature; and though I have no means of judging how far they may be founded and am always an advocate for careful & dispassionate examination before accusations are allowed to influence, yet there have been symptoms which impress me with an idea, that it will deserve serious investigation whether it be the interest of the Society to continue Mr. Hall.

Marshall[5] is an essential, and, I believe, a very deserving man. I think his salary ought to be increased.

Pearce[6] has valuable qualities & some ill ones. He is prone to new projects & will require a watchful eye on that score. Probably it may be good policy to secure him, till further experiment of his discretion and *real* skill, by an augmentation of Salary.

I have heard in different ways the proposed change in the plan, to which you refer. Perhaps I do not appreciate all the circumstances which ought to decide—But I acknowlege I feel a strong disapprobation of it. Perseverance in almost any plan is better than fickleness & fluctuation.

I wish these remarks to be considered as so far confidential that they may not be formally communicated to the Board but you are at liberty, if you think it of any use to make them known to such members of it as you may judge expedient.

With esteem I am Sir   Your Obed Se   A Hamilton

Peter Colt Esqr

ALS, The Passaic County Historical Society, Lambert Castle, Paterson, New Jersey.

1. William Duer's agent in Philadelphia was Francis Ingraham, a Philadelphia merchant. Duer had served as governor of the Society for Establishing Useful Manufactures until his business failure in 1792.

2. Benjamin Walker was a director of the Society for Establishing Useful Manufactures and served as the society's "Accomptant."

3. Joseph Mort.

4. William Hall.

5. Thomas Marshall.

6. William Pearce.

From Tench Coxe

Walnut Street [Philadelphia] Wednesday Evening
April 10th. 1793.

Sir,

Having completed the purchase of Lands lying in the State of Pennsylvania from sundry individuals, for the joint and equal account of John Barker Church[1] and myself, to the amount of the Sum of Ten Thousand Dollars, as originally proposed and agreed between us, I communicate to you an account of the Purchases. They are as follows

1st. Sixteen thousand acres of Land in the counties of Northampton and Luzerne, agreeably to a contract of the twelfth day of March past, between Blackall William Ball & Francis Joseph Smith, and myself.

2ly. Eight thousand acres of Land in the Counties of Northumberland & Luzerne agreeably to Contracts of the 30th March & 1st & 4th days of April between William Stedman and myself.

3ly. Twenty three thousand acres of land in the counties of Northampton and Luzerne, agreeably to a contract of the tenth day of April Instant, between Alexander and William Alexander Patterson & Daniel Stroud, and myself.

These Lands according to the best estimate I can form, will amount to about ten thousand dollars.

You will remember that I mentioned to you, that Four thousand acres, a part of the first parcel of 16,000 acres, was under an offer to a friend well known to you, and whose name shall be communicated. I daily expect his decision. Should he not elect to take the Lands within the course of the current month, they shall remain a part of the joint purchase for Mr Church and myself. Should he elect to take them, I shall endeavor to be prepared for securing another equivalent parcel.

I have the honor to be Sir Your most obedient Servant

Tench Coxe.

Memorandum of the lands referred to above and their presumed Costs according to the provisions of the contracts.

	Dolls.
16,000 Acres bought of Ball & Smith—expected to cost 22½d—or 25 Cents ⅌ acre—patented	4000
8000 Acres bought of William Stedman ditto 16⅞d or 18¾ Cents	
23,000 ditto bought of Pattersons & Stroud ditto	5812.50
31,000 Acres (16⅞ or 18¾ Cents)	
47,000 As. Total	
Expence of Inspection	300.00
	Dolls 10,112.50

One undivided moiety of the said 47,000 Acres purchased for and the property of John Barker Church Esqr. and the other the property of Tench Coxe—on account of the above Contract, there were paid to me by you five hundred dollars on the 9th day of April 1793, and five hundred dollars on the 10th day of April 1793.

Alexander Hamilton Esquire
Agent for John Barker Church Eqr. of London.

Copy, RG 21, Records of the United States Circuit Court for the Eastern District of Pennsylvania, Equity Records, Case Files, 1790–1911, National Archives.
  1. During the American Revolution John Barker Church had married Angelica Schuyler, Elizabeth Hamilton's sister. After the war Church returned to his home in England, and H handled his American business affairs.
  The early transactions for the partnership which Church and Coxe formed for the purchase of Pennsylvania lands are described in a statement which Coxe made under oath on April 22, 1799. According to this statement, Coxe conferred several times during March, 1793, with H as agent and attorney in fact for Church. H first spoke of investing ten thousand pounds sterling in the purchase of Pennsylvania lands, but later the amount was reduced to ten thousand dollars. Coxe agreed that H should furnish the money between March and September, 1793. On his part Coxe would purchase the lands without an agent's fee and would repay Church one half of the original amount with interest after an unspecified date. H advanced the full amount during 1793 (D, signed by Coxe, RG 21, Records of the United States Circuit Court for the Eastern District of Pennsylvania, Equity Records, Case Files, 1790–1911, National Archives).

From Stephen Higginson [1]

Boston Apr. 10. 1793

Dr Sir
  France having declared War against Britain &c, Questions may arise tending to involve us in their disputes. I know indeed that

attempts will be made to procure Aid to France from us, on the grounds of policy interest & obligations from Treaties &c. Such an attempt may be made through the medium of our Legislature in their May Sessions; & very sound Assertions will be made which may not be easily refuted without more information than I find any one here at present possesses.

Are there any Articles existing between us & France involving such an Obligation beside the 11 & 12 in the Treaty of Alliance? [2] —Have those Articles been in part or wholly done away since the Treaty was made & how? Do general guarrantys like that in those articles, without any provision for specific Aid, imply or involve any obligations to give Aid? If there be no political or moral obligation on us to take a part, it is a pity We should not know it, & be able to convince every one of it.

Your Situation must have led you to examine those Questions; & if there will be no impropriety in doing it, I should request you to give me some information on this Subject. It is important I think to prevent any general impressions, which may lead to a popular call to become Parties in European quarrels & I wish to know the true State of things, so as to meet assertions with facts, & to form Sentiments upon them.

You will excuse this application if it has any appearance of impropriety in your mind, & will comply with the request so far only as may appear proper.

If the Executive could by proclamation inform the public on this Subject it would do great good, or prevent much mischief. Will not the Citizens be prohibited from taking any part under cover or openly? Some of our old adventurers in privateering who are again reduced will require a tight Rein to prevent them.

I am with respect Sir your hum Servant   Stephen Higginson

ALS, Hamilton Papers, Library of Congress.

1. Higginson was a Boston merchant whose business interests included an extensive foreign trade.

2. See H to John Jay, first letter of April 9, 1793, note 2.

To Thomas Willing [1]

[Philadelphia, April 10–May 31, 1793]

DSir

You will receive with this the Draft of an agreement for the loan heretofore arranged [2]—which if approved I request may be made out into duplicates *indented* so as to correspond with each other.

You will observe an option to the UStates as to the *time of receiving.* I understood that this would not be agreeable; but as it has not been formaly objected to it is proper for me to insert it. Should it appear objectionable, it may be struck out—but in this case I shall wish for my justification a line expressive of the objection. I understood it to be that it was not deemed consistent with a due regard to the interest of the Bank to leave the periods of receiving the interest of the money optional as the Bank must in such case hold funds on hand ready to be advanced for an unknown & indefinite term for which it would receive no consideration.

With respect & esteem   I am Dr sir   Your obed ser

A. Hamilton

It is proper the instrument should be executed to day.

Thomas Willing Esq

ADfS, anonymous donor.
    1. For background to this letter, see H to George Washington, March 18, second letter of March 20, 1793; Washington to H, March 20, 21, 1793; H to the President and Directors of the Bank of the United States, March 26, 1793; H to Rufus King, April 2, 1793; William Bingham to H, April 9, 1793; H to Bingham, April 10, 1793.
    2. The draft has not been found. For the final agreement between H and the Bank of the United States, see "Agreement with the President, Directors, and Company of the Bank of the United States," May 31, 1793.

From John Jay

New York 11 ap. 1793

Dr Sir

Your Letters of the 9th. Inst. were this Day delivered to me, as I was preparing to go out of town. The Subject of them is important.

ALS, Hamilton Papers, Library of Congress.

I have not Time to judge decidedly on some of the points. The enclosed will shew what my present Ideas of a proclamation are—it is hastily drawn—it says nothing of Treaties—it speaks of neutrality, but avoids the Expression because in this country often associated with others. I shall be at Pha. in my way to Richmond. I think it better at present that too little shd. be said, than too much. I wd. not recieve any Minister from a Regent untill he was Regent *de facto;* and therefore I think such Intention shd. be inferable from the proclamn. Let us do every thing that may be right to avoid war; and if without our Fault we shd. be involved in it, there will be little Room for apprehensions about the Issue. It is happy for us that we have Presid. who will do nothing rashly—and who regards his own Interest as inseparable from the public good.

Yours sincerely   John Jay

Col. Hamilton

[ENCLOSURE]1

By George Washington President of the U. S. of am⟨erica⟩
a Proclamation.

Whereas every nation has a right to change and modify their constitution and Govt., in such manner as they may think most

1. D, in the handwriting of John Jay, Hamilton Papers, Library of Congress.

This document should be compared with a somewhat different version printed in Henry P. Johnston, ed., *The Correspondence and Public Papers of John Jay* (New York, 1891), III, 474–77, and with the proclamation drafted by Edmund Randolph and issued by Washington on April 22, 1793. Washington's proclamation reads as follows:

"Whereas it appears that a state of war exists between Austria, Prussia, Sardinia, Great Britain, and the United Netherlands, of the one part, and France on the other; and the duty and interest of the United States require, that they should with sincerity and good faith adopt and pursue a conduct friendly and impartial towards the belligerent Powers:

"I have therefore thought fit by these presents to declare the disposition of the United States to observe the conduct aforesaid towards those Powers respectively; and to exhort and warn the citizens of the United States carefully to avoid all acts and proceedings whatsoever, which may in any manner tend to contravene such disposition.

"And I hereby also make known, that whosoever of the citizens of the United States shall render himself liable to punishment or forfeiture under the law of nations, by committing, aiding, or abetting hostilities against any of the said Powers, or by carrying to any of them those articles which are deemed contraband by the *modern* usage of nations, will not receive the protection of the United States, against such punishment or forfeiture; and further, that I have

c⟨onducive⟩ to their welfare and Happiness. And Whereas they who a⟨ctually⟩ administer the governmt. of any nation, are by foreign nations ⟨to⟩ be regarded as its *lawful Rulers*, so long as they continue to b⟨e⟩ recognized and obeyed *as such*. by the great Body of their ⟨people.⟩

And Whereas monarchy has been in fact abolished in Fra⟨nce, and⟩ a Government, recognized and obeyed by the great Body of the ⟨people⟩ does there *actually* exist and operate; it is proper as well a⟨s⟩ necessary that the political Intercourse between that nation & ⟨this⟩ should be conducted thro the medium of that government wh⟨en⟩ it shall so continue to be recognized and obeyed.

Altho the misfortunes (to whatever Cause they may be impute⟨d⟩ which the late King of France and others have suffered in the Co⟨urse⟩ of that Revolution or which that nation may yet experience are to be regretted by the friends of Hum⟨anity,⟩ and particularly by the People of america, to whom both th⟨e king⟩ and that Nation have done essential Services; yet it is no less ⟨the⟩ Duty than the Interest of the United States, strictly to observe th⟨at⟩ conduct towards all nations, which the Laws of nations prescr⟨ibe.⟩

And whereas war actually exists between France on the one ⟨side⟩ and Austria Prussia Great Britain and the united Netherlands, on ⟨the⟩ other; and to avoid being involved in that Calamity, it is necessar⟨y⟩ that the United States should by a conduct perfectly inoffensiv⟨e⟩ cultivate and preserve the Peace they now enjoy; with a firm Determination nevertheless, always to prefer War to Inj⟨ustice⟩ and Disgrace.

I do therefore most earnestly advise and require the Ci⟨tizens of⟩ the United States to be circumspect in their conduct towards all nations ⟨and⟩ particularly towards those now at war—to demean themselves ⟨in every⟩ Respect in the manner becoming a nation at Peace with all the wor⟨ld, and to⟩ unite in rendering thanks to almighty God for the peace & Prosperity ⟨that under a⟩ beneficent Providence we enjoy, and in devotely entreatin⟨g Him⟩ to continue to us these invaluable Blessings.

I do also recommend to my fellow Citizens in general, that ⟨to

---

given instructions to those officers, to whom it belongs, to cause prosecutions to be instituted against all persons, who shall, within the cognizance of the courts of the United States, violate the law of nations, with respect to the Powers at war, or any of them." (*ASP, Foreign Relations*, I, 140.)

omit⟩ such public Discussions of certain questions foreign to us, as mus⟨t⟩ tend not only to cause Divisions and Parties among ourselves, and ⟨thereby⟩ impair that union on which our Strength depends, but also giv⟨e unnecessary⟩ cause of offence and Irritation to foreign powers. And I can⟨not forbear⟩ expressing a wish, that our Printers may study to be impartial ⟨in the⟩ Representation of Facts, and observe much Prudence relative t⟨o such⟩ Strictures and animadversions as may render the Disposition of foreign governments & Rulers, unfriendly to the People of the uni⟨ted States.⟩

I do expressly require that the Citizens of the U. S. do abs⟨tain from⟩ acting hostilely against any of the belligerent powers, under Co⟨mmissions⟩ from either of them. Such Conduct would tend to provoke Hos⟨tilities⟩ against their Country, and be in every Respect highly reprehens⟨ible,⟩ for while the people of all other States abstain from doing Injury ⟨to any⟩ of our People, it would be unjust and wicked in any of our People ⟨to do⟩ Injuries to them.

I do also enjoin all Magistrates and others in authority to be watchful and diligent in preventing aggressions against foreign nati⟨ons⟩ and their people; and to cause all offenders to be prosecuted & pun⟨ished⟩ in an Exemplary manner.

From Gouverneur Morris

Paris 11 April 1793.

Dear Sir

In mine of the sixteenth of February I mentioned to you the Case of Colo. Laumoy and that I would write in Answer to his Applications that I am not authoriz'd to make payment but on Production of the Certificate. I do not know how I came to misunderstand you so egregiously as I find upon reading over your Letter [1] to have been the Case. In the present State of the Business however I think it will be as well to adhere to the line adopted because the Communication between this and other Countries being interrupted a power of Attorney falling into bad Hands might be used to defraud the Party: and further it is decreed long since by the Convention that those who remit to Emigrants shall be punished with Death so that the Bankers and Agents of every Kind are either afraid to act or else disposed to betray their Trust. Wherefore it is more simple that such as are under this disagreable Predicament, should receive their Whole Demand in America. That being the only Way to avoid very disagreable questions. Genl. Koskiusko was here some Time ago and not having his Certificate did not receive his Interest, but I desired Messrs. Grand [2] to Enquire after him and pay him if he still be in France.[3]

LC, Gouverneur Morris Papers, Library of Congress.
  1. Morris is apparently referring to H's letter to him of September 13, 1792, which contained a description of the procedures to be followed for the payment of both the principal and the interest of the debt owed to foreign officers who had served in the American Revolution.
  2. The Paris banking house of Ferdinand Le Grand.
  3. See Thomas Jefferson to H, October 31, 1792, note 26.

To George Washington

Treasury Department, April 11, 1793. Encloses "a communication of the 9 instant from the Commissioner of the Revenue,[1] this morning received, transmitting a Contract with Abishai Woodward [2] as Superintendant of the workmen to be employed in completing the Lighthouse at Bald-Head." [3] Recommends that the contract be approved.

LC, George Washington Papers, Library of Congress.
  1. Letter from Tench Coxe not found.
  2. Woodward was a carpenter in New London, Connecticut.
  3. See Coxe to H, March 22, 1793.

From Charles Lee

Alexandria [Virginia] 12th. April, 1793

Sir!

Having resigned the Office of Collector, at the District of Alexandria, my successor who I have heard is to be John Fitzgerald, will to-morrow commence his official duties. To him, I have supposed myself bound to pay the balance of public monies and of public bonds due from me at this time, and his receipt I shall transmit to the Comptroller, that he may be debited with the amount. To him also I shall deliver all the laws and instructions heretofore received from the Treasury Department, and in his hands I shall leave all the Books containing any matters of public account. Wishing to be finally discharged from all the demands of the United States against me, I shall send on my accounts ending with the last quarter, and from that to the present time, and I hope they will upon examination be found to be correct, and that I shall soon receive an acquittance.

There were some prosecutions commenced by my orders against offenders of the Revenue Laws, and the costs in some instances, will be and are payable out of the public money, but not being demanded they remain unpaid. I wish you to make some arrangements for paying whatever sums of money would have been payable on account of prosecutions before mentioned by me as Collector, if I had continued in Office.

I shall be thankful to you if you will transmit to me your directions respecting the paying and delivering to my successor, the various matters herein before mentioned, in order that I may conduct myself in a manner agreeable to you, and safe to myself.

I am Sir!   with the most respectful considerations   Your Obedt. Humble Servant   Charles Lee, Collector

Copy, RG 56, Letters to and from the Collector at Alexandria, National Archives.

From Henry Lee

In Council [Richmond] April 12th. 1793.

Sir,

I had the honor to receive your letter of the 22d. Ultimo and submitted the same to the Council of State.

In conformity with their advice, I have given directions to the proper officer of this Commonwealth to Supply the loan officer of the United States [1] with the information requested.

Some doubts arise with respect to the propriety of the measure adopted, but our Solicitude to prevent any interruption to the laws of the United States and a thorough confidence in your declaration of rectifying when required any inconveniencies which may result from our decision should the construction of the law under which you act be found erroneous produced a compliance with your request.

To understand unequivocally the law on the case, I beg leave to propose to you, that the matter be brought before the Supreme judiciary of the United States at their next term, and hope you will favour me with your reply to this proposition. I have the honor &c.

Henry Lee

LC, Archives Division, Virginia State Library, Richmond.
1. John Hopkins was commissioner of loans for Virginia.

From Gouverneur Morris

Paris 12. April 1793.

Dear Sir

I wrote to you Yesterday and mentioned the affair of General Laumoy. A View of that Gentlemans very disagreable Situation and the sincere Desire of releiving him from it have suggested to my Mind an Expedient and I have in Consequence written the Letter to our Bankers in Amsterdam of which a Copy is enclosed and by which he will be I hope enabled to receive his Due. For his Capital however he must be indebted to your kind Interposition.

[ENCLOSURE]

Gouverneur Morris to Wilhem and Jan Willink, Nicholaas and Jacob Van Staphorst, and Nicholas Hubbard [1]

Paris 12. April 1793.

Gentlemen

I expect that this Letter will be delivered to you by Major General Laumoy who will produce to you some others which I have formerly written so as to certify to you that there is no mistake as to the Person. My last to him was of the sixteenth of February mentioning the Necessity of an Application in America for the Object a part of which it is my Intention to effectuate by this Letter. Be pleased therefore Gentlemen to pay to General Laumoy the Sum of five thousand nine hundred and ninety seven florins banco and pass the same to account of the Sum plac'd at my Disposition by Mr. Short. Take triplicate Receipts and forward two of them to me.

LC, Gouverneur Morris Papers, Library of Congress.
1. LC, Gouverneur Morris Papers, Library of Congress.

Treasury Department Circular
to the Collectors of the Customs

Treasury Department, April 12, 1793.

Sir,

The Collectors stand charged with the sealed blank Certificates of Registry which have been furnished from this Department under the act, entitled, "An act for registering and clearing of Vessels, regulating the coasting Trade, and for other purposes." [1]

It will therefore be proper that all such blank Certificates as may have remained on hand after the last day of March past (the time when the operation of the act, entitled, "An act concerning the Registering and Recording of Ships or Vessels" commenced) [2] be forthwith returned to the Register of the Treasury; accompanied with an account, agreeably to the annexed form, shewing the number of Registers which have been received by you from the Treasury, and the number issued and returned.

With consideration, I am,   Sir, your obedient Servant,

A Hamilton

LS, Office of the Secretary, United States Treasury Department; L[S], RG 36, Collector of Customs at Boston, Letters from the Treasury and Others, 1789–1809, Vol. 1, National Archives; LC, RG 56, Circulars of the Office of the Secretary, "Set T," National Archives; LC, United States Finance Miscellany, Treasury Circulars, Library of Congress.

1. 1 *Stat.* 55–65 (September 1, 1789).
2. 1 *Stat.* 287–99 (December 31, 1792).

From George Washington

Mount Vernon 12 April 1793.

Dear sir,

In due course of Post I have received your Letters of the 5 and 8 instant. & thank you for the information contained in them.

Tomorrow I leave this for Philadelphia. The advices which I may receive this Evening by the Post, will fix my route by Baltimore (as usual)—or by the one I intended to have come—that is, by Reading, the Canals between the rivers, Harrisburgh, Carlisle &c. In either case ten days, I expect, will land me in the City.

Hostilities having commenced between France & England, it is incumbent on the Government of the United States to prevent, as far as in it lies, all interferences of our Citizens in them; and immediate precautionary measures ought, I conceive, to be taken for that purpose, as I have reason to believe (from some things I have heard) that many vessels in different parts of the Union are designated for Privateers & are preparing accordingly. The means to prevent it, and for the United States to maintain a strict neutrality between the powers at war, I wish to have seriously thought of, that I may, as soon as I arrive at the Seat of the Government, take such steps, tending to these ends, as shall be deemed proper & effectual.

With great esteem, I am &c. Geo: Washington

LC, George Washington Papers, Library of Congress.

To John Davidson [1]

Treasury Department, April 13, 1793. ". . . I shall regret your final determination to resign at the same time, that I should be wanting in candour were I to hold out to you the probability of any material increase of your present official emoluments. Yet it is expected that the subject of compensations at large will engage the consideration of the Legislature at their next session, and it is impossible to forsee what alterations they may make. Should you persevere in your intention to resign it will be proper for you to communicate it to the President & at the same time to transmit your Commission to him."

Copy, RG 56, Letters to and from the Collectors at Bridgetown and Annapolis, National Archives; LC, RG 56, Letters to Collectors at Small Ports, "Set G," National Archives.
1. Davidson was collector of customs and inspector of the port of Annapolis.

From Alexander Macomb [1]

New york April 13th. 1793

Dear sir

I take the Liberty of enclosing you an order of Mr Udney Hay to receive the Sum allowed to Mr. Simon Frazer of Quebec upon Mr Hay's petition in his behalf [2] which I learn is 400 Ds. and I will take kind your forwarding it to me as soon as possible, as an opportunity for Quebec offers in the course of the ensuing week, to which place I wish to Remit it.

I have just rec'd a Letter dated 27 feby from Mr Robert Hamilton [3] of Niagara, wherein he mentions that Genl. Hull [4] is in very good winter quarters at Mr Stedmans [5] & that he will esteem himself happy if he can by any means aid in his negotiation or add to his comforts. If my services can in any wise be essential to you in the business of the treaty, you may freely command them.

I remain very respectfully   Dr. Sir   Yr. obt Servant

Alex Macomb

ALS, Hamilton Papers, Library of Congress.

1. Macomb, a native of Ireland, had engaged in trade with the Indians in the American West during the American Revolution and was a partner in the Detroit firm of Macomb, Edgar, and Macomb, which supplied the British Indian Department. After the Revolution he settled in New York where he became a leading land speculator.

2. See "Report on the Petition of Udny Hay," November 21, 1792.

3. Robert Hamilton and Richard Cartwright operated a trading station at Niagara. Hamilton held several official positions and was one of Canada's wealthiest men.

4. For an account of William Hull's mission to Canada, see H to George Hammond, December 29, 1792; "Draft of Instructions for William Hull," January 14, 1793; H to William Edgar, January 17, 1793; Hull to H, February 6, 1793.

5. John Stedman was a trader at Fort Schlosser on the Niagara River.

From Joseph Whipple [1]

Portsmouth [*New Hampshire*] *April 13, 1793.* Writes concerning "a Small Seizure in this district of one bag of Cocoa and four bags of Coffee." Discusses the details of the case. Asks for "instructions on this matter."

LC, RG 36, Collector of Customs at Portsmouth, Letters Sent, 1792–1793, Vol. 4, National Archives; copy, RG 56, Letters from the Collector at Portsmouth, National Archives.

1. Whipple was collector of customs at Portsmouth, New Hampshire.

From James McHenry [1]

Fayetteville near Baltimore 14 April 1793

My dear Hamilton

Though exceedingly mortified and hurt at Mr. Perry's being refused that inspectorship I did not once think of blaming you. I ascribed it to the peculiarity of your situation and the enmity of those who were near you, originating in the part that gentleman had taken against them. The Tilghmans I believe influenced Coxe. Coxe made the thing an object and you had those of greater magnitude to attend, till it was too late to counteract your assistant. I perceive he understands his business, or rather the intrigues of a court. He appears to present Eccleston as the most intitled; all the recommendations run hig[h]est for Eccleston, and yet Richardson, who was then treasurer of the Eastern shore is appointed inspector; which some how or other fell in with the views of the Tilghmans much better than Ecclestons appointment, and short of the wishes of Henry and Murry. It is true as I have mentioned before to you Mr. Richardson is a very worthy man and very deserving of the office, but not more worthy and less active than Perry as far as I have been able to investigate character.

I know not what to say to Perry when I may see him. I cannot tell him what you have told me; and from the impressions made against him I cannot flatter him with being remembered in future. What impressions the disappointment may excite and how they may issue is impossible to foresee. However as I shall not see him soon I shall have time for meditation.[2]

I did not forget you during the late storm,[3] and had the pleasure to find that the merchantile interest in Baltimore entertained corresponding opinions. Perhaps you may contrive to visit me sometime in the summer, should the President return again to his seat and you should have any business with him to cover a journey.

Our people wish to be able to carry our produce freely to all the parties at war who may want it, without having any thing further to do with the war.

Yours affectionately & truly   James McHenry

I cannot get the whole of your communications to Congress during the late session. If convenient I beg you will send them.

ALS, Hamilton Papers, Library of Congress.

1. For background to this letter, see McHenry to H, November 18, 1792; H to McHenry, April 5, 1793.

2. On the back of H's letter to McHenry, April 5, 1793, McHenry wrote the following undated note to William Perry: "I have had a communication upon a recent subject. Mr. [George] Gale actually gave you the preference in his recommendation and the head of the treasury handed in your name to the President under circumstances which did not seem to leave a doubt as to your

appointment. The intrigues against you began then to appear. Delay was proposed till further information could be obtained and it was supposed was acquiesced in: but it so happened notwithstanding, that before my letter Mr Gales letter or any other letter arrived the nomination was made to the Senate. You see I cannot be particular. One day I may be so. In the mean while rest assured that every thing was done by my little friend, and that his regret and disappointment was not less than mine. 'Patience and shuffle the cards'" (AL, The Huntington Library, San Marino, California).

3. See the introductory note to "Report on the Balance of All Unapplied Revenues at the End of the Year 1792 and on All Unapplied Monies Which May Have Been Obtained by the Several Loans Authorized by Law," February 4, 1793.

From Henry Knox

[*Philadelphia, April 15, 1793.* On April 18, 1793, Hamilton wrote to Knox: "The requests contained in your letter of the 15 of April have been complied with." *Letter not found.*]

To Nicholas Low [1]

[Philadelphia, April 15, 1793]

My Dear Sir

I send you the inclosed rather because I promised you I would think of the subject than because I expect that the result of so little thinking on my part in a case in which I know much more serious reflection will have been bestowed. Take it however for so much as it may be worth.

I have many reasons to think that Hall & Mort may be parted with without inconvenience to the Society. I doubted whether either have its interests at all at heart. Yet latter circumstances will enable you better to judge than I can.

Marshall I believe is essential to you; and I think it is proper and necessary to secure him by a better salary.

It is some time since I have been led to doubt whether Pearce has not given himself for much more than he is worth. He is unsteady, & I fear incapable of being kept within any bounds of order or œconomy. I believe it will not be difficult to have all the realy useful Machines he can make made by others. Yet he is ingenious & inventive—And ought not precipitably to be dismissed. What I here say is only to intimate my opinion that he may be spared and that the Society ought not to receive the law from him.

Perkinson [2] was engaged experimentally. If any competent utility does not appear to attend his stay there is nothing to hinder his being sent away. It will be well however to see his articles.

Tell Mr. Colt I shall shortly write to him. The chief part of the money advanced by me for the Society was my own. Except what I had of Mr. Walker, I do not recollect to have received more than four or 500 Dollars which was paid me in this City upon Duers order by Mr. Ingraham.[3]

Truly & with much esteem   Yrs   A Hamilton

April 15th. 1793

There is a Mr. Taylor a man of whom I have had a good character a Calli[c]oe Printer who has been some time in the Country—& has carried on the business—who offers himself to the Society as a Director of the Branch.[4]

I am informed he has executed some good work.

This letter is not intended for formal communication to the Board. Tis for yourself.

ALS, Columbia University Libraries.
    1. For background to this letter, see Low to H, March 4, 1793; Peter Colt to H, February 28, March 27, 1793; H to Colt, April 10, 1793; Elisha Boudinot to H, March 26, 1793.
    2. George Parkinson. See Colt to H, February 28, 1793.
    3. See Colt to H, February 28, March 27, 1793; H to Colt, April 10, 1793.
    4. An entry in the minutes of the board of directors of the Society for Establishing Useful Manufactures for November 5, 1793, reads as follows: "A Letter from Mr Robert Taylor of Philadelphia to Peter Colt, respecting employment as a Callicoe Printer was read—on which Resolved, that the Society cannot in the present State of their affairs engage with him in the printing business" ("Minutes of the S.U.M.," 91).

To the President and Directors of the Bank of New York

[*Philadelphia, April 15, 1793*.[1] The catalogue description of this letter reads: "Notifying them that the bank's notes would not be received by port collectors." *Letter not found.*]

LS, sold by Swann Galleries, February 26, 1943, Lot 42.
    1. This letter may be incorrectly dated in the dealer's catalogue, for in "Treasury Department Circular to the Collectors of the Customs," February 21, 1792, H had instructed the collectors not to accept the notes of the Bank of New York and the Bank of North America. See also William Seton to H, June 25, 1793.

From Jeremiah Olney [1]

Custom-House
District of Providence 15th. April 1793

Sir

I have the Honour to acquaint you that the Suit commenced against me by Mr. Edward Dexter in the Case of the Brigantine Neptune, was taken up and argued before the Superior Court in this Town on Saturday afternoon the 13th Instant and continued untill 9 o'Clock in the Evening, when Mr. Howell [2] Counsel for the Plaintiff moved for an adjournment of the Cause untill the next Term to be held here in September, assigning for reason that he was much fatigued and should not be able to close the cause that evening! But to avoid a delay calculated to give them an advantage (by an expected and probable change of the Court in May next) I proposed that the cause should be removed to the County of Kent, and the pleadings closed before the same Court which meets there in course on the 22d. Instant, which was objected to by my opponents, but the Court adopted my proposition.

Judgment was not given in the Case of Mr. Arnold, as that of Mr. Dexters being Similar; the Court deemed it expedient to defer their Opinion untill the Pleas of the latter were closed at Kent when both would be decided upon, and I have no doubt of a favorable Issue. The District Attorney [3] has Promised me (after the rising of the Court at Kent) he will give you a particular Statement of the principles on which these Causes have been conducted and Decided upon, this I presume will prove satisfactory to you.

I have the Honor to be very Respectfully Sir Your Most Obedt. Hume. Servt.   Jereh. Olney Collr.

Alexander Hamilton Esqr.
Secretary of the Treasury

LS, Rhode Island Historical Society, Providence.

1. For background to this letter, see William Ellery to H, September 4, October 9, 1792; Olney to H, September 8, 13, October 4, 25, November 7, 28, December 10, 13, 27, 1792, March 14, 25, 1793; H to Olney, September 19, 24, October 12, November 27, 1792.

2. Presumably David Howell, a prominent Providence attorney who had served in the Continental Congress from 1782 to 1785 and had been attorney general of Rhode Island in 1789.

3. William Channing was United States attorney for the District of Rhode Island.

From Isaac Holmes

[*Charleston, South Carolina, April 16, 1793.* On May 10, 1793, Hamilton wrote to Edmund Randolph and referred to a letter "of the 16th of April from the Collector of the District of Charlestown." *Letter not found.*]

To John Kean [1]

[Philadelphia] April 17. 1793

D Sir

A warrant lately issued for money for the Quarter Master's department 40000 Dollars which Mr. Hodgsdon [2] will receive by a Check from the Treasurer as usual. He is instructed to receive & forward the money in *Post Notes of the Bank.* I mention this that in case contrary to instruction, he may call for specie, you may be able to state your knowlege of the arrangement & refer it to me. I have some suspicions that sometimes the intention of the Department in this particular has not been strictly pursued.

Yrs.   A Hamilton

ALS, New-York Historical Society, New York City.
  1. Kean was cashier of the Bank of the United States.
  2. Samuel Hodgdon.

To Nathaniel Appleton

[*Philadelphia, April 18, 1793.* Letter listed in dealer's catalogue. *Letter not found.*]

LS, sold by Birchs's Sons, March, 1893, Lot 1627.

From Tench Coxe

[*Philadelphia, April 18, 1793.* On May 22, 1793, Hamilton wrote to George Washington: "The Secretary of the Treasury has the honor to transmit to the President of the UStates a communication of the 18 of April, from the Commissioner of the Revenue." *Letter not found.*]

From Samuel Hodgdon

[*Philadelphia, April 18, 1793.* On April 20, 1793, Hamilton wrote to Hodgdon and referred to "your letter of the 18 inst." *Letter not found.*]

To Henry Knox

Treasury Department
April 18. 1793

Sir

The requests contained in your letter of the 15 of April have been complied with.[1]

There are two points arising out of the Estimate of the Qr. Master General,[2] which you transmitted, to which I beg leave to call your attention.

One Item of Expenditure in the estimate is 450 Pack-Horses. It has been noticed to me by the Accounting Officers of the Treasury, that there appear to have been already expended in the purchase of this article a large sum by the present Qr. Master's Department. And it is recollected that a very considerable number of horses were purchased and paid for, for the use of the Campaign under General St Clair,[3] a great part of which survived the Campaign and it is understood were put out to be recruited for future service.

This renders it desireable that Inquiry should be made what ultimately became of those horses—what are the calculations of the quantity of transportation for which so extensive a provision of pack-horses is intended?

I submit also to your consideration whether under the prospects of the Campaign the provision need be made at once to the extent contemplated or may be made successively, so always as to be in measure for ulterior operations. The maintenance of a superfluous number of Packhorses, when not required for service, has an objectionable side on the score of expence. Whether the procuring them much sooner than they will be wanted may not have other inconveniences is for you to determine.

In making these suggestions, I certainly do not mean to throw any impediment in the way of timely preparation. This is a primary idea.

But if expence can be saved by a delay in providing not injurious, it is of course to be desired.

Another item in the estimate of the Qr. Master General is 12000 Dollars for *pay* of his Department to the 1st of July.

This sum appears considerable especially as seperate sums are estimated for Horse Masters Waggon Masters and Drivers. No light on this head can be obtained from any accounts heretofore rendered at the Treasury. I understood you that none was possessed by your department.

Hence the necessity of an inquiry into the circumstances.

With respect & esteem I have the honor to be Sir Your Obedt serv

The Secretary at War

ADf, Connecticut Historical Society, Hartford.
    1. Letter not found. H had acquired the responsibility for "all purchases and contracts for supplying the army with provisions, clothing, supplies in the quartermaster's department, military stores, Indian goods, and all other supplies or articles for the use of the department of war" in 1792 when these functions had been removed from the War Department and lodged in the Treasury Department under the terms of "An Act making alterations in the Treasury and War Departments" (1 *Stat.* 279–81 [May 8, 1792]). See also H to George Washington, August 10, 1792.
    2. James O'Hara had replaced Samuel Hodgdon as quartermaster general of the Army in April, 1792. O'Hara and his deputy quartermaster general, John Belli, were engaged in supplying provisions to the troops at Pittsburgh and at the forts along the Ohio and Great Miami rivers.
    3. After the defeat of Major General Arthur St. Clair by the Indians in November, 1791, plans had been made for a new campaign against the western tribes. "An Act for making farther and more effectual Provision for the Protection of the Frontiers of the United States" (1 *Stat.* 241–43 [March 5, 1792]) had increased the forces on the frontier and provided for a virtual reorganization of the Army. In April, 1792, Major General Anthony Wayne was appointed commanding officer to superintend the reorganization and training of the Army in preparation for a new Indian campaign. Although Indian attacks continued on the frontier during 1792, the campaign was delayed awaiting the outcome of peace negotiations with the Indians at a proposed conference in the summer of 1793. See George Washington to H, February 17, 1793; "Conversation with George Hammond," November 22, December 15–28, 1792; H to Hammond, December 29, 1792; "Cabinet Meeting. Opinion Respecting the Proposed Treaty with the Indians Northwest of the Ohio," February 25, 1793.

From Tobias Lear

[Philadelphia] April 18th: 1793

T. Lear has the honor to return to the Secretary of the Treasury the Contract made with Abijah Woodward [1] to superintend the building of the Light-House on Bald Head, which is approved of by the President. T. L. has likewise enclosed a memorandum of such letters &c. as are in the possession of the President relative to loans &c agreeably to the wish of the Secretary.[2]

AL, Hamilton Papers, Library of Congress.
    1. Abishai Woodward. See H to George Washington, April 11, 1793.
    2. AD, Hamilton Papers, Library of Congress. This enclosure lists the dates and contents of forty-five letters exchanged by H, Washington, and Lear between March 29, 1790, and March 25, 1793.

From Jeremiah Olney

Custom House
District of Providence 18th April 1793.

Sir

I have been honored with your Letter of 2nd. Instant on the Subject of Exportation permits;[1] from the Tenor of which it appears, that your construction of the law is similar to mine;[2] and that the want of more full information has led you to conceive my practice to be erroneous. To form, therefore, a right judgement of the Case, it is Necessary you should know, that for lading of Merchandize (other than Fish and provisions) for Exportation never more than *one* permit is given, because the whole are always contained in *one* Notice; but the practice in this district is very different in regard to Fish and Provisions: The Merchant rarely has by him the whole Quantity of those articles which he means to Export in any one vessel; but wishing to forward the Lading, without waiting for the arrival of, or an opportunity to *purchase*, the remainder, he applies at the Office, notices the Quantity on hand, and demands A permit to take it on Board; I then "cause an Inspection to be had, and if the Number of Barrels of each corresponds with the Notice, the Permit is granted and they are seen on Board by an Inspector."[3] In a few days perhaps, or, which is as common, a Fortnight, the exporter obtains another Quantity, again applies, gives notice thereof, and, after the same precaution is taken as before, another Permit is granted. Tho' this in a very few instances has been repeated from Three to six times in Loading one Vessel, yet Twice is scarcely every exceeded. This practice appears to me to be perfectly Consistant with the Law, and I think agrees with your conception of it, for "only *one* permit is granted for one notice given by *one* Exporter, whether an Individual or a Copartnership." If however, either, by a modification of the Law, or Instructions from the Treasury, I could be warranted in adopting a mode more convenient and less expensive to the Exporter, believe me, Sir, I would do it with Pleasure.

I have the Honor to be &c.   Jereh. Olney Collr.

Alexander Hamilton Esqr.
Secretary of the Treasury

ALS, Rhode Island Historical Society, Providence; ADfS, Rhode Island Historical Society. The draft differs slightly in wording from the ALS.
    1. On April 2, 1793, H wrote to Olney both a private and an official letter. The official letter has not been found.
    2. In his official letter to Olney of April 2 H apparently referred to "An Act to provide more effectually for the collection of the duties imposed by law on goods, wares and merchandise imported into the United States, and on the tonnage of ships or vessels" (1 *Stat.* 145–78 [August 4, 1790]).
    3. Section 58 of "An Act to provide more effectually for the collection of the duties imposed by law on goods, wares and merchandise imported into the United States, and on the tonnage of ships or vessels" reads in part as follows: "And in respect to the said dried and pickled fish and salted provisions, proof shall be made to the satisfaction of the said collector, according to the circumstances of the case, that the same, if fish, are of the fisheries of the United States; if salted provisions, were salted within the United States. And the said collector shall inspect or cause to be inspected, the goods, wares or merchandise so notified for exportation; and if they shall be found to correspond with the notice and proof concerning the same, the said collector shall grant a permit for lading the same on board the ship or vessel named in such notice, which lading shall be performed under the superintendence of the officer by whom the same shall have been so inspected" (1 *Stat.* 173–74).

From Jean Baptiste de Ternant [1]

[Philadelphia] du 18 avril [1793]

Le M. f. previent le S. d. la t. des E. U. qu'il a donné à Conyngham Nesbit et compe.[2] deux mandats dont un de 40624 Doll. 33/oo à vue faisant le reliqua du payement echu au 15 du present et l'autre de 9980 Dol. 28/oo payable au lr. de may prochain.

T.

LC, *Arch. des Aff. Etr., Corr. Pol., Etats-Unis,* Supplement Vol. 20.
    1. For background to this letter, see Tobias Lear to H, February 8, 1793; "Cabinet Meeting. Opinion on Furnishing Three Million Livres Agreeably to the Request of the French Minister," February 25, 1793; H to Ternant, February 26, 1793.
    2. The Philadelphia merchant firm of David H. Conyngham and John M. Nesbitt acted as purchasing agents in the United States for the French government.

George Washington to Alexander Hamilton, Thomas Jefferson, Henry Knox, and Edmund Randolph

Philadelphia April 18th. 1793.[1]

Sir,

The posture of affairs in Europe, particularly between France and Great Britain, places the United States in a delicate situation; and requires much consideration of the measures which will be proper for them to observe in the War betwn. those Powers. With a view to forming a general plan of conduct for the Executive, I have stated and enclosed sundry questions[2] to be considered preparatory to a meeting at my house to morrow; where I shall expect to see you at 9 'o clock, & to receive the result of your reflections thereon.

Go: Washington

[ENCLOSURE]

Question   I. Shall a proclamation issue for the purpose of preventing interferences of the Citizens of the United States in the War between France & Great Britain &ca? Shall it contain a declaration of Neutrality or not? What shall it contain?

Questn.   II. Shall a Minister from the Republic of France be received?

Questn.   III. If received shall it be absolutely or with qualifications; and if with qualifications, of what kind?

Questn.   IV. Are the United States obliged by good faith to consider the Treaties heretofore made with France as applying to the present situation of the parties.[3] May they either renounce them, or hold them suspended 'till the Government of France shall be *established?*

Questn.   V. If they have the right is it expedient to do either—and which?

Questn.   VI. If they have an option—would it be a breach of Neutrality to consider the Treaties still in operation?

Questn.   VII. If the Treaties are to be considered as now in operation is the Guarantee in the Treaty of Alliance[4] appli-

cable to a defensive war only, or to War either offensive
or defensive?

VIII. Does the War in which France is engaged appear to
be offensive or defensive on her part? or of a mixed &
equivocal character?

IX. If of a mixed & equivocal character does the Guarantee in any event apply to such a War?

X. What is the effect of a Guarantee such as that to be
found in the Treaty of Alliance between the United
States and France?

XI. Does any article in either of the Treaties prevent
Ships of War, other than Privateers, of the Powers
opposed to France, from coming into the Ports of the
United States to act as Convoys to their own Merchant-
men?—or does it lay any other restraints upon them
more than wd. apply to the Ships of War of France?

Questn. XII. Should the future Regent of France send a minister to
the United States ought he to be received?

XIII. Is it necessary or advisable to ask together the two
Houses of Congress with a view to the present posture
of European Affairs? If it is, what should be the particular objects of such a call?

Philada. April 18th. 1793.   Go: Washington

ALS, George Washington Papers, Library of Congress; DS, Hamilton Papers,
Library of Congress; LC, George Washington Papers, Library of Congress;
LC, RG 59, State Department Correspondence, 1791–1796, National Archives.
    1. Washington had returned from Mount Vernon to Philadelphia on April
17, 1793.
    2. According to Jefferson, the President was not the author of the questions
enclosed in this letter. Jefferson stated: "Apr. 18. The President sends a set of
Questions to be considered & calls a meeting. Tho' those sent me were in his
own hand writing, yet it was palpable from the style, their ingenious tissu &
suite that they were not the President's, that they were raised upon a prepared
chain of argument, in short that the language was Hamilton's, and the doubts
his alone. They led to a declaration of the Executive that our treaty with
France is void. E. R. the next day told me, that the day before the date of
these questions, Hamilton went with him thro' the whole chain of reasoning of
which these questions are the skeleton, & that he recognized them the moment
he saw them" (AD, Thomas Jefferson Papers, Library of Congress). This statement is printed in the "Anas" (Ford, Writings of Jefferson, I, 226). Jefferson
was probably correct, for on April 9, 1793, H had sent very similar questions to
John Jay.
    3. For a description of the provisions of the 1778 treaties of Alliance and

Amity and Commerce with France which affected the diplomatic position of the United States in 1793, see H to John Jay, first letter of April 9, 1793, note 2.

4. This is a reference to Article 11 of the Treaty of Alliance, which guaranteed "the present Possessions of the Crown of france in America as well as those which it may acquire by the future Treaty of peace" (Miller, *Treaties*, II, 39).

Cabinet Meeting. Opinion on a Proclamation of Neutrality and on Receiving the French Minister

[Philadelphia, April 19, 1793]

At a meeting of the heads of departments & the Attorney general at the President's Apr. 19. 1793. by special summons to consider of several questions previously communicated to them in writing by the President.[1]

Qu. I. Shall a Proclamation issue &c.? (see the questions)

agreed by all that a Proclamation shall issue, forbidding our citizens to take part in any hostilities on the seas with or against any of the belligerant powers, and warning them against carrying to any such powers any of those articles deemed contraband according to the modern usage of nations, and enjoining them from all acts and proceedings inconsistent with the duties of a friendly nation towards those at war.[2]

Qu. II. Shall a Minister from the Republic of France be received?

agreed unanimously that he shall be received.

Qu. III If received, shall it be absolutely &c.

[The Attorney general & Secretary of state are of opinion he shoud be received absolutely & without qualifications.

The Secretaries of the Treasury & War?][3]

This & the subsequent questions are postponed to another day.[4]

D, in the handwriting of Thomas Jefferson, George Washington Papers, Library of Congress; LC, RG 59, State Department Correspondence, 1791–1796, National Archives.

1. Washington to H, Thomas Jefferson, Henry Knox, and Edmund Randolph, April 18, 1793.

2. The neutrality proclamation was issued on April 22, 1793. For the text, see John Jay to H, April 11, 1793, note 1.

3. The bracketed words were crossed out on the MS. For the opinion of H and Knox on this point, see H and Knox to Washington, May 2, 1793.

4. An account of the debate in the cabinet meeting on this date was kept by Jefferson, who wrote: "We met. The 1st. question whether we should receive the French minister Genest was proposed, & we agreed unanimously that he

should be received, Hamilton at the same time expressing his great regret that any incident had happnd. which should oblige us to recognize the govmt. The next question was whether he shd. be received absolutely, or with qualificns. Here H. took up the whole subject, and went through it in the order in which the questions sketch it. . . . Knox subscribed at once to H's opn that we ought to declare the treaty void, acknoleging at the same time, like a fool as he is, that he knew nothing about it. I was clear it remained valid. E. R. declared himself of the same opn. but on H's undertaking to present to him the authority in Vattel (which we had not present) & to prove to him that, if the authority was admitted, the treaty might be declared void, E. R. agreed to take further time to consider. It was adjourned. We determd Unanimly. the last qu. . . . Congress shd nt be called . . ." (AD, Thomas Jefferson Papers, Library of Congress). This statement, on which Jefferson wrote "May 6 written," is printed in the "Anas" (Ford, *Writings of Jefferson*, I, 226–27).

In his opinion on the treaties sent to Washington on April 28, 1793, Jefferson described the position taken by H at this cabinet meeting as follows: "In the Consultation at the President's on the 19th. inst. the Secretary of the Treasury took the following position's & consequences. 'France was a monarchy when we entered into treaties with it: but it has now declared itself a Republic, & is preparing a Republican form of government. Os it may issue in a Republic or a military despotism, or in something else which may possibly render our alliance with it dangerous to ourselves, we have a right of election to renounce the treaty altogether, or to declare it suspended till their government shall be settled in the form it is ultimately to take; & then we may judge whether we will call the treaties into operation again, or declare them forever null. Having that right of election now, if we receive their minister without any qualifications, it will amount to an act of election to continue the treaties; & if the change they are undergoing should issue in a form which should bring danger on us, we shall not be then free to renounce them. To elect to continue them is equivalent to the making a new treaty at this time in the same form, that is to say, with a clause of guarantee; but to make a treaty with a clause of guarantee, during a war, is a departure from neutrality, and would make us associates in the war. To renounce or suspend the treaties therefore is a necessary act of neutrality'" (ADS, George Washington Papers, Library of Congress).

To Samuel Hodgdon

T.D. April 20th 1793

Sir

I think it will be proper for you to address the inquiry concerning the public buildings alluded to in you letter of the 18 inst [1] to the Secretary at war, as I presume they have been built for the use of that Department. This will put the matter in a regular train of consultation between the Secretary at war and myself.

I am Sir   Yr Obedt Servt

Samuel Hodgdon Esqr

Df, Connecticut Historical Society, Hartford.
1. Letter not found.

From Stephen Higginson

Boston Apr. 21. 1793

D Sir

The Event of a general War in Europe may give rise to some Questions which the Collectors will think necessary to be referred to you for decision. I will state a case that may soon arise. A Cargo of Sugars may be sent here from Hispaniola for Sale in an American Vessel. I may buy it & want to send it to market in the same Vessel without unlading or being at additional expence.[1] But an Entry & Clearance [2] from here will be desireable, as a collateral & strong Evidence of the property being neutral; it will be a new Security against detention trouble & expence. Every ground of suspicion as to the property being neutral is very much against us, & to be avoided if possible. Now why may not an Entry be admitted in such case without unlading? In a bulky heavy Cargo much expence may thereby be saved, & the Security wished for acquired without any injury or danger to the Revenue. The Duty on the Cargo & the drawback being equal, save the 1 ⅌ Ct deducted,[3] no loss to the public can arise, there being an actual exportation; & of this you will have the same Evidence as in other cases where drawback is claimed, & smugling will be checked by the usual guards. There is indeed much more room for fraud in case of landing the Cargo, it being much easier to obtain a drawback on Goods not reshipped, than to smuggle Goods out of a heavy Cargo.

Why may not an Entry be made by the Invo. attested by the Importer, as is done by dry Goods? Will there not be the same Check in both Cases? If the Oath of the Party is taken as to the amount, where Duties are to be paid, may it not be admitted where no Duties are expected, & no loss or injury can arise but from smugling? And if the risk of smugling is to prevent such an Entry, will it not operate as strongly against admitting Vessels to report, & after laying some time to go away? If the Letter of the Law be already against such an Entry, the Spirit of it may not be; & the general principle of giving facility to Trade, compatible with the interest & safety of the Revenue pleads in favour of it.

I am the more induced to state this to you, & to wish for a decision, because I may very probably wish to purchase a Cargo under those circumstances, & I shall certainly be glad to save the expences which must attend the unlading & relading, which will be great. But I shall prefer increasing that expence, rather not have the Evidence wanted. With much haste I am respectfully

Sir your very hum Serv   Stephen Higginson

PS: The Vessel with my Geneva has not yet arrived & will exceed this month probably. I may land it under care of the Officer to reship, if nothing better, in another Vessel. The Vessel it is in can not be trusted any farther, She has been so torn & injured already. Perhaps it may in your mind be recivable & may be marked. The Officers will do nothing here without your direction.[4]

ALS, Hamilton Papers, Library of Congress.

1. Section 18 of "An Act to provide more effectually for the collection of the duties imposed by law on goods, wares and merchandise imported into the United States, and on the tonnage of ships or vessels" provided in part "That it shall be lawful for the said ship or vessel to proceed with any goods, wares and merchandise brought in her which shall be reported by the . . . master . . . to be destined for any foreign port or place from the district within which such ship or vessel shall first arrive, to such foreign port or place, without paying or securing the payment of any duties upon such of the said goods, wares or merchandise, as shall be actually re-exported in the said ship or vessel accordingly; any thing herein contained to the contrary notwithstanding. *Provided always,* That the said master . . . shall first give bond with one or more sureties, in a sum equal to the amount of the duties upon the said goods, wares and merchandise, as the same shall be estimated by the collector to whom the said report shall be made, to the satisfaction of the said collector, with condition that the said goods, wares and merchandise, or any part thereof, shall not be landed within the United States, unless due entry thereof shall have been first made, . . . which bonds shall be cancelled in like manner as bonds herein after directed to be given for obtaining drawbacks of duties . . ." (1 *Stat.* 159 [August 4, 1790]).

2. Section 73 of the same act provided in part "That the master or person having the charge or command of a ship or vessel bound to a foreign port or place, shall deliver to the collector of the district from which such ship or vessel shall be about to depart, a manifest of the cargo on board the same, and shall make oath or affirmation to the truth thereof, whereupon the said collector shall grant a clearance for the said ship or vessel, and her cargo . . ." (1 *Stat.* 177).

3. Section 57 provided in part "That all drawbacks . . . on the exportation of goods, wares and merchandise imported, shall be paid or allowed by the collector at whose office the said goods, wares and merchandise were originally entered, . . . retaining one per centum for the benefit of the United States . . ." (1 *Stat.* 173).

4. H endorsed this letter "Answered May 8." Letter not found.

To John Hopkins

[*Philadelphia, April 21, 1793.* On April 29, 1793, Hopkins wrote to Hamilton: "In compliance with your letter of the 21st of April." *Letter not found.*]

To Tench Coxe [1]

[Philadelphia, April 22, 1793]

The President is of opinion that it will be adviseable to close the purchase & to extend it to a years supply taking due precaution as to preservation &c.

April 22, 1793
A Hamilton

ALS, RG 26, "Segregated" Lighthouse Records, Hamilton, National Archives.
1. This letter is attached to "A Note of a contract for two parcels of oil for the use of the light Houses of the United States, made by Thomas Randall of New York with Benjamin Seixas on the 2d of April 1793."

From Jeremiah Olney

Providence, April 22, 1793. "As it may, in some measure, affect arrangements made at the Treasury, on the probable amount of the Revenue for twelve or Eighteen Months hence, I take leave to inform you, that the difficulty of paying Duties, owing to the scarcity of Specie, has induced the Owners of Two or Three Ships, expected here this Season from the East Indies, to forward Orders to such foreign Ports as it is probable they may touch at on their passages, directing the Supercargoes to dispose of the principal part of the Effects on board, before their return to the United States; fixing the prices so extremely low that there is but little doubt of its being accomplished. This will probably reduce the Duties, which would otherwise have been secured at this Office, about 50,000 Dollars. . . ."

ADfS, Rhode Island Historical Society, Providence.

From Jeremiah Olney [1]

Private.   Providence 22nd. April 1793.

My Dear Sir

By the last Post I acknowledged the receipt of your confidential, and very Friendly Letter of the 2nd Instant,[2] and I embrace the first leisure moment to express my Gratitude, and return my sincere Thanks for the kindness of the motives which prompted you to write it.

Your flattering approbation of my official Conduct in general, and the intimation you have been pleased to give of the great confidence you have in my Intentions, afford me the sincerest satisfaction; and I hope my future Behavior, as a public officer, will furnish you with no cause to alter your good opinion, I will at least *endeavor* that it shall not.

Your acquainting me, in this *private* manner, with the "Idea of some good Men who have expressed to you that in some Instances, my conduct has been too punctilious, and not sufficiently accommodating," I esteem an unequivocal proof of your Regard; and which is greatly enhanced by your favorable construction of those intimations. On this point I beg leave, Dear Sir, respectfully to observe, that it is more than probable the introduction of punctuality and exactness, in the execution of the revenue Laws, may appear to some Gentlemen like vigour; especially when it is considered, and which I assert as a Fact, that the Merchants in General, in this District, were *before* strangers to an honorable punctuality and exactness, as they respected the collection and payment of the Duties imposed by the State Legislature; for it is a well known Truth, that the Merchants paid but little regard to the law when it clashed with their Interest; and that the officers of the Customs being annually chosen, were perfectly under their controul; hence they were permitted to make such Entries as they pleased (very seldom exceeding half the cargoes;) to regard the law in other respects, (particularly in *altering registers at their pleasure &c.*) so far only as it suited their own convenience; and to clear out their Vessels even on the Sabath! It is therefore, easy to conceive, that so great a change, in being suddenly restricted from this *pleasing* liberty, is the real and only sourse of the illiberal and unmerited Censure against me,

I have never ventured to exercise a discretionary power in the execution of the Duties of my office, not authorised, by the Law or your instructions; because I considered it dangerous to establish a precident, which might, from the imperfection of human nature, of which perhaps, I possess too great a share, lead me beyond the line of Prudence and my Duty to the public. But Sir, since you have been pleased to place such confidence in me, as to permit a *discreet* exercise of it, on urgent occasions, I will venture upon the expedient, with great caution, as those occasions may arise, taking particular care to execute every *essential* part of the Law. With such views I shall not doubt but your candour will induce you to make every allowance for any unintentional deviation from the law in my exercise of Discretion.

The good will of the Merchants is very important and desirable, as you observe; and it shall be secured, if a fair and Just discharge of my duty will obtain it: indeed, I possess it already, from a greater part of the Gentlemen.

With every sentiment of Esteem and Gratitude, I have the honor to be, Dear Sir, Your much obliged, and Most Obedt. Servant

Jereh. Olney

Alexander Hamilton Esquire.

ALS, Hamilton Papers, Library of Congress.
  1. For background to this letter, see Olney to H, March 18, 1793; H to Olney, April 2, 1793.
  2. On April 18, 1793, Olney acknowledged H's official letter of April 2, but Olney's letter acknowledging H's "confidential, and very Friendly Letter of the 2nd Instant" has not been found.

From Wilhem and Jan Willink, Nicholaas and Jacob Van Staphorst, and Nicholas Hubbard

[*Amsterdam, April 22, 1793.* On August 12, 1793, Hamilton wrote to Willink, Van Staphorst, and Hubbard: "I have lately the pleasure of your letters of the 22d of April and first of may." *Letter of April 22 not found.*]

To Tobias Lear

[*Philadelphia*] *April 23, 1793.* Asks "whether Mr Lee's [1] resignation was purely voluntary on his part, or was occasioned by any circumstance dissatisfactory to the President."

LC, George Washington Papers, Library of Congress.
1. Charles Lee, collector of customs at Alexandria, Virginia. See Lee to H, April 12, 1793.

From Thomas Jefferson

Philadelphia, April 24, 1793. Requests a warrant "for the sum of six hundred fifty one Dollars, sixty seven Cents, the Balance of the appropriation for my office, to be applied to defray its contingent expenses."

LS, letterpress copy, Thomas Jefferson Papers, Library of Congress; LC, RG 59, Domestic Letters, Vol. V, National Archives.

From Rufus King [1]

[New York] 24 Ap. 1793

Averse to any connexion with the war beyound what may be permitted by the laws of strict neutrality, we are pleased to see the Proclamation.[2] I have no precedents with which to compare it, but I could have wished to have seen in some part of it the word "Neutrality," which every one would have understood and felt the force of.

Having anxiously considered the point respecting which we conversed when I was with you last, I hope you are founded in your opinions. The change which has happened will not perhaps justify us in saying "the Treaties are void"—and whether we may contend in favor of their suspension is a point of delicacy and not quite free from doubt. The authority of the present government is as extensive with their Territory, which is free from the possession of their antagonists.

Prudence would seem to require us to move with caution, and by delay to insure a safe decision. The mere reception of the minister will do us no injury, although I am in Mind to believe, that in order to avoid being pressed on points we may wish not to decide, it will be best to qualify the reception of the Minister in such manner, as will save our commitment in reference to those questions, we wish to stand open.

Our Treaty with Holland may be used with advantage.[3] The report of Mr. Le Brun [4] to the convention respecting perfidy of the monarchy towards us is proof of such a want of good Faith as poinsons the whole Treaty. Have you noticed that the 16th. article of the Treaty of commerce between Eng. and France,[5] is in the Teeth of the 22d. article of the Treaty of commerce between France & us? [6] On the principle that all the articles of a Treaty have the force of conditions, the violation of this article by France, wd. give us the power to renounce the whole Treaty.

Examining our Laws respecting the registry of our Ships & vessels [7] I was struck with a difficulty which will luckily be in the way of our purchasing Prizes brought into our ports by any of the powers at war. It is worth your attention. As the law stands, I do not perceive that any such vessels can be protected by the *american Flag*, even though owned bona fide by american Citizens. Of this point however I will not be confident—such vessels will beyound doubt be liable to pay the foreign Tonnage.

The conduct of England in searching our ships, and impressing seamen engaged under our Flag, is very different in the present armament from what it was in the late armament against Spain.[8] The masters of our ships which have arrived here from England, as also those who have arrived from Ireland, speak with the appearance of national pride, when they mention the hotness of the Press, and the intire exemption of Ships which sail under our Flag. The circumstance is one from which we may make pretty certain inferences. Farewel, I wish I could give assistance to the measures & maxims you will pursue. We must not become intangled with this mad War.[9]

Yours &c   Rufus King

ALS, Hamilton Papers, Library of Congress.

1. For background to this letter, see George Washington to H, Thomas Jefferson, Henry Knox, and Edmund Randolph, April 18, 1793; "Cabinet Meeting. Opinion on a Proclamation of Neutrality and on Receiving the French Minister," April 19, 1793.

2. Washington's proclamation of neutrality, dated April 22, 1793, was pub-

lished in the [Philadelphia] *Gazette of the United States* on April 24, 1793. For the text, see John Jay to H, April 11, 1793, note 1.

3. King is referring to the Treaty of Amity and Commerce concluded between the United States and the Netherlands on October 8, 1782.

4. Pierre Henri Hélène Marie Lebrun-Tondu was French Minister of Foreign Affairs from August 12, 1792, to June 2, 1793. The "report" was a letter from Lebrun to the president of the National Assembly, dated December 20, 1792. In this letter Lebrun, in commenting on the relationship between the monarchy and the United States, wrote that "dans le temps même où ce bon peuple nous exprimait de la manière la plus touchante son amitié et sa reconnaissance, Vergennes et Montmorin pensaient 'qu'il ne convenait pas à la France de lui donner tout la consistance dont il était susceptible, parce qu'il acquerrait une force dont il serait probablement tenté d'abuser'" (*Archives Parlementaires*, LV, 349).

5. The commercial treaty between France and England was signed at Versailles on September 26, 1786. Article XVI reads as follows: "It shall not be lawful for any foreign privateers, not being subjects of either crown, who have commissions from any other Prince or State, in enmity with either nation, to arm their ships in the ports of either of the said two kingdoms, to sell what they have taken, or in any other manner whatever to exchange the same; neither shall they be allowed even to purchase victuals, except such as shall be necessary for their going to the nearest port of that Prince from whom they have obtained commissions" (George Chalmers, *A Collection of Treaties Between Great Britain and Other Powers* [London, 1790], I, 528).

6. King is referring to Article 24 of the Franco-American Treaty of Amity and Commerce of 1778. For a discussion of the discrepancies in the numbering of the articles of this treaty, see H to John Jay, April 9, 1793, note 2. Article 24 reads as follows: "It shall not be lawful for any foreign Privateers, not belonging to Subjects of the most Christian King nor Citizens of the said United States, who have Commissions from any other Prince or State in enmity with either Nation to fit their Ships in the Ports of either the one or the other of the aforesaid Parties, to sell what they have taken or in any other manner whatsoever to exchange their Ships, Merchandizes or any other lading; neither shall they be allowed even to purchase victuals except such as shall be necessary for their going to the next Port of that Prince or State from which they have Commissions" (Miller, *Treaties*, II, 19–20).

7. See "An Act concerning the registering and recording of ships or vessels" (1 *Stat.* 287–99 [December 31, 1792]).

8. This is a reference to the Nootka Sound controversy of 1790.

9. An undated and unsigned copy of an essay on the position of the United States in reference to the French treaties, which is in the Hamilton Papers, Library of Congress, touches upon some of the points raised by King in this letter. Although this document is in an unidentified handwriting, it is an earlier version of an essay by King which is printed in Charles R. King, *The Life and Correspondence of Rufus King* (New York, 1894), I, 440–54. Since the copy in the Hamilton Papers contains many alternative words and phrases, King had apparently submitted it to H for his opinion.

From William Loughton Smith

Winsborough [South Carolina] April 24th. 93

Dear Sir

Allow an old acquaintance to interrupt for a few minutes your attention & to divert it from the great affairs of State to a hasty Epistle written from the back woods.[1] Availing myself of a little repose at this place after a long & fatiguing Journey, I have determined to give you some account of the Situation in which I found affairs on my arrival in the State because I conceived the Detail would not be uninteresting. It is with much pleasure I acquaint you that on landing in Charleston I found a very general satisfaction pervading the City on the Triumph we had recently obtained over the Sons of Faction at Philada:[2] I received congratulations from all Quarters & particy. from the respectable part of the mercantile interest, who considered your Cause as their own. My Stay in Charleston was but a week; having a long Tour in Contemplation I was anxious to commence it; I began with Augusta in Georgia & went from thence thro Wilkes County to Washington, crossed the Savannah River at Petersburgh about 60 miles above Augusta, proceeded up the Carolina side to the Kiowee & went to Hopewell, the Seat of my new Colleague, Genl. Pickens,[3] with whom I passed a day; thence continued thro the remotest part of our state & the new settled Country to Rocky Mount & this place, which I shall leave to morrow for Charleston, passing thro' Columbia. At Augusta I waited on the Governor,[4] who knowing my Sentiments, was cautious in delivering his own, but I perceived in his Discourse about the Creeks,

ALS, Hamilton Papers, Library of Congress.

1. When Smith wrote this letter, he was traveling through the backcountry of South Carolina and Georgia in an effort to secure support for Federalist policies. See Joseph Nourse to H, March 18, 1793, note 2.

2. For the "Triumph," see the introductory note to "Report on the Balance of All Unapplied Revenues at the End of the Year 1792 and on All Unapplied Monies Which May Have Been Obtained by the Several Loans Authorized by Law," February 4, 1793.

3. Andrew Pickens had recently been elected to the House of Representatives as a Republican.

4. Edward Telfair.

who have been lately very troublesome about St. Mary's, that he was not much pleased with Seagrove's [5] having the managemt. of Indian Affairs. In passing thro Wilkes County I travelled among Baldwin's [6] neighbours & Constituents; I was within a few miles of him, but missed seeing him; I am sorry I can't give a very good Accot. of their people, who are the strangest mixture of emigrants from other Countries I ever met with. I passed part of a Day at Washington a considerable inland place where I found the County Court (Wilkes) sitting; there was a great concourse of people, & many of them were much at a loss to discover what brought me among them; not conceiving it in the line of probability that a Gentleman or a Member of Congress shod. travel so far from home, merely to see a Country, they set me down as a *Land-Speculator*. Bad as they are I am told they are considy. ameliorated, & that a few years ago they were such a set of bandetti that it was less safe for a Gentleman to be among them than in the midst of the Wabash Tribes. I understood they were extremely exasperated against the President for his Proclamation against the Depredators on the Indian Land,[7] & that the Fellow who was apprehended would have been rescued had he not desired his friends not to interpose. I lodged & past the night at the House of one of the County Court Judges, a very good & respectable Man & (to give the Devil his due) a Virginian; I there met with the first newspaper I had seen since I left Chars. & as I expected, the National Gazette, which I saw regularly filed over the Mantlepeice. I took occasion to remark that I was Surprised at his countenancing such a party paper; he was no less surprised at my giving it that epithet, assuring me that he had been informed it was the most *liberal* paper printed at Philada. & that *Fenno's* was the party paper; on my entering into an historical explanation of the business, he said he was sorry to find that such a paper shod. be introduced by a Member of Congress; I explained to him Baldwin's Conduct & assured him that the

5. James Seagrove was United States agent to the Creeks.

6. Abraham Baldwin, a member of the House of Representatives and a prominent Georgia politician, consistently opposed H's policies in Congress.

7. Washington's proclamation, dated December 12, 1792, concerning "certain lawless and wicked persons, of the western frontier in the State of Georgia" who "did lately invade, burn, and destroy a town belonging to the Cherokee nation," is printed in *GW*, XXXII, 260–61.

Nat. Gaz. was stuffed with lies & propagated by a malicious party. I am in hopes my stay at his House will have not been without some benefit. In Abbeville County in S.C. I past a night in a Col. Baird's; [8] he said the people in that Country, which is one of the most numerous Counties in Ninety Six District, had been violently opposed to the Excise, but that they began to be reconciled to it; however he thought the Conduct of some of the Officers would give disgust & set the people against it; he mentioned an instance of rough & menacing conduct on the part of one Wright, an Inspector. I assured him that I would acquaint the Supervisor [9] with the circumstance & was persuaded he wod. direct his Officers to conduct themselves otherwise as He knew as well as myself, that it was the wish of the federal Governt. to execute it's Laws with mildness. I passed a Day with Genl. Pickens; from his conversation I have hopes he will do well. I left with him the whole of the Debate on the Treasury business & one of the Pamphlets. At Union Court House I found a smart young County Court Lawyer, who had been reading (in the Nat. Gaz.) a part of the Debates. He was desirous of understanding the business well in order to explain it to the people, with whom he is a kind of oracle, & as I found in him very good dispositions (for he is a New England-man) I left with him a duplicate of the speeches, which I had carried with me & a Pamphlet; before I left him, he was quite one of us. He told me the people in that part were much prejudiced agt. the Secy. of the T. but that he saw it was all party-work & he wod. do away the impressions. I aftds. passed a Day with Col Winn [10] & part of another with his brother, my new Colleague, the General.[11] They are influential men in this part of the State; they are both much in favor of the Excise; the General told me he had been reading the Debates on the Secys conduct & that it appeared to him his opponents had been censuring him for only having done his Duty. I have great hopes he will go right: I haven't seen Benton &

8. Jonas Beard of Orangeburg District had served as a colonel during the American Revolution and had been elected sheriff of Lexington County in 1790.

9. Daniel Stevens was supervisor of the revenue for South Carolina.

10. John Winn of Winnsboro, South Carolina, had served in the American Revolution and had been a member of the South Carolina House of Representatives in 1775.

11. Richard Winn was a newly elected member of the House of Representatives from Fairfield County, South Carolina.

Hunter:[12] I saw Gillon[13] in Town; he says he understands there are parties in Congress & that he will judge for himself.

I am now at the House of a Mr Evans[14] who is Inspector of the Excise for this part of the Country—he is an intelligt. man, & informs me the Thing goes on very well. Wherever I have been & have had an opporty. I have explained the nature of the Contest in Congress & the cause of the abuse & censure in the Nat. Gazette, which I am sorry to say circulates too extensively in the back parts of this State.

I suppose you have heard of the French Frigate coming off our Bar &c. Monsr. Genet is expected at Camden today on his way to Philada.[15] A gentleman arrived from that place this morng. tells me they mean to compliment him with a public Dinner, a foolish thing entre nous.

By the paper I find all the old members are reelected in Virginia, except White,[16] the only good one: it is what I apprehended; it was suffict. for him to have voted right once for them to have turned him out: When Col. Bland was the only good member in that Delegatn. he died;[17] & now we have lost White! But what good can we hope from that quarter? Should you have any thing material to communicate & leisure to write, direct to me in Charleston where I expect to be in about a week or ten days, & which I shall not leave for Philada. until the end of June.

Present me respecty. to Mrs Hamilton & mention me to my friends. Should you see the fair Lady of Walnut Street, in admiring whose amiableness our Tastes have united (& it is not in Politics alone that they concur) please to present my best respects to her.

With unfiegned esteem I remain Dear Sir   Yours &c   Wm Smith.

12. Lemuel Benton and John Hunter had been elected to the House of Representatives from South Carolina in March, 1793.

13. Alexander Gillon was a newly elected member of the House of Representatives from South Carolina.

14. Presumably David Reid Evans.

15. Edmond Charles Genet had arrived at Charleston, South Carolina, on April 8, 1793. On April 19, 1793, he left Charleston for Philadelphia, proceeding by way of Camden, Richmond, and Baltimore.

16. Alexander White had served as a member of the House of Representatives from Virginia from March 4, 1789, to March 3, 1793.

17. Theodorick Bland had been elected to the First Congress and had served until his death in June, 1790.

From Jeremiah Olney [1]

Custom House
District of Providence 25th April 1793.

Sir

Agreeably to the information contained in my Letter of the 15th Instant, I have attended the Superior Court which met at East Greenwich for the County of Kent on the 22nd. Instant, and am sorry to acquaint you that the Causes of Messrs. Arnold and Dexter, against me, in the Case of the Brigantine Neptune, remain undecided, the Chief Justis [2] being indisposed and unable to attend the Court declined acting on this Business in his absence, this will unavoidably postpone a decision of it, untill the Court meets here in Septr. next. There will be some Change in the Court, one new Judge at least, will be added in the place of one some time Since Deceased, which will be the cause of additional Expence, as the pleadings must then Necessarily be Taken up a Second time.

I have the Honor to be &c.   Jereh. Olney Collr.

A. Ander Hamilton Esqr.
Secy. Treasury

ADfS, Rhode Island Historical Society, Providence.
  1. For background to this letter, see William Ellery to H, September 4, October 9, 1792; Olney to H, September 8, 13, October 4, 25, November 7, 28, December 10, 13, 27, 1792, March 14, 25, April 15, 1793; H to Olney, September 19, 24, October 12, November 27, 1792.
  2. Daniel Owen.

From David Ross [1]

Baltimore April 25. 1793

Dear Sir

As it is probable the enclosed [2] might not have come to your knowledge from its contracted circulation I have sent it and you will see my reply to it in the Baltimore Journal of Monday next.[3] Co Mercer has lodged the communications, with Mr. Angell [4] except *your last*. Mr Angell does not mean to publish them unless he shall give more explicit directions than are contained in his of the 18th of April. Co Mercer will I expect be sufficiently known to prevent the necessity of any thing personal between you. I have not let any one see or know of yours & Co Mercers last [5] nor shall I without your permission.

Yours in haste   David Ross

ALS, Hamilton Papers, Library of Congress.

1. For background to this letter, see the introductory note to H to John F. Mercer, September 26, 1792. See also H to Mercer, November 3, December 6, December, 1792, March 1, 14, 1793; Mercer to H, October 16–28, December, 1792, January 31, March 5, 26, 1793; H to Ross, September 26, November 3, 1792; Ross to H, October 5–10, November 23, 1792, March 13, April 8, 1793; Uriah Forrest to H, November 7, 1792.

2. The enclosure to which Ross is referring is a statement by Mercer published in *The* [Annapolis] *Maryland Gazette*, April 18, 1793. It reads as follows:

"Major Ross, restless to display the splendour of his literary accomplishments beyond the limits of Maryland, has pursued me to my farm in a retired part of Virginia, with more of his works, republished from the Baltimore paper, in one of the Gazettes of that state. No jaded horse ever returned to a beaten track and endless journey, with more reluctance than I do, to this tiresome man and exhausted controversy.

"A sound heart is seldom united with an unsound mind—and the perversion of the understanding almost invariably deranges the morality of a man; hence it is that we frequently observe the folly of a weak and vain head blended with the apparent malice and low cunning of a very wicked heart—where this compound exists, it is to be cautiously guarded against—it operates like a masked battery—it is dangerous because it is unsuspected.

"Major Ross accuses me of a design to mislead the public, by some inference that may be drawn from my last publication in Mr. [James] Angell's paper. When every document relative to the transaction had been previously deposited with the Printer, who could have supposed that I meant to create an impression not warranted by those papers, and thus to expose myself to the contempt of every ingenuous mind that should make the examination? He did not surely see in my publication a mirror that reflected back so disordered a mind and half witted a policy! . . .

"But major Ross's publication alone would not have dragged me again into the news-papers, had I not both written and published *that matter of opinion only, and not matter of fact, were now at issue between Mr. Hamilton and myself,* posterior to which I have received a letter from that gentleman, wherein he asserts, *that there has been a general denial of the facts that are the basis of the exceptionable suggestions on my part, and that there is not one of them that is not wholly or substantially unfounded.* I had before declared, that I would enter into no farther *epistolary* explanation with him, as I considered the question as to facts to have ceased. But it is now necessary that this matter should be so far understood at least, that if there has been a departure from veracity, the public, to whom the assertion has been thus committed, may be enabled to decide with whom and on whom that departure rests. If there has been any such general denial before, it has escaped me—but a general denial is always admitted to be no answer to a specific charge—the papers must speak for themselves—but as they cannot well be all now published, or taken in one view, I shall offer a brief recapitulation of the different points that have occurred in this controversy, the whole of which I pledge myself will be found to be unequivocally established by the testimony lodged with Mr. Angell, in Baltimore. The original foundation of Mr. Hamilton's first letter to me, and that to major Ross, which was published in hand bills during my election, was grounded solely, as it will appear, on this single fact, 'That I had accused Mr. Hamilton, ⟨to the citizens of⟩ this district, of buying and selling stock on his private account.' This assertion, resting altogether on the veracity or comprehension of major Ross, which thus became the basis of so exceptionable a procedure, was fully and unequivocally disproved by the certificates of six as respectable characters as any in the union, both with regard to my public address at the time and place specified, as well as my private and confidential communications—they were Mr. [David] Craufurd, Mr. [Walter] Bowie and Mr. [Clement] Hill, as to my public address; Mr. [William] Paca and the two Mr. Chases [Jeremiah and Samuel] as to my private conversation—and as far as I can recollect, not one of the numerous certificates procured by major Ross from the most virulent of my opponents, furnishes the slightest evidence of the fact which he had asserted, and which, as it was the ground-work of the procedure he was called on to authenticate in the most peculiar and pressing manner, could it have been effected with the least regard to truth—but on the contrary, they entirely corroborate the certificates of the gentlemen above named as to that fact—and the whole district at this day know that this assertion of major Ross was entirely without foundation.

"In reply then to Mr. Hamilton's letter, used as it was during my election— I stated clearly and precisely what I said, in which two facts only were asserted. The one, that of the public money laid out in the purchase of stock, on account of the sinking fund, more had been given than others had purchased for, at the open market, at the same time. In making this assertion, I quoted at the time, (as my sole authority) the public news-papers of Philadelphia and New York, from which I stated that I had read extracts in my place in congress to that effect, and I added, that the fact was not then controverted or denied in congress, nor had it been since, to my knowledge, although my speech to that effect had long appeared in print. The other fact—that when three parcels of stock were offered under sealed proposals, at three different prices, that part was taken of each, and part returned of each, by which means the public gave more than they were offered at. I have lodged with Mr [John] Beckley, clerk of the house of representatives, a certificate of Mr. [Benjamin] Hawkins, a senator from North Carolina, with respect to two parcels at different prices, parts of each of which were taken, and part of each returned, and the name of the witness, (who was in Philadelphia when I mentioned the fact in congress)— Mr. Hawkins will also (I have no doubt) add, that he gave me fully the information I have above stated with regard to three parcels of stock, at three different prices, although, when he gave me the certificate, as he could not recollect the authority for this latter case, he did not then insert it. Mr. Hamilton has no where, I assert, denied these specific facts—the latter was admitted and justified by one of my opponents, as may also be proved from good authority. These were all the facts that I had asserted—afterwards, by the disclosure of a private conversation, major Ross introduced another fact into discussion— that I had asserted, that Mr. Hamilton had interfered in my election previous to the letter. At the time I mentioned this as fact, I also stated to major Ross my authority—that authority is well known in this part of the district, it was not confined to the gentleman who was my immediate informant; and although the person who informed him may have been incorrect, yet the authority was sufficient justification of my belief and consequent conduct, and Mr. Hamilton will not assert, that his opinion on my election was withheld in this district previous to his letter. There is still another fact that has grown out of this discussion, that Mr. Hamilton offered me money to vote for the assumption. As this is a delicate subject, I will not hazard any thing respecting it, but the statement of the transaction, authenticated by unexceptionable testimony, together with a letter relative thereto from Mr. Hamilton, admitting fully the fact as I stated it, and my reply to his letter, all of which are among the papers in the hands of Mr. Angell, which I request him to publish. As to the other subjects, that the administration of Mr. Hamilton was unfriendly to the interests of the southern states—that his funding system was founded on false and ruinous principles of public credit, and admitted of dangerous interferences to raise and depress the value of that property, and sacrificed occasionally and unjustly other property to the interest of stockholders. That he had engrossed the legislative functions of government. They were all matters of opinion, on which I had a right, nay, was sacredly bound to form my judgement, from a great complexity of views, that from their nature will admit of no entire demonstration, or direct proof—they are the result of a variety of data that terminate in an opinion, which must and will remain disputable.

"There is one other point, respecting a preference shewn by Mr. Hamilton to Mr. [William] Duer, which I really considered as the only remaining subject of discussion reserved by that gentleman in his letter to me of March 2d. With regard to any pecuniary connexion between these two persons, I have always disavowed having suggested such in or out of this district. I did consider the connexion and consequent preference as the result of intimate and long established habits of intercourse and friendship—as such I consider my suggestion essentially a matter of opinion—but as it is a sole object, it will admit of a direct reference to those facts on which that opinion was founded. I hold myself therefore justified in that opinion by the supplementary report of the committee of inquiry, which in this instance, states facts fully before the committee at their first session; by that it will appear, that the transfer of the contract from [Theodosius] Fowler to Duer, on which transfer Mr. Hamilton rests and justifies the connexion of the public with Duer, was notified to him and lodged in his office long posterior to an official correspondence with Mr. Duer as contractor, and it was also long posterior to a consultation between Mr. Hamilton, the secretary at war, general [Arthur] St. Clair, and Mr. Duer as contractor, and that no correspondence was produced to the committee between the public offices and Fowler as contractor, although Fowler's contract subsisted above six months before the notification and lodging of the transfer.

"Let my anxiety to retain any confidence that may have been reposed in me, justify this tedious detail. About to retire for the greater part of the summer to attend to a much neglected farm in a secluded part of the country, it must be a wanton attack that will interrupt pursuits, which, as a citizen, in the recess from public duties, I have some right to enjoy. Let it be also remembered, that captain [William] Campbell commenced an opposition of my re-election, grounded in a great measure, as appears from his own certificate, on the part I took in congress against the measures of Mr. Hamilton—that my defence of that conduct, when called before the citizens of the district, was confined to a reiteration of those reasons which I had given in my place in congress, and long published to the world. That Mr. Hamilton commenced an attack on me during my election, grounded on an unfounded assertion of major Ross—and that all these parties persist in pursuing the most malevolent objects against all rule, decorum and right."

3. Ross's reply, dated April 20, 1793, to Mercer's article of April 18 appeared in *The Maryland Journal and Baltimore Advertiser* for April 30, 1793. After reiterating his charges against Mercer, Ross closed his statement with this observation: "Colonel Mercer appears to be so much in earnest when he wishes not to be again recalled to this subject, that otherwise it might have been a doubt with some, whether he had sensibility enough left to be really hurt by any thing that could be related of him; but since he has some left, it is a matter

of course that this subject should be so disagreeable to him, and that he should feel himself like a 'jaded horse,' whenever he is again forced into it, since no view of it can possibly excite any agreeable sensation in him, and disagreeable ones must be as tiresome to the Colonel as to every other person, and the only thing that can now be recommended to make him feel more like a man and less like a 'jaded horse,' is to change the nature of his late pursuits, that have led him into this dilemma; and there can be no doubt but such a change of conduct would not only be advantageous to himself and his 'neglected farm,' but please numbers who have confidence in our government, and the present measures and officers of the administration."

4. James Angell, formerly associated with William Goddard in the publication of *The Maryland Journal and Baltimore Advertiser,* had become sole publisher of that paper with the issue of February 22, 1793.

5. H to Mercer, March 14, 1793, and Mercer to H, March 26, 1793.

To George Washington

Treasury Department, April 25, 1793. Submits "two communications from the Commissioner of the revenue; [1] one enclosing a Contract entered into by the Superintendant of the Delaware Lighthouse with Matthew Van Dusen, for a mooring Chain for one of the floating beacons in the Delaware bay [2]—the other transmitting an offer of Samuel Wheeler concerning two Iron Lanterns for the Lighthouses on Tybee & Cape Fear Islands." [3] Recommends approval. Suggests that "A House for the Keeper & an Oil Vault" for the Baldhead lighthouse be made "concurrent operations."

LC, George Washington Papers, Library of Congress.

1. Letters from Tench Coxe not found.

2. William Allibone was superintendent of lighthouses, beacons, buoys, public piers, and stakage for Philadelphia, Cape Henlopen, and the Delaware River. A copy of this contract, signed on March 16, 1793, and approved by Washington on April 27, 1793, may be found in RG 26, Lighthouse Deeds and Contracts, Vol. A, National Archives.

3. A copy of Wheeler's proposals may be found in RG 26, Lighthouse Deeds and Contracts, Vol. A, National Archives.

From Edward Carrington

Richmond Apl. 26. 1793

My dear Sir,

I am favored with your[s] of the 10th. Instant.[1] Your determination to persevere with patience in your labors to establish a per-

ALS, Hamilton Papers, Library of Congress.

1. Letter not found.

manent and successful system of Revenue & credit for the United States, must give satisfaction to all who feel that these are the only supports of public safety and private prosperity. I am well assured that, in private life, you experienced pecuniary advantages, and personal ease, both of body & mind, not to be found in your present office, even were all hands to Unite for your assistance; great indeed then must be your sacrifices when, instead of this generous assistance, you are beset with numerous hostilities.

To your enquiries concerning the public mind in Virginia in regard to the events which are happening in Europe, I will give the most satisfactory answers I can; it is not however unknown to you, that upon things so remote, but few are heard actually to speak, and these generally take the liberty to affix the name of the people to their own suggestions. The truth is, that the great body of the people desire nothing that will interrupt the freedom, peace, and happiness, they now enjoy. With regard to the Cause of France, I believe the general wish is, for its success. My own sentiments are in favor of such reforms in most of the Governments in Europe, & indeed in the World, as will give to the human race the most Free Goverments it can enjoy. The experiments in France have not however, been very flattering. This applies to your first question.

As to the second. I believe the decapitation of the King is pretty generally considered as an Act of unprincipled Cruelty, dictated by neither justice nor policy. In my own mind, it was an horrible transaction in every view, and, to an American who can even yeild to its propriety, it ought to be felt as a truly sorrowful event.

As to the third. I have no doubt, that the sense of this Country is for a perfect neutrality, if it can possibly be had. My own sentiments are, that the French, from having commenced one of the noblest causes that ever presented itself in any country, have lost themselves in the wildest quixotism: my wish is, that they may recover their reason, and establish for themselves a good government, leaving other Countries to judge for themselves. If they will do this, they need not fear the combinations of their Enemies.

As to the 4th. & 5th. So far as I have heard observations upon the subject of the Treaty between France & America, it appears to be considered that no alteration in the Government of either Country, changes the obligations of preexisting Treaties; [2] at the same time, it is generally held, that, should we in consequence of Treaty, be bound to take any other than a Neutral station in the business of France, it will be an unfortunate circumstance, as we could do them no real service, and would involve ourselves in distress. I have no doubt of its being the general opinion, that if we, of right, have an option, the most perfect neutrality ought to be observed. We have in this, as there are, no doubt, in every State, some characters to whom any thing but quiet would be agreeable—this, however, is not the case with the great body of our fellow Citizens, and the few who are desirous of new adventures, will, doubtless, have the consent of their Countrymen to go to France in quest of them. My own sentiments on these two questions are, that, in determining what is to be done in regard to the Treaty, several considerations present themselves. Ist. its applicability to the present State of the parties. 2dly. the reasonableness of calling, on the part of the French, for a performance of it, on ours, in reference to the original motives for entering into it. 3dly. the probable consequences to both parties from an attempt to fulfil the required service. The first consideration I shall leave to those well versed in the Laws of Nations; and, perhaps, the sentiments of the people in the Islands concerned, may claim some regard in the determination. If they are desirous of adhering to the old government, it may not be an insupportable opinion, that theirs is the claim upon us for the guarantee promised in the Treaty. Upon the principles of liberty and equality, it would seem that this distinct part of the old Kingdom, should have a free choice upon the subject of the Revolution. The american Confederacy, as well as I recollect, demanded not the co-operation of Georgia until she, sometime after the commencement of our opposition to Britain, voluntarily joined her Sister Colonies; nor did we during the War, claim the allegiance of Canada: and our connection with these colonies in a common subjection under the British Monarchy, was as compleat, and, locally, more so, than France and the French Islands under the French Monarchy. To this it may with some pluasibility be said, that the american case was not a Revolution of the national supreme power,

2. For a description of the articles of the 1778 Franco-American treaties of Alliance and Amity and Commerce which affected the diplomatic position of the United States in 1793, see H to John Jay, first letter of April 9, 1793, note 2.

but only a separation of a part from it, and therefore not applicable in the present instance; granting this, we have a more recent one which, the principle of this objection, renders certainly applicable in our late change of government, when a sufficient number of States had adopted the new form to give it effect, the constituted power did not claim right of government over the two non-adopting States, until they, voluntarily, reconsidered the subject and adopted.[3] There can be no doubt but, that at the time of this event, we were an entire Nation, bound together under one government, and that the change was a Revolution of the national supreme power, as compleatly as that which has taken place in France. I should suppose that, should these Islands elect to place themselves in a situation independent of the French Republic, or even to place themselves under the protection of any other power, such election would be in perfect consistency with the avowed principles of that Republic, & when we consider the actual situation of the Islanders, as well in regard to the nature of their property, as their dependence upon foreign protection, it is highly probable that, if they be taken by any of the maritime powers now combined against the French, the event will be a consequence of their desiring it. Upon the 2d. consideration, it must be concluded, that each of the contracting parties had regard to the extent of its engagement, and relied as much on mutual good faith in reasonable constructions of, as compliances with the stipulations contained in the Treaty; and it would seem that, upon either involving itself in War by voluntary acts, which thing cannot be supposed to have been contemplated at the time of Contract, there can be no equitable claim upon the other for performance. Could it be, at the time of the Treaty, in the contemplation of the United States that a revolution, such as has happened in France was possible, and that the new power, before organizing itself upon a rational form, would be *crusading* it after the liberties of other countries, and by that means arising all Europe against it? Had they foreseen that such was to be the state of French affairs, would they have bound themselves to guarantee the Islands under the consequent Wars? I presume that had the United States at any time after the peace thought proper to attempt the freeing of Canada from Britain, or the Spanish Colonies

3. North Carolina ratified the Constitution on November 21, 1789, and Rhode Island ratified it on May 29, 1790.

from Spain, neither the King, nor even the Republic of France, would have thought we had a reasonable claim upon that Nation for a participation in the war on accounts of her having, in general terms, guaranteed our "liberty and independence as well in government as Commerce." Upon the third consideration, could our attempting a compliance with the Treaty produce good to the French Cause? We have not, nor had ever, at the time of the contract, a Navy, the only means by which the Islands can be protected against naval powers; we could, therefore, give no immediate defence in that quarter. We might attack Canada, and, upon the same principle, the Spanish Colonies also; but any offensive operation, would, at once, involve us in war with them, and all the combined powers; this must, inevitably, interrupt our Trade, which neither America nor France is in a situation to protect, and prevent those supplies of provisions, now sent to Europe, of which France is in greater need than any of her Enemies. This consequence would follow, although even should no part of the Forces destined to act against the Republic, be diverted to Act in America; and, should such deversion take place, the scenes here would be so considerable as to interrupt our agriculture, and abridge, if not totally, prevent, a surplussage of provisions for exportation. These would undoubtedly be the consequences to France from any attempt on our part to assist her as an ally, and, it does appear to me, that her true policy, if she can be in temper to reflect on it, is, to be vigilant in keeping the United States clear of the War, leaving them to enjoy of the Mare liberum as fully as possible. This is the only Country from which she can expect supplies of provisions, and if we can retain the free use of the seas, she will be more certain of receiving them in the course of Trade, than by a feeble attempt of government to supply her against the fleets of her Enemies. The consequences to the United States, from an attempt to comply with the Treaty, need not be mentioned; they must be evident to all who will think at all on the subject; nor will any one, whose happiness is connected with that of his Country, be willing to encounter them, but under the pressure of inevitable necessity. This, I am inclined to think, will not occur, if we are wise. The Inhabitants of the United States ought to rejoice, that, being no longer adventurers for their own liberties, they are too remote from the Countries which have the desperate game yet to play, to be brought into hazard with them.

In answer to your 6th. question, I suppose the Embassador from the French Republic, might be received *in form* without the least impropriety upon the ground of neutrality.[4] He comes from the prevailing Authority of the nation, and it would seem, that any government refusing a reception, would manifest more than a spirit of neutrality. The Conduct of England on this point was followed by effective measures against the Republic. The expediency of a reception in form, I have no doubt of, upon more considerations than the mere propriety of it. It will prevent many cavils against our Administration. It is proper for me to inform you, that we have amongst us, those who are preparing the people for such an event as a refusal, under the old Story of an Eastern influence in favor of Monarchy in America, and, consequently, unfriendly to the liberties of France. You will readily perceive that the motive for this, arises less from a zeal in the cause of France, than a desire to destroy the confidence of the people in their own Government.

I would be for receiving an Embassador from the French Republic, and from any other of the beligerent powers, but would be *publicly explicit,* as to a perfect neutrality. The French, I suppose, have a good pretext for business with us, not connected with a participation in the War. The Debt, which it appears to be understood, ought to be paid to the existing Authority is certainly no unimportant ground of intercourse.

The only chance, that I can now perceive, for the United States being lugged into the War is, that great Britain may attempt to restrain, by force, the passage of their ships into the French Ports with provisions, and our feeling it necessary, for the public honor, to resent the injury. Should such a circumstance happen, we shall, I suppose, have a delicate, and, perhaps, difficult, part to act. I cannot however be very apprehensive of our being brought into the difficulty, if we, *evidently,* preserve a neutrality. If we leave our Trade open to all Countries, and our Citizens free to visit all ports, I see not how Great Britain can have a pretext to meddle with our vessels going into France, unless laden with what are called contraband articles, or approaching places beseiged &c. Some of our hotheads throw out opinions that we should attempt, by an order of Govern-

4. See "Cabinet Meeting. Opinion on a Proclamation of Neutrality and on Receiving the French Minister," April 19, 1793.

ment, an exclusive exportation to France; these however are few and contemptible. The nation that would attempt this, without even one armed ship, and in behalf of a nation too, whose naval force is impaired, and far inferior to that of her Enemies, would indeed entitle itself to the ridicule of the whole world. It is certain that France could derive no benefit from such an attempt, which she may not secure without our infringing the rights of neutrality. Having no navy, we must rely altogether, in the effort, upon her Convoys; and if these could cover our trading ships, their own might, under the same convoys, pass safely home with the provisions purchased in our ports.

I have, my dear Sir, complied with your request in giving the result of my observations and reflections upon the present very important crisis, and have indeavored to render them worth your trouble in asking for them. Your own judgement will direct you how far to rely upon their accuracy. With every sentiment of private friendship, and the fullest confidence in your public administration,

I am your afft. Hl. sr.   Ed. Carrington

Alexander Hamilton Esq

From Thomas Pinckney

London, April 26, 1793. Introduces "Mr. Archdekue and Mr. Godfrey . . . Gentlemen of independent Fortune who purpose visiting as Travellers several parts of the United States."

ALS, Hamilton Papers, Library of Congress.

Conveyance by Lease and Release to Gulian Verplanck [1]

[Philadelphia] April 27, 1793. ". . . Alexander Hamilton and Elizabeth his wife for and in consideration of the sum of Two thousand four hundred pounds current money of the State of New York . . . paid by the said Gulian VerPlank . . . HAVE granted, bargained, sold, aliened, released and confirmed, and by these Presents DO grant, bargain, Sell, alien, release, and Confirm unto the said Gulian VerPlank . . . and to his heirs and assigns for ever ALL that certain

messuage or Dwelling House and the Store House thereunto ad-
joining, as also a Lot of Ground whereon the said Dwelling House
and Stone House do stand, . . . situate lying and being in the ward
lately called the South ward of the City of New York, pointing to a
certain Street called Wall Street. . . ."

D, signed by Elizabeth Hamilton and H, New Haven Colony Historical Society, New Haven, Connecticut.
    1. For background to this document, see Verplanck to H, September 10,
1792, and March 17, 1793.

From Tobias Lear [1]

[*Philadelphia*] *April 27, 1793.* Returns "with the President's approbation annexed, the Contract made by the Superintendant of the
Lighthouse &c. on the Delaware, with Matthew Van Dusen, for a
mooring chain for one of the floating beacons & the proposal of
Samuel Wheeler to make two iron lanterns—one for Tybee & one for
Cape Fear lighthouse." States that "The President approves of the
suggestion . . . to make the building of a House for the Keeper & a
vault for the oil, at the Baldhead Lighthouse concurrent operations."

LC, George Washington Papers, Library of Congress.
    1. For background to this letter, see H to George Washington, April 25, 1793.

To George Washington

Philadelphia, April 27, 1793. ". . . The enclosed Letter just received
from the Collector of Charleston contains information & raises a
question, which are proper for the eye of the President." [1]

LC, George Washington Papers, Library of Congress.
    1. Letter from Isaac Holmes not found. This letter is described in an entry in
JPP for April 29, 1793, as follows: "The Secretary of the Treasury laid before
me a letter he had recd from the Collector of Charleston S.C. respecting the
prizes sent in there by the French Frigate L'Ambuscade—Whether the duties
are to be paid as upon other Vessels? He has secured the duties by bond payable in 4 mos. but wishes instructions thereon. Encloses to the Secy a letter he
had recd on the subject from the French Consul at Charleston & his answer
thereto" (JPP, 103).
    On April 30, 1793, Washington returned Holmes's letter to H and observed
that H "shd. consider well the subject, & if necessary consult the Attorney
Genl. upon it. The Secretary observed that it was not a matter requiring to be
acted upon immediately—and that some other points which were now under
consideration were necessary first to be decided upon" (JPP, 103).

From Tench Coxe

[*Philadelphia, April 28, 1793.* On May 4, 1793, Hamilton wrote to George Washington and referred to "a letter of the 28 of April received yesterday from the Commissioner of the Revenue." *Letter not found.*]

From Stephen Higginson

Boston Apr. 28. 1793

Dr Sir

In the present State of things new cases every day arise that require a referrence to you.

It is a very desireable thing to have our Vessels & Our Seamen so guarded, as to prevent any interruption in Our Commerce that shall appear unreasonable & affrontive. There are men among us who will make the most of every injury done to our property, or insult offered to Our flag. I wish there were Sea Letters or other proper Documents issued by the Officer of the Union, to serve as uniform mode of Evidence as to the property &c. For want of this every man follows his own fancy as to the manner of doing it, & each foreign Consul is tenacious of his own forms & modes of legalising or authenticating. Why may not the Secretary, to whom it belongs, consult with the ministers or Residents from the different powers, & decide on the form of such Documents to be sent signed, & countersigned or not, to the several Collectors to be issued by them; & also on the mode of authentication by the Consuls? We shall have a vast number of Vessels, scattered every where over the face of the Deep; & I fear much uneasiness may arise, & real injury be sustained for want of a proper & uniform mode of evidencing the property, beside what results from the common custom house papers. The Dutch Treaty contains a form settled & required by the 25th Article,[1] it may serve as a model, but I should prefer ours more simple & clear.

This Object may not fall within your department, but you can put the business in train & help it forward.

I am in haste but with respect   Yours &ca   Stephen Higginson

ALS, Hamilton Papers, Library of Congress.
1. Higginson is referring to the Treaty of Amity and Commerce between the United Netherlands and the United States concluded on October 8, 1782. Article 25 provided that "in case that one of the Two Parties happens to be at War, the Vessells belonging to the Subjects or Inhabitants of the other Ally, shall be provided with Sea-Letters or Passports" (Miller, *Treaties*, II, 80). Attached to the treaty was "The Form of the Passport which shall be given to Ships and Vessells, in consequence of the 25th. Article of this Treaty" and a "Form of the Sea-Letter" (Miller, *Treaties*, II, 85–88).

From George Thacher [1]

[*Biddeford, District of Maine, April 28, 1793.* On May 18, 1793, Hamilton wrote to Thacher: "Your letter of the 28th. of April has been received." *Letter not found.*]

1. Thacher, a resident of Biddeford, District of Maine, was a Federalist member of the House of Representatives from Massachusetts.

From Wilhem and Jan Willink, Nicholaas and Jacob Van Staphorst, and Nicholas Hubbard

[*Amsterdam, April 28, 1793.* On May 1, 1793, Willink, Van Staphorst, and Hubbard wrote to Hamilton and referred to "our Respects of 4 & 28 Ulto." *Letter of April 28 not found.*]

From William Ellery

[*Newport, Rhode Island*] *April 29, 1793.* "I acknowledge the Receipt of your Circular Letter of the 29th. of March last. . . . As a War has been declared between the French and British Nations, the Port of Newport is easily accessible, and it may be convenient for the Ships of War and Privateers of the French Nation to bring into it Vessels which they may capture from the British on this coast, and they are not prohibited by the Treaty of Amity and Commerce [1] from selling such Vessels and their cargoes in any port of the United States, it is probable that some British Vessels which may be captured by them, may be brought into & sold in this District, and it is uncertain how soon this may take place. I should therefore be happy to be informed how I am to conduct on such an occasion. The Duties imposed by Law on goods, wares & merchandize imported into the United States I imagin would be demandable on such prize goods, and that of course they must be reported and entered at the Custom House; but what, upon this supposition, should be the form of the Report and Entry I am at a loss to determin, and whether the duties should be paid down or secured to be paid, and, if secured to be paid, what time should be allowed for payment. Be pleased to favour me with such directions in this respect, and in general with regard to my Official conduct towards the Ships of War & Privateers belonging to either of the powers which may be at war, and the Vessels and their cargoes captured by them and brought into this District as shall be judged proper; and with such Sea Letters or Pass Ports as you may deem will be for the security of our navigation & commerce."

LC, Newport Historical Society, Newport, Rhode Island.
   1. See H to John Jay, first letter of April 9, 1793, note 2.

From John Hopkins [1]

United States Loan Office
[Richmond] State of Virga. April 29. 1793.

Sir

In compliance with your letter of the 21st of April 1792,[2] I have to inform you that James Brown this day applied for the purpose of transferring the Stock standing in his name in trust for William Short Esqr to the said William Short; and considering that the object of Mr. Jeffersons letter to you of the 19th of April[3] would be fully answered by this Transfer, I have accordingly permitted it to take place and the Stock now stands in the name and to the Credit of Mr Short.

   I have the honor to be,   Sir,   Your Mo. Obedt Servant.

John Hopkins,
Commr Loans for Virga.

The Honble
Alexander Hamilton
Secretary of the Treasury.

Copy, William Short Papers, Library of Congress.
   1. For background to this letter, see Thomas Jefferson to H, April 9, 1793.
   2. Letter not found. This should be 1793.
   3. Hopkins apparently meant to refer to Jefferson's letter of April 9, 1793.

To William Seton

[*Philadelphia, April 29, 1793.* On May 3, 1793, Seton wrote to Hamilton: "I did not answer your Letter of the 29th." *Letter not found.*]

Treasury Department Circular
to the Collectors of the Customs

Treasury Department,
April 29th, 1793.

Sir,

It having been deemed expedient, to commit to the Commissioner of the Revenue the business of preparing certain documents, respecting commerce, navigation, and manufactures, with a view to the public service, I request that you will regularly transmit to his office the quarterly Returns of Exports. It is also my request, that you furnish him from time to time with such other papers and pieces containing information relative to those objects, arising from materials in your office, or matters under your immediate observation, as he may desire. This, however, is not meant to include any official returns or documents which you have been or shall be directed to transmit to any other office of this Department.

With great consideration, I am, Sir, Your Obedient

A Hamilton

LS, to John Fitzgerald, John Fitzgerald Papers, Library of Congress; LS, to Samuel Gerry, Indiana Historical Society Library, Indianapolis; LS, Office of the Secretary, United States Treasury Department; LC, RG 56, Circulars of the Office of the Secretary, "Set T," National Archives.

To Edmund Randolph [1]

Treasury Department
April 30, 1793

Sir

On a reperusal of the letter from the Governor of Virginia which I mentioned to you, I find that the proposal is to submit the Question to the Supreme Court of the United States at its next term.[2]

With the approbation of the President and in conformity to your opinion I have informed the Governor that the Question would be submitted as proposed.[3]

It will therefore remain for you to concert with the proper law Officer of the State of Virginia the most fit effectual and summary mode of obtaining the opinion of the Court on the point in Question.

The Comptroller has been directed to possess you of the facts as communicated to the Treasury. Should any difference in this respect appear, it can easily be settled on the spot by the Cooperation of the Commissioner of Loans.

With respectful consideration I have the honor to be Sir Yr Obed

The Atty General
of The Ustates

ADf, Connecticut Historical Society, Hartford.
1. For background to this letter, see H to Henry Lee, March 22, 1793, and Lee to H, April 12, 1793.
2. On February 13, 1794, the case of the *United States* v *John Hopkins* was heard in the Supreme Court. A motion was made that the court "grant a rule to shew cause . . . why a Mandamus should not issue directed to John Hopkins Esquire Commissioner of Loans for the District of Virginia requiring him to admit Richard Smyth to subscribe to the Loan proposed by the United States in and by an act of the Congress of the United States entitled 'An Act supplementary to the Act making provision for the debt of the United States' passed the 8th: day of May 1792 a certain certificate for the sum of 23,454 Dollars 76 Cents issued by the Commonwealth of Virginia bearing date prior to the 1st. day of January 1790 which Certificate after having been paid into the Treasury of the said Commonwealth was re-issued thereout in pursuance of an Act of the legislature of the said Commonwealth passed the 26th: day of December 1792." On February 14 the Attorney General "proceeded to shew cause why a Mandamus should not issue against the Defendant," and on February 15 "the Court after argument and full consideration are of opinion that the right claimed by the petitioner in the present case does not appear sufficiently clear to authorize the Court to issue the Mandamus moved for" (RG 267, Minutes of the Supreme Court of the United States, National Archives).
3. Letter not found.

From John Steele [1]

Salisbury [North Carolina] April 30th. [1793]

My dear sir,

This morning Mr. Genet the French Minister set out from this place for Philada.[2] His route is by Richmond thence to Mont Vernon, where he hopes to see the President. It will require 18 or 20 days for him to reach Philada. tho: he professes, and really seems to be in haste. You have heard much of *this Citizen* no doubt, and therefore any thing of him from me will seem superfluous; but as I am writing of the man that we are all affraid of, permit me to say, that he has a good person, fine ruddy complection, quite active and seems always in a bustle, more like a busy man than a man of business. A French man in his manners, he announces himself in all companies as the Minister of the Republic &ca. talks freely of his Commission, and like most Europeans seems to have adopted mistaken notions of the penetration, and knowledge of the people of the United States. He is, or affects to be, highly gratified by the affectionate treatment he has thus far experienced from the Americans, except of Charleston where an insult was offered to a French seaman which he attributes to the Merchants, who seem in his opinion almost wholly attachd to the Brittish. The Minister, notwithstanding his good nature, spoke angrily of this insult, and for a moment deviated from his system which is I think, to laugh us into the war if he can. The best informed men in this State, who are wholly disinterested continue uneasey, from an aprehension that our political connection with France, and our commercial intercourse with England will place the United States in a delicate, if not a dangerous situation during the war. My own mind has been at ease since the communication which you were pleased to make to me of your sentiments of that subject in Philada. This conversation having been confidential, I have never considered myself at liberty to repeat any part of it, but I have often said, on proper occasions, that the friends to Neutrality, & peace would find in the Secty. of The Treasury, an able and zealous friend. In short the best men in this country rely chiefly upon your talents, and disposition to avoid the rocks which lie upon the right hand, and upon the left, ready to dash our young government to pieces upon the least unskilfull pilotage.

This part of the country affords nothing worth your attention, except the prospect of plentiful harvests, and good share of political contentment. Those who have usually been most clamourous, are now in Congress, where you may be assured, they can do less evil than at home. With these *honorable Citizens* I am perfectly acquainted, and cou'd give you a more certain description of their characters, than of *the illustrious Republican* who occupies a considerable space in this letter. But you will know them soon enough.

Perhaps I may say a word, or two of each of the new Ones, sometimes before next December, as it is certainly important that a man in your situation should know what sort of Materials he has the misfortune to work with.

Commend me to the remembrance of Mrs. Hamilton, and believe me to be

With perfect respect   Your most humble servt.   Jno. Steele

ALS, Hamilton Papers, Library of Congress.
1. Steele, a leading North Carolina Federalist, had served in the North Carolina House of Commons in 1787 and 1788, as North Carolina commissioner to the Cherokee and Chickasaw Indians from 1788 to 1790, and as a member of the House of Representatives from March 4, 1789, to March 3, 1793.
2. Edmond Charles Genet had arrived at Charleston, South Carolina, aboard the French frigate *L'Embuscade* on April 8, 1793. On April 19, 1793, he left Charleston for Philadelphia and proceeded by way of Camden, Richmond, and Baltimore.

From Jean Baptiste de Ternant

Philadelphie le 30 Avril 1793
l'an 2 de la République francoise

Le Ministre plénipe. soussigné prie le Sécretaire de la tresorerie des Etats Unis, de vouloir lui faire payer la somme de vingt mille livres turnois,[1] à compte de la dette des dits Etats envers la france, ainsi qu'il a eté prècédement arreté par le President.   Ternant.

Copy, James Madison Papers, Library of Congress.
1. For background to this letter, see Thomas Jefferson to H, May 1, 1793; H to Jefferson, May 3, 1793.

To _____

[Philadelphia, April, 1793][1]

Dr. Sir

I request the favour of you to present for me the inclosed Bill & when paid to remit the amount in bills of the Bank of the UStates.
Yrs.   A Hamilton

ALS, Yale University Library.
1. This letter is undated but is endorsed "April, 1793" in an unidentified handwriting.

Statement on Remarks by John F. Mercer [1]

[April, 1793]

Mr. Mercer after amusing with his financial reveries the House of Representatives, during the last session, has thought fit to serve them up a second time, for the entertainment or instruction of the electors of Prince Georges and Anne Arundel counties, in the State of Maryland.[2] And as if the Editors of certain Gazettes thought doctrines worthy of propagation in proportion to their absurdity, we have seen the wild paradoxes of that Gentleman handed from paper to paper with no less attention than would be due to the most precious truths.

To follow Mr. Mercer, through all the incoherent ravings of a sublimated and excentric imagination, that often indulges itself in more than poetic fiction, would far exceed the leisure I have to bestow upon him. But he shall be examined in a few palpable particulars—the result of which will serve to shew his entire ignorance of the subject he undertakes to speak and write about, and his total incapacity to be the reformer of the public administration and the instructor of his fellow Citizens.

To effect this, in the clearest and simplest manner, I shall state each suggestion meant to be examined distinctly and shall connect with it its answer.

1 Suggestion   The present advantageous rate of the loans made abroad is not to be attributed to prudent management: For the old Congress, without the command of any fund whatever, in the midst of an unequal war, on the doubtful event of which all payment depended, borrowed of the Dutch once at four per Cent, and never at more than five per Cent. While the Secretary of the Treasury, in full possession of all the productive funds of the Continent has borrowed at five ꝑ Cent and never till lately so low as four.

Answer   The low rates of the loans made under the old government were for the most part *nominal;* those made under the present government are *real.* The only four per Cent loan made by the UStates on their own Credit of Individuals under the former government was in fact a   [3] per Cent loan. This arose from

The 4 ℔ Cent loans made under the present government[4] are incumbered with nothing but a charge of 5 ℔ Cent for brokerage and commissions and upon strict calculation allowing for the deduction to satisfy this charge, they will actually cost the United States   per Cent and no more. The difference is nearly   per Cent in favour of the present Government.

From the manner of expression used by Mr. Mercer, it would be supposed by one unacquainted with facts, that much time had been spent in bringing the reduction to this point. Whereas the provision for borrowing was only made the   [5] and as early as   a loan was effected at Antwerp[6] at 4½ per Cent in   one was effected at Amsterdam at four [per] Cent and a subsequent one has been made at the same place, at the same rate.[7] So that this important point was accomplished in   .

And from the facts stated it is evident that the present advantageous rate of loans is a consequence of the sound credit established by the measures of the present Government; contrary to the ignorant or deceptive assertion of Mr. Mercer. *Now is there a* truth which every channel of correspondence between this country and Europe conforms.

2 Suggestion. Were it not for the irredeemable quality of the debt, we might at this moment reduce the interest upon it to 4 ℔ Cent by borrowing the money in Holland at that rate.

Answer 1 The thing asserted is not practicable. Exertions have been making for   to borrow money abroad to pay of the arrears of our foreign debt and change the form of the residue advantageously; and in all that time the total amount of the loans effected does not exceed[8]

ADf, Hamilton Papers, Library of Congress.

1. For background to the Mercer-Hamilton dispute, see the introductory note to H to Mercer, September 26, 1793. The details of the controversy may be found in the following documents: H to Mercer, September 26, November 3, December 6, December, 1792, March 1, 14, 1793; Mercer to H, October 16-28, December, 1792, January 31, March 5, 26, 1793; H to David Ross, September 26, November 3, 1792; Ross to H, October 5-10, November 23, 1792, March 13, April 8, 25, July 23, August 30, 1793; Uriah Forrest to H, November 7, 1792.

It is uncertain when H prepared this document, but presumably it was written sometime before or shortly after the end of the direct correspondence between H and Mercer. If H had originally intended to publish this document, he apparently thought better of it, for the MS is endorsed in his handwriting: "This matter is dead. I will not revive it."

2. At the beginning of this document H wrote and crossed out: "Mr. Mercer, whose imagination delights in more than poetic fiction."

3. This and following spaces left blank in MS. This is a reference to the 1784 Holland loan. This loan carried only four percent interest but provided for additional premiums and "gratifications" which raised the real rate of interest. See William Short to H, September 1, 1790, note 22.

4. H is referring to the Holland loan of December, 1791, and the Holland loan of 1792. See Short to H, December 23, 28, 1791, June 28, 1792, note 17.

5. The foreign loans were authorized by "An Act making provision for the (payment of the) Debt of the United States" (1 *Stat.* 138–44 [August 4, 1790]) and "An Act making Provision for the Reduction of the Public Debt" (1 *Stat.* 186 [August 12, 1793]).

6. For a description of the Antwerp loan of 1791, see Short to H, November 8, 1791, note 4, and November 12, 1791.

7. See note 4.

8. The MS is incomplete.

From Thomas Jefferson

Philadelphia. May. 1. 1793.

Sir

When you mentioned to me yesterday that M. de Ternant proposed to apply for a sum of money,[1] & founded himself on a letter of mine which gave him reason to expect it, I thought I could not have written such a letter, because I did not recollect it, & because it was out of the plan which you know had been adopted that when we furnished one sum of money we should avoid promising another.[2] I have now most carefully examined all my letters to M. de Ternant, as far back as Mar. 7. 1792. the date of the first on the subject of furnishing money, & can assure you there is not a word, in one of them, which can be construed into a promise, express or implied, relative to the present subject, or which can have committed the government in the smallest degree to a departure from the rules it has laid down. I am equally confident that I have never said a word which could do it. Upon the ground therefore of any such commitment by me, the proposition will not be supported.

With respect to these applications in general, they were of course to pass through me: but I have considered them as depending too much on the arrangements of your department to permit myself to take & be tenacious of any particular ground, other than that whatever rule we adopt, it be plain & persevered in uniformly in all cases where the material circumstances are the same, so that we never refuse to one what has been done for another. It is, & ever has been my opinion & wish that we should gratify the diplomatic gentlemen in every way in which we can do it, without too great inconvenience or commitment of our own government. I think it our interest to do so; and am under this impression in the present case so much that I should readily concur, if it be the pleasure of the President, in reconsidering the rule adopted on a late occasion, & substituting any other consistent with our public duties, more adapted to the gratification of the diplomatic gentlemen, & uniformly to be applied where the material circumstances shall be the same: for it would reverse our aim were we to put ourselves in the case of disobliging one by refusing what we have done to gratify another. In these sentiments, I will hand to the President any application which M. de Ternant shall think proper to communicate to me in writing.

I have the honor to be with great respect, Sir   Your most obedt. humble servt.   Th: Jefferson

The Secretary of the Treasury.

ALS, letterpress copy, Thomas Jefferson Papers, Library of Congress.
1. See Jean Baptiste de Ternant to H, April 30, 1793.
2. See H to George Washington, November 19, 1792.

To William Seton

[*Philadelphia, May 1, 1793.* On May 3, 1793, Seton wrote to Hamilton: "I received your . . . Letter of the 1st." *Letter not found.*]

From Wilhem and Jan Willink, Nicholaas and Jacob Van Staphorst, and Nicholas Hubbard

Amsterdam 1 May 1793

The Situation of affairs here, as we had the honor to point it out to you in our Respects of 4 & 28 Ulto.[1] naturally urged our every attention, to provide for the support of the Credit of the United States, at the fast approaching Period of the first of June, when was to be paid f.1.000.000.—Reimbursement
  "   470.000.—Interest [2]

All the monies in our hands, having been more than absorbed by the Bills you had ordered to be drawn upon us, and which we must at all Events hold ourselves ready to honor, The Demands against the United States, required a Loan for Two Millions of Guilders, to face, the payments of June; the sums that we every Day expect your orders to apply to the Department of State, whose Funds are exhausted; and the Interest due next September, for which the last Instalments of the Loan would but just have been in time. Circumstances, which joined to the strong probability of our Advices of the State of affairs in Europe, not reaching you early enough, to enable you to make the Provision in Season, seemed to prescribe absolutely the Recourse to a Loan of that Extent; notwithstanding which, the disagreeable Consequences of giving five per Cent Interest for a new Loan, after we had assured our undertakers the United States would borrow no more at that rate, and the difficulty such a step would lay in the way of a future Reduction of the Interest, operated so forcibly upon us, that after having protracted the Decision of the matter, to the last moment Prudence warranted, We determined only to propose a prolongation of the Reimbursment, and to assume the advance ourselves of the large sum of Interest, which in such a critical Juncture, is an object of very great consequence indeed. By this means, We should maintain the appearance, of not borrowing any fresh Sums at an increased Interest, avoid Stretching the Credit of the United States to the utmost under such unfavorable Circumstances, and thereby facilitate the obtainments hereafter at a lower Interest, should events render such in any wise practicable.

It was therefore only on the 27th. April, that we closed with the undertakers, for the prolongation of the Reimbursment of the one Million of florins due the 1st. June 1793 by the United-States, at the same Interest of five per Cent per Annum for Ten years, reserving however unto the united States, the faculty to discharge same, as much sooner as they shall please: It was totally impossible, to stipulate for a Lower Interest, A Point you will easily concede, upon our informing you, that the five Per Cent American Bonds were not Saleable at more than par, and the four per Cents were not above 91 Per Cent.

We succeeded to fix the Charges at 3½ Per Cent, because It was a Prolongation, which is an half Per Cent lower than the last five

Per Cent Loan, and extraordinarily favorable, considering the State of affairs here and all over Europe: You Sir! we are persuaded will judge the same of them.

On the 29th. ultimo, we received your Respected favors of 1 February, 15 & 16 March,[3] advising your having arrested the Negotiation of ƒ495000. of the Bills you had directed to be drawn upon us, and of your Intention to remit us further, by the British April Packet ƒ975000. in Bills upon London and Amsterdam, Exertions on your part, not only active and praiseworthy in the extreme, but likewise beyond what we could have deemed or supposed probable: The last Letters had a very quick passage, yet arrived a few days too late, to prevent the prolongation of the Reimbursment.

The Treasurer of the United States has remitted us, Robert Morris's Bill at Sixty Days Sight on Bourdieu Chollet & Bourdieu, of London £12096.15. Stg. for which the united States shall be Credited.

We rejoice in the Determination we took not to open a New Loan, and likewise at the Intelligence of your Remittances coming forward at such a crisis, which have tended to raise an high Idea here, of the Credit and Resources of your Country, and of the judicious management of them; This can but operate very favorably, upon the future Loans to be raised here for the United States.

We are even at a loss to decide, whether the Prolongation is really to be regretted, since from the present Posture of the Powers of Europe, Events may proceed, of a Nature to render future Loans for some time to come, very difficult if not totally impracticable, as is actually the case with Austria and Russia, whose Agents here have Powers to borrow at five per Cent Interest, the very first moment they can push a Loan upon the market: If so or even in the prospect thereof, the Honor and permanent Advantages, flowing from the Provision your Remittances will make, for discharging regularly the large Amount of Interest, that is constantly falling due hereby the United-States, can greatly preponderate over any temporary Sacrifices, that such Provision may have occasioned.

We are respectfully &c.   W & J. Willink

                 N & J van Staphorst & Hubbard

Copy, William Short Papers, Library of Congress.
1. Letter of April 28, 1793, not found.

2. These sums were the first installment and interest due on the Holland loan of 1782. For a description of this loan, see Willink, Van Staphorst, and Hubbard to H, January 25, 1790, note 15.

3. Letters of February 1 and March 16, 1793, not found.

Alexander Hamilton and Henry Knox
to George Washington

Philadelphia
May 2. 1793

Sir

A conformity of opinion, and upon the same grounds, enables us to submit to you a joint Answer to the third of the Questions, which you were pleased to propose on the 18th. of April to the Heads of Departments and the Attorney General.

We have concluded that this mode would be more agreeable to you than a *repetition* of the same ideas and arguments in seperate answers.

With perfect respect & the truest attachment   We have the honor to be Sir,   Your most Obedt & hum servan⟨ts⟩   Alexander Hamilton
H Knox.

The President of The UStates

[ENCLOSURE]¹

Answer to Question the 3d. proposed
by the President of the UStates,
April 18th. 1793 viz

"If received" meaning a Minister from the Republic of France "shall it be absolutely or with qualifications, and if with qualifications of what kind"?

LS, in the handwriting of H, George Washington Papers, Library of Congress; copy, Hamilton Papers, Library of Congress; copy, in the handwriting of Knox, Massachusetts Historical Society, Boston.

1. DS, in the handwriting of H, George Washington Papers, Library of Congress; Df, in the handwriting of H, dated April, 1793, Hamilton Papers, Library of Congress. Although this opinion was officially that of H and Knox, H alone signed the document submitted to the President.

For background to this document, see Washington to H, Thomas Jefferson, Henry Knox, and Edmund Randolph, April 18, 1793, and "Cabinet Meeting. Opinion on a Proclamation of Neutrality and on Receiving the French Minister," April 19, 1793.

It is conceived to be adviseable, that the reception of the expected Minister from the Republic of France should be qualified by a previous declaration substantially to this effect—"that the Government of the United States uniformly entertaining cordial wishes for the happiness of the French Nation, and disposed to maintain with it an amicable communication and intercourse, uninterrupted by political vicissitudes, does not hesitate to receive [2] him in the character which his credentials import; yet considering the origin, course and circumstances of the Relations contracted between the two Countries, and the existing position of the affairs of France, it is deemed adviseable and proper, on the part of the United States, to reserve to future consideration and discussion, the question—whether the operation of the Treaties, by which those relations were formed,[3] ought not to be deemed temporarily and provisionally suspended—and under this impression, it is thought due to a spirit of candid and friendly procedure to apprize him before hand of the intention to reserve that question, lest silence on the point should occasion misconstruction." [4]

The grounds of this opinion are as follow—

Jefferson submitted his opinion on the treaties to the President on April 28, 1793 (ADS, George Washington Papers, Library of Congress). Randolph's opinion was submitted on May 6 (DS, partly in Randolph's handwriting, George Washington Papers, Library of Congress). The evident familiarity that Jefferson and Randolph showed with H's arguments can be explained by the fact that H stated them at some length in the cabinet meeting of April 19 ("Cabinet Meeting. Opinion on a Proclamation of Neutrality and on Receiving the French Minister," April 19, 1793, note 4).

2. At this point in the draft H wrote and crossed out: "the representative of the present Government of France provisionally instituted." Only substantive changes in the draft have been noted.

3. For a description of the articles of the 1778 Franco-American treaties of Alliance and Amity and Commerce which affected the diplomatic position of the United States in 1793, see H to John Jay, first letter of April 9, 1793, note 2.

4. Randolph stated: "It has been suggested, however, that Mr. Genest ought to be received with such a qualification as to reserve to the U. S. the liberty of renouncing the treaties with France, if at some future day they shall be found useless, dangerous or disagreeable; as Vattel expresses himself (Book 2. c. 12. S. 197).

"A qualification of this kind is not necessary; not a duty from candor; nor expedient. It is not necessary; because his title to be received does not depend upon those treaties; and therefore they will not gain the shadow of a confirmation from that act. It is not a duty from candor; because his mere reception excites no false hopes concerning the treaties. It is not expedient; since the right to renounce, whatsoever it may be, will not be impaired by a prudent forbearance on an irritating subject, which if not prematurely stirred, may possibly sleep for ever. Vigilance in government is undoubtedly wisdom; but it is equally wise not to create an evil for the gratification of subduing it."

The Treaties between the United States and France were made with His Most Christian Majesty, his heirs and successors. The Government of France which existed at the time those treaties were made, gave way, in the first instance to a new constitution, formed by the Representatives of the nation, and accepted by the King, which went into regular operation. Of a sudden, a tumultuous rising took place—the King was seized, imprisoned, and declared to be suspended by the authority of the National Assembly; a body delegated to exercise the legislative functions of the already established Government—in no shape authorised to divest any other of the constituted authorities of its legal capacities or powers.[5] So far then, what was done was a manifest assumption of power.

To justify it, it is alleged to have been necessary for the safety of the nation; to prevent the success of a counter-revolution,[6] meditated or patronized by the King.

On the other side it is affirmed, that the whole transaction was merely the execution of a plan, which had been for some time projected, and had been gradually ripening, to bring about an abolition of the Royalty and the establishment of a Republican Government.

No satisfactory proof is known to have been produced, to fix upon the King the charges, which have been brought against him.

On the other hand, declarations have escaped [from] [7] characters, who took a lead in the measure of suppressing the Royalty, which seem to amount to a tacit acknowlegement, that the events of the tenth of August were the result of a premeditated plan of the republican party, to get rid of the monarchichal power—rather than a necessary counteraction of mischievous designs on the part of the King.

Mr. Deseze [8]—one of the Counsel for the King makes these striking observations on the point—

5. At this point in the draft H wrote and crossed out: "in no shape qualified to do what they did that is to imprison the person of the King and suspend the Kingly power."
6. At this point in the draft H wrote and crossed out: "to defeat a conspiracy against its liberty on the part of the King."
7. The word within brackets has been taken from the draft.
8. Romain Deseze was one of the three lawyers who defended Louis XVI at his trial in December, 1792, and January, 1793. The observations H quotes were made by Deseze in his speech in defense of the King on December 26, 1792. The relevant section reads as follows:
"Je sais qu'on a dit que Louis avait excité lui-même l'insurrection du peuple, pour remplir les vues qu'on lui prête ou qu'on lui suppose.

"I know it has been said that he excited the Insurrection to gain the end of his plan. But who is now ignorant that this insurrection had been planned ripened—that it had its agents, its Counsul, its Directory? Who knows not, that there had been signed Acts and treaties on this subject?"

"*Within this Hall* has been contested the *glories* of the 10th of August. I do not come to dispute the glory; but since it has been *proved* that *this day was meditated,* how can it be attributed as a Crime to him?"

The events of the tenth of August were followed on the second and third of September with the massacre of a great number of persons in different parts of France including several distinguished individuals, who were known to be attached either to the ancient Government or to the constitution, which had succeeded it.

The suspension of the King was accompanied by a call upon the primary assemblies to depute persons to represent them in a Convention, in order to the taking of such measures as the exigency of the conjuncture might require.

Under circumstances not free from precipitation violence and awe deputies to a National Convention were chosen. They assembled on the   9 of September at Paris, and on the very day of their Meeting, decreed the abolition of Royalty.

They proceeded in the next place to organise a temporary provisional Government; charged with managing the affairs of the nation, till *a constitution should be established.*

"Et qui donc ignore aujourd'hui, que longtemps avant la journée du 10 août, on préparait cette journée, qu'on la méditait, qu'on la nourrissait en silence, qu'on avait cru sentir la nécessité d'une insurrection contre Louis, que cette insurrection avait ses agents, ses moteurs, son cabinet, son directoire?

"Qu'est-ce qui ignore qu'il a été combiné des plans, formé des ligues, signé des traités?

"Qu'est-ce qui ignore que tout a été conduit, arrangé, exécuté pour l'accomplissement du grand dessein qui devait amener pour la France les destinées dont elle jouit?

"Ce ne sont pas là, législateurs, des faits qu'on puisse désavouer: ils sont publics; ils ont retenti dans la France entière; ils se sont passés au milieu de vous; dans cette salle même où je parle, on s'est disputé la gloire de la journée du 10 août. Je ne viens point contester cette gloire à ceux qui se la sont décernée, je n'attaque point les motifs de l'insurrection, je n'attaque point ses effets; je dis seulement que, puisque l'insurrection a existé, et bien antérieurement au 10 août, qu'elle est certaine, qu'elle est avouée, il est impossible que Louis soit l'aggresseur." (*Archives Parlementaires,* LV, 633.)

9. Space left blank in MS. The National Convention met and decreed the abolition of royalty on September 21, 1792.

As a circumstance that gives a complexion to the course of things, it is proper to mention that the Jacobin Club at Paris (a society which with its branches in different parts of France appears to have had a prevailing influence over the affairs of the Country) previous to the meeting of the Convention entered into measures with the avowed object of *purging* the Convention of those persons, favourers of Royalty, who might have escaped the *attention* of the *primary assemblies.*

In the last place, the late King of France has been tried and condemned by the Convention, and has suffered death.

. Whether he has suffered justly or unjustly—whether he has been a guilty tyrant or an unfortunate victim is at least a problem. There certainly can be no hazard in affirming, that no proof has yet come to light sufficient to establish a belief, that the death of Louis is an act of National Justice.

It appears to be regarded in a different light throughout Europe, and by a numerous and respectable part, if not by a majority, of The People of the United States.

Almost all Europe is or seems likely to be armed, in opposition to the present Rulers of France—with the declared or implied intention of restoring if possible the Royalty, in the successor of the deceased monarch.

The present war, then, turns essentially on the point—what shall be the future Government of France? Shall the royal authority be restored in the person of the successor of Louis, or shall a republic be constituted in exclusion of it?

Thus stand the material facts, which regard the origin of our connections with France, and the obligations or dispensations that now exist. They have been stated, not with a view to indicate a definitive opinion concerning the propriety of the conduct of the present Rulers of France, but to shew, that the course of the Revolution there, has been attended with circumstances, which militate against a full conviction of its having been brought to its present *stage,* by such a *free, regular* and *deliberate* act of the nation, and with such a spirit of justice and humanity, as ought to silence all scruples about the validity of what has been done, and the morality of aiding it, even if consistent with policy.

This great and important question arises out of the facts which have been stated.

Are the United States bound, by the principles of the laws of nations, to consider the Treaties heretofore made with France, as in present force and operation between them and the actual Governing powers of the French Nation? or may they elect to consider their operation as suspended, reserving also a right to judge finally, whether any such changes have happened in the political affairs of France as may justify a renunciation of those Treaties? [10]

It is believed, that they have an option to consider the operation of the Treaties as suspended, and will have eventually a right to renounce them, if such changes shall take place as can *bona fide* be pronounced *to render* a continuance of the connections, which result from them, disadvantageous or dangerous.

There are two general propositions which may be opposed to this opinion. I. That a Nation has a right, in its own discretion, to change its form of Government; to abolish one, and substitute another. II That *real* Treaties [11] (of which description those in ques-

10. Jefferson stated: "I consider the people who constitute a society or nation as the source of all authority in that nation, as free to transact their common concerns by any agents they think proper, to change these agents individually, or the organisation of them in form or function whenever they please: that all the acts done by those agents under the authority of the nation, are the acts of the nation, are obligatory on them, & enure to their use, & can in no wise be annulled or affected by any change in the form of the government, or of the persons administering it. Consequently the Treaties between the US and France, were not treaties between the US. & Louis Capet, but between the two nations of America & France, and the nations remaining in existance, tho' both of them have since changed their forms of government, the treaties are not annulled by these changes."

11. On the distinction between "real" and "personal" treaties Vattel wrote:
"By another general division of treaties or alliances they are distinguished into *personal* and *real:* the first are those that relate to the person of the contracting parties, and are restrained and in a manner attached to them. *Real alliances* relate only to the things of which they treat, without any dependence on the person of the contracting parties.

"The *personal alliance* expires with him who contracted it.
"The *real alliance* is affixed to the body of the state, and subsists as long as the state, if the time of its duration is not limited. . . .

"Every alliance made by a republic is in its own nature real, for it relates only to the body of the state. When a free people, a popular state, or an Aristocratical republic concludes a treaty, it is the state itself that contracts; and its engagements do not depend on the lives of those who were only the instruments: the members of the people or of the regency change and succeed each other; but the state is always the same.

"Since then such a treaty directly relates to the body of the state, it subsists, though the form of the republic happens to be changed, and though it should be even transformed into a monarchy. For the state and the nation are always the same, whatever changes are made in the form of the government, and the treaty concluded with the nation, remains in force as long as the nation exists. But it is manifest that we ought to except from this rule all the treaties that relate to the form of the government. Thus two popular states that have treated expressly, or that appear evidently to have treated with the view of maintaining themselves in concert in their state of liberty and popular government, cease to be allies at the very moment when one of them has submitted to be governed by a single person.

"Every public treaty concluded by a king or any other monarch, is a treaty of the state; it lays under an obligation the intire state, the nation which the king represents, and whose power and right he exercises. It seems then at first that every public treaty ought to be presumed real, as concerning the state itself. There is no doubt with respect to the obligation to observe the treaty, this relates only to its duration. Now there is often room to doubt whether the contracting parties have intended to extend the reciprocal engagements beyond the term of their own lives, and to bind their successors. Conjunctures change; a burthen that is to day light, may in other circumstances become insupportable or too heavy: the manner of thinking among sovereigns is no less variable; and there are things which it is convenient that each prince should dispose of freely according to his own plan. There are others that are freely granted to a king and would not be permitted to his successor. It is necessary then to consider the terms of the treaty, or the design of it, in order to discover the intentions of the contracting powers.

"Treaties that are perpetual, and those made for a determinate time, are real; since their duration does not depend on the lives of the contracting parties.

"In the same manner when a king declares in the treaty that it is made for himself and his successors, it is manifest that the treaty is real. It is affixed to the state and made in order to last as long as the kingdom itself.

"When a treaty expressly declares, that it is made for the good of the kingdom, it is a manifest indication that the contracting powers have not intended to make it depend on the duration of their lives; but rather to affix it to the duration of the kingdom itself: the treaty is then real.

"Independently even of this express declaration, when a treaty is concluded to procure an advantage to the state that will always subsist, there is no reason to believe that the prince who has concluded it, was willing to limit it only to the duration of his life. Such a treaty ought then to be considered as real, unless very strong reasons shew, that he with whom it was concluded, granted the advantage to which it relates only out of regard to the prince then reigning, and as a personal favour; in this case the treaty terminates with the life of the prince, the reason of the concession expiring with him. But this reserve is not easily presumed; for it would seem that if contracting parties had this in their view, they would have expressed it in the treaty.

"In case of doubt, when nothing clearly establishes, either the personality or the reality of a treaty, it ought to be presumed real if it turns on things that are favourable, and personal in matters that are odious. The things favourable are here those that tend to the common advantage of the contracting powers, and that equally favour the two parties; things odious are those that burthen one party alone, or that are a greater grievance to one than the other. . . . But if the engagement has something odious, if one of the contracting states finds itself overburthened, how can it be presumed that a prince who entered into such engagements, was willing to lay that burthen forever upon his kingdom? Every sovereign is presumed to desire the safety and advantage of the state with which he is entrusted, it cannot then be supposed, that he has consented to load it forever with a burthensome obligation. . . .

tion are) bind the NATIONS, whose Governments contract and continue in force, notwithstanding any changes, which happen in the forms of their Government.[12]

The truth of the first proposition ought to be admitted in its fullest latitude. But it will by no means follow, that because a Nation has a right to manage its own concerns, as it thinks fit, and to make such changes in its political institutions as itself judges best calculated to promote its interests—that it has *therefore* a right to involve other nations, with whom it may have had connections, *absolutely* and *unconditionally*, in the consequences of the changes, which it may

---

"Since public treaties, and even those that are personal, concluded by a king or by any other sovereign who is invested with sufficient power, are treaties of state and obligatory with respect to the whole nation; . . . real treaties, made to subsist independently of the person who has concluded them, doubtless, oblige his successors; and the obligation imposed on the state passes successively to all its conductors, in proportion as they assume the public authority. It is the same with respect to the rights acquired by these treaties: they are acquired for the state, and successively pass to its conductors.

"It is at present a pretty general custom for the successor to confirm, or renew even real alliances, concluded by his predecessors: and prudence requires, that this precaution should not be neglected, since men lay a greater stress on an obligation they themselves have contracted, than on one imposed on them by others, or to which they have only tacitly agreed. This is because they believe their word engaged in the first, and only their conscience in the other." (Vattel, *Law of Nations*, I, 182–85.)

12. Randolph stated: ". . . the treaties need not shun an investigation.

"In their origin, they were dear to the U.S., for the critical relief, which the connection with France administered. They were rendered still more dear by the rescinding of the two obnoxious clauses. They were fulfilled by the French with fidelity, and would have remained sacred in the eyes of the Americans, but for the new order of things in France. This new order has produced many changes; the most influential of which on the present inquiry are, the dissolution of the old monarchy, the erection of a republic with an hereditary executive, the dethronement and decapitation of that hereditary executive, the annihilation of every germ of monarchy, and a government, at this moment unsettled. We are led to ask . . . whether the treaties have been annulled by these circumstances? . . . Perhaps the position is true, that if the U.S. have an option to declare the treaties void, or even to hold them in suspence, they ought not *now* to assert to their operation. For the provisions, contained in them are of such a nature, that, if they were *created* during *this* war, they would amount to a breach of neutrality. The guarantee, and the preference to French privateers wear too much of the air of a military succour, to be consistent with impartiality; were they now for the first time stipulated; and to *elect* without being absolutely bound, in favor of treaties having those articles, is equal to the original formation of them.

"But the U.S. are absolutely bound, with out the privilege of election.

"They are real treaties, not personal. These two species are so well defined and distinguished by Vattel in the 12th chapter of his second book, from the 183d to the 191st. sections inclusive, as to deserve transcription at length."

think proper to make. This would be to give to a nation or society, not only a power over its own happiness, but a power over the happiness of other Nations or Societies. It would be to extend the operations of the maxim, much beyond the *reason* of it—which is simply, that every Nation ought to have a right to provide for its *own happiness*.[13]

13. On the right to suspend treaties Jefferson observed: "The Moral duties which exist between individual and individual, in a state of nature, accompany them into a state of society, & the aggregate of the duties of all the individuals composing the society constitutes the duties of that society towards any other; so that between society & society the same moral duties exist as did between the individuals composing them while in an unassociated state, their maker not having released them from those duties on their forming themselves into a nation. Compacts then between nation & nation are obligatory on them by the same moral law which obliges individuals to observe their compacts. There are circumstances however which sometimes excuse the non-performance of contracts between man & man: so are there also between nation & nation. When performance, for instance, becomes *impossible*, non-performance is not immoral. So if performance becomes *self-destructive* to the party, the law of self-preservation overrules the laws of obligation to others. For the reality of these principles I appeal to the true fountains of evidence, the head & heart of every rational & honest man. It is there Nature has written her moral laws, & where every man may read them for himself. He will never read there the permission to annul his obligations for a time, or for ever, whenever they become 'dangerous, useless, or disagreeable.' Certainly not when merely *useless* or *disagreeable*, as seems to be said in an authority which has been quoted, Vattle. 2. 197. and tho he may under certain degrees of *danger*, yet the danger must be imminent, & the degree great. . . .

"The danger which absolves us must be great, inevitable & imminent. Is such the character of that now apprehended from our treaties with France? What is that danger. 1. Is it that if their government issues in a military despotism, an alliance with them may taint us with despotic principles? But their government, when we allied ourselves to it, was a perfect despotism, civil & military. Yet the treaties were made in that very state of things, & therefore that danger can furnish no just cause. 2. Is it that their government may issue in a republic, and too much strengthen our republican principles? But this is the hope of the great mass of our constituents, & not their dread. They do not look with longing to the happy mean of a limited monarchy. 3. But says the doctrine I am combating, the change the French are undergoing may possibly end in something we know not what, and bring on us danger we know not whence. . . . it is not the *possibility of danger*, which absolves a party from his contract: for that possibility always exists, & in every case. It existed in the present one at the moment of making the contract."

Randolph stated: "This quotation [from Vattel], applied in its most essential doctrines to the treaties with France, may be affirmed without being minute, to justify in the most conclusive manner, that they are *national* and *real*, not *personal*, and will therefore survive the prince, who in the character of chief magistrate was only the organ, thro' which they were made. In the language of politics, our gratitude towards him ought to be showed by the nation, which enabled him to be so beneficient to us. The change of government is from a less, to a greater degree of congeniality with our own, as far at least, as it has been yet established. The treaties are as capable of being executed now, as ever; and had it been in our choice to have contracted with a monarch or a republic; had it been foretold, that the commonwealth of France was to rise on the ruins of its despotism, we should have courted its alliance with equal avidity. Sympathy with the unhappy Lewis need not be concealed by us, as *men;* but it is the nation, which put him to death; it is the nation, which abolished kingly government; and their will in their own internal affairs cannot be rightfully controuled by foreigners.

"Except in bloodshed, has not America exhibited examples of altering constitutions, with constant recognitions of old engagements? Did not many of the obligations under the royal, descend on the state-governments? Have not the state governments observed the same conduct in all their mutations? Did not the present government of the U. S. avow its own liability to the debts of the confederation? The national convention indeed are said to have invalidated some ancient treaties, but to what extent is unknown here. Thus much, however, is certain; some of them, such as the family-compact, and those, which related to the prince *personally,* might well be proclaimed void; but the American treaties are treated with reverence.

"The U.S. then have no excuse for presuming them to be cancelled at this time; and even if they had, the President would probably not bring upon himself alone the responsibility of hazarding a war, by a declaration of their nullity.

"2. The second point for examination is, whether the U. S. may hold the treaties with France suspended?

"She will quickly collect the meaning of such a measure to be, that her destiny is, in our judgment, so precarious, as to exact the utmost scrupulousness in admitting her old claims to subsist. She will discern, that it has been dictated by our fear of her enemies, and a disregard of herself. What process of reasoning will be adopted by her in such an exigency? She will ask, whether the treaties be void? The answer will be, that they are not void. Are they in force? No. They must then be in a kind of middle, or dormant state, until some important change shall be effected. Must this change, which is to call the treaties into life, be a restoration of the former tyranny? No man insinuates it. Must the change be to the constitution accepted by the late king? During its operation, the binding quality of the treaties was not suspected. We are assured, that the future government, if it shall not be a monarchy, absolute or limited, must be a republic or democracy. Mark then the inference. While despotism lasted, America thought herself bound: While an hereditary king presided, America thought herself bound: as soon as the tincture of monarchy was suppressed, America kept herself equipoized to renounce or confirm. It partakes of the nature of a threat to France to reestablish monarchy in some form or other, at the peril of our alliance. Such a conduct would be coloured only by alledging the apprehension of too much tumult and distraction in the French government to merit our confidence. But this pretext would be driven to flight, by shewing, that the nation, for whom and by whose officer, the treaties were made, are now wielding their own power; and therefore is upon as respectable a footing, as with a prince at its head.

"Even if the U.S. should be ultimately reduced to the extremity of renouncing the treaties, France could reproach them, with but an illgrace, for suffering them still to operate. Her remonstrances, so far as they might be built on the charge of a fraudulant acquiescence at this time, might be repelled by the delicacy of our deportment, in discarding wanton conjectures of the possibility of her being unable hereafter to perform her contract. Besides if to abolish a treaty unjustly is a cause of war, to suspend it unjustly is also a cause of war, tho' inferior in degree."

If then a Nation thinks fit to make changes in its Government, which render treaties that before subsisted between it and another nation useless or dangerous or hurtful to that other nation, it is a plain dictate of reason, that the *latter* will have a right to renounce those treaties; because *it* also has a right to take care of its own happiness, and cannot be obliged to suffer this to be impaired by the means, which its neighbour or ally may have adopted for its own advantage, contrary to the ancient state of things.

But it may be said, that an obligation to submit to the inconveniencies that may ensue, arises from the other maxim, which has been stated, namely, that real treaties bind nations,[14] notwithstanding the changes which happen in the forms of their Governments.

All general rules are to be construed with certain reasonable limitations. That which has been just mentioned must be understood in this sense—that changes in forms of Government do not of course abrogate *real* treaties; that they continue absolutely binding on the party, which makes the change, and will bind the other party, unless in due time and for just cause he declares his election to renounce them—that in good faith he ought not to renounce them, unless the change which happened does really render them useless or materially less advantageous, or more dangerous than before. But for good and sufficient cause,[15] he may renounce them.

Nothing can be more evident, than that the existing forms of Government of two Nations may enter far into the motives of a real treaty. Two republics may contract an alliance—the principal inducement to which may be a similarity of constitutions, producing common interest to defend their mutual rights and liberties. A change of the Government of one of them into a monarchy or despotism may destroy this inducement, and the main link of common interest. Two monarchies may form an alliance on a like principle, their common defence against a powerful neighbouring republic. The change of the Government of one of the allies may destroy the source of common sympathy and common interest, and render it prudent for the other ally to renounce the connection, and seek to fortify itself in some other quarter.

14. At this point in the draft H wrote and crossed out: "not merely the contracting Government and attach themselves to them, whatever mutations attend the forms of their Governments."

15. At this point in the draft H wrote and crossed out: "of which he is to be the judge."

Two nations may form an alliance, because each has confidence in the energy and efficacy of the Government of the other. A revolution may subject one of them to a different form of Government— feeble fluctuating and turbulent, liable to provoke wars & very little fitted to repel them. Even the connections of a nation with other foreign powers may enter into the motives of an alliance with it. If a dissolution of ancient connections shall have been a consequence of a revolution of Government, the external political relations of the parties may have become so varied as to occasion an incompatibility of the alliance with the Power, which had changed its constitution with the other connections of its ally; connections perhaps essential to its welfare.

In such cases, Reason which is the touchstone of all similar maxims, would dictate, that the party whose government had remained stationary would have a right under a *bona fide* conviction that the change in the situation of the other party would render a future connection detrimental or dangerous, to declare the connection dissolved.

Contracts between nations as between Individuals must lose their force where the considerations fail.

A Treaty *pernicious* to the State is of itself void, where no change in the situation of either of the parties takes place. By a much stronger reason, it must become *voidable*, at the option of the other party, when the voluntary act of one of the allies has made so material a change in the condition of things, as is always implied in a radical revolution of Government.

Moreover, the maxim in question must it is presumed, be understood with this further limitation—that the Revolution be *consummated*—that the new Government be *established* and recognised among nations—that there be an *undisputed* organ of the national Will, to claim the performance of the stipulations made with the former Government.

It is not natural to presume, that an ally is obliged to throw his weight into either scale—where the war involves the very point, what shall be the Government of the Country; and that too against the very party with whom the formal obligations of the alliance have been contracted.

It is more natural to conclude, that in such a case, the ally ought either to aid the party, with whom the contract was immediately made—or to consider the operation of the alliance as suspended. The latter is undoubtedly his duty, rather than the former, where the Nation appears to have pronounced the change.

A doctrine contrary to that here supported may involve an opposition of moral duties, and dilemmas of a very singular and embarrassing kind.

A Nation may owe its existence or preservation intirely, or in a great degree, to the voluntary succours, which it derived from the Monarch of a Country—the then lawful organ of the national Will —the director of its sword and its purse—the dispenser of its aids and its favours. In consideration of the good offices promised or afforded by him, an alliance may have been formed—between the Monarch his heirs and successors and the country indebted to him for those good offices—stipulating future cooperation and mutual aid. This monarch, without any particular crime on his part, may be afterwards deposed and expelled by his nation, or by a triumphant faction, which may perhaps momentarily direct the national voice. He may find in the assistance of neighbouring powers friendly to his cause the means of endeavouring to reinstate himself.

In the midst of his efforts to accomplish this purpose—the ruling powers of the Nation over which he had reigned, call upon the Country, which had been saved by his friendship and patronage to perform the stipulations expressed in the alliance made with him and embark in a war against their friend and benefactor on the suggestion, that the treaty being a *real* one the actual rulers of the nation have a right to claim the benefit of it.

If there be no option in such case—would there not be a most perplexing conflict of opposite obligations?—of the faith supposed to be plighted by the treaty, and of justice and gratitude, towards a man, from whom essential benefits had been received, and who could oppose the *formal* and *express* terms of the contract to an abstract theoretic proposition? Would genuine honor, would true morality permit the taking a hostile part against the friend and benefactor, being at the same time the original party to the contract?

Suppose the call of the actual rulers to be complied with and the war to have been entered into by the ally—Suppose the expelled Monarch to have reentered his former dominions, and to have been joined by one half of his former subjects—how would the obligation then stand? He will now have added to the title of being the formal party to the contract that of being the actual possessor of one half the country and of the wishes of one half the Nation.

Is it supposeable, that in such a case the obligations of the alliance can continue in favour of those, by whom he had been expelled? Or would they then revert again to the Monarch? Or would they fluctuate with the alternations of good and ill fortune attending the one or the other party? Can a principle which would involve such a dilemma be true? Is it not evident, that there must be an option to consider the operation of the alliance as suspended during the contest concerning the Government—that on the one hand there may not be a necessity of taking part with the expelled Monarch, against the apparent will of the nation, or on the other, a necessity of joining the ruling powers of the moment against the immediate party with whom the contract was made and from whom the consideration may have flowed?

If the opinions of writers be consulted, they will, as far as they go, confirm the sense of the maxim, which is here contended for.[16]

16. Jefferson stated: "The doctrine then of Grotius, Puffendorf & Wolf is that 'treaties remain obligatory notwithstanding any change in the form of government, except in the single case where the preservation of that form was the object of the treaty.' There the treaty extinguishes, not by the election or declaration of the party remaining in statu quo; but independantly of that, by the evanishment of the object. Vattel lays down, in fact, the same doctrine, that treaties continue obligatory, notwithstanding a change of government by the will of the other party, that to oppose that will would be a wrong, & that the ally remains an ally, notwithstanding the change. So far he concurs with all the previous writers. But he then adds what they had not said, nor would say 'but if this change renders the alliance *useless,* dangerous, or *disagreeable* to it, it is free to renounce it.' It was unnecessary for him to have specified the exception of *danger* in this particular case, because that exception exists in all cases & it's extent has been considered. But when he adds that, because a contract is become merely *useless* or *disagreeable,* we are free to renounce it, he is in opposition to Grotius, Puffendorf, & Wolf, who admit no such licence against the obligation of treaties, & he is in opposition to the morality of every honest man, to whom we may safely appeal to decide whether he feels himself free to renounce a contract the moment it becomes merely *useless* or *disagreeable* to him? We may appeal too to Vattel himself, in those parts of his book where he cannot be misunderstood, & to his known character, as one of the most zealous & constant advocates for the preservation of good faith in all our dealings. Let us hear him on other occasions; & first where he shews what degree of danger or injury will authorize self-liberation from a treaty. 'If simple lezion' (lezion means the loss sustained by selling a thing for less than half value, which degree of loss rendered the sale void by the Roman law), 'if simple lezion, says he, or some degree of disadvantage in a treaty does not suffice to render it invalid, it is not so as to inconveniences which would go the *ruin* of the nation. As every treaty

ought to be made by a sufficient power, a treaty pernicious to the state is null, & not at all obligatory; no governor of a nation having power to engage things capable of *destroying* the state, for the safety of which the empire is trusted to him. The nation itself, bound necessarily to whatever it's preservation & safety require, cannot enter into engagements contrary to it's indispensable obligations.' Here then we find that the degree of injury or danger which he deems sufficient to liberate us from a treaty, is that which would go to the absolute *ruin* or *destruction* of the state; not simply the lesion of the Roman law, not merely the being disadvantageous, or dangerous. For as he says himself S. 158. 'lezion cannot render a treaty invalid. It is his duty, who enters into engagements, to weigh well all things before he concludes. He may do with his property what he pleases, he may relinquish his rights, renounce his advantages, as he judges proper: the acceptant is not obliged to inform himself of his motives, nor to weigh their just value. If we could free ourselves from a compact because we find ourselves injured by it, there would be nothing firm in the contracts of nations. Civil laws may set limits to lezion, & determine the degree capable of producing a nullity of the contract. But sovereigns acknolege no judge. How establish lezion among them? Who will determine the degree sufficient to invalidate a treaty? The happiness & peace of nations require manifestly that their treaties should not depend on a means of nullity so vague & so dangerous.'

"Let us hear him again on the general subject of the observance of treaties S. 163. 'It is demonstrated in Natural law that he who promises another confers on him a perfect right to require the thing promised, & that, consequently, not to observe a perfect promise, is to violate the right of another; it is as manifest injustice as to plunder any one of their right. All the tranquillity, the happiness & security of mankind rest on justice, on the obligation to respect the rights of others. The respect of others for our rights of domain & property is the security of our actual possessions; the faith of promises is our security for the things which cannot be delivered or executed on the spot. No more security, no more commerce among men, if they think themselves not obliged to preserve faith, to keep their word. This obligation then is as necessary as it is natural & indubitable, among nations who live together in a state of nature, & who acknolege no superior on earth, to maintain order & peace in their society. Nations & their governors then ought to observe inviolably their promises & their treaties. This great truth, altho' too often neglected in practice, is generally acknoleged by all nations: the reproach of perfidy is a bitter affront among sovereigns; now he who does not observe a treaty is assuredly perfidious, since he violates his faith. On the contrary nothing is so glorious to a prince & his nation, as the reputation of inviolable fidelity to his word.' Again S. 219. 'Who will doubt that treaties are of the things sacred among nations? They decide matters the most important. They impose rules on the pretensions of sovereigns: they cause the rights of nations to be acknoleged, they assure their most precious interests. Among political bodies, sovereigns, who acknolege no superior on earth, treaties are the only means of adjusting their different pretensions, of establishing a rule, to know on what to count, on what to depend. But treaties are but vain words if nations do not consider them as respectable engagements, as rules, inviolable for sovereigns, & sacred through the whole earth. S. 220. The faith of treaties, that firm & sincere will, that invariable constancy in fulfilling engagements, of which a declaration is made in a treaty, is then holy & sacred among nations, whose safety & repose it ensures; & if nations will not be wanting to themselves, they will load with infamy whoever violates his faith.

"After evidence so copious & explicit of the respect of this author for the sanctity of treaties, we should hardly have expected that his authority would have been resorted to for a wanton invalidation of them whenever they should

Grotius, while he asserts the general principle of the obligation of real treaties upon nations, notwithstanding the changes in their Governments—admits the qualification, which has been insisted upon—and expressly excepts the case where it appears that the motive to the Treaty was "peculiar to the form of Government, *as* when free States enter into an alliance for the defence of their liberties." Book II Chapt. 16. §XVI. No. 1.[17]

And *Vatel* who is the most systematic of the writers on the laws of nations lays down the qualification in the greatest latitude. To give a correct idea of his meaning it will be of use to transcribe the entire section with its marginal note. It is found Book II. Chapt: XII. §197.[18]

"The same question" (says he, to wit, that stated in the margin) [19] "presents itself in *real* alliances, and in general in all alliances made with the State, and not in particular with a King for the defence of his person. An Ally ought doubtless to be defended against every invasion, against every foreign violence, and even against his rebellious subjects; in the same manner, a republic ought to be defended against the enterprizes of one, who attempts to destroy the public liberty. But it ought to be remembered that an ally of the State or the nation is not its judge. If the nation has deposed its King in form, if the people of a republic have driven out their Magistrates and set themselves at liberty, or acknowleged the authority of an usurper,

---

become merely *useless* or *disagreeable*. We should hardly have expected that, rejecting all the rest of his book, this scrap would have been culled, & made the hook whereon to hang such a chain of immoral consequences. Had the passage accidentally met our eye, we should have imagined it had fallen from the author's pen under some momentary view, not sufficiently developed to found a conjecture what he meant: and we may certainly affirm that a fragment like this cannot weigh against the authority of all other writers, against the uniform & systematic doctrine of the very work from which it is torn, against the moral feelings & the reason of all honest men. If the terms of the fragment are not misunderstood, they are in full contradiction to all the written & unwritten evidences of morality: if they are misunderstood, they are no longer a foundation for the doctrines which have been built on them."

17. Grotius, *The Rights of War and Peace*, 360. Jefferson also cites this passage in his opinion.

18. Vattel, *Law of Nations*, I, 188. Jefferson also quotes this passage in his opinion.

19. A marginal note opposite this paragraph reads as follows: " 'What is the obligation of a *real alliance*, when the King who is the ally is driven from the throne?' " This also appears in Vattel, *Law of Nations*, I, 188, as a marginal note to the paragraph quoted by H.

either expressly or tacitly; to oppose these domestic regulations by disputing their justice or validity would be to interfere with the Government of the nation and to do it an injury. The ally *remains the ally of the State*, notwithstanding the change that has happened in it. *However* when this change renders the alliance *useless, dangerous*, or *disagreeable*, it may renounce it, for it may say upon a good foundation, that it would not have entered into an alliance with that nation, had it been under the present form of Government."

It is not perceived, that there is any ambiguity of expression, or any other circumstance to throw the least obscurity upon the sense of the author. The precise question he raises is what is the obligation of a *real* alliance when the King, who is the ally is driven from the throne? He concludes, after several intermediate observations, that the *ally remains the ally of the State*, notwithstanding the change which has happened. Nevertheless, says he, when the change renders the alliance *useless, dangerous* or *disagreeable*, it may be renounced.

It is observable, that the question made by writers always is whether, in a real alliance, when the King who is the ally is deposed, the ally of the deposed King is bound to súccour and support him. And though it is decided by the better opinions, as well as by the reason of the thing, that there is not an obligation to support him, against the will of the nation, when his dethronement is to be ascribed to that source—yet there is never a single suggestion on the other hand of the ally of such dethroned King being obliged to assist his nation against him. The most that appears to be admitted in favour of the decision of the nation is that there is no support due to the dethroned Prince.

Puffendorf puts this matter upon very proper ground. Referring to the opinion of Grotius, who with too much latitude lays it down "that a league made with a King is valid though that King or his successors be expelled the Kingdom *by his subjects;* for though he has lost his possession the right to the crown still remains in him" [20] —makes the following observation. "To me so much in this case seems to be certain, that if the terms of the league *expressly mention* and *intend* the defence of the Prince's *person* and *family*, he ought to be assisted in the recovery of his Kingdom. But if the league was

20. Grotius, *The Rights of War and Peace*, Book II, Ch. XVI, Section XVII, p. 362.

formed for *public good* only, 'tis a *disputable* point, whether the exiled Prince can demand assistance in virtue of his league. *For the aids mentioned are presumed to have been promised against foreign enemies, without view of this particular case.* Not but that still such a league leaves *liberty* to assist a *lawful Prince* against an *Usurper.*" [21]

The presumption here stated is a natural and a proper one, and in its reason applies to both sides, to the exiled Prince, who should demand succours against his nation, and to the nation, who having dethroned its Prince should demand succours to support the act of dethronement and establish the revolution. The ally in such case is not bound to come in aid of either party—but may consider the operation of the alliance as suspended, till the competition about the Government is decided.

What a difference is there between asserting it to be a *disputable* point, whether the ally of a dethroned Prince, in the case of a real Treaty, is not bound to assist him against the Nation—and maintaining that the ally is bound at all events to assist the Nation against him? For this is the consequence of asserting, that such a Treaty *ipso facto* attaches itself to the body of the nation, even in the course of a pending Revolution, and without option either to suspend or renounce.

If the practice of Nations be consulted—neither will that be found to confirm the proposition—that the obligation of real treaties extends unconditionally to the *actual Governors* of Nations, whatever changes take place. In the books which treat the subject, numerous examples of the contrary are quoted. The most prevailing practice has been to assist the *ancient* sovereign. In the very instance to which this discussion relates, this is the course, which a great part of Europe directly or indirectly pursues.

It may be argued by way of objection to what has been said—that admitting the general principle of a right for sufficient cause to renounce; yet still, as the change in the present case is from a monarchy to a Republic and no sufficient cause hitherto exists for a renunciation—the possibility of its arising here after in the progress of events, does not appear a valid reason, for resorting to the principle in question.

21. Pufendorf, *Of the Law of Nature and Nations,* Book VIII, Ch. IX, Section IX, p. 862.

To this the answer is, that no government has yet been instituted in France, in lieu of that which has been pulled down—That the existing political powers are by the French themselves denominated provisional, and are to give way to a constitution, to be established.

It is therefore impossible to foresee what the future Government of France will be—and in this sttae of uncertainty, the right to *renounce* resolves itself of course into a right to *suspend*. The one is a consequence of the other; *applicable* to the *undetermined* state of things. If there be a right to renounce, when the change of Government proves to be of a nature to render an alliance useless or injurious—there must be a right, amidst a pending revolution, to wait to see what change will take place.

Should it be said that the Treaty is binding now, no objectionable change having yet taken place, but may be renounced hereafter if any such change shall take place? The answer is, that it is not possible to pronounce at present, what is the *quality* of the change. Every thing is in *transitu*. This state of suspense as to the object of option, naturally suspends the option itself. The business may in its progress assume a variety of forms. If the issue may not be waited for, the obligations of the country may fluctuate indefinitely, be one thing to day, another to morrow; a consequence which is inadmissible.

Besides: the true reasoning would seem to be, that to admit the *operation* of the Treaties while the event is pending, would be to take the chance of what that event shall be, and would preclude a future renunciation.

Moreover: the right to consider the operation of the treaties as suspended, results from this further consideration—that during a *pending Revolution*, an ally in a real Treaty is not bound to pronounce between the competitors or contending Parties.

The conclusion from the whole is, that there is an option in the United States to hold the operation of the Treaties suspended—and that in the event, if the form of Government established in France shall be such as to render a continuance of the Treaties contrary to the interest of the United States, they may be renounced.

If there be such an option, there are strong reasons to shew, that the character and interest of the United States require, that they should pursue the course of holding the operation of the Treaties suspended.

Their character—because it was from Louis the XVI, the then sovereign of the Country, that they received those succours, which were so important in the establishment of their independence and liberty—It was with him his heirs and successors, that they contracted the engagements by which they obtained those precious succours.

It is enough on their part to respect the right of the nation to change its government, so far as not to side with the successors of the dethroned Prince—as to receive their ambassador and keep up an amicable intercourse—as to be willing to render every good office not contrary to the duties of real neutrality.

To throw their weight into the scale of the New Government, would it is to be feared be considered by Mankind as not consistent with a decent regard to the relations which subsisted between them and Louis the XVI—as not consistent with a due sense of the services they received from that unfortunate Prince—as not consistent with National delicacy and decorum.

The character of the United States may be also concerned in keeping clear of any connection with the Present Government of France in other views.

A struggle for liberty is in itself respectable and glorious. When conducted with magnanimity, justice and humanity it ought to command the admiration of every friend to human nature. But if sullied by crimes and extravagancies, it loses its respectability. Though success may rescue it from infamy, it cannot in the opinion of the sober part of Mankind attach to it much positive merit or praise. But in the event of a want of success, a general execration must attend it.

It appears thus far but too probable, that the pending revolution of France has sustained some serious blemishes. There is too much ground to anticipate that a sentence uncommonly severe will be passed upon it, if it fails.

Will it be well for the United States to expose their reputation to the *issue*, by implicating themselves as associates? Will their reputation be promoted by a successful issue? What will it suffer by the reverse? These questions suggest very serious considerations to a mind anxious for the reputation of the Country—anxious that it may emulate a character of sobriety, moderation, justice, and love of order.

The *interest* of the United States seems to dictate the course recommended in many ways.

I. In reference to their character, from the considerations already stated.

II. In reference to their peace.

As the present Treaties contain stipulations of military succours and military aids in certain cases which are likely to occur, there can be no doubt, that *if* there be an option, to consider them as not binding, as not in operation—the considering them as binding, as in operation, would be equivalent to making new treaties of similar import—and it is a well settled point, that such stipulations entered into pending a war or with a view to a war is a departure from Neutrality.

How far the parties opposed to France may think fit to treat us as enemies, in consequence of this, is a problem which experience only can solve—the solution of which will probably be regulated by their views of their own interest—by the circumstances which may occur —and it is far from impossible, that these will restrain them so long as we in fact take no active part in favour of France.

But if there be an option to avoid it, it can hardly be wise to incur so great an additional risk and embarrassment—to implicate ourselves in the perplexities which may follow.

With regard to the good effect of the conduct which is advocated, upon the Powers at War with France, nothing need be said.

Considering our interest with reference even to France herself, some reasons may be urged in favour of considering the Treaties as suspended.

It seems to be the general, if not the universal sentiment, that we ought not to embark in the war.

Suppose the French Islands attacked and we called upon to perform the Guarantee.[22]

22. Jefferson expressed his views on the American guarantee of the French West Indies as follows: "If *possibilities* would avoid contracts, there never could be a valid contract. For possibilities hang over everything. Obligation is not suspended till the danger is become real, & the moment of it so imminent, that we can no longer avoid decision without forever losing the opportunity to do it. But can a danger which has not yet taken it's shape, which does not yet exist, & never may exist, which cannot therefore be defined, can such a danger I ask, be so imminent that if we fail to pronounce on it in this moment we can never have another opportunity of doing it? The danger apprehended, is it that, the treaties remaining valid, the clause guarantying their West India islands

will engage us in the war? But Does the Guarantee engage us to enter into the war in any event? Are we to enter into it before we are called on by our allies? Have we been called on by them?—shall we ever be called on? Is it their interest to call on us? Can they call on us before their islands are invaded, or imminently threatened? If they can save them themselves, have they a right to call on us? Are we obliged to go to war at once, without trying peaceable negotiations with their enemy? If all these questions be against us, there are still others behind. Are we in a condition to go to war? Can we be expected to begin before we are in condition? Will the islands be lost if we do not save them? Have we the means of saving them? If we cannot save them are we bound to go to war for a desperate object? Will not a 10. years forbearance in us to call them into the guarantee of our posts, entitle us to some indulgence? Many, if not most of these questions offer grounds of doubt whether the clause of guarantee will draw us into the war. Consequently if this be the danger apprehended, it is not yet certain enough to authorize us in sound morality to declare, at this moment, the treaties null."

Randolph stated: "We cannot be embraced in the war by confessing the obligation of the treaties.

"Whether France will press the guarantee or not, is a problem, not yet solved. On the one hand, if she could involve the U. S. in the war, their force would be let out at large; their privateers might supply some of the naval defects of France: their ports would be *wholly* shut against the English. On the other, the French nation can now by the means of neutral American bottoms be relieved from a famine, which the scantiness of their own harvests too strongly predict. But suppose that a compliance with the guarantees be demanded: it will be adviseable, and in no manner derogate from the public honor, to decline the guarantee. If it were allowed (which however might, if this were the proper place for dilating on it, be safely denied) that Vattel is consistent with himself, consistent with principle, and conformable with other writers, when he vindicates the renunciation of whole treaties, which are useless or disagreeable; a *part* of those treaties may surely be renounced for the same causes. If he be right, only in assigning danger, as a justifying cause of renouncing a treaty, it may equally invalidate any article of that treaty, And in fact he is very explicit in B. 2. S. 160 and B. 3. S. 92, when he lays it down as to guarantees that, if the 'state, which has promised succours, finds itself unable to furnish them, its very inability is its exemption; and if the furnishing of succours would expose it to an evident danger, this also is a lawful dispensation.' Whosoever shall cast his eye over the U. S., will immediately discover, that a war, in which they should be engaged, would convulse them to the center. It will be the deathwound of public credit, the surest pledge of attachment to the general government. It will strike home at our trade, the only source of revenue, which the general temper of our country will yet permit to be used. It will give a scope to those discontents, which, from the opportunities, incident to the best-conducted war, will be concentrated against government, and will burst upon the Union itself. In a word the calamities of war are immeasurable. It may be humiliating to confess our weakness. But would it not be a hazardous experiment to be bickering with France immediately, by alternating the right of suspending the treaties, in order to counteract the possible necessity of refusing a guarantee, by telling a fact, which France and all the world know? Again: the alliance is defensive only; and an offensive war on the part of France would absolve us from the guarantee, pending that war. I own, that altho' the first blow has been struck by her in most instances, her war is not in my estimation thereby conclusively of an offensive nature. Still an additional prospect may open from this quarter, to cover us from the guarantee. Why then shall we risque an instantanious quarrel

To avoid complying with it—we must either say—

That the war being *offensive* on the part of France the *casus fœderis* does not exist.

Or, that as our cooperation would be *useless* to the object of the Guarantee and attended with more than ordinary danger to ourselves, we cannot afford it.

Would the one or the other be satisfactory to France?

The first would probably *displease*—the last would *not please*. It is moreover the most questionable & the least reputable of all the

---

with France? Why, when the design of holding the treaties in suspence is to guard against unfriendly events, may we not take the chance of friendly ones, to fortify us in withdrawing from the guarantee? If we be faithful in executing every other stipulation in the treaty, France herself, impressed with the awfulness of our situation, will acquit us. Upon principle she cannot condemn; and against an outrage on principle no uprightness of conduct can afford protection.

"As little is a war to be apprehended from the 17th and 22d. articles of the commercial treaty. It is true, that they provide for an inequality of measure in two particulars; first by cutting off shelter or refuge to the enemies of France, who shall have made prize of the people or property thereof; and secondly by prohibiting the privateers of those enemies from fitting their ships in the ports of the U. S., selling what they may have taken, exchanging their ships, merchandizes or any other lading, or purchasing victuals, except such, as shall be necessary for their going to the next port of their sovereign. The contrary privileges are allowed to the French.

"1. This treaty was made many years ago without relation to the present war; and it is therefore no breach of neutrality to fulfil it in both points.

"2. The 17th article has been copied almost verbatim, and intirely in substance, into the 40th. article of the commercial treaty between France and Great Britain on the 22d. of September 1786, with a reservation of preceding treaties. This disables Great Britain from complaining.

"3. In the 22d. article of the treaty with the Netherlands, it is specially declared, that it shall not derogate from the 17th and 22d articles of our treaty with France. This disables the Dutch from complaining.

"4. In the 19th. article of the treaty with Prussia, arrangements are fixed, similar to those in our treaty with France, in respect to prizes; and the latter treaty is recognized, as intitled to a preference. This disables Prussia from complaining.

"5. Further: neither the 17th. nor 22d. article of our treaty with France, imposes any disability on the *public* ships of war of any prince, except where they may have captured the French. The belligerent powers will not imagine, that the U. S. can have a predilection for the commercial treaty, which is not as advantageous, as might now be obtained, if the subject were new. Nor will they ascribe our adherence to it, to any desire of being unsocial to them; but rather to the pure motives of a young nation, seeking the general esteem by acts of good faith. In the vicissitudes, which may befal those powers, the U.S. will incur the blame of fluctuation and caprice, unless they pursue some stable principle; and none can be more stable, than this, that the nation, which does in fact exercise the supreme power for their own benefit, is to be considered, as justly exercising it."

objections, which a nation is allowed to oppose to the performance of its engagements. We should not therefore be much more certain of avoiding the displeasure of the present ruling Powers of France, by considering the Treaties as in operation, than by considering their operation as suspended; taking it for granted that we are in either case to observe a neutral conduct *in fact*.

But suppose the contest unsuccessfull on the part of the present Governing Powers of France. What would be our situation with the future Government of that Country?

Should we not be branded and detested by it, as the worst of Ingrates?

When it is added, that the restoration of the Monarchy would be very materially attributed to the Interposition of Great Britain—the reflection, just suggested, acquires peculiar weight and importance.

But against this may be placed the consideration—that in the event of the success of the present Governing Powers we should stand on much worse ground, by having considered the operation of the Treaties as suspended, than by having pursued a contrary conduct.

This is not clear, for the reasons just given; unless we are also willing, if called upon, to become parties in the war.

But admitting, that the *course* of considering the Treaties as in present operation, would give us a claim of merit with France, in the event of the establishment of the Republic—our affairs with that Country would not stand *so much the better* on this account as they would *stand worse*, for giving operation to the Treaties—should the monarchy be restored.

We should still have to offer a better claim to the friendship of France than any other power—the not taking side with her enemies —the early acknowlegement of the Republic, by the reception of its Minister—and such good offices as have been and may be rendered, consistently with a sincere neutrality.

The reasons too, which induced us not to go further, will have their due weight in times, that shall restore tranquillity, moderation, and sober reflection! They will justify us even to France herself.

Is there not however danger, that a refusal to admit the operation of the Treaties might occasion an immediate rupture with France?

A danger of this sort cannot be supposed without supposing such a degree of intemperance on the part of France as will finally force us to *quarrel* with her, or to *embark* with her.

And if such be her temper, a fair calculation of hazards will lead us to risk her displeasure in the first instance.

An inquiry naturally arises of this kind—Whether from the nature of the Treaties, they have any such intrinsic value, as to render it inexpedient to put them in jeopardy—by raising a question about their operation or validity?

Here, it may freely be pronounced, there is no difficulty. The military stipulations, they contain, are contrary to that neutrality in the quarrels of Europe, which it is our true policy to cultivate and maintain. And the commercial stipulations to be found in them present no peculiar advantages. They secure to us nothing or scarcely any thing, which an inevitable course of circumstances would not produce. It would be our interest, in the abstract, to be disengaged from them, and take the chance of future negociation, for a better treaty of commerce.

It might be observed by way of objection, to what has been said— that an *admission* of the *operation* of the Treaties has been considered as equivalent to taking part with France.

It is true, that the two things have been considered as *equivalent* to each other—and in strict reasoning this ought to be the case. Because—

I. If there be an option, the effect of not using it would be to pass from a *state* of *neutrality* to that *of being an ally*—thereby *authorising* the Powers at War with France to treat us as an enemy.

II. If under the operation of the Treaties, we are not bound to embark in the war, it must be owing either to *casualty* or *inability*.

If the war is not *offensive* on the part of France, an attack on the West India Islands would leave us no escape but in the plea of Inability.

The putting ourselves in a situation, in which it might so happen, that we could preserve our neutrality under no other plea than that of *inability* is in all the political legal relations of the subject—to make ourselves a party. In other words, the placing ourselves in a position, in which it would depend on casualty, whether it would not become our duty to engage in the war—ought in a general question of *establishing* or *recognising* a political relation with a foreign power embarked in war—to be regarded in the same light as taking part with that Power in the War. To do a thing, or to contract or incur an obligation of doing it, are not in such a question materially different.

There remain some miscellaneous views of the subject, which will serve to fortify the general reasoning.

I. The conduct of the present Government of France gives a sanction to other Nations to use some latitude of discretion in respect to their treaties with the former Government. That Government, it is understood, has formally declared null various stipulations of the ancient Government with Foreign Powers—on the principle of their inapplicability to the new order of things. Were it to be urged that an erroneous conduct on the part of France will not justify a like conduct on our part, it might be solidly replied—that a rule of practice formally adopted by any nation for regulating its political obligations towards other nations may justly be appealed to as a standard for regulating the obligations of other Nations towards her. Suppose this general ground to have been explicitly taken by France, that all treaties made by the old Government became void by the Revolution, unless recognised by the existing authority. Can it be doubted that every other nation would have had a right to adopt the same principle of conduct towards France? It cannot. By parity of reasoning, as far as France may in practice have pursued that principle, other Nations may justifiably plead the example.[23]

II. In addition to the embarrassment heretofore suggested, as incident to the admission of the present operation of the Treaties— this very particular one may attend our case. An *Island* may be taken by Great Britain, or Holland, with the avowed intention of holding it for the future King of France, the successor of Louis the XVI. Can it be possible, that a Treaty made with Louis the XVI. should *oblige* us to embark in the war to rescue a part of his dominions from his immediate successor? Under all the circumstances of the case, would the national integrity or delicacy permit it? Was it clear, that Louis merited his death as a perfidious Tyrant, the last question might receive a different answer, from what can now be given to it?

Ought the United States to involve themselves in a dilemma of this kind?

III. In national questions the general conduct of nations have great weight. When all Europe is or is likely to be armed in opposition to

23. In the margin opposite this paragraph H wrote: "Note. The fact on which this argument turns is stated from memory & is therefore the less relied upon. There has not been leisure to examine."

the authority of the present Government of France, would it not be to carry Theory to an extreme, to pronounce, that the United States are under an *absolute* indispensable obligation, not only to acknowlege respectfully the authority of that Government, but to admit the immediate operation of Treaties which would constitute them at once its ally?

IV. Prudence at least seems to dictate the course of *reserving* the question, in order that further reflection and a more complete developement of circumstances may enable us to make a decision both *right* and *safe*. It does not appear necessary to precipitate the fixing of our relations to France beyond the possibility of retraction. It is putting too suddenly too much to hazard.

It may be asked—Does an unqualified reception of the Minister determine the point?

Perhaps it does not. Yet there is no satisfactory guide by which to decide the precise import and extent of such a reception—by which to pronounce, that it would not *conclude* us, as to the Treaties. There is great room to consider the epoch of receiving a Minister from the Republic as that, *when* we ought to explain ourselves on the point in question—and silence, at that time, as a waver of our option.

It is probable that on the part of France it will be urged to have this effect, and if it should be truly so considered by her, to raise the question afterwards would lead to complaint, accusation, ill humour.

It seems most candid and most safe to anticipate—not to risk the imputation of inconsistency. It seems adviseable to be able to say to foreign Powers, if questioned—"In receiving the Minister of France, we have not acknowledged ourself its ally. We have reserved the point for future consideration." [24]

24. Jefferson stated: "But the reception of a Minister from the Republic of France, without qualifications, it is thought will bring us into danger: because this, it is said, will determine the continuance of the treaty, and take from us the right of self-liberation when at any time hereafter our safety would require us to use it. The reception of the Minister at all (in favor of which Colo. Hamilton has given his opinion, tho reluctantly as he confessed) is an acknolegement of the legitimacy of their government: and if the qualifications meditated are to deny that legitimacy, it will be a curious compound which is to admit & deny the same thing. But I deny that the reception of a minister has any thing to do with the treaties. There is not a word, in either of them, about sending ministers. This has been done between us under the common usage of nations, & can have no effect either to continue or annul the treaties.

It may be asked, whether the reception at any rate is not inconsistent with the reservation recommended.

It does not appear to be so. The acknowlegement of a Government by the reception of its ambassador, and the acknowledgment of it, *as an ally*, are things different and *separable* from each other. However the first, where a connection before existed between two nations may imply the last, if nothing is said; this implication may clearly be repelled, by a declaration, that it is not the intention of the party. Such a declaration would be in the nature of a protest against the implication—and the declared intent would govern. It is a rule, that *"Expressum facit cessare tacitum."*

It may likewise be asked, whether we are not too late for the ground proposed to be taken—whether the payments on account of the debt to France subsequent to the last change, be not an acknowl-

---

"But how can any act of election have the effect to continue a treaty which is acknoleged to be going on still? For it was not pretended the treaty was void, but only voidable if we chuse to declare it so. To make it void would require an act of election, but to let it go on requires only that we should do nothing. And doing nothing can hardly be an infraction of peace or neutrality.

"But I go further & deny that the most explicit declaration made at this moment that we acknolege the obligation of the treaties could take from us the right of non-compliance at any future time when compliance would involve us in great & inevitable danger.

"I conclude then that few of these sources threaten our danger at all; and from none of them is it inevitable: & consequently none of them give us the right at this moment of releasing ourselves from our treaties."

Randolph stated: "The policy of the proposed qualification can hardly be supported, after the justice of it is disavowed.

"To induct Mr. Genest into all the rights and immunities of a public minister, and hang over his head the terror of abrogating the treaties, will agitate him with perpetual jealousy towards the U. S. He will want that cordiality, without which rancour will sooner or later ensue.

"It is certainly reconcileable with the firmness of government to watch the state of the public mind on such an occasion. It probably is in this train; that the U. S. should, if possible, embark her happiness upon an association with no power on earth; but since such an independency is impracticable, France is the nation, to which our affections tend, and from which we have the greatest expectations. The truth and wisdom of this idea might be developed to a wide extent; but the President possesses the different views so amply, that a recapitulation of them would be superfluous. I own, without reserve, that I contemplate a danger of magnitude, hovering over the U.S., from the ardour of some, to transplant French politics, as fresh fuel for our own parties. The very instant it shall be known, that government has, without the most palpable grounds, betrayed even a distinct inclination to sever us from France, no argument nor influence can oppose itself with success to this new hotbed of dissension."

egement, that all engagements to the former Government are to be fulfilled to the present.[25]

The two objects of a debt in money—and a Treaty of Alliance, have no necessary connection. They are governed by considerations altogether different and irrelative.

The payment of a debt is a matter of perfect and strict obligation. It must be done at all events. It is to be regulated by circumstances of time and place—and ought to be done with precise punctuality.

In the case of a nation—whoever acquires *possession* of its political power, whoever becomes Master of its *goods*, of the national property, must pay all the debts which the government of the nation has contracted.

In like manner, on the principle of reciprocity the Sovereign in possession, is to receive the debts due to the Government of the nation. These debts are at all events to be paid—and *possession* alone can guide as to the party to whom they are to be paid.

Questions of property are very different from those of *political connection.*

Nobody can doubt, that the debt due to France is at all events to be paid, whatever *form* of Government may take place in that Country.

Treaties between nations are capable of being affected by a great variety of considerations, casualties and contingencies. Forms of Government it is evident, may be the considerations of them. Revolutions of Government, by changing those forms, may consequently vary the obligations of parties.

Hence the payment of a debt to the sovereign in possession does not imply an admission of the present operation of political treaties. It may so happen, that there is a strict obligation to pay the debt, and a perfect right to withdraw from the Treaties.

And while we are not bound to expose ourselves to the resentment of the GOVERNING POWER of France by refusing to pay a debt at the time and place stipulated; so neither are we bound, pending a con-

25. For the negotiations on the payment to the French revolutionary government of the American debt to France, see William Short to H, August 30, September 25, October 27, November 29, 1792; Gouverneur Morris to H, September 25, December 24, 1792; H to Short, October 1–15, 16, November 5, 1792.

tested revolution of Government, to expose ourselves to the resentment of other nations, by declaring ourselves the ally of that Power, in virtue of Treaties contracted with a former sovereign, who still pursues his claim to govern, supported by the general sense and arm of Europe.[26]

Philadelphia May 2d. 1793.
Alexander Hamilton

26. Jefferson concluded his statement as follows: "Upon the whole I conclude "That the treaties are still binding, notwithstanding the change of government in France: that no part of them, but the clause of guarantee, holds up *danger,* even at a distance, & consequently that a liberation from no other part could be proposed in any case: that if that clause may ever bring *danger,* it is neither extreme, nor imminent, nor even probable: that the authority for renouncing a treaty, when *useless* or *disagreeable,* is either misunderstood, or in opposition to itself, to all other writers, & to every moral feeling: that were it not so, these treaties are in fact neither useless or disagreeable.

"That the receiving a Minister from France at this time is an act of no significance with respect to the treaties, amounting neither to an admission nor denial of them, foreasmuch as he comes not under any stipulation in them:

"That were it an explicit admission, or were an express declaration of their obligation now to be made, it would not take from us that right which exists at all times of liberating ourselves when an adherence to the treaties would be *ruinous,* or *destructive* to the society: and that the not renouncing the treaties now is so far from being a breach of neutrality, that the doing it would be the breach, by giving just cause of war to France."

Randolph concluded his statement as follows: "From these premises, which might be diversified into many other forms, the attorney-general submits it, as his opinion.

"Upon the 2d., 3d., and 12th., questions, that Mr. Genest ought to be received absolutely, and without qualifications; and that no minister ought to be received from any regent of France, *against the will of the French nation:*

"Upon the 4th., 5th. and sixth questions, that altho' it would be an infraction of neutrality to *elect,* (if we had the power of choosing) the operation of the treaties, the U. S. are *bound* to admit them to be applicable to the present situation of the parties:

"Upon the 7th., 8th., 9th. and 10th. questions, that the guarantee, even if exacted, will not oblige us to become a party to the war, and abandon our neutrality:

"and upon the 11th. question, that public ships of war, hostile to France are under no other impediment in our ports, than those of France herself, except where they may have captured the French.

"The 1st. & 13th. questions as to the proclamation and calling of congress, having been already settled, are here passed over."

To Rufus King

Philadelphia May 2d. 1793

The failures in England will be so seriously felt in this Country as to involve a real crisis in our money concerns.[1] I anxiously wish you could be here to assist in the operations of the Bank of the UStates [2] —never was there a time, which required more the Union of Courage & Prudence, than the present and approaching Juncture. You can imagine all that I could add on this subject. Is it impossible for you to spend a month with us?

Yrs. truly   A Hamilton

R King Esqr

ALS, New-York Historical Society, New York City.
    1. A severe commercial crisis occurred in England soon after the outbreak of war between that country and France. The financial panic beginning in March, 1793, resulted in numerous failures among British banks and in a steadily increasing number of bankruptcies throughout the spring of that year. David Macpherson describes this crisis as follows: "The funds immediately felt the shock. The three-per-cents, which had been at 97⅛ in March 1792, and had been gradually depressed by the apprehension of war, now, on the certainty of it, fell almost instantaneously from 79⅞ to 70½. But they rose again as soon as April to 81; and, though they never afterwards came near to 80, yet they kept for a long time at prices rather higher than could be expected, owing to the men of property on the continent pouring their money into our funds, which they thought the most secure deposit in Europe" (David Macpherson, *Annals of Commerce, Manufactures, Fisheries, and Navigation, with Brief Notices of the Arts and Sciences Connected with Them. Containing the Commercial Transactions of the British Empire and Other Countries, From the Earliest Accounts to the Meeting of the Union Parliament in January 1801; and Comprehending the Most Valuable Part of the Late Mr. Anderson's History of Commerce* ... [London, 1805], IV, 264).
    2. King was a director of the Bank of the United States.

To Jeremiah Olney

Treasury Department, May 2, 1793. "Your letter of the 18th of April was duly received. The practice which obtains in your District with respect to *Exportation permits* ... appears to me to be right."

LS, Rhode Island Historical Society, Providence.

To George Washington [1]

[Philadelphia, May 2, 1793] [2]

Answers to remaining Questions proposed by the President of
The United States on the Question the   [3]

Answer

The War is plainly an *offensive war* on the part of France.
BURLAMAQUI,[4] an approved Writer Vol II Part IV Chap III Sections
IV & V thus defines the different species of War "Neither are we to
believe (says he) that he who *first injures another* begins by that an
offensive War, and that the other, *who demands satisfaction for the
injury* received is always upon the *defensive. There are a great many
unjust acts, which may kindle a war and which however are not the
war; as the ill treatment of a Prince's Ambassador, the plundering of
his subjects &c.* If therefore we take up arms to revenge such an unjust Act, we commence an offensive, but a just war; and the Prince
who has done the injury and will not give satisfaction makes a defensive but an unjust war. An offensive war is therefore unjust only,
when it is undertaken without a lawful cause, and then the defensive
War, which on other occasions might be unjust, becomes just."

ADf, Hamilton Papers, Library of Congress.

1. For background to this letter, see Washington to H, Thomas Jefferson,
Henry Knox, and Edmund Randolph, April 18, 1793; "Cabinet Meeting. Opin-
ion on a Proclamation of Neutrality and on Receiving the French Minister,"
April 19, 1793; H and Knox to Washington, May 2, 1793.

2. The draft of this document is undated. The date has been taken from
JCHW, IV, 382.

3. Space left blank in MS. According to the version of this document printed
in *JCHW*, the original of which has not been found, the question answered by
H in this document was the fourth question submitted by Washington to his
cabinet on April 18, 1793: "Are the United States obliged by good faith to
consider the Treaties heretofore made with France as applying to the present
situation of the parties. May they either renounce them or hold them suspended
'till the Government of France shall be *established*." H and Knox, however,
had already taken up this point in their letter to George Washington of May 2.
The second opinion, printed above, deals more specifically with Washington's
eighth question of April 18: "Does the War in which France is engaged appear
to be offensive or defensive on her part? Or of a mixed & equivocal character?"

4. Jean Jacques Burlamaqui, *The Principles of Political Law: Being a Sequel
to the Principles of Natural Law. By J. J. Burlamaqui, Counsellor of State, and
Late Professor of Natural and Civil Law at Geneva. Translated into English
by Mr. Nugent* (Dublin: Printed for J. Sheppard, and G. Nugent, No. 7 in
Anne Street, Stephen's Green, 1776), II, 189–90.

"*We must therefore affirm, in general, that the first who takes up arms, whether justly or unjustly, commences an offensive war; and he who opposes him, whether with or without reason begins a defensive war.*"

This definition of *offensive* and *defensive* war is conformable to the ideas of Writers on the Laws of Nations, in general, and is adopted almost verbatim by Barbeyrac in his Notes on §III & IV of Book the VIII Chap VI of Puffendorfs "Law of Nature and Nations." [5]

France, it is certain, was the first to declare war against every one of the Powers with which she is at War. Whether she had good cause or not therefore in each instance, the War is completely *offensive* on her part.

The forms, which she has employed in some of her declarations (whereafter reciting the aggressions she alleges to have been committed against her by a particular power [6] she proceeds to pronounce that war exists between her and such power) cannot alter the substance of the thing. The aggressions complained of, if ever so well founded, and however they may have been of a Nature *to kindle a war were not the War itself.* The war was begun, in each case, by the declaration, & by the commencement of hostilities on the part of France. It was therefore clearly offensive on her part.

With regard to the causes that led to the War, in each case, it requires more exact information than I have to pronounce upon them with confidence. As it regards Austria & Prussia, the suggestion on one hand is that a combination was formed to overthrow the new constitution of France, and that the declaration on the part of the latter Country was only an anticipation of what would soon have proceeded from the confederated powers. On the other hand it is affirmed that the preparations and arrangements on their part were merely provisional and eventual; and that the Republican party in France precipitated a War under the idea that it would furnish opportunities for accusing and criminating the Kings administration and finally overthrowing the Royalty.

Mr. Short [7]

5. H is referring to the notes of Jean Barbeyrac, translator and editor of the works of Samuel Pufendorf (*Of the Law of Nature and Nations*, 825).

6. See *Archives Parlementaires*, LVIII, 118–19.

7. After the words "Mr. Short" H left several lines blank in the MS. Presumably he planned to insert information given to him by William Short.

Waving all definitive opinion on this point, better guides will enable us to pronounce with more certainty in the other cases.

In respect to Holland, there seems to be no doubt, that the aggression began with France.

France in different Treaties, had recognised a right in the Dutch to the exclusive Navigation of the River Scheldt.

It appears, that she had a leading agency in adjusting a controversy on the point, between the late Emperor Joseph & the U Netherlands.

The XXVIII Article of a Treaty between those parties concluded at Fontainebleau the 8th. of November 1785 is in these words:

"The Most Christian Majesty contributed to the completion of the arrangement made between the High-Contracting parties (namely the Emperor & States General), by *his friendly intervention and his effectual and just mediation*, his said Majesty is requested by the High Contracting Parties to charge himself likewise with being the Guarantee of the present Treaty."

Nevertheless the Provisionary Executive Council, by a decree of the 16 of November 1792, break through all these formal and express engagements, on the pretext of their being contrary to natural right, and declare the Navigation of the *Scheldt* & Meuse *free*.[8]

Such an infraction of Treaties on such a ground cannot be justified without subverting all the foundation of positive and pactitious right among Nations. It is equally agreeable to the doctrine of theorists and to the practice of Nations that rights to the common use of Waters of the description in question may be relinquished and qualified by Treaty. To resume them therefore on the ground of the *imprescriptibility* as it is called, of natural rights—is to set up a new rule of conduct contrary to the common sense and common practice of mankind, amounting in the party, which attempts the resumption, to an unequivocal injury to the party against which it is attempted.

In respect to Great Britain, the case is not equally clear; but there is sufficient ground to pronounce, that she had cause of complaint, prior to any given on her part.

It is known that in the early periods of the French Revolution she

8. See *Archives Parlementaires*, LIII, 512–13.

adopted the ground of neutrality and nothing is alleged against her till after the 10th of August.

That event led her to withdraw her Minister from the Court of France; but before his departure he left a note declarative of the intention of Great Britain to pursue still a pacific course; accompanied indeed with a cautious intimation, that personal violence to the King would excite the general indignation in Europe.[9]

But it will hardly be affirmed, that this procedure amounted to an aggression. To recal a minister from or not to keep one at any Court is of itself an Act of indifference. The recall under such circumstances as took place on the 10th: of August was not an extraordinary step. Every Government had a right to deliberate, and was bound for its own safety to consider well—when it would recognize a new order of things, which had been produced by a National Revolution. None was obliged by a hasty determination to expose itself to the ill will of other powers who might be at war with that new order of things. The keeping of a Minister at France, after the deposition of the King, might be deemed a sanction of the change and indeed was useless until it was intended to give that sanction. It was not therefore incumbent upon any power to pursue this course; especially one which was not in the condition of an ally.

The intimation with regard to the King, to characterise it in the most exceptionable light, was at most an act of officiousness. Relating to a thing not at the time in agigation, it could only be considered as a caution to avoid a measure which might beget misunderstanding.

9. George Granville Leveson-Gower, British Minister to France, was recalled on August 17, 1792. The letter of recall was written by Henry Dundas, Secretary of State for Home Affairs. This letter, which Gower submitted to the French Ministry, reads in part as follows: "In all the conversations that you may have occasion to hold before your departure, you will take care to express yourself in a manner conformable to the sentiments herein communicated to you; and you will take special care not to neglect any opportunity of declaring, that at the same time his Majesty means to observe the principles of neutrality in every thing which regards the arrangement of the internal government of France, he does not conceive that he departs from these principles in manifesting, by every possible means in his power, his solicitude for the personal situation of their Most Christian Majesties and the Royal Family. He most earnestly hopes that his wishes in that respect will not be deceived; that the Royal Family will be preserved from every act of violence; the commission of which would not fail to excite sentiments of universal indignation throughout all Europe" (*Annual Register* [State Papers], 1792, 184).

The conduct of France shews that she did not at the time consider this step as an injury; for she continued a Minister at the Court of London, and continued to negotiate.[10]

The next step of Great Britain in order of time, which is complained of by France, and the first of a really hostile complexion is the restriction on the exportation of Corn to France, by way of exception to a general permission to export that article.[11]

10. The French Ministry's reaction to the recall of the British Minister is contained in the reply of Pierre Henri Hélène Marie Lebrun-Tondu, French Minister of Foreign Affairs, to Dundas's letter of August 17, 1792. It reads in part as follows: "The council has seen with regret, that the British Cabinet has resolved to recal[l] an Ambassador whose presence attested the favourable disposition of a free and generous nation, and who has never been the organ but of friendly expressions, and of benevolent sentiments. If anything can abate this regret, it is the renewed assurance of neutrality made on the part of England to the French nation. This assurance seems to be the result of an intention wisely considered and formally expressed by his Britannic Majesty, not to meddle with the interior arrangements of the affairs of France. . . . The French nation has good grounds to hope, that the British cabinet will not, at this decisive moment, depart from that justice, moderation, and impartiality which it has hitherto manifested. Full of this confidence, which rests on facts, the undersigned renews to his Excellency Earl Gower, in the name of the Provisional Executive Council, the assurances which he has had the honour to give him, *viva voce*, that whatever relates to commerce between the two nations, and all affairs in general, shall be carried on, on the part of the French government, with the same justice and fidelity. The Council flatter themselves that there will be a full reciprocity on the part of the British government, and that nothing will interrupt the good understanding which subsists between the two nations" (*Annual Register* [State Papers], 1792, 184–85).

In the declaration of war against England on February 1, 1793, however, the French Ministry advanced as a grievance the fact that the British King had ordered "son ambassadeur à Paris de se retirer, parce qu'il ne voulait pas reconnaître le conseil exécutif provisoire, créé par l'Assemblée législative" (*Archives Parlementaires*, LVIII, 118).

11. An order in council of November 9, 1792, prohibited the exportation of corn from Great Britain. In a letter to Lord Grenville of January 7, 1793, Bernard François, Marquis de Chauvelin, French Minister to Great Britain, expressed France's views concerning this policy as follows: "the king of England has prohibited . . . the exportation of grain and flour. Several vessels lawfully freighted, and ready to depart for France . . . have been stopped. . . . Another proclamation, which soon followed the first, except all foreign wheat from the prohibition of exportation. . . . Four weeks after that declaration, some vessels laden with foreign grain, on account of France, were stopped in the English ports; and when the merchants who were commissioned made their claims, they were coldly answered, that it was by order of government. . . . the English government itself took care to prove to Europe that it had no other motive than an hostile partiality against France, if it is true that the custom-houses received orders to permit the exportation of foreign wheat to all ports, except those of France" (*The Parliamentary History of England, From the Earliest Period to the Year 1803* [London: Printed by T. C. Hansard, Peterborough-

This was an unfriendly measure. It happened as far as I am able to trace it in the latter part of December 1792.

But prior to these causes of dissatisfaction an alarm had been given by France to Great Britain.

The Convention on the 19th. of November passed a Decree in these words—

"The National Convention declare, in the name of the French Nation, that they will grant FRATERNITY and ASSISTANCE TO EVERY PEOPLE, who wish to recover their Liberty; and they charge the Executive Power to send the necessary orders to the Generals to give assistance to such People, and to *defend* those *citizens who may have been or who may be vexed for the cause of Liberty*" which Decree was ordered to be printed IN ALL LANGUAGES.[12]

This decree might justly be regarded in an exceptionable light by the Government of every country. For though it be lawful and meritorious to assist a people in a virtuous and rational struggle for liberty, *when the particular case happens;* yet it is not justifiable in any government or Nation to hold out to the world a *general invitation* and *encouragement* to *revolution* and insurrection, under a promise of *fraternity* and *assistance*. Such a step is of a nature to disturb the repose of mankind, to excite fermentation in every country, to endanger government every where. Nor can there be a doubt that wheresoever a spirit of this kind appears it is lawful to repress and repel it.

But this generally exceptionable proceeding might be looked upon by Great Britain as having a more particular reference to her from some collateral circumstances.

It is known that various societies were instituted in Great Britain with the avowed object of reforms in the Government. These societies presented addresses to the Convention of France and received answers; containing an interchange of sentiments justly alarming to the British Government.

Court, Fleet-Street, 1817], XXX, 259–60). See also 33 Geo. III, C. III (1793). When the National Convention declared war against Great Britain on February 1, 1793, the effort of the British government to "impede the different purchases of corn, arms, and other commodities, ordered in England, either by French citizens, or the agents of the republic" was given as one of the causes of the conflict (*Annual Register* [State Papers], 1793, 139).

12. See *Archives Parlementaires*, LIII, 474.

It will suffice by way of illustration to cite passages from two of these answers, each given by the President of the Convention, at a *sitting* on the 28 of November, one to a deputation from "The Society for constitutional information in London" the other to a deputation of English and Irish Citizens at Paris.

1   "The shades of PENN of HAMPDEN and of SYNDNEY hover over your heads; and *the moment without doubt approaches, in which the French will bring congratulations to the National Convention of Great Britain.*"

2   "Nature and *principles* draw *towards us* England Scotland & Ireland. Let the cries of friendship resound through the two REPUBLICS." Again "Principles are waging war against Tyranny, which will fall under the blows of philosophy. *Royalty in Europe is either destroyed or on the point of perishing*, on the ruins of Feodality; and the declaration of rights placed by the side of *thrones is a devouring fire which will consume them.* WORTHY REPUBLICANS &c" [13]

Such *declarations* to such *societies* are a comment upon the Decree —are in every sense inconsistent with what was due to a just respect for a Neutral Nation and amounted to so direct a patronage of a Revolution in the essential principles of its government as authorised even a declaration of War.

It is true that Mr. Chauvelin in a Note to Lord Grenville of the 27 of December 1792 [14]—declares that the "National Convention never meant that the French Republic should *favour insurrections,* should espouse the quarrels of a *few seditious persons* or should endeavour to *excite disturbances* in any neutral or friendly country; the decree being only applicable to a People, who after having *aquired* their liberty, should *call for the fraternity, the assistance of the Republic,* by the *solemn* and *unequivocal expression of the general Will.*"

But this explanation could not change the real nature and tendency of the decree, which holding out a general promise of fraternity and *assistance* to every people who *wished to recover* their liberty did

---

13. For these addresses and the replies of Henri Gregoire, president of the National Convention, see *Archives Parlementaires*, LIII, 635–37.

14. Chauvelin's letter is printed in the *Annual Register* [State Papers], 1793, 114–16.

favour insurrections, was calculated to excite disturbances in neutral & friendly countries.

Still less could it efface the exceptionable and offensive nature of the reception which was given and the declarations which were made to the Revolutionary—or Reforming—Societies of G B.

The answer of Lord Grenville [15] very justly observes that "Neither satisfaction nor security is found in the terms of an explanation, which still declares to the promoters of sedition, in every country, what are the cases in which they may count *beforehand* on the support and succour of France; and which reserves to that Country the right of mixing herself in the internal affairs of another, whenever she shall judge it proper, and on principles incompatible with the political institutions of all the Countries of Europe."

Besides the Declarations, which have been mentioned, to the different English societies, and which apply particularly to Great Britain, there are other acts of France which were just causes of umbrage and alarm to all the Governments of Europe.

Her Decree of the 15 of December [16] is one of them. This decree, extraordinary in every respect, which contemplates the total subversion of all the antient establishments of every country into which the arms of France should be carried—has the following article—

"The French Nation declare—That *it will treat as enemies the People, who refusing or renouncing Liberty and Equality, are desirous of preserving their Prince and privileged Casts, or of entering into an accommodation with them.* The Nation promises and engages not to lay down its arms, until the Sovereignty and Liberty of the People, on whose Territory the French Armies *shall have entered* shall be established and not to consent to any *arrangement or Treaty with the Prince and privileged persons* so dispossessed, with whom the Republic is at war."

This Decree cannot but be regarded as an outrage, little short of a declaration of war, against every Government of Europe, and as a violent attack upon the *freedom of opinion of all Mankind.*

15. Grenville's reply, dated December 31, 1792, is printed in the *Annual Register* [State Papers], 1793, 116–19, and in *Archives Parlementaires*, LVIII, 148–50.

16. See *Archives Parlementaires*, LV, 70–76. This decree concerned "la conduite des généraux français dans les pays occupés par les armées de la République." The section quoted by H appears in Article 11.

The *incorpation* of the territories, conquered by the arms of France with France herself is another of the acts alluded to, as giving just cause of umbrage and alarm to neutral Nations in general. It is a principle well established by the laws of Nations, that the property and dominion of conquered places do not become *absolute* in the conquerors 'till they have been ceded or relinquished by a Treaty of peace or some equivalent termination of the War. Till then it is understood to be in a state of suspense, (the Conqueror having only a possessory and qualified title) liable to such a disposition as may be made by the compact which terminates the War. Hence the citizen of a neutral nation can acquire no final or irrevocable title to land by purchase of the Conqueror during the continuance of the War. This principle, it is evident, is of the greatest importance to the peace and security of Nations—greatly facilitating an adjustment of the quarrels in which they happen at any time to be involved.

But the *Incorporation*, which has been mentioned, and which actually took place, in respect to the territories of different Powers, *Savoy Antwerp* &c. was a direct violation of that very important and fundamental principle; and of those rights which the laws of war reserve to every Power at War; a violation tending to throw insuperable difficulties in the way of peace. After once having adopted those territories *as part of herself*, she became bound to maintain them to the last extremity by all those peremptory rules which forbid a Nation to consent to its own dismemberment.

That *incorporation* therefore changed intirely the principle of the War on the part of France. It ceased to be a war for the defence of her rights, for the preservation of her liberty. It became a war of acquisition, of extension of territory and dominion, and in a manner altogether subversive of the laws & usages of Nations, and tending to the aggrandisement of France, to a degree, dangerous to the Independence & safety of every Country in the world.

There is no principle better supported by the Doctrines of Writers, the practice of Nations, and the dictates of right reason, than this—that whenever a Nation adopts maxims of conduct tending to the disturbance of the tranquillity and established order of its neighbours, or manifesting a spirit of self-aggrandisement—it is lawful for other Nations to combine against it, and, by force, to controul the effects of those maxims and that spirit. The conduct of France, in the instances which have been stated, calmly and impartially viewed, was an *offence* against *Nations,* which naturally made it a common cause among them to check her carreer.

The pretext of propagating liberty can make no difference. Every Nation has a right to carve out its own happiness in its own way, and it is the height of presumption in another, to attempt to fashion its political creed.

These acts and proceedings are all prior in time to the last aggressive step of Great Britain, the ordering out of the Kingdom the person who was charged with a diplomatic mission to that Court from the Government of France. The stile and manner of that proceeding rendered it undoubtedly an insult—and if the conduct of France before that time had been unexceptionable, the war declared by France, though *offensive* in its nature, would have been justifiable in its motive.[17]

With regard to Spain, the War was likewise declared by France and is consequently *offensive* on her part. The conduct of the former towards the latter, previous to this event, appears not only to have been moderate but even timid.

The War on the part of Portugal appears to have been *offensive.*

The result from what has been said is that the War in which France is engaged is in *fact* an offensive war on her part against all the Powers with which she is engaged, except one; and in *principle,* to speak in the most favourable terms for her, is *at least* a mixed case—a case of mutual aggression.

The inference from this state of things is as plain, as it is important.

17. This is a reference to the circumstances under which Chauvelin had been ordered out of Great Britain by the British government after the execution of Louis XVI. On January 24, 1793, Grenville sent the following letter to Chauvelin: "I am charged to notify to you, Sir, that the character with which you had been invested at this court, and the functions of which have been so long suspended, being now entirely terminated by the fatal death of his most Christian majesty, you have no longer any public character here.

"The king can no longer, after such an event, permit your residence here. His majesty has thought fit to order, that you should retire from this kingdom within the term of eight days; and I herewith transmit to you a copy of the order which his majesty in his privy council has given to this effect.

"I send you a passport for yourself and your suite; and I shall not fail to take all the other necessary steps, in order that you may return to France with all the attentions which are due to the character of minister plenipotentiary from his most Christian majesty, which you have exercised at this court." (*Annual Register* [State Papers], 1793, 128.)

The *casus fœderis* of the guarantee in the Treaty of alliance between the UStates and France cannot take place, though her West India Islands should be attacked.

The express Denomination of this Treaty is "Traité D'Alliance eventuelle et *defensive*" Treaty of Alliance *Eventual* and *Defensive*.

The 2 Article of the Treaty also calls it a *"Defensive* Alliance." This then constitutes the leading feature—the *characteristic quality* of the Treaty. By this principle, every stipulation in it is to be judged.

To George Washington

[*Philadelphia*] *May 2, 1793.* "The Secretary of the Treasury has the honor to enclose for the information of the President a Letter of the 26 of February from our Bankers at Amsterdam. . . ." [1]

LC, George Washington Papers, Library of Congress.
  1. Willink, Van Staphorst, and Hubbard to H, February 26, 1793.

To George Washington

[*Philadelphia*] *May 2, 1793.* ". . . encloses . . . a letter from the Commissioner of the Revenue on the subject of a Keeper of the Lt House for Cape Henlopen." [1]

LC, George Washington Papers, Library of Congress.
  1. Letter from Tench Coxe not found. In an entry in JPP for May 2, 1793, Coxe's letter is described as follows: ". . . a letter from the Commisr. of the Revenue, stating that the person, Lemuel Cornick, who had been appointed Keeper of the Light Ho. on Cape Henry had resigned & that Laban Geoffigan, had been appointed to fill the place till the president's pleasure could be known" (JPP, 106).

To Joseph Whipple

[*Philadelphia, May 2, 1793.* On May 16, 1793, Whipple wrote to Hamilton and referred to Hamilton's "directions of the 2d instant." *Letter not found.*]

To Wilhem and Jan Willink, Nicholaas and Jacob Van Staphorst, and Nicholas Hubbard

[*Philadelphia, May 2, 1793*. On July 1, 1793, Willink, Van Staphorst, and Hubbard wrote to Hamilton: "The letter you wrote us the 2d. May has . . . come to hand." *Letter not found.*]

To Thomas Jefferson [1]

Treasury Department
May 3d. 1793

Sir

I regret extremely, that I did not receive your letter respecting Mr. Ternant's application till two oClock yesterday; after a warrant had issued in his favour for the sum requested.[2]

Agreeing intirely in opinion with you, that all applications from Diplomatic characters, as well those relating to pecuniary matters as others, ought to be addressed to your Department—I should have taken no step on the present occasion had it not been put on the footing of a previous arrangement (as you will perceive by the copy of Mr. Ternant's note to me) [3] and had I not myself carried along in my mind a general impression, that the spirit of what had passed would comprise the advance requested in the *individual case.*

For greater caution, however, I thought it adviseable to mention the matter to the President—which was followed (if I remember right upon my own suggestion) by the conversation which I had with you.

You will remember that though your recollection, at the time, of what had passed from you agreed with what has been the result of your subsequent examination—yet you expressed an opinion that in the special case (adhering as a general rule to the spirit of your late communication) it might be adviseable to make the advance desired —as it would be well "*to part friends.*" And it was at my request, subsequent to this declaration, that you engaged to review your communications to Mr. Ternant.

Having told Mr. Ternant that the matter would be terminated the day succeeding his application—not having heard from you on that day—understanding it to be your opinion that on the whole it would be well to make the advance—I waited on the President yesterday Morning, stated what had passed between us, and obtained his consent for making the advance.

I am thus particular from a desire that you may see the ground upon which I have proceeded; as it would give me pain that you should consider what has been done, as the infringement of a rule of official propriety. I assure you this was not my intention.

With great respect I have the honor to be   Sir   Your Obed ser

A Hamilton

The Secretary of State

ALS, James Madison Papers, Library of Congress.
1. For background to this letter, see Jefferson to H, May 1, 1793, and Jean Baptiste de Ternant to H, April 30, 1793.
2. On May 2, 1793, a warrant for $3,630 was issued in favor of Ternant ("Statement of the Payments at the Treasury on Account of the debt due to France," December 20, 1793, D, RG 53, Register of the Treasury, Estimates and Statements for 1793, National Archives).
3. Ternant to H, April 30, 1793.

From Tobias Lear

[*Philadelphia*] *May 3, 1793*. Returns "the letters from our Bankers at Amsterdam which were laid before the President yesterday." States "that the President approves of the appointment of Laban Goffigan to be Keeper of the Light House on Cape Henry."[1]

ALS, RG 26, Lighthouse Letters Received, "Segregated" Lighthouse Records, Cape Henry, National Archives.
1. See H to Washington, second and third letters of May 2, 1793. This letter was endorsed by H "For the Commissioner of The Revenue."

From John Murray [1]

New York 3 May 1793

Alexr. Hamilton Esqr
Sir!

My particular Friend Mr. Philip Mark [2] is now about to take up his residence in Germany; he has informed me that it would be a very pleasing thing to him to have an appointment to a Consulate from the United States to some part of the German Empire; as I have been long acquainted with him, I can with fredom recommend him as a man well qualified to fill that Office; I know him to be a man of abilities, & integrity. I am with respect

Sir   Your most obedt. hble. Sert.   John Murray

ALS, George Washington Papers, Library of Congress.

1. Murray was a New York City merchant who engaged in extensive shipping operations.

2. Marck, a New York City merchant, was a native of Germany. On May 29, 1794, he was appointed consul for the United States in Franconia, Germany (*Executive Journal*, I, 158).

From William Seton

New York 3d May 1793

My Dear sir

I did not answer your Letter of the 29th.[1] till I should see Mr. Verplanck, which I did just as I receivd your further Letter of the 1st.[2] He says in a few days he will pay the money on your account, as soon as some error in the Deed &c which had been returned was corrected.[3] Your draft for 500 has not appeared but shall be punctually honored. Enclosed is a Sketch of your account with the Bank, the balance of Dolls. 524.$^{6\%}$/100 will be chargeable with Interest from the 29th September the amount agreable to your desire shall be retained out of the Money to be received of Mr. Verplanck & the remainder remitted you in U. States Bank Notes.

The drain of Specie having stopt,[4] we now go on tolerably smooth, & upon the whole rather get a head of the Branch on the Exchange of Notes. Mr Meredith[5] drew one Check upon us the 25th. for 10,000 Dollars which went to their credit—this would be a good time to lessen the balance of the Public money in our hands if it is necessary as the Branch still owes us 45,000. The great failures in England[6] may perhaps cause Specie to be shipt from hence which is the only thing we have to dread for our Stocks will no longer answer for a remittance, tho the prices here are so distressingly low.

I am with the greatest respect & esteem   Dear sir   Your obliged obed Hube Servt   Wm Seton

Alexr. Hamilton Esqr

ALS, Hamilton Papers, Library of Congress.
   1. Letter not found.
   2. Letter not found.
   3. See "Conveyance by Lease and Release to Gulian Verplanck," April 27,
1793.
   4. See Seton to H, January 22, December 20, 1792; March 5, 1793.
   5. Samuel Meredith, treasurer of the United States.
   6. See H to Rufus King, May 2, 1793, note 1.

To George Washington

Treasury Depart: 4 May 93

The Secretary of the Treasury respectfully communicates to The President of the United States a letter of the 28 of April received yesterday from the Commissioner of the Revenue.[1] In the early part of the ensuing week he will have the honor of waiting upon the president to submit his ideas on the several points raised, & take the President's orders thereupon.   A. Hamilton

LC, George Washington Papers, Library of Congress.
   1. Letter from Tench Coxe not found.

To George Washington

[Philadelphia, May 4, 1793]

The Secretary of the Treasury presents his respects to the President. It has appeared to him that a circular letter of the enclosed form to the several Collectors would be a measure of utility.[1] If not disapproved by the President it will be forwarded.

May 4 1793.

The enclosed paper is sent lest the president should not have received it otherwise. It contains intelligence *critically* important, tho' requiring confirmation.

LC, George Washington Papers, Library of Congress.
   1. This draft of a circular letter to the collectors of the customs has not been found. It apparently was a first draft of the circular letter sent to the collectors on August 4, 1793, telling them how to deal with violations of the neutrality proclamation. The correspondence between Thomas Jefferson and Edmund Randolph, however, reveals at least one major difference between this draft and the version sent to the collectors in August. The August 4 circular directed the collectors to report violations of United States neutrality to the governor of the state and the United States attorney of the district involved. In the original

draft submitted to Washington reports of infractions of neutrality were to be submitted by the collectors directly to the United States Treasury. This clause in the draft encountered serious opposition from the Secretary of State. Jefferson stated on May 6 that "The President shews me a draught of a lre from Colo. H. to the Collectors of the customs, desirg them to superintend their neighborhood, watch for all acts of our citizens contrary to laws of neutrality or tending to infringe those laws, & inform him of it; & particularly to see if vessels should be building pierced for guns. I told the Pr. that at a conference a few days before Colo. H. & E. R. had concurred in opn agt. me that for us to build and sell vessels fit for war would be a breach of neutrality, but that I understood them as agreeing that no opn should go from the public on that question as not being now necessary: that as the 1st part of the letter I did not of a sudden decide it to be improper.—he, on this, returned the (draught) to Ham. with a desire that he, E. R. & myself would confer on it" (Ford, *Writings of Jefferson*, I, 227-28). Jefferson soon had second thoughts concerning his agreement, and on May 8, 1793, he wrote to Randolph as follows:

"I have been still reflecting on the draught of the letter from the Secretary of the Treasury to the Custom house officers, instructing them to be on the watch as to all infractions or tendencies to infraction of the laws of neutrality by our citizens & to communicate the same to him. When this paper was first communicated to me, tho' the whole of it struck me disagreeably, I did not in the first moment see clearly the improprieties but of the last clause. The more I have reflected, the more objectionable the whole appears.

"By this proposal the Collectors of the customs are to be made an established corps of spies or informers against their fellow citizens, whose actions they are to watch in secret, inform against in secret to the Secretary of the Treasury, who is to communicate it to the President. . . . This will at least furnish the collector with a convenient weapon to keep down a rival, draw a cloud over an inconvenient censor, or satisfy mere malice & private enmity.

"The object of this new institution is to be to prevent infractions of the laws of neutrality, & preserve our peace with foreign nations. Acts involving war, or proceedings which respect foreign nations, seem to belong either to the department of war, or to that which is charged with the affairs of foreign nations. But I cannot possibly conceive how the superintendance of the laws of neutrality, or the preservation of our peace with foreign nations can be ascribed to the department of the treasury, which I suppose to comprehend merely matters of revenue. It would be to add a new & a large field to a department already amply provided with business, patronage, & influence. . . ." (AL, letterpress copy, Thomas Jefferson Papers, Library of Congress.)

On May 9, 1793, Randolph replied as follows:

"You recollect, that I was on the point of making your very objection, as deserving consideration, when you mentioned it. It was impossible not to have heard, that the revenue-officers have been suspected to be a corps, trained to the arts of spies, in the service of the Treasury. Awake as I was to this conjecture, I wished not only to guard against the practice, but to submit it to an accurate inquiry.

"I accordingly asked Colo. H. whether his correspondence has at any time been directed to the prying into the conduct of individuals, or even an inspection over the legislatures. He solemnly appealed to his letter-books for a proof of the negative.

"Viewing then his draught, as unconnected with past suspicions, I could discover nothing, opposed to my judgment.

"Was there ever a government, which hesitated to gather information from its *executive* officers? If their duties are defined; still it may reasonably be expected, that they will readily transmit *general* intelligence to the fountainhead. A refusal might not be the ground of an impeachment; but under the strictest constitution it would be deemed an indecorum. . . . the collectors are, from their position near the water, the scene of those violations, best qualified to assist congress. . . .

"Why too, may not the collectors be requested, to represent any unlawful actions, which fall more immediately under their notice, to the district attornies? . . . .

"It is true, that the original draught proposed, that a report should be made to the secretary of the treasury, But this was agreed to be erased upon my suggestion; so that the intercourse was confined to the attorney alone. This correction goes very far into your main objection. . . ." (AL, Thomas Jefferson Papers, Library of Congress.)

The dispute was settled in accordance with Randolph's suggestion. Jefferson wrote to James Madison on May 13 that Randolph "found out a hair to split, which, as always happens, became the decision. H. is to write to the collectors of the customs, who are to convey their information to the Attornies of the districts, to whom E. R. is to write to receive their information & proceed by indictment. The clause respecting the building vessels pierced for guns was omitted. For tho' 3. against 1. thought it would be a breach of neutrality, yet they thought we might defer giving a public opinion on it as yet" (AL, Thomas Jefferson Papers, Library of Congress).

From George Washington

[Philadelphia] Sunday Noon—5th May 1793.

Dear Sir,   (Private)

Before you dispatch the circular letter (of wch you enclosed me a Copy) to the several Collectors, I would speak to you respecting a particular clause in it.[1]

In the conversation you may have with a certain Gentleman to day*—I pray you to intimate to him gently, & delicately, that if the letters, or papers wch. he has to present, are (knowingly to him) of a nature which relates to public matters, and not particularly addressed to me—or if he has any verbal communications to make of a similar kind, I had rather they should come through the proper channel—add thereto, generally, that the peculiar situation of European affairs at this moment my good wishes for his Nation agregately —my regard for those of it in particular with whom I have had the honor of an acquaintance—My anxious desire to keep this Country in Peace—and the delicacy of my situation renders a circumspect conduct indispensably necessary on my part. I do not, however, mean by this that I am to with-hold from him such civilities as are *common*

* Viscount de Noailles [2]

to others. Those *more marked*, notwithstanding our former acquaintance, would excite speculations which had better be avoided. And if
the characters (similarly circumstanced with his own) could be
introduced by any other than *himself;* especially on tuesday next in
the public room when, it is presumed, the Officers of the French
Frigate will be presented it would, unquestionably be better. But
how this can be brot. about as they are strangers without embarrassment as the F—— M——[3] is shy on the occasion I do not at this
moment see, for it may not escape observation (as every movement
is watched) if the head of any department should appear prompt in
this business in the existing state of things.

    I am always   Yours &ca.   G W——n

ADfS, George Washington Papers, Library of Congress.
    1. See H to Washington, May 4, 1793, note 1.
    2. Louis Marie, Vicomte de Noailles, hero of Yorktown, had arrived in
Philadelphia on May 3, 1793, with several other French Royalist refugees. Soon
after his arrival he had sought a private interview with the President.
    3. The French Minister to the United States, Jean Baptiste de Ternant. In a
letter to James Monroe, dated May 5, 1793, Jefferson wrote: "When Ternant
received certain account of his appointment thinking he had nothing further to
hope from the Jacobins, he . . . put on mourning for the king, & became a
perfect Counter-revolutioner. A few days ago he received a letter from Genest
[Edmond Charles Genet] giving him a hope that they will employ him in the
army. On this he has tacked about again, become a Jacobin, & refused to present
the Viscount Noailles & some French aristocrats arrived here" (Ford, *Writings
of Jefferson*, VI, 240).
    That French suspicions of Noailles were warranted is indicated by a state-
ment in a letter from Lord Grenville to George Hammond, July 25, 1793. This
letter reads as follows: "Before M. Noailles left England for America he made
some offers of service here which were civilly declined on account of his former
connections and conduct. . . . He expressed however a desire of being of service
to you when he got there, and stated himself to have the means of being so,
desiring at the same time that his disposition to that effect might be mentioned
to you" (Historical Manuscripts Commission, *The Manuscripts of J. B. For-
tescue, Esq., Preserved at Dropmore*, Fourteenth Report, Appendix, Part V
[London, 1894], II, 408).

From Tench Coxe

[*Philadelphia, May 6, 1793.* On May 8, 1793, Hamilton wrote to
George Washington: "The Secretary of the Treasury has the honor
to submit to the consideration of the President of the U States a
communication from the Commissioner of the Revenue of the 6
instant." *Letter not found.*]

From Henry Lee [1]

Richmond 6th. May [1793]

My Dear sir

I had your letter delivered to me last evening [2] & feel myself hurt at the suggestions it contains concerning your own situation. [3]

Knowing you as I do I should ever give to your political conduct the basis of truth honor & love of country however I might have differed from you on some measures.

When therefore I feel undiminished regard to you, I cannot help lamenting the misery to which you continue to be exposed & I wish to god they could be averted—our countrys prosperity will ever be with me the first object & next to that (speaking as to public matters) the happiness of my friends. Unfortunately those I most love have taken different sides in American questions & this discord in sentiment has issued in personal disgust & hate.

This event kept me from Congress & will confine me to my own state. I had once cherished a hope of finding full employment corresponding with my feelings in France, to which place I was almost in the act of embarkation 7 weeks ago, but the confusions there & the interposition of some of my best friends here arrested my project. [4] I mean now to become a farmer & get a wife as soon as possible. [5]

When I let you have my own riding horse, [6] I did not mean to receive any thing for him save the expence which attended him in Alexa. previous to my obtaining an opportunity of conveying him, & your small advance exceeded this sum, but as you make a serious point of it I will draw on you for the ballance of his price which is 16 guineas. I would censure the delicacy which your ltr. exhibits on this subject [did] I not know that to one exposed to such a portion of incrimination from his foes would not be relished even ironical censure from his friends. Your attention to me in Philad. was as usual —friendly & affectionate tho' your situation forbad us mingling much together. Was I with you I would talk an hour with doors bolted & windows shut, as my heart is much afflicted by some whispers which I have heard. [7] Yours ever   H. Lee

ALS, Hamilton Papers, Library of Congress.
    1. Lee was governor of Virginia.

2. Letter not found.

3. This is a reference to the congressional attack on H's fiscal policies. See the introductory note to H's "Report on the Balance of All Unapplied Revenues at the End of the Year 1792 and on All Unapplied Monies Which May Have Been Obtained by the Several Loans Authorized by Law," February 4, 1793.

4. Lee was considering going to France for military service. On September 21, 1792, he wrote to William S. Smith inquiring about conditions in France and about the possibility of offering to that "Nation my humble services as a soldier" (*Archivo del General Miranda, Negociaciones 1770–1810* [Caracas, 1938], XV, 147). Lee wrote to George Washington concerning his plans on April 29, 1793 (ALS, George Washington Papers, Library of Congress). On May 6 the President answered Lee's letter, pointing out the difficulties attending the enlistment of the governor of a state in the service of a foreign power (ADf, George Washington Papers, Library of Congress). On May 15 Lee wrote to Washington that he had given up the idea (ALS, George Washington Papers, Library of Congress).

5. Lee's first wife, his cousin Matilda Lee, had died in 1790. On June 18, 1793, he married Ann Hill Carter, a member of one of Virginia's most prominent families.

6. See Lee to H, October 18, 1791.

7. H endorsed this letter "Answered June 15." Letter not found.

To Robert Morris [1]

[*Philadelphia*] *May 6, 1793.* "Mr. Winstanley [2] who will deliver you this, is a Young Gentleman from England, who has lately turned his attention to Landscape painting. . . . He wishes to say something to you about your House now occupied by Mr. Trumball." [3]

ALS, Pierpont Morgan Library, New York City.

1. Morris at this time was a Senator from Pennsylvania.

2. William Winstanley. See H to ———, April 10, 1793.

3. Presumably Jonathan Trumbull of Connecticut, speaker of the House of Representatives.

Treasury Department Circular to the Commissioners of Loans

Treasury Department
May 6 1793

Sir

The Comptroller of the Treasury [1] being in an ill state of health— I have found it necessary to avoid an interruption of business to direct Henry Kuhl his principal Clerk to countersign the warrants which may be issued during the Comptroller's illness for transfering stock to the Books of your office. You will therefore regard his signature (a specimen of which is inclosed) as sufficient to authorise you to pass the Credits directed by the warrants thus countersigned.

The recovery of the Comptroller of which you will be advised, will terminate the object of this Instruction.

I am with Consideration   Sir your Obed Servt

Alexander Hamilton

LS, to John Cochran, Charles Roberts Autograph Collection of the Haverford College Library, Haverford, Pennsylvania.
   1. Oliver Wolcott, Jr.

To Joseph Ward [1]

Treasury Department
May 6. 1793.

Sir

Some very serious difficulties incident to the species of paper mentioned in your letter of the 18th of February last,[2] which produced a real embarrassment in my mind as to a mode of treating them, at once proper and safe, have been the principal causes of the delay which has happened in reporting upon the Petitions relating to that subject.[3]

It was nevertheless fully my intention to have done it at the last Session, but circumstances not unknown which unexpectedly intervened to occupy my time put it out of my power.[4]

I regret any inconveniences which may have resulted to the holders of the paper.

With much consideration & esteem,   I am, Sir, your Obed Servant

A Hamilton

Joseph Ward Esqr.

LS, Chicago Historical Society.
   1. For background to this letter, see H to Ward, May 26, 1791.
   2. Letter not found.
   3. See H to Ward, May 26, 1791, note 1.
   4. For the "circumstances," see the introductory note to H's "Report on the Balance of All Unapplied Revenues at the End of the Year 1792 and on All Unapplied Monies Which May Have Been Obtained by the Several Loans Authorized by Law," February 4, 1793.

From Peter Colt

Hartford 7th May 1793

Sir

Your favour of 10th April only reached me *here* the last Mail. I had left Paterson the 17th. of April, on the Evening of the Day that the Board of Directors left Town, in consequence of Letters from Hartford, stating the critical Situation of my Family, Sick with the Small pox. It has proved fatal to one of my children, & another has been confined to the Hospital for upwards of five Weeks; & is yet so weak as not to be removed. This unexpected Circumstance will necessarily detain me longer from Paterson than I had calculated. I hope however no serious difficulty will arrise, or disadvantage accrue to the affairs of the Society in consequence of this detention.

Your Letter not coming to hand before the meeting of the Directors, will prevent my obtaining the Money to discharge the Balance of your account, so soon as would otherways have been done.[1] I will attend to it as soon as I get back to Paterson.

The Directors at their last meeting discharged Mort[2] from their Service—his Salary to cease the first Instant. They advanced the Salary of Marshall & Pearce[3] to £200 Sterlg ℔ ann. for *one Year*, at which period, it is contemplated our Works will be in compleat operation; & when they may be put upon their first establishment. They reduced the Salary of Hall[4] to the same sum. As I set out for home immediatly after this was declared to him, I had not time to see how this effected him; I only know he has not quit their Service in consequence of this reduction.

I am well aware that many persons, & even some of the Directors, consider him not only as a *bad Man*, but particularly unfriendly to the Interest of the Society. That he is an imprudent Man I can have no doubt. He does not conceale his want of confidence in the plans of the Society, respecting the mode adopted for geting command of the water &c.[5] It is very possible that his supposed disaffection to the Interest of the Society may arrise from imprudent observations respecting this Business, & the deranged State of their Funds. It is very possible he may have calculated on a general Superintendance of the affairs of the Society; & that the appointment of Majr L'Enfant to construct the Canal & the Mills & other works has mortifyed not only him, but Marshall & pearce also. An *English manufacturer* cannot bring himself to believe that a *French Gentleman* can possibly know anything respecting manufactures. From this quarter I believe has orriginated much of the uneasiness amongst the head work men, who appear equally to consider the *Factory* sacrifised to the *Town*.

Pearce is certainly a very injenious Man, & at present very necessary to the Society but he has Substantial failings. He is intemperate; & I fear this evil will grow on him. From his natural temper he is easily led to hasty & inconsiderate Measures respecting his workmen &c—& He seems too much prone to new projects.

The Directors at their last meeting Seemed Seriously alarmed at the extensive plans & views of Major L'Enfant. They came together seeminly determind to confine his operations Strictly to *the Canal;*[6] and to place everything else under my Sole direction. But he wishing to have the compleating his plan of the Town, & stating the impropriety of puting that under any other direction it was agreed to. On further conversation it appeard he considered the *Cotton Mills* as a part of the Canal—at least necessarily connected with it—and shewed the greatest reluctance at having that part of the Business taken out of his Management. After much conversation the Board seemed to acquiese in his having the superintendance of the *Cotton Mill,* altho they had passed a formal vote to restrict him to the Canal, which is to be compleated on the orriginal plan. He has assured them he will give them the entire command of the water this Season; & yet leave them some thing to operate with in future. Everything depends on his accomplishing this promise.

We have much to fear from the present State of the Funds of the Society. It is probable that the *third* payment which falls due the 13 Instant will be made wholly in the *funded Debt of the united States,* as well as the last, which falls due the 13 July next—& that these payments will be compleated only on *about one half of the orriginal Shares*. Should this prove to be the case, it must add greatly to our present embarrassments; as this debt could not be turned into Cash without great loss; and it will be even difficult to obtain Money, on the Credit of those Funds, in the different Banks, Sufficient for the Expenditures of this summer & fall.[7]

I have serious fears that Majr L'Enfant will not be able to reduce his plans & operations, so as to square with the present Situation of the Funds of the Society. As he has the greatest relyance on you, it may be of essential Service to the affairs of the Society for you to press on him the necessity of the greatest Oeconomy in executing his plans; & confining his views to those things which are *essential* instead of what is *ornimental* in forming his works.

I am with great regard   Sir   your most obedt humble Servant

P. Colt

Honl Alexr. Hamilton Esqr

ALS, Hamilton Papers, Library of Congress.

1. See Colt to H, February 28, March 27, 1793.

2. Joseph Mort.

3. On April 16, 1793, the directors of the Society for Establishing Useful Manufactures adopted the following resolution: "Mr. Colt having reported to the Directors, that in his opinion the Salaries of Thomas Marshall and William Pearce ought to be raised; and the Board taking the same into consideration, Resolved, That the Salary of the said Thomas Marshall be at the rate of Eight Hundred and eighty eight dollars and eighty eight cents for one year to commence from the date hereof; on condition that he undertake and obliges himself to instruct such persons as the Superintendent may point out, in the art and mystery of making and erecting the Cotton Mill Machinery, and Spinning thereon by Water, within the said term of one Year. And that the Salary of William Pearce shall be at the rate of Eight hundred and Eighty eight dollars and Eighty eight Cents for one Year to commence from the date hereof" ("Minutes of the S.U.M.," 83–84).

4. On April 16, 1793, the directors of the society "Resolved that the Salary of William Hall be reduced from the date hereof to the sum of Eight hundred and Eighty eight dollars and Eighty eight cents per Annum" ("Minutes of the S.U.M.," 84).

5. See Elisha Boudinot to H, March 26, 1793; Pierre Charles L'Enfant to H, March 26, 1793.

6. For L'Enfant's views on the construction of the proposed canal, see L'Enfant to H, September 17, 1792; March 26, 1793. On April 16, 1793, the directors of the society passed the following resolution: "Whereas Mr. Colt has been appointed Superintendent & no particular duty has hitherto been assigned to him; and Whereas it is essential to the Interest of the Society, that the Aquaduct be constructed in the Speediest Manner possible, consistant with a due regard to Œconomy, Therefore Resolved that Major L'Enfant be requested to confine his attention entirely to the completion of the Aquaduct for the use of the Works, . . . and that the erection of the buildings and other works devolve on Mr. Colt" ("Minutes of the S.U.M.," 83).

7. Joseph S. Davis has described the society's financial problems as follows: "Throughout the period of construction the problem of finance was a serious one. The ingenious plan originally devised . . . [was] to have the subscriptions invested in stock of the United States or the Bank of the United States; to finance both construction and operation by loans on these stocks as collateral, at rates more than covered by the income from the securities; to reserve a considerable part of the authorized capital stock of the company for sale when its marketability was assured. Experience, however, soon disclosed weaknesses in

this plan, although, with Hamilton's effective support, it worked better than might have been expected.

"The subscriptions totalled 6388 shares. On most of these the first instalment (one-fourth) was paid with few delinquencies in January and February, 1792. Since United States stocks ruled at this time higher than their cash equivalents, payments were largely made in cash; $127,185.08 ($19.91 per share) was therefore due. That most of this was received may be inferred from the fact that in April, 1792, 'Accomptant' [Benjamin] Walker accounted for $118,000; and from the statement made to the stockholders in October, 1792, of a sum received 'in full of the first payment, and in part of the second.'

"The Society was financially injured by the panic in three ways. Through directors who were made bankrupt . . . it lost large sums. Many of its subscribers were speculators who were hard hit or made more cautious by the disaster and were thus unable or unwilling to risk more for the Society. And the prestige of the Society, whereby it had been able to secure subscribers among less speculative men, was so injured that new contributors were not to be had and some former ones doubtless deserted the ship. Despite, therefore, the leniency of the board in permitting postponements in paying the second instalment, the total received up to October, 1792, amounted to only $160,200.93, which means that the second instalment was paid on only about one-third of the shares.

"Up to this time the penalties of forfeiture of shares for non-payment, though established by the board in January, 1792, had not been enforced, partly at least because objection was raised that the board could not enact such a by-law. An act amending the charter in this respect was passed Nov. 27, 1792. Still the board hesitated to use this power freely and went to an extreme of leniency in granting till April 13, 1793, to pay the second instalment, and extending the time of payment for the third to May 13 (from January 13), 1793." (Joseph Stancliffe Davis, *Essays in the Earlier History of American Corporations* ["Harvard Economic Studies," XVI (Cambridge, 1917)], I, 473–75.)

From George Washington

Philadelphia May 7th. 1793.

Dear Sir,

As I perceive there has been some mis-conception respecting the building of Vessels in our Ports wch may be converted into armed ones; and as I understand from the Attorney General there is to be a meeting to day, or tomorrow of the Gentlemen on another occasion,[1] I wish to have that part of your circular letter which respects this matter reconsidered by them before it goes out.[2]

I am not disposed to adopt any measures which may check Ship-building in this Country. Nor am I satisfied that we should too promptly adopt measures—in the first instance—that is not indispensably necessary. To take *fair* and *supportable* ground I conceive to be our best policy, and is all that can be required of us by the

Powers at War; leaving the rest to be managed according to circumstances and the advantages which may be derived from them.

I am always Yours &ca.   Go: Washington

Quere,

Is it not expedient that the District Attornies should be written to, requiring their attention to the observance of the Injunctions of the Proclamation?

Colo. Hamilton

ALS, Hamilton Papers, Library of Congress.
1. There was a meeting of the commissioners of the sinking fund on May 7, 1793 (Ford, *Writings of Jefferson*, I, 228).
2. Washington is referring to a draft by H of a circular letter to the collectors of the customs which H had sent to the President. See H to Washington, May 4, 1793; Washington to H, May 5, 1793.

To Stephen Higginson

[*Philadelphia, May 8, 1793.* On the cover of a letter that Higginson wrote to Hamilton on April 21, 1793, Hamilton wrote: "Answered May 8." *Letter not found.*]

From Thomas Jefferson

Philadelphia May 8. 1793.

Sir

I had wished to have kept back the issuing passports for sea vessels, till the question should be decided whether the treaty with France should be declared void,[1] lest the issuing the Passport prescribed by that treaty[2] might be considered as prejudging the question. The importunities however of the owners obliging me to give out a few, I had them printed in the Dutch form[3] only. Not then having sufficiently considered on the best mode of distributing them, I took the liberty, as an expedient of the moment, of sending 7. (the number of vessels then waiting in this port) to mr Delany[4] asking the favor of him to fill them up & deliver them for me. Application for another parcel coming, and the applicant not being able to wait himself till I could send them to be signed by the President, he desired I would lodge them with mr Coxe [5] on whom it would be convenient for him to call for them. I did so; & afterwards sent a second parcel of a dozen, which were pressingly requested.

The President having now decided that the French passport [6] may also be issued, it is at this time in the press, & the whole instrument compleat with the two passports, sea-letters, & certificates in it's final form, will be ready for signature tomorrow. It has therefore now become necessary to determine on the ultimate channel of distributing them. I am not the judge whether the task of distribution might interfere too much with the other duties of the collectors of the customs. If it would not, their position seems best accomodated to that distribution. I took the liberty therefore to-day of proposing to the President that, if you should think there would be no inconvenience in charging them with the distribution, the blanks might be lodged with them; of which he approved: and I have now the honor of submitting that question to you. If you find no inconvenience in it, I will send 300 blanks, as soon as they shall be signed, either to your office or to that of the Commissioner of the revenue, whichever you shall prefer, to be forwarded to the collectors of the different ports; & from time to time afterwards will keep up a supply. Should it however, in your opinion, interfere too much with the other duties of those officers, I will submit to the President the depositing them with the deputy marshals appointed or to be appointed in every port. I will ask the favor of your answer, as the applications are numerous & pressing, & I am unwilling to be further troublesome to the gentlemen who have hitherto been so kind as to fill up & deliver them for me till some arrangement could be made which might relieve me personally from a business with the details of which I was not acquainted. I have the honor to be with great respect, Sir,

Your most obedt & most humble sert   Th: Jefferson

The Secretary of the Treasury

ALS, letterpress copy, Thomas Jefferson Papers, Library of Congress.

1. See H to John Jay, first letter of April 9, 1793, note 2; George Washington to H, Jefferson, Henry Knox, and Edmund Randolph, April 18, 1793; "Cabinet Meeting. Opinion on a Proclamation of Neutrality and on Receiving the French Minister," April 19, 1793; H and Knox to Washington, May 2, 1793; H to Washington, May 2, 1793.

2. Article 25 of the Franco-American Treaty of Amity and Commerce of 1778 provided "that in case either of the Parties hereto should be engaged in

War, the Ships and Vessels belonging to the Subjects or People of the other Ally must be furnished with Sea Letters or Passports expressing the name, Property and Bulk of the Ship as also the name and Place of habitation of the Master or Commander of the said Ship, that it may appear thereby, that the Ship really & truely belongs to the Subjects of one of the Parties. . . . It is likewise agreed, that such Ships being laden are to be provided not only with Passports as above mentioned, but also with Certificates containing the several Particulars of the Cargo, the Place whence the Ship sailed, and whither she is bound, that so it may be known, whether any forbidden or contraband Goods be on board the same: which Certificates shall be made out by the Officers of the Place, whence the Ship set sail, in the accustomed Form" (Miller, *Treaties*, II, 23–24).

3. See "Treasury Department Circular to the Collectors of the Customs," May 13–16, 1793.

4. Sharp Delany, collector of customs at Philadelphia.

5. Tench Coxe, commissioner of the revenue.

6. See "Treasury Department Circular to the Collectors of the Customs," May 13–16, 1793.

To Richard Morris [1]

[*Philadelphia, May 8, 1793*. On May 20, 1793, Morris wrote to Hamilton: "I am favoured with your letter of the 8th. instant." *Letter not found.*]

1. Morris had been supervisor of the revenue for the District of New York until April, 1793.

From William Vans Murray [1]

Cambridge, Dorset, E. S. Maryland.
8. May. 1793.

Dear Sir,

A little event has taken place here which must be my apology for intruding on you.

A report circulated here that a prize taken from british subjects at sea by a french privateer has actually past this town (on Choptank) [2] under the command of a citizen of this District. [3] This took place on the 3d or 4th inst. I sent an express to Oxford to Col. Banning [4] of that port to inform him of the circumstance with the substance of the treaty of commerce on the point. He came hither & we went on board. The Captn. show'd a *power* signed by a certain Baptst. Ferey, (with a recital of Ferey's commission from the French Republic), authorising "*Citizen* Hooper" (that is the Capt's. Name) to carry the prize into the nearest port. The spirit & letter of the 17th. article of the Commercial Treaty [5] seemed the best ground—& Col. Banning not thinking this power A *Commission* in the hands of a *Citizen* sufficient to protect the prize with the U.S.—*Seized the Vessel.* In the mean time by the same express I wrote to Mr. Paca [6] the Judge of the District. In so retired a situation where no light flows from reciprocated opinions I had no clue but the treaty—strictly to be construed by the spirit of the Proclamation & the essential principles of good faith in Neutrality—but being the only member on the spot & finding people imagined I ought to do something, I hazarded this step as the most decisive & exemplary. It has given, I believe complete satisfaction, as the public here are with the Proclamation & though friendly to the French Revolution, decided friends & supporters of Neutrality.

You will pardon me, Sir, when I suggest the idea that some *leading impression,* by way of official communication perhaps will be found convenient, from the High Departments of the Executive to the Officers of ports &c. We had not a man in the county who could lawfully enter on board the prize till Banning (who is a very excellent officer) came from another county which is divided from this (Dorsset) by a river as wide as the Delaware off Wilmington. So extremely naked is the body of the Federal Govt. so wanting in not only cloathing, but in limbs.

I will observe the paper purporting to be a *commission* wh. by way of recital preceded Hooper's authority, was not signed by any name of the Executive Council of France—& that it struck me that though Hooper might have been a french officer on the ocean his arrival in his own country, then under the obligation of Neutrality, would instantly divest him of any power from the French to act contrary to the declared rights of Neutrality within the Dominions of the U.S.—& that a prize *lawfully* taken if sent *without a commission & unlawfully* into a neutral country became subject to all the rights of Dominion (as protection) inherent in the neutral State.

Whatever you communicate will be considered as confidential & will not be made use of as anticipating opinions which time & policy might undermine. Hooper means to go down the bay to order the privateers to send their prizes to the Islands. He is suspected to own a share of the privateer which took the prize. Two of the crew (prisioners!) had left the schooner before we reached her. She was from N. Providence to Philada. Captn. Tucker commander. I am respectfully & with sincere esteem Dear Sr. Yrs.

W. V. Murray.

N B: Hooper came from Charles Town—so did the privateer. The privateer was, it is by every body understood, fitted out there! & was sold by Hooper to the french he retaining a share—so is the *report*. He is much alarmed—is an ignorant young man—& declares that the great men of Charles Town led him to error & particularly the *Governor:* which is incredible. He says a great number have fitted out there & will be.[7]

ALS, Hamilton Papers, Library of Congress.
    1. Murray was a Federalist member of the House of Representatives from Maryland.
    2. The Choptank is a river in eastern Maryland.
    3. This vessel was the *Eunice*, captured and sent into port by the French privateer *Sans Culotte*, commanded by Captain Baptiste André Ferey. In a deposition forwarded to Thomas Jefferson by Thomas Newton, Jr., inspector of the revenue for Virginia, and William Lindsay, collector of customs at Norfolk, Virginia, on May 5, 1793, Henry Tucker, the master of the *Eunice*, reported that "he was on the 29th last month taken by a privateer schooner called the San Culotte commanded by Capt. Farre . . . that after being in possession of the privateer the name of his schooner was erased from the Stern and a Mr Hooper of Cambridge in the State of Maryland was put on board as prize master. . . . Mr. Hooper own'd the schooner Eagle & plied from this to Georgia & Charleston as a packet. She Was fitted originally from Cambridge. From every circumstance Capt Tucker was of opinion they wou'd take vessels in the Bay of Cheasapeake . . ." (copy, RG 59, Miscellaneous Letters, 1790–1799, National Archives). On May 7, 1793, John Hamilton, the British consul at Norfolk, complained to Governor Thomas Sim Lee of Maryland concerning the "capture of a Vessel belonging to British Subjects residing at New Providence and trading to this country. . . . The Schooner Eunice of New Providence, Henry Tucker Master, having 2,000 Dollars in specie and a few boxes of Sugars, bound for Philadelphia was taken off Virginia . . . on the 29th of April last, by an American built armed Schooner under french colours, said to be French property, and the greatest part of her crew Americans" (ALS, RG 59, Miscellaneous Letters, 1790–1799, National Archives).
    4. Jeremiah Banning was collector of customs and inspector of the port of Oxford, Maryland.
    5. This article is also cited as Article 19 of the 1778 Franco-American Treaty of Amity and Commerce. For an explanation of the discrepancy in the numbering of the articles of this treaty, see H to John Jay, first letter of April 9, 1793, note 2. Article 17 provided that the commanders of ships of war or privateers of either party might "carry whithersoever they please the Ships and Goods taken from their Enemies, without being obliged to pay any Duty to the Officers of the Admiralty or any other Judges; nor shall such Prizes be arrested or seized, when they come to and enter the Ports of either Party; nor shall the Searchers or other Officers of those Places search the same or make examination concerning the Lawfulness of such Prizes, but they may hoist Sail

at any time and depart and carry their Prizes to the Places express'd in their Commissions, which the Commanders of such Ships of War shall be obliged to shew . . ." (Miller, *Treaties*, II, 16–17).

6. William Paca.

7. According to Gouverneur Morris, United States Minister Plenipotentiary to France, when Edmond Charles Genet sailed from France he "took out with him three hundred blank commissions, which he is to distribute to such as will fit out cruisers in our ports to prey on the British commerce" (*ASP, Foreign Relations*, I, 354). In a discussion with Jefferson in May, 1793, concerning the vessels fitted out in Charleston, Genet told the Secretary of State "that on his arrival there he was surrounded suddenly by Frenchmen full of zeal for their country, pressing for authority to arm with their own means for it's assistance, that they would fit out their own vessels, provide everything, man them, and only ask a commission from him: that he asked the opinion of Govr [William] Moultrie on the subject, who said he knew no law to the contrary, but begged that whatever was to be done, might be done without consulting him, that he must know nothing of it &c" (Ford, *Writings of Jefferson*, I, 248–49).

To George Washington

Treasy. Departmt. 8 May 93.

The Secretary of the Treasury has the honor to lay before the President sundry papers relating to Ephraim Kirby,[1] which is done merely on the score of propriety, as it is not perceived that any special provision in the case, can be consistently made.

Alexander Hamilton

LC, George Washington Papers, Library of Congress.

1. An entry in JPP for May 9, 1793, reads as follows: "The Secretary of the Treasury sent me . . . sundry papers (merely as a matter of form) for my perusal, relating to Ephm. Kirby Collect. of one of the Divisions in the Dist. of Connecticut for indemnification for expenses incurred in the discharge of his duty" (JPP, 112).

To George Washington

[Philadelphia, May 8, 1793]

The Secretary of the Treasury has the honor to submit to the consideration of the President of the UStates a communication from the Commissioner of the Revenue of the 6 instant [1]—respecting a contract provisionally entered into with Moses M. Hayes for a further supply of Oil for the Light Houses.[2] It is respectfully conceived that the arrangement is in every view eligible.   A. Hamilton

8 May 1793.

LC, George Washington Papers, Library of Congress.

1. Letter from Tench Coxe not found.

2. An entry in JPP for May 9, 1793, reads as follows: "The Secretary of the Treasury sent me a bond of Moses M. Hayes as principal & Jno. C. Jones as surity (both of Boston) in the sum of 10,545 Dolls. to furnish 14,000 Gals. of Oil for the Light Houses in the Eastern States" (JPP, 112). A copy of the contract between Hayes and the United States, approved by Washington on May 16, 1793, may be found in RG 26, Lighthouse Deeds and Contracts, National Archives.

To Thomas Jefferson

Treasury Department
May 9. 1793

Sir

I have this moment received your Letter of yesterday.

It appears to me, as it does to you, that the position of the Collectors of the Customs will render them the most convenient channel of distribution for the Passports; nor do I perceive, that it can interfere with their other duties.

It will be equally agreeable to me, that they be transmitted either directly from your office, or through this department. If you prefer the latter, which I shall with pleasure facilitate, I will request you to cause them to be sent in the first instance to me—when I will put them in the usual course of conveyance. With great respect

I have the honor to be   Sir   Your obedient servant

Alexander Hamilton

P.S.   Inclosed is the copy of a letter from the Collector of New York to Mr. Coxe of the 7th instant, which is transmitted for your consideration.[1]

The Seretary of State

ALS, James Madison Papers, Library of Congress.

1. This letter from John Lamb to Tench Coxe concerned sea letters for United States vessels (copy, Thomas Jefferson Papers, Library of Congress).

To John Kean

[Philadelphia, May 9, 1793]
D Sir

As soon as the term of the inclosed Note shall have come within your rule of Discount you will oblige me by having it presented for that purpose.

It is often my Lot to distress myself to accommodate friends. This is my present situation.

Yrs truly   A Hamilton

Philadelphia May 9. 1793

ALS, Historical Society of Pennsylvania, Philadelphia.

From Joseph Nourse

Treasury Department, Register's Office, May 10, 1793. Encloses "a Certified Copy of a Letter received from Stephen Hussuy Collr. of the District of Nantucket. . . .¹ Enclosing 2 Ship Registers issued from that Port in the year 1791."

LS, Thomas Jefferson Papers, Library of Congress.
    1. Hussey's letter, dated April 23, 1793, is addressed to Nourse and reads in part as follows: "Inclosed is the registers of the Ships Beaver & Washington given up at this Office to be cancelled, both rendered useless by reason of a written Declaration in Spanish on the Back of the same. Capt. [Paul] Worth of the Ship Beaver being in Latitude 13 So. on the coast of Peru and about 12 Leagues from the Land, fell in with a Spanish Frigate named the Hare. Capt. Worth was ordered on Board the said Frigate, and to take with him his Papers and Log Book, when on Board the Capt. of the Frigate asked him if he had any Passport, being told he had not, the Captain of the Frigate then said to Capt. Worth, if he had no Passport from the Spanish King he had no right to navigate in their seas. The Capt. of the Frigate then wrote in Spanish on the Back of the Ship Beavers Register, authorizing all other vessels, that shou'd first meet said Ship to sieze her and then sent an Officer in his Boat on Board the Beaver to serch the Ship. Finding she was not on that Coast upon a Fishing Voyage, the spanish Capt. said he woud let the Beaver go, but, at the same time advised Capt. Worth to leave that Coast immediately, for the Ship woud be seizd and made a Prize by the next armd Spanish Vessel that shoud find her. . . . It appears from the Circumstances abovementioned, that the Whale Fishery in the Southern Ocean must be lost to American Vessels unless some Credentials can be obtain sufficient to protect them against Insults and Injuries from Spanish armed Vessels. It is the Wish of many Persons concernd in the Whale Fishery to be informd by the Secretary, whether any further Aid can

be obtaind for the Use of American vessels to be Employd in the Southern Ocean on the Whale Fishery . . ." (copy, Thomas Jefferson Papers, Library of Congress).

Copies of the registers are also in the Thomas Jefferson Papers, Library of Congress.

To Thomas Pinckney

[Philadelphia, May 10, 1793]

The Secretary of the Treasury presents his compliments to Mr Pinckney and takes the liberty of troubling him with the charge of the enclosed letter for the Commissioners of the United States at Amsterdam.[1]

Treasury Departmt.
May 10. 1793.

Copy, Pinckney Family Papers, Library of Congress.
1. The letter to Willink, Van Staphorst, and Hubbard has not been found.

To Edmund Randolph

Treasury Department
May 10. 1793

Sir

Inclosed are two letters one of the 16th of April from the Collector of the District of Charlestown,[1] the other of the 29 of April from the Collector of the District of New Port [2]—raising certain questions concerning the conduct to be observed in respect to prizes brought into the ports of the UStates by the Powers of Europe now at War with each other.

I request your opinion on the points of law which they suggest; marking the distinctions if any which arise out of Treaties with any or either of the parties.

The case requires that some precise and explicit instruction should be transmitted to the several Collectors as soon as possible; with a view to which your opinion as soon as convenient is desired.

This course, I understand [from] Mr Lear, was indicated by the President.[3]

With respectful consideration   I am Sir   Your obed servant

The Atty General

ADf, Connecticut Historical Society, Hartford.
  1. Isaac Holmes. Letter not found, but see H to George Washington, April 27, 1793, note 1.
  2. William Ellery to H, April 29, 1793.
  3. This sentence is in an unidentified handwriting.

From William Short

Private   (Duplicate)   Aranjuez [Spain] May 11th. 1793

Sir

Your private letter of the 5th. of febry. forwarded to me by Mr. Pinckney [1] was recieved yesterday. I hasten to reply to it because you observe therein that an investigation intended to prejudice you was begun with respect to the circumstances attending the last payment on account of the French debt, which in its progress might draw my conduct into question. Although as you observe very justly for the reasons you mention in your letter that I should have no anxiety for the result; & although the only step I took in the whole business, namely the asking of a receipt of a particular kind of the French agents,[2] for greater security, under the circumstances of France, which as soon as known to the President & yourself, had induced you to direct a suspension of the payments,[3] yet at the distance I am from the scene of investigation, I cannot help hoping you will be so good as to take the trouble to expose fully the whole of my conduct as contained in my tedious & prolix correspondence with you, if any part of it should be considered as questionable by any body. It seems to me that nothing more can be necessary to shew that whatever I did under the circumstances I was placed, would be absolutely out of the reach of the most captious, & the more so as except in the instance abovementioned I cannot be said to have had any alternative for the exercise of my will—& of course did only what was unavoidable.

ALS, letterpress copy, William Short Papers, Library of Congress.
  1. Thomas Pinckney.
  2. The "French agents" were Hogguer, Grand, and Company. For the controversy over the payment by the United States of the installment due on the French debt in the summer of 1792, see Gouverneur Morris to H, September 25, 1792; Short to H, September 25, October 27, November 29, 1792; Thomas Jefferson to H, October 31, 1792.
  3. See H to Short, October 1–15, 1792.

In this instance also I exercised my judgment only to a certain degree in consequence of the then state of the French government— before you knew what part I had taken & as soon as that state of the French government was known to you, you directed me & afterwards repeated by the President's approbation, to go still further than I had of myself undertaken to go, & consequently what I had done met your approbation & it still seems to me impossible that any government under those circumstances could have given different orders from those which you communicated to me—but even if that were possible, certainly no subordinate agent of a government, however enterprizing he might be, or however confident of the infallibility of his own opinions, could with propriety act otherwise or go further than I did. It suffices only to recall those circumstances to shew this beyond the question of any body.

You are acquainted fully with the causes of the delay in the payments to France until Mr. Morris made an arrangement with the commissioners of the national treasury.[4] When I recd. his letter informing me of this arrangement made a few days before the King's suspension, I recieved also an account of that suspension & the government being no longer in the hands of those to whom I was directed by my powers [5] from the President to make the payment. I received at the same time your letter of June the 14th. informing me that it was the President's intention that whatever related to the re-imbursement to France should still remain under my direction. This was certainly flattering, but nothing could be more unexpected after my having been removed from Paris & Mr. Morris being sent there, & the President's original instructions being to you that you should *employ me to make loans* & for the arrangements with respect to the French debt should employ *the Minister of the U.S. for the time being at Paris*.[6] As soon as I knew that the President had nominated another minister for Paris, delicacy & propriety certainly forbad my taking any further steps in such arrangement, as I have repeated to you in my letters even to satiety & the more so when I considered the circumstances of Mr. Morris's nomination which

4. See Morris to Short, August 6, 9, 1792, and Short to Morris, August 17, 1792. These letters are printed as enclosures to Morris to H, September 25, 1792.
5. See H to Short, September 1, 1790.
6. See George Washington to H, August 28, 1790.

could not but leave an impression, that it must have been in some degree with a view to the financial arrangements of the U.S. with France, as his abilities, far surpassing mine in all subjects, have still a greater superiority in this than any other.

You know also that it was necessary to settle with France the depreciation on former payments before proceeding to make any other. Consequently when I left Paris for the Hague, I became nothing more with respect to the payments to France than Mr. Morris's agent to recieve & transmit his orders to our commissioners at Amsterdam.[7] This was perfectly understood between us to be the case as I have often mentioned to you. My anxiety on account of the increasing sums in the hands of our commissioners at a dead interest, has also been often mentioned to you.[8]

Thus situated I recieved at length Mr. Morris's letter desiring me to direct the commissioners to make a payment to the French bankers at Amsterdam of 1.625.000 florins.[9] This letter was previous to the King's suspension. I recd. at the same time an account of the King's suspension. It was known also at the Hague that the Duke of Brunswick was marching towards Paris, & in the eyes of every observer there seemed no doubt of his arriving there—& of course of the members of the then government being obliged to leave that place. Supposing then I had had a right to make payments to those who had overturned the government to which alone I had been authorized to make payments (which however cannot be supposed without the absurdity of establishing that I as a subordinate agent had a right to cancel the powers given me by the President & to substitute new ones of my own) still prudence would have dictated the taking precautions under these circumstances, & the being sure at least that those for whom it was intended should recieve it. Several circumstances contributed to render my situation peculiarly embarassing. I had hitherto supposed myself the passive agent of M. Morris in these payments, & his letter written before the suspension giving these orders, not being contradicted by one he wrote two or three days after,[10] might therefore rigorously have sufficed for my ordering

7. Willink, Van Staphorst, and Hubbard.
8. See Short to H, October 27, December 17, 1792, and H to Short, November 26, 1792.
9. See note 4.
10. Morris to Short, August 13, 1792 (ALS, William Short Papers, Library of Congress).

the payment—but I had now recieved your letter of June 14th. which shewed that it would be expected that I should not be totally passive.

I weighed the whole with the anxiety you may suppose & the deepest attention I was capable of. It seemed to me the principal desideratum, was the arranging this payment in such a manner as that the U.S. might be exempted from paying a further interest thereon, & yet so as no future government in France could question the legality of the payment & of course despute it, if not applied in the manner they might wish. This seemed to me to be attained by the reciept which I desired our commissioners to ask of the French agents, as formerly mentioned to you—namely that *the payment was on* account of the debt due by the U.S. to France, & to be held at the disposition of His Most *Christian Majesty* (which I put by inattention instead of the King of the French & was of no consequence).[11] Under this rect. all questions were removed from the U.S. & placed between the Agents of France at Amsterdam & the French government—& let what government be established that might be, Republican, Aristocratical, or Monarchical, still the payment would have been valid & indisputable as to the U.S. whatever the French agents might have done with the money paid them. From their desire to recieve these payments & from being Merchts. of Amsterdam, I thought they would give this reciept. They chose however to take time to consider of it; this occasioned delay—& at length the payment was made for the reasons & in the manner you have been so often informed of on the 4th of Sept:—The whole delay therefore of this payment which can in any way be attributed to me is from Aug. 17th. to Sep. 4th. & of this you see a part was occasioned by the French agents themselves. I am willing thereon to refer it to the most censorious & captious, & think I may defy even a disposition to blame what was done. I trust you will have been so kind as to have taken the trouble to have placed this subject in its full & clear light, & I rely with as much certainty on exemption from blame by my fellow citizens in this instance, as the approbation of the President & your own which you have been so good as to express, & which I place in the highest degree of estimation, as being the most consoling circumstance I have experienced for all the anxiety I have undergone since being employed in these delicate concerns of the U.S.

11. See Short to Morris, August 21, 1792, and Morris to Short, August 27, 1792. These letters are printed as enclosures to Morris to H, September 25, 1792.

I will not add to the length of this letter by recapitulating the causes of the delay in the French payments, which took place after monies became disposible in the hands of the bankers from about the first of March 1792 until Mr. Morris's arrangement with the commissaries of the treasury. My letters written to [12]

agents could had an example, were conducted to the satisfaction of government, it would entitle me to the permanent mission at Paris where as yet I was only employed by interim. I was encouraged in this hope from reflecting that that mission would probably present nothing more delicate or confidential than those money concerns of the U.S.—from supposing that none of the characters who had been formerly abroad would accept this mission—from having been so long employed myself at Paris—& from the observation of the weight which that circumstance has with all the governments of Europe in their foreign appointments, except where counteracted by the longer experience of others in the same line, or by the privileges which high birth sometimes give to those without experience, in those countries where different orders of citizens exist. I mention these considerations by no means with a view to complain of what has taken place, but merely that you may not accuse me of too much vanity in the idea, I had taken up. I respect too much the President's unquestionable right to place his confidence on those whom he may judge most worthy of it, & most capable of serving the U.S.—to have any pretensions to complaint—& never doubted after learning that this confidence was placed on another, that he had very sufficient reasons for overweighing the considerations abovementioned. Until I had learned this however, by a letter from Mr. Morris himself, it was natural for me to give more & more weight to them in my own mind, from the flattering manner in which you had been pleased to express to me the Presidents & your approbation of my manner of conducting the business at Amsterdam,[13] & from the increasing length of time I had been continued to be employed at Paris. However willing or desirous I might be to be employed in that mission, I was never reconciled to be employed alone in the money concerns at Amster-

12. At this point in the MS a page or pages are missing.
13. See H to Short, April 2, 1792.

dam,[14] & the arrangements which might be made with respect to the debt to France. I was conscious of my own ignorance on such subjects, & was persuaded that many advantageous arrangements would present themselves, which few individuals would have sufficient confidence in their own skill, or sufficient boldness to make the most of for the U.S.—whilst acting alone & unaided. At least I felt this with respect to myself & had the honor of mentioning it to you uniformly —& I assure you with the same unreserve with which I have written the rest of this letter, that the most agreeable reflexion which presented itself in being removed from Paris was that I was relieved from any further active agency in this business. I need not mention that I could discover nothing particularly agreeable in the appointment as Resident at the Hague (except its being a mark of the President's confidence which no person can rate higher than I do in every instance) as it was being sent with the same grade to an inferior court —& also as this character from the modern usage of nations is no longer in fact, what it appears to be in diplomatick authors, & has now gone into disuse except at places of the lowest importance, such as the little principalities of Germany—& also as the grade of chargés des affaires, ministers resident, or any others of this class, when accidentally employed, are exposed to many disagreeable circumstances at the Hague, & in some other places, from which they are exempted totally at Paris, from local considerations; which probably escape the attention (of those whose more extensive observations induce them only to generalize their ideas) merely from their being local.

The principal not to say the only inducement wch. I could have to accept the mission at the Hague instead of returning to America, was that at the same time that I was informed of my being named for it, & recieved my orders to repair there, I was informed also that the President had done me the honor to nominate me for a special commission at Madrid.[15] Although I did not know precisely the nature of the business I was informed by the Secy. of State that it was urgent & that I should recieve my instructions at the Hague. From the delay which this annunciation of my appointment to the

14. See Short to H, October 9, 27, 1792.
15. On March 18, 1792, Short and William Carmichael had been appointed "joint Commissioners Plenipotentiary, on the part of the U. S. to treat with the Court of Madrid on the subjects of the navigation of the Mississipi, arrangements on our limits, & commerce . . ." (Ford, *Writings of Jefferson*, V, 456–57).

Hague had experienced in the way,[16] I had reason to believe that I should find my instructions wd. arrive at the Hague, as soon as I shd. In this instance I had no alternative left either but to accept the mission or expose government to a delay which the business, as far as I could then judge, seemed not to admit of. I accordingly repaired immediately to the Hague. I remained there several months in the daily expectation of recieving those instructions, & in the expectation of setting out for Madrid. As it turned out, my having declined this business from the beginning could have occasioned no delay—but this I could not know until it was too late—& as soon as I recd. the second of these instructions I set off for this country [17]—the hope of serving my own & returning to it with that advantage my leading motive. In this I have found myself also mistaken from a combination of circumstances which afterwards took place, & also from a circumstance which I learned immediately on my arrival here, & which had it been made known to me at the Hague as it might have been, would have shewn me that there was little foundation for the hope which I had entertained—& induced my suggesting the propriety of waiting for this business being negotiated at Philadelphia by the minister that C. de Florida Blanca had engaged to send there for that purpose [18]—& which would have been better for all parties—at least for

16. Short did not receive notice of his appointment as commissioner until November, 1792. See Short to H, November 29, 1792, note 33.

17. See Short to H, November 29, December 17, 1792.

18. José de Monino y Redono, Count de Floridablanca, had been Spanish Minister of Foreign Affairs in 1791 when the subject of negotiations between the United States and Spain had been opened. Before Short's arrival in Spain in February, 1793, however, Floridablanca had been replaced successively by Pedro Pablo Abarca de Bolea, Conde de Aranda, and by Manuel de Goday. At this time Spanish affairs in the United States were under the direction of two commissioners, Josef de Jaudenes and Josef de Viar.

On February 3, 1793, Short wrote to Jefferson from Madrid informing him that he had assumed that the Spanish Court had given assurances of its willingness to open negotiations. On his arrival in Spain, however, Short had found that his co-commissioner, William Carmichael, had taken it for granted "that the Spanish agents in America must have been instructed to give such assurances although you have not thought it worth while to mention is to us yet it seems to me by no means indifferent for us to know with precision and particularly in the present situation of affairs on what our mission was grounded. Mr. Carmichael knows of no other ground than a letter of Count Florida to him, sent to you, saying the King had resolved to send a person authorised to treat and verbal assurances from the same Minister of the good dispositions of this Court. He was told by Ct. Aranda during his short administration in speaking on this subject that the assurances given by one Minister were not an obligation

us—& particularly for me as it would have saved me the mortification of being sent so far & at a considerable expence to the U.S. without any prospect of rendering them the service I wished to do—& without any means for the present of relieving myself from it without risking to do an impropriety & injury, as has been in our joint letters fully explained to the Sec. of State. I beg a thousand pardons for this tedious letter—& trust that my great distance from America, under the information you gave me in your letter will be its apology. I have the honor to be with the most perfect respect, Sir, your most obedt. & humble servt.   W: Short

The Honble. Alexr. Hamilton Esqr. &c &c.

———

on his successor. I cannot yet know in what light the present Minister who is a remove further from the *Count Florida will consider the assurances he gave* ..." (LC, RG 59, Despatches from United States Ministers to Spain, 1792–1825, Vol. I, August 15, 1792–February 2, 1796, National Archives). The words in italics were written in cipher and deciphered above the line.

To Thomas Jefferson

Philadelphia, May [12] [1] *1793.* Transmits "the Copy of a letter of the 23d of April last from the Collector of the District of Nantucket to the Register of the Treasury" and "Copies of the declarations on the Registers, therein referred to." [2]

LS, Thomas Jefferson Papers, Library of Congress.
    1. Although this letter is dated May 8, the enclosures were not submitted to H by Joseph Nourse until May 10. The letter is endorsed as having been received by Jefferson on May 13.
    2. See Nourse to H, May 10, 1793, note 1.

Alexander Hamilton and Edmund Randolph to Thomas Jefferson [1]

[Philadelphia, May 13–15, 1793]

A   Perhaps the Secretary of State, revising the expression of this member of the sentence, will find terms to express his idea still more clearly and may avoid the use of a word of doubtful propriety "Contraventions."

B   "but be attentive"

C   "mere" to be omitted

D   Considering that this Letter will probably become a matter of publicity to the world is it necessary to be so strong? Would not the following suffice as a substitute?

"but our unwillingness to believe that the French Nation could be wanting in respect or friendship to us upon any occasion suspends our assent to and conclusions upon these statements 'till further evidence." It will be observed that the words "conclusions upon" are proposed to be added to indicate that some further measure is contemplated, conformably to the declaration to Mr. ⟨– – – – –⟩ measures will be taken, ⟨– – –⟩ may be in lieu of General Knox's amendment

E   Suppose the words "bay of" were omitted

F   "Expectation" is proposed to be substituted to "*desire*"

G   For the sentence between [   ] [2] It is proposed to substitute this—

"They consider the rigorous exercise of that virtue as the surest means of preserving perfect harmony between the UStates and the Powers at War"

A Hamilton
Edm: Randolph

DS, in the handwriting of H, Thomas Jefferson Papers, Library of Congress.
1. This document contains H's and Randolph's suggested changes for a letter to Jean Baptiste de Ternant, dated May 15, 1793, discussing memorials presented to the United States Government by George Hammond. See the introductory note to H to Washington, May 15, 1793. The draft of Jefferson's letter to Ternant which contained the passages for which H and Randolph suggested substitutions has not been found. The final version of the letter incorporating most of the suggestions is printed in *ASP, Foreign Relations*, I, 147–48, and copies may be found in the Thomas Jefferson Papers, Library of Congress; Edmond C. Genet Papers, Library of Congress; RG 59, Domestic Letters of the Department of State, Vol. 5, February 4, 1792–December 31, 1793, National Archives.
2. These brackets appear in the MS.

From Henry Knox

War Department, May 13, 1793. Approves payment of a bill "drawn by Israel Ludlow on William Duer 29 January 1792." [1]

LS, RG 217, Miscellaneous Treasury Accounts, 1790–1894, Account No. 4118, National Archives.

1. Duer had served as contractor for the Army for the campaign against the Indians in the Northwest Territory in 1791, and Ludlow had acted as his agent in purchasing supplies and services on the frontier. The bill was for two hundred and fifty-five dollars and three ninetieths to be paid to John Duncan for his services as a packhorse driver during the campaign.

To Henry Knox

Treasury Department
May 13. 1793

Sir

I have the honor to inclose an extract of a letter from me of this date to General Wilkinson,[1] on a question of some importance lately raised by the Contractors.[2]

I need not observe of how much moment it is, that the Commanding General should without delay establish with the Contractors the construction which I put on the Contract; about which I have no idea that they can mean any serious difficulty.

With respect   I have the honor to be &c

Secy of War

ADf, Connecticut Historical Society, Hartford.

1. James Wilkinson, a brigadier general in the United States Army, had served as a lieutenant colonel and deputy adjutant general for the northern department during the American Revolution. In 1784 he settled in Kentucky, where he engaged in business and politics and during the seventeen-eighties was involved in the so-called "Spanish Conspiracy" for the separation of Kentucky from the Union. In March, 1791, he commanded a band of Kentucky volunteers in an expedition against the Ohio Indians. In October, 1791, he received a commission as lieutenant colonel in the regular Army and the next year was promoted to brigadier general.

2. The contractors were Robert Elliot and Elie Williams, who had contracted to furnish supplies to the Army on the western frontier during the preparations for a new campaign against the western Indians. Knox forwarded the extract of Wilkinson's letter to Major General Anthony Wayne on May 17, 1793. See H to Wilkinson, May 13, 1793. According to Knox's letter to Wayne, the question raised by the contractors was "whether they are bound to transport the rations of provisions and furnish them daily to the Troops while on their march" (LS, Historical Society of Pennsylvania, Philadelphia).

Treasury Department Circular
to the Collectors of the Customs [1]

Treasury Department, May [13–16] 1793

Sir,

It being necessary in the present state of War among the principal European powers, that all ships and vessels belonging to the citizens of the United States, should be furnished as soon as possible with sea letters, for their more perfect identification and security, you will find within this inclosure   [2] copies of two several documents of that kind, signed by the President of the United States, and undersigned by the Secretary of the Department of State, which have been received from that Department for the purpose of being transmitted to the several Custom-houses. One of each of these letters is to be delivered to every ship or vessel, being actually and bona fide, the property of one or more citizens of the United States, after the captain shall have duly made oath to the effect, and according to the tenor of the certificate printed under that which is in Dutch and English, the substance and purport of which oath is comprised in the 10th, 11th, 12th, 13th, 14th, and 15th, lines of the said printed certificate. To this the captain is to be duly sworn before some officer qualified to administer oaths, such as a justice of the peace, an alderman, or any superior judicial officer, preferring the Mayor, chief Burgess, or other officer (if any there be) who is the *chief* Magistrate of the city, town or borough in which the issuing Custom-house is

LS, dated May 14, 1793, to Otho H. Williams, Office of the Secretary, United States Treasury Department; copy, dated May 16, 1793, to Nathaniel Fosdick, RG 56, Letters to and from the Collector at Portland, National Archives; copy, dated May 16, 1793, to Nathaniel Fosdick, RG 56, Letters to Collectors at Small Ports, "Set G," National Archives; copy, dated May 13, 1793, to John Lamb, Bureau of Customs, Philadelphia; copy, dated May 13, 1793, to John Lamb, RG 56, Circulars of the Office of the Secretary, "Set T," National Archives; copy, dated May 13, 1793, to John Lamb, United States Finance Miscellany, Treasury Circulars, Library of Congress; copy, dated May 13, 1793, to John Lamb, Office of the Secretary, United States Treasury Department; copy, dated May 14, 1793, to Otho H. Williams, RG 56, Circulars of the Office of the Secretary, "Set T," National Archives. Copies of this circular were also issued from the office of the commissioner of the revenue over the signature of Tench Coxe (LS, Thomas Jefferson Papers, Library of Congress).

1. For background to this letter, see Thomas Jefferson to H, May 8, 1793; H to Jefferson, May 10, 1793.

2. In the original documents, words pertinent to the particular collector to whom each circular was sent were inserted in the spaces left blank in the MS.

situated. The certificate is then to be signed by the Magistrate, and the public seal (or if he has no public one his private seal) is to be affixed. The blanks are to be filled up, both in the English and in the Dutch copies of the sea letter, by the Collector, and in both the English and Dutch copies of the certificate by the Magistrate or Judge.[3] The English language may be used in filling the blanks in

3. The form for the certificate and sea letter, with the blanks filled in by Joseph Hiller, collector of customs at Salem, Massachusetts, is printed below. The material supplied by Hiller is indicated by italics.

"DOEN TE WEETEN dat by deezen vryheiden permissie gegeeven werd aen *Herbert Woodberry* Schipper en Bevelhebber van het Schip (of vaartuig:) genaamt *Leopard* van de *Port* van *Salem* groot *156* Tonnen of daar omtrent, leggende teegenswoordig in de Haaven van *Salem* gedestineert naar *West Indies* en beladen met *Dry Goods Candles, Lumber Fish & Soap* omte vertrekken, en met zyn voornoemd Schip of vaartuig deszelfs gemelde reize voort te zetten, zodanig Schip of Vaartuig gevisiteert zynde, en de voornoemde Schipper of Bevelhebber onder Eede, voor den daar toe gestelden officier verklaart hebbende dat het gemelde Schip of vaartuig aan een of meerder onderdanen, volk, of Ingezeetenen van de Vereenigde Staaten van America, toebehoort, enaan hem (of hun:) alleen.

"IN GETUIGENIS WAAR VAN ik deese teegenswoordige met myne naam hebbe onderteekent, en het Zeegel van onse Veereenigde Staaten van America daar aan gehegt, en het Zelve doen contrasigneeren door *Joseph Hiller Collector of the Customs* tot *Salem* den *18* dag van *June* in het yaar van onzes Heeren Christi, een duysend seven hondert en *three* negentig.

"BE IT KNOWN, That leave and permission, are hereby given to *Herbert Woodberry* master or commander of the *Brigantine* called *Leopard* of the burthen of *one hundred fifty six* tons or thereabouts, lying at present in the port of *Salem* bound for *West Indies* and laden with *Dry Goods Candles, Lumber, Fish & Soap* to depart and proceed with his said *Brigantine* on his said voyage, such *Brigantine* having been visited, and the said *Herbert Woodberry* having made oath before the proper officer, that the said *Brigantine* belongs to one or more of the citizens of the United States, and to him or them only.

"IN WITNESS WHEREOF, I have subscribed my name to these Presents, and affixed the Seal of the United States of America thereto, and caused the same to be countersigned by *Joseph Hiller, Collector of the Customs* at *Salem* the *eighteenth* day of *June* in the Year of our Lord Christ, one thousand seven hundred and ninety *three*.

Go: Washington
By the President
Thomas Jefferson
Countersigned. Jos. Hiller

"ALDER Doorluchtigste, Doorluchtigste, Doorluchtige, Grootmachtigste, Grootmachtige, Hoogh ende welgeboorne, wel Edele, Erentfeste, Acht baare, wyze, voorsienige, Heeren, Keizeren, Koningen, Republiquen,

"MOST Serene, Serene, most Puissant, Puissant, High, Illustrious, Noble, Honourable, Venerable, wise and prudent, Lords, Emperors, Kings, Republics, Princes, Dukes, Earls, Barons, Lords, Burgomasters, Schepens, Coun-

both the English and Dutch papers. The blanks in the two papers vary, owing to a little difference in the words which bound them. This is produced by the want of a perfect similarity between idiom of our language and that of the Dutch; wherefore the following instruction to fill the Dutch copy is to be precisely followed, in regard both to the sea letter, and the certificate annexed thereto.

Princen, Fursten, Hertogen Graeven, Baronnen, Heeren, Burgemeesteren, Scheepenen, Raden, mitsgaders, Rechteren, Officieren, Justicieren ende, Regenten aller goede steeden en plaatzen, het zy geestelyke of waereldlyke die deeze opene Letteren zullen sien ofte hooren leezen: Doen wy Burgemeesteren en Regeerders der Stad *of Salem* te weeter dat Schipper *Herbert Woodberry* van *Salem* (voor ons compareerende) by solemneelen Eede verklaart heeft, dat het schip genaamd *Leopard* groot omtrent *Seventy Eight* lasten t'welk hy thans voert in de Verenigde Staaten van America t'huys behoort, en dat geen onderdaanen vandenteegenwoordige oorlogende moogendheeden daar in direct of indirect eenig deel of gedeeite hebben: Soo waarlyk helpen hem God Almagtig: En terwyl wy den voorz. Schipper gaarne gevorderd zagen in zyne wettigen zaaken zoo is ons verzoek, aan alle voornoemde en een yder in't byzonder alwaar den voornoemde schipper, met zyn schip en lading aankomen zal hem alle bystand gelieven te verleenen, en behoorlyk te behandelen vergunnende hem ophet betaalen der gewoonlyke Toolen en ongelden in het heen en weeder vaaren der havenen stroomen en gebied te laaten passeeren vaaren en frequenteeren, omme zyn handel te dryven alwaar en in wat manner hy zig zal geraadenvinden en best oordeelen zal, war aan wy ons gaarne willen schulig agten.

"Des t'oirconde hebben het zelve bekragtigt met het zegel van den.

"the said Justice   Isaac Osgood."

sellors, as also Judges, Officers, Justiciaries and Regents of all the good cities and places, whether Ecclesiastical or Secular, who shall see these patents, or hear them read. We *Issac Osgood Justice of the Peace* make known, that the master of *the Brigantine Leopard* appearing before us, has declared upon oath, that the vessel, called the *Leopard* of the burthen of about *one hundred & fifty six* tons, which he at present navigates, is of the United States of America, and that no subjects of the present belligerent powers have any part or portion therein, directly nor indirectly, so may God Almighty help him. And, as we wish to see the said master prosper in his lawful affairs, our prayer is, to all the before mentioned, and to each of them separately, where the said master shall arrive, with his vessel and cargo, that they may please to receive the said master, with goodness, and to treat him in a becoming manner, permitting him, upon the usual tolls and expences, in passing and repassing, to pass, navigate, and frequent the ports, passes and territories, to the end to transact his business, where, and in what manner he shall judge proper: Whereof we shall be willingly indebted.

"In Witness and for cause whereof we affix hereto the Seal of *the said Justice   Isaac Osgood."*

(DS, RG 36, French Spoilation Claims, National Archives.)

On the reverse side of this certificate and sea letter is a certificate in French and English guaranteeing that the ship for which the certificate was issued was the property of American citizens and that the captain of the ship would "keep

The first blank after the word "*aen*" and before the word "*schipper*" is to be filled with the name of the Captain, (say *John Thomas*, or whoever may be the Captain.)

The second, after "*genaamt*" and before "*van de*" with the name of the vessel, (say *the Juno*, or whatever may be the name of the vessel.)

The third, after "*van de*" and before "*van*" is to be filled up with the word "*port*."

The fourth, after "*van*" and before "*groot*" is to be filled with the name of the port to which the vessel belongs (say *Philadelphia*, or whatever may be the port in the United States.) This, in the case of American built ships, is always painted on their sterns.

The fifth, after "*groot*" and before "tonnen" is to be filled with the number of tons in the vessel's certificate of Registry, (say 150, or whatever may be her measurement.)

The sixth, after "*haaven van*" and before "*gedestineert*" is to be filled with the port of the United States in which the vessel is at the time, which will be the port of   in which you (the issuing Collector) have authority.

The seventh, after "*naar*" and before "*en*" is to be filled with the port of destination (say *Cadiz*, or whatever it may be.)

The eighth, after "*met*" and before "*omte*" is to be filled with the names of the articles composing the cargo (such as *flour, pickled fish, tobacco, staves, boards,* and *bricks*, or whatever the lading of the vessel may consist of.) You will be careful to include *each species* of article, the design being to exhibit to the belligerent powers such articles as by the laws of War are deemed contraband; and the Government being desirous to act fairly in this particular. Indeed the safety of the vessel and other parts of the cargo will probably require exactness in this particular.

The ninth, after "*door*" and before "*tot*" with your own name and style of office, viz. Collector of the Customs.

---

and cause to be kept by his crew on board, the marine ordinances and regulations, and enter in the proper office a list signed and witnessed, containing the names and surnames, the places of birth and abode of the crew . . . and of all who shall embark on board . . . whom he shall not take on board without the knowledge and permission of the *proper officers;* and in every port or haven where he shall enter . . . he shall shew this present leave to the *proper officers,* and shall give a faithful account to them of what passed and was done during his voyage, and he shall carry the colours, arms, and ensigns of the United States during his voyage."

The tenth, after *"tot"* and before *"den"* with the name of your port, viz.   .

The eleventh, after *"den"* and before *"dag van"* with the day of the month on which you shall issue the sea letters respectively.

The twelfth, after *"dag van"* and before *"en"* with the name of the month in which you shall issue the said sea letters.

The thirteenth, after *"en"* and before *"negentig"* with the word *"three."*

Below the signature of the President, and likewise below the undersigning of the Secretary of State, you are to write the word "countersigned" and to add your name thus—*Countersigned*   .

The blanks in the English copy of the sea letter will be filled *substantially* with the same names of vessels and persons, dates of time and place, &c. though some parts of the mere wording will vary a little from the difference in the nature of the two languages, as before observed.

The blanks in the certificate remain to be noticed.

The first of those blanks after the word *"stad"* and before the word *"te,"* is to be filled with the word *"of"* and with the name of the city, town, or borough, whose chief or other Magistrate administers the oath, and in which place the issuing collector's office is situated, namely   .

The second, after *"schipper"* and before *"van,"* with the name of the Captain, *"John Thomas,"* or as in the sea letter.

The third, after the word *"van"* and before the word *"voor,"* with the name of the place to which the vessel may belong, and which (if she be a registered vessel) is always painted on her stern.

The fourth, after *"genaamd"* and before *"groot,"* with the vessel's name, (*Juno*), or as mentioned in the sea letter.

The fifth, after *"omtrent,"* and before *"lasten,"* with a number equal to *half* the number of tons, the Dutch last being equal to two of our tons. Thus, for the vessel mentioned in the sea letter, the blank would be filled with *"seventy five."*

And, the sixth and last blank, being that after the last word *"den,"* in the printed certificate, will be filled with the same words, which will follow the word *"of,"* at the end of the English copy, which written words will mention what public seal (or private one) is affixed to the certificate. The manner of filling the blanks in the other sea letter, that which is in French and English, will be indicated by what precedes and follows in each case. You will only observe, that in the French counterpart, the word *"navire"* is in each case used for "vessel," while in the copy in English a blank is left, wherever that word is used in the French, to be filled with the denomination of the particular kind of vessel, as whether ship, brig, snow, sloop, &c. &c.

You will be pleased *particularly to observe*, that these sea letters are to be issued to all vessels, bound to *foreign ports*, which are, really and bona fide, *wholly* the property of one or more citizens of the United States, including those which are registered as ships built in the said States, and foreign built ships owned on the 15th of May, 1789, by the citizens thereof, and foreign built ships, since actually and truly acquired by the said citizens.

No vessel in which any foreigner is interested wholly, or even in part, directly, or indirectly, either by holding the legal title to her, or by any trust, or other device, is entitled to the benefit of one of these documents; and *you will take the most especial care to prevent deceptions and collusions in that respect.*

Some delay has necessarily arisen in making the arrangements of so nice, new, and important a business.

You will acknowledge the receipt of all the sea letters you shall receive from time to time, and you will keep a record thereof, and of your disposition of them, shewing the names of the vessels, (with their masters and owners) for which they were issued, the ports of the United States to which the vessels shall belong, the date at which you issue them, the officer before whom the Captains shall be sworn, the burdens or tonnage of the vessels, and the ladings on board them. Of these you will be pleased to make an abstract by way of return, up to the last day of every revenue quarter, and to transmit the same to this Office, with a note of the sea letters, received and issued during such quarter, and of the quantity remaining on hand.

These documents being of great importance to the United States, not only as they regard the benefits to be derived from a state of peace by the owners, navigators and builders of ships, but also as they affect the importation of our supplies, and the exportation of our produce at peace charges, you will execute the business in relation to them with proportionate circumspection and care.

I am, Sir,   With consideration,   Your obedient servant,

A Hamilton

To James Wilkinson [1]

[Philadelphia, May 13, 1793]

My understanding of the Contract has always been different from that which seems to be intimated by Messrs. Elliott and Williams and constant usage hitherto furnishes a comment agreeable to my construction.

I entertain no doubt that the Contractors are not only to supply stationary posts, but are to keep measure with the movements of the Army or any detachment of it—in other words are to furnish the troops on their march as occasion may require—as well as in Garrison or at predetermined places. Where the scenes of supply are designated they are to receive the prices specified—Where they are not designated they are to receive such prices as shall be afterwards agreed upon between them and the Treasury.

In the first instance certain points are given, and they are to furnish what shall be required at any *place* or *places* between the given points —Wherever the Army or any detachment of it happens to be, there is a *place* at which they are to make the requisite supply and must be prepared accordingly. Nothing is said about posts or places previously known or fixed.

The same principle will apply to any places not between given points, with this only difference that in this case a price will be to be afterwards settled between the Contractors and the public.

In all such cases no doubt a reasonable course of practice must govern. It will always be incumbent upon the commanding Officer to give such due previous information to the Contractors of the supplies which will be wanted in any scene as will enable them with due diligence to be prepared for the demand. This attended to, it will be their duty in measure for answering it—whether on the march, in Camp or in Garrison.

The prices of the rations announce that an adequate calculation has been made for the casualties incident to this construction of the Contract and I doubt not the Contractors will readily accede to its being the true one.

Extract, Historical Society of Pennsylvania, Philadelphia.

1. This extract was enclosed in a letter from Henry Knox to Anthony Wayne, May 17, 1793 (LS, Historical Society of Pennsylvania). For background to this document, see H to Knox, May 13, 1793.

On the Reception of Edmond Charles Genet in Philadelphia [1]

[Philadelphia, May 14–16, 1793]

It is observable, that attempts are making to engage the good citizens of this place, to give some public demonstrations of satisfaction, on the arrival of M. Janet, the expected Minister Plenipotentiary from France.

The good sense and prudence of the Citizens of Philadelphia, it is hoped, will guard them against being led into so unadvised a step.

Every discreet man must perceive at once that it is highly the interest of this country to remain at peace and as a mean to this to observe a strict neutrality in the present quarrel between the European Powers.

Public manifestations even of strong wishes in our citizens in favour of any of the contending parties might interfere with this object; in tending to induce a belief that we may finally take a side.

If done, at the seat of the general Government, it may be suspected to have been done with the countenance of the Government. Tis easy to see, that such a supposition might not be without inconvenience.

The step recommended would be the more delicate, as nothing of the kind happened on the arrival of Mr. Ternant, the immediate predecessor of the expected Gentleman. Mr. Ternant, having served with reputation & usefulness, in our armies, during the late war,[2] had a personal claim to marks of esteem, as far as on considerations of public propriety, it would have been right to bestow them. None were bestowed. To distinguish his successor would savour as little of kindness towards him as of prudence towards ourselves.

If we feel kind dispositions towards France for the assistance afforded us, in our revolution, it will not do us honor to forget that Louis the XVI was then the sovereign of the Country—that the succour afforded depended on his pleasure. *Of this we are sure—* there is no ambiguity. Whether he has suffered justly the melancholy fate, which he has recently experienced, is *at least a question.* No satisfactory evidence of the affirmative has yet appeared in this Country. We have seen strong assertions but no proof. To the last awful moment, he persevered in declaring his innocence.

In such a state of things, any extraordinary honors to the representative of those who consigned him to so affecting a doom, would be as little consonant with decorum and humanity, as with true policy.

It will not be difficult, either, to perceive that in such a state of things [3]

ADf, Hamilton Papers, Library of Congress.
    1. This article was presumably written for publication in one of the Philadelphia newspapers. Genet had left Charleston, South Carolina, on April 19 for Philadelphia to present his credentials to the President. He had received enthusiastic receptions at towns and villages along his route, and extensive plans were being made by Republicans in Philadelphia to give him an elaborate welcome in Philadelphia. Genet arrived in Philadelphia on May 16 and, as Jefferson wrote to James Madison on May 19, "arrangements were taken for meeting him at Gray's ferry in a great body. He escaped that by arriving in town with the letters which brought information that he was on the road" (ALS, letterpress copy, Thomas Jefferson Papers, Library of Congress).
    2. Jean Baptiste de Ternant had served during the American Revolution as a lieutenant colonel with Pulaski's Legion and as a colonel with Armand's Partisan Corps.
    3. The MS is incomplete.

To George Washington

[Philadelphia, May 14, 1793]

The Secretary of the Treasury presents his respects to the President & sends for his information & direction two letters, one from the Collector of Oxford,[1] the other from mr Murray member from Maryland.[2] The Secretary, if not directed otherwise, will by the post of tomorrow, desire the Collector to detain the prize until further order; lest not receiving early instruction he may surrender her to one or the other party, contrary to the final determination of the Executive.

May 14 1793.

LC, George Washington Papers, Library of Congress.
    1. The letter from Jeremiah Banning has not been found.
    2. William Vans Murray to H, May 8, 1793.

To Richard Harrison [1]

Treasury Department, May 15, 1793. "Mr. Bailey [2] sometime since made a number of Seals for the use of the Supervisors. . . . it is proper that his claim be settled. . . ." [3]

ALS, RG 217, Miscellaneous Treasury Accounts, Account No. 4092, National Archives.
  1. Harrison was auditor of the Treasury.
  2. Francis Bailey was a Philadelphia printer.
  3. A warrant for one hundred and sixty dollars was issued to Bailey on May 18, 1793.

From Gulian Verplanck [1]

New York, May 15, 1793. "I have paid to Mr Seton two thousand Dollars on Acct. & will be prepared to discharge the remainder of the Ballance with the further Interest that will have accrued to the time of the Deeds being returned. . . ."

ALS, Hamilton Papers, Library of Congress.
  1. For background to this letter, see Verplanck to H, September 10, 1792, March 17, 1793; "Conveyance by Lease and Release to Gulian Verplanck," April 27, 1793; William Seton to H, May 3, 1793.

To George Washington

Introductory Note

According to Gouverneur Morris, United States Minister Plenipotentiary to France, Edmund Charles Genet had sailed from France in February, 1793, "with . . . three hundred blank commissions, which he is to distribute to such as will fit out cruisers in our ports to prey on the British commerce." [1] In July, 1793, Genet told Thomas Jefferson that on his arrival at Charleston on April 8 "he was surrounded suddenly by Frenchmen full of zeal for their country, pressing for authority to arm with their own means for it's assistance, that they would fit out their own vessels, provide everything, man them, and only ask a commission from him." [2] While in Charleston Genet armed and sent to sea four privateers—the *Republican,* the *Sans Culotte,* the *Anti-George,* and the *Patriot* or *Citizen Genet.*

On May 2 and May 8, 1793, George Hammond, British Minister to

ALS, George Washington Papers, Library of Congress.
  1. *ASP, Foreign Relations,* I, 354.
  2. Ford, *Writings of Jefferson,* I, 248.

the United States, presented memorials to Jefferson protesting the depredations by these vessels on British shipping along the coast of the United States. On May 2 he complained to Jefferson of the capture on April 25 of the British ship *Grange,* which *"having a Delaware Pilot on board, was lying at anchor near the Buoy of the Brown* in the Bay of Delaware, a Frigate appeared off the Capes under British Colours, which she continued to display until she approached within half a mile of the Grange at which time they were struck, the colours of France hoisted in their place, and the Frigate proved to be the French Frigate Embuscade. . . . The Captain of the Frigate then sent his boat with thirty or forty men, who took possession of the Grange as a prize to the French Republic, and sent the crew prisoners on board of the Frigate. The Grange arrived in the harbour of this city [Philadelphia] yesterday evening. . . . it is manifest that the French Frigate Embuscade captured the British Ship Grange, as she was lying at anchor within the Territory and jurisdiction of the United States, in direct violation of the Law of Nations." [3] On May 8 Hammond informed Jefferson that he had "received intelligence from his majesty's Consul at Charleston South Carolina, that two privateers have been fitted out from that port under French Commissions. They carry six small guns and are navigated by forty or fifty men, who are for the most part Citizens of the United States. . . . [Hammond] does not deem it necessary to enter into any reasoning upon these Facts, as he conceives them to be breaches of that neutrality which the United States profess to observe, and direct Contraventions of the Proclamation which the President issued upon the 22d. of last month." [4] Further memorials from Hammond, also dated May 8, reported two additional prizes taken by *L'Embuscade* and complained that "considerable quantity of arms and military accoutrements, which an agent of the French Government has collected and purchased in this Country, is now preparing to be exported from New York to France." The memorials also stated that the French consul in Charleston had condemned as legal prizes and presented for sale in that city two British ships seized by French privateers. [5]

Jefferson submitted Hammond's memorials to the President, who ordered "These Memorials to undergo a *consideration before they are answered."* [6] In order to decide on a reply to the British Minister's charges, a meeting of the cabinet was called for May 15, 1793, at which time a draft of a letter to Hammond was approved. This letter reads in part as follows:

"Your several memorials of the 8th. instant, have been laid before the President, as had been that of the 2d, as soon as received. They have been considered with all the attention and the impartiality which a firm determination could inspire to do what is equal and right between all the belligerent powers.

3. Copy, Thomas Jefferson Papers, Library of Congress.
4. Copy, Thomas Jefferson Papers, Library of Congress.
5. Copies, Thomas Jefferson Papers, Library of Congress.
6. JPP, 111.

"In one of these, you communicate on the information of the british consul at Charleston, that the Consul of France, at the same place, had condemned, as legal prize, a british vessel, captured by a french Frigate, and you justly add, that this judicial act is not warranted by the usage of nations, nor by the stipulations existing between the United States and France. I observe further, that it is not warranted by any law of the Land. It is consequently a mere nullity, as such it can be respected in no Court, can make no part in the title to the Vessel, nor give to the purchaser any other security than what he would have had without it. . . . The proceeding, indeed, if the British Consul has been rightly informed . . . has been an act of disrespect towards the United States, to which its Government cannot be inattentive. . . .

"The purchase of arms and military accoutrements by an agent of the french Government, in this Country, with an intent to export them to France, is the subject of another of the memorials. Of this fact we are equally uninformed, as of the former. Our citizens have been always free to make, vend, and export arms. It is the constant occupation and livelihood of some of them. To suppress their callings, the only means perhaps of their subsistence because a war exists in foreign and distant countries, in which we have no concern, would scarcely be expected. It would be hard in principle, and impossible in practice. The law of nations, therefore, respecting the rights of those at peace, does not require from them such an internal derangement in their occupations. It is satisfied with the external penalty pronounced in the President's proclamation, that of confiscation of such portion of these arms as shall fall into the Hands of any of the belligerent powers on their way to the ports of their enemies. To this penalty our Citizens are warned that they will be abandoned, and that even private contraventions may work no inequality between the parties at war, the benefits of them will be left equally free and open to all.

"The capture of the British ship Grange, by the French frigate l'Embuscade, has, on inquiry been found to have taken place within the Bay of Delaware and Jurisdiction of the United States, as stated in your memorial of the 2d instant. The government is therefore, taking measures for the liberation of the Crew and restitution of the ship and cargo.

"It condemns in the highest degree the conduct of any of our citizens, who may personally engage in committing hostilities at sea against any of the nations, parties to the present war, and will exert all the means with which the laws and constitution have armed them to discover such as offend herein and bring them to condign punishment. Of these dispositions I am authorized to give assurances to all the parties, without reserve. . . . Instructions are consequently given to the proper law officer to institute such proceedings as the laws will justify for apprehending and punishing certain individuals of our Citizens suggested to have been concerned in enterprises of this kind, as mentioned in one of your memorials of the 8th instant.

"The practice of commissioning, equipping and manning Vessels, in our ports to cruise on any of the belligerent parties, is equally and entirely disapproved, and the government will take effectual measures to prevent a repetition of it. The remaining point in the same memorial, is reserved for further Consideration." [7]

The question which remained to be considered was that of restoring to their proper owners prizes captured by privateers fitted out in American ports,[8] and on this question the members of the cabinet submitted written opinions.

Jefferson in his opinion, dated May 16, 1793, stated that "considering that the present is the first case which has arisen, that it has been in the first moment of the war, in one of the most distant ports of the U S., and before measures could be taken by the government to meet all the cases which may flow from the infant state of our government and novelty of our position, it ought to be placed by Great Britain among the accidents of loss to which a nation is exposed in a state of war, and by no means as a premeditated wrong on the part of the Government." [9] Randolph in his opinion, dated May 17, 1793, also maintained that the United States was not required to make restitution to Great Britain but observed that it had been agreed "to advise the President to direct a remonstrance to Mr. Genet against what is passed, and a repetition of it in future, So that the dignity of the government will be asserted." [10] Knox's opinion, dated May 16, 1793,[11] closely corresponded to Hamilton's.

[Philadelphia, May 15, 1793]

State of facts as supposed.

Mr. Jenet Minister Plenipotentiary from the Republic of France arrives at charsletown. There he causes two privateers to be fitted out, to which he issues Commissions, to cruise against the enemies of France. There also, the Privateers are manned and partly with citizens of the United States, who are inlisted or engaged for the purpose, without the privity or permission of the Government of this Country; before even Mr Jenet has delivered his credentials and been recognized as a public Minister. One or both these Privateers make captures of British Vessels, in the neighbourhood of our Coasts, and bring or send their prizes into our Ports.

The British Minister Plenipotentiary among other things demands a restitution of these prizes. Ought the demands to be complied with?

I am of opinion that it ought to be complied with, and for the following reasons.

The proceedings in question are highly exceptionable both as they

7. Copy, Thomas Jefferson Papers, Library of Congress.
8. JPP, 118.
9. ADS, George Washington Papers, Library of Congress.
10. ADS, George Washington Papers, Library of Congress.
11. DS, George Washington Papers, Library of Congress.

respect our rights and as they make us an instrument of hostilities against Great Britain.

The jursidiction of every *Independent* Nation, within its own territories, naturally excludes all exercise of authority, by any other Government, within those Territories, unless by its own consent, or in consequence of stipulations in Treaties. Every such exercise of authority therefore not warranted by consent or treaty is an intrusion on the jurisdiction of the Country within which it is exercised; and amounts to an injury and affront, more or less great, according to the nature of the case.

The equipping manning and commissioning of Vessels of War, the inlisting, levying or raising of men for military service, whether by land or sea—all which are essentially of the same nature—are among the highest and most important exercises of sovereignty.

It is therefore an injury and affront of a very serious kind, for one Nation to do acts of the above description, within the territories of another, without its consent or permission. This is a principle so obvious—in itself—that it does not stand in need of confirmation from authorities.

Yet the following passage from VATEL, as to one of the points, included in the case, is so pertinent and forcible that it cannot be improper to quote it. It is found Book III Chapt II §15 in these words.

"As the Right of levying soldiers belongs solely to the Nation, so no person is to inlist soldiers in a foreign country without the permission of the sovereign. They who undertake to inlist soldiers in a foreign Country, without the sovereign's permission; and, in general, *whoever alienates the subjects of another* violates one of *the most sacred rights*, both of the Prince and the state. Foreign *Recruiters are hanged immediately* and very justly, as it is not to be presumed, that their sovereign ordered them to commit the crime; and if they did receive such an order they ought not to obey it: their sovereign having no right to command what is contrary to the law of Nature. It is not, I say apprehended that these Recruiters act by order of their sovereign, and usually they who have practiced seduction only are, if taken, severely punished. If they have used violence and made their escape, they are claimed and the men they carried off demanded. *But if it appears, that they acted by order, such a proceeding in a foreign sovereign is justly considered as an injury, and as a*

*sufficient cause for declaring war against him, unless he condescends
to make suitable Reparation."* [12]

The word soldiers here made use is to be understood to mean all
persons engaged or inlisted for military service—seamen as well as
landmen. The principle applies equally to the former as to the latter.
This, it is imagined, will not be questionned.

In the case under consideration there was neither Treaty, nor consent, to warrant what was done. And the case is much stronger than
a mere levying of Men.

The injury and insult to our Government then, under the facts
stated, cannot be doubted. The right to reparation follows of course.

It remains to inquire whether we are under an obligation to redress
any injury which may have accrued to Great Britain, from the
irregularity committed towards us.

The existence of such an obligation is affirmed upon the following
grounds.

It is manifestly contrary to the duty of a Neutral Nation to suffer
itself to be made an *instrument* of hostility, by one power at war
against another. In doing it, such Nation becomes an Associate, a
Party.

The United States would become effectually an instrument of hostility to France against the other powers at War—if France could
ad libitum build equip and commission, in their ports, vessels of War
—man those vessels with their seamen—send them out of their ports
to cruise against the enemies of France—bring or send the vessels and
property taken from those enemies *into* their ports—dispose of them
there; with a right to repeat these expeditions as often as she should
find expedient.

By the same rule, that France could do these things—she could
issue Commissions among us at pleasure for raising any number of
troops—could march those troops towards our frontiers attack from
thence the territories of Spain or England—return with the plunder,
which had been taken within our territories—go again on new expeditions, and repeat them as often as was found advantageous.

There can be no material differences between the two cases—
between preparing the means in, and carrying on from our Ports
naval expeditions—and preparing the means in and carrying on from

12. Vattel, *Law of Nations*, II, 7–8.

our territories land expeditions, against the enemies of France. The principle in each case would be the same.

And from both or either would result a state of war between us and those enemies of the worst kind for them, as long as it was tolerated. I say a state of war of the worst kind because while the resources of our Country would be employed in annoying them, the instruments of this annoyance would be occasionally protected from pursuit, by the privileges of our ostensible neutrality.

It is easy to see, that such a state of things would not be tolerated longer than 'till it was perceived—and that we should quickly and with good reason be treated as an associate of the power whose instrument we had been made.

If it is inconsistent with the duties of neutrality to permit the practices described to an indefinite extent, it must be alike inconsistent with those duties to permit them to any extent. The quality of the fact, not the degree, must be the Criterion.

It has indeed been agreed, that we are bound to *prevent* the practices in question in future, and that an assurance shall be given to the British Minister, that *effective measures* will be taken, for that purpose.

But it is denied, that we are bound to interpose, to remedy the effects which have hitherto ensued.

The obligation to prevent an injury usually, if not universally, includes that of repairing or redressing it, when it has happened.

If it be contrary to the duty of the UStates as a Neutral Nation to suffer cruisers to be fitted out of their ports to annoy the British Trade, it comports with their duty to remedy the injury, which may have been sustained, when it is in their power so to do.

If it be said that what was done took place before the Government could be prepared to prescribe a preventative; and that this creates a dispensation from the obligation to redress—

The answer is—

That a Government is responsible for the conduct of all parts of the community over which it presides; that it is to be supposed to have at all times a competent police every where to prevent infractions of its duty towards foreign Nations—that in the case in question the Magistracy of the place ought not to have permitted what was done—and that the Government is answerable for the consequences of its omissions.

It is true that in a number of cases a Government may excuse itself for the nonperformance of its duty—on account of the want of time to take due precautions—from the consideration of the thing having been unexpected and unforeseen &c. &c. And justice often requires that excuses of this kind bona fide offered should be admitted as satisfactory.

But such things are only *excuses* not *justifications*, and they are only then to be received when a remedy is not within the reach of the party.

If the Privateers expedited from Charletown had been sent to the French dominions, there to operate out of our reach, the excuse of want of time to take due precautions ought to have been satisfactory to Great Britain. But now that they have sent their prizes into our Ports, that excuse cannot avail us. We have it in our power to administer a specific remedy, by causing restitution of the property taken—and it is conceived to be our duty to do so.

It is objected to this, that the Commissions, which were issued, are valid between the parties at War, though irregular with respect to us—that the captures made under it are therefore valid Captures, vesting the property in the Captors; of which they cannot be deprived without a violation of their rights, and an aggression on our part.

It is believed to be true that the Commissions are in a legal sense valid as between the parties at War. But the inference drawn from this position does not seem to follow.

It has been seen, that what has been done, on the part of the French, is a violation of our rights—for which we have a *claim to reparation* and a right to make war, if it be refused.

We may reasonably demand then, as the reparation to which we are intitled, restitution of the property taken, with or without an apology for the infringement of our sovereignty. This we have a right to demand, as a species of reparation, consonant with the nature of the injury, and enabling us to do justice to the party, in injuring whom we have been made instrumental.

It can therefore be no just cause of complaint, on the part of the Captors, that they are required to surrender a property, *the means of acquiring which took their origin in a violation of our rights.*

On the other hand, there is a claim upon us to arrest the effects of the injury or annoyance to which we have been made accessory. To insist therefore upon the restitution of the property taken will be to enforce a *right*, in order to the performance of a *duty*.

The effects of captures under the Commissions, however valid between the parties at War, have no validity against us. Originating in a violation of our rights, we are no wise bound to respect them.

Why then (it may be asked) not send then to the animadversion and decision of the Courts of Justice?

Because, it is believed, they are not competent to the decision. The whole is an affair between the Governments of the parties concerned —to be settled by reasons of state, not rules of law. Tis the case of an infringement of our sovereignty to the prejudice of a third party; in which the Government is to demand a reparation, with the double view of vindicating its own rights and doing justice to the suffering party.

A comparison of this case with that of contraband articles can only mislead. A neutral Nation has a general right to Trade with a power at War. The exception of contraband articles is an exception of necessity; it is a qualification of the general right of the neutral Nation in favour of the safety of the Belligerent party. And from this cause and the difficulty of tracing it in the course of commercial dealings that for the peace of Nations, the external penalty of confiscation is alone established. The Neutral Nation is only bound to abandon its subjects to that penalty not to take internal measures to prevent and punish the practice. The state of peace between two Nations on the other hand makes it intrinsically criminal in either nation or in the subjects of either to engage in actual hostilities against the other. The sovereign of each Nation is bound to prevent this by internal regulations and measures—and of course to give redress where the offence has been committed.

What has been agreed to be done in the present case acknowleges the distinction and establishes the consequences. While it was refused to interfere to prevent the shipment of arms, it has been agreed that measures should be taken towards punishing our citizens who engaged on board the privateers; and to assure the British Minister that effectual measures would be taken to prevent a repetition of the thing complained. Hence a recognized distinction of principle and a virtual recognition of the consequences contended for.

As little to the purpose is the example of cases in which particular Nations permit the levying of Troops among them by the parties at War. The almost continually warlike posture of Europe can alone have produced the *toleration* of a practice so inconsistent with morality and humanity; but allowing these examples their full force; they are at an *infinite distance from* the case of raising equipping and organising within the neutral territory an armed force sending it on expeditions against a party at War & bringing back their spoils into the Neutral Country.

If the view which has been taken of the subject is a just one, Great Britain will have a right to consider our refusal to cause restitution to be made, as equivalent to our becoming an accomplice in the hostility—as a departure from neutrality—as an aggression upon her.

Hence we shall furnish a cause of War and endanger the existence of it.

I infer then, that we equally owe it to ourselves and to Great Britain to cause restitution to be made of the property taken. In the case of so palpable and serious a violation of our rights, aggravated by several collateral circumstances, the mention of which is purposely waved, a decided conduct appears most consistent with our honor and with our future safety.

Philadelphia   May 15. 1793
Alex Hamilton

From Andrew G. Fraunces [1]

Introductory Note

This letter from Andrew Fraunces initiated a controversy over the payment of two warrants issued by the Board of Treasury in 1787 and 1789. Although Fraunces maintained that he had purchased these war-

---

An Appeal to the Legislature of the United States, and to the Citizens Individually, of the Several States. Against the Conduct of the Secretary of the Treasury. By Andrew G. Fraunces, Citizen of the State of New-York, Late in the Treasury of the United States. "E tenebris elucidit lux." Printed for Andrew G. Fraunces, Esq. (n. p., 1793), 11.

1. Fraunces was a resident of New York City and a son of Samuel Fraunces, George Washington's steward and the erstwhile proprietor of Fraunces Tavern. He had been dismissed in March, 1793, from a clerkship in the Treasury Department and returned to New York to open an office as a notary public, offer-

rants in early May, 1793, it cannot be stated with certainty just how he obtained them or whether he ever actually owned them.[2] During June, July, and August, 1793, Fraunces wrote to both Hamilton and George Washington demanding payment,[3] and in a pamphlet dated August 25, 1793, he published his correspondence with both men.[4] On December 18, 1793, he submitted the pamphlet to Frederick A. C. Muhlenberg, Speaker of the House of Representatives, as a memorial to Congress.[5] After Congress had dismissed his memorial on February 19, 1794,[6] he approached various officials in the Treasury Department in an unsuccessful effort to secure payment.[7] Finally, in December, 1795, when the disposition of the payment of all such warrants was lodged in Congress,[8] Fraunces's case was closed, for he could no longer appeal to the Treasury Department and he had already been refused by Congress.

In his memorial to Congress Fraunces argued that the Treasury had paid similar warrants in the past and that in his conduct of the Treasury

---

ing his services in drawing up legal forms and in acting as a real-estate agent and stockbroker. Fraunces advertised his former experience in the Treasury Department in the following terms: "Having been for several years employed in the Treasury of the United States, and perfectly understanding the routine of public business, he informs those who have claims on the United States, of whatever description they may be, that he will advise them gratis; or if they prefer that he should undertake and go through with their business, he will do it on reasonable terms" (*The* [New York] *Daily Advertiser*, March 19, 1793).

2. Fraunces's own testimony on this point is not clear. In the letter printed below he states that the warrants "are put into my hands, in order that I may obtain a settlement from the Treasury of the United States." On July 30, 1793, in a letter to Washington he stated: ". . . early in the month of May, I purchased in New-York, two warrants" (Fraunces, *An Appeal*, 9). In July, 1794, Fraunces attempted to obtain payment once more at the Treasury, stating that he had purchased the warrants from Jasper Murdock. The warrants were apparently the property of William Duer and had been "improperly" sold "by the Agency of Azariah Williams" (Richard Harison to H, July 10, 1794). At the same time, it might be noted that while Fraunces was still attempting to obtain payment for them in the summer of 1794, the certificates themselves had already been deposited with the auditor of the Treasury by John M. Taylor, a Philadelphia stockbroker, as his own property (*ASP, Claims*, I, 174, 181).

3. See Fraunces to H, June 10, July 1, August 2, 4, 1793; H to Fraunces, May 18, July 2, August 2, two letters of August 3, 1793; Washington to H, August 3, 1793; Taylor to H, August 6, 1793; Oliver Wolcott, Jr., to H, August 7, 1793; H to Washington, August 9, 1793.

4. Fraunces, *An Appeal*.

5. *Journal of the House*, II, 18.

6. *Journal of the House*, II, 67.

7. Edmund Randolph to H, June 26, 1794; Wolcott to Fraunces, July 7, 1794 (ADfS, Connecticut Historical Society, Hartford); Harison to H, July 10, 1794.

8. On December 23, 1795, Wolcott submitted to Congress the auditor's report of January 19, 1795, concerning claims submitted under "An Act relative to claims against the United States, not barred by any act of limitation, and which have not been already adjusted" (1 *Stat.* 301–02 [February 12, 1793]; *ASP, Claims*, I, 172–81).

Department Hamilton had permitted personal considerations to influence his decisions. In an effort to substantiate these charges Fraunces cited Hamilton's part in the purchase of Baron Glaubeck's claim against the United States.⁹ Although Hamilton did not directly refute Fraunces's

9. Peter William Joseph Ludwig, Baron de Glaubeck, a foreign officer during the American Revolution, was an "imposter," according to Anne César, Chevalier de La Luzerne. Glaubeck had added to General Nathanael Greene's financial difficulties at the close of the war by obtaining Greene's signature on bills for more than five thousand livres tournois which were protested for nonpayment (Greene to La Luzerne, May 20, 1783, ALS, William L. Clements Library of the University of Michigan; Joseph and William Russell to Greene, December 29, 1793, LS, William L. Clements Library of the University of Michigan; Greene to James Lacaze and Michael Mallet, January 14, 1784, ALS, William L. Clements Library of the University of Michigan). On September 29, 1789, Washington approved "An Act to allow the Baron de Glaubeck the pay of a Captain in the Army of the United States" (6 *Stat.* 1), which added Glaubeck to the list of foreign officers who were eligible for United States certificates granted for service during the American Revolution. On October 1, 1789, Glaubeck, in an effort to avoid his creditors, assigned his pay as a foreign officer, amounting to $701.33, to Thomas Bazen, a New York City storekeeper and merchant, for $273. The assignment is written in Fraunces's handwriting, and one word, "interest," may be in H's handwriting. According to Jacob Clingman, H paid Fraunces fifty dollars for his part in the transfer of Glaubeck's pay (Clingman to John Beckley, June 27, 1793, copy, Mr. Pierce Gaines, Fairfield, Connecticut). A certificate for the total amount of the principal for his pay as a foreign officer was made out in the auditor's office on November 3, 1790 (DS, Hamilton Papers, Library of Congress). Slightly more than two weeks later Thomas Bazen assigned Glaubeck's claim to Royal Flint, attorney for Catharine Greene, for the amount which Bazen had originally given to Glaubeck (DS, Hamilton Papers, Library of Congress). On March 16, 1790, Henry Aborn of New York City received a certificate of registered debt for $561.07 for Flint, who lived at the same address as Aborn (DS, Hamilton Papers, Library of Congress). On March 19, 1790, the accounts for Glaubeck's pay were written up in the office of Joseph Nourse, register of the Treasury (D, RG 39, Blotters of the Register of the Treasury, 1782–1810, National Archives; D, RG 217, Journals of the Office of the Register of the Treasury, 1776–1799, Journal "C," National Archives). On June 1, 1790, Fraunces obtained from the register of the Treasury Warrant No. 498 for Flint, as attorney for Catharine Greene, in the amount of $140.26, which, as one fifth of Glaubeck's compensation, was collectible in specie in the United States under the plan to enable foreign officers to return to Europe after the war. On June 26, 1792, Catharine Greene wrote to H for information on the proceeding, and on February 14, 1793, her agents at Philadelphia, Joseph Anthony and Son, returned the original certificate to the Treasury (DS, Hamilton Papers, Library of Congress) in order to take advantage of the new regulations enabling foreign officers to receive payment for their certificates and for the interest at Philadelphia (H to Gouverneur Morris, September 13, 1792) instead of receiving the interest at Paris as had been stipulated in the certificates issued to foreign officers. A new certificate was issued and given to H. On February 15, 1793, Warrant No. 2480 for $909.59 was issued to Catharine Greene in full payment of principal and interest on the Glaubeck claim (extract, Hamilton Papers, Library of Congress). The conclusion of the report which the committee of the House of Representatives delivered on December 29, 1793, stated that "At the request of the Secretary of the Treasury, the committee have . . . proceeded to examine the charge

accusations, he did collect what he considered relevant information for both Washington and the House committee appointed to consider Fraunces's memorial.[10] The material assembled by Hamilton provided the essential facts covering his role in the transactions involving Baron Glaubeck and a description of the problems that had arisen in connection with the warrants issued under the Board of Treasury.

Fraunces was correct in his assertion that warrants similar to those which he had presented had been paid. One of the two warrants for which he wished to receive payment was the first of three warrants (Warrants No. 1155, 1156, 1157) that had been drawn on the treasurer, Michael Hillegas, on May 29, 1789, payable to James O'Hara "or order... on account of provisions issued to the Indians from 1 Decr. 1787 to 30th June 1788 and on account of 41,789½ Rations of Provisions furnished the Governor of the Western Territory for Indian Treaties in 1788." [11] When the third of these warrants (Warrant No. 1157) was presented by William Constable to the Treasury Department on July 19, 1790, Constable received payment [12] under the act of September, 1789,[13] which had appropriated one hundred and ninety thousand dollars for warrants that had been issued by the Board of Treasury and that had not been paid. In somewhat the same fashion on March 5, 1790, Warrant No. 237, dated November 19, 1787, was paid to Royal Flint as assignee of Michael Hillegas.[14] Fraunces, on the other hand, was refused payment on Warrant No. 236.[15]

---

made against him, relative to the purchase of the pension of Baron de Glaubeck, and are of opinion that it is wholly illiberal & groundless" ([Philadelphia] *Gazette of the United States & Evening Advertiser*, January 9, 1794). Fraunces had, however, merely used the Glaubeck affair to bolster his main thesis that H had shown favoritism in office when he refused payment for the warrants which Fraunces had presented.

10. Wolcott to H, August 7, 1793; H to Washington, August 9, 1793; H to Catharine Greene, September 3, 1793; H to Jeremiah Wadsworth, September 3, 1793; Wadsworth to H, September 13, 1793; Robert Affleck to H, September 7, 1793; William Willcocks to H, September 1, 5, 1793; Joseph Nourse to H, November 29, 1793; Robert Troup to H, December 25, 1793; John Laurance to H, December 25, 1793; Catharine Greene to H, May 10, 1794.
Washington also consulted Edmund Randolph on the Fraunces affair, for on August 13, 1793, Randolph wrote to Washington: "I am perfectly satisfied, that the conduct of the treasury as to Mr. Fraunces has been right in all its parts" (ALS, George Washington Papers, Library of Congress).
11. These warrants were recorded by the register of the Treasury in the Blotter, Page 4279 (D, RG 39, Blotters of the Register of the Treasury, 1782–1810, National Archives).
12. See "Report on the Receipts and Expenditures of Public Monies to the End of the Year 1791," November 10, 1792 (*Hamilton Papers*, XIII, 43).
13. "An Act making Appropriations for the Service of the present year" (1 *Stat.* 95 [September 29, 1789]).
14. For the payment to Flint, see "Report on the Receipts and Expenditures of Public Monies to the End of the Year 1791," November 10, 1792 (*Hamilton Papers*, XIII, 43).
15. Warrants No. 236 and 237 were recorded by the register of the Treasury in the Blotter, Page 3716 (D, RG 39, Blotters of the Register of the Treasury, 1782–1810, National Archives).

Fraunces's case, which rested in part on the point that warrants similar to his had been paid in the past, was weakened by the fact that by May, 1793, when he presented his warrant, the Treasury's policy toward warrants had changed. Originally the Treasury Department had paid all warrants without question, but by 1793 Hamilton had become aware that the records for many specie transactions under the Board of Treasury were not available and that it was impossible to judge the validity of any particular warrant without such records.[16] The inadequacy—or even lack—of records can be attributed to the fact that the accounts of William Duer, who had served as secretary to the Board of Treasury, were not available. Duer had been imprisoned for debt in March, 1792, and he had submitted neither his accounts nor the warrants which he had insisted would substantiate these accounts.[17]

The regulations of the Board of Treasury [18] required the register of the Treasury to record before issuance all warrants drawn on the receivers of taxes or commissioners of loans and all warrants drawn on the treasurer. If this had been done, the final account of the two sets of warrants would have balanced and left a clear record of all receipts and expenditures. During the last years of the Confederation, however, these regulations were frequently ignored, and procedures for recording and canceling warrants can best be described as haphazard. On numerous occasions Hillegas was not at the seat of government,[19] and warrants on the treasurer were paid by the secretary to the Board of Treasury,[20] who delivered the receipts to the treasurer at some unspecified later date. Warrants on the receivers of taxes were often not recorded until such warrants had been returned by the receivers as vouchers for their specie accounts.[21] These warrants were, however, recorded by the register when the treasurer had no cash to pay a warrant drawn upon him. In that case, two warrants were drawn at the same time: one on the treasurer to be receipted by the payee and one on the receiver of taxes in the same amount, payable to the treasurer and endorsed for the benefit of the individual to whom the government owed money. The second warrant presented by Fraunces (Warrant No. 236) was one on a receiver of taxes which had been endorsed for this purpose.

On November 19, 1789, Warrant No. 236 had been drawn on Nathaniel Appleton, receiver of taxes for Massachusetts, in the amount of three

16. Fraunces, *An Appeal*, 6, 19; Wolcott to H, August 7, 1793; H to Washington, August 9, 1793.

17. See Duer to H, March 12, 1792; H to Duer, March 14, 1792.

18. On June 11, 1789, the Board of Treasury furnished Washington with an outline of procedures and some of the forms it used (LC, George Washington Papers, Library of Congress).

19. Michael Hillegas accepted the office of treasurer of the United States on September 22, 1781. After Congress moved from Philadelphia to New York, Hillegas offered to resign if he could not be permitted to remain in Philadelphia (JCC, XXI, 995; XXIX, 499, 651).

20. Duer had served as secretary to the Board of Treasury from 1785, when he had been hired by the board, until September, 1789, when H asked him to serve as Assistant Secretary of the Treasury.

21. Wolcott to H, August 7, 1793.

thousand five hundred dollars. On July 26, 1793, John M. Taylor wrote to Fraunces that he had "made every possible research into the actual situation of your Treasury warrant, and I find an account current of Nathaniel Appleton's *stated by Mr. Hillegas, late Treasurer of the United States,* in the Comptroller's office, certified by the Register, that of 18,000 dollars and odd of warrants drawn on Appleton in said Hillegas's favor by the Board of Treasury, of which yours is one, but 600 remain unpaid. If this be true, it will appear that William Duer has stolen them off the files and put them into circulation. . . . Mr. [William] Simmons [a clerk in the auditor's office] tells me he will do all in his power to search this out. I shall call on him to day, and if he has made the intended search, I will communicate the result thereof. . . ." [22] Fraunces enclosed this letter from Taylor in his letter to Washington of July 30, 1793.[23] On August 2, 1793, Joseph Nourse wrote to Richard Harrison, the auditor of the Treasury: "Upon Reference to the Copies of certain Statements made in this Office . . . I have Certified that *no* Payment was ever made by Nath: Appleton the late Commissioner of the Loan Office for the State of Massachusetts upon a Warrant *No. 236* . . . whereas it woud appear by a Paper furnished about the same Time Entitled 'List of Warrants drawn by the Board of Treasury on Nathaniel Appleton Receiver of Continental Taxes Massachusetts' that *it had been paid:* this apparent Contradiction may be easily Explained: Both were official Papers and were given to the Clerk (who perfectly understood them) to Enable him to Settle the Accounts of the late Commissioners of the Loan Office and also of the Treasurer of the United States. The Use therefore that has been made of a Referrence to one Document without having a Connection with the Other was improper. With Respect to my first Statement . . . it is a fact that the said Warrant No. *236 was never paid* by Mr. Appleton altho' by Mr. Hillegas's Account upon which the second Statement was made it is Considered by *him as an Absolute Receipt.* . . . The Mode of doing Business at the Treasury when that Warrant issued was this. The Board from the Want of Funds at the immediate Seat of Government drew warrants on the Commissioners of the Loan Offices. This warrant No. 236 for Instance was drawn on Mr. Appleton: at the same time another Warrant issued on the Treasurer in favour of the Person to whom Payment was to be made. As it was to Arnold Henry Dorhman Esqr. the Treasurer therefore Endorses to Dorhman the warrant upon Appleton and takes Dorhman's Receipt upon the warrant which the Board had drawn in his favour. . . ." [24]

This warrant on Appleton had been presented to Hamilton for payment on December 26, 1792, by Jasper Murdock.[25] On April 14, 1794,

22. Fraunces, *An Appeal,* 11–12.

23. Fraunces, *An Appeal,* 8–11.

24. LC, RG 53, Register of the Treasury, Estimates and Statements for 1793, Vol. "135-T," National Archives.

25. The published copy of this warrant does not contain any note that it had been previously presented (Fraunces, *An Appeal,* 12–13). The report of December 29, 1793, by the committee of the House of Representatives quotes the endorsement ([Philadelphia] *Gazette of the United States & Evening Adver-*

it was presented to the auditor of the Treasury by John M. Taylor in his own right [26] under "An Act relative to claims against the United States, not barred by any act of limitation, and which have not been already adjusted." [27] The auditor's report of January 19, 1795, on claims filed under this act states that "This warrant appears to have been presented at different times and by different persons, at the Treasury, but payment there has been uniformly refused, from an opinion that it had, with others of the same complexion, been already discharged out of funds belonging to the public." [28]

The dispute between Hamilton and Fraunces also became a part of the continuing attempt of certain Republican politicians to discredit Hamilton by uncovering corruption in the Treasury Department.[29] Fraunces had been a clerk under the Board of Treasury and had continued in that capacity from the organization of the Treasury Department in 1789 until March, 1793, when he was dismissed.[30] Fraunces was of particular interest to Hamilton's Republican opponents, for he had considerable firsthand knowledge of Treasury procedures and had left the Treasury Department with a grudge against the Secretary. On June 22, 1793, John Beckley, clerk of the House of Representatives, began a letter to an unnamed addressee which he completed on July 2. The letter reads as follows:

"Some information, which I have received from Mr. [Jacob] Clingman,[31] seems to be so connected with what you already possess in relation to Mr. Hamilton, that I cannot withhold communicating it. He says that Andrew G. Fraunces was here, about ten days ago, with letters from Duer to Hamilton, and carried back answers. That Fraunces brought with him, and received payment, at the Treasury, for two Warrants issued by the old Board of Treasury, which he purchased in New York, on speculation, and by which he cleared fifteen hundred dollars: that before he purchased those warrants, and when they were offered to him, they were indorsed on the back with red ink, in a date which he did not then recollect 'presented at the Treasury of the United States, and refused payment—Jos: Nourse, Regr.' Whereupon, that he, Fraunces, wrote to Hamilton to know whether they would be paid, and if so, to send him a Certificate under his hand to that effect; which Hamilton did, and Clingman says that he has seen both Fraunces's letter, and Hamilton's answer and certificate.

---

tiser, January 9, 1794). A copy of this warrant certified by a New York notary public on June 19, 1793, is endorsed: "Presented to the Secretary of the Treasury On the 25th: December 1792 by Jasper Murdock" (copy, RG 59, Miscellaneous Letters, 1790–1799, National Archives).

26. *ASP, Claims*, I, 181.

27. 1 *Stat.* 301–02 (February 12, 1793).

28. *ASP, Claims*, I, 174.

29. See James Reynolds to H, November 13–15, 1792, note 1.

30. Fraunces to Washington, June 3, 1789 (ALS, George Washington Papers, Library of Congress); Fraunces, *An Appeal*, 22–23.

31. Clingman was a former employee of Frederick A. C. Muhlenberg, who was speaker of the House of Representatives in the First Congress.

"Clingman also says, that Fraunces told him, he could, if he pleased, hang Hamilton. And altho' he considers Fraunces as a man of no principle, yet he is sure that he is privy to the whole connection with Duer, and is the agent between them, for supplying the latter with money, and that he saw him when last in New York, pay money to Duer's Clerk (who brought a note to him for it) and took his receipt. He tells me too, that Fraunces is fond of drink and very avaricious, and that a judicious appeal to either of those passions, would induce him to deliver up Hamilton's and Duer's letters and tell all he knows.

"Clingman further informs me, that Mrs. Reynolds has obtained a divorce from her husband, in consequence of his intrigue with Hamilton to her prejudice, and that Colonel Burr obtained it for her: he adds too, that she is thoroughly disposed to attest all she knows of the connection between Hamilton and Reynolds: This, if true, is important.

"Clingman has been sent for by Hamilton, and had an interview with him this week, in which he used every artifice to make a friend of him, and asked many leading questions about, who were his friends? What he would do to serve him &c &c. &c. He is to be with him again tonight, and has promised to call on me tomorrow morning, and inform me of all that passes. If he should, I will add it to this letter.

"June 25th. The proposed interview did not take place till today; it was to the following effect.

1st Was he (Clingman) intimate with Mr. A. G. Fraunces of New York?

Answer. He knew him.

2nd Did he ever board at his house?

Answer. He never did.

3d. Did he not frequently dine and sup with him?

Answer. He had once dined with him at a stranger's house.

4th. Did he not frequently visit Mr. Fraunces's Office?

Answer. He had been there several times.

5th. Did he not visit Mr. Beckley sometimes?

Answer. He knew Mr. Beckley, as he had seen him at Mr. Muhlenberg's.

"Mr. Hamilton then observed that Clingman did not put that confidence in him that he ought, as every thing that he (Clingman) said, was as secret as the grave.

"Mr. Hamilton then asked if Mr. Beckley did not visit at Mr. Muhlenberg's, and what other persons frequented Mr. Muhlenberg's house.

"Mr. Hamilton said that Clingman should not mind what Fraunces said, as he spoke much at random and drank.

"June 27th. Mr. Clingman left this yesterday morning for New York, and, I expect, will, as well as Fraunces, be well watched by Hamilton's Spies. I do not think it will be advisable that Clingman should be applied to, or in any manner, made acquainted with any thing here communicated respecting Fraunces or Hamilton, as he will continue to give me every information, or evidence, he can collect respecting them. You will make such a confidential use of the contents of this letter, as you may deem proper. . . ." [32]

32. Copy, Mr. Pierce W. Gaines, Fairfield, Connecticut.

On June 27 Clingman wrote to Beckley:

"I got to York only late last night, and this morning called on Mr. A. G. Fraunces, who is just agoing to Philada. Mr. A. G. Fraunces seems to be vexed with Colo H—— and shewed me a power of Attorney of his own writing corrected by Colo. H—— and which correction is in his hand writing for the purchase of the Baron De Glaubeck's pay, which he the said Fraunces purchased for Colo. H—— and D——er, from one Bazel,[33] and for which they gave him fifty dollars for doing the business. He further told me, that Colo. H—— had agents in Philada. who purchased Stock for him, and in a few days after, the stock was sold to the Commissioner of the United States, which was appointed to purchase Stock, at a higher price, which agents name he mentioned to me; and further said, that he had carried checks to the said agents from Colo. H—— and he hath promised me, that the moment he gets to Philadelphia, to get a certificate from one of those agents, to certify that he had transacted such business, and that he had received money from him, A. G. Fraunces, for that business: and further told me, that he could prove and was known to a connection in speculation with D——er. All which A. G. Fraunces is willing to swear to and can bring other witnesses beside himself.

"Now, my dear Sir, if you think that these facts will be sufficient to do his business, I would wish you to stay in Philada. and write me word, and I will come on immediately.

"I am somewhat afraid, that Fraunces will fall back from what he has said, but he declares, that he will stick to what he has told me, and that beside his own oath, he can bring proof to support it: and as to the power of Attorney, I have seen it myself, and know that the corrections is in Colo. H—— own handwriting." [34]

Beckley enclosed a copy of Clingman's letter in his letter of June 22 to an unknown correspondent and added the following postscript, dated July 1:

"A. G. Fraunces is now here, and, I am told, in treaty with Hamilton for delivering up to him all such letters and papers, as he (Fraunces) may be possessed of, in relation to Hamilton's speculations and connection with Duer; and for which, Hamilton is to pay him two thousand dollars. I have written to Clingman, and expect him here this night. Should he come, I think it probable, he may so far counterwork Hamilton, as to possess himself of some further, and corroborating evidence to that of Fraunces's. If he does not come this evening, or by tomorrow night at farthest, I shall conclude that he has declined it, and shall therefore set off the next day, with my family, for the Virginia Springs, and expect to be absent from this until the tenth of September. In the mean time, I hope it will be in your power, from the information now given you, so to manage Fraunces, thro' the influence of Clingman (whom, I now think, it will be advisable for you to confide in, seeing how far he has committed himself in his letter to me) as to obtain some decisive proof, during my absence. When I return, should it be necessary, and you will

33. Thomas Bazen. See note 9.
34. Copy, Mr. Pierce W. Gaines, Fairfield, Connecticut.

drop me a line thro' our common friend, Melancton Smith,[35] I will come on to New York, and aid, with my best endeavors, to unravel this scene of iniquity.

"Perhaps the following hints may be worth attention.

1st   To urge Clingman to get from Fraunces the power of Attorney for Glaubeck's pay, with Hamilton's correction.

2d: To obtain Bazel's[36] deposition respecting that transaction.

3d   To get Fraunces's letter to Hamilton, and Hamilton's answer respecting the two Treasury Warrants, mentioned in the beginning of this letter.

4th   To obtain the original, or copies of any receipts of Duer's, for monies paid to him by Fraunces.

5th   To enquire respecting Mrs. Reynolds's divorce, and to obtain her certificate or affidavit of all she knows.

6th.   To make like enquiry, and obtain like evidence from Mr. Reynolds.

7th.   To obtain some corroborating evidence from Fraunces, besides his own, of Hamilton's having purchased public stock on his private account.

8th.   To obtain any like corroborating evidence respecting the connection with Duer.

9th   To obtain Fraunces's certificate or affidavit of all that passed at his late and present interview with Hamilton.

"The *instrumentality* of Clingman in this business, you see, will be highly important; but in your communications with him, I do not wish that he should see any thing that I have written to you: altho' you must necessarily acquaint him with the source of your information. My own opinion is, that *he* may be *fully depended* on; but you know human nature too well, not to observe every proper caution. Nor can I forbear to hint, how quickly Hamilton will take alarm, at the remotest appearance of your concern in the business."[37]

In New York several of Hamilton's supporters watched the Fraunces affair develop with some uneasiness. William Willcocks, Robert Affleck, and Robert Troup wrote to Hamilton concerning the publication of Fraunces's pamphlet, the arrival of a lawyer from Philadelphia who questioned Thomas Bazen as a witness in the question of Baron Glaubeck's pay, and the various affidavits and charges which Fraunces had made.[38] There were also occasional newspaper references to the dispute between Fraunces and Hamilton during September, October, and November, 1793.[39]

35. A New York merchant and Antifederalist, Smith was United States Army supply contractor for West Point.

36. Thomas Bazen. See note 9.

37. Copy, Mr. Pierce W. Gaines, Fairfield, Connecticut.

38. Willcocks to H, August 25, September 1, 5, 1793; Affleck to H, September 7, 1793; Troup to H, December 25, 1793.

39. Fraunces cited an advertisement dated August 3 that he published which reads as follows:

"Two warrants of the late Board of Treasury, under the old government, amounting to 5500 dollars specie, for the payment of which the faith of the

On December 18, 1793, "The Speaker informed the House that he had received a letter subscribed A. G. Fraunces, inclosing a petition against the management of the Secretary of the Treasury, addressed to the House of Representatives, accompanied by sundry documents."[40] The memorial was read on December 19, 1793, and referred to a committee. The committee's report was given on December 30, 1793, and considered on January 6, 17, 1794. On February 19 the House adopted two resolutions commending the Secretary of the Treasury.[41]

New-York May 16, 1793.

Sir,

Warrants for a considerable amount of the late Treasurer of the United States, and on certain Loan-Officers, drawn by the late Board

---

United States is pledged, and has been confirmed by the first Congress, under the new government, by their having granted an appropriation therefor, and by the Secretary of the Treasury having paid nearly 158,000 dollars, out of 190,000 of the same.

"For particulars enquire of Andrew G. Fraunces, Filbert-Street, between Eighth and Ninth-Streets, and Market and Arch-Streets." (Fraunces, *An Appeal*, 16.)

On October 17, 1793, Wolcott wrote to his father: "Perhaps the New York papers may fall in your way, in which is contained an address of A. G. Frauncis to the people, containing an attack upon the Secretary of the Treasury and insinuations which may affect me. You may be assured and may assert on my credit, if the subject is mentioned, that Frauncis is a villain—that his claim is a fraudulent one—that the whole affair proceeds from party enmity and disappointed avarice—and that when the matter is understood, as it will be, by the public, it will appear that the Treasury have conducted with propriety, and that they have the merit, if performing a duty can be called merit, of resisting a deliberate fraud upon the public" (George Gibbs, *Memoirs of the Administrations of Washington and John Adams: Edited from the Papers of Oliver Wolcott, Secretary of the Treasury* [New York, 1846], I, 111). See also H to Fraunces, October 1, 1793.

On October 9, 1793, the [Philadelphia] *National Gazette* published the following account:

"A gentleman from New-York informs me, that Mr. Andrew G. Fraunces has published a pamphlet, entitled 'An Appeal to the Legislature of the United States, on the conduct of the Secretary of the Treasury, respecting a demand of payment of some Treasurer's warrants: with a Literary Correspondence that took place between these two gentlemen, on that subject.'

"It being believed by some, that a gentleman who lodged at the city-tavern in New-York, was in possession of the original papers, whereon the calumniating pamphlet was founded; hence arose a report, *that this gentleman had sold a tract of land that belonged to a prior claimant*. In consequence of which report, the Mayor went in person to the city-tavern, with the sheriffs and constables of the city, to apprehend the gentleman, and take possession of his papers—but, from some unfortunate delay, the gentleman had previously set out for the neighbourhood of Philadelphia, that being his place of abode; and my informant farther saith, that several gentlemen in New-York are determined to pursue him as soon as the *yellow fever abates*."

40. *Journal of the House*, II, 18.
41. *Journal of the House*, II, 18, 23, 27, 41, 42, 67.

of Treasury, are put into my hands, in order that I may obtain a settlement from the Treasury of the United States.

In turning over the laws relative to appropriations, I observe provision was made in the year 1789, for this purpose.[42] As I do not wish to make a journey to Philadelphia, unless the business could be done, I have taken the liberty of troubling you in this way, and of requesting you to favor me, by saying whether they will be paid on presentment or not.

I have the honor to be, with respect and esteem,   Sir, your most obedient servant,   Andrew G. Fraunces.

The Hon. A. Hamilton, Esq. Secretary
of the Treasury of the United States.

42. "An Act making Appropriations for the Service of the present Year" (1 *Stat.* 95 [September 29, 1789]).

To Benjamin Lincoln

Treasury Department, May 16, 1793. Authorizes payment to Moses Hays for "14,000 Gallons best pressed spermaceti oil, supplied for the Northern & Eastern light houses."[1]

LS, RG 36, Collector of Customs at Boston, Letters and Papers re Lighthouses, Buoys, and Piers, 1789–1819, National Archives.
1. See H to George Washington, second letter of May 8, 1793.

From Joseph Whipple

Portsmouth [*New Hampshire*] *May 16, 1793.* "Agreeably to your directions of the 2d instant . . . .[1] I enclose you a Copy of the manifest of the Cargo of the Brig Rising Sun, as exhibited by the Master on the day of the Vessels arrival—also Schedules of the articles Seized and of those found on board the Vessel after the delivery of the Cargo, agreeing with the Masters mem: produced after the Seizure. . . . The goods taken out in the night time being of the Value of 80 dollars only, the Vessel is not liable to Seizure—those that were found on board & not contained in the Manifest are of the Value of 292½ Dollars & were undoubtedly withheld from the Manifest or corrected by the Sailors with fraudulent intentions,[2] but I do not find they are liable to Seizure although the master is subject to penalties on account of their omission. . . ."

Copy, RG 36, Collector of Customs at Portsmouth, Letters Sent, 1792–1793, National Archives; copy, RG 56, Letters from the Collector at Portsmouth, National Archives.

1. Letter not found.

2. For Sections 9 and 10 of "An Act to provide more effectually for the collection of the duties imposed by law on goods, wares and merchandise imported into the United States, and on the tonnage of ships or vessels" (1 *Stat.* 148–78 [August 4, 1790]), see Charles Lee to H, January 11, 1792, note 2.

From Otho H. Williams

Baltimore, May 16, 1793. "This is to acknowledge the receipt of your letter of the 14th Instant. . . .¹ The instructions contained in your letter relative to this important business shall be attentively observed."

Copy, RG 45, Unbound Records, Area 7 Files, National Archives.

1. "Treasury Department Circular to the Collectors of the Customs," May 13–16, 1793.

From John Fitzgerald

Alexandria [Virginia] May 17th. 1793

Sir!

Last evening a British Schooner, from New Providence bound to Norfolk arrived here as prize to the Privateer Sans Culotte.¹ The Prize Master says, she was taken off Cape Hatteras, and by application of the French Vice Consul here is desirous of being admitted to an entry; this I refused until I could hear from you.

The necessity of some general rule of conduct on this and similar occasions is too obvious to escape the attention of our Executive, I therefore trust that general instructions will soon be received; in the mean time I will be thankful for your sentiments on this particular occasion. With sentiments of great respect and consideration I am Sir!

Your most Obedt. Servt.   John Fitzgerald

Copy, RG 56, Letters to and from the Collector at Alexandria, National Archives.

1. The *Sans Culotte* was one of four privateers commissioned by Edmond Charles Genet after his arrival in Charleston, South Carolina, in April, 1793. See the introductory note to George Washington to H, May 15, 1793.

To ——————— [1]

[Philadelphia, May 18, 1793]

You ask me if the News-papers of Philadelphia give a true picture of the conduct of its citizens on the occasion of the arrival of Mr. Genet, and whether the great body of them are really as indiscreet as those papers represent them.[2]

It gives me pleasure to be able to answer you in the negative. I can assure you upon the best evidence that comparitively speaking, but a small proportion of them have had an agency in the business.

Though the papers in the morning of the day of Mr. Genets arrival announced his approach and at　　　[3] oClock　　[4] three guns were fired from the Frigate as a signal to those who were disposed to go to meet him at Gray's ferry, as had been previously concerted and notified in the papers—and though we are *told* by some of the printers that all the outlets from the city were crouded with persons going out to meet Mr. Genet—the fact is that a very inconsiderable number indeed went out. It is seldom easy to speak with absolute certainty in such cases but from all I could observe or have been able to learn, I believe the number would be stated high at a hundred persons.

In the evening of the same day, according to notice in an evening paper, which came out earlier than usual for the purpose, a Meeting was convened at the State House Yard, under the direction of the same persons who had projected the going out to Gray's.[5] This

ADf, Hamilton Papers, Library of Congress.

1. In *HCLW*, X, 42–46, this letter is dated "May, 1793." For background to this letter, see "On the Reception of Edmond Charles Genet in Philadelphia," May 14–16, 1793, note 1.

2. Some Philadelphia newspapers printed greatly exaggerated accounts of the reception accorded Genet. See, for example, *The* [Philadelphia] *General Advertiser* for May 16, 1793, which reported that thousands of cheering Philadelphians carried Genet into the city.

3. Space left blank in MS. According to *The Federal Gazette and Philadelphia Daily Advertiser,* May 16, 1793, "About one o'clock this afternoon three guns, fired on board the French frigate in our harbour, announced the arrival of Mr. Genet, in the neighbourhood of this city. Many citizens immediately set out to meet him."

4. Space left blank in MS.

5. An entry in *The Federal Gazette and Philadelphia Daily Advertiser* for May 16, 1793, states: "The Citizens of Philadelphia, well wishers to the cause of

Meeting was also inconsiderable. From forty to 100 persons give you the extremes of the numbers present, as reported by those who were at the Meeting or in a situation to observe it.

Here a Committee was appointed to prepare an address to Mr. Genet—and another Meeting of the Citizens was advertised for the ensuing Evening at   [6] at the same place the object of which it seems was to consider & approve the address.[7]

This last Meeting is stated differently, from 300 to 1000. An accurate observer, who was a byestander and paid particular attention to the matter assures me that there were between five and six hundred assembled. I rely upon this as about the truth.

The persons who were met approved the address, which had been prepared, and as you have seen nominated a Comittee to present it, whom they accompanied to Mr. Genets lodgings at the City Tavern.

On their way to the City Tavern, their number was, as you will imagine, considerably increased. A croud will always draw a croud, whatever be the purpose. Curiosity will supply the place of attachment to or interest in the object.

What number may have been assembled in the vicinity of the City Tavern it is impossible to say. The Evening being pretty far advanced was alone an obstacle to judging.

But the true test was the Meeting in the State House Yard. Tis there we are to look for the real partisans of the measure. And according to this standard it may be pronounced that not a tenth part of the City participated in it.

You ask who were its *promoters*.

I answer, that with *very few exceptions*, they were the same men who have been uniformly the enemies and the disturbers of the Government of the UStates. It will not be surprising if we see ere long a curious *combination* growing up to controul its measures, with regard to foreign politics, at the expence of the peace of the Country—perhaps at a still greater expense. We too have our dis-

France, are requested to meet at the State House this afternoon, at 6 o'clock, to proceed from thence to the City Tavern, to congratulate Mr. Genet with three cheers."

6. Space left blank in MS.

7. Both the address of "the Citizens of Philadelphia," which welcomed Genet to the city, and Genet's reply are printed in *The Federal Gazette and Philadelphia Daily Advertiser*, May 18, 1793.

organizers. But I trust there is enough of virtue and good sense in the people of America to baffle every attempt against their prosperity—though masked under the specious garb of an extraordinary zeal for liberty. They practically, I doubt not, adopt this sacred maxim, that without government, there is no true liberty.

I agree with you in the reflections you make on the tendency of public demonstrations of attachment to the cause of France. Tis certainly not wise to expose ourselves to the jealousy and resentment of the rest of the world, by a fruitless display of zeal for that cause—it may do us much harm—it can do France no good (unless indeed we are to embark in the War with her, which nobody is so hardy as to avow, though some secretly *machinate* it). It cannot be without danger and inconvenience to our interests to impress on the Nations of Europe an idea that we are actuated by the *same spirit,* which has for some time past fatally misguided the measures of those who conduct the affairs of France and sullied a cause once glorious and that might have been triumphant.

The cause of France is compared with that of America during its late revolution. Would to Heaven that the comparison were just. Would to heaven that we could discern in the Mirror of French affairs, the same humanity, the same decorum the same gravity, the same order, the same dignity, the same solemnity, which distinguished the course of the American Revolution. Clouds & Darkness would not then rest upon the issue as they now do.

I own, I do not like the comparison. When I contemplate the horrid and systematic massacres of the 2d. & 3d. of September—When I observe that a Marat and a Robertspierre, the notorious prompters of those bloody scenes—sit triumphantly in the Convention and take a conspicuous part in its measures—that an attempt to bring the assassins to justice has been obliged to be abandonned—When I see an unfortunate Prince, whose reign was a continued demonstration of the goodness & benevolence of his heart, of his attachment to the people, of whom he was the Monarch—who though educated in the lap of despostism, had given repeated proofs, that he was not the enemy of liberty—brought precipitately and ignominiously to the block,—without any substantial proof of guilt, as yet disclosed—without even an authentic exhibition of motives, in decent regard to the opinions of mankind—When I find the doctrines of Atheism openly advanced in the Convention and heared with loud applauses—When I see the sword of fanaticism extended to force a political creed upon citizens who were invited to submit to the arms of France as the hargingers of Liberty—When I behold the hand of Rapacity outstreched to prostrate and ravish the monuments of religious worship erected by those citizens and their ancestors. When I perceive passion tumult and violence usurping those seats, where reason and cool deliberation ought to preside—

I acknowlege, that I am glad to believe, there is no real resemblance between what was the cause of America & what is the cause of France —that the difference is no less great than that between Liberty & Licentiousness. I regret whatever has a tendency to confound them, and I feel anxious, as an American, that the ebullitions of inconsiderate men among us may not tend to involve our Reputation in the issue.

To Andrew G. Fraunces [1]

Treasury Department, May 18, 1793.

Sir,

Your letter of the 16th instant has been duly received. The want of sufficient light with regard to the warrants in question must defer the payment of them. I advise the holders to notify them as claims under the act of the last session, entitled, "An Act relative to claims against the United States not barred by any act of limitation, and which have not been already adjusted." [2]

I am, Sir, with esteem,   Your most obedient servant,

Alexander Hamilton

Mr. Andrew G. Fraunces,
New-York.

Fraunces, *An Appeal,* 4.
   1. For background to this letter, see Fraunces to H, May 16, 1793.
   2. 1 *Stat.* 301–02 (February 12, 1793).

To George Thacher

Philadelphia
May 18. 1793

My Dear Sir

Your letter of the 28th. of April has been received.[1]

The complaint against Mr. Cook[2] has lately come forward under a more precise form—so as to have rendered a precise inquiry necessary for his character and for my justification. The making of it has been committed to Mr. Jonathan Jackson[3]—as a man of sense probity & delicacy & whose impartiality will be drawn into question by no local circumstance.

Should it unfortunately issue against Mr. Cook, I will not fail to pay proper attention to your suggestion.

With sincere regard   Yr Obed ser.   A Hamilton

G Thatcher Esq

ALS, courtesy of the Trustees of the Boston Public Library.
  1. Letter not found.
  2. Francis Cook was collector of customs at Wiscasset, District of Maine.
  3. Jackson, a resident of Newburyport, had served as United States marshal for the District of Massachusetts from 1789 to 1791.

From Gouverneur Morris

Sain Port near Paris 20. May 1793

My dear Sir

You have annexed Copies of my Letters of the eleventh and twelfth of last month since which I have received from Amsterdam the receipts of Col. Laumoy[1] which are lodged with Mr. Grand.[2] I learn at the same Time that the Creditors of the United States have consented to postpone the reimbursement due to them in June[3] so that the Difficulties in that quarter are removed to my no small Satisfaction for I had received from Mr. Short very alarming Letters on the Subject[4] pressing me to go forward to Amsterdam where he conceived it necessary to take Steps to which if on the Spot *his* Powers were inadequate and which he supposed I who had no Powers whatever might take upon me to do. As this could have

answered no good End to the public and would have exposed me to
Suspicion here and to Censure on your Side of the Water besides the
Inconveniencies which my Absence might Occasion to our Countrymen whose Affairs oblige them frequently to apply to me I thought
it better to avoid that Journey and try what Resources might be
found in the disjointed State of things here. Accordingly I prepared
Matters for a Loan of £.300000. Stg to be paid about 14 years hence
and that for £150000 Cash which is you know at the rate of 5. p%
Interest. I will not trouble you with all the particulars they being
unnecessary. Only this the Commission of Bankers and every Thing
else was to be included so as to produce the simple Effect above
stated. My Engagements were of Course only eventual but suspended
on the Intelligence I should get from Amsterdam and this was long
delayed and of Course I was in a State of considerable Anxiety which
was most happily releieved by the Intelligence that my Efforts were
unnecessary.

LC, Gouverneur Morris Papers, Library of Congress.
  1. See Morris to H, February 16, 1793.
  2. The Paris banking house of Ferdinand Le Grand.
  3. See Willink, Van Staphorst, and Hubbard to H, May 1, 1793.
  4. William Short to Morris, February 16, March 25, April 1, 1793 (ALS,
Columbia University Libraries).

From Richard Morris

New York, May 20, 1793. "I am favoured with your letter of the
8th. instant [1] and am happy my conduct touching the Seized Gina.[2]
mett your Approbation. . . . I am Making up all my Accounts [3] and
Could forward them with the Abstracts this day but upon Examining
I find that the whole Emoluments that Rest with me for 13 Months
and 20 Days is only 526 dollrs. and 52 Cents. which will not Indemnify me for my Actual Expences in living in town for that time, but
if you Approve I think I may be Saved. The Contingencies for
printing, paper, &c, &c, &c, &c, in the whole if charged by Each
particular will Amount to 317.45 Cts. This will Leave a Saving of
482.55 from the 800 Appropiated by the presidents Arrangement for
the Contingencies of this State. My Attentions to those Expences has
had Some Share in Increasing the Savings and if I should be Justified

and permitted in the place of Chargeing the particular Contingencies to charge the 800 dollars as Allowed by the President for Contingencies of this State, it will do a little more than make me Whole for my Expences. I mention this to you as my friend if it can be done without Giveing you trouble I shall be glad, I do not mean that it Should produce Solicitation I had rather put up with the first loss. Your letter shall be my Guide. The Sooner the Better. . . ." [4]

ALS, Hamilton Papers, Library of Congress.
1. Letter not found.
2. This is a misspelling of the abbreviation for geneva, i.e., gin.
3. Morris had requested that he be relieved as supervisor of the revenue. See H to John Armstrong, Jr., April 1, 1793.
4. H endorsed this letter as follows: "Richard Morris Esq. to converse with commissioner. Ansd. May 28." The answer of May 28, 1793, has not been found.

To George Washington

[Philadelphia] May 20, 1793. Submits "a communication of the 15 inst: [1] from the Collector & Naval officer of Baltimore,[2] concerning the conduct of the third Mate of the Revenue Cutter, Active." [3]

LC, George Washington Papers, Library of Congress.
1. Letter not found.
2. Otho H. Williams and Robert Purviance.
3. James Forbes.

To George Washington

Treasury Depart: May [22] 1793.[1]

The Secretary of The Treasury has the honor to transmit to The President of the U: States a communication of the 18 of April, from the Commissioner of the Revenue,[2] & respectfully submits it as his opinion that the public service will be promoted by the acceptance of the resignation offered, and the appointment of the person recommended as a substitute.

With regard to what concerns the Lighthouse at Montock Point,[3] measures are taking towards a comparison of what has been done in other cases, to enable the President to take a collective view of the business. A: Hamilton.

LC, George Washington Papers, Library of Congress.
1. Although this letter is dated May 23 in the George Washington letter

books, an entry in JPP for May 22, 1793, reads as follows: "The Secretary of
the Treasury sent me a letter from the Commissioner of the Revenue, dated
18th of April enclosing the Commission of Samuel Tredwell who had been
Appointed Inspector of the Revenue in Survey No. 2 in No. Carolina and
mentioning that Hardy Murfree had been recommended to fill his place. The
Secy being asked why this letter of the 18th of April had not been laid before
the President sooner; observed, that from the multiplicity of important business
in which he had been lately engaged, it had escaped his memory & lain 'till this
time; but, however, that no evil could result therefrom" (JPP, 125). Washington signed Murfree's commission on May 23 (JPP, 125).

2. Letter from Tench Coxe not found.

3. See Coxe to H, January 3, 1793; Edmund Randolph to H, January 7, 1793.

From Joseph Whipple

Portsmouth [*New Hampshire*] *May 22, 1793.* ". . . Capt. Yeaton [1]
informs me he has sustained considerable loss in furnishing provisions
for the Cutter at 12 cents per Ration for several quarters past &
requests an augmentation of the Stipend if he continues the Supply
and desires also the deficiencies of past quarters, since his Contract
expired may be made up—his application on this Subject I now
inclose—his proposal of one shilling or 16⅔ cents per Ration considering the Advanced price of provision I do not think beyond its
Value. . . ." [2]

LC, RG 36, Collector of Customs at Portsmouth, Letters Sent, 1792–1793, National Archives; copy, RG 56, Letters from the Collector at Portsmouth, National Archives.

1. Hopley Yeaton was the master of the New Hampshire revenue cutter
Scammell.

2. For the arrangements concerning the rations allowed for the revenue cutters, see "Treasury Department Circular to the Collectors of the Customs,"
September 21, November 17, 1791.

To Thomas Jefferson

Treasury Department May 23. 1793.

Sir

I have the honor of your note, transmitting the copy of one from
mr. Genet of yesterday.[1]

As our laws stand no transfer of any part of her cargo from one
vessel to another within our Ports, can take place 'till after a regular
entry and the paying or securing the payment of the duties.[2] You

are sensible, Sir, that I have no discretion to dispense with their requisitions.

If the wines are to be carried to any foreign port and there landed, a drawback of the duties, essentially, may be obtained, under the usual securities for their due transportation to the place for which they are destined.[3]

I have the honor to be very respectfully, Sir your obedient Servant.   Alex. Hamilton.

The Secretary of State

Copy, Thomas Jefferson Papers, Library of Congress; LC, RG 59, Domestic Letters, 1792–1793, Vol. 5, National Archives.

1. Neither Jefferson's note nor the letters from Edmond Charles Genet to Jefferson has been found. On May 24, 1793, Jefferson wrote to Genet: "TH: Jefferson having forwarded to the Secretary of the Treasury the application of mr Genet on behalf of mr [James] Vanuxem, has now the honor to inclose to mr Genet the answer he has received, and of assuring him of his respect" (AL, Thomas Jefferson Papers, Library of Congress).

2. Sections 13, 14, and 16 of "An Act to provide more effectually for the collection of the duties imposed by law on goods, wares and merchandise imported into the United States, and on the tonnage of ships or vessels" (1 Stat. 145–78 [August 4, 1790]) contained the regulations concerning the unloading of vessels.

3. Sections 57, 58, 60, and 61 of the "Collection Law" state the terms under which drawbacks on wine could be paid.

To Benjamin Lincoln

Treasury Department, May 23, 1793. "You will herewith receive a package of Sea letters, which I request you to distribute among the Collectors of your State, as they shall apply for them.[1] A further and a larger parcel will be forwarded to you, for the same purpose in a few days. . . ."

L[S], RG 36, Collector of Customs at Boston, Letters from the Treasury, 1789–1807, National Archives; copy, RG 56, Letters to the Collector at Boston, National Archives; LC, RG 56, Letters to Collectors at Small Ports, "Set G," National Archives.

1. See "Treasury Department Circular to the Collectors of the Customs," May 13–16, 1793.

To William Short

[*Philadelphia, May 23, 1793.* The catalogue description of this
letter reads: "Introducing Major Jackson [1] to the United States Minister at the Hague." *Letter not found.*]

ALS, sold by Stan V. Henkels, Jr., October 9, 1914, Lot 774.

1. William Jackson, who had served as secretary of the Constitutional Convention in 1787 and as George Washington's secretary from 1789 to 1791, was a business partner of William Bingham of Philadelphia. In 1793 he went to Europe as a land agent for Bingham.

From Otho H. Williams

[*Baltimore, May 24, 1793.* On June 12, 1793, Hamilton wrote to Williams: "Your letter of the 24th Ultimo was received some time ago." *Letter not found.*]

To Edmond Charles Genet

Philadelphia May 25. 1793

Mr. Hamilton presents his Compliments to Mr. Genet—has the honor to inclose him a sketch of the state of payments on account of the three Millions for which an arrangement was made with Mr. Ternant [1]—shewing a sum yet to be paid of One hundred and seventy six thousand three hundred and Eighty three Dollars and Eight-Nine Cents, beyond those heretofore paid and those for which collateral engagements have been entered into by the Treasury. How far Mr. Ternant's operations may have anticipated this ballance is a point unknown to Mr. Hamilton and concerning which Mr. Genet will no doubt have received precise information from Mr. Ternant.

The ballance still remaining to be paid of the 4000000 promised for St Domingo is not necessary to be specified for the immediate purpose; as it is understood to be pledged for the payment of the Bills drawn by the Administration of that Colony & virtually accepted by the late Consul-General of France [2]

AL, *Arch. des Aff. Etr., Corr. Pol., Etats-Unis,* Supplement Vol. 20.

1. For information on the payment of three million livres to France, see

Tobias Lear to H, February 8, 1793; "Cabinet Meeting. Opinion on Furnishing Three Million Livres Agreeably to the Request of the French Minister," February 25, 1793; Jean Baptiste de Ternant to H, February 26, 1793; H to Ternant, February 26, 1793.

2. For background to United States advances for the relief of Santo Domingo and for a discussion of the bills issued by the administration of the colony, see the introductory note to George Latimer to H, January 2, 1793, and H to Ternant, January 13, 1793, note 2.

To Henry Knox

Treasury Department
May 25 1793

Sir

Inclosed is a letter from Mr Stephen Bruce,[1] on the subject of certain articles furnished by him upon the order of Lieutenant Greaton[2] and disallowed in the settlement of his accounts on the principle of their not having been conformable to instructions— together with a copy of the settlement at the Treasury shewing what those articles were.

I request to be informed whether the requisition of these articles by the officer or officers concerned be justified by any instruction or license from your department; or by any usage in like cases; and if not whether there are any & what reasons to induce their being paid for by the Public. I request your particular attention to the article of room-hire.

The practice appears to the Treasury to be of a nature to involve a danger of double supplies complexity in the public accounts— opportunities of abuse and such as without cogent reasons ought not to be countenanced.

If it can plead no authority license or usage—will not the good of the public service require that any inconveniences to be sustained should fall on the Officer concerned—that his conduct should be animadverted upon and that an injunction should be incorporated with the instructions of the Recruiting Officers against demanding any articles of a similar nature, or any not strictly within the letter of the instructions?[3]

I have the honor to be very respectfully Sir   Your Obedient & humble servant   A. Hamilton

The Secy at War

ADfS, Connecticut Historical Society, Hartford.

1. Letter not found. Stephen Bruce supplied the United States Army at Boston.

2. Richard H. Greaton of Massachusetts was a lieutenant in the Second United States Regiment.

3. The papers dealing with Bruce's accounts may be found in RG 217, Miscellaneous Treasury Accounts, Account No. 3865 and 4977, National Archives. Among these papers is a statement by Knox, dated January 24, 1794, which reads as follows: "It is my opinion that as the twenty Blankets and Clothing, which Mr. Stephen Bruce, furnished to the order of Capn. R. H. Greaton at Boston in the year 1792, were actually Supplied to the recruits, that Mr. Bruce is entitled to receive compensation for them." Below Knox's statement H wrote the following undated note to Richard Harrison, auditor of the Treasury: "In consequence of a special explanation from the Secretary at War, I am [of] opinion, that the claim should be admitted for such articles as are proved to have been delivered."

To Tobias Lear

[Philadelphia, May 25, 1793]

Dear sir,

The proper fund for the payment of the enclosed is the 10,000 Dollars for defraying the contingent Expences of the Government.[1] Will you add a few words directing it to be paid out of that fund?

Yours

A Hamilton

25 May 1793.

LC, George Washington Papers, Library of Congress.

1. See H to George Washington, May 25, 1793.

To George Washington

[Philadelphia, May 25, 1793]

The Secretary of the Treasury presents his respects to the President; submits the draft of an Act relative to the points lately determined upon by the President.

May 25 1793

[E N C L O S U R E] [1]

[Philadelphia, May 25, 1793]

An act making allowances for certain services & contingencies in the collection of the Revenue during the year ending on the 30 day of June 1792.

Whereas it has been found necessary to provide a compensation for the legal admeasurement of Stills during the year ending on the 30 day of June 1792. it is hereby established & declared, that there may & shall be allowed to the Collectors of the Revenue on spirits distilled in the United States and upon Stills, for each & every Still by them respectively measured according to law on or before the said 30 day of June 1792. the Sum of Thirty Cents.

And whereas it has also been found necessary that certain services & expences of divers officers of inspection & persons actually employed in the business of the Revenue wch. have unavoidably arisen out of the first operations of the Act of the 3d. day of March 1791,[2] and in the year aforesaid, & certain compensations to the same should be allowed & defrayed.

The Supervisors of the Revenue for the several Districts herein after mentioned are hereby authorised to allow to the officers & persons employed within their respective Districts, for services & Duties actually by them performed and expences paid during the year aforesaid & not yet compensated or defrayed, the sums set against the said Districts respectively—that is to say

In the District of South Carolina a sum not exceeding	600 Dollars
In the District of North Carolina	100.
In the District of Virginia	350.
In the District of Maryland	150.
In the District of Delaware	150.
In the District of Pennsylvania	300.
In the District of New York	400.
In the District of Connecticut	200.

Given under my hand at Philadelphia on the 25 day of May 1793.

Geo: Washington [3]

LC, George Washington Papers, Library of Congress.

1. LC, George Washington Papers, Library of Congress.

2. "An Act repealing, after the last day of June next, the duties heretofore laid upon Distilled Spirits imported from abroad, and laying others in their stead; and also upon Spirits distilled within the United States, and for appropriating the same" (1 *Stat.* 199–214 [March 3, 1791]).

3. An entry in JPP for May 25, 1793, notes that Washington "Signed & retd: sd. Act" (JPP, 127).

From William Ellery

Newport [*Rhode Island*] *May 27, 1793.* "... Last saturday evening
I recd. a letter from you dated   [1] containing directions for filling Sea Letters, and enclosing four of these Letters. The day before
I received them, I received two Sea-Letters in a blank wrapper directed to me and freed Oliver Wolcott. It gave me great Satisfactn
to receive your particular directions for filling Sea Letters, and I wish
that one of all the forms of documents which may be sent to me may
be either completely filled fictitiously so that such particular directions may be given concerning the filling thereof as may prevent
errors, and promote Uniformity. . . . Please to inform me what fees
I am to receive for each Sea-Letter issued."

LC, Newport Historical Society, Newport, Rhode Island.
  1. Space left blank in MS. Ellery is referring to "Treasury Department Circular to the Collectors of the Customs," May 13–16, 1793.

From Jeremiah Olney

Custom-House,
District of Providence 27th May 1793.

Sir.

I have recd. your circular Letter of the 14th instant,[1] covering
Four blank Sea Letters; together with Two more from the Comptroller's Office: more of which will be speedily wanted.

I am entirely at a loss to know what *Office* the list of Mariners &
others, on board any Vessel clearing for a foreign Port, is to be
lodged; and who the "proper Officers" are, by whose *knowledge and
permission* they are to be taken on board; nor can I comprehend who
is the proper Person to visit such Vessels, nor for what purpose: You
will Sir, much oblige me by a speedy reply to these questions; also
by informing me how the blank in the Magistrate's Certites between
"Master of" and "appearing", is to be filled up; and by explaining
the word "We", it appearing that only *one* Magistrate is to sign it.[2]

Those Sea Letters encreasing the time and trouble of clearing out
a Vessel, at least Eight fold, (the general Clearance containg. no
other specification of the Cargo than "Sundry Merchandize;") their

not being contemplated by the Legislature in fixing the Fees for clearing Vessels; together with their great importance in securing the property of American Vessels, induces me respectfully to submit to your consideration, the propriety and *justise* of demanding for every Sea Letter, granted by the Collectors, a sum, (in proportion to the size of the Vessel,) which will be a more adequate compensation for the Service than the *Twenty Cents,* allowed in the Collection Law,[3] for an official Document, other than those enumerated.

I have the honor to be &c.   Jereh. Olney Collr.

Alexr. Hamilton Esqr.
Secy. of the Treasury.

ADfS, Rhode Island Historical Society, Providence.
 1. "Treasury Department Circular to the Collectors of the Customs," May 13–16, 1793.
 2. See "Treasury Department Circular to the Collectors of the Customs," May 13–16, 1793, note 3.
 3. This sum was stipulated by Section 53 of "An Act to provide more effectually for the collection of the duties imposed by law on goods, wares and merchandise imported into the United States, and on the tonnage of ships or vessels" (1 *Stat.* 171–72 [August 4, 1790]).

From Oliver Wolcott, Junior [1]

T D C O. May 27. 1793

Sir

I herewith transmit an extract from a Law of the Commonwealth of Virginia passed on the 26th. of Decr. 1792.[2] Also extracts from a Letter written by Jno. Hopkins Esq. dated Jany 3d. 1793. & from a Letter written to him from this office dated February 22d 1793.[3]

These papers will shew, that the Commonwealth of Virginia authorised the Treasr. to *issue* from the State Treasy. certain Certificates of the Sinking Fund, in payment of debts due to *foreign Creditors,* & also to *exchange* Certificates of said Fund dated prior to the 1st. of Jany. 1790, for Certificates of a subsequent date.

The question for consideration is, whether the Certificates so issued or exchanged may be admitted in Loan to the United States, under the Acts of the 4th. of Aug. '90 [4] & of the 8th of May 1792.[5]

I have the honor to be &c.

A Hamilton

ADf, Connecticut Historical Society, Hartford.

1. For background to this letter, see H to Henry Lee, March 22, 1793; Lee to H, April 12, 1793; H to Edmund Randolph, April 30, 1793.

2. See H to Lee, March 22, 1793, note 1.

3. Hopkins was commissioner of loans for Virginia. Neither of these letters has been found, but on March 18, 1793, Wolcott wrote to Hopkins the following letter on certificates previously redeemed by Virginia: ". . . It is much regretted that any discontents Should exist in the minds of the public Creditors: but it is hoped that none of them will imagine that there is any want of attention to their rights on the part of the Treasury. . . .

"While the transactions under the Act of Aug 4th. 1790 were depending & unsettled this question was fully considered. The Attorney General of the United States was consulted & his opinion now on file in this Office fully supports the instructions which have been issued from this Department.

"It may also be well for them to consider the effects which would have followed from a contrary opinion—in the first place an artificial accumulation of the public debt—secondly an injury to the Creditors, from the necessity which would have been produced in many instances of proportioning the sums to be admitted on Loan, among the subscribers in consequence of the unexpected ⟨reissues⟩ from the State Treasuries—& thirdly a derangement of the system established by Congress for adjusting the account of the several States with the Union.

"It is however reasonable that every accomodation should be granted to the Creditors which is compatible with the public Interest & a due ⟨execution⟩ of the Law. If therefore the whole sum which has been subscribed in your office does not exceed the balance of the sum Assumed & which remained unsubscribed under the Act of Augt. 4th. 1790 you are authorized hereby to issue Certificates of Funded Debt for such subscriptions as were made *prior* to the passing of the late Act for issuing Certificates from the State Treass. If however the sum subscribed exceeds the said balance, it will be necessary that you suspend issuing any Certificates untill farther instructions are recd.

"In case any of the Creditors prefer having Certifs. of Funded Debt bearing Interest from the 1st. of Jany 1793; to a settlement in the manner proposed in my letter of Feb: 20th. 1793, it will in my opinion be proper to comply with their request—as in either mode the purpose intended will have been substantially accomplished." (ADf, Connecticut Historical Society, Hartford.)

4. "An Act making provision for the ⟨payment of the⟩ Debt of the United States" (1 *Stat.* 138–44).

5. "An Act supplementary to the act making provision for the Debt of the United States" (1 *Stat.* 281–83).

From Henry Dufouer [1]

New York May 28th. 1793

Sir

I intend going into the Merchantile line of Business and have a good prospect before me of doing well had I any Begining. When I was at Philadelphia you was so generous as to make me an Offer of some Cash if I had any Inclination of going into Business, an Oppertunity now Offers and if you will be so kind and send the Cash to my Friend Mr. Robert Lenox[2] I will give him my Obligation for the Same. I am

Sir   Your Most Obt. & Verry hume. Servt.   Henry Dufouer

Honbe. Alexander Hamilton Esqr.

ALS, Hamilton Papers, Library of Congress.
1. Dufouer had been employed in the New York customhouse during the American Revolution and had held a minor post as a port official in 1792. He had written to H for a position in the Federal Government on June 23, 1792.
2. Lenox was a New York City merchant.

To Richard Morris

[*Philadelphia, May 28, 1793.* Hamilton endorsed a letter of May 20, 1793, from Morris: "Ansd. May 28." *Letter not found.*]

From Otho H. Williams

Collectors Office Baltr. 28 May 93

Sir

Inclosed are, *A*, a copy of my letter to the Surveyor of the port[1] respecting a French Privatier and her prize lately arrived; *B*, a Copy of the Surveyors report and, *C*, a translation of the French Commission in possession of the commander of the Privateer.[2]

As the laws of Congress, which govern the conduct of the Officers of the customs have no reference to the present case, and as we have received no instructions relative to the construction of existing treaties I am forced to hesitate about the proper conduct to be observed upon this new occasion.

I am Sir,   Your most obedient   Humble Servant   O H Williams

A Hamilton Esqr.
Secretary of the Treasury

ADf, RG 45, Unbound Records, Area 7 Files, National Archives.
1. Robert Ballard.
2. These enclosures, which concerned "the arrival of a french privateer called the Sans Coulote, with a prize at Baltimore," were submitted to the President on May 31, 1793, together with "a letter from Saml. Smith Esqr starting the apprehensions of the people of Maryland on acct of the captures made by the french Privateers which had been fitted out from the U.S." Washington "Sent the . . . letters &c. to the Atty Genl. for his consideration & desireing him to

lay them before the Secretary of State & let the President Know their opinion of the steps wh. shd. be taken by the Governmt. in the case" (JPP, 135). On May 31, 1793, Edmund Randolph referred the papers to Thomas Jefferson (AL, Thomas Jefferson Papers, Library of Congress), who wrote: "On the letters & papers from Genl. Williams & Colo. Smith. It is the opinion that the writers be informed that with respect to vessels armed & equipped in the ports of the US. before notice to the contrary was given, the President is taking measures for obliging them to depart from the ports of the US. and that all such equipments in future are forbidden: but that as to the prizes taken by them, no power less than that of the legislature can prohibit their sale" (ADf, Thomas Jefferson Papers, Library of Congress).

Cabinet Meeting. Opinion on the Depredations of the Creek Indians Upon the State of Georgia

Introductory Note

Throughout 1792 and the early months of 1793 the Washington Administration had received reports of Indian depredations and Spanish intrigue on the southern frontier. In 1790 the Creek Nation under the leadership of Alexander McGillivray had signed a treaty of peace and friendship with the United States at New York, which among other stipulations had provided for a survey of the boundary between the United States and Creek territory. A similar treaty was signed with the Cherokee in 1791.[1] The Creek treaty, moreover, placed the Indian towns within the United States territory under the protection of the Federal Government and prohibited all but licensed traders from entering the Creek country. By 1793 the survey for the boundary had not been run, and there was an open frontier between Georgia and the Creek country.

The Treaty of New York and the 1791 treaty with the Cherokee constituted a direct challenge to Spain's view that the Indian tribes on the southwestern frontier were under her direct protection. Francisco Louis Hector, Baron de Carondelet, who on December 30, 1791, succeeded Esteban Miró as governor and intendant of Louisiana and West Florida, began a series of vigorous efforts to weld the southern tribes into an effective unit to halt American expansion. To prevent the running of the boundary between the United States and Creek territory and to draw the Indians more closely under Spanish influence Carondelet employed a number of agents among the tribes in the area: Pedro Olivier was sent to reside among the Creeks, Juan de la Villebeuvre to the Chickasaw and Choctaw, and John McDonald to the Chickamauga. He also made extensive use of the British trading firm of Panton, Leslie, and Company, which in exchange for the governor's protection of its trading privileges

DS, George Washington Papers, Library of Congress.

1. These treaties are printed in C. J. Kappler, ed., *Indian Affairs: Laws and Treaties* (Washington, 1904), II, 19–25.

was more than willing to aid in the furtherance of Spanish ambitions. Carondelet, however, was not solely responsible for the delay in the settlement of the boundary and other outstanding problems between the Creeks and the United States. He was aided by the opposition of many Creek factions to the New York treaty, by the reluctance of McGillivray to effect a final settlement, and by the attempts of the adventurer William Bowles to create a pro-British faction among the Creeks. The result was that on July 6, 1792, McGillivray signed a treaty with the Spanish at New Orleans. This treaty virtually abrogated the Treaty of New York.

In the early months of 1793 the Federal authorities in Philadelphia were deluged with reports of Indian raids on the southern frontier settlements, particularly those on the Georgia frontier. On April 29 Edward Telfair, the governor of Georgia, informed Henry Knox that "there is little expectation of avoiding a general war with the Creeks and Cherokees. Blood has been spilt in every direction on the extended frontier of this State, and one man killed in the State of South Carolina. . . . If I find the pressure become great, the opposition must keep pace with the several emergencies. I shall make the necessary communications to the Governor of the State of South Carolina, in order to obtain aid, as I have every reason to hope that provident measures have been taken to that effect. Should general hostilities continue, it will be well to give Governor [William] Blount [of the Southwest Territory] the needful instructions, to cause a co-operation on his part." [2] On May 8 Telfair reported that the situation continued to deteriorate: "Such is the havoc and carnage making by the savages, in every direction on our frontier, that retaliation by open war becomes the only resort. The horrid barbarities committed . . . have impelled me to cause the additional aid of six troops of horse to be drawn into service, to range on the frontiers, and also to establish a camp at Shoulderbone, to consist of three battalion companies; and I have directed a general officer to repair to the said camp, to be reinforced as circumstances may require. The late respite is only to be attributed to the height of the waters, and, so soon as they subside, I have nothing to expect but an immediate renewal of the like barbarities. Every measure in my power to repel and annoy shall be taken, and, as far as means will extend, shall be carried into effect. Let no idea of peace so far amuse as to divert the necessary and immediate preparations for war. Every information you may receive tending thereto must proceed from ignorance or design. The field is now taken; the people must be protected, and a failure, in this juncture, will affect the operations of Government in a serious degree. . . ." [3]

The Federal Government was somewhat skeptical of Georgia's complaints. Although it was evident that Creek depredations on the Georgia frontier were increasing at an alarming rate, it was equally apparent that they were not unprovoked by residents of Georgia. The Georgians were as dissatisfied as the Creeks with the tentative boundary suggested by the Treaty of New York and on numerous occasions ignored the provision of the treaty forbidding entry into Creek territory and conducted retalia-

2. *ASP, Indian Affairs,* I, 368–69.
3. *ASP, Indian Affairs,* I, 369.

tory raids into Indian country. Georgia, indeed, was never reconciled to the possibility that a final settlement of the boundary would exclude her permanently from the tempting Creek lands, and on more than one occasion James Seagrove, United States Indian agent to the Creeks, implied that Telfair was exaggerating the crisis on the frontier in order to promote a general Creek war. Similar reports came from Major Henry Gaither, the ranking Federal Army officer in Georgia, who maintained a running battle with Telfair on the question of calling out militia to protect the settlements and on the issuing of arms from Federal stores to equip them.[4]

Because the United States was planning a major campaign under the leadership of Major General Anthony Wayne against the northwestern tribes, the Washington Administration wished to avoid a war in the south. On November 26, 1792, in response to requests from officials on the southern frontier for permission to send punitive expeditions against the Indians, Knox wrote to Blount: "I can ... with great truth assure you that the extension of the Northern Indian War to the Southern tribes would be a measure into which the Country would enter with extreme reluctance. They view an Indian War in any event of it as unproductive either of profit or honor. ... the President ... for great political reasons ardently desires a general tranquillity in the Southern quarter. He is exceedingly apprehensive that the flame of War once kindled in that region upon the smallest scale, will extend itself, and become general."[5] On May 14, 1793, Knox again presented the Government's position in a letter to Blount: "You have been fully informed of the difficulties which have existed to prevent the President of the United States from giving orders in consequence of your representations, for the most vigorous offensive operations against the hostile indians. If those difficulties existed while the Congress were in Session, and which it was conceived they alone were competent to remove, they recur in the present case with still greater force, for all the information received at the time Congress were in session were laid before both houses, but no order was taken thereon nor any authority given to the President of the United States, of consequence his authority remains in the same situation it did on the commencement of the last session. It is indeed a serious question to plunge the nation into a war with the southern tribes of Indians, supported as it is said they would be. But, if that war actually exists, if depredations are repeated and continued upon the frontier inhabitants, the measure of protection is indispensible, but that protection can only be of the defensive sort. If other, or more extensive measures shall be necessary, they must probably result from the authority expressly given for that purpose."[6]

Any decision concerning Federal intervention on the southern frontier was complicated by the necessity of considering its effect on the delicate discussions under way between the United States and Spain. In 1793 William Short and William Carmichael were in Madrid attempting with indifferent success to negotiate with Spain on the southern boundary,

4. *ASP, Indian Affairs*, 305–07, 411–12, 417.
5. Carter, *Territorial Papers*, IV, 221.
6. Carter, *Territorial Papers*, IV, 257.

the navigation of the Mississippi, and Spanish-American commerce.[7] By the end of May, 1793, however, the acrimonious discussion between Jefferson and Josef de Viar and Josef de Jaudenes, the representatives of Spain in the United States, threatened to present a serious obstacle to negotiations between the two powers. On November 3, 1792, in a letter to Carmichael and Short, Jefferson wrote: ". . . although we have been constantly endeavoring, by every possible means, to keep peace with the Creeks; that in order to do this, we have even suspended, and still suspend the running a fair boundary between them and us, as agreed to by themselves . . . and that we have constantly endeavored to keep them at peace with the Spanish settlements also; that Spain, on the contrary, or at least the officers of her Government . . . has undertaken to keep an agent among the Creeks, has excited them and the other southern Indians to commence a war against us, has furnished them with arms and ammunition for the express purpose of carrying on that war, and prevented the Creeks from running the boundary which would have removed the source of differences from between us."[8] Viar and Jaudenes replied on May 25, 1793, with a statement that Blount had distributed medals to the Indians and had asked their aid for the United States in the event of a war with Spain.[9] On June 18, 1793, they accused the United States of inciting "the Chicakasaws to commence war against the Creeks with the palpable views, that they, being less numerous than the Creeks, may be under the necessity to ask the protection of Govr. Blount & his troops, & so give him then a good occasion of asking a recompense from the Chickasaws lands to form an establishment at the place called the Encores Amargas . . . & have a source whence to incommode & intercept the communication between New Orleans & the establishments of Spain at the Illinois & New Madrid. . . ."[10]

On June 30, 1793, Jefferson presented the Government's views on the Spanish charges concerning the situation on the southern frontier in a letter to Carmichael and Short. After refuting the claims of the Spanish representatives, Jefferson concluded: "And lastly, these gentlemen say, that, on a view of these proceedings of the United States, with respect to Spain and the Indians their allies, they forsee that our peace with Spain is very problematical in future. The principal object of the letter being *our* supposed excitements of the Chickasaws against the Creeks, and *their* protection of the latter, are we to understand from this, that, if we arm to repel the attacks of the Creeks on ourselves, it will disturb our peace with Spain? That if we will not fold our arms, and let them butcher us without resistance, Spain will consider it as a cause of war? This is indeed so serious an intimation, that the President has thought it could no longer be treated of with subordinate characters, but, that his sentiments should be conveyed to the government of Spain itself, through you. . . . If we

7. See "Notes on Thomas Jefferson's Report of Instructions for the Commissioners to Spain," March 1-4, 1792.

8. *ASP, Foreign Relations*, I, 259.

9. *ASP, Foreign Relations*, I, 263-64.

10. Translation, in the handwriting of Jefferson, Thomas Jefferson Papers, Library of Congress.

cannot otherwise prevail on the Creeks to discontinue their depredations, we will attack them in force. If Spain chooses to consider our self defence against savage butchery as a cause of war to her, we must meet her also in war. . . ." [11]

[Philadelphia] May 29th 1793

The President of the United States having assembled the heads of the respective departments and the attorney General, laid before them for their advice thereon, sundry communications from the Governor of Georgia, and others, relatively to the recent alarming depredations of the creek Indians upon the state of Georgia.[12]

Whereupon after the subject was maturely considered and discussed it was unanimously advised

That the Governor of Georgia be informed that [13] from considerations relative to foreign powers, and the pending treaty with the Northern Indians,[14] it is deemed adviseable for the present, to avoid offensive expeditions into the Indian Country. But from the nature of the late appearances, it is thought expedient to encrease the force to be kept up for defensive purposes. The President therefore authorises, the calling into, and keeping in service, in addition to the troops heretofore stationed in Georgia, one hundred horse, and one hundred infantry, to be employed in repelling inroads as circumstances shall require. As it does not yet appear that the whole nation

11. *ASP, Foreign Relations*, I, 265–67.

12. On May 25, 1793, Knox sent to the President several letters which had recently arrived from Georgia indicating the hostile temper of the Creeks. Two days later Knox submitted to Washington letters from South Carolina providing further evidence of the warlike intentions of the tribe (JPP, 128–29). Washington then called a meeting of the cabinet on May 28 to "take into consideration certain communications relative to the state of our affairs with the Southern Indians." H, who "was detained in the Country," did not attend. As no decision was reached at this meeting, the cabinet reassembled on the following day (JPP, 133).

13. Knox wrote to Telfair on May 30, 1793, informing him of the President's decision concerning military operations against the Creeks. The letter follows closely the opinions expressed by the cabinet at this meeting (LS, letterpress copy, George Washington Papers, Library of Congress).

14. See "Conversation with George Hammond," November 22, December 15–28, 1792, February 24–March 7, 1793; H to Hammond, December 29, 1793; "Draft of Instructions for William Hull," January 14, 1793; Hull to H, February 6, 1793; Washington to H, February 17, 1793; Washington to H, Jefferson, Knox, and Randolph, February 24, 1793, March 21–22, 1793; "Cabinet Meeting. Opinion Respecting the Proposed Treaty with the Indians Northwest of the Ohio," February 25, 1793.

of the creeks, is engaged in hostility, it is confided that this force will be sufficient for the object designated. The case of a serious invasion of the territory of Georgia, by large bodies of Indians must be referred to the provisions of the constitution. The proceeding with efficacy in future requires absolutely, that no unnecessary expence should be incurred in the mean time.

The above corps of horse to be raised for any period of time not exceeding twelve Months as may be found most practicable, subject to be dismissed at any time sooner as the government may think fit. The infantry to be called into service according to the course of the militia Laws endevoring to secure their continuance in service for the like time.

That General Pickens [15] be invited to repair to the seat of Government, for the purpose of information and consultation; a proper compensation for his expences, and loss of time to be allowed.

That a further supply of one thousand arms with correspondent accoutrements be forwarded to the state of Georgia. Arms and accoutrements, for the cavalry to be also provided and forwarded.

That an Agent be sent to the Creeks to endevor to adjust the surrender of those Indians who have lately committed murders on the citizens of Georgia; to conciliate, and secure such of the Indians as may be well disposed to the United States, in the event of a war with the Creek nation, and if possible to prevent that extremety.[16]

Th: Jefferson
H Knox
Edm: Randolph
Alexander Hamilton

15. Andrew Pickens, who was a brigadier general in the South Carolina militia during the American Revolution and a member of the South Carolina legislature after the war, had on several occasions served as representative of the Confederation government in negotiations with the southern Indians. In 1793 Pickens was elected to Congress.

16. Washington recommended that Marinus Willett of New York be appointed as agent. As Willett could not undertake the mission because of a broken leg, James Seagrove, an experienced Indian agent, was instructed to offer peace terms to the Creeks.

From Oliver Wolcott, Junior

Treasury Department
Comptroller's Office May 29th. 1793.

Sir

I have the honor of communicating to you the information which has been received for the subscriptions to the loan payable in the principal and interest of certificates or notes issued by the respective States, and of the amount admitted on loan, under the Acts of August 4th. 1790 [1] and May 8th. 1792 [2]

In certificates of the State of
New Hampshire

subscribed under the act of august 4: 1790	242,501.14	
do May 8: 1792	40,094.37	
Amount admitted on loan		282,595.51
Massachusetts		
subscribed under the act of august 4: 1790	4,473,851.61	
Amount admitted on loan		3,981,733.05
Rhode Island		
subscribed under the act of august 4: 1790	344,262.78	
Amount admitted on loan		200,000.
Connecticut		
subscribed under the act of august 4: 1790	1,446,463.16	
do May 8: 1792	248,304.94	
Amount admitted on loan		1,600,000.
New York		
subscribed under the act of august 4: 1790	1,107,580.58	
do May 8: 1792	76,136.11	
Amount admitted on loan		1,183,716.69
New Jersey		
subscribed under the act of august 4: 1790	599,182.09	
do May 8: 1792	96,033.53	
Amount admitted on loan		695,215.62
Pennsylvania		
subscribed under the act of august 4: 1790	674,675	
do May 8: 1792	103,308.48	
Amount admitted on loan		777,983.48

Subscriptions were also made under the last-mentioned act, of certificates of this State, commonly called New Loan certificates [3] to the amount of sixty five thousand two hundred and ten dollars & twenty eight cents, in principal and interest, which however will not be admitted on loan.

Delaware		
subscribed under the act of august 4: 1790	53,305.64	
do May 8: 1792	5,857.54	
Amount admitted on loan		59,163.18

Maryland
subscribed under the act of august 4: 1790   302,524
    do   May 8: 1792   214,968.
          Amount admitted on loan   517,492
Virginia
subscribed under the act of august 4: 1790   2,552,570.88

No statement has been received of the amount subscribed under the act of May 8: 1792, one however will be shortly transmitted by the Commissioner.[4] The delay has been occasioned by the subscription of certificates which had been reissued from the Treasury of the State,[5] the admission of which to the loan is not yet determined.

North Carolina
subscribed under the act of august 4: 1790   1,686,563.18
    do   May 8: 1792   107,233.22
          Amount admitted on loan   1,793,796.40
South Carolina
subscribed under the act of august 4: 1790   4,634,578.52

The Commissioner[6] has not yet transmitted a Statement of the amount admitted on loan, but it is presumed that the sum assumed has been admitted.

Georgia
subscribed under the act of august 4: 1790   220,140.33
    do   May 8: 1792   25,890.40
          Amount admitted on loan   246,030.73[7]

Enclosed are the certificates of the Commissioners of loans for the States of New Hampshire, Massachusetts, Connecticut, New York, New Jersey, Pennsylvania, Delaware, Maryland, North Carolina & Georgia of the amount subscribed and admitted on loan in their offices, from which the above statement is formed.[8] The amount subscribed and admitted on loan in the State of Rhode Island is taken from the account of the Commissioner, settled at the Treasury. The subscriptions in the States of Virginia, & South Carolina, are ascertained from communications made by the Commissioners at the close of the year 1791, and the beginning of the year 1792, copies of which are also enclosed.[9]

You will likewise receive herewith a copy of a letter of the 27th. instant from the Register of the Treasury, & a statement therein referred to, relative to a credit claimed by the State of Pennsylvania—

The auditor of the Treasury[10] is causing an examination to be made in his office, whether any further information remains to be given, of charge account or credits in favour of any of the States. The result of the examination will be communicated to you.

I have the honr. to be with the greatest respect   Sir etc

The Hon. A. H., Esq.
Secy Treasy

Df, Connecticut Historical Society, Hartford.

1. "An Act making provision for the (payment of the) Debt of the United States" (1 *Stat.* 138–44).
2. "An Act supplementary to the act making provision for the Debt of the United States" (1 *Stat.* 281–83).
3. For information concerning these certificates, see John Nicholson to H, July 26, 1792, note 1.
4. John Hopkins.
5. See H to Henry Lee, March 22, 1793; Lee to H, April 13, 1793; H to Edmund Randolph, April 30, 1793; Wolcott to H, May 27, 1793.
6. John Neufville.
7. At this point in the draft, the following was written and crossed out: "besides which there was subscribed by the Treasurer of the State under this act, but not admitted on loan by the Commissioner, thirty nine thousand one hundred and nineteen dollars & forty nine Cents."
8. Copies of these certificates are appended to a statement of the assumed debt prepared by Joseph Nourse, June 12, 1793 (D, RG 53, Register of the Treasury, Estimates and Statements for 1793, Vol. "135–T," National Archives).
9. Neufville's letter to the Treasury Department is dated November 5, 1791 (copy, RG 53, Register of the Treasury, Estimates and Statements for 1793, Vol. "135–T," National Archives). Although Hopkins's letter has not been found, a copy of his statement, dated June 13, 1793, may be found in RG 53, Register of the Treasury, Estimates and Statements for 1793, Vol. "135–T," National Archives.
10. Richard Harrison.

From John Addison and Peter Van Gaasbeck [1]

[*Kingston, New York, May 30, 1793.* On June 15, 1793, Hamilton wrote to Addison and Van Gaasbeck: "I received two or three days since your letter of the 30th. of May." *Letter not found.*]

1. Both Addison and Van Gaasbeck were residents of Kingston. Van Gaasbeck was elected to the House of Representatives from New York in March, 1793.

Treasury Department Circular
to the Collectors of the Customs [1]

Treasury Department,
May 30, 1793.

Sir,

It being the opinion of the Executive, that there is no general law of the land, prohibiting the entry and sale of goods captured by foreign powers at war—and consequently that such entry and sale are lawful; except in cases where a prohibition is to be found in the treaties of the United States—

It becomes the duty of this Department to make known to you, that the *entry* of vessels captured and brought into our ports by the ships of war and privateers of France, and of their cargoes, is to be received in the same manner, under the same regulations, and upon the same conditions, as *that* of vessels and their cargoes which are not prizes. One of these conditions is, of course, the payment or securing the payment of the duties imposed by law on goods, wares and merchandize imported, and on the tonnage of ships and vessels.

But the same privilege will not extend to any of the other Belligerent Powers, being contrary to the 17th and 22d articles of our Treaty with France.[2]

With consideration, I am, Sir, Your obedient servant,

L[S], to Benjamin Lincoln, RG 36, Collector of Customs at Boston, Letters from the Treasury, 1789–1807, Vol. 4, National Archives; LS, to William Ellery, sold at Parke-Bernet Galleries, Inc., October 17, 1961, Lot 120; LS, Office of the Secretary, United States Treasury Department; L[S], Circulars of the Treasury Department, 1789–1814, Library of Congress; LC, RG 56, Circulars of the Office of the Secretary, "Set T," National Archives.

1. On May 17, 1793, John Fitzgerald, collector of customs at Alexandria, Virginia, had written to H and had raised a question concerning the subject which H discusses in this circular.

2. See H to John Jay, first letter of April 9, 1793, note 2.

Agreement with the
President, Directors, and Company of the
Bank of the United States [1]

[Philadelphia, May 31, 1793]

Articles of Agreement between Alexander Hamilton, Secretary of the Treasury, on behalf of the United States of the one part, and the president Directors & Company of the Bank of the Ud. States of the other part, made & concluded the 31st day of May in the year of our Lord one thousand seven hundred & ninety three. Whereas by the third section of the Act entitled, an Act making appropriations for the support of Government for the year 1793 the President of the U: States is authorised to borrow on accot. of the said States, any sum or sums, not exceeding in the whole 800,000 Dollars, at a rate of interest not exceeding 5 ℔ Centum pr. annum, & reimbursable at the pleasure of the United States, and it is also thereby declared to be lawful for the Bank of the UStates to lend the said Sum.[2] And whereas the President of the United States by an Instrument under his hand bearing date the 21st day of March 1793, did empower the Secretary of the Treasury to carry into execution the authority so vested in him.

Now therefore these presents witness, that pursuant to the authority & provisions aforesaid it hath been & hereby is agreed, by & between the said parties of the first & second part as follows, vizt. 1st—The said President, Directors & Company shall lend to the United States the said sum of 800,000 Dollars, to be advanced & paid into the Treasury of the United States in four equal monthly installments; the first, on the first day of June; the second, on the first day of July; the third, on the first day of August; & the fourth, on the first day of September of this present year. 2d. The several sums which shall be from time to time advanced, shall respectively bear interest from the time of each advance, at the rate of five ℔ Centum ℔ annum, & shall each be reimbursed, or repaid within the term of six months after the advance thereof, reserving nevertheless, to the UStates the right at their pleasure to reimburse the whole, or any part of the monies which shall have been so lent & advanced, as much sooner as they shall think fit.

In testimony whereof the said Secretary of the Treasury hath caused the Seal of the Treasury to be affixed to these presents, & hath hereunto subscribed his hand; & the said President, Directors & Company have also caused the Seal of the Bank of the UStates to be affixed to the same the day & year aforesaid. Alexander Hamilton, Secretary of the Treasury (L.S.). witness to signing by the Secy. of the Treasury Henry Kuhl. Thos. Willing, prest. (L.S.). signed in the presence of Henry Clymer. Thos. M. Willing. attest John Kean, Cashr.

LC, George Washington Papers, Library of Congress; LC, RG 39, Letter Book, 1789–1795, National Archives; copy, RG 59, Records Relating to Foreign Accounts, 1782–1797, Letters, Accounts, and Contracts, National Archives.

1. This document is taken from George Washington's ratification of the agreement. The agreement was submitted to the President on June 12, 1793 (JPP, 145). Washington approved it on June 17, 1793, and it appears under that date in his letter book. The two copies in the National Archives are also dated June 17.

For background to this document, see H to Washington, March 18, second letter of March 20, 1793; Washington to H, March 20, 21, 1793; H to the President and Directors of the Bank of the United States, March 26, 1793; H to Rufus King, April 2, 1793; William Bingham to H, April 9, 1793; H to Bingham, April 10, 1793; H to Thomas Willing, April 10–May 31, 1793.

2. 1 Stat. 328–29 (February 28, 1793).

To Nathaniel Appleton

[Philadelphia] May 31st. 1793

Sir,

I have directed the Treasurer of the United States to furnish you with draughts for Sixty five Thousand Dollars, on the Office of Discount & Deposit of the Bank of the United States at Boston, to be applied by you towards discharging the Interest which will become due the 30th. of the ensuing month on the several species of Stocks standing on your Books.

I have further to add, that if the remittances made at any time to you on account of Interest shall prove inadequate to the Object, it will be highly expedient that you give me the earliest intelligence thereof.

I am with Consideration   Sir   Your most obedient Servant
Alexander Hamilton

Nathaniel Appleton Esquire
Commissioner of Loans
for Massachusetts

LS, Massachusetts Historical Society, Boston.

Defense of the President's Neutrality Proclamation

[Philadelphia, May, 1793]

1. It is a melancholy truth, which every new political occurrence more and more unfolds, that there is a discription of men in this country, irreconcileably adverse to the government of the United States; whose exertions, whatever be the springs of them, whether infatuation or depravity or both, tend to disturb the tranquillity order and prosperity of this now peaceable flourishing and truly happy land. A real and enlightened friend to public felicity cannot observe new confirmations of this fact, without feeling a deep and poignant regret, that human nature should be so refractory and perverse; that amidst a profusion of the bounties and blessings of Providence, political as well as natural, inviting to contentment and gratitude, there should still be found men disposed to cherish and propagate disquietude and alarm; to render suspected and detested the instruments of the felicity, in which they partake; to sacrifice the most substantial advantages, that ever fell to the lot of a people at the shrine of personal envy rivalship and animosity, to the instigations of a turbulent and criminal ambition, or to the treacherous phantoms of an ever craving and never to be satisfied spirit of innovation; a spirit, which seems to suggest to its votaries that the most natural and happy state of Society is a state of continual revolution and change—that the welfare of a nation is in exact ratio to the rapidity of the political vicissitudes, which it undergoes—to the frequency and violence of the tempests with which it is agitated.

ADf, Hamilton Papers, Library of Congress.

2   Yet so the fact unfortunately is—such men there certainly are —and it is essential to our dearest interests to the preservation of peace and good order to the dignity and independence of our public councils—to the real and permanent security of liberty and property —that the Citizens of the UStates should open their eyes to the true characters and designs of the men alluded to—should be upon their guard against their insidious and ruinous machinations.

3   At this moment a most dangerous combination exists. Those who for some time past have been busy in undermining the constitution and government of the UStates, by indirect attacks, by labouring to render its measures odious, by striving to destroy the confidence of the people in its administration—are now meditating a more direct and destructive war against it—a⟨nd⟩ embodying and arranging their forces and systematising their efforts. Secret clubs are formed and private consultations held. Emissaries are dispatched to distant parts of the United States to effect a concert of views and measures, among the members and partisans of the disorganising corps, in the several states. The language in the confidential circles is that the constitution of the United States is too complex a system— that it savours too much of the pernicious doctrine of "ballances and checks" that it requires to be simplified in its structure, to be purged of some monarchical and aristocratic ingredients which are said to have found their way into it and to be stripped of some dangerous prerogatives, with which it is pretended to be invested.

4   The noblest passion of the human soul, which no where burns with so pure and bright a flame, as in the breasts of the people of the UStates, is if possible to be made subservient to this fatal project. That zeal for the liberty of mankind, which produced so universal a sympathy in the cause of France in the first stages of its revolution, and which, it is supposed, has not yet yielded to the just reprobation, which a sober temperate and humane people, friends of religion, social order, and justice, enemies to tumult and massacre, to the wanton and lawless shedding of human blood cannot but bestow upon those extravagancies excesses and outrages, which have sullied and which endanger that cause—that laudable, it is not too much to say that holy zeal is intended by every art of misrepresentation and deception to be made the instrument first of controuling finally of overturning the Government of the Union.

5 The ground which has been so wisely taken by the Executive of the UStates, in regard to the present war of Europe against France, is to be the pretext of this mischievous attempt. The people are if possible to be made to believe, that the Proclamation of neutrality issued by the President of the US was unauthorised illegal and officious—inconsistent with the treaties and plighted faith of the Nation—inconsistent with a due sense of gratitude to France for the services rendered us in our late contest for independence and liberty —inconsistent with a due regard for the progress and success of republican principles. Already the presses begin to groan with invective against the Chief Magistrate of the Union, for that prudent and necessary measure; a measure calculated to manifest to the World the pacific position of the Government and to caution the citizens of the UStates against practices, which would tend to involve us in a War the most unequal and calamitous, in which it is possible for a Country to be engaged—a war which would not be unlikely to prove pregnant with still greater dangers and disasters, than that by which we established our existence as an Independent Nation.

6 What is the true solution of this extraordinary appearance? Are the professed the real motives of its authors? They are not. The true object is to disparage in the opinion and affections of his fellow citizens that man who at the head of our armies fought so successfully for the Liberty and Independence, which are now our pride and our boast—who during the war supported the hopes, united the hearts and nerved the arm of his countrymen—who at the close of it, unseduced by ambition & the love of power, soothed and appeased the discontents of his suffering companions in arms, and with them left the proud scenes of a victorious field for the modest retreats of private life—who could only have been drawn out of these favourite retreats, to aid in the glorious work of ingrafting that liberty, which his sword had contributed to win, upon a stock of which it stood in need and without which it could not flourish—endure—a firm adequate national Government—who at this moment sacrifices his tranquillity and every favourite pursuit to the peremptory call of his country to aid in giving solidity to a fabric, which he has assisted in rearing—whose whole conduct has been one continued proof of his rectitude moderation disinterestedness and patriotism, who whether the evidence of a uniform course of virtuous public actions be con-

sidered, or the motives likely to actuate a man placed precisely in his situation be estimated, it may safely be pronounced, can have no other ambition than that of doing good to his Country & transmitting his fame unimpaired to posterity. For what or for whom is he to hazard that rich harvest of glory, which he has acquired that unexampled veneration and love of his fellow Citizens, which he so eminently possesses? [1]

7   Yet the men alluded to, while they contend with affected zeal for gratitude towards a foreign Nation, which in assisting us was and ought to have been influenced by considerations relative to its own interest—forgetting what is due to a fellow Citizen, who at every hazard rendered essential services to his Country from the most patriotic motives—insidiously endeavour to despoil him of that precious reward of his services, the confidence and approbation of his fellow Citizens.

8   The present attempt is but the renewal in another form of an attack some time since commenced, and which was only dropped because it was perceived to have excited a general indignation. Domestic arrangements of mere convenience, calculated to reconcile the œconomy of time with the attentions of decorum and civility were then the topics of malevolent declamation. A more serious article of charge is now opened and seems intended to be urged with greater earnestness and vigour. The merits of it shall be examined in one or two succeeding papers, I trust in a manner, that will evince to every candid mind to futility.

9   To be an able and firm supporter of the Government of the Union is in the eyes of the men referred to a crime sufficient to justify the most malignant persecution. Hence the attacks which have been made and repeated with such persevering industry upon more than one public Character in that Government. Hence the effort which is now going on to depreciate in the eyes and estimation of the People the man whom their unanimous suffrages have placed at the head of it.

10   Hence the pains which are taking to inculcate a discrimination between *principles* and *men* and to represent an attachment to the one as a species of war against the other; an endeavour, which has a tendency to stifle or weaken one of the best and most useful feelings

1. In the margin at this point H wrote "veneration & love of his Country."

of the human heart—a reverence for merit—and to take away one of the strongest incentives to public virtue—the expectation of public esteem.

11 A solicitude for the character who is attacked forms no part of the motives to this comment. He has deserved too much, and his countrymen are too sensible of it to render any advocation of him necessary. If his virtues and services do not secure his fame and ensure to him the unchangeable attachment of his fellow Citizens, twere in vain to attempt to prop them by anonymous panygeric.

12 The design of the observations which have been made is merely to awaken the public attention to the views of a party engaged in a dangerous conspiracy against the tranquillity and happiness of their country. Aware that their hostile aims against the Government can never succeed til they have subverted the confidence of the people in its present Chief Magistrate, they have at length permitted the suggestions of their enmity to betray them into this hopeless and culpable attempt. If we can destroy his popularity (say they) our work is more than half completed.

13 In proportion as the Citizens of the UStates value the constitution on which their union and happiness depend, in proportion as they tender the blessings of peace and deprecate the calamities of War—ought to be their watchfulness against this success of the artifices which will be employed to endanger that constitution and those blessings. A mortal blow is aimed at both.

14 It imports them infinitely not to be deceived by the protestations which are made—that no harm is meditated against the Constitution—that no design is entertained to involve the peace of the Country. These appearances are necessary to the accomplishment of the plan which has been formed. It is known that the great body of the People are attached to the constitution. It would therefore defeat the intention of destroying it to avow that it exists. It is also known that the People of the UStates are firmly attached to peace. It would consequently frustrate the design of engaging them in the War to tell them that such an object is in contemplation.

15 A more artful course has therefore been adopted. Professions of good will to the Constitution are made without reserve: But every possible art is employed to render the administration and the most zealous and useful friends of the Government odious. The reasoning

is obvious. If the people can be persuaded to dislike all the measures of the Government and to dislike all or the greater part of those who have [been] [2] most conspicuous in establishing or conducting it—the passage from this to the dislike and change of the constitution will not be long nor difficult. The abstract idea of regard for a constitution on paper will not long resist a thorough detestation of its practice.

16 In like manner, professions of a disposition to preserve the peace of the Country are liberally made. But the means of effecting the end are condemned; and exertions are used to prejudice the community against them. A proclamation of neutrality in the most cautious form is represented as illegal—contrary to our engagements with and our duty towards one of the belligerent powers. The plain inference is that in the opinion of these characters the UStates are under obligations which do not permit them to be neutral. Of course they are in a situation to become a party in the War from duty.

17 Pains are likewise taken to inflame the zeal of the people for the cause of France and to excite their resentments against the powers at War with her. To what end all this—but to beget if possible a temper in the community which may overrule the moderate or pacific views of the Government.

2. In MS "men."

Cabinet Meeting. Opinion on Sending an Agent to the Choctaw

[Philadelphia] June 1. [-5] [1] 1793

That an Agent be sent to the Choctaw nation to endeavor secretly to engage them to support the Chickasaws in their present war with the Creeks,[2] giving them for that purpose arms and ammunition sufficient: and that it be kept in view that if we settle our differences amicably with the Creeks, we at the same time mediate effectually the peace of the Chickasaws & Choctaws, so as to rescue the former from the difficulties in which they are engaged, and the latter from those into which we may have been instrumental in engaging them.

Th: Jefferson

H Knox

Altho' I approve of the general policy of employing Indians against Indians; yet I doubt greatly, whether it ought to be exercised under the particular existing circumstances with Spain; who may hold herself bound to take the part of the Creeks, and criminate the U. S. for some degree of insincerity.

Edm: Randolph.

My judgment ballanced a considerable time on the proposed measure; but it has at length decided against it, and very materially on this ground that I do not think the UStates can honorably or morally or with good policy embark the Chocktaws in the War, without a determination to extricate them from the consequences even by force. Accordingly it is proposed that in settling our differences with the Creeks "we *mediate effectually* the peace of the Chickesaws and Choctaws" which I understand to mean, that we are to insist with the Creeks on such terms of peace for them as shall appear to us equitable, and if refused will exert ourselves *to procure them by arms.* I am unwilling, all circumstances foreign and domestic considered, to embarrass the Government with such an obligation.

Alex Hamilton

DS, George Washington Papers, Library of Congress. The first paragraph of this document is in the handwriting of Jefferson, the second in the handwriting of Randolph, and the third in the handwriting of H.

1. According to an entry in JPP, a cabinet meeting was held on June 1, 1793, but H did not attend. As Washington noted in an entry of June 5 that he "Recd. the Opinions of the Heads of Depts. & Atty Genl. on sending an Agent among the Choctaws &c." on that day, it can be assumed that H added his opinion sometime between June 1 and June 5 (JPP, 137, 140).

2. Hostilities had broken out between the Creeks and the Chickasaw early in 1793. On February 13, 1793, a group of Chickasaw chiefs wrote to James Robertson, a brigadier general in the militia of the Southwest Territory and a United States agent to the Chickasaw, announcing the outbreak of the new Indian war and requesting aid for themselves and the Choctaw (*ASP, Indian Affairs,* I, 442–43).

From *Thomas Jefferson*

Philadelphia June 1. 1793

Sir

I have the honor to inclose you the following portion of a Draught of a letter to M. Genet in answer to his ⟨– – –⟩.[1]

do. to order away the privateers fitted out in our ports.[2]

do.   to Messrs Carmichael & Short on the letter of Viar & Jaudenes.[3]

do.   to Viar & Jaudenes in answer to their letter.[4]

with these are all the preceding letters respecting the same subject.

The ideas are in the form approved by Genl. Knox, Mr. Randolph & myself and we have agreed to meet at my office on Monday at 12 oclock to consider of any alterations which you would wish to impose on my giving them my signature.

I also inclose two other papers for your signature; the third which relates to the letters of Genl Williams [5] which is merely in the form of a memorandum to which no signature was thought to be requisite.

I have the honor to be with great respect Sir   Th: Jefferson

The Secretary of the Treasury

ALS, letterpress copy, Thomas Jefferson Papers, Library of Congress.

1. Jefferson's letter to Edmund Charles Genet, June 1, 1793, reads as follows: "I have to acknolege the receipt of your Note of the 27th. of May on the subject of Gideon Henfield, a citizen of the US. engaged on board an armed vessel in the service of France. It has been laid before the President & referred to the Attorney general of the US. for his opinion on the matter of law, and I have now the honour of inclosing you a copy of that opinion. Mr Henfield appears to be in the custody of the civil magistrate, over whose proceedings the Executive has no controul. The act with which he is charged will be examined by a jury of his countrymen, in the presence of judges of learning & integrity, and if it is not contrary to the laws of the land, no doubt need be entertained that his case will issue accordingly. The forms of the law involve certain necessary delays; of which however, he will assuredly experience none but what are necessary. It will give me great pleasure to be able to communicate to you that the laws (which admit of no controul) on being applied to the action of mr Henfield, shall have found in them no cause of animadversion" (ADf, Thomas Jefferson Papers, Library of Congress).

The last sentence in this draft was eventually deleted since both H and Randolph took exception to it. In a note on the reverse side of the draft Jefferson wrote: "E.R. objected to it as conveying a wish that the act might not be punishable, and proposed it should be 'it will give me a great pleasure to be able to communicate to you that on his examination he shall be found to be innocent.' It was done. The letter with this alteration was sent into the country to Colo. Hamilton, who found the clause, even as altered, to be too strong & proposed it should be omitted. It was therefore struck out altogether."

This letter concerns the celebrated Henfield case. Gideon Henfield, an American citizen and a native of Salem, Massachusetts, had signed as a crew member on the French privateer *Citizen Genet* at Charleston, South Carolina. Upon the arrival of the French ship at Philadelphia in May, 1793, Henfield was arrested by order of William Rawle, United States attorney for the District of Pennsylvania, for breach of United States neutrality. He was tried at Philadelphia in July, 1793, at a special session of the Circuit Court of the United States with the prosecution maintaining that an American citizen did not have the right to engage in a hostile action against a friendly power. The case quickly became a *cause célèbre*. Henfield was represented by three prominent Republican lawyers, Peter S. Duponceau, Jared Ingersoll, and Jonathan Dickinson Sergeant. On July 29, 1793, he was acquitted.

2. This enclosure was a draft of Jefferson to Genet, June 5, 1793 (ADf, Thomas Jefferson Papers, Library of Congress).

3. Jefferson to William Carmichael and William Short, May 31, 1793 (LS, letterpress copy, Thomas Jefferson Papers, Library of Congress). This letter concerns a letter of May 25, 1793, from the Spanish attachés to the United States, Josef de Jaudenes and Josef de Viar, to Jefferson (letterpress copy, Thomas Jefferson Papers, Library of Congress).

4. This was a draft of Jefferson to Jaudenes and Viar, June 5, 1793 (ADf, Thomas Jefferson Papers, Library of Congress), which was written in reply to Jaudenes and Viar to Jefferson, May 25, 1793.

5. See Otho H. Williams to H, May 28, 1793, note 2.

From John Nicholson [1]

Comptroller General's Office [Philadelphia] June 1st. 1793

Sir

A suit hath been commenced against me in the Supreme Court for recovery to the State of the Amount of New Loans subscribed to the United States whether by myself or others.[2] In this Cause the Attorney General of the United States with other Able Counsel are engaged in my defence the decision therein will determine also the question as to their assumability in the Loan of the United States for State debts. There are sundry Laws which have not come before you which I have no doubt would induce your determination in the Affirmative but as in this way the question will have all the advantage of legal discussion on both sides and Judicial determination, I would wish your postponment of the decision thereon until after that hath taken place. As this debt is not like other assumed debts chargeable to the State unless a Credit be also given for a like amount of Principal and Interest respectively which the Act of Congress [3] requires to be surrendered therefor, no injury can arise from the postponement on this part of the Subscription made with Mr. Smith.[4] However if you should determine to decide previously I wish an Opportunity of laying before you Laws, Sections of Laws of Pennsylvania posterior to March 1789—which abundantly prove their assumability.

I am with very great Respect, &c   J N

The Honble A. Hamilton Esqr.
Secretary of the Treasury U states

LC, Division of Public Records, Pennsylvania Historical and Museum Commission, Harrisburg.

1. For background to this letter, see Nicholson to H, July 26, 1792, note 1; H to Edmund Randolph, March 20, 1793; Randolph to H, March 30, 1793; and Nicholson to H, April 5, 1793.

2. Nicholson's case came before the Pennsylvania Supreme Court during the December term, 1795. The court advised that "The jury should either find a verdict for the amount of the money paid by the state treasurer to the defendant, or by affirming the new loan certificates to be the property of the state, find for the commonwealth, a sum of money equal to the difference between the real value of the amount of the new loan certificates produced by the defendant and the sum he has received from the treasury" (*Reports of Cases Adjudged in the Supreme Court of Pennsylvania: with Some Select Cases at Nisi Prius, and in the Circuit Courts. By the Honorable Jasper Yeates, One of the Judges of the Supreme Court of Pennsylvania. Vol. II.* [Philadelphia: Printed and Published by John Bioren, No. 88, Chestnut Street, 1818], II, 15).

3. Nicholson is referring to Section 18 of "An Act making provision for the (payment of the) Debt of the United States" (1 *Stat.* 144 [August 4, 1790]). For this section, see Alexander Dallas to H, January 15, 1793, note 7.

4. Thomas Smith was commissioner of loans for Pennsylvania.

From William Bell [1]

Philadelphia June 2. 1793

Sir

The note, which I endorsed for Mr. Edmund Randolph for twenty five hundred dollars,[2] and is now in your hands, I acknowledge to be as binding on me, as if a demand had been made from me for the same, when it became due or at any time since.

William Bell

To Alexander Hamilton esqr.

LS, in the handwriting of Edmund Randolph, New-York Historical Society, New York City.

1. This letter was enclosed in Edmund Randolph to H, June 4, 1793. For information on Randolph's financial difficulties, see Randolph to H, April 3, 1793.

2. This note, which is dated April 5, 1793, and was written and signed by Randolph, is located in the New-York Historical Society. It reads as follows:

"Thirty days after date, I promise to pay to Mr. Wm. Bell or order twenty five hundred dollars for value received.

Dolls. 2500   Edm: Randolph"

H endorsed this note as follows: "Pay the contents to Alexander Hamilton or order." These words are followed by Bell's signature.

From William Ellery

[*Newport, Rhode Island*] *June 3, 1793.* "When Aaron Usher returned I made all the inquiry I could into the cause of his departure from the American coast, and the sale of his Vessel at Port au Prince.[1] I asked for his protest. He answered he had made none. I told him it would have been proper to have made one at Hispaniola. He said it might; but it would have cost him as much as his vessel was worth. His mate did not return with him, otherwise I should have called upon him and examined him. . . . Before I received your letter of the 29th. of April [2] Samuel Slocum master of the Sloop Ranger of Bristol arrived here in said Sloop from St. Domingo, and delivered his License, declaring that he had been [driven] from the American coast by adverse and violent winds. I asked him whether he had protested at St. Eustatia the place where he said he first arrived, or at St. Domingo the second place of his arrival. He said he had not, and assigned for reason that one of his owners who was on board the vessel did not direct it to be done, and the owner declared that he did not think it was necessary, as neither the Vessel nor Cargo was insured, and it would have been expensive. . . . About the same time that Samuel Slocum appeared at my offe. appeared also John Hull late master of the Sloop Wallow of Newport and delivered up his Register and License, declaring that he had been driven by a violent gale of wind from the American coast, and proceeded to the island of St. Thomas where he sold said Sloop. I asked him questions similar to those I had asked Slocum & Usher, and received for answer that he did not know that it was necessary to protest, that his vessel was not insured &c. . . ."

LC, Newport Historical Society, Newport, Rhode Island.
1. See Ellery to H, April 8, 1793.
2. "Treasury Department Circular to the Collectors of the Customs," April 29, 1793.

From Edmond Charles Genet

[*June 3, 1793.* An extract [1] of this letter reads as follows: "I pray you to put hereafter in the disposition of Citizen Bournonville, Secretary of Legation of the Republic,[2] the funds destined to the acquittal of the drafts of the Colony of St. Domingo, according to the order of payments settled between you & my predecessor." [3] *Letter not found.*]

1. This extract has been taken from H to George Washington, January 4, 1794.
2. Charles François Bournonville.
3. See the introductory note to George Latimer to H, January 2, 1793, and H to Jean Baptiste de Ternant, January 13, 1793, note 2.

To William Heth [1]

[*Philadelphia, June 3, 1793.* On June 14, 1793, Heth wrote to Hamilton: "I am favor'd with your private address of the 3d. Inst." *Letter not found.*]

1. Heth was collector of customs at Bermuda Hundred, Virginia.

To Thomas Jefferson

Treasury Department
June 3d. 1793

Sir

It was not till within an hour, that I received your letter of the 1st with the papers accompanying it. I approve all the drafts of letters, as they stand, except that I have some doubt about the concluding sentence of *that* on the subject of *Henfield*. If the *facts* are (as I presume they are) established—may it not be construed into a wish, that there may be found no law to punish a conduct in our citizens, which is of a tendency dangerous to the peace of the Nation and injurious to powers with whom we are on terms of peace and neutrality?

I should also like to substitute to the words "have the *favourable* issue you desire" these words "issue accordingly."

I retain till tomorrow the paper relating to an Agent to the Choctaws.[1] My judgment is not intirely made up on the point—the state of my family's and of my own health for some days having

prevented due reflection upon it. With great respect I have the honor
to be Sir

Your obedient servant   A Hamilton

The Secretary of State

ALS, Thomas Jefferson Papers, Library of Congress.
1. See "Cabinet Meeting. Opinion on Sending an Agent to the Choctaw,"
June 1, 1793.

From George Washington

United States 3d. June 1793.

Pay to the Director of the Mint,[1] or his order, five thousand
Dollars for the purposes of that Establishment.   Go: Washington

5,000 Ds.

LC, George Washington Papers, Library of Congress.
1. On June 3, 1793, David Rittenhouse, the director of the Mint, transmitted
his accounts to Thomas Jefferson and wrote: "I was unwilling to ask a further
Sum of money on account of the Mint until the Treasurer had obtained a
Settlement of his Accounts at the Comptrollers office, which is now done to the
1st. of April last. This has obliged me to advance considerably for the Expendi-
tures of the Mint, and I must request you to apply to the President for his
Warrant for 5000 Dollars, in favour of the Mint" (ALS, RG 59, Miscellaneous
Letters, 1790-1799, National Archives). Jefferson sent Rittenhouse's letter to
Washington on June 3, 1793 (AL, RG 59, Miscellaneous Letters, 1790-1799,
National Archives).

From George Washington

[Philadelphia, June 3, 1793]

Sir,

The question of admitting modifications of the debt of the US. to
France, having been the subject of consultation with the heads of the
Departments & the Attorney General, and an unanimous opinion
given thereon which involves the enclosed propositions from the
French Minister,[1] you will be pleased, under the form of a report to
me, to prepare what may serve as an answer, making it conformable
to the opinion [2] already given.[3]

Go Washington

3d. June 1793.

LC, George Washington Papers, Library of Congress; Df, letterpress copy, in the handwriting of Thomas Jefferson, Thomas Jefferson Papers, Library of Congress.

1. On May 22, 1793, Edmond Charles Genet wrote to Thomas Jefferson and enclosed copies of his instructions from the French republic "to solicit the American Government for the payment of the sums remaining due to France by the said States, tho' all the terms stipulated for the reimbursement have not yet expired" (translation, RG 59, Notes from the French Legation in the United States to the Department of State, Vol. I, June 7, 1789–March 1, 1805, National Archives).

Genet's letter reads in part as follows: "The Executive council of the French republic has learnt through my precedessor, the citizen [Jean Baptiste de] Ternant, the readiness with which the government of the US. of A. attended to the facilitation of the purchases which that minister was charged to make in the US. on account of the French republic, as also the acquittal of the draughts of the colonies for which imperious circumstances obliged it to provide. The Executive council, Sir, has charged me to express to the American government the acknolegement inspired by all the marks of friendship which it has given on this subject to the French nation; & to prove to it the reciprocity of our sentiments it has determined to give at once a great movement to the commerce of France with America, in drawing henceforth from the US. the greatest part of the subsistences & stores necessary for the armies, fleets, & colonies of the French republic.

"The Executive council has entrusted me with the direction of these great & useful operations, & has given me particular powers comprehended in the reports, & in the resolutions now inclosed, in virtue of which I am authorized by the council & by the national treasury of France to employ the sums of which the US. can effect the paiment (towards their debt to France) or those which I can procure on my personal draughts payable by the national treasury in purchasing provisions, naval stores, & in fulfilling other particular services, conformably to the orders which have been given to me by the ministers of the Interior, of war, of the Marine, & of foreign affairs.

"The government of the US. is too enlightened not to perceive the immense advantages which will result from this measure to the people of America, & I cannot doubt that, knowing the difficulties which different circumstances might oppose at this moment to the execution of the pressing commissions which have been given to me, if it should not facilitate to us still the receipt of new sums by anticipation, it will find in it's wisdom & in the reports now inclosed, of the Minister of the public contributions of France, measures proper to answer our views, & to satisfy our wants.

"It does not belong to me to judge if the President of the US. is invested with powers sufficient to accede to our request, without the concurrence of the legislative body: but I will permit myself to observe to you, Sir, that the last anticipated payments, which took place, prove it, & that this question appears equally decided by the act of Congress which authorizes the Executive power not to change the order of the reimbursements of the foreign debt of the US. unless it shall find therein an evident advantage. Now what advantage more sensible can we offer to you, than that of discharging your debt to us with your own productions, without exporting your cash, without recurring to the burthensome operations of bankers? It is furnishing you at the same time with the means of paying your debts, & of enriching your citizens: in short it is to raise the value of your productions, & consequently of your lands, in establishing a necessary competition between us & a nation which has in a measure reserved with a great deal of art & of sacrifices, the monopoly of your own productions. . . ."

Translations of Genet's instructions and various pertinent decrees of the French National Convention were transmitted by Jefferson to the President on May 27, and on May 30 Washington received from Jefferson "a Copy, in french, of Mr. Genet's communication cn the subject of the debt, to be referred, if I shd. think proper, to the Secretary of the Treasury" (JPP, 129–132, 134). On May 31 Washington "Returned to the Secretary of State the . . . copy of Mr Genet's communication (which had been sent to me yesterday) with a request that he would prepare the draught of a letter for the Presidt. to send to the Secy of the Treasury with these communications from Mr. Genet" (JPP, 135).

2. This is apparently a reference to the decision of the cabinet on William S. Smith's proposals for the settlement of the United States debt to France. See H to Washington, March 1, 1793, note 1; "Cabinet Meeting. Opinion on Proposals Made by William S. Smith Relative to the French Debt," March 2, 1793.

3. Jefferson's draft of this letter concludes with the following sentence: "If however the instalments of the present year can be made a matter of accomodation, & it be mutual, their near approach may perhaps admit it within the spirit of the opinion given."

To George Washington

Treasury Departmt. 3d. June 1793.

Sir,

The failure of the late enterprize against the United Netherlands [1] may be expected to have made a favourable alteration, in regard to the prospects of obtaining Loans there for the United States. Such an expectation is also countenanced by a late letter from our bankers at Amsterdam,[2] which however as yet gives no certainty, that can be a basis of operation.

The existing instructions from this Department to mr Short do not extend beyond two millions of florins.[3] A comprehensive view of the affairs of the United States, in various relations, appears to me to recommend a still further loan, if obtainable. Yet I do not think it adviseable to take the step, by virtue of the general powers from you, without your special approbation; particularly as there is little probability that the loan can be effected on better terms than five per Cent Interests and four per cent charges. The further loan which I should contemplate would embrace 3,000,000 of florins.

With perfect respect   I am &c.   A Hamilton

LC, George Washington Papers, Library of Congress; letterpress copy, in the handwriting of Jefferson, Thomas Jefferson Papers, Library of Congress.

1. This is a reference to the French invasion of Holland in the spring of 1793.
2. Willink, Van Staphorst, and Hubbard to H, April 4, 1793.
3. See H to William Short, November 5, 1792.

From Tench Coxe

[*Philadelphia, June 4, 1793.* On June 22, 1793, Hamilton wrote to George Washington and referred to a letter "of the 4 inst. from the Commissioner of the Revenue on the subject of compensations to Keepers of Light houses." *Letter not found.*]

To Edmond Charles Genet

Treasury Department
June 4. 1793

Sir

Absence from Town, occasionned by circumstances of ill health, prevented my receiving the letter, which you did me the honor to write me yesterday,[1] till today.

I shall with pleasure conform to the arrangement you indicate, for the future payments of the monies destined for the acquittal of the Drafts of the Colony of St Domingo, according to the order of payment settled with your predecessor.[2]

Very respectfully   I have the honor to be   Sir   Your obedient servant   Alexander Hamilton

The Minister Plenipotentiary
of the French Republic

ALS, *Arch. des Aff. Etr., Corr. Pol., Etats-Unis,* Supplement Vol. 20.
  1. Letter not found, but see extract printed under date of June 3, 1793.
  2. See the introductory note to George Latimer to H, January 2, 1793, and H to Jean Baptiste de Ternant, January 13, 1793, note 2.

From Edmund Randolph

Philadelphia, June 4, 1793. ". . . Inclosed is Mr. Bell's paper.[1] From Baltimore I shall remit that Sum, which I mentioned to you in part of your kind favor. . . ."

ALS, New-York Historical Society, New York City.
  1. For background to this letter, see Randolph to H, April 3, 1793, and William Bell to H, June 2, 1793.

Draft of a Report on the French Debt[1]

[Philadelphia, June 5, 1793]

The Secy. of the Treasury, to whom were referred by the President of the US. sundry documents communicated by the Min. Plenipy. of the Republic of France, respectfully makes the following report thereupon.

The object of the communication appears to be to engage the US. to enter into arrangements for discharging the residue of the debt which they owe to France by an *anticipated* payment of the instalments not yet due, either in specie, bank bills of equal currency with specie, or Government bonds, bearing interest & payable at certain specified periods, upon condition that the sum advanced shall be invested in productions of the US. for the supply of the French dominions.

This object is the same which came under consideration on certain propositions lately made by Colo. W. S. Smith who appeared to have been charged by the Provisional Executive Council of France with a negociation concerning it; in reference to which it was determined by the President with the concurring opinions of the heads of department & the Attorney general that the measure was ineligible, & that the proposer should be informed that it did not consist with the arrangements of the government to adopt it.[2]

The grounds of the determination were purely political. Nothing has hitherto happened to weaken them. The decision on the application of the min. pleny. of France will therefore naturally correspond with that on the propositions of Col. Smith. This indeed is signified to be the intention of the President.

It consequently only remains to make known the determination to the minister, in answer to his application with or without reasons.

The following considerations seem to recommend a simple communication of the determination without reasons, viz.

I. The US. not being bound by the terms of their contract to make the anticipated payments desired, there is no necessity for a specification of the motives for not doing it.

II. No adequate reasons but the true ones can be assigned for the non-compliance, & the assignment of these would not be wholly without inconvenience. The mention of them might create difficulties in some future stage of affairs, when they may have lost a considerable portion of their force.

The following answer in substance, is presumed then to be the most proper which can be given.

"That a proposition to the same effect was not long since brought forward by Col. Smith, as having been charged with a negociation on the subject, by the Provisional Executive Council of France. That it was then, upon full consideration, concluded not to accede to the measure, for reasons which continue to operate, & consequently lead at this time to the same conclusion. That an explanation of these reasons would with pleasure be entered into, were it not for the considerations that it would have no object of present utility, & might rather serve to occasion embarrasment in future." [3]

Letterpress copy, in the handwriting of Thomas Jefferson, Thomas Jefferson Papers, Library of Congress.

1. For background to this report, see George Washington to H, June 3, 1793, note 1.

2. See H to Washington, March 1, 1793, note 1; "Cabinet Meeting. Opinion on Proposals Made by William S. Smith Relative to the French Debt," March 2, 1793.

3. An entry in JPP for June 6, 1793, reads as follows: "The Secretary of the Treasury sent me a sketch of his report in answer to Mr. Genet's communication relative to the French debt. This is not according altogether with my ideas, as being rather too dry & abrupt an answer. I sent it to the Secretary of State for his remarks thereon" (JPP, 140).

At the bottom of his copy of H's report Jefferson wrote: "The above having been communicated by the President to me, I wrote the following letter." Jefferson's letter to Washington, dated June 6, 1793, reads as follows:

"I cannot but think that to decline the proposition to mr Genet on the subject of our debt, without assigning any reason at all would have a very dry and unpleasant aspect indeed. We are then to examine what are our good reasons for the refusal, which of them may be spoken out, & which may not. 1. want of confidence in the continuance of the present form of government, and consequently that *advances* to them might commit us with their successors. This cannot be spoken out. 2. since they propose to take the debt in produce, it would be better for us that it should be done in moderate masses yearly, than all in one year. This cannot be professed. 3. when M. [Charles-Alexandre] de Calonne was minister of finance, a Dutch company proposed to buy up the whole of our debt, by dividing it into actions or shares. I think mr [Etienne] Claviere, now minister of finance, was their agent. It was observed to M. de Calonne that to create such a mass of American paper, divide it into shares, and let them deluge the market, would depreciate them, the rest of our paper, and our credit in general. That the credit of a nation was a delicate and important thing & should not be risked on such an operation. M. de Calonne, sensible of the injury of the operation to us, declined it. In May, 1791, there came, thro' mr [Louis Guillaume] Otto, a similar proposition from Schwizer, Jeanneret & co. We had a representation on the subject from mr [William] Short, urging this same reason strongly. It was referred to the Secretary of the Treasury, who in a letter to yourself assigned the reasons against it, and these were communicated to mr Otto, who acquiesced in them. This objection then having been sufficient to decline the proposition twice before, & having been urged to the two preceding forms of government (the antient & that of 1791) will not be considered by them as founded in objections to the present form. 4. The law allows the whole debt to be paid only on condition it can be done on terms *advantageous* to the US. The minister foresees the objection & thinks he answers it by observing the *advantage* which the paiment in *produce* will occasion. It would be easy to shew that this was not the sort of advantage the legislature meant, but a *lower rate of interest*. 5. I cannot but suppose that the Secretary of the Treasury much more familiar than I am with the money operations of the treasury would on examination be able to derive practical objections from them. We pay to France but 5. per cent. The people of this country would never subscribe their money for less than 6. If to remedy this, obligations at less than 5 per cent were offered & accepted by mr Genet, he must part with them immediately at a considerable discount to indemnify the loss of the 1. per cent: and at a still greater discount to bring them down to par with our present 6. per cents: so that the operation would be equally disgraceful to us & losing to them &c. &c. &c.

"I think it very material myself to keep alive the friendly sentiments of that country as far as can be done without risking war, or double payment. If the instalments falling due this year can be advanced, without incurring those dangers, I should be for doing it. We now see by the declaration of the prince of Saxe-Cobourg on the part of Austria & Prussia that the ultimate point they desire is to restore the constitution of 1791. Were this even to be done before the pay-days of this year, there is no doubt in my mind but that that government (as republican as the present except in the form of it's executive) would confirm an advance so moderate in sum & time. I am sure the *nation* of France would never suffer their government to go to war *with us* for such a bagatelle, & the more surely if that bagatelle shall have been granted by us so as to *please* and not to *displease the nation;* so as to keep their affections engaged on our side. So that I should have no fear in advancing the instalments of this year at epochs convenient to the treasury. But at any rate should be for assigning reasons for not changing the form of the debt. These thoughts are very hastily thrown on paper, as will be but too evident." (ALS, letterpress copy, Thomas Jefferson Papers, Library of Congress.)

Jefferson then stated: "The President concurring with the Preceeding letter, and so signifying to Colo. Hamilton he erased the words 'which is humbly submitted' on the former report, & added on the same paper as follows:

" 'If nevertheless the President should be of opinion that reasons ought to be assigned the following seem to [be] the best which the nature of the case will admit, viz.

" 'Two modes of reimbursing or discharging *by anticipation* the residue of the debt which the US. owe to France are proposed.

" 'The first by a payment in specie, or bank bills having currency equal with specie which amounts to the same thing.

" 'The second by government bonds, bearing interest, & payable at certain specified periods.

" 'With regard to the first expedient the resources of the Treasury of the US. do not admit of it's being adopted. The government has relied for the means of reimbursing the foreign debt of the country on loans to be made abroad. The late events in Europe have thrown a temporary obstacle in the way of these loans producing an inability to make anticipated payments of sums hereafter to grow due.

" 'With regard to the second expedient, it has repeatedly come under consideration, & has uniformly been declined, as ineligible. The government has perceived, & continues to perceive great inconveniences to it's credit tending to the derangement of it's general operations of finance in every plan which is calculated to throw suddenly upon the market a large additional run of it's bonds. The present state of things, for obvious reasons, would serve to augment the evil of such a circumstance; while the existing & possible exigencies of the US. admonish them to be particularly cautious, at the present juncture, of any measure which may in any degree serve to impair or hazard their credit.

" 'These considerations are the more readily yielded to, from a belief that the utility of the measure to France might not on experiment prove adequate to the sacrifices which she would have to make in the sale of the bonds.

" 'All which is humbly submitted.' " (D, in the handwriting of Jefferson, Thomas Jefferson Papers, Library of Congress.)

The report was again submitted to Jefferson, and on June 7, 1793, he wrote to Washington: "Th. Jefferson has the honor of returning to the President the Report of the Secretary of the Treasury on the proposition of Mr. Genet. He is of the opinion that all may be omitted which precedes the words, 'Two modes of reimbursing,' etc., which follows 'of the reasons that are proper and not offensive.' The following passage should perhaps be altered: 'It has repeatedly come under consideration, and has uniformly been declined as ineligible.' The present proposition varies from that repeatedly offered in the circumstances which are of some importance, and is accordingly made by the minister, viz., the offer to take the payment in the produce of the United States. A very slight alteration will qualify this expression—thus agreeing to the fact without abating the force of the argument" (HCLW, IV, 425-26). An almost illegible letterpress copy of this note may be found in the Thomas Jefferson Papers, Library of Congress.

On June 8, 1793, Washington "Put into the hands of the Secretary of the Treasury the observations of the Secretary of State on his Report on Mr. Genet's communication & desired him to alter his report in some measure to conform to the suggestions of the Secretary of State" (JPP, 141).

From Jeremiah Banning [1]

[Oxford, Maryland, June 6, 1793. On June 21, 1793, Hamilton wrote to Banning "In answer to your letter of the 6th instant." Letter not found.]

1. Banning was collector of customs and inspector at the port at Oxford, Maryland.

From George Washington

Sir,

[Philadelphia, June 6, 1793]

Upon a mature consideration of your communication to me of the 3d. instant,[1] recommending a still further Loan in Holland, if obtainable, to the amount of 3,000,000 florins—and stating, that in case the recommendation should meet my ideas, my special approbation thereof would be proper, I have thought it necessary, in order to make the subject clear to my mind, before any steps are taken in it, to request you to give me information on the following points—vizt.

1st—Whether all the monies, borrowed under the Acts of the 4. & 12. of Augt. 1790,[2] have been expended on their respective objects? If not, what is the balance?

2d.—Under which of the two Laws do you propose that a loan should be opened?

3d.—If under one, or the other, or both, what is the balance remaining unborrowed, of the two sums allowed to be borrowed? [3]

4. To what use is the money, proposed to be borrowed, to be applied?

Go. Washington

Philadelphia
6. June 1793.

LC, George Washington Papers, Library of Congress.
1. Upon receipt of H's letter of June 3, 1793, Washington submitted it on June 4 to Thomas Jefferson for his opinion (*GW*, XXXII, 487). In his opinion on the proposed loan, dated June 5, 1793, Jefferson stressed the need for additional information on the purposes of the loan and on the necessity of borrowing to meet the payments on the French debt, since "uncertainty with respect to the true state of our account with France & the difference of the result from what has been understood, shows that the gentlemen, who are to give opinions on this subject, must do it in the dark . . . " (AD, letterpress copy, Thomas Jefferson Papers, Library of Congress).
2. "An Act making provision for the (payment of the) Debt of the United States" (1 *Stat.* 138–44 [August 4, 1790]); "An Act making Provision for the Reduction of the Public Debt" (1 *Stat.* 186–87 [August 12, 1790]).
3. The August 4, 1790, act authorized the President to borrow a sum not exceeding twelve million dollars (1 *Stat.* 139); the August 12, 1790, act stipulated that the sum of two million dollars might be borrowed (1 *Stat.* 187).

To Joseph Whipple

[*Philadelphia, June 7, 1793.* On June 19, 1793, Whipple wrote to Hamilton: "I had the honor to receive . . . your letter of the 7th. instant." *Letter not found.*]

To Otho H. Williams

Treasury Department, June 7, 1793. "I duly received your letter of the 28th Ultimo. . . . In reply to this letter, I have to refer you to my Circular one of the 30th Ultimo."

LS, Columbia University Libraries.

To Samuel Smith [1]

[*Philadelphia, June 8, 1793.* On June 16, 1793, Smith wrote to Hamilton: "I receivd your Letter of the 8 Inst." *Letter not found.*]

1. Smith was a Baltimore merchant who had been an officer in the American Revolution and a member of the Maryland House of Delegates from 1790 to 1792. In March, 1793, he was elected to Congress.

From John Cleves Symmes

[*June 8, 1793.* "The Secretary of the Treasury put into my hands a letter from Judge Symmes,[1] dated 8th June on the subject of the land granted to him & his associates." *Letter not found.*]

JPP, 142.
1. See H to William Rawle, January 6, 1793, note 2.

To George Washington [1]

Treasury Departmt. 8 June 1793.

Sir,

I have the honor to send you a report on the communication from the Minister plenipotentiary of France respecting the reimbursement of the residue of the Debt of the United States to that Country,[2] altered in conformity to your desire; and to be with perfect respect &c.   Alexander Hamilton

[ENCLOSURE] [3]

The Secretary of the Treasury to whom was referred a Communication from the Minister Plenipotentiary of the Republic of

France, on the subject of the Debt of the United States to France, respectfully makes thereupon the following Report.

The object of this communication is to engage the United States to enter into an arrangement for discharging the residue of the Debt, which they owe to France; by an anticipated payment of the Instalments not yet due, either in specie or bank bills of equal currency with specie, or in Government Bonds bearing interest & payable at certain specified periods; upon condition, that the sum advanced shall be invested in productions of the UStates for the supply of the French Dominions.

With regard to the first expedient, namely a payment in specie or bank bills, the resources of the Treasury of the United States do not admit of its being adopted. The Government has relied for the means of reimbursing its foreign Debt on new Loans to be made abroad. The late events in Europe have thrown a temporary obstacle in the way of these loans—producing consequently an inability to make payment, by anticipation, of the residue of the Debt hereafter to grow due.

With regard to the second expedient, that of Government bonds payable at certain specified periods, this in substance, though in other forms, has repeatedly come under consideration & has as often been declined, as ineligible. Great inconveniences to the credit of the Government, tending to derange its general operations of finance, have been & must continue to be perceived, in every plan which is calculated to throw suddenly upon the market a large additional sum of its bonds. The present state of things, for obvious reasons, wou'd serve to augment the evil of such a circumstance; while the existing & possible exigencies of the United States admonish them to be particularly cautious, at this juncture, of any measure, which may tend to hazard or impair their Credit.

These considerations greatly outweigh the advantage, which is suggested, as an inducement to the measure, (the conditions respecting which is the principal circumstance of difference between the present & former propositions) to arise from an investment of the sum to be advanced in the products of the Country; an advantage on which, perhaps little stress can be laid, in the present & probable state of foreign demand for these products.

The motives which dissuade from the adoption of the proposed measure, may, it is conceived, be the more readily yielded to from the probability that the utility of it to France might not, on experiment, prove an equivalent for the sacrifices, which she might have to make in the disposition of the bonds.

All which is humbly submitted,   Alex: Hamilton
                                                  Secy. of the Treasury.

Treasury Departmt.
8 June 1793.

LC, George Washington Papers, Library of Congress.
    1. For background to this letter, see Washington to H, June 3, 1793, note 1; "Draft of a Report on the French Debt," June 5, 1793.
    2. An entry for June 10, 1793, in JPP states that Washington referred H's report to Thomas Jefferson (JPP, 142). On June 11, 1793, Jefferson sent this report to Edmond Charles Genet (ALS, letterpress copy, Thomas Jefferson Papers, Library of Congress).
    3. LC, George Washington Papers, Library of Congress, copy, Columbia University Libraries; copy, in the handwriting of Tobias Lear, Thomas Jefferson Papers, Library of Congress; copy, *Arch. des Aff. Etr., Corr. Pol., Etats-Unis,* Supplement Vol. 20; LC, Domestic Letters of the Department of State, Vol. 5, February 4, 1792–December 31, 1793, National Archives.

Conversation with George Hammond [1]

[Philadelphia, June 10–July 6, 1793]

For this purpose,[2] I waited on a very influential member of the American administration,[3] who informed me that the fact was much as it had been communicated to the public, and that Mr. Genêt's conduct was a direct violation of a formal compact, originally entered into with Mr. Ternant and subsequently confirmed by himself both in conversation and in writing, and on the faith of which the last payment of the installment due had been made: but notwithstanding the precise conditions of the contract, Mr. Genêt had not only refused payment of the bills in question, but had treated all the remonstrances of the government on the subject, with the utmost arrogance, and contempt. My informant farther said that this circumstance was extremely embarassing to the government, as it stood pledged to its own citizens that these bills should be paid. In consequence of which it would be under the necessity of anticipating as much of the installment due next September as would discharge these bills. Upon this, I took the liberty of remarking that Mr. Genêt's conduct unworthy as it was, seemed to me to have originated in the design of entrapping the government into the last mentioned measure, as the best mode of remedying his failure in the proposition he had himself made to this government (the particulars of which have been stated in some of my former dispatches) to incline it to grant him some money in advance: [4] for it was evident that he had occasion for a large sum to supply some urgent necessities, that he had directed to them the money he had received for other purposes, and had imagined that he should thereby compel the government to anticipate a part of the next installment, in order to fulfil its engagements to its own citizens, and that the disgrace attendant on his breach of contract would soon be forgotten after the claims of the merchants had been satisfied. Upon this account I thought it below the dignity of any government to be the dupe of such an artifice, or be forced by it into the abandonment of a system that it had wisely formed after the most mature deliberation. I also added that, however manifest the necessity of the measure might appear to those, who were not unacquainted with it, it might in others create a suspicion that the whole transaction had been concerted with Mr. Genêt, in order to afford this government a colourable pretext for partly gratifying the wishes, which the French government had expressed to effect an alteration in the mode of liquidating the debt oweing by the United States. These observations appeared to make some impression upon the Gentleman with whom I was conversing, and whom I again saw yesterday,[5] when he acquainted me that in consequence of what had fallen from me, it had been determined to adhere to the resolution of not anticipating the next installment, and that the merchants, holding these bills, had been informed that they would not be paid until September next—the period, at which the installment would become due. . . .[6] I have been informed, *most confidentially and secretly*,[7] that he [Genêt] has lately delivered a memorial to the executive government, couched in language the most offensive and intemperate, and containing, the most pointed animadversions in the conduct of the government since his arrival, as well as some direct menaces. The President, is at present in the country, but he will return on Wednesday next, and I shall then endeavor to discover the light, in which he may regard this singular performance, and the consequent measures that he may think it expedient to pursue.

D, PRO: F.O., Series 5, Vol. 1.

1. This conversation has been taken from Hammond to Lord Grenville, July 7, 1793, Dispatch No. 16.

2. Hammond described his reason for meeting H at an earlier point in his letter of July 7 to Grenville, when he wrote: "In the beginning of this year, Mr. [Antoine René Charles Mathurin de] Laforêt, the late Consul General of France, published, with the concurrence of Mr [Jean Baptiste de] Ternant, an advertisement, purporting that certain bills, drawn by the colonial government of Saint Domingo on the Minister of France in Philadelphia, would be paid this month, when due; and it was at the time universally understood that this notification was made, in consequence of a stipulation on the part of this government, that a certain portion of the sums arising from the installments of last year, should be appropriated to the payment of these particular bills, all of which were held by American citizens, and now amount to about ninety three thousand dollars. The functions of Mr. Ternant and Mr. Laforêt having ceased on the arrival of Mr. [Edmond Charles] Genet and on the appointment of a new Consul, these bills, part of which to the amount of forty-five thousand dollars had been previously accepted by Mr. Laforêt, were the week before last presented to Mr. Genêt, who premptorily refused to pay any of them."

For information on these bills issued by the administration of Santo Domingo, see the introductory note to George Latimer to H, January 2, 1793; H to Ternant, January 13, 1793, note 2; Genet to H, June 3, 4, 1793.

On June 18, 1793, Genet wrote the following letter to Jefferson: "I have examined the correspondence which has taken place between you and my predecessor, relatively to the requisition of funds which he has made on the Federal Government, to pay off certain drafts of the administrators of Saint Domingo, and to procure provisions for that colony. I pay due respect, sir, to the justness of the observations which you transmitted to the citizen Ternant, on the subject of this request. Forced from his circumspection by the pressing instances of the administrators of Saint Domingo, I conceive that this requisition must have embarrassed your government infinitely; and, under this view, I feel all the obligations we owe you, for having, as you yourself expressed it, less consulted prudence than friendship in yielding to it. You have with propriety remarked, sir, that the decree, which appropriated for the necessities of the colonies four millions from the debt of the United States to France, not being yet transmitted to the Federal Government, in the usual official form, should not have an application so positive, so determined as that which the commissioners of the administration of Saint Domingo had given it; and that it was probable the ministers of France had had recourse, in order to supply the wants of this colony, to operations of another nature than those which took place. In fact, sir, the drafts for the payment of which the commissioners of Saint Domingo, pressed by imperious circumstances, have, in some degree, obliged the citizen Ternant to demand funds of you, have neither been authorized by the National Convention, nor by the Executive Council; and I must even inform you, that I am forbidden to pay, out of the funds placed at my disposal, any other than those drafts which shall have been accepted by the consul La Forest, in virtue of orders from my predecessor. But, on my arrival here, I was informed that this consul had received orders from the minister plenipotentiary to register all drafts issued by the administration of Saint Domingo, and to pay them out of the new funds which the Federal Government had provisionally granted, on the basis of the decree of the 26th June, although it was not officialy notified. I have not thought proper, sir, to stop suddenly the payment of these drafts, in the hope that the mode of reimbursing your debt, which you at my request have laid before the President of the

United States, would be adopted by him, and give me the means, first, to honor the drafts registered by my predecessor, the payment of which had been ordered by him; secondly, to provide, at the same time, for the urgent necessities of France and her colonies; but having been deceived in my expectation, by motives which are not for me to examine, I find myself deprived of the advantage of conciliating all interests, and constrained to obey only the empire of circumstances, which prescribe me to suspend the payment of the colonial drafts, and to employ the funds destined for their acquittal to the purchase of provisions for France and her colonies. This arrangement, sir, need not alarm either the bearers of the registered drafts, or those of the other drafts issued and not registered, of the administrators of Saint Domingo, and other colonies of the French republic. The nation will certainly fulfil towards them the engagements contracted by its agents. I know that they have destined particular funds for this purpose. I also know that the colonies have made contributions in kind to fulfil their obligations, and provide themselves for a part of their wants; and it is according to these ideas that I have determined to have inserted in the public papers the enclosed information, the intention of which is to calm inquietudes of the bearers of the drafts which I am obliged to set aside, and to encourage the citizens of the United States to continue to carry succor to their brothers the French republicans of the Antilles . . ." (*ASP, Foreign Relations,* I, 158).

Genet also sent to Jefferson an announcement, dated June 17, 1793, which he planned to insert in the newspapers to inform citizens who held bills drawn by the administration of Santo Domingo that these bills would not be paid until Genet had been authorized to discharge them (*ASP, Foreign Relations,* I, 158).

3. In the postscript Hammond wrote in code: "The information relative to St. Domingo Bills, and to Mr. Genet's Memorial was communicated to me by Mr. Hamilton."

4. See George Washington to H, June 3, 1793; "Draft of a Report on the French Debt," June 6, 1793; H to Washington, June 8, 1793.

5. July 6, 1793.

6. See note 2.

7. See note 3.

From Andrew G. Fraunces [1]

Philadelphia, June 10, 1793.

Sir,

I had the honor of receiving your letter of the 18th ult. I observe what you advice with respect to the warrants of the late Board of Treasury, and shall lodge those I possess in the proper office, agreeably to the act quoted by you.[2]

Having purchased these warrants from an idea that they would immediately be paid on presentation, I feel a little embarrassed at receiving information that they must wait the issue of a regular adjustment, with other claims against the United States, notwithstanding I am willing to dispose of them as you advise in your letter aforesaid.

It will be satisfactory to me, however, to receive an answer to the following, and it will relieve in some measure the inconvenience I labor under from advances I made when I purchased them.

Whether those warrants will be paid, if it be found from the accounts of the late Treasurer [3] and Receiver of Taxes,[4] that they never have been taken up by those officers, or that the United States have never been charged with the payment of them? When and at what time they will be taken under consideration, and the claim finally determined on by the present officers of the United States? [5] Whether I as the present holder, owner, and presenter of them, (and not any one else, unless legally empowered by me) will receive the amount of them, if it should be found that they are a legal claim against the United States? And whether there are any steps necessary to be taken by me that can throw further light on the business, and thereby expedite their final adjustment?

Notwithstanding I ask these questions, I must confess I feel myself perfectly satisfied that they are a substantial claim against the United States; yet, as there is another person to be satisfied as well as myself,[6] I wish them answered as fully as the present state of things will admit, and as you may please to favor me from the above statement.[7]

I have the honor to be, Sir,   Your obedient servant,

Andrew G. Fraunces.

Hon. A. Hamilton, Esq. Secretary
of the Treasury of the United States.

Fraunces, *An Appeal*, 5–6.

1. For background to this letter, see Fraunces to H, May 16, 1793; H to Fraunces, May 18, 1793.

In introducing the letter printed above, Fraunces in his pamphlet stated that H's letter of May 18 had not satisfied him. He wrote: "I repaired early in June last to Philadelphia; I waited on Mr. Hamilton at his office; I represented to him the hardship of his detaining from me monies justly due, and of his not pointing out the reasons why they were detained, since provision had been made for them. He then, (as I then thought) *graciously condescended* to say, *if I could point out a mode for him to proceed upon satisfactory to me, he would adopt it:* He then desired, (in the mean time while I considered) that I would write him a letter by way of answer to his of the 18th of May; some further conversation took place which will be seen in my letter of the 19th of August to the President. Mr. Hamilton then requested he should *dictate* the following letter to himself. I submitted to this mode of doing the business, merely in order to see to what lengths he would go.

"This said letter so dictated was nearly in these words" (Fraunces, *An Appeal*, 5).

2. Section 2 of "An Act relative to claims against the United States, not

barred by any act of limitation, and which have not been already adjusted" provided "That it shall be the duty of the Auditor of the Treasury, to receive all such claims aforesaid as have not been heretofore barred by any act of limitation, as shall be presented before the time aforesaid, with the certificates, or other documents in support thereof, and to cause a record to be made of the names of the persons, and of the time when the said claims are presented; which record shall be made in the presence of the person or persons presenting the same, and shall be the only evidence that the said claims were presented, during the time limited by this act" (1 *Stat.* 301–02 [February 12, 1793]).

3. Michael Hillegas.

4. Fraunces is referring to Nathaniel Appleton, receiver of taxes for Massachusetts. On November 19, 1787, Warrant No. 236 had been drawn on Appleton. Under an ordinance of Congress of September 30, 1785, commissioners of the continental loan offices were required to act as receivers of public moneys in their respective states (*JCC*, XXIX, 692–93).

5. Section 3 of "An Act relative to claims against the United States, not barred by any act of limitation, and which have not been already adjusted" made the officers of the Treasury responsible for making a report to Congress on any claims which were disallowed, but set no deadline for their account (1 *Stat.* 302). On December 23, 1795, Oliver Wolcott, Jr., submitted a report of "Proceedings of the Accounting Officers of the Treasury on Certain Claims" (*ASP, Claims,* I, 172–81).

6. Fraunces was in need of money. When he opened his office in New York, he had advertised for a loan (*The* [New York] *Daily Advertiser,* March 19, 1793).

7. In his pamphlet following the letter printed above Fraunces wrote: "I called upon him shortly after, (and agreeably to his direction) for an answer to this, and with an assurance at which I was astonished, he told me he had consulted with the Comptroller, who with himself had determined to give me for the present, no further satisfaction; however, said he, in a *low voice,* 'If you will pledge to me your honor not to purchase any more of them, I will secure to you the amount of those you hold.' I told him I could not, in justice to my fellow-citizens, holders of this kind of debt, accept payment in any other mode than that which had been already officially adopted by him, and in which he had paid the greater part of the 190,000 dollars appropriated by Congress for this purpose. He then begged me to postpone the business for some time, and return to New-York, that on my arrival again in Philadelphia, he would satisfy the demand in the manner I insisted. I agreed to this; my presence being necessary for a short-time in that city. He further assured me, that if I would continue *silent,* my demand should not only be satisfied, but he would make me a handsome compensation for my loss of time, expences, &c. &c. He then offered me a sum in advance, from his private funds, to be reimbursed when the warrants should be regularly paid. I accepted a sum upon these conditions, and accordingly departed . . ." (Fraunces, *An Appeal,* 6–7).

To Thomas Jefferson [1]

Treasury Department
June 10th 1793.

Sir

The Comptroller of the Treasury has reported to me that [2] "On examining the subsisting contracts between the United States and the Government of France and the Farmers General and a comparison thereof with the foreign accounts and documents transmitted to the Treasury the following facts appear.

That, previous to the Treaty of February 1778, the sum of Three millions of livres had been advanced by the Government of France to the Agents of the United States, under the title of gratuitous assistance for which no reimbursement was to be made.

That the payments which composed the before mentioned sum of Three millions of Livres are stated in a letter of Mr Durival to Mr Grand, dated in 1776, to have been made at the following periods.

One million delivered by the Royal Treasury the 10th of June 1776, and two other millions advanced also by the Royal Treasury in 1777, on four receipts of the Deputies of Congress of the 17th of January, 3d of April, 10th of June and 15th of October of the same year.

In the accounts of Mr Ferdinand Grand, Banker of the United States, the following sums are credited. viz—

1777	January 31st	Livres	500,000
"	April 28th		500,000
"	June 4th		1.000,000
"	July 3rd		500,000
"	October 10th		500,000
Amounting, in the whole, to Livs			3,000,000

The Farmers General of France claim a large balance from the United States on account of one million of Livres which they contend was advanced in June, 1777, in consequence of a special contract with Messrs. Franklin and Deane, to be repaid by the delivery of Tobacco at certain stipulated prices—and the advance made by the Farmers General is said to be the same money as is credited by Mr Grand on the 4th of June 1777.

After a careful examination of the foreign accounts, it is found that no more than Three millions of Livres have been credited by any Agents of the United States.

An opinion was entertained by the late Officers of the Treasury, that the sum claimed by the Farmers General, composed a part of the sum supplied as a gratuitous aid by the Government. Subsequent explanations have, however, rendered it probable, that, including the claim of the Farmers General, the sum of four millions of livres were in fact received: it is, however, indispensable, that it should be known to whom the money was paid.

The most direct mode of obtaining this information will be to call for Copies of the receipts mentioned in Mr Durivals letter of 1786,[3] and, more particularly, a Copy of that said to have been given on the 10th of June 1776"—and, as explanatory of the Transaction, has sent me the documents herewith transmitted.

The most likely conjecture, in my mind, considering the period of the advance and the circumstances of that period is that the unaccounted for million went into the hands of M De Beaumarchais. The supplies which he furnished to the United States exceeded his own probable resources, besides the imprudence of having hazarded so much at that stage of our affairs upon our ability to pay—and there were many symtoms at the time of his having been secretly put in motion by the Government.

It is now become urgent that the truth of the case should be known. An account has recently passed the Auditor's Office, admitting, in favor of Mr De Beaumarchais, a balance of 422,265 Dollars and 18 Cents—with a reservation only of the question of the Million. If he has received that Million, which has been acknowledged as a free gift from the French Government, it is unjust that he should be able to establish a claim against the United States for supplies which must have been the proceeds of that sum. If he has never received the million every days suspension of his claim, after the immense delays heretofore incurred, is a grievous hardship upon him. It concerns, materially, the Interests and more the Justice, the Credit and the Character of the United States, that as speedy a solution, as possible, of the enigma may be obtained.

With a view to this I have the honor to make you the present communication, that you may be pleased to take such steps as shall appear to you the most proper and efficacious, to procure, as speedily as the nature of the case will admit, the requisite explanations.[4]

With great respect,   I have the honor to be,   Sir, your Mo. Obedt Servant,   Alexander Hamilton

The Secretary of State.

LS, Thomas Jefferson Papers, Library of Congress; letterpress copy, Thomas Jefferson Papers, Library of Congress; LC, RG 59, Diplomatic and Consular Instructions, 1791–1801, January 23, 1791–August 16, 1793, National Archives.

1. This letter concerns the so-called "lost million." See the introductory note to Oliver Wolcott, Jr., to H, March 29, 1792.

2. The material within H's quotation marks consists of extracts from Wolcott to H, March 29, 1792.

3. See Wolcott to H, March 29, 1792, note 6.

4. On June 13, 1793, Jefferson wrote to Gouverneur Morris, United States Minister Plenipotentiary to France, instructing him to make inquiries concerning the "lost million" and enclosing copies of H's letter and the correspondence mentioned in it (ALS, letterpress copy, Thomas Jefferson Papers, Library of Congress).

To John Chaloner [1]

[Philadelphia, June 11, 1793]

Mr. Hamilton presents his Compliments to Mr Chaloner requests to be informed what is the amount of the Mortgage on Holkers land in which Mr. Church is interested principal & interest & what proportion belongs to Mr. Church.[2] The inquiry demands dispatch.

June 11. 1793

AL, Historical Society of Pennsylvania, Philadelphia.

1. Chaloner was a Philadelphia merchant who formerly handled the business affairs of Jeremiah Wadsworth and John B. Church in that city. Church, who was the husband of Elizabeth Hamilton's sister Angelica, was at this time living in England. H managed Church's business interests in the United States.

2. John Holker was a Philadelphia merchant and speculator, who during the American Revolution was French consul in Philadelphia and agent for supplying the French navy. See H to Thomas FitzSimons, June 20, 1792, note 2.

This document concerns a tract of twenty-one thousand acres of land in Croghan's Patent in Otsego County, New York, which was purchased by Holker from Henry Hill in 1783. In 1783 and 1784 Holker had drawn two sets of bills of exchange on London and Paris banking houses. These bills eventually came into the possession of William Price and Company and were protested for nonpayment in September, 1784. Price entered suit against Holker in the Philadelphia County Court of Common Pleas and in September, 1784, sold his interest in one set of bills to John B. Church. As a result of judgments against him, Holker mortgaged the twenty-one thousand acres of land in Croghan's Patent to Price and Church on January 15, 1789. According to the terms of the agreement the mortgage would be discharged if Holker paid the sums due (Recital in indenture, January 15, 1789, between Holker and Price and Church, anonymous donor). In May, 1793, preparations were being made to sell at a sheriff's sale the lands mortgaged by Holker (Cornelius Bogert to William Cooper, May 20, 1793, anonymous donor). On June 23, 1793, however, Robert Troup wrote to Judge William Cooper of Otsego County requesting that the sale be canceled since an agreement had been reached with Price and H, who was acting on behalf of Church, for the discharge of the mortgage (Troup to Cooper, June 23, 1793, anonymous donor). Cooper eventually contracted with Holker's representative, Thomas FitzSimons, to purchase the land and Price's shares of the January, 1789, mortgage and promised to pay the mortgage held by Church (Indenture, William Cooper and Samuel and Miers Fisher, February 7, 1797, anonymous donor; William Cooper in account current with Thomas FitzSimons, February 7, 1797, anonymous donor).

To George Washington

[Philadelphia, June 11, 1793]

The Secretary of the Treasury presents his respects to The President, sends him for consideration, two letters [1] on the subject of a proper site for a Custom House, on the New York side of Lake Champlain. The Secretary will have the honor of waiting on the President in a day or two to submit whatever further may occur & take his orders.

11 June 1793.

LC, George Washington Papers, Library of Congress.
   1. These enclosures have not been found, but an entry in JPP for June 12, 1793, reads: "Secy of the Treasury sent me two letters—one from Stephen Keyes the Collector of Vermont—and one from M. L. Woolsey the Collector of Champlain—both recommending Cumberland Head as the most proper place to establish the port of Entry to be fixed on Lake Champlain, agreeably to a law of Congress" (JPP, 145). On the following day Washington wrote: "Retd. to the Secy of the Treasy the letters relative to fixing the Port of Entry on Lake Champlain and informed him of my approving of Cumberland Head for this Port, and desired that he would have a proper notification thereof drawn up for my signature" (JPP, 146).

Cabinet Meeting. Opinion Respecting the Measures to Be Taken Relative to a Sloop Fitted Out as a Privateer

[Philadelphia] June 12. 1793.

The President having required the opinions of the heads of the three departments on a letter from Governor Clinton of the 9th. inst.[1] stating that he had taken possession of the sloop Polly, now called the Republican, which was arming, equipping & manning by French & other citizens to cruize against some of the belligerent powers, and desiring to know what further was to be done, and they having met & deliberated thereon, are unanimously of opinion, that Governor Clinton be desired to deliver over to the civil power the said vessel & her appurtenances, to be dealt with according to law: and that the Attorney of the US. for the district of New York be desired, to have such proceedings at law instituted as well concerning the sd vessel and her appurtenances, as against all the persons citizens or aliens participating in the armament or object thereof as he shall think will be most effectual for punishing the said offenders, & preventing the sd vessel & appurtenances from being applied to the destined purpose: and that if he shall be of opinion that no judiciary process will be sufficient to prevent such application of the vessel to the hostile purpose intended that then the Governor be desired to detain her by force till the further advice of the General government can be taken.

The President having also required the same opinions on the Memorial of the British minister of the 11th. inst.[2] on the subject of the British brigantine Catherine captured by the French frigete the Embuscade within the limits of the protection of the US. as is said, and carried into the harbour of New York, they are of opinion unanimously, that the governor of N. York be desired to seize the said vessel in the first instance, and then deliver her over to the civil power, and that the Attorney of the US. for the district of New York be instructed to institute proceedings at law in the proper court for deciding whether the sd capture was made within the limits of the protection of the US. & for delivering her up to her owners if it be so decided: but that if it shall be found that no court may take cognisance of the sd question, then the said vessel to be detained by the Governor until the further orders of the general government can be had thereon.[3]

Th. Jefferson

H Knox

Alexander Hamilton

DS, in the handwriting of Thomas Jefferson, George Washington Papers, Library of Congress.

1. Letterpress copy, Thomas Jefferson Papers, Library of Congress.

2. An entry in JPP for June 11, 1793, reads as follows: "The Secy of State sent me a memorial wh. he had recd from Mr [George] Hammond relative to the Capture of the Brigantine Catharine by the French Frigate Ambuscade on the 8th Inst. and respecting the Brig Morning Star which had been captured & carried into Charleston. Encloses deposition of sailors & a pilot respecting the Brig Catharine" (JPP, 144). Hammond's memorial reads as follows:

"The Undersigned, his Brittanic Majesty's Minister Plenipotentiary to the United States, has the honor of submitting to the Secretary of State the annexed deposition; from which it appears that the British brigantine Catharine, James Drysdale Master bound from Jamaica to the Port of Philadelphia, was on Sunday last the 8th inst captured by the French frigate the Embuscade off

Hereford at the distance of not more than two miles and a half from the state of New Jersey.

"The Undersigned can entertain no doubt that the executive government of the United states will consider the circumstances of this capture as an aggression on the territory and jurisdiction of the United States, and will consequently pursue such measures as to its wisdom may appear the most efficacious for procuring the immediate restitution of this vessel to its owners as soon as it shall arrive at New York (for which port is understood to have been sent as prize) or within any other harbour of the United States.

"The Undersigned ventures to hope that the annexed deposition will be regarded by the executive government of the United States as evidence sufficient to authenticate the fact of the capture and the circumstances by which it has been accompanied. When he is informed of the actual arrival of the brigantine Catharine, within any part of the United States, he will obtain the corroborating testimony of the master and pilot now on board of the vessel, which testimony he will not fail to transmit without delay to the Secretary of State.

"The Undersigned thinks it expedient to add that he has lately received information, on which he can depend, from Charleston, that the brig the Morning Star, which on the 9th of last month was condemned as legal prize by Mr [Michel Ange Bernard de] Mangourit the French Consul at that place, was taken by the French frigate the Embuscade (on the 15th of April) at the distance of *not more than two miles from the bar of Charleston,* and within sight of the town. The Undersigned is taking the proper measures to collect the proof of this fact, which, if substantiated will, added to the capture of the present vessel, and that of the Ship Grange within the bay of Delaware constitute the third instance of similar aggression on the territory and jurisdiction of the United States, that has been committed by the French frigate the Embuscade within the short period of two months." (LS, Notes from the British Legation in the United States to the Department of State, Vol. I, October 26, 1791–August 15, 1794, National Archives.) The deposition mentioned by Hammond may also be found in the location cited above.

3. The version of this cabinet meeting in JPP reads as follows: "The Secy of State was directed to write to the Atty. of the district of New York on the Subject agreeably to said opinion—and the Secy of War to the Govr. of N York. The Memorial of Mr Hammond was also considered, and it was determined that the Dist Atty of N. York shd. be written to on this subject likewise, in the way stated in the opinions" (JPP, 144-45).

From James Hamilton [1]

St. Vincent [Danish West Indies] June 12th. 1793

Dear Alexander

I wrote you a letter in June 1792 [2] inclosed in one to Mr. Donald [3] of Virginia Since which I have had no further accounts from you. My bad State of health has prevented my going to Sea at this time being afflicted with a complication of disorders.

The war which has lately broke out between France & England makes it very dengerous going to Sea at this time, however we daily expect news of a peace & when that takes place provided it is not too late in the Season I will embark in the first Vessel that Sails for Philadelphia.

I have now Settled all my business in this part of the World, with the assistance of my good freind Mr. Donald who has been of every Service to me that lay in his power in contributing to make my life Easy, at this advanced period of life. The bearer of this, Capt. Sherref of the Brig, Dispatch Sails direct for Philadelphia & has promised to deliver you this letter with his own hands, & as he returns to this Island from Philadelphia I beg you will drop me a few lines letting me know how you & your family keeps your health as I am uneasy at not having heard from you for some time past.

I beg my respectfull Compliments to Mrs. Hamilton & your Children, & wishing you health & happiness, I remain, with esteem

Dear Alexander   Your very Affectte. Father   James Hamilton

ALS, Hamilton Papers, Library of Congress.
1. H's father had remained in the West Indies after H had come to North America. He had lived on several islands during this period and sometime before 1793 had moved to St. Vincent. H had hoped to bring him to the United States. See H to William Seton, August 17, 1792.
2. Letter not found.
3. Presumably Alexander Donald, a Richmond merchant who was in the tobacco trade.

To George Washington

[Philadelphia, June 12, 1793]

The Secretary of the Treasury has the honor to transmit to the President a Letter which he has just received from Judge Symmes,[1] together with certificates of the payments [2] which have been made. On Monday he will wait upon the President on the subject.

12 June 1793

LC, George Washington Papers, Library of Congress.
1. Letter not found, but see John Cleves Symmes to H, June 8, 1793. For background to the Symmes purchase, see H to William Rawle, January 6, 1793, note 2.
2. These certificates were "two Certificates of the paymts. which had been made by Judge Symmes for his land" (JPP, 145).

George Washington to Alexander Hamilton, Thomas Jefferson, and Henry Knox

[Philadelphia] June 12th. 1793.

Gentlemen,

As you are about to meet on other business,[1] it is my desire, that you would take the enclosed application [2] into consideration. It is not my wish, on one hand, to throw unnecessary obstacles in the way of gratifying the wishes of the applicants. On the other, it is incumbent on me to proceed with regularity. Would not the granting a Patent then, which I believe is always the concluding Act and predicated upon the Survey (as a necessary document) have too much the appearance of placing the Cart before the horse? [3] And does not the Law enjoin something on the Attorney General of the U. States previous to the Signature of the President? What can be done with propriety I am willing to do. More I ought not to do.

Go: Washington

To the Secretaries of State Treasury & War.

ALS (photostat), George Washington Papers, Library of Congress; LC, George Washington Papers, Library of Congress; LC, RG 59, State Department Correspondence, 1791–1796, National Archives.

1. The "other business" was presumably the topic discussed in "Cabinet Meeting. Opinion Respecting the Measures to Be Taken Relative to a Sloop Fitted Out as a Privateer," June 12, 1793.
2. See H to Washington, June 12, 1793.
3. See H to William Rawle, January 6, 1793, note 2.

To Otho H. Williams

Treasury Department
June 12th 1793.

Sir

Your letter of the 24th Ultimo [1] was received some time ago.

You will make the arrangement in question, as to Boats, combining the accomodation of the Cutter with that of the Port.

It does not appear that there is sufficient reason for complying with the wishes of the Boatmen, as to wages. If there be inconveniences, there are counterbalancing advantages in their situation.

With consideration, I am, Sir, your Obed Servt. A Hamilton

Otho H Williams Esqr.
Collector, Baltimore.

LS, Columbia University Libraries.
1. Letter not found.

To Richard Harison [1]

[Philadelphia, June 13–15, 1793]

Private & Confidential

Dear Harrison

You will receive a letter this Morning from the Secretary of State.[2] The occasion requires vigour and a decisive resort to *principles*.

Tis clear that no foreign nation can without the consent of our government *organize* within our territory and jurisdiction the means of military expeditions by land or sea. To do it is an offence against the law of Nations—the law of Nations is a part of the law of the land. Hence such an act must on principle be punishable. Vatel Book III Chapt II Section 15th is strong as to the point of inlisting men [3]—this is a part of the present case. The other circumstances aggravate the offence.

Our own citizens are guilty of a breach of the peace stipulated by our Treaties with England Holland & Prussia.[4] The Citizens of France are guilty of a violation of our Sovereignty and Jurisdiction, tending to endanger and disturb our Peace.

An intention to commit Piracy may be *charged*. It will serve to bring out the Commissions, under which the vessel is armed. This is very desireable for many reasons.

With regard to the vessel I am puzzled to see how you will get her into the custody of the law. Can it be done as an Instrument of this Offence? You will perceive that if she cannot be put into civil she is to remain in Military custody.

Yr. friend & ser A Hamilton

R Harrison Esq

ALS, New-York Historical Society, New York City.

1. For background to this letter, see "Cabinet Meeting. Opinion Respecting the Measures to Be Taken Relative to a Sloop Fitted Out as a Privateer," June 12, 1793.

2. In his letter to Harison, dated June 12, 1793, concerning the *Polly*, Jefferson asked him "to take up the business on the part of the U.S.; instituting such proceedings at law against the vessel & her appurtences as may place her in the custody of the law, and may prevent her being used for purposes of hostility against any of the belligerent powers." Harison was directed to have the governor seize and turn over to the civil authority the brig *Catharine*, which had been captured by the French frigate *L'Embuscade* and carried into New York Harbor. Jefferson also asked Harison to institute proceedings to determine whether the *Catharine* had been taken in American territorial waters (ALS, letterpress copy, Thomas Jefferson Papers, Library of Congress).

3. This section reads as follows: "As the right of levying soldiers belongs solely to the nation (sec. 7) so no person is to enlist soldiers in a foreign country, without the permission of the sovereign, and even with this permission none but volunteers are to be enlisted; for the service of their country is out of the question here, and no sovereign has a right to give or sell his subjects to another. They who undertake to enlist soldiers in a foreign country, without the sovereign's permission; and in general, whoever alienates the subjects of another, violates one of the most sacred rights both of the prince and the state. It is the crime distinguished by the name of *Plagiat* or man-stealing, and accordingly is punished with the utmost severity in every policied state. Foreign recruiters are hanged immediately, and very justly, as it is not to be presumed that their sovereign ordered them to commit the crime; and if they did receive such an order, they ought not to obey it; their sovereign having no right to command what is contrary to the law of nature. It is not, I say, apprehended that these recruiters act by order of their sovereign, and usually they who have practised seduction only, are, if taken, severely punished. If they have used violence, and made their escape, they are claimed, and the men they carried off demanded. But if it appears that they acted by order, such a proceeding in a foreign sovereign is justly considered as an injury, and as a sufficient cause for declaring war against him, unless he condescends to make suitable reparation" (Vattel, *Law of Nations*, II, 7–8).

4. Both the Treaty of Amity and Commerce of October, 1782, with the Netherlands and the treaty with Prussia of September, 1785, contained specific prohibitions against the nationals of either signatory power accepting commissions or letters of marque from any power hostile to the other contracting party on pain of being "punished as a Pirate." See Article 19 of the treaty with the Netherlands (Miller, *Treaties*, II, 76–77) and Article 20 of the treaty with Prussia (Miller, *Treaties*, II, 175–76). Article 20 of the treaty with Prussia also stipulated that neither party should "hire, lend, or give Any part of their naval or military force to the enemy of the other to aid them offensively or defensively against that other."

Treasury Department Circular to the Collectors of the Customs

Treasury Department, June 13, 1793.

Sir,

I have to desire that you extend my Instructions, of the 2d of January, 1792,[1] relatively to the Receipt of the Cash and Post Notes of the Bank of the United States, to the Notes of the several Branches of this Institution, the Offices of Discount and Deposit, at Boston, New-York, Baltimore, and Charleston.

The Signatures of the Presidents of these Offices are, herewith, transmitted to you, to serve as a Check against the Imposition of Counterfeits.

With Consideration, I am, Sir, Your Obedient Servant,

A Hamilton

LS, MS Division, New York Public Library; LC, RG 56, Circulars of the Office of the Secretary, "Set T," National Archives; copy, Office of the Secretary, United States Treasury Department.

1. "Treasury Department Circular to the Collectors of the Customs," January 2, 1792.

From William Heth

Bermuda Hundred [Virginia] 14th June 1793

Dear Sir

I am favor'd with your private address of the 3d. Inst.[1] Instead of making use of the Mayor of Petersburg to perfect the Sea letters [2]—I got the favor of a County Magistrate to come down, who very readily, and without scruple, signed & sealed as many as I wished, being a more proper & consistent expedient, than the one suggested before.

If I may Judge of the *public-pulse*, respecting the questions which you ask, from the opinions & sentiments of the *best informed*, and *best characters* within the small circle to which I am confined, I can inform you pretty accurately, how *it beats*. First respecting *War*.

ALS, Hamilton Papers, Library of Congress.

1. Letter not found.

2. See "Treasury Department Circular to the Collectors of the Customs," May 13–16, 1793.

No man of *common sense*, & *common honesty*, *wishes*, I believe, to
See America engaged in the present European contest. It is a *calamity*,
on which, no virtuous, or good Man; or one, who *really* prays for
the happiness and prosperity of this Country, can reflect, but with
extreme concern & horror: and the few among us—and thank God,
they are *very few*—who talk with great calmness & ease about *War*,
and of our being bound by gratitude to take an immediate and decided part in favor of France, are not those, I assure you, who are held
in estimation, either for *their talents*, their *Virtue*, or their *property;*
nor are they those, who—if we should be *obliged* to *fight*, or be
kicked—will be found to meet the Enemy in the hour of danger.
They are Men, either desperate in their circumstances, of unprincipled and envious characters, or, who have been uniformly & violently opposed to the present constitution, and all the measures of
government; and some of whom—in case of a general convulsion—
may expect to *better* their fortunes, for *worse* they cannot well be;
but whose buzzing, & insignificate clamor, only serves to render them
more contemptible. These, you may rely are the sentiments of every
man of information, & acknowledgd probity, within my acquaintance,
and whose names, if mentioned, would command your respect, and
esteem. But, at the same time—However much the horrors of war
ought to be dreaded—and those who pass'd thro' the late glorious
revolution, can form some tolerable Idea of its calamities—If we
must either take up Arms, or remain in peace, on such terms as
GBritain may be pleased to prescribe to us; or, as I have said before—
if we must either *fight*, or be *kicked* by G Britain, then, it will be
found, that those who are now most averse to War, will be the *first
in the field*, and in the *front of the battle*. In that case, it will be found
that the resentment of our much injured Country towards that proud,
haughty nation, which—so much to the honor & credit of human
nature—was sinking fast into oblivion, will be rekindled in a moment,
and the noble enthusiatic spirit of 75. 76. & 77, will, I trust, in Heaven
like a stroke of electricity, fill at the same instant, the breast of every
American.

The aforegoing answer may be apply'd to your second question
respecting *Neutrality*—for those who deprecate the Idea of a War,
as the greatest evil which could befall us; must, of course, pray de-
voutly, that the most *pure* & *strict neutrality*, may be observed by
our government; not only, from the most pacific motives, but from

the fullest conviction, that it is a line of conduct which the soundest policy would urge us to observe, and Such, as if America hast not lost her Guardian Angel, will unquestionably be recommended to every council and department in the United States, in terms, which cannot be disobeyed; unless indeed *dire necessity* Should justify a different conduct, and then I trust, the same Guardian Angel will not be less careful of us than heretofore. But before I leave the subject of *Neutrality* I must observe, that I should hold myself a very uncandid, & unworthy confidential correspondent, if I did not tell you that, the instructions contained in your circular of the 30th Ulto, are not altogether approved by those, whose opinions I so highly respect, & whom, I have already described, as being *now* much averse to the *very Idea* of *War*—tho' they entertain not the least doubt of the Wisdom & propriety of the decision of the Executive of the United States. But they cannot see *how*—if the Treaty with France, can Justify, such a partiality in favor of *that* Nation—*why*, the Dutch are not entitled to the same *marks of Neutrality;* since, the article in the Treaties with both, on that particular question, are *precisely* the same. And it is apprehended, or rather, *feared*, that this decision, will draw from G. Britain, such language and conditions, as cannot be submitted to, so long as America possesses the smallest degree of pride or national spirit, *whatever may be the Consequences.*

3dly—French Revolution. Until the Execution of Louis 16th there *appeared*, but *one wish* on this subject; and that was, that the French might succeed. But Since that period, or rather, since *Great Britain* has taken a decided part in the contest, there has been a very considerable *outward change* of opinion, not among the *natives*, or those *foreigners* who were attached to, or took a part *with* us, in the late American revolution. No: *they* are still on our side, in favor of the French; notwithstanding the many acts of licentiousness which they have committed. The others, are those, who adhered to the British Army & government, & who fell under the denomination of *Tories* & *Refugees* during the late War, and who now, almost openly deprecate every measure of the National Convention. Beleiving, as I do, my religious creed, that *no man* who joind the British in the late War, can really love the American government, or, will remain a true & steady friend to America, in case of another Rupture with G Britain: and moreover, that Such men, can never pray cordially for the establishment of a republican Government in any part of the

World; * I could not help using & marking as above, the words *"appeard"* and *"outward change"*—for I deem it impossible, that any man, who really wish'd well to the French Revolution *before* the Decapitation of Louis the 16th, can wish otherwise *now*, notwithstanding he may view that affair, in so criminal a point of view, as to feel himself Justified, if it was in his power—to order the same measure to every man, who voted for the death of the unfortunate King. This Massacre then, as it is called, is only a pitiful pretext for change of Sentiment. The true cause is, that their old friend *John Bull*, has again bellowed and steped forth on the Theatre of War.

I wrote you a long private, and confidential letter in April last,[4] congratulating you on the Victory which you obtained at the close of the last,[5] and giving you some account of the new forces likely to be employ'd against you the ensuing Campaign—with some cursory

---

* If I am not greatly mistaken by dear Sir, you have a Man near you whose pen—notwithstanding the magnanimity of his Country, in so far forgeting his crimes, as to give him an important office with a handsome salary; and notwithstanding *your* personal friendship towards him—has been employd in abusing the measures of government, and particularly, your Official conduct; and whose study has been to sap, and undermine *you*, in hopes of filling your place, through the Interests of ———[3] you know who. You may imagine, that this is a suspicion, proceeding altogether from the vile opinion in which I must ever hold such traitorous scoundrels beleiving them capable of every species of perfidy and ingratitude. But do not I beseech you. The time may come, when I may feel myself at liberty to be more explicit. In the mean time, neglect not the advice of one who loves you. Watch him narrowly. Attend closely to the motions of his eyes, & changes of countenance when he may suppose you are placeing confidence in him, & you will not be long in discovering the *perfidious, & ungrateful* friend.

3. Heth may be referring in this paragraph to Tench Coxe, commissioner of the revenue and formerly Assistant Secretary of the Treasury. Although Coxe was apparently a neutral rather than a Loyalist during the American Revolution, he was strongly suspected of Tory sympathies, and his name was included in a list of persons charged with treason issued by the Supreme Executive of Pennsylvania after the departure of the British from Philadelphia in 1778 (*Pennsylvania Archives*, 4th ser. [Harrisburg, 1900], III, 676). Although at this time Coxe was still a Federalist, he eventually shifted his allegiance from the Federalist to the Republican party. The phrase "through the Interests of ———" may well be a reference to either Thomas Jefferson or James Madison. Coxe had long been a friend of Madison, and he had aided Jefferson in the preparation of several of his reports to Congress during the early Federal period. See Harold Hutchinson, *Tench Coxe: A Study in American Economic Development* (Baltimore, 1938), 29–36.

4. Letter not found.

5. For H's "Victory," see the introductory note to "Report on the Balance of All Unapplied Revenues at the End of the Year 1792 and on All Unapplied Monies Which May Have Been Obtained by the Several Loans Authorized by Law," February 4, 1793.

observations on the temper of the times. But having deliverd my opinions—and which are the Same with those whom you esteem in this quarter—with my usual freedom I have been unwilling to risque it, even in the Mail as it sometimes gets rob'd and, in such a case, a letter of mine might perchance—as *a curiosity*—find its way into the Public prints—and tho', I Should not hesitate one second, to tell *every Man* to his face, whose character I have drawn—what I think of him—yet, I should be unwilling to be thus exhibited to the public, lest even *knaves* & *fools,* might attribute my giving you such communications to motives, which my soul abhors—viz. *that,* of paying court to *you,* or any Man under Heaven! If I can meet with such a private oppy. as I like, I will forward it—or if you will assure me, that it shall be burnt so soon as it is read, I will trust it by stage. Has any person whatever access to your private correspondence? I ask this question, because I am well convinced, that observations of mine, respecting certain men, have been communicated to them, but perhaps, they were made in Official letters.

Having answered your questions with great sincerity & freedom, may I hope to be indulged with your private opinions on the same subject? Such, as you may wish to remain with me, as secret as the grave; or *such,* as you may not be unwilling I should communicate to those who esteem & admire you, and with whom I am upon an intimate footing—Viz.—Our Governor[6]—John Marshall,[7] & Colo. Innis[8] & Carrington.[9] As to my own private opinion about the War, I am so apprehensive that We shall be drawn into it, that I am seriously thinking of disposing of what little stock, I have left, for Valuable lands—to put myself into keeping for Military employment, and to make such an arrangement of my affairs, as to be ready to take the field at the shortest Notice. If you really think that my apprehensions, are not sufficiently grounded to Justify the first step —pray my dear friend, advise me; for I would not willingly come altogether out of the funds. I fear, I have exhausted your patience. Adieu

Yrs truly   W Heth

6. Henry Lee.

7. At this time Marshall was practicing law in Richmond.

8. James Innes, who had served as a lieutenant colonel during the American Revolution, was a Federalist politician in Virginia.

9. Edward Carrington was supervisor of the revenue for Virginia.

From Rufus King

[*New York, June 14, 1793.* On June 15, 1793, Hamilton wrote to King: "The ideas expressed in your letter of the 14th correspond with my view of the subject." *Letter not found.*]

To Nicholas Low [1]

[Philadelphia, June 14, 1793]

Sir

The bearer of this is a Mr Campbell who has lately brought from Europe some Machinery to hand for establishing a Cotton Manufactory at Patterson. He wants to ascertain when & how soon the proper accommodation & Materials can be found there.[2] Be so good as to aid him with all the necessary lights.

Yrs. with much esteem   A Hamilton

ALS, The Turner Manuscript Collection at the Torrington Library, Torrington, Connecticut.

1. For background to this letter, see "Contract with James and Shoemaker," November 5, 1792; "Agreement with John Campbell and Receipt from John Campbell," November 9, 1792.

2. An entry in the "Minutes of the S.U.M." for July 16, 1793, reads as follows: "The Governor laid before the Board a letter from John Campbell stocking weaver relative to the accomodating him with the necessary buildings and lotts for his Factory. Resolved, that the Superintendant be authorized to accommodate Mr Campbell with the necessary buildings and lotts for his Factory as far as he thinks will be consistant with the Interest of the Society; at an Interest not less than Seven ⅌ Cent ⅌ Annum for the Money laid out; and the rent of the lott at such a reasonable rate to encourage his settling in the Town" ("Minutes of the S.U.M.," 87–88).

To John Addison and Peter Van Gaasbeck

Treasury Department
Philadelphia June 15. 1793

Gentlemen

I received two or three days since your letter of the 30th. of May.[1]

The Intention of Mr. Tappen [2] to resign is not yet known to the Assistant of the Post Master General,[3] who in his absence [4] represents him. But you may depend, that when the event you mention shall happen, I shall take care to bring under the consideration of the Post Master General the Gentleman whom you recommend and in a manner corresponding with the decided terms in which you speak of his pretensions. With sentiments of great consideration and esteem I am

    Gentlemen   Your obedient servt   A Hamilton

Peter Van Gaasbeck ⎫
               ⎬   Esquires
John Addison   ⎭

ALS, Museum of the City of New York.
  1. Letter not found.
  2. Christopher Tappan was postmaster at Kingston.
  3. Charles Burrall.
  4. Timothy Pickering, the Postmaster General, had been appointed one of the three commissioners to negotiate with the western Indians and was at this time on his way to the proposed meeting place at Sandusky.

To Edward Carrington

[*Philadelphia, June 15, 1793.* On July 2, 1793, Carrington wrote to Hamilton: "I am favored with yours of the 15th. June." *Letter not found.*]

To Rufus King

[Philadelphia, June 15, 1793]

The ideas expressed in your letter of the 14th[1] correspond with my view of the subject, in general. I did not perceive that any process could be devised to detain the Privateer and concluded that the issue would be to leave her in military custody. Indeed I believe this was rather the expectation with all, though it was thought adviseable to make the experiment of a reference to the Civil Tribunal.

With regard to the Catharine[2] I also entertain the doubt you appear to have. In the case of the Grange,[3] the surrender was brought about by a demand of Mr. Genet and his interposition. But it was in contemplation of employing the Military in case of refusal.

Yet since that time a libel has been filed in the District Court in the case of another vessel[4] alleged to have been captured within the limits of our Jurisdiction. And both Mr. Lewis [5] and Mr. Rawle [6] Atty of the District hold that the District or Admiralty Court will take cognizance of this question. They argue that it would be a great *chasm* in the law that there should not be some competent judicial authority to do justice between parties in the case of an illegal seizure within our jurisdiction. That the Court of Admiralty has naturally cognizance of *tortious takings* on the high seas & as she gives relief *in rem,* may cause a redelivery. That though as a general principle a Court of a *Neutral Nation* will not examine the question of prize or not prize, between belligerent Powers—yet this principle must except the case of the infraction of the Jurisdiction of the Neutral Power itself. Quoad this fact its Courts will interpose & give relief.

This is their reasoning and it has much force. The desire of the Executive is to have the point ascertained & if possible to put the affair in this train. There may arise nice disputes about the *fact* and nice points about the extent of jurisdiction at sea which the Courts had best settle.

The Contest in form must as you say be between the *Owners* and the Captors. For this purpose Mr. *Hammond* is to cause the proper instructions to be given.

Yrs. truly   A Hamilton

June 15. 1793.

There is a letter from *me* to *Harrison.*[7] If Troupe [8] has not opened it, let him do it.

R King Esq

ALS, Hamilton Papers, Library of Congress.
    1. Letter not found.
    2. See "Cabinet Meeting. Opinion Respecting the Measures to Be Taken Relative to a Sloop Fitted Out as a Privateer," June 12, 1793.
    3. See the introductory note to H to Washington, May 15, 1793.
    4. This is a reference either to the *William,* a British merchantman captured by the *Citizen Genet* on May 3, 1793, or to the *Fanny,* a British brigantine captured on May 8 by the *Sans Culotte.* British officials maintained that both ships were captured within United States territorial waters. In a letter to Thomas Jefferson, dated June 5, 1793, George Hammond, the British Minister to the United States, described the complications arising out of the capture of these ships as follows:
    ". . . The Ship William of Glasgow, Captain Leggett, was some time ago captured by a privateer Schooner named Le Citoyen Genêt fitted out at Charleston, and was sent as prize to this port, but some doubts having been

entertained with respect to the validity of the commission of the Schooner which made the capture (and which is now also in this harbour) a suit was instituted by the agent for the Owners of the Ship William in the district federal Court of this state, for the purpose of obtaining its opinion on this subject. Another point will also I understand be submitted to the court viz. that the Ship William was captured within the jurisdiction of the United States. Of the truth of this last mentioned fact of which I had prior information, I have now obtained such corroborating testimony as I am persuaded will be satisfactory to the general government of the United States should the district Court deem itself incompetent either to the requisition or enforcement of the restitution of the vessel captured. In consequence of this suit the Ship William and the property on board are now under attachment by the Marshall of the district Court. The Court will give judgment on this question on Friday next. But if its decision be unfavorable to the restoration of the Ship, I am apprehensive lest attachment being taken off, the vessell may be sent to sea so speedily as to preclude the effect of any application relative to it which I may deem it expedient to make. I therefore venture to hope that the general government of the United States will either direct the attachment now subsisting to be continued or will adopt any other measures that may tend to prevent the vessel from departing until it shall have investigated and formed some determination on the evidence which I shall lay before it without delay, in order to substantiate the fact of the Ship William having been captured within the jurisdiction of the United States.

"As I expect at the same time to be enabled to offer testimony establishing a similar state of facts relative to the brig Fanny Captain Pyle now lying in this harbour, as a prize to another privateer fitted out at Charleston named the Sans Culottes, and also under an attachment from the Marshall of the district Court, I hope that the general government will prevent that vessel also from sailing until that point can be ascertained." (LS, RG 59, Notes from the British Legation in the United States to the Department of State, Vol. 1, October 26, 1791–August 15, 1794, National Archives.)

5. William Lewis was United States judge for the District of Pennsylvania.
6. William Rawle was United States attorney for the District of Pennsylvania.
7. H to Richard Harison, June 13-15, 1793.
8. H and Robert Troup had been close friends since the time when both had been undergraduates at King's College. In 1793 Troup was a New York City attorney and clerk of the New York District Court.

From Henry Lee

Richmond June 15th. 93.

My dear sir

We have heard here that a circular ltr. from you to the several collectors relative to French prizes [1] has given great offence to the British minister [2] & that this conduct on the part of the U.S. will contribute to produce a rupture with G.B. I should be very much obliged to you for the truth on this point & its expected consequences.

Peace to America is in one word, our all. A set of clamorous desperadoes in their fortunes or political hopes cry aloud for war & I fear G.B is not indisposed to take advantage of every event to injure us. What the intemperance of some among us & her solicitude to avenge past disgrace may produce time alone can unfold, but I hope that the true friends to their country will every where & on every occasion unite to prevent the calamitys of war.

What is the real state of things in france, & will not her enemys after victory there, feel the exploit but half accomplished, unless we also be politically changed. On this ground I sometimes apprehend danger, but am revived again when I look at the sea which divides us & reckon on the exhausted state of their finances. Farewel [3]

H L

ALS, Hamilton Papers, Library of Congress.
　1. "Treasury Department Circular to the Collectors of the Customs," May 30, 1793.
　2. George Hammond was the British Minister to the United States.
　3. H endorsed this letter as follows: "For the information of the President as evidence of the public Disposition."

To Henry Lee

[*Philadelphia, June 15, 1793.* On the back of Lee's letter to him of May 6, 1793, Hamilton wrote: "Answered June 15." *Letter not found.*]

To George Washington [1]

Private   Philadelphia June 15. 1793

Sir

　The inclosed report will I trust make it appear, that there are good reasons relative to the execution of the purposes specified in the laws [2] for making a further loan to the extent proposed.

　But bottoming the proceeding upon the direct object of the laws, as the legal and primary inducement, it appears to me justifiable and

ALS, George Washington Papers, Library of Congress; copy, Hamilton Papers, Library of Congress.
　1. For background to this letter, see H to Washington, June 3, 1793; Washington to H, June 6, 1793.
　2. For the provisions for the payment of the foreign and domestic debt, see "An Act making provision for the (payment of the) Debt of the United States" (1 *Stat.* 138–44 [August 4, 1790]) and "An Act making Provision for the Reduction of the Public Debt" (1 *Stat.* 186–87 [August 12, 1790]).

wise to embrace as secondary and collateral motives the probable operation of the measure on the public interests in ways not immediately indicated in the laws. On this ground I think the legal considerations for a further loan are enforced by the general state of affairs at the present Juncture. Should a general Indian War ensue [3] & still more should we unfortunately be involved in a European War, nothing could be more convenient than to have anticipated such a resource, which the Legislature might apply to the new exigencies, as far as regards the purchase of the Debt, without any violation of principle.

In the event of a European War breaking out, it would probably be too late to attempt what before hand would be practicable without difficulty.

With perfect respect   & the truest attachment   I have the honor to be Sir   Your most Obedt & humble servant   A Hamilton

The President of The UStates

[ENCLOSURE] [4]

[Philadelphia, June 15, 1793]

The Secretary of the Treasury in obedience to the order of the President of the U States of the 6. instant, respectfully makes the following Report.

The statement herewith transmitted marked A shews, on the credit side thereof, the amount of the fund arising from foreign Loans transferred to the United States, amounting to 2,965,643. Dollars & 47 Cents; and on the debit side thereof the amount of the sums which have been *actually* disbursed and are in a *course of disbursement* out of that fund for specific purposes, being 2,400,159 Dolls. & 19 Cents.

There of course remains free for and subject to application, according to the Laws authorising the Loans, a balance of 565,484 Dollars & 28 Cents.

3. At this time preparations were being made for a campaign against the western Indians. See "Report on the State of the Treasury at the Commencement of Each Quarter During the Years 1791 and 1792 and on the State of the Market in Regard to the Same Years," February 19, 1793, note 13.

4. LC, George Washington Papers, Library of Congress; copy, in the handwriting of Thomas Jefferson, Thomas Jefferson Papers, Library of Congress.

To this will be to be added, when ascertained, certain sums of interest subsequent to the year 1790 which will have been included in the payments to France & Spain out of the proceeds of the foreign Loans; & which will thereby have been virtually transferred to the United States—provision having been made for that object out of domestic funds. The addition however will not be large.

Hence results an answer to the first question stated by the President.[5]

In answer to the Second Question, the Secretary has the honor to observe that it would be, in his opinion, expedient, for the reason which has governed hitherto, the convenience of which has been fully experienced, namely, the *power of applying the funds to the purposes of either Law according to circumstances*—that the proposed Loan should be made upon the authority of both acts, & not upon the seperate authority of either of them.

The following summary answers the third Question proposed.

The sum allowed to be borrowed by the two Acts of the 4. & 12. of August 1790 is 14.000,000 of Dollars. The whole amount of the Loans hitherto made is 19,550,000 Guilders, equal, at 36$\frac{4}{11}$ ninetieths of a Dollar ₱ Guilder, to 7,898,989 Dollars & 88 Cents; consequently "the balance remaining unborrowed of the two Sums allowed to be borrowed" is 6,101,010 Dollars and 12 Cents.

Which leaves much more than sufficient latitude for a Loan of 3,000,000 of florins in addition to that for 2,000,000, already directed & probably set on foot.[6]

The immediate main object of this further loan would be the purchase of the Debt.

The Installments of the Debt to France falling due in September & November next, & the interest for a year upon so much of the Debt, as by the terms of Contract would fall due after the present time, amount to 3,335,000 Livres, or Dollars 605,302, and 50 Cents which, *if to be wholly paid*, will more than absorb the balance on hand of the foreign fund.

Supposing the application of this balance to that purpose there would remain to be borrowed for the purpose of purchases of the Debt, Dollars 1,715,098 and 11 Cents.

5. Washington had submitted four questions concerning the proposed new loan in his letter to H of June 6, 1793.
6. See H to William Short, November 5, 1792.

The two millions of Guilders already directed to be borrowed, & the three millions, the loan of which is proposed to be authorised, would amount together to 2,020,202. Dollars & 2 Cents, which would exceed the sum requisite for purchases of the Debt by 305,103 Dollars and 91. Cents.

But it is so possible that events may arise which would render it desirable to the United States to encrease its payments to France, as in that view alone to make such an excess not inconvenient. Besides that on the first of June 1794 another installment of the Dutch loans becomes payable, & it is probable if instructions to set on foot the loan, should go at this time, the entire payment of the sums subscribed to the loan would not be completed much sooner than June next. Add to this that it is frequently possible to get the periods of payments protracted.

It would have been fortunate in every sense, if the state of the Treasury had permitted the entering the market for purchases, in force; but the detail which has been given, shews that it could not have been done, under the obstacles which the state of European Affairs lately threw in the way of Loans, without materially hazarding the credit of the United States.

While it is prudent to wait, 'till it is experimentally ascertained, that these obstacles have been removed by the change of affairs, it is desireable to be provided to the extent of the authority given, with means of prosecuting purchases.

It is probable that for a considerable time to come the prices of stock will remain at a point which will render purchases extremely advantageous.

The further consideration which has been stated with reference to France & the next installment of the Dutch Loans, may not be found unworthy of attention.

All which is humbly submitted.   Alexander Hamilton
                                                  Secy. of the Treasy.

Treasury Department
June 15. 1793.

[A]

Dr. State of Monies transferred to The United States out of the proceeds of Foreign Loans.

To this sum expended in purchases of the public Debt	284,901.89.
To this sum paid & to be paid to France for the use of St. Domingo [7]	726,000.
To this sum paid & to be paid to France on accot. of the 3,000,000 of Livres promised [8]	544,500.
To this sum paid to France for miscellaneous purposes	49,400.
To this sum paid & to be paid to Foreign Officers [9]	191,316.90
To this sum appropriated for the 1st installment due to the Bank of the U S [10]	200,000.
To this sum remitted to Europe for paying an installment due the 1st June on the Dutch Debt 1,000,000 of Guilders at 36⁴⁄₁₁ ninetieths pr. Guilder	404,040.40.
	2,400,159.19.
Balce. subject to future disposition	565,484.28.
	2,965,643.47.

Pr. Contra. Cr.	
By the Sum drawn for by Saml. Meredith, Treasurer	2,305,769.13.
By this sum applied in Amsterdam to the payment of interest for which provision was made out of domestic funds & thereby virtually drawn to the U. States 1,633,189 guilders & 2 stivers @ 36⁴⁄₁₁ ninetieths per guilder	659,874.34
D.	2,965,643.47.

Treasy. Depmt. 15 June 1793.

Alex: Hamilton
Secy of ye. Treasy

7. See the introductory note to George Latimer to H, January 2, 1793.

8. See "Cabinet Meeting. Opinion on Furnishing Three Million Livres Agreeably to the Request of the French Minister," February 25, 1793; Jean Baptiste de Ternant to H, February 26, 1793; H to Ternant, February 26, 1793.

9. For a description of this debt, see Short to H, August 3, 1790, note 5. Section 5 of "An Act supplementary to an act making provision for the Debt of the United States" (1 *Stat.* 282 [May 8, 1792]) authorized the President "to cause to be discharged the principal and interest of the said debt, out of any of the monies which have been or shall be obtained on loan." For the negotiations on the payment of these officers, see H to Short, August 16, September 13, 1792; H to Washington, August 27, 1792; Washington to H, August 31, 1792; H to Gouverneur Morris, September 13, 1792.

10. This was the first installment due on the two million dollars borrowed from the Bank of the United States. See H to the President and Directors of the Bank of the United States, January 1, 1793, note 1.

INDEX

COMPILED BY JEAN G. COOKE